D0743490

CANADIAN
PUBLIC POLICY

IDEAS, STRUCTURE, PROCESS

CANADIAN PUBLIC POLICY
IDEAS, STRUCTURE, PROCESS

G. Bruce Doern & Richard W. Phidd

ⓝ METHUEN

Toronto   New York   London   Sydney   Auckland

Canadian Public Policy: Ideas, Structure, Process

Canadian Cataloguing in Publication Data

Doern, G. Bruce, 1942-
    Canadian public policy

Bibliography: p.
ISBN 0-458-94850-0

1. Policy sciences.   2. Canada—Politics and government.   I. Phidd, Richard W.   II. Title.

JL108.D6   354.710072   C83-098364-3

Table 5.3 on p. 119 and Figure 5.2 on p. 121 reproduced with permission from the Economic Council of Canada, *Responsible Regulation*, An Interim Report (Ottawa: Minister of Supply and Services, Canada, 1979).

Printed and bound in Canada

1   2   3   4   5   83   88   87   86   85   84

TO JOAN, KRISTIN AND SHANNON

AND

TO ISKAH, KARENA, RICHARD, EASTON AND NADIA-ELENA

CONTENTS

DETAILED TABLE OF CONTENTS

CANADIAN PUBLIC POLICY

IDEAS, STRUCTURE, PROCESS

PREFACE

In the French language the word "politique" means both politics and policy. The frequent separation of politics and policy in the English language has unfortunate implications. When it is said that something is done for "political" reasons, too often the implication for the layman is that this stands for excessive partisan behaviour, personal power seeking or even lower forms of skullduggery. When it is said that something is done for reasons of policy, a loftier image emerges, one which reaches beyond personalities and Machiavellian manoeuvring into the world of principle. While there is obviously some basis in human experience and in the study of politics for this separation, in the final analysis it is a day-to-day dichotomy which blocks a full understanding of Canadian political life. Policy and politics are in many respects the same thing, since both deal with ideas and with the power to actually implement ideas in a world of large structures and institutions and in the face of numerous uncertainties.

Ottawa's decisions are often perplexing and contradictory, coloured by long years of Liberal party dominance both before and during the Trudeau era and perplexed by a future that increasingly refuses to cooperate. This book examines Canadian public policy through an approach that stresses the interplay among ideas, structures and processes. Federal policies are the product of numerous decisions, including decisions to do nothing. The book provides the first reasonably integrated examination of public policy making in Canada, one which systematically links ideas and substantive policy fields with structures and processes. Though focused on Ottawa's decisions, the analysis deals with federal-provincial relations and with analagous policy ideas and problems at the provincial level. The book locates the policy process firmly within the broadest historical, economic, social and institutional features of the Canadian political system, including the central importance of federal-provincial, government-industry-labour and foreign policy relations. It show the essential intellectual links among Canadian public administration, political science and economics by critically examining the influence of ideas and approaches emanating from these fields of study.

The book requires the reader to look at public policy fields (social and economic) in two contexts: in terms of the historical drift or evolution of policy ideas, structures and processes; and in relation to the constraints on decisions at a particular time. It thus attempts to develop an appreciation of the fact that the modern state and Canada's political decision makers are neither all-powerful or powerless. Rather, Ottawa's politicians must deal with an uncertain future and function in a complex setting of structures and interdependent institutions where ideas are *always* in action.

Our analysis is a reflection of years of research, writing and teaching in the field of Canadian as well as comparative public policy and public administration. It builds on our previous work on several fields of public policy, including economic policy, industrial policy, science and technology policy, communications policy, occupational and environmental health policy, agricultural policy, energy and nuclear policy and regional development policy, as well as on public expenditure, regulation, taxation, and Crown corporations. It also benefits from over three hundred interviews and discussions carried out over the past three years with officials, ministers, interest group leaders and journalists. Above all, it reflects an effort to respond to criticisms of our previous books and articles conveyed to us by friends and colleagues, students, professors, and practitioners. It hopefully reflects an appreciation of, and an indebtedness to, the burgeoning literature on public policy produced by numerous individuals of widely varying ideological and disciplinary persuasions across Canada and abroad. Much of this literature was not available as recently as ten years ago, but it greatly enriches the field.

It must also be said that our two academic home bases force a healthy exposure to different aspects of public policy thought and action. The School of Public Administration at Carleton University is an interdisciplinary graduate institution. Located in Ottawa, it forces one to deal with the insights of different disciplines and to consider the connections, usually much closer than some may think, between theory and practice. The great advantage of the University of Guelph is, first, that it is not in Ottawa and that it is located in a smaller urban and rural setting. Second, its students, faculty and traditions offer a different view, including a focus on scientific, physical and human resource fields embracing studies on policy fields such as agricultural and food and family and consumer studies. We owe much to our colleagues and students who have taught us not only by gentle persuasion and osmosis but also through the occasional application of the intellectual equivalent of the proverbial "two by four" across the head.

We thank several colleagues and friends who in general discussion or in the reading of early drafts of the manuscript contributed greatly to our work. These include Peter Aucoin, Sharon Sutherland, Vince Wilson, Allan Maslove, Michael Prince, Harvey Lithwick, Gene Swimmer, Donald Swartz, Stan Winer, Brian Tomlin, Rick Van Loon, Glen Toner, O.P. Dwividi, Ken Woodside, Brian Woodrow, Pat Kyba, Henry Wiseman, Bill Christian and Jack Happy. Any weaknesses in the final product, however, are ours alone. We are also especially grateful to Monica Wright for her excellent and always cheerful typing and editing services. Thanks are also owed to Jay and Liz Spence whose cottage in the Gatineau provided a quiet place for thought and writing. Finally, we thank our two families for support and devotion well beyond the call of normal affection and family duty.

G. Bruce Doern and Richard W. Phidd
Ottawa, January 1983

CHAPTER 1

INTRODUCTION:
PUBLIC POLICY IN THE CANADIAN POLITICAL
SYSTEM

The making of public policy in the age of media politics is too often
portrayed as being dominated by key personalities or as the slow tortuous
crawl of pragmatism. This is primarily because of the decidedly
unhealthy tendency of some commentators to separate ideas from
leaders and of the failure to place modern policy issues in a historical
context. We do not wish to downplay the role of personalities. Indeed, we
show that ideas and people are inseparable both at an individual leader's
level and in relation to public policy structures and processes. Nor do we
argue that gradual adjustment does not characterize many policy fields.
Pragmatism, however, is a useful adjective for the policy process only if it
does not imply the presence of idea-less politics.

The best antidote to the narrow "personality-cum-pragmatism"
school of public policy analysis is to develop an appreciation of the social
and economic environment and of the political system in which
Canadian public policy is formulated. The environment and the political
system affect the nature of the policies and decisions produced in a
constant interactive way. The government as public policy maker is
neither a feeble political eunuch nor an all-powerful leviathan.

The main purpose of this chapter is to review briefly the main
attributes of Canada's social and economic environment and of the
Canadian political system. There are numerous primary sources of
analysis on each of these attributes which examine them in great detail.
Our intention is to highlight their critical importance for all that follows
in this book, and to show how we link these attributes in later chapters to
the ideas, structures and processes of the Canadian public policy system.
Following this initial review the chapter defines the main characteristics
of the public policy-making system and examines recent trends and
perspectives in the study and practice of public policy in Canada. It is in
the context of these trends that we set out the approach used in this book,

an approach which focuses on the interplay between ideas, structures and processes.

The Environment of Canadian Politics

Canada consists of an evolving amalgam of social and economic characteristics, institutions and ideas. These environmental features continue to be of critical importance in understanding how and why policies and decisions are made.[1] The major features to be stressed are: Canada's historical origins in relation to the United States and the United Kingdom; French-English relations and Canada's evolving ethnic composition; the role of geographical and spatial/physical realities; the uneasy co-existence of capitalism, economic classes and traditions of statism; Canada's dependence on foreign trade and the extensive foreign ownership of major sectors of the economy.

Canada's political origins demonstrate an explicit rejection of the American revolution and an acceptance of the "peace, order and good government" offered by British traditions and institutions reflected especially in Parliamentary government. At a basic constitutional level this also led to the adoption of a system of responsible Cabinet-Parliamentary government as opposed to the American system which constructed an elaborate array of "checks and balances" between the three branches of government: the executive, the legislature and the judiciary.[2] Canadian political leaders rejected the excesses of the American belief in individual liberty and distrust of government and authority. Even in the 1981 debate which led to an entrenched Charter of Rights, the Canadian system balanced its adherence to basic rights by providing for the right of legislative bodies to override these rights for a limited period of time. While Canada evolved into a liberal democratic state, it did so with a strong adherence to collectivist norms, whether of the Tory organic community variety or of a later social democratic kind.

The magnetic pull of the American giant has always been important—economically, politically and culturally. The earliest definition of Canada's national and industrial policies after Confederation was an act of political will to counter American expansionism. It involved the deliberate creation of an east-west continental axis, physically and politically, to counter the efficiency of the north-south continental axis. In the last decades of the twentieth century the American influence, aided by mass communication, has exerted an even larger cultural pressure which Canadians have simultaneously welcomed and resisted. Canada is not, however, a carbon copy of the United States. This seemingly obvious point deserves repeated emphasis since it affects the content of Canadian ideologies and dominant ideas examined in Chapter 2; the much more limited degree of legitimacy accorded in Canada to interest group pluralism analyzed in Chapter 3; the approaches to social policy and economic policy assessed in Chapter 14; attitudes to regulatory and tax reform surveyed in Chapter 12; and even the acceptance and use of formal models in the study of public policy evaluated in Chapter 6.

The strong collectivist traditions in Canada are also a reflection of the central role of the relationships between French Canadians and English Canadians. In particular, the deeply rooted desire by French Canadians since "the Conquest" to preserve and enhance their collective cultural, religious and linguistic independence, and even nationhood, is a central fact of Canadian political life.[3] The constant need to seek a new delicate accommodation with French Canada affects many policy fields in ways that are not always obvious. Consequently, not only are policies on language and education so affected, but also policies tied to broader social issues (family allowances, for example), industrial location and foreign policy.

The tension in French-English relations has been increased by the growth and changing composition of Canada's ethnic peoples including Canada's original citizens, the Indians and Inuit. As a nation of immigrants, where immigration and settlement policy was once the centrepiece of industrial policy, the emergence of German, Italian, Ukrainian and Polish Canadians, to name only a few of the ethnic groups, challenged the very definition of Canada, especially as viewed in Western Canada where a large proportion of these peoples were located and whose work and sacrifice opened the western frontier.

The enormous continental size and geographical composition of Canada, especially when contrasted with the thin ribbon of humanity that hugs the 49th parallel, imposes a spatial and physical reality to Canadian political life and public policy that even modern communications and the mass media cannot fully alter. Canada's most innovative contribution to social science, the work of Innis and others, was founded on an appreciation of this fundamental reality.[4] It focused on the importance of communication relationships between the centre and the periphery. As well, Innis showed the importance to Canadian economic development of basic staple resources from furs and fish, to grain and mineral resources. He also pointed out the limits and dependence created by reliance on a staples approach to economic development. In practical day-to-day public policy terms, the spatial and geographical realities cannot be underestimated. They affect the importance of staple resources as a central element of economic and industrial policy and of Canada's economic wealth and dependence; the importance of transportation and communication policy as a vehicle of national integration (with the infrastructure usually supplied by the state); the changing definition and response to demands for sensitive regional policy; the emotional and normative attachment, especially in Western Canada but also in Atlantic Canada, to the question of resource ownership and the management of nonrenewable resources; and the perception by Canada's trading partners, especially the United States, of Canada as a stable supplier of basic resources.

Canada's economy is essentially a capitalist one and thus is rooted in a belief in the value and efficiency of the market and in the individual freedom and defence of property rights which capitalism helps sustain. The right to own property was a particularly important value to the immigrant settlers. Though linked to the values of liberalism and individualism, there has always existed in Canada an ambivalence about the idea of effiency inherent in capitalism. The numerous rough edges of Canadian capitalism have always been moderated by an inclination to use the state. Statism was reflected not only in the frequent use of public enterprise or Crown corporations, but even earlier in the extensive public subsidization and financing of major transportation networks.[5]

It must also be stressed that Canada's economy, like that of any continental country, is a regionally varied one. This reality arises from the physical and geographical attributes noted above. The geographic dispersal of natural resources such as fish, forests, grain and minerals, the existence of different energy dependencies in each region, the proximity of different regions to population concentrations and therefore markets, and the widely varying modes and costs of transportation generate a need for regional policies and responses. They also result in distinctly different and often contradictory views about the soundness and appropriateness of national economic policy. These economic features are not ones which can be simplistically attributed to capitalism. They are influenced by capitalism, but they also predate and affect what capitalists and government entrepreneurs can do in the market place and in the exercise of political power.

Capitalism, however, does produce relations of dependence and economic subordination between those who own capital and those who supply their labour.[6] It also increasingly produces other "classes" such as government workers whose class orientations are at best vague and subject to other regional, ethnic and individual cross pressures. The presence of capitalism raises fundamental questions about the role of class politics in the policy process. Several recent studies in Canada make it evident that the class aspects of Canadian politics cannot be viewed at the simplistic level of capitalists and workers in perpetual conflict, with the state operating as the agent of the owners of capital. It is increasingly acknowledged that the state has considerable autonomy. Nor can it be argued, on the basis of voting data and the failure of left-wing political parties such as the New Democratic Party (NDP) to gain power at the national level, that class politics is irrelevant in electoral and party politics and hence in public policy. The truth lies somewhere in between. Class analysis, as a formal approach to studying policy and to practising politics, does offer a distinctly different view of public policy, but also suffers from numerous weaknesses as an explanation of public policy in Canada. These strengths and weaknesses are shown in more practical terms in the review of social and economic policy in Chapter 14. Existing literature already indicates several important ways in which the role of capitalism, and the class issues which eminate from it, influences the making of policy. The presence of even ill-defined classes in Canada suggests the limitations of American-style interest group pluralism as a descriptive or normative attribute of Canadian politics. The concept of interest group pluralism suggests a system of politics in which policies are the product of a competition among more-or-less equal interest groups. Class analysis casts serious doubt on the implicit pluralist notion that the state is a neutral referee carefully balancing interests.[7] At the same time it recognizes that government has some degree of autonomy and must deal with the often contradictory demands of different elements of capital (for example, resource capital, financial capital, foreign capital) as well as between capital and labour. It has relevance, as we see in Chapter 9, for the analysis of intrabureaucratic policy structures and processes as well, since it poses questions about how different elements of the business community and of labour are represented or excluded from representation in government agencies in an unequal way.

The presence of capitalism and the ideas and beliefs associated with it and in opposition to it, raises the age-old debate about efficiency versus equality. Since capitalism helps generate political parties of the left or socialist variety, it brings into organized political life a concern for the redistribution of income and power between rich and poor, between capital and labour and among interests and regions.

A final but critical dual feature of Canadian capitalism and the Canadian economy is the considerable dependence on foreign trade and the extensive foreign ownership of the Canadian industrial and resource sectors, especially by American business interests.[8] About 25 to 30 percent of the income of Canadians is dependent upon foreign trade, much of it with the United States. These percentages may be even higher in certain regions and subregions of Canada. As Chapters 15 and 16 demonstrate in more detail, the trade and foreign ownership imperatives affect and constrain Canada's conduct of policy both in foreign policy terms vis-à-vis the United States, and in domestic policy in fields such as energy, industrial and regional policy. The presence of large blocks of concentrated foreign capital also affects the internal deliberations of major business interest groups which must take positions that accommodate both indigenous capital and foreign-owned capital. Thus foreign ownership and trade dependence is a political and policy issue, not just because it implies possible control by foreign enterprises operating through active support of their own foreign government, but because they are a strong influence in the domestic counsels of Canadian federal and provincial governments and within major Canadian economic interest groups. These imperatives are reinforced by close relations among Canadian and American unions and by conflicts within the Canadian labour movement, relationships we examine in greater detail in Chapter 3.[9]

The Canadian Political System and Political Institutions

The broader environmental features outlined above have combined to produce the Canadian political system. This system comprises several major institutions that help resolve conflict and differences of view among Canadians and that allocate values in an authoritative way. These institutions include federalism, Cabinet-Parliamentary government, interest groups, the electoral system and political parties and the mass media. These institutions are not dry appendages of some extinct dinosaur which one can conveniently separate from "behaviour" and ideas. Institutions are forged around key ideas to form entrenched patterns of behaviour. They are themselves embued with ideas that are important not only in relation to the content of policy but also in relation to the policy process and to how policy *should be* made. We examine these institutions briefly here but will review them again in Chapters 2, 3, 7 and 8. The institutions interact with each other. One cannot understand their role in policy formulation by viewing each of them in isolation. Federalism and Cabinet-Parliamentary government interact with each other, partly through electoral competition and political party alliances and personalities. The media interact with all of the institutions since they are both an essential part of democratic life and a necessary forum for modern political communication and leadership. Interest groups seek to influence all the major institutions since they play a crucial intermediary role between the citizen and the state.

In examining institutions it is also essential not to confuse them with the concept of "institutionalism." The latter refers to a label applied to earlier Canadian scholars by latter-day social science "behaviouralists." The behaviouralists were critical of the excessive emphasis by a few scholars in the 1940s and 1950s on traditional institutions such as Parliament, the executive and the judiciary. While some of these criticisms were valid, we see below that they often led to a dangerous and utterly false separation between behaviour and ideas on the one hand, and institutions on the other.[10]

Institutions, central political ideas and beliefs, and behaviour are in many ways the same thing. Federalism is based on a belief in the need to balance national integration and unity with regional and cultural differences. It incorporates ideas of centralization and decentralization. It imposes a dominant reality on the Canadian policy process, namely the need to practise some form of cooperative federalism regardless of the short-term rhetoric of day-to-day politics. Parliamentary government is founded on a belief in responsible government, allied with the democratic concept of "one man—one vote." It rejects, in part at least, the idea of the rigid separation of powers between the executive, the legislature and the judiciary, a matter of no small importance in understanding the policy process in Canada compared to the United

States. Interest groups evolve out of the belief in freedom of association and the practical need to create institutions which mediate between individuals and society as a whole, including the state. The mass media are also forums for the free expression of views and a belief in a free but responsible press. Each of the institutions are surveyed below in these fundamental terms.

The physical, cultural and ethnic realities of Canada, more than any other, combined to produce the need for a federal system of government. Federalism is first an article of belief, not just a document containing the deathless prose of the British North America Act or the more inspiring ideals of the 1981 Constitution Act and its charter of rights.[11] It legitimizes the existence of separate, but interdependent, realms of political power. In particular, sections 91, 92 and 95 enumerate federal and provincial legislative powers and thus, in part, constrain what each level of government can do. Federalism sanctifies the right of constituent governments to pursue different policy priorities at different times. It also makes possible public policy experimentation and "learning" where one province or the federal government adopts an approach tried elsewhere and adapts it to its own situation. But policy and program interdependence between the two levels of government is also an evident feature of federalism. Public policy is profoundly affected by joint statutory agreements on taxation, equalization payments, and major social programs such as medicare, education, welfare and manpower training. Interdependence is a reality in environmental regulation, agricultural policy, labour relations, and in the industrial, resource and energy policy fields, to mention only a few.

The growing dominance since the 1960s of "executive federalism" where policy is made in a series of "behind-the-scenes" multilateral bargains struck among ministers and senior officials has led to concern about the process itself, about the policies it produces, and about the demoralizing inaction or mere tinkering it often produces. Although the focus of this book is on the federal government, the analysis will show in very concrete ways the influence of federalism and federal-provincial relations on: the ideas inherent in public policy (Chapters 2, 14, 15 and 16); calculations about instrument choice (Chapter 5); the priority-setting process (Chapter 10); policy information and knowledge (Chapter 13); and the evaluation of policies (Chapter 18).

Cabinet-Parliamentary government exists at both the federal and provincial levels of Canadian government. It is a system of government which has significant implications for the relations between the executive, the legislature and the judiciary. The executive, comprising the Crown, the prime minister, the Cabinet and the bureaucracy, has the main powers of initiation in matters of policy, finance and legislation. Parliament and provincial legislatures represent public opinion, legislate, oppose and criticize. But legally, and by convention, they do not initiate policy per se. The courts have some independence to uphold the rule of law and render judgements on constitutional propriety, especially given a federal system of government. The courts have not played the major role they perform in the American congressional system. It is likely that Canadian courts will have a more active role in the public policy process because of the entrenched charter of rights, but this remains to be seen.

In recent years there has been a strong tendency to attribute a declining, low or even nonexistent policy role to Parliament or the legislature itself.[12] Nonetheless, it is patently evident that the *existence* of an assembly, democratically elected by voters in geographically based constituencies and charged with holding the majority party (expressed in votes in the assembly) accountable, has important implications for policy formulation. Under a parliamentary system, governed by rigid rules of confidence and party discipline, the government majority party has the main power to initiate policy, especially through taxation and spending. This fact, coupled with the growing complexity and technological nature of public policy, has contributed further to the view that Parliament has virtually no policy role—only the power to oppose, criticize and scrutinize. The policy role of Parliament is held to be that of a mere "refinery" or, somewhat more grandly, the ultimate source of legitimacy through its exercise of legislative procedures in the passage of bills.[13] While, as we have seen, it is difficult to argue that Parliament has much power—almost by definition this is so—the refinery concept and other similar labels nonetheless seriously underplay the role of Parliament, particularly the role it plays when governments have to "anticipate" the opposition political parties' views and strategies expressed and forged in the House of Commons. In Chapter 2 and 10, we draw attention to other particular attributes of Parliament that are essential in understanding policy formulation.

There is of course little dispute that the executive branch of Cabinet-

Parliamentary government is the fulcrum of policy making. This applies to the role of the prime minister and other Cabinet ministers but also to the role of the senior bureaucracy and the central agency apparatus that supports the Cabinet.[14] The policy structures and processes of the executive-bureaucratic arena are examined primarily in Part II of the book. Policy is influenced by the central personal preferences and beliefs of the prime minister and of other ministers; by the inevitable and unavoidable need to delegate tasks to over three dozen ministers and hundreds of agencies; by the need to actually rank or balance ideas and to allocate resources of time, money, personnel and political energy; by the size and representative composition of the Cabinet; by the advice, expertise and longevity in office of senior officials, and by the presence, or lack, of resources, information and knowledge.

As a country with a strong belief in the right of persons to associate freely in groups, it is axiomatic that interest groups are important elements of Canadian politics and hence of public policy formulation.[15] However, as we stressed above, interest-group pluralism has never reached the sanctity of belief and practice that it has in the United States. While interest groups serve many important purposes for their members, our concern in this book is with their role in influencing policy development, by advocating change or marshalling political action to prevent changes unfavourable to them, by providing information to and withholding it from government, and by acting as a source of support for government. Interest groups are active in lobbying ministers and senior officials of the key departments and agencies that concern them. In Chapter 3 we highlight particular attributes of the evolving structure of interest groups including questions about the changing composition of business and worker interests, the unequal power among such groups and the role of the government in using groups to its own advantage. We will also refer to the role of and positions taken by interest groups in several later chapters which deal with the tax, expenditure and regulatory processes and with substantive policy fields.

The role of the electoral and party system in the development and formulation of public policy presents some puzzling paradoxes for the student of public policy, especially regarding the contrasting perspectives supplied by economists and political scientists. The latter have tended to downplay the formal policy role of parties by asserting that political parties are primarily agents for the recruitment of political leaders and the aggregation and mobilization of interests and voters for electoral purposes.[16] The two major Canadian parties, the Liberals and Progressive Conservatives, are often viewed as cadre parties lacking even the British party traditions of the serious party "mandate" or platform and with only periodic policy meetings whose resolutions are not binding on the party leaders. The New Democratic party, it is acknowledged, is more of a mass-based party and takes policy more seriously, but only, it is said by some, because it has no serious chance of gaining national office.

In contrast, while economists tend not to say much about parties per se, they nonetheless hold strongly to the adage that "voters are to politicians what the price system is to the market"—the basic, explanatory variable. In this regard parties as electoral vehicles are the key link between voters and officeholders. Chapters 5 and 6 illustrate that excessively simplistic models of political and policy behaviour have been derived from this otherwise central point.[17] A particularly important feature of this economic view of the politicians' electoral market is the policy importance (especially on key issues) ascribed to the efforts by governmental and opposition parties alike to cater to the views and perceptions of the *marginal* swing voter in the swing constituency (electoral seats that were won or lost by a small plurality of votes). Political leaders, including central party advisors, often through the use of extensive public opinion polls, are particularly sensitive to the potential marginal vote changes in the fifty or so swing constituencies that make or break an election. In Chapters 2, 5, 8 and 10 we examine the relative importance of this trait in relation to other elements of electoral and party behaviour and to relations among institutions. In particular, there is a need to appreciate how political parties define what is to be viewed as "political" and how certain conceptions of politics, and therefore policies, can be successfully screened out of policy debates, out of the list of national priorities, and out of the very definition of the national interest. The central example of this is the capacity of the dominant Liberal party to define politics in terms of French-English or interregional relations, thus blurring and as some claim "distorting" the concern for such issues as the distribution of income between rich and poor.[18] The role of elections and parties in policy making is a subtle one, not easily captured by the scorecard approach (that is, efforts to gauge how much of the party's policy platform the government adopted) or by concepts linked to the swing voter in the swing constituency.

As with the other main institutions, the issue of the mass media's role is important and complex.[19] Television and mass communication influence politics and public policy in several ways. An ability to communicate through the media is a prime factor in the selection and evaluation of leaders. It is said that a prime minister's dominance over policy and over the setting of the agenda is enhanced by his ability to command the media's attention. It is also evident that the media's short attention span makes it all the more difficult for government to hold any set of policy priorities constant for any extended period of time. Policies and decisions are often strategically timed either to minimize unfavourable coverage or to maximize coverage. The alleged bias of the media is held to be the major reason why governments and interest groups alike feel the need to spend increasing millions on policy advocacy advertising and on the marketing of their policies and leaders. Some assert glibly that Question Period in the House of Commons could not function without *The Globe and Mail*.

Judgements about the political rise and fall of ministers and their strengths and weaknesses are formed partly by a tight network of gossip and information exchanged among journalists, ministers, ministerial aids and senior bureaucrats. The media's role is held by many policy practitioners to be a central reason why, in public policy making, *perception* may be more important than reality. It contributes to the pressure which both politicians and officials feel constantly and which propels them to try at least to "be seen" doing "something" about a problem. This in turn contributes to excessive tinkering with policy and, it is suggested, to a growing disillusionment with government. Too many policies are "for show" and not "for real," a proposition we examine in some detail. There are few good studies of the media's role in the policy process. This book does not rectify this gap, but we refer again in several chapters to the media's undoubted importance.

The Public Policy System:
Ideas, Structures and Processes

Different definitions of public policy can arise depending on the formal model or approach used by a particular author. The general definition of public policy suggested by William Jenkins serves as a useful guide:

> A set of interrelated decisions taken by a political actor or group of actors concerning the selections of goals and the means of achieving

them within a specified situation where these decisions should, in principle, be within the power of these actors to achieve.[20]

This definition fits in with our view of public policy system provided that it is linked with a detailed understanding of the key features discussed below. The public policy system is a subsidiary but central part of the Canadian political system. It consists of an amalgam and interplay of *ideas*; numerous *structures* headed by individual elected and appointed persons who are engaged in ranking, balancing and allocating scarce resources of money, personnel, political energy and time; and *processes*. Ideas refer to the broad normative content of policy including ideas which are the central basis for the existence of the key institutions surveyed above. Structures refer to organizations and bureaucracies and the persons who head them, including those in public and private sector institutions. Processes refer to the changing dynamics which arise when decision makers are required to deal with uncertainty and with a changing environment, an ever present feature of policy making. Both structures and processes are embued with the key ideas of political life.

The essential need to view policy as an interplay between ideas, structures and processes flows logically and practically from the main features of public policy and of the policy system. Public policy involves:

- expressions of normative intent and therefore of ideas, values and purposes;
- the exercise and structuring of power, influence and legitimate coercion.
- process, including not only the need to deal with uncertainty but also with equally normative judgements about the legitimacy and fairness of the dynamic processes used to develop policy;
- changing or sustaining human behaviour in desired ways, in short, with implementing desired behaviour; and
- a series of decisions and nondecisions.

Thus the public policy system is a central part of the larger political system but the two are not fully coterminous. The larger political system is also concerned with issues such as preventing tyranny and ensuring orderly changes of leadership, holding elections, selecting and recruiting political participants of many kinds within political parties and interest groups, and inculcating and socializing citizens, voters, and leaders with views and ideas about Canada's problems and prospects. We focus on the public policy elements listed above throughout the book, both in the general analysis of public policy concepts in Part I, in the examination of executive policy structures and processes in Part II, and in the assessment of policy fields (social, economic, foreign, energy, etc.) in Part III. Each element requires a brief introductory presentation.

The normative content of political life is the central element of public policy. In Chapter 2 we stress the need to distinguish different levels of normative content, including general ideologies and dominant ideas, as well as more specific goals or objectives. We focus on how these ideologies, ideas and objectives change or are sustained over long periods of time. The ideologies include the historical and current Canadian interpretations of liberalism, conservatism and socialism. The dominant ideas include the enduring concern for efficiency, individual freedom, equity, stability, redistribution, national unity and identity and regional sensitivity. In addition, the normative content often includes major "paradigms" which influence particular policy fields and which affect the education of professional policy advisers. An obvious example of a paradigm is Keynesian economics but there are others as well which we examine in different policy fields. An understanding of ideas is also the essential ingredient to bring some order to the dozens of different policy fields or issue areas from agricultural to youth policy. One cannot possibly understand the details of all of these fields, but can appreciate the relatively short list of dominant ideas that are contained within each of them.

Public policy is the product of the need to structure and organize power and influence by political leaders and by other elected persons and appointed officials. The policy system consists of numerous structures which embody ideas. Headed by elected or appointed individuals who come and go, these structures have a stake in the policy process and in its results. These include governmental structures and private structures. Power and influence can be directed both to getting things done and to preventing things from happening. Public policy involves some degree of legitimate coercion of a majority over a minority, or vice versa, of one region's preferences over another, or of one class or group over another. The state (the sum of the legislature, executive, bureaucracy, courts, police and military authorities) is that unit of society to which is accorded the legitimate right to exercise coercive powers. We show in Chapter 2 that there are widely varying views about what the role of the state is and should be. It is held by some to be an omnipotent leviathan, and by others to be impotent or at least with only limited spheres of "autonomy." Coercion and perceptions of coercion, as Chapter 5 shows, are also contentious. Levels and degrees of coercion are not always easy to discover, study and quantify, but they are obviously essential elements in the formulation of public policy. It must also be stressed that because structures include both collective organizational forms and individuals, and because structures must interact legally and politically with each other, there are paradoxes that must be confronted in analyzing public policy.

It is a fact of Canadian democratic political life that policy *processes* are as much valued and are the object of as much dispute as are the substantive purposes and outcomes of policy. Moreover, to understand these dynamics one has to deal not only with the overall policy routine, as we do in Chapter 4, but with numerous subsidiary and interlocking dynamics. These can be expressed not only in terms of substantive policy content such as the *social* or *economic* policy process but also in terms of policy instruments—the *tax* process, the *expenditure* process or the *regulatory* process. In addition, one must appreciate the central importance of Parliamentary, federal-provincial, and foreign policy and interest group processes because each involves an idea about institutions that must be "consulted" or somehow involved in the policy process and whose often uncertain responses and counteractions must be anticipated but cannot necessarily be controlled. The policy processes are valued not only for what they produce but also because the processes must be legitimate in some general way or in specific ways. That is, they must operate in such a way that they produce authorative decisions that are accepted by Canadians as a whole and/or by those most affected by them. Processes inherently involve dynamics and uncertainty. Public policy makers cannot avoid the future and the inevitable uncertainties. They are endowed with an ordinary distribution of intelligence, foresight and attitudes towards risk, as well as capacity to integrate information, analysis and social pressure.

Ideas, structures and processes are linked to the fourth feature of public policy. Policy always involves the need to change or sustain human behaviour.[21] Those who advocate a policy change do so presumably because they wish to see a *desired* change in human behaviour occur and be *sustained over time* in a reliable, predictable way. Or, alternatively, they wish to see the status quo preserved. Because of this, the study and practice of policy formulation cannot avoid grappling with models of human behaviour, with beliefs about what makes human behaviour change, and hence with causality and its limits, the understanding of which is also central to social science. We show in Chapter 6 and elsewhere how these models and *beliefs about* causality are central to an understanding of how policy is studied, analyzed, formulated and implemented and to why policy often fails or is perceived to have failed.

The formulation and implementation of public policy also involve the need to describe and understand a series of decisions. This includes so-called nondecisions. Public policy and political life always involves a struggle between change and the status quo. The serial nature of policy making is such that policy is often "revealed" by a decision or decisions to do nothing or merely to express symbolic concern. It also means that a policy or policies must be examined over a long period of time to be understood properly, especially, as we stressed at the beginning of this chapter, to place the role of personalities and the alleged pragmatism of decisions in some perspective. We see in Chapter 6 and elsewhere that the term "policy" and "decision" is used interchangeably. We will undoubtedly succumb to this grammatical habit from time to time, but in general we prefer to use decision as a smaller unit of analysis. Several decisions may or may not add up to a policy.

It is customary to think of the public policy system as having an "input" side and an "output" side. The former involves the various institutions and interests (political parties, interest groups, ministers, bureaucrats) whose actions and views affect the "formulation" of public policy. The latter side takes us into the realm of the implementation of public policy and involves both the outputs and outcomes of policy.

Our focus is on the formulation of policy rather than on its detailed implementation. This emphasis is a product of both design and necessity. The focus is deliberate in that there is a need in the basic Canadian literature to link and integrate the broader aspects of the input side (ideologies, parties, interest groups) with the executive-bureaucratic aspects (Cabinet, central agencies, line departments) and with ideas and broad policy fields.[22] The focus is also a matter of necessity in that it is very difficult in practice, keeping in mind the length of the book, to deal with both policy formulation and detailed implementation. At the same time, however, the later implementation stages of the policy process clearly affect policy formulation in significant ways. We therefore deal indirectly with policy implementation in several ways, especially when we examine how policy is evaluated or, in short, how the political system "learns" about success and failure. We also deal with implementation when we examine the role that private behaviour and theories of how to change behaviour plays in policy formulation. In general, however, we focus on overall policy formulation rather than detailed implementation.

The Study and Practice of Public Policy

Anyone contemplating the study of public policy for the first time has a right to feel somewhat bewildered. In addition to being familiar with the environment of Canadian politics, the Canadian political system itself and the public policy system outlined above, it is also necessary to sort out the different perspectives on the study and practice of public policy supplied by academics, applied policy makers, advisors and analysts, and policy advocates.

The academic perspective of public policy can perhaps best be viewed as one which focuses on the attempt to *explain* the evolution of public policy or a particular policy field *over a significant period of time*. The search for such explanation is an elusive but necessary one. The overriding purpose of this book is academic in this sense. For example, the analysis in Part III of policy fields seeks to present a longitudinal look at policy since World War II. It seeks to examine public policy in general and in selected policy fields in the broadest sense possible by focusing on the evolution and persistence of dominant ideas and by showing how these often transcend, but at the same time are always represented and articulated by, structures and personalities. We examine causes but we show also how difficult it is usually to "prove" causality. This is not to suggest that academics are not also often applied analysts as well. Rather, we are at this stage merely distinguishing this broader academic perspective.

It is useful to contrast the academic perspective from the more applied perspective. A public policy decision maker, analyst or advisor, whether located in a government department, interest group or corporation, is usually more preoccupied with the applied task of deciding what to do or not to do or what to advise *at a particular point in time*. The policy analyst is severely constrained by role, position, power, information, time and resources and may or may not be aware of broader causal forces in the policy field concerned. The applied perspective puts a higher premium on techniques of analysis. Sometimes this may include so-called "hard" techniques such as cost-benefit analysis or even econometrics. More often, it includes softer "techniques," including talking and consulting with the right people. In Chapter 18 we portray the world of analysis as both an intellectual process and as a process of social interaction. To do justice to the study of public policy one must appreciate both of these perspectives—the academic and the applied— and relate one to the other. This requires a certain amount of intellectual schizophrenia. We try to show, however, the importance of viewing public policy through both of these perspectives.

In this regard it is important to note another feature of the link between theory and practice. One often thinks of the academic perspective as being "theoretical" and the decision makers' perspective as "applied." Often the former perspective is mistakenly equated with "abstract" thinking while the latter is supposedly concrete and practical. But policy "theory" and policy formulation and implementation are not the separate worlds that we are often led to believe they are. This is because both theory and practice are ultimately concerned with causality and its limits. The academic perspective wants to know if policy X is caused by factors, a, b and c. The policy advisor and practitioner want to achieve policy result X by changing behaviour a, b, and c. The academic and applied perspectives are not identical, but they are linked by their vital common concern with causality. Many practitioners would agree with the proposition that most public policies are hypotheses waiting to be tested. In this regard it can be said that if there is no policy "theory" there is likely to be no policy practice in the sense of achieving desired causal results. Several chapters show that many public policy makers and analysts lack both theory and knowledge in this important sense. Hence, they necessarily "muddle through," much like the rest of us, making small marginal changes that help them avoid making large errors.

A third important perspective is that of the policy advocate. A policy advocate could be a politician, a bureaucrat, an editorial writer, a union leader, or anyone advocating his or her preferred solution to a problem or preferred policy result. Such a person may be only partly interested in, or informed by, the analysis of public policy per se or of the intricate interdependencies among policy fields. The focus of the policy advocate, especially those for single issue advocates (for example, abortion or nuclear power), is on the normative condition to be rectified, changed, or re-established. In one sense all policy change starts with some kind of aggressive policy advocacy, sometimes informed by analysis, sometimes in opposition to "objective facts," and sometimes propelled by an affinity for both current facts and a preferred idea or future state.

Because of the main elements of public policy and the contending perspectives outlined above, it follows that within the academic setting public policy is not the preserve of any single academic discipline. The study of public policy is influenced by several academic fields, including public administration, political science, economics, management, sociology and law. This presents further problems for students since the primary literature is a minefield of both intra- and interdisciplinary quarrels and controversies, some important and substantive, but others trivial and frustrating for both the novice and the seasoned reader alike. Each academic discipline, however, makes important contributions to the study of public policy. The biases and value assumptions of political science, economics and public administration and of the mixed concoction that some call "political economy" (class analysis from the political left or public choice from the political right) will be more evident when we examine the formal models of policy and decision making in Chapter 6.

An appreciation of the disciplinary orientation is all the more necessary because many policy analysts in government and elsewhere are the products of these disciplines and of interdisciplinary graduate schools of public administration, public policy and business administration. There is admittedly a danger in stereotyping the core disciplines, but the increasing number of economists, lawyers and social scientists occupying these positions makes it a necessary task. Indeed, the emergence of a so-called policy analysis industry in the 1970s and 1980s is a major feature of the Canadian policy process. We show in Chapters 13 and 18 that the industry is reflected visibly in the emergence of such public and private policy advisory and research bodies as the Economic Council of Canada, the Science Council of Canada, the C.D. Howe Research Institute, the Institute for Research on Public Policy, the Conference Board of Canada, the Fraser Institute and the Canadian Institute for Economic Policy. We refer to the work of these bodies at some length since they cover a broad ideological spectrum of Canadian politics. The policy analysis industry is reflected also within government in the growth of formal policy and planning units or branches in line departments and central agencies.

The Approach

There have been many broad approaches or more or less precise models used in the academic study of public policy and politics in Canada and elsewhere.[23] Inevitably, they all seek to simplify reality. These include the four examined in some detail in Chapter 6: the rational model, incrementalism, public choice and class analysis. In addition, approaches such as systems theory, interest-group pluralism and elite theories have been utilized in Canada and elsewhere. Versions of these latter approaches have influenced our work in a limited sense. Thus, system theory can be usefully applied at a very general level, as we have in this chapter, in distinguishing the political system from the public policy system.[24] It is also evident in our periodic reference to comparative studies of public policy that quantitatively compare the policy outputs and inputs of different countries, provinces or states. Interest group pluralism is noted and largely rejected in our analysis of interest groups in Chapter 3, but the important influence of "interests" and interest groups is not. Elite theories provide insights into such phenomenon as "nondecisions" where governmental leaders and others choose not to act in order to sustain the status quo.[25]

In general, however, our approach, while paying a necessary and deserved debt to these other approaches (particularly because they embody basic ideas), is on the interplay of ideas, structures and processes as outlined earlier in this chapter. Such an approach captures more of the reality of public policy making than do these other approaches. We are not the first to suggest the need for such an approach but, in the Canadian context, we are the first to try to carry out this task in an integrated way across several policy fields and in an historical context. Moreover, we do so in a way which re-emphasizes the core ideas inherent in institutions and which does not assume that public administration, structure and bureaucracy, as many public policy critics of "public administration" have too easily suggested, is a mere sideshow. Structure and process are populated by ideas in action and do not represent the mere "to-ing and fro-ing" of bureaucrats. In one sense our approach may be viewed by some as a defence of institutionalism, but not the narrower institutionalism referred to earlier in this chapter. This is because it recognizes that the direction of causality and explanation operates both ways, from society and economy to government and vice versa. Policies are neither the product of a powerless state automatically responding to powerful external, including capitalist, forces nor is it the behemoth that makes society and economy march to its drum beat. There is ample evidence, as several chapters show, that constant interaction and influence of a two-way kind occurs. We reserve until Chapter 19 other aspects of our defence of the approach used in this book, an approach that has several advantages over other books published to date in the field of Canadian public policy, including our own earlier work.

First, by focusing on the interplay between ideas, structures and processes one is forced to deal more rigourously with the historical continuity, persistence and drift of public policy over recent decades. In several chapters we view priority setting and individual policy fields in this way. One therefore sees public policy as constituting both choice *and* governing relationships more clearly. Within the context of political science, the book also allows the reader to see how different parts of the public policy system in Ottawa interact and relate to the broader political system.

Second, we examine policies in several different fields, both social and economic and foreign and domestic. It is obvious that there are dozens of different policy fields, from agriculture to fisheries, and from policies on the status of women to policies for youth and the aged, to name only a few. People have different interests in different policy fields. For example, we include individual chapters on industrial, energy and labour market policy. Does this mean the student of competition policy or environmental policy or medicare should not use the book? We believe our approach offers one way of coming to grips with these and other policy fields as well. It does so first by requiring the reader to look at policy in relation to the existence in Canadian political life of a small number of dominant ideas. These ideas as enumerated briefly above are present in virtually all policy fields, especially when one seriously searches beyond the rhetoric that often accompanies policy debate and analysis. Because of this focus on ideas our approach requires the reader to look for the social, economic and foreign policy content of *all* policy fields. We also discuss several other particular policy fields in illustrative ways and suggest from time to time how our approach could be used in specific policy fields which we do not examine. Appendix A provides further bibliographical guidance.

Third, the approach used provides a closer look at actual resource allocation, not only within the economic and social policy fields, but also in relation to the role of governing instruments such as taxation, spending, regulation, public enterprise and symbolic acts or exhortation, as well as an understanding of the role of knowledge and analysis. We have not, however, used our approach in an intellectual vacuum. We critically review other approaches but also use them to illuminate all three dimensions of our approach—ideas, structures and processes.

Fourth, the book explicitly links process to uncertainty and thus begins to deal with a yawning and obvious gap, one which is scarcely ever acknowledged by Canadian political science critics of public policy literature. Economists have had a healthier realism about the role of uncertainty though it has been usually expressed in a narrow context. Uncertainty is created not only by the limits of knowledge, analysis and the lack of causality, but by the difficult political calculus of anticipating how other interests and realms of private behaviour will actually react to policy initiatives.

Finally, we believe our approach provides a useful antidote for those who see all or most policies in terms of personalities and individuals and as remorseless pragmatism. Not surprisingly, journalists and even senior bureaucrats and businessmen often ascribe much to the personality or leadership variable. Even economists who advocate a public choice approach attempt to reduce the behaviour of whole organizations to the self-interested dictates of their leaders. We do not wish to argue that individual leaders and their power do not matter. Quite the contrary. Leaders and ideas are inextricably linked. But a focus on ideas, structures and processes viewed in a historical time period requires us to confront the existence and persistence of ideas and policies which sometimes do not change or which drift along slowly despite many changes of leadership. Our approach also requires the reader to deal with organizational structures, whose behaviour and role cannot be reduced to, or summed up by, their leaders only.

Organization
The book is organized into four parts. Part I introduces the basic public policy concepts. These are, first, an appreciation of the normative

content of policy, ideologies and ideas, including those that lie at the core of political institutions; second, an understanding of interests and interest groups; third, an outline of the general routine of policy formulation; and fourth, knowledge of the role of the basic instruments of governing (exhortation, expenditure, regulation, taxation and public enterprise). The first part concludes with a critical review of other formal approaches for studying and analyzing public policy, each of which simplifies reality but nonetheless contributes some insights into how and why public policy in Canada is made.

Part II describes and critically examines the structures and processes of the executive core of the public policy system. It examines the major executive actors and structures such as the prime minister, the Cabinet and the central agencies, including the leadership styles and policy preferences of several recent Canadian prime ministers. This is followed by a critical review of the role of departments, agencies and senior bureaucrats. Chapter 10 presents an empirical look at priorities and priority setting over the past two decades. The next three chapters explore resource allocation in three ways or contexts: the overall resource allocation process; allocation problems generated by the dynamics of expenditure, taxation, regulation, public enterprise and exhortation; and, finally, allocation problems reflected through the use of information, knowledge and analysis.

The third part of the book examines selected policy fields. This is done first through a review of the elusive problems of defining and categorizing the umbrella policy fields, economic versus social, and foreign versus domestic. The review encompasses both a historical and contemporary time period and is linked to the analysis of dominant ideas in Part I and to executive structures and processes in Part II. Individual chapters are then devoted to industrial policy, energy policy and labour market policy. These fields are examined in an illustrative way to show their evolving economic-social and foreign-domestic policy content in both a contemporary and historical time frame.

The final part of the book brings the policy process full circle. It examines the enumerable ways in which policies are "evaluated" by institutions and actors both within, and external to, government. By evaluation, the book does not refer just to narrow efforts to secure program evaluation. Rather, evaluation is treated in its broadest sense as feedback and "learning," as Canadians attempt to judge the elusive successes and failures of the policies made on their behalf. Thus, we examine evaluations that occur through Parliamentary debate, media coverage, advisory councils, private policy institutions, the criticism of other governments, as well as central agencies and the Auditor General of Canada. Such evaluation brings us invariably back to the political contest over several recurring dominant ideas and to concerns about structure and process as well. Finally, in Chapter 19 we offer several concluding observations both about Canadian public policy and about our approach in studying it.

NOTES

1. See R. Van Loon and M. Whittington, *The Canadian Political System*, Third Edition (Toronto: McGraw-Hill Ryerson, 1981), Chapters 1 to 13.
2. T.A. Hockin, *Government in Canada* (Toronto: McGraw-Hill Ryerson, 1976) and R.M. Dawson, *The Government of Canada*, revised by N. Ward (Toronto: University of Toronto Press, 1970). See also Reg Whitaker, "Images of the State in Canada" in Leo Panitch, ed., *The Canadian State* (Toronto: University of Toronto Press, 1977), Chapter 2.
3. See Leon Dion, *Quebec: the Unfinished Revolution* (Montreal: McGill-Queen's University Press, 1976); Hubert Guindon, "The Modernization of Quebec and the Legitimacy of the Canadian State," *Canadian Review of Sociology and Anthropology*, Vol. 15, no. 2, 1978, pp. 227-245; Ramsay Cook, *Canada and the French Canadian Question* (Toronto: Macmillan of Canada, 1976); and Denis Moniere, *Ideologies in Quebec* (Toronto: University of Toronto Press, 1981).
4. See Donald Creighton, *Harold Adams Innis: Portrait of a Scholar* (Toronto: University of Toronto Press, 1978) and Harold Innis, *Essays in Canadian Economic History* (Toronto: University of Toronto Press, 1956).
5. See Herschel Hardin, *A Nation Unaware: The Canadian Economic Culture* (Vancouver: J.J. Douglas, 1974); W.L. Morton, *The Canadian Identity*, Second Edition (Toronto: University of Toronto Press, 1972); and H.G. Aitken "Defensive Expansionism: The State and Economic Growth in Canada," in W.T. Easterbrook and M.H. Watkins, eds., *Approaches to Canadian Economic History* (Toronto: McClelland and Stewart, 1967).
6. See Leo Panitch, *op. cit.*
7. John Porter, *The Vertical Mosaic* (Toronto: University of Toronto Press, 1965), Chapter 12.

8. See Robert Bothwell, Ian Drummond and John English, *Canada Since 1945: Power, Politics and Provincialism* (Toronto: University of Toronto Press, 1981), Chapter 5; and J. Fayerweather, *Foreign Investment in Canada* (Toronto: Oxford University Press, 1973).

9. See Gad Horowitz, *Canadian Labour in Politics* (Toronto: University of Toronto Press, 1968); John Anderson and Morley Gunderson, eds., *Union Management Relations in Canada* (Toronto: Addison-Wesley, 1982) and G. Swimmer and M. Thompson, eds., *Public Sector Industrial Relations in Canada* (Montreal: Institute for Research on Public Policy, 1983).

10. See D.V. Smiley, *Canada in Question,* Third Edition (Toronto: McGraw-Hill Ryerson, 1980), Chapter 1.

11. See Smiley, *op. cit.,* and Garth Stevenson, *Unfulfilled Union* (Toronto: Macmillan of Canada, 1979).

12. See Van Loon and Whittington, *op. cit.,* Chapter 19; Robert J. Jackson and M. Atkinson, *The Canadian Legislative System,* Second Edition (Toronto: Macmillan of Canada, 1980); and T. d'Aquino, G. Bruce Doern and C. Blair, *Parliamentary Government in Canada: A Critical Assessment and Suggestions for Change* (Ottawa: Intercounsel Ltd., 1979).

13. Van Loon and Whittington, *op. cit.,* Chapter 19.

14. G. Bruce Doern and Peter Aucoin, ed., *Public Policy in Canada* (Toronto: Macmillan of Canada, 1979) and T. Hockin, ed., *Apex of Power,* Second Edition (Toronto: Prentice-Hall, 1980).

15. A. Paul Pross, *Pressure Group Behavior in Canadian Politics* (Toronto: McGraw-Hill Ryerson, 1975).

16. See, for example, H. Thorburn, ed., *Party Politics in Canada,* 4th Edition (Toronto: Prentice-Hall, 1979). For a broader view see M.J. Brodie and Jane Jenson, *Crisis, Challenge and Change: Party and Class in Canada* (Toronto: Methuen, 1980) and Conrad Winn and J. McMenemy, *Political Parties in Canada* (Toronto: McGraw-Hill Ryerson, 1976).

17. Douglas Hartle, *Public Policy Decision Making and Regulation* (Montreal: Institute for Research on Public Policy, 1979).

18. Brodie and Jenson, *op. cit.,* Chapter 1.

19. See Edwin R. Black, *Politics and the News* (Toronto: Butterworths, 1982); and Hartle, *op. cit.,* Chapters 3 and 4.

20. W.I. Jenkins, *Policy Analysis* (London: Martin Robertson, 1978), p. 15. For other views see Y. Dror, *Public Policy Making Reexamined* (San Francisco: Chandler, 1968); Ellen F. Paul and Phillip A. Russo Jr., *Public Policy: Issues, Analysis and Ideology* (Chatham, N.J.: Chatham House, 1982); and Ira Sharkansky, *Public Administration: Policy Making in Government Agencies* (Chicago: Markham, 1972).

21. See Aaron Wildavski, *Speaking Truth to Power: The Art and Craft of Policy Analysis* (Boston: Little Brown, 1979) and Charles E. Lindblom, *Politics and Markets* (New York: Basic Books, 1977).

22. See Richard Simeon, "Studying Public Policy," *Canadian Journal of Political Science.* Vol. 9 (December 1976), pp. 547-580.

23. For general reviews, see Simeon, *op. cit.;* Jenkins, *op. cit.;* Peter Aucoin, "Public Policy Theory and Analysis" in G. Bruce Doern and Peter Aucoin, eds., *Public Policy in Canada, op. cit.,* Chapter 1; V. Seymour Wilson, *Canadian Public Policy: Theory and Environment* (Toronto: McGraw-Hill Ryerson, 1981), Chapter 6; Leo Panitch, *op. cit.,* Chapter 1; and Thomas Dye, *Understanding Public Policy,* Fourth Edition (New York: Prentice-Hall, 1982), Chapter 1.

PART I

PUBLIC POLICY CONCEPTS

- Normative Content: Ideas and Institutions

- Interests, Interest Groups and Consultation

- The General Policy Formulation Routine: The Problems of Doing First Things First

- Governing Instruments

- Models and Approaches: Simplifying Reality

CHAPTER 2

THE NORMATIVE CONTENT OF PUBLIC POLICY: IDEAS AND INSTITUTIONS

To study Canadian public policy is to inquire into the purposeful nature of democratic political activity or, in other words, its normative content. We are first required to develop an appreciation of the major contending ideologies and dominant ideas which exist in Canadian political life including those which reside as the core ideas of the main institutions of the Canadian political system. These ideas both influence and are embedded in the structures and processes of public policy. The student of public policy must grapple therefore with both the "ends" and "means" of political life, recognizing, however, that there is no tidy basis on which to separate ends and means since both are valued, hold normative content and are themselves the object of political dispute. This reality is also evident in Chapter 5 when we show the ideas involved in the choice of governing instruments, that is, the decision to exhort, to tax, to spend or to regulate.

The central tenet of democratic politics, especially in a Cabinet-Parliamentary system, is that political parties offer a program of policies to the electorate and that the victor at the polls, expressed in Parliamentary seats, possesses a majoritarian mandate to carry out its policies. The assumption is that democratic life is purposeful and that public policy and policy structures and processes are first and foremost normative, a peaceful contest over contending ideas, preferences and objectives. The assumption is that political power or the gaining of political office is a means to carry out policies, not that policies are a means to gain office.

In this chapter we examine the normative content in two ways. In the first part we examine the normative basis of public policy in a general way by differentiating ideologies from other dominant ideas and from narrower objectives. In the second part we build on the brief review of institutions begun in Chapter 1 by focusing on several ways in which the core ideas of major institutions directly affect policy formulation.

Ideologies, Ideas and Objectives

In examining any public policy field or public policy in general it is essential to look for and attempt to differentiate different levels of normative content, ideologies, dominant ideas and objectives. This three-level typology begins at the most general level with ideologies and ends with more specific objectives. It is evident that the boundaries between the levels can be only approximate. Each level of normative content will be discussed in turn. The purpose of the review is to show why each is important to look for when analyzing any policy field. Our overall view is that to understand the formulation of public policy, one must first look at the evolution or drift of a policy field over a long period of time. What are the central ideas in the policy field in question? Where do they conflict and how have these ideas changed, if at all? In respect of all policy fields, how and why do some ideas and proposals gain acceptance and stay on the public priority list of governments while others do not get there at all, or emerge only for a brief period of time?

Ideologies

Ideologies encompass the broadest level of normative public policy content. An ideology is an umbrella of belief and action that helps provide political and social identity to its adherents and that serves to integrate and coordinate their views and actions on a wide range of political issues. Given the inherent breadth and nature of ideologies and their role in determining views about the role of the state, it should not be surprising that they evoke contentious debate about power and control in society. Critics on the political left, for example, often regard liberal ideology as an instrument of class control designed to mystify and distort reality. The political right often regards socialism in a similar vein.[1] We equate ideologies with the broad "isms" of Canadian political life: liberalism, conservatism and socialism. We reserve our discussion of nationalism to later parts of the chapter where we treat it as a dominant territorial and spatial idea which cuts across all the left-right political ideologies in the same way that regionalism does. There are, of course, many subtleties, nuances and contradictions in these ideologies, many of which were reflected in the review in Chapter 1 of Canada's political environment and of the main institutions of the Canadian political system. Other nuances will be more evident in later chapters, particularly when ideologies are related to policy fields such as economic and social policies or to issues such as tax and regulatory reform.

Liberalism encompasses a belief in the central role of the individual in a free society. Rooted in a defence of private property and a free market capitalist economy, twentieth century liberalism has also sought to smooth over the rough edges of capitalism through moderate amounts of government intervention, including measures to ensure the sharing and redistribution of wealth to the disadvantaged. In addition, liberalism encompasses a belief in scientific and technological progress. In relation to the role of the state liberalism has often implied that the state plays a benevolent reformist referee-like role, balancing the ideas and power of contending interests in an even-handed way.

Conservatism, as the name implies, encompasses a belief in the need to preserve valued and proven traditions and hence places the burden of proof on those who advocate change. Despite a strong contemporary belief in the market (which is, in reality, a nineteenth century liberal view) and an adherence to minimum government intervention, progressive conservatism also suggests a belief in an organic paternal view of society, of the need for the state and the community to care for those who cannot care for themselves.

Socialism rests on a class analysis of society and posits a collective view of society and a de-emphasis of individualism. It favours much more government intervention, particularly to achieve a significant amount of redistribution of both wealth and power to disadvantaged classes and groups. Accordingly, it sees less to defend in the status quo and is more disposed to see rapid change. While seeing the need for a socialist state that will redistribute income, the socialist view is ambivalent about centralized power. Power must be concentrated to achieve redistribution in a capitalist society, but at the same time there is a fear among social democrats about the possible bureaucratization of that power.

A capsule summary of the ideologies obviously does not capture all of the beliefs, partial contradictions and nuances present in them. Moreover, as reflected over time in the positions of Canadian political parties, there has been a cumulative adoption or at least acceptance of major parts of one ideology by another. For example, the New Democratic party supported an entrenched Charter of Rights in the Canadian constitution. The Liberals' dominance in power at the federal level has been partly the product of their willingness to borrow and use as their own items ostensibly more at home in a competing ideology (for example, compulsory medical care).

Equally evident has been the presence of ideological mixtures *within* each of the major political parties. The nomenclature is both familiar and seemingly endless. The mixtures include red-Tories, right-wing Socialists, social democrats, left-wing Liberals, the "radical centre," prairie populists, etc.[2] These mixtures are even more difficult to interpret when they are combined with, or opposed by, regional variations within a political party and in the country as a whole. Prairie populism, for example, combined both a regional grievance and an agrarian class-based criticism of Eastern capitalism.[3] It has arisen both in the form of so-called third parties such as the Progressives, the Social Credit party and the Western Canada Concept and as a movement within the Progressive Conservative party.

It has often been argued that the crazy quilt ideological mixtures of Canada's political parties, coupled with regionalism and the technological complexity of modern decisions, has brought with it the end of ideology. It is even argued that "middle of the road" liberalism is nonideological and pragmatic. The "ideologues," it is often suggested, are only on the extreme left or right of the political spectrum. Both of these strands of the "end of ideology" argument are highly questionable and involve the same dangers that we stressed in the opening paragraph of this book regarding personalities and pragmatism.

Ideologies remain an important element of political life not because ideologies "cause" or automatically lead to policy preferences and action by governments in power, but because ideologies can help foreclose certain policy options or reduce levels of commitment to particular courses of action and to particular ideas. They can help screen out ideas which are unacceptable or which will only be used as a last resort. Canada's political parties do coalesce roughly around different portions of the ideological spectrum.[4] Because of this they frequently advocate different policies, and they judge the policies of others according to different criteria. The presence of these ideologies in varying minority or majority concentrations *within* the major political parties is also of critical importance since, as beliefs, they represent a normative test against which policies to act, or not act, are "evaluated." They also affect party leadership strategies and coalitions both within and among parties since leaders must often appeal to or react to the presence of these basic ideologies both among their own supporters and among voters or interests whose support they would like to attract.

Perhaps the worst aspect of the view that ideologies no longer matter is that it quickly leads to the bland and blanket assertion that policies are made on pragmatic grounds. Pragmatism implies an idea-less political world. Nothing could be further from the truth nor do more to dull one's analytical senses.

Dominant Ideas

We refer to the second level of normative content as dominant ideas. While obviously related to the larger ideologies, these ideas often have a separate normative force of their own in that, rather than being always grouped or combined into a larger ideological view, the ideas may be combined or used to embody a particular normative preference in a particular policy field. Several ideas of this magnitude exist. These include:

- efficiency
- individual liberty
- stability (of income and of other desired conditions)
- redistribution and equality
- equity
- national identity, unity and integration, and
- regional diversity and sensitivity

We comment below on each of these ideas. Their importance arises out of the fact that any one or all of them can be part of the normative agenda of a particular policy field regardless of how they are defined by governments or even in the statutes that create them. They are one of the main ways in which one can provide some common ground among diverse policy fields from tariff policy to police and corrections policy. Later, in several chapters we relate these ideas to the evolution of social, economic and foreign policy (Chapter 14), to formal policy models (Chapter 6), and to the problems of priority setting (Chapter 10) and resource allocation (Chapters 11 and 12).

Efficiency is an enduring market-based idea which places a high value on the realization of a goal at the least cost, with costs measured both absolutely and in terms of opportunity costs (alternatives fore-gone).[5] It is an idea rooted in the very notion of a free market where capitalists maximize wealth by mobilizing the factors of production. capital, land, knowledge and labour to produce optimum returns. It is an idea that places a premium on change, particularly for those whose lives are "mobilized" to produce the desired goal.

Efficiency is also linked to the idea of individual liberty, though the latter is rooted in more than just economic freedom and embraces religious and other freedoms as well.[6] Individualism implies a belief in the social value of self-interest and self-development. An entrenched Charter of Rights suggests in formal terms a belief that the purpose of the state is to serve the individual and not vice versa. While efficiency and individualism are important ideas, we have stressed in Chapter 1 that Canadians have not embraced them as enthusiastically as have Americans.

Stability of income (and of other desired conditions) over time is an idea which places a high value on predictability and reliability, the opposite of change. As an idea it takes many forms. It can take the form of a general appeal for order and continuity in social relations such as in the call for law and order, energy security, strong defence forces or the right to live and work in one's home region, near family and friends. It can show up in demands to protect income, as many agricultural commodity producers have requested, to smooth out the uncertainties of income caused by the vagaries of climate and foreign markets. It is an essential idea in Keynesian economics.[7] As we see in Chapters 10 and 14, the Keynesian view advocated the need for stabilization policies to even out the uncertainties of the business cycle.

Redistribution and equality is an idea that places the highest preference on the need to redistribute income and power from the rich and powerful to the poor and politically weak. It may imply a concept of absolute equality and a sharing of property, but at the very least it endorses the need for a significant reduction in the gap between rich and poor. One may be tempted to think that this is what social policy should be about. We see in Chapters 12, 14 and 18 that social policy embraces far more than the idea of redistribution and equality.[8]

The concept of equity reinforced by ideas about the rule of law and equality before the law simultaneously enjoins policy makers to:

- treat people in equivalent situations equally, *and* to
- treat people who are not in equivalent situations unequally (that is, be fair and reasonable).

Equity, in a broad sense, forms a consistent philosophical and democratic concept. In practice, however, its component injunctions often conflict.

When formulating policy, decision makers frequently have to "treat people equally" and "treat people unequally" within the framework of the same policy or program. This is because the practical physical situations of the object of the policy (a business, a person, a province or a region) are rarely uniform or homogenous. These ideas are present in devising environmental, drug, and health and safety policies and regulations; developing and implementing welfare policies; devising tax policies; and allocating industrial subsidies and grants.[9] We show how, in several policy fields, this delicate balancing act is a continuing necessity.

National unity and nationalism is an idea which flows from the territorial imperatives of politics, including foreign policy needs, sovereignty and international relations. It places the highest value on decisions that enhance the identity of individuals and groups within Canada as a whole, its traditions, symbols, institutions and collective memory. Nationalism may also be the dominant concern of territorially concentrated religious, cultural and linguistic minorities such as French Canadians in the Province of Quebec and therefore easily embraces the possibility or the threat of separatism.[10] Many, of course, would place nationalism alongside the ideologies discussed above. National unity as an idea is thus linked to national independence and hence to foreign policy, but it may also be based on policies against domestic threats such as provincial governments or other narrower intepretations of the collective political will.[11]

The converse of national unity is the idea of regional diversity and sensitivity. It is an idea rooted in a spatial or territorial view of policy whether the region is defined as a province, the North or the Gaspé. The idea of regionalism pervades Canadian politics and affects the very definition, as well as the administrative delivery, of many public policies.[12]

One could think of the foregoing ideas in many ways. For example, one could visualize them separately corresponding to single voters, each with one of these idea preferences. Alternatively, one could imagine a government comprising separate departments headed by ministers in charge of these ideas (a Minister of Efficiency, a Minister of Redistribution, etc.). Or one could envision separate political parties formed to appeal to voters who have each of these preferences.

One could go on to construct an even more complex and realistic model of the public policy system. The points we wish to stress would be the same. To understand public policy one has to appreciate the enduring existence of several dominant ideas. These ideas influence political debate and the "evaluation" of public policy *regardless* of the particular preferences stated in the legislation or the ministerial speech accompanying the particular policy or decision. These ideas are each desirable. They also often totally or partially contradict each other (efficiency versus regional sensitivity or redistribution versus stability of income). We see this in practical terms in our later review of economic, social and foreign policies and in more particular policy fields such as industrial, energy and labour market policies as well.

The constant need to rank, balance or otherwise deal with the relations and contradictions among dominant ideas is a central aspect of public policy. It is indeed the feature which puts the "politics" in public policy. Politics is the "authoritative allocation of values"[13] or, as we have expressed it here, of "dominant ideas." The public policy system must not only continuously rank them but actually allocate scarce resources among them in a manner which gives meaning to these ideas.

Ideas and Paradigms

In addition to the ideas surveyed above, the student of public policy should be aware of the existence of another type of policy idea. Manzer has referred to these as paradigms.[14] Policy paradigms are also a type of dominant idea but can be distinguished from those discussed above, at least in part, because they tend to be somewhat more associated with a particular policy field. In some policy fields there may be one obvious dominant paradigm while in others the field may be occupied by a dominant and a contending paradigm.

A well-developed paradigm provides a series of principles or assumptions which guide action and suggest solutions within a given policy field. Paradigms can become entrenched and thus change very slowly because they become tied to the education and socialization of professionals or experts and perhaps of the larger public as well. Thus, Keynesian economics, even though it has not been practised with any consistency, nonetheless was the dominant paradigm for macroeconomic policy makers from the 1940s to the early 1970s.[15] Since then Monetarism has emerged, not to replace it, but certainly to challenge it.[16] Similarly, health care policy is said to be dominated by a "curative" approach (helping those who are already sick) and is doctor-dominated.

Some advocate a more "preventative" approach which would prevent illness before it occurs.[17] Since this would relate to broader lifestyles and environmental concerns, it would be less doctor-oriented.

Somewhat like the broader ideologies, policy paradigms often screen out policy options. They may help to explain why some policies do not change or change very slowly. They also alert us to the role of professional experts who have power partly because they are the successful purveyors of the dominant paradigm. Within the confines of a policy field the student of policy formulation should look for, and be aware of, the existence of such paradigms. For example, in Chapters 11 and 16 we show that industrial policy formulation has always been influenced by contending paradigms, albeit not all as congealed or well-formulated as the Keynesian macroeconomic policy paradigm was. Thus, industrial policy has been influenced by concerns about a "resources first" or "resource sell-out" approach as opposed to an approach that focused on manufacturing and industry. In the field of labour market policies, "manpower" needs can be and have been viewed through either an "education" paradigm or a "training" paradigm. These paradigms partly conform to and reflect the exigencies of federal-provincial jurisdiction, but they also embody different combinations of ideas.

It will be obvious that by defining a policy paradigm primarily in terms of it being confined to a single policy field we are being somewhat arbitrary, especially because the boundaries between policy fields are themselves not watertight. Paradigms can also be linked to ideologies and to the dominant ideas discussed above. For example, Keynesianism is viewed by many to be a policy prescription necessary to justify state intervention to help maintain a capitalist market economy, as well as to stabilize economic activity.

Specific Objectives

The third level of normative content is, in a sense, a residual category but not an unimportant one. We refer to it simply as "specific objectives." It includes the more specific purposes that may be debated or be in dispute within a policy field. The periodic enunciation of objectives also reflects the existence of specific structures and organizations in the public policy system. Thus, economic policy may be concerned with holding inflation to a particular rate of increase, or achieving a specific decrease in the level of unemployment. In energy policy the specific objectives may be over how much conversion from oil to gas or electricity is desirable and possible in different regions of the country.

We have set out the above three levels of normative content precisely to disabuse the reader of the simplistic assumption that one can understand public policy and can even later evaluate policies if one can only find out what the "objectives" are.[18] We suggest that the study of public policy must begin with an appreciation of the broader levels of normative content and the purposeful nature of democratic political life. It does not begin with a search for "objectives" only. The three levels we have identified in this section should be the first three items in one's mental checklist as one carries out the task of studying public policy formulation.

Institutions and Ideas

Public policy both shapes and is influenced by institutions and the ideas which give these institutions life. Because of this central fact, our three-level typology is not in itself a sufficient inventory of ideas. A focus on the connection between ideas and institutions deserves emphasis because there has been a tendency to discard the role of institutions and to regard them as rather archaic. Indeed, in the so-called behavioural revolution that inflicted the social sciences in the past two decades, institutions were often viewed to be nonbehavioural, unempirical and seemingly unreal. We have stressed in Chapter 1, however, how institutions such as federalism, Cabinet-Parliamentary government, interest groups and the mass media are forged on core ideas. Table 2.1 shows the need, in fact, to have two checklists or columns of ideas—the dominant ideas we have already discussed and the institutional ideas surveyed in Chapter 1 and which we are about to discuss in a somewhat more detailed way in this chapter and in Chapters 3 and 7.

All institutions, moreover, are "interests" capable of exercising influence and power. They develop and articulate a normative rhetoric that is used in public debate to defend their most central ideas. The rhetoric is both real and mythical at the same time. For example, for the media the rhetoric includes a defence of freedom of press and the sanctity of one's sources of information; conversely, for business capitalists it is free enterprise and a ritualistic opposition to government intervention even though intervention may be actively sought by individual business

TABLE 2.1
A CAPSULE VIEW OF PERSISTENT AND RECURRING
PUBLIC POLICY IDEAS

Dominant Ideas	*Ideas Central to Key Political Institutions*
• efficiency • individual liberty • stability (of income and other conditions) • redistribution and equality • equity • national identity, unity and integration • regional diversity and sensitivity	• centralization and decentralization • "one man—one vote" and majoritarian government • responsible and accountable Cabinet-Parliamentary government • individual and collective ministerial responsibility • the policy-administration dichotomy and political control of bureaucrats by elected officials • freedom of a responsible press and media • freedom of association and the right to be consulted

interests. We need, however, to take these ideas one step beyond our treatment of them in Chapter 1.

This section therefore highlights selected *policy formulation* implications of the ideas which emanate from the major institutions introduced in Chapter 1. We exclude here only the role of interest groups in policy making which is examined in Chapter 3 and the Cabinet and bureaucracy which is the subject of Chapters 8, 10, 11 and 12. Our treatment of the major institutions is brief and is intended only to highlight some selected attributes of each institutional idea that are particularly important in understanding policy formulation. We stress again that we are interested not just in each institution and its core ideas in isolation, but in relation to other institutions. The reader should consult the other sources cited for a more detailed analysis of these institutions, particularly to appreciate their other nonpolicy formulation roles and attributes.

We summarily highlight only selected attributes of each institution that have a particularly important connection to policy formulation. We refer again to many of these attributes in later chapters. Our larger purpose, however, is to develop in the reader an appreciation of the on-going importance of institutions in policy formulation and their inextricable link to ideas, structures and processes.

Capitalism

Two attributes of capitalism as an idea and as a system of economic production are especially important in relation to policy formulation. The first is the influence capitalism has in blurring and de-emphasizing the issue of redistribution and inequality in Canadian political life and public debate. The second attribute is the selective views held by business interests about what constitutes government intervention.

It is argued by many that business interests have succeeded in having Canadian political issues viewed through the dominant idea of regional conflict and national integration, and/or French-English relations. Thus, redistribution as a dominant political idea has had to take a secondary role in the definition and evolution of economic and social policy. A number of writers since the mid-1960s in particular have pointed out the capacity of capitalist interests to "distort" political debate in this way. They argue that business interests have succeeded by securing the support of both the major political parties through financing elections and leadership expenses and also through media ownership.[19] John Porter bemoaned the dominance of "brokerage" politics, the name he gave to regional politics and piecemeal accommodation.[20] Brody and Jensen stress the historical capacity of the major parties to define what is political and to exclude a class interpretation of policy issues.[21]

We have already stressed above that redistribution is one of a handful of dominant ideas that pervade Canadian political debate. The question is whether the blurring of redistributive issues is a "distortion" of how Canada's politics does and *should* occur. There is clearly no "technical" answer to this question. Answers are rooted in the ideas various segments of the political system have and how they use them to interpret evidence or history. Defenders of liberal capitalism avowedly place a higher value on individual freedom and on efficiency than they do on equality, especially equality as expressed in income levels. The approach used in this book suggests that several dominant ideas do govern political life in Canada. Accordingly, it is evident that capitalism helps explain why redistribution is only one of these dominant concerns. We are by definition less inclined to argue that this distorts political life, since it is clear that the other dominant ideas have real as opposed to "distorted" roots in Canada's political history and political institutions.[22]

A second attribute of capitalism and its core ideas is the issue of government intervention. We discuss this issue in Chapters 5 and 12 when we review the growth of government and the role of governing instruments. It is important to stress at the outset, however, the degree of selectivity that exists when the business community engages in political debate as opposed to actual political behaviour. Therefore, the general "ideology" of business is to oppose intervention and to urge that the free market be allowed to flourish. There can be little doubt that this is a genuine article of belief for the business community in general. This does not prevent particular segments of business, because of their particular stake in the competitive struggle at particular points in time, from wanting to secure favours or protection from the state to stabilize or augment their incomes. When capital is mobilized, some segments of capital often lose and seek protection. Businesses covet stability of income over time as much as anyone else. If governments respond favourably, these actions will rarely be called "interventions" by business interests or by the individual business corporations involved. Rather, they will be referred to as "incentives" or, even more generally, as actions which will create a stable "climate for investment."

The business community rarely wants untrammelled free enterprise. It prefers a controlled form of entrepreneurial climate—in short, the provision of a high degree of certainty by the state so that "risks" can be taken. The relations between business and government are thus at one and the same time both simple and complex, monolithic and heterogenous, consistent and contradictory. They flow from the contradictory relations between capitalism, its modern business interest groups and liberal democracy.

Capitalism also raises important issues about the labour movement and trade unions and about how they are visualized in the policy process. The majority of workers in Canada are not members of unions. In Chapter 3 we focus on labour unions, including their major federation, the Canadian Labour Congress, seemingly as if they were an ordinary interest group. Is labour then a class? The class analysis approach and a socialist view of politics would invite such a conclusion. But how then does one deal with divisions within the labour movement, with the CLC's own ambivalence about government intervention and with the fact that most union members do not vote for the New Democratic party? Can all or most of the evident lack of class cohesion be due to "distortion" propagated by liberal capitalist ideologies? These are questions to which we also return, especially in Chapters 3 and 6.[23]

Federalism

Federalism institutionalizes the idea of regional diversity within the confines of a larger political union. Federal-provincial relations have evolved through several phases, the most recent of which have combined elements of executive and "province building" federalism.[24] Executive federalism is characterized by the bargaining of ministers and officials behind closed doors in numerous conferences of the eleven governments. There can be little doubt that post-World War II federalism of the bureaucratic executive kind is different than federalism of earlier eras when governments functioned somewhat more independently and less interdependently. Federal-provincial relations are a dominant element of Ottawa's policy process both because of the interdependent effect of each level of government's decisions and because of the competition, partisan and otherwise, for citizen loyalty and the acquisition of political credit.

"Province building" refers to the pronounced expansionist tendencies by major provincial governments since the mid-1960s to construct an elaborate state apparatus, including sophisticated bureaucracies, state enterprises and legislative controls to protect and manage regional and provincial economies and to guard themselves against Ottawa's incursions. The data on the growth of government presented in Chapter 5 show this expansionist activity. Despite the "province building" realities, however, there has been a tendency in the general model of executive federalism to characterize the intergovernmental policy process as a general diplomacy and/or bargaining process between the federal government and "the provinces." The more one relates province building to what is now known about particular policy fields, the less useful is the general bargaining notion of executive federalism. This is not to suggest that general bargaining aspects (such as the funding of established social programs) are not crucial in understanding public policy. Rather, we are suggesting that this view does not adequately allow us to understand either the *bilateral* (for example, Alberta-federal or Quebec-Ottawa) and multilateral (for example, federal-maritime provinces) bargains that are struck or the particular effects of federal policies on particular provincial settings.

In one sense, of course, this is merely the equivalent phenomena at the intergovernmental level to that stressed above regarding equity and equality. There we discussed the enduring political importance of the idea of "treating people equally" and "treating people fairly." The provinces have to be treated equally, and yet everyone knows that each is different and that policy circumstances are different in different policy fields. But the need for bilateral bargaining and sometimes stalemating activity arises from more than just the dichotomy inherent in the idea of justice and equity. It is also a product of the different economies, market dependencies and interests in each province, and the different partisan relations and political party configurations in each province vis-à-vis Ottawa. In the early 1980s it was also a product of overt and deliberate strategy on the part of the federal government to "divide and conquer," so to speak—to play one province off against another. An even broader version of this strategy emerged when the Trudeau government, bemoaning its lack of political credit and identity and attacking the Clark government's view of Canada as a decentralized "community of communities," sought to redirect some of its policies so as to increase the *direct* contact of Canadians with the federal government, rather than *through* the provinces. Indeed, at one point, in 1982, Trudeau pronounced the death of cooperative federalism.[25]

All of the above also suggest that on-going ideas of centralization and decentralization are inherent in federalism, but that they cannot be interpreted merely as aggregate swings of the federal-provincial pendulum. What centralization and decentralization mean can be truly understood only in the context of bilateral relations between Ottawa and particular provinces.

The more evident bilateral aspects of the federal-provincial policy process are a product of deeper forces in Canadian society and changes in the types of policy that are in dispute. The cause-effect relations here are complex and multidimensional. For example, it may now be seen in retrospect that the Pearsonian era of cooperative federalism was cooperative not just because Canada's political leaders inherently bickered less, but because they were essentially dividing up a *growing* public expenditure and tax pie. Politics was a benevolent nonzero-sum game. Since then, federalism has involved the need to allocate a pie that is not growing. The issues in dispute, moreover, are more broadly regulative (energy, transportation, communication). Thus, conflict emerges over a broader front, out of scarcity itself, out of legal and political concern about the power to control and regulate, as well as over the dominant ideas inherent in these policy fields.[26]

We are hardly the first to point out that federalism is complex or that executive federalism increasingly has to take into account the particular bilateral and idiocyncratic concerns of provinces. We think, however, that this bilateral aspect of federalism deserves a concrete emphasis which it has not received in the existing literature on federalism in Canada.

Cabinet-Parliamentary Government

In Chapter 1 we stressed the tendency of many commentators to regard Parliament's policy role as marginal, even though the idea of majoritarian responsible government is the central idea of this institution. This view is understandable in a certain context since the constitutional powers of the executive are dominant. Moreover, numerous studies have shown the litany of weaknesses in the role of Parliament as a crucial link in the accountability of government, especially financial accountability.[27] These general views seriously underestimate other attributes of Parliament's role in policy formulation which arise less out of the things Parliament *does*, than out of the fact that Parliament is simply *there.* Two attributes deserve emphasis: the government's tactical and political need to consider in advance the substantive views, priorities and tactics of the opposition political parties in Parliament—a form of policy evaluation "by anticipation"; and the relationship between tough political partisan criticism and more formal policy and program evaluation.

The art of anticipating the opposition political parties in Parliament is a central feature of policy making for any government. At a general level, priorities are forged in the context of what other contenders are proposing. We see this in Chapter 10 when we review past priorities expressed through Throne Speeches and Budget

Speeches. The priority-setting process undoubtedly involves a constant search for the broad centre of political life, for the consensus that will hold a majority or win one at the next election. Parliament (and the coverage of it by the media) is the main stage on which this ultimate political theatre is presented. The longevity of Liberal governments at the federal level and Tory governments in Ontario is evidence of the successful practice of this consummate political art. Its importance in policy formulation cannot be underestimated.

A practical example of Parliament's role in this anticipatory sense is found in the relationship between legislative priorities and general priorities. There are often fewer obstacles to a policy decision if it does not require new legislation but can be carried out under an existing statute. Where new legislation is required even for an item that is a high priority for the government, it may receive a lower priority ranking *in legislative terms* because of the issues of timing and the expected Parliamentary tactics and priorities of the opposition parties. In this sense priorities are influenced by the mood of the country as reflected in, and judged by, the House of Commons. In recent years this has often been reflected in virtually ritualistic opposition pressure for a new Budget Speech to cure an ailing and depressed economy, but it also occurs over other items of legislation as well.

Parliament is first and foremost a place of aggressive adversarial partisanship and party discipline. The rigid rules regarding "want of confidence" ensure that partisanship is rampant. This is both a strength and a weakness. It allows more or less stable governments to be formed and criticized, but it also produces a frequently stultifying debate, where political truth is often the first victim. The partisanship of the House of Commons makes it particularly difficult for the government and opposition parties alike to acknowledge errors or to change when change is probably desirable.

The twin issues, anticipating the opposition and the partisan nature of debate, raise important questions about how policies and programs are and should be evaluated. The partisan cut and thrust of debate is viewed by rationalists as a messy and unsophisticated form of evaluation. Indeed, professional program evaluators would not regard it as "evaluation" at all.[28] In their view it lacks the controlled cerebral quality of objective thought. While there is no doubt that the Parliamentary struggle is often not ideal in "speaking truth to power,"[29] it is by far the best democratic forum we possess for reflecting the broad ideas and preferences of Canadians. This is the ultimate form of rough-and-ready evaluation for which we have fortunately found no adequate substitutes. We refer again to these intrinsic roles of Parliament in policy formation and evaluation in Chapters 10, 13 and 18.

The Mass Media

It has been glibly asserted that Ottawa practises "government by *Globe and Mail*"! While this is happily yet another example of Ottawa hyperbole, the media's role is very important in politics and policy making. In Chapter 1 we focused on the core idea of a "free press" and on several features of the media's influence. Here we highlight two elements of the media's role in policy making, both of which flow from this idea. These elements are its influence in causing politicians to respond to *perceptions* as opposed to reality, and its influence in communicating policy information, the weaknesses of which have led governments, political parties and interests into the use of advocacy advertising to market or sell their policies.

The media has played a major role in the process that some call the "overload" of governments and others call the revolution in rising entitlements.[30] It helps fuel the increased pace of demands on government and contributes through its persistent criticism to a climate where it is often next to impossible for a politician "to be seen" doing nothing. Given the inevitability of scarce resources (money, time, expertise, etc.), this has helped lead to an increasing tendency to devise policies "for show" rather than "for real." Thus, as we discuss in greater detail in Chapters 5 and 12, governments have had to devise an even more elaborate array of ways in which they can express symbolic concern (studies, announcements, royal commissions, inquiries, conferences, reorganizations). The choice the politician often faces, at a minimum, is to "do something" or "do nothing." The latter is less and less viable in an era of intensive media scrutiny, since the politician is expected to at least show concern even though he or she cannot always respond in other more concrete ways through actual expenditure or regulatory programs.

There has been, of course, a reaction to this important policy phenomenon. It has resulted in a growing cynicism about government's capacity to solve real problems. It is one among many factors that has led small "c" conservatives to advocate less government and to assert that governments cannot solve all or even most of society's problems. It has also shortened the time frame of decision making, forcing private decision makers to play the same game as they postpone decisions to wait for a more favourable "priority" change from government, six or twelve months in the future.

Of particular importance to the policy formulation process is the impact of the media-induced "perception versus reality" issue on the communication of policy. In Chapter 13 we show how information, knowledge and analysis interact in the policy process, but it is essential in this review of major institutions to link the marketing of public policy to the perception versus reality issue. Increasingly, government, opposition parties, and interests (for example, oil companies) have become more and more distrustful of the media to impart "objective" information about leaders, programs and positions. They are spending vastly increased sums on advocacy advertising to reach "the people" in a direct way.[31]

It is evident that there are no easy answers to the above issues. There has always been and will always be a difficult tension between "freedom of the press" and the right and duty of a government to inform the public and carry out its policies, in short, between "information" and "propaganda," and there is clearly a fine and debatable line between what is reality and what is perception as viewed by different interests, regions and classes.

The Electoral and Party System

In Chapter 1 we referred to the importance of the electoral and party system as institutions. The electoral system incorporates not just the type of voting system (single member constituencies elected on a first past-the-post basis), but also includes the importance of electoral politics and calculus by political parties at the time of actual elections and in anticipation of an election. In this regard we highlight two attributes of the electoral and party system broadly defined, namely, the absence of national political parties, and the importance of the swing voter in the swing constituency in policy formulation, particularly in the "between elections" stages of the policy process.

No one can understand the Canadian policy-making process without a deep appreciation of the fact that Canada's party system has become increasingly regionalized.[32] Neither the Liberals nor the Progressive Conservatives can claim to span or accommodate the major sources of political cleavage in Canada. This can be partly attributed to the voting system itself, which exacerbates the regional underrepresentation as expressed in seats in the House of Commons.[33] As a result the Parliamentary caucus of the two major parties, and of the NDP, distorts the policy process because certain regional views are not *continuously* represented in day-to-day and week-to-week debate and discussion. While we do not concern ourselves here with proposals for proportional representation and other reforms designed to rectify this problem, we certainly wish to emphasize the importance of this question in policy development.[34] Chapters 15 and 16 show this influence on the definition and conduct of industrial and energy policy. Its ongoing importance in defining policies, or the lack thereof, on Western Canada and Quebec are also identified in Chapter 11.

The importance of the analytical debate about the influence of the swing voter in the swing constituency on public policy deserves attention. We noted in Chapter 1 how much importance this electoral calculus is given by economists who study public policy.[35] It corresponds to the laymen's instinctive and often heard view that you can understand the politician best by realizing that he or she is just "looking for votes." Moreover, formal public opinion polls are carried out by the Prime Minister's Office and party headquarters precisely to learn as much as possible about voter views on particular policies and on priorities.

Clearly then, to ignore electoral politics is to take a lot of the politics out of policy. Proximity to an election is therefore an important factor in explaining both the content and the timing of policy. One is left, however, with the "between election" phase, a considerable period of time during which other institutions and other determinants of policy are at least equally important. The high degree of determinism in the voter calculus model of political life is a central issue in the use of the public choice approach examined in Chapter 6 and in Chapter 5's review of the theories of instrument choice. Thus, we return to this point which is contentious both in the practice of making policy and in the way different academic disciplines try to explain policy choices.

Concluding Observations

Our two-step survey of the normative content of public policy, one focusing on levels of content and the other on more precise institutional reflections of core ideas, has been presented to help develop an appreciation of the complexity and yet the persuasiveness of the purposeful nature of democratic politics in Canada and of Canadian public policy. This need to rigourously appreciate and dissect the normative content is important because of the tendency to describe all policy as being remorselessly pragmatic. The policy process does involve the need for pragmatic balance, but it is not done without ideologies or ideas. The evaluation of policy cannot proceed by happily focusing on one or two "objectives" without reference to the interdependence of ideas and the historical drift or evolution of these ideas over time. Nor have we treated here all the ideas present in the policy process. We have left some for later chapters, including the Cabinet-Parliamentary idea of individual ministerial and collective Cabinet responsibility, the idea that elected politicians make policy and bureaucrats carry it out, and the idea of freedom of association and the right to be consulted in the policy process.

NOTES

1. See W. Christian and C. Campbell, *Political Parties and Ideologies in Canada,* Second Edition (Toronto: McGraw-Hill Ryerson, 1983); and Denis Moniere, *Ideologies in Quebec* (Toronto: University of Toronto Press, 1981).
2. See Christian and Campbell, *op. cit.,* and Charles Taylor, *Radical Tories* (Toronto: Anansi, 1982).
3. See S.M. Lipset, *Agrarian Socialism* (New York: Anchor Books, Doubleday, 1968) and C.B. MacPherson, *Democracy in Alberta* (Toronto: University of Toronto Press, 1953).
4. Christian and Campbell, *op. cit.* See also M.J. Brodie and Jane Jenson, *Crisis, Challenge and Change: Party and Class in Canada* (Toronto: Methuen, 1980); and Conrad Winn and J. McMenemy, *Political Parties in Canada* (Toronto: McGraw-Hill Ryerson, 1976).
5. See for example Richard B. McKenzie and Gordon Tullock, *Modern Political Economy: An Introduction to Economics* (New York: McGraw-Hill, 1978), Chapters 1 and 2.
6. See Milton Friedman, *Capitalism and Freedom* (Chicago: University of Chicago Press, 1962).
7. See Robert Campbell, *Grand Illusions: The Keynesian Experience in Canada* (Trent University—Manuscript, in press).

8. See James Rice and Michael Prince, *Social Policy and Administration in Canada* (Ottawa: Manuscript). For more detailed references see Chapter 14.

9. See, for example, G. Bruce Doern, Michael Prince and Garth McNaughton, *Living with Contradictions: Health and Safety Regulation and Implementation in Ontario* (Toronto: Ontario Royal Commissions on Matters of Health and Safety Arising from the Use of Asbestos in Ontario, 1982).

10. See Moniere, *op. cit.;* Christian and Campbell; *op. cit.,* Chapter 6; Peter Russell, ed., *Nationalism in Canada* (Toronto: McGraw-Hill, 1966); and David Cameron, *Nationalism, Self-Determination and the Quebec Question* (Toronto: Macmillan of Canada, 1974).

11. See Michael Tucker, *Canadian Foreign Policy: Contemporary Issues and Themes* (Toronto: McGraw-Hill Ryerson, 1980) and Peyton V. Lyon and Brian W. Tomlin, *Canada as an International Actor* (Toronto: Macmillan of Canada, 1979). See also Mildred Swartz, *The Environment for Policy Making in Canada and the United States* (Washington: National Planning Association and the C.D. Howe Research Institute, 1981).

12. See Richard Simeon, "Regionalism and Canadian Political Institutions," *Queens Quarterly,* Vol. 82, Winter 1975; Donald V. Smiley, *Canada in Question,* Third Edition (Toronto: McGraw-Hill Ryerson, 1980); Canada West Foundation, *Regional Representation* (Calgary: Canada West Foundation, 1981); David J. Elkins and Richard Simeon, *Small Worlds* (Toronto: Methuen, 1980).

13. David Easton, *A Systems Analysis of Political Life* (New York: John Wiley and Sons, 1965), Chapter 1.

14. Ronald Manzer, "Public Policies in Canada: A Development Perspective." Paper presented to the Canadian Political Science Association, Edmonton, June 1975. See also Ronald Manzer, "Social Policy and Political Paradigms," *Canadian Public Administration,* Vol. 24, No. 4 (Winter 1981), pp. 641-648.

15. See Campbell, *op. cit.*

16. Thomas J. Courchene, *The Strategy of Gradualism* (Montreal: C.D. Howe Research Institute, 1978); Thomas J. Courchene, *Money, Inflation and the Bank of Canada,* Vol. II (Montreal: C.D. Howe Research Institute, 1981); and Arthur W. Donner and Douglas D. Peters, *Monetarist Counter-Revolution* (Ottawa: Canadian Institute for Economic Policy, 1979).

17. For a case study of a failed attempt to sell an alternative health care paradigm, see Betty Muggah, "A New Perspective: The Making and Fate of a New Paradigm for Health Policy," *Ian Macdonald Essays* (Ottawa: School of Public Administration, Carleton University, 1981), pp. 1-42.

18. See Royal Commission on Financial Management and Accountability, *Final Report* (Ottawa: Minister of Supply and Services, 1979), Chapter 9. For a critique of the management by objectives concept, see Aaron

Wildavsky, *Speaking Truth to Power* (Boston: Little Brown, 1979), Chapter 9.

19. Brodie and Jenson, *op. cit.*, Chapter 1.

20. John Porter, *The Vertical Mosaic* (Toronto: University of Toronto Press, 1965), Chapter 12.

21. Brodie and Jenson, *op. cit.*

22. *Ibid.*, Chapter 1.

23. See A. Shonfield, *Modern Capitalism: The Changing Balance of Public and Private Power* (London: Oxford University Press, 1965); David I. Langille, "From Consultation to Corporatism? The Consultative Process Between Canadian Business, Labour, and Government, 1977-1981." (Ottawa: Masters Research Essay, Department of Political Science, Carleton University, 1982); and Anthony Giles, "The Politics of Wage Controls: The Canadian State, Organized Labour and Corporatism," (Masters Thesis, School of Public Administration, Carleton University, 1980).

24. See D.V. Smiley, *Canada in Question*, Third Edition (Toronto: McGraw-Hill Ryerson, 1980), Chapter 4; Edwin R. Black, *Divided Loyalties* (Montreal: McGill-Queen's University Press, 1975); John Richards and Larry Pratt, *Prairie Capitalism* (Toronto: McClelland and Stewart, 1979); Richard Simeon and David J. Elkin, "Regional Political Cultures in Canada," *Canadian Journal of Political Science*, Vol. III (September 1974), pp. 397-437; and Allan Cairns, "The Governments and Societies of Canadian Federalism," *Canadian Journal of Political Science*, Vol. X, pp. 695-725.

25. See G. Bruce Doern, ed., *How Ottawa Spends Your Tax Dollars 1981* (Toronto: James Lorimer Publishers, 1981), Chapter 1.

26. See Smiley, *op. cit.*, Chapter 8 and Richards and Pratt, *op. cit.*

27. See Royal Commission on Financial Management and Accountability, *op. cit.*, Chapters 1, 2 and 3; and T. d'Aquino, G. Bruce Doern and C. Blair, *Parliamentary Government in Canada: A Critical Assessment and Suggestions for Change* (Ottawa: Intercounsel Ltd., 1979).

28. See Len Rutman, *Planning Useful Evaluations* (Beverley Hills: Sage Publications, 1980).

29. See Aaron Wildavsky, *op. cit.*, Chapter 5.

30. See Richard Simeon, "The 'Overload Thesis' and Canadian Government," *Canadian Public Policy*, Volume II, No. 4 (Autumn 1976), pp. 541-552; and Edwin R. Black, *Politics and the News* (Toronto: Butterworths, 1982).

31. See W.T. Stanbury, "Government Advertising Expenditures: The Critical .001 Percent" in G. Bruce Doern, ed., *How Ottawa Spends: The Liberals, the Opposition and National Priorities* (Toronto: James Lorimer, 1983), Chapter 5.

32. See R. Van Loon and M. Whittington, *The Canadian Political System*,

Third Edition (Toronto: McGraw-Hill Ryerson, 1981), Chapters 10 and 11.

33. See Allan C. Cairns, "The Electoral System and the Party System in Canada 1921-1965," *Canadian Journal of Political Science,* Volume 1, No. 1, 1968, pp. 55-80; and William P. Irvine, *Does Canada Need a New Electoral System* (Kingston: Institute of Intergovernmental Relations, 1979).

34. See William P. Irvine, *op. cit.,* and Canada West Foundation, *Regional Representation* (Calgary: Canada West Foundation, 1981).

35. See Douglas G. Hartle, *Public Policy Decision Making and Regulation* (Montreal: Institute for Research on Public Policy, 1979); and M.J. Trebilcock, R.S. Prichard, D.G. Hartle and D.N. Dewees, *The Choice of Governing Instruments* (Ottawa: Ministry of Supply and Services, 1982).

CHAPTER 3

INTERESTS, INTEREST GROUPS AND THE DILEMMA OF CONSULTATION

Although the focus of this chapter is on interest groups, the role of such groups can only be understood in the broader institutional context presented in Chapters 1 and 2. This is because all the major institutions are also "interests," and interests therefore include political actors that are not synonymous with interest groups, as one would conventionally think of such groups. There is a second overriding reason to distinguish interests from interest groups, namely, to recognize the role of particular entities that may belong to interest groups but that have, in some respects, power that exceeds the formal group itself. Thus, many individual corporations have command over resources that exceeds that of some of the smaller provinces. McMillan Bloedel is a dominant interest in the Province of British Columbia in ways that vastly exceed their membership in the Canadian Pulp and Paper Association. Inco Canada Limited is a major interest in the life of Sudbury and North Bay, as are other companies in many hinterland "company towns." Imperial Oil of Canada and Dome Petroleum are interests of no small importance in the energy industry because of the investment decisions they make or do not make. While interest groups can often take positions on issues and can *sometimes* act as a group, interests can often act without taking positions.

The concept of interests is also important in relation to our comments in Chapter 2 about the role of labour. Not all workers are members of unions, and yet many issues or positions are presented or taken to be in the "interests of labour" or to help the "working class." Such workers are also consumers and members of families and perhaps churches or religious groups. Interests intersect and overlap and exert cross pressures on individual Canadians and in turn on elected politicians. In the case of labour and capital one also encounters the difficulties of the class analysis approach examined in Chapter 6. In a broad sense it is appropriate to speak of the existence of the interests of capitalist and labouring classes. In other respects such categories are not subjectively what appears to cause interests to act in various ways, and thus a "class" becomes vague as a unit of political behaviour.

Interests are important in relation to our later discussion of information, knowledge and power. Policies often fail not because one merely lacked knowledge or did not get the analysis quite right, but because interests will not let policies succeed or can partially counteract them. Provincial governments as interests have the power to act within limits. So do foreign governments, corporations and large labour unions.

Finally, as we show in the last section of this chapter, interests represented by the core institutions often present competing and yet overlapping bases of legitimacy in Canadian politics. They profoundly affect the idea of democratic consultation in policy making and the elusive search for institutional consensus reflected in such concepts and ideas as "tripartism," "corporatism," "participatory democracy," an "industrial strategy" and "voluntary incomes" policies.

In all of the above, interests, interest groups and the dilemmas of consultation are linked. The first part of the chapter deals with interest groups. The second part examines the limits and prospects of formal consultation as a central idea in policy making.

Interest Groups

Interest groups are an integral part of the democratic policy process reflecting the fundamental idea of the right to associate freely. They range in their spectrum of interests from the Civil Liberties Association to the Canadian Manufacturers Association. Every department of government must deal with a number of such groups. Interest groups compete with political parties, the media, and others "for the privilege of interpreting the public will to key decision makers."[1] They also exist to provide goods and services to their members, as well as to represent the interests of their members to various levels of government. They act as a buffer between the individual and the state. In this chapter we are primarily interested in their role in policy formulation rather than in their internal service roles.

Paul Pross's analysis shows that Canadian interest groups perform two major politically relevant functions—communication and legitimation.[2] In addition, they act to regulate their members and to supplement governmental administration. The communications function includes everything from furnishing technical data to government to the communication of the intensity of the views of its members, which may range from apathy to concern or even anger. Groups also communicate the concerns of policy makers and officials to their members. The legitimating function relates to the role interest groups play in broadening the base of information and the number of people involved in discussing policy problems. Interest groups are used also by government to test policy ideas, to obtain visible support, and to neutralize extreme opposition. The role of interest groups as formal or informal agents of government is also important. Numerous voluntary organizations provide services which are an essential complement to those supplied by public social service agencies.[3] Some interest groups are given public funding to help them to better intervene in the policy process. The recognized leading professions such as medicine and law are in a very formal way conferred powers to regulate their members and to make policy decisions.[4]

While there is a mutual dependence in the relationships that develop between interest groups and public policy makers, there are also a number of normative and practical tensions and concerns. The first rests on the danger perceived by interest groups that they will be coopted by governments, contrary to their own interests. Labour federations have been especially concerned about both the substance and the appearance of cooptation in wage control programs by government and business.[5] Unions are pulled in two directions by the pressure to cooperate and to maintain social peace, and by a knowledge that they will become an instrument of the state to enforce wage restraint. Labour federations have been somewhat ambivalent because of the normal desire of any group and its leaders to have influence on, and to be consulted by, other power centres in Canadian society. At the same time they must deal with these power centres from a position of strength and, hence, a premium is placed on the appearance of solidarity and the need for a common front.

The ideas espoused by interest groups and the tensions among interest groups are essential to understand. Interest groups, moreover, do not necessarily see the ideas that concern them as being properly handled even though they may have regular or even cordial relations with "their" department. They are cognizant of the complexity of government and of the fact that they must interact at both the federal and provincial levels with several ministers and officials, including the burgeoning central agencies. The interest group-departmental relations are rarely of a simple one-to-one kind. They change as policy fields change and are redefined. For example, for several decades agricultural policy was essentially synonymous with farm policy. In the mid and late 1970s it increasingly became defined and aligned with a broader concept of food policy. The latter embraces a larger number of interest groups, including food retailers and distributors as well as farm producers.[6]

In this chapter we examine the role of interest groups in four ways. First, we distinguish between producer groups and public interest groups or collective rights associations. In the next two sections we examine the evolution of macro umbrella associations, first for the business-producer sector and secondly for labour unions and other collective rights associations. Finally, we relate the overall role of these groups and broader interests to the demands for, and the processes of, consultation in the public policy process. The right to be consulted is an important democratic idea, but it is demanded not only by interest groups but by other major institutions as well.

Producer Versus Collective Rights Associations

An essential first task is to distinguish between producer interest groups and broader collective rights associations. The former include business, agricultural producers, and professions such as law and medicine. The latter are often referred to as public interest groups and include groups that coalesce around broader nonproducer definitions of a group. These include labour unions, consumer and environmental groups, as well as groups such as women, students, tenants or youth. In some respects the former are viewed to be involved in "economic" policy while the latter are engaged in "social" policy. This is in many ways a false and arbitrary distinction, but such a dual view of interest groups does reflect one reality of political organization, the "free rider" problem.

As economists have pointed out, all interest groups must grapple in varying degrees with the "free rider" problem or the "logic of collective action."[7] To organize politically is to incur significant costs. These usually have to be recovered through membership fees. But, as Hartle puts it, "if others are going to pay to advance your interests in pursuit of their own, why pay the fee?"[8] In short, why not be a "free rider." This is the nub of the problem for sustaining groups, especially for broadly based groups. The narrower the group with the common producer interest, the easier it is to exclude free riders. Otherwise, if normative belief is not enough to secure paying adherents, then the group must often offer other remunerative services or, alternatively, have the capacity to coerce their members, such as through the compulsory check-off of dues.

As Hartle's and other economic analyses suggest, the "free rider" problem is a major reason why some groups are weaker and less cohesive than others. There are, however, other explanations offered for this weakness. Those who use a class analysis approach would attribute the weakness of nonproducer groups to their dependent place in a capitalist system of production and to the role of the state which supports that system. Both the "free rider" and the class analysis diagnosis stress economic determinants. The free rider notion basically suggests that producer groups in industry and agriculture have far greater incentives and capability in organizing to exert pressure about a government policy essential to their livelihood than do broader labour, consumer, health, safety and environmental groups.

> Here, "everybody's interest is nobody's interest" and association fees are correctly treated as a charitable contribution. These collective rights groups have, for obvious reasons, great difficulty in staying alive despite the fact that they play an invaluable role.[9]

By analogy, one could use the "free rider" insights to see why other large social groupings such as political parties or the working "class"would be less cohesive in sustaining both action and membership.

The sparse literature on Canadian interest groups appears to agree that while interest groups exert some countervailing influence on each other, there has never been in Canada the interest group pluralism alleged to exist in the United States. The "separation of powers" system of government and politics provides many more points of influence and power for such groups.[10] A significant inequality of power among groups in Canada is readily acknowledged to exist, as we show in greater detail below. But it is the institutional realities engendered by, and inherent in, the relations between Canadian federalism and Cabinet-Parliamentary government that also help explain the different roles of interest groups in the Canadian setting.

In contrast to the open debate inherent in electoral and Parliamentary politics, interest group pressure is exerted primarily in closed, behind-the-scenes meetings and discussions. Successful groups seek to earn and obtain such access to ministers and senior officials, while those who do not have such access rely more heavily on broader appeals to the media or through public campaigns.[11] It is obvious, however, that there are many factors which influence group tactics, including their level of resources and expertise, as well as tactical concerns about the particular range of issues on the agenda at any given time.

It is instructive to note at this point how Hartle relates the combined characteristics of the "free rider" problem and the closed nature of interest group pressure to the question of the choice of regulation as a governing instrument. He concludes:

> What does seem beyond question is that in choosing the instrumentality for intervention ministers are not unmindful of the fact that regulation, as distinct from tax or expenditure intervention, has certain political advantages when seeking to satisfy strong special interests. One of those advantages is that the regulatory route may proclaim the government's awareness of a problem of widespread public concern, yet not greatly damage the special interest group because it can marshall the resources (lawyers, accountants, experts) to protect its interest in a regulatory forum much more effectively than can those whose interests are nominally being served by the regulation. From a politician's point of view this is the best of both worlds: credit is obtained for acting "in the public interest" while, at the same time, not greatly hurting the interest that is ostensibly being damaged.[12]

While we argue in Chapter 5 that propositions about the choice of instruments such as the one enunciated by Hartle are usually too simplistic and narrow, Hartle is right in showing the need to link the characteristics of the two types of interest groups to the actual instruments of governing, rather than leaving them in splendid isolation.

There is no satisfactory way to gauge the relative influence of interest groups in all policy fields relative to other institutions and centres of power such as the media, individual large businesses, political parties or Parliament. How would one aggregate such evidence even if one had it? One cannot simply add up the few case studies of interest groups because, even when well done, they relate to a mere handful of policy case studies at specific points in time. Moreover, many such studies do not deal well with the problem of analyzing "nonevents" such as those inactions designed to maintain the status quo.

Interest Groups, Ideas and Policy Fields

While interest groups undoubtedly initiate many demands for changes in policy, they also play a significant role in persistently "massaging" ministers and officials to preserve the status quo, or to prevent unfavourable acts from occurring. Many business groups, for example, spend considerable time trying to ensure that a favourable overall policy climate is maintained. Often this is a function of their own internal political needs. Public positions must be taken at a sufficient level of generality so as to paper over the inevitable cracks in the internal consensus of the interest group. The broader based the group, the more general the rhetoric must become. The generality of the rhetoric is also a function of the breadth of the policy occasion. For example, the ritual of pre-Budget Speech consultations between the Minister of Finance and business interests induces a high level of predictable rhetoric spiced with a few specifics, depending on the state of the economy and the industry in question. On the other hand, a discussion of foreign investment policy or competition policy may bring out more specifics. The existence of rhetorical generalities does not make the process any less real, especially when it is seen as part of a broader process of persistently asserting values and dominant ideas so as to *prevent* change that offends them.

There should be no doubt that interest groups, particularly cohesive producer groups, exert a significant influence both in preserving the status quo and in promoting manageable change favourable to their interests. Several examples can be easily cited. Canada's banks, through the Canadian Banking Association, have been instrumental in shaping the evolution of the Bank Act, reviewed approximately every ten years through a formal White Paper process and its accompanying consultative mechanisms.[13] They have, of course, not been the only groups in the process; trust companies, the cooperatives, foreign banks and consumers seek to influence the content of the Bank Act and other banking legislation.

In the energy policy field major oil and gas associations, such as the Canadian Petroleum Association, dominated by the large multinational companies, and the Independent Petroleum Association of Canada composed of smaller Canadian firms, successfully influenced energy policy in the 1960s and 1970s. They found themselves in strident opposition to the main features of the interventionist National Energy

Policy initiated in 1980, a policy which caused them, in part, to eschew their quiet behind-the-scenes lobbying and to adopt aggressive public advocacy advertising.[14]

Analyses by Bill Stanbury show the power of the business lobby in watering down and/or derailing successive Competition Policy bills.[15] This political success is partly due to the vagueness and contradictions inherent in competition policy (particularly those between encouraging competition, on the one hand, and the need to allow mergers to achieve an internationally competitive scale of operations on the other), but it was also due to the classic free rider dilemma. The proponent consumer interest groups were weaker than the coherent producer groups. This was true even when one took into account the division of views among industrial groups such as energy companies on the one hand and grocery and food distributors on the other.

In the food and agricultural policy field, interest groups such as the Canadian Federation of Agriculture, the National Farmer's Union and the prairie cooperatives, often operating in concert with provincial governments, succeeded until the early 1980s in preserving the subsidies to grain transportation first entrenched in the historic Crow's Nest Pass agreement.[16] It was not until the early 1980s that a new and broader coalition of "interests" centred in resource companies, and actively fostered by the federal Liberals, succeeded in making changes to the Crow system of subsidies. These changes were ultimately needed to give the railways, the CNR and CPR, more revenue so that they would invest in the new track and infrastructure needed to meet the high volume demands of the booming resource trade in grain, coal, potash and sulphur. Farm groups have also succeeded in persuading governments to create numerous marketing boards to protect and stabilize their incomes.[17]

Perhaps the most dominant producer group interests in their respective policy fields are the professions of medicine and law, in the health care and justice policy fields, respectively.[18] They are overtly conferred a state monopoly over many aspects of decision making. As with other groups, the professions seek to cultivate a certain mystique and set of ideas. These are both the product of genuine belief and conviction by their adherents and by many in the general public, but at the same time are intended to foster a sense of indispensability as to the social need of the producer group in question. For doctors and lawyers, part of the mystique centres on the need to protect the sanctity of the doctor-patient and lawyer-client relationships, respectively, and on the need to produce properly qualified people embued with proper professional ethics.

Doctors and lawyers are not the only groups to engage in this practice. In a slightly less explicit way, farmers have cultivated the notion that food producers, as custodians of the vital Canadian bread basket, are subject to the vagaries of both climate and international market fluctuations. They have argued that they are especially deserving of measures to stabilize their incomes and to make their lives more predictable. Similarly, airline pilots and air traffic controllers seek to create an elevated rhetoric about the importance of public safety and their crucial role in preserving it.[19]

The collective rights associations have not been without their moments of political success. The emergence in the 1970s of a significant amount of health, safety and fairness regulation—so-called "social" regulation—can be attributed to their political influence.[20] On the other hand, their political weakness can be seen in the effort to roll back, or at least "correct," some of these social regulation measures in the late 1970s and in the 1980s. Women's groups have pushed women's issues onto the political agenda, culminating with their remarkable lobbying of first ministers in the hectic constitutional debate of 1981. However, women's issues are still in many ways on the fringes of official priorities and resource allocation.

Public interest associations have also managed to persuade governments to introduce some new structures in the decision process, some temporary and some permanent. These include: special inquiries such as the famous Berger Commission on the Mackenzie Valley pipeline and several provincial inquiries into uranium mining and nuclear power; statutorily based and nonstatutorily based environmental assessment processes for reviewing major projects; the establishment of consumer and environmental departments; and selected public funding of public interest intervenors involved in different regulatory tribunals.[21]

Thus, the nonproducer associations have managed to secure a place for themselves in the policy process and in the departments of government. However, their organized political base is, on the whole, much weaker, less stable and less coherent than producer associations.

It is important to stress the different levels of aggregation and differentiation inherent among producer groups. Business and producer groups are obviously not a homogeneous mass. Moreover, they interact with different departments and agencies of government. There are indeed different segments or fragments of capital that find it necessary to organize in different ways and that find themselves in opposition with each other as they seek to invest, introduce new technologies, protect themselves from intolerable uncertainty, and seek favours from government. Conflicts arise between foreign-owned and Canadian firms, between private firms and Crown enterprises in the same industry, among firms in different regions, and between large firms and small firms.[22] This is why regulators and policy makers, while dutifully reading industry association briefs, and listening to the positions taken in numerous meetings, must ultimately develop policies which deal with these divisions, many of which will be papered over in the industry association's communications. The policy maker must devise, as we stressed in Chapter 2, a policy that both treats people and firms equally (even when they are patently different) and which treats them fairly (even though some firms are clearly more powerful and better endowed economically than others).

The multiple levels of business and producer associations must also be appreciated. At the macro level there are general associations such as the Canadian Manufacturers Association, the Canadian Chamber of Commerce, the Business Council on National Issues and the Canadian Federation of Independent Business. At the middle level there are dozens of specific associations such as for banking, oil and gas and mining, to name only three. At the micro level there are thousands of more localized associations for even smaller industrial or producer units (for instance, tobacco growers in Ontario) or as chapters of the larger organizations. We cannot possibly deal with all of these levels in our brief treatment here, but it is essential to highlight trends in the development of the four macro associations as the umbrella organizations of the "business community." This is particularly necessary in view of the perpetual effort in recent years to find out how to bring business, labour and government "together" or, less ambitiously, how to find out "what business wants" from government. We will do the same later in the chapter in relation to labour and other collective rights associations.

The Evolution of Macro Business Interest Groups

None of the four macro business interest groups can individually claim to speak for the business community. The Canadian Chamber of Commerce

(CCC) is probably the most broadly based. The CCC is a federation of six hundred Chambers of Commerce and Boards of Trade, which in turn embrace 130,000 businesses across Canada.[23] It also represents 2,900 firms which have direct corporate memberships. Over 70 vertical trade associations are also affiliated. The breadth of its membership forces the CCC to shift its lobbying strategy from narrow issues of concern to specific segments of its membership to broad brush positions (for example, general criticisms of greedy unions and aggressive bureaucrats) that will not offend any of its members. In the early 1980s, especially in Western Canada, the CCC began a Legislative Action Program to improve lobbying efforts by their local members with Members of Parliament.

The Canadian Manufacturers Association (CMA) comprises nine thousand members covering a wide range of industries. It is not, however, as disposed as the CCC to establishing a network at the grass root level. As its name implies, it is focused much more on the manufacturing sector per se. Because of this, it faces the normal problems of accommodating the views of foreign-owned and Canadian-owned firms. It has consistently argued that economic policy, whether at the level of macro fiscal policy or at the level of an industrial strategy, must be oriented to encouraging an incentive-oriented market system, albeit one "compatible with social responsibility and the political integrity of the country and that preserves maximum personal freedom."[24]

The Business Council on National Issues (BCNI) comprises about 150 chief executive officers of major Canadian-based corporations. Established in 1976 in the midst of the 1975–1977 wage and price controls program, BCNI has attempted to differentiate itself from the other business associations by taking a more "statesman-like" approach to national policy by operating quietly behind the scenes and with well-prepared positions and papers. Its work on competition policy extended to the point of actually preparing a draft bill incorporating its views.[25] The BCNI directly involves the chief executive officers of its member firms and hence has a flexibility and an authoritative aura about it that other associations cannot match. It also saw itself as eventually being the fulcrum for the elusive but long sought after consultative forum with government and labour. Thus, it has gone out of its way to foster more sympathetic relationships with labour through the Canadian Labour Congress. This highly tentative cooperation has been most in evidence in a joint BCNI-CLC proposal to create an independent Labour Market Institute. Its wooing of labour, however, has not prevented the BCNI from being a strong advocate of public sector wage controls.[26] The BCNI has not been immune to its own internal divisions, particularly between Canadian-owned and foreign-owned firms. It also lacks adequate representation among Western Canadian and French-Canadian chief executive officers.

If the BCNI represents an elite behind-the-scenes business lobby, then it is the opposite of the second business association to emerge in the 1970s, the Canadian Federation of Independent Business (CFIB). It comprises over sixty thousand small, primarily Canadian businesses, especially in the rapidly growing service and small manufacturing sectors.[27] It evolved into an aggressive public lobby for the concerns of small business. Openly suspicious and often critical of the other business associations, the CFIB has used the media as well as numerous briefs and meetings to criticize policies harmful to small businesses. The establishment of the Ministry of State for Small Business can be directly attributed to the CFIB lobby. As well, the CFIB has spearheaded concern about excessive regulation, the governmental paper burden on small business and the effects of taxation, interest rates, postal strikes and increased postal rates. It continuously reminds the government that small businesses have created the largest number of new jobs in the Canadian economy.

It is evident from the above survey of macro business associations that the business community is not monolithic. Business interests, moreover, are not represented only through business interest groups. Major corporations and individual chief executive officers have their own network of access points and personal friends and contacts. Foreign and provincial governments serve as vigourous behind-the-scenes defenders of individual companies and industries as the political circumstances require. The several economic and resource departments of government play similar roles in Ottawa.

Despite the numerous tensions and disputes among industries and between segments of industry and government, the business community does share a broad official series of values and ideas, including a belief in efficiency and profit and in the freedom of the market, in individual freedom and the work ethic, and in a suspicion of organized labour and of bureaucratic government.

The Evolution of Labour Unions and Macro
Collective Rights Associations

As noted above, the nonproducer or nonbusiness interest groups have been variously labelled as public interest groups or collective rights associations. They include groups such as labour unions, environmental, health, and safety interests, consumer associations, women's and native interests, and social, community and welfare voluntary associations. All of these groups are likely to suffer more than producer groups from the vagaries of the "free rider" problem enunciated earlier and are financially weaker. Some are funded by the state. All of them, more often than not, are likely to be instinctively associated by the public with social policy issues, including social regulation.[28] All of them are suspicious of the established producer groups as well as the other centres of legitimacy—federal-provincial relations, Parliament and executive government. They are far more inclined to use the media to attract political attention to their causes.

As a result, this grouping of interests has a much greater problem in creating and sustaining its macro associations. There is no supra public interest group coalition. The labour movement has come closest to constructing one, but even its major association, the Canadian Labour Congress (CLC), is a fragile federation of labour unions only.[29] Despite some congealment of the CLC in the wake of wage and price controls in the late 1970s, it remains an organization beset by internal division between industrial and craft unions, between international unions and Canadian unions, between rapidly growing public sector unions and private sector unions, and between English- and French-Canadian labour groups and federations. In 1982 construction unions left the CLC to form a new smaller macro body, the Canadian Federation of Labour (CFL).

Even the effort to construct an electoral and political alliance between the CLC and the New Democratic party has not borne fruit since the majority of individual workers do not vote for the NDP. At the same time this overt alliance with the NDP has made successive federal Liberal governments suspicious of the CLC and all the more unwilling to consult with the CLC, much less enact policies favourable to the CLC. The CLC's flirtation with proposals for tripartism (or what some even loosely called corporatism) in the midst of the wage and price controls debate in 1976 reflected the CLC's ambivalence and its political dilemma.[30] It wanted access and influence, but it did not want to become an instrument of the state.

Formal Consultation: Limits and Prospects

The role of interest groups immediately invokes ideas of consultation in the policy process. Consultation is itself an idea of no small importance.[31] Often, governments are charged with a failure to consult, or to consult adequately, with interest groups and interests which are affected by a particular decision or policy. Alas, the purposes of formal (and informal) consultation in a democratic setting are many. The politics of consultation means different things to different interest groups, not to mention governments, regions, and classes in Canadian political life. Formal consultation can be and has been used:

- to learn, to be informed, and to *understand* in the best democratic and human sense of the word;
- to secure or conclude an agreement (sometimes);
- to agree to disagree;
- to delay;
- to coopt interests and/or to facilitate "voluntary" compliance;
- as a symbolic act to show concern, or as a substitute for other more substantive action.

Canadian governments in the last two decades have experimented in various ways with formal consultation with different economic interests. The National Productivity Council, the Economic Council of Canada and the Science Council of Canada were formed in the early and mid-1960s; the Prices and Incomes Commission had a consultative role in the late 1960s, as did several other consultative efforts to secure "voluntary" wage and price restraint in the early 1970s. The Labour Relations Council was formed in the mid-1970s and in the late 1970s; "tripartism" was discussed in the wake of the AIB experiment. A system of 23 sector task forces involving business and labour was attempted in 1978. Efforts at reorganizing or creating new economic departments in the federal government were also linked to finding new ways to consult and to seek consensus. As examples one can cite agencies for regional development, small business, science and technology and economic development. These bodies, all headed by Cabinet ministers, emerged from concern about genuine problems. However, as we see in Chapters 11 and 15, they have increased the problems of coordination and consultation *within* government.

Because consultation serves many purposes and the motives and expectations of the parties engaged in consultation often differ, it is not surprising that there is frequently much talk about failures or weaknesses in consultative exercises. The rhetoric of "failed consultation" is standard fare in politics, and one of the truly scarce political skills is the art of differentiating bogus from legitimate claims in this regard.

The need to talk, to consult, and to learn is central in democratic government. However, consultation is made particularly difficult in Canada because there are different ideas and bases of political and institutional legitimacy, and these compete.

First, Canada is a federal state in which legitimacy rests on a regional base, a geographic base and a cultural/ethnic base. This requires consultation of a costly but usually necessary kind. Second, legitimacy resides in a Cabinet held accountable in theory and sometimes in practice by a popularly elected House of Commons. Third, legitimacy rests in part on interest group participation. It is accorded in proportion to the real power and influence exercised by major economic interests. Big business ranks at the top, but agriculture and, to a certain extent, unions share this base of legitimacy.

These bases of legitimacy intersect and overlap in numerous ways and so are often difficult to disentangle. That the competing bases affect both the appearance and the reality of consultation in Canada there can be no doubt. It is next to impossible for any single formal consultative body to adequately embrace all these bases, and efforts to do so are destined to disappoint. Worse still, such efforts may add to the disillusionment with governmental and private institutions that already prevails.

It is also evident that consultation is not a uniform game in which the rules are the same for all the players. Numerous multilateral and bilateral bargains are struck. The "interests" involved are not just monolithic ones such as "government," "industry" and "labour," but must be seen more realistically to include:

- big business and small business;
- foreign-owned business and Canadian-owned business;
- organized labour and unorganized labour;
- public sector unions and private sector unions;
- agriculture and consumers;
- strong provinces and weak provinces;
- established professions and professions that would like to be established;
- those who have expertise and those who do not;
- those who have and those who have not.

Even this list does not encompass all the players and does nothing to alert us to the problem of the inequality of access to the consultative process. It tells us nothing, moreover, about informal consultation. It *does* alert us to the complexity of governing, to the need to be suspicious of exaggerated claims for new consultative eras, and to the potential costs of excessive consultation.

Consultation in an era of fiscal restraint and economic decline also makes more visible another critical aspect of the policy process, namely, the relationships between consultation and governing instruments. When governments wish to secure compliance with, or support for, whatever ideas or objectives they are pursuing, they have to choose from a list of basic instruments available to them. They can exhort, spend, regulate, tax or resort to public ownership. An era of restraint shows more sharply and vividly just how politicians trade in a "market of governing instruments." If the "price" of one or another instrument is politically too high, politicians will turn to other instruments. For example, if spending is denied them as an instrument because the political costs of spending are too high, they will probably regulate *more* not less because they have to do *something*.

The assertion that there is a need to trade in a market of governing instruments is based on the point stressed earlier that politicians *cannot be seen to be doing nothing*. The pressure of interest groups, the appetite of the media and the realities of electoral politics and other institutional forces are such that doing *something*, even at a minimum, expressing concern or consulting with interests is almost always preferable to doing nothing.

Consider the following: In the latter half of the 1970s the neoconservative revival in Canada led to a call for less taxation, less regulation and less spending. The former Liberal government through its document, *The Way Ahead*, published in 1976, and the Clark government of 1979 both asserted that henceforth government would have to attempt to achieve objectives in "less interventionist" ways. Accordingly, both governments said they would try to secure support and compliance through consultation and exhortation.

Their frustrations and failures point out the paradox of consultation in a "less government" (taxation, regulation, spending) ethos or era. However useful and necessary consultation and gentle persuasion are in democratically *learning* about *problems* and issues, they are probably, more often than not, unreliable as a way to achieve long-run support for the practical resolution of most of these problems.

Yet if one denies politicians spending, regulating and taxing, then *only* exhortation and consultation are left. The likelihood, therefore, is that politicians will turn to these other instruments because "doing something" through consultative forums will simply not be good enough. Politicians know in their souls that the carrot and the stick are as necessary in the modern context of democratic politics as speaking softly and listening attentively!

Politicians, of course, are not the only ones trading in this market of governing instruments. Interest groups do too in their efforts to exert pressure or secure favours from government. There is thus a considerable hidden agenda that lies beneath the rhetoric of "less government" and more consultation. These strains and contradictions quickly surfaced in the late 1970s and 1980s.

Consultation in an era of restraint also requires a careful examination of the rhetoric, or "language," of consultation and public position-taking by various interest groups and institutions. An example will illustrate the point.

It is often said that governments must create a suitable "climate for investment." While there is undoubtedly truth in this, it is also true that what this often really means is that governments should "plan" in order to make one group's situation more predictable and prosperous by making other people's lives more unpredictable and less prosperous (for example, energy tax write-offs versus the tightening of unemployment insurance eligibility).

The nature and time frames of many policy controversies (energy, resources, food, transportation) are such that consultation in a time of restraint raises starkly the issue of "planning"—usually a four-letter word studiously avoided in Canadian political discussion. Instead, we use words like "industrial strategy" or "strategy for economic development." Ultimately these terms imply a longer time frame and predictability and raise questions about in whose interests such predictability (planning?) will be secured.

To summarize, it can be seen through any serious analysis of institutions, interests and interest groups that there is clearly a legitimate place for formal consultation in the policy formulation process. It is needed to identify ideas, to *learn* about problems and, with luck and goodwill, to achieve *some* solutions. It is equally clear that no single formal consultative mechanism can adequately embrace the federal-provincial, Parliamentary, media, producer interest group, and public interest group elements of the political system. There will always have to be a number of forums.

Finally, it is evident that too much formal consultation, especially when other instruments of governing (regulation, taxation and spending) are denied politicians, can result in enormous costs, including economic costs. But more importantly, too much consultation helps cause increasing cynicism about the capacity of democratic government to take concrete action when required.

NOTES

1. A. Paul Pross, ed., *Pressure Group Behaviour in Canadian Politics* (Toronto: McGraw-Hill Ryerson, 1975), p. 7. See also Robert Presthus, *Elite Accommodation in Canadian Politics* (Toronto: Macmillan of Canada, 1973).
2. Pross, *op. cit.,* Chapter 1.
3. See James Rice and Michael Prince, *Social Policy and Administration in Canada* (Manuscript in progress).
4. See Phillip Slayton and Michael J. Trebilcock, *The Professions and Public Policy* (Toronto: University of Toronto Press, 1978).
5. See David Langille, *From Consultation to Corporatism? The Consultative Process Between Canadian Business, Labour and Government, 1977-1981* (Ottawa: Master Research Essay, Department of Political Science, Carleton University, 1982); Anthony Giles, *The Politics of Wage Controls: The Canadian State, Organized Labour and Corporatism* (Ottawa: Masters Thesis, School of Public Administration, Carleton University, 1980); and William Dodge, ed., *Consultation and Consensus: A New Era in Policy Formulation?* (Ottawa: Conference Board of Canada, 1978).
6. Richard W. Phidd, "The Agricultural Policy Formulation Process in Canada." Paper presented to the Canadian Political Science Association Meetings (Montreal: June 2-4, 1980).
7. See Mancur Olson, *The Logic of Collective Action* (Cambridge, Mass.: Harvard University Press, 1965). For a critique of this view as applied to trade unions, see Leo Pantich, "Trade Unions and the Capitalist State," *New Left Review,* No. 125 (January-February, 1981), pp. 21-43.

8. Douglas Hartle, *Public Policy Decision Making and Regulation* (Montreal: Institute for Research on Public Policy, 1979), p. 66.

9. *Ibid,* p. 66.

10. See Paul Pross, *op. cit.,* Chapter 1; and A. Paul Pross, "Governing Under Pressure: the Special Interest Groups," *Canadian Public Administration,* Vol. 25, no. 2, (Summer 1982), pp. 170-182.

11. For example in the environmental field, see G. Bruce Doern, *The Politics of Risk: The Identification of Toxic and Other Hazardous Substances in Canada* (Toronto: Royal Commission on Matters of Health and Safety Arising from the Use of Asbestos in Ontario, 1982).

12. Hartle, *op. cit.,* p. 67.

13. See R.M. Rickover, "The 1977 Bank Act: Emerging Issues and Policy Choices," *Canadian Public Policy,* Vol. II, No. 3 (Summer, 1976), pp. 368-379; and D.E. Bond and R.A. Shearer, *The Economics of the Canadian Financial System: Theory, Policy and Institutions* (Toronto: Prentice-Hall of Canada, 1972).

14. See David Crane, *Controlling Interest* (Toronto: McClelland and Stewart, 1982); and G. Bruce Doern and Glen Toner, *The NEP and the Politics of Energy* (Toronto: Methuen, 1984), Chapter 5.

15. W.T. Stanbury, *Business Interests and the Reform of Canadian Competition Policy, 1971-1975* (Toronto: Methuen, 1977).

16. See David R. Harvey, *Christmas Turkey or Prairie Vulture?* (Montreal: Institute for Research on Public Policy, 1981); Howard Darling, *The Politics of Freight Rates* (Toronto: McClelland and Stewart, 1980); V.C. Fowke, *Canadian Agricultural Policy: The Historical Pattern* (Toronto: University of Toronto Press, 1946); and V.C. Fowke, *The National Policy and the Wheat Economy* (Toronto: University of Toronto Press, 1957).

17. See Grant Vinning, "Regulation and Regulatory Modes in Canadian Agriculture" (Ottawa: M.A. Thesis, School of Public Administration, Carleton University, 1978), J.D. Forbes, R.D. Hughes and T.K. Warley, *Economic Intervention and Regulation in Canadian Agriculture* (Ottawa: Ministry of Supply and Services, 1982). See also Don Mitchell, *The Politics of Food* (Toronto: Lorimer, 1975); and J.D. Forbes, *Institutional and Influence Groups in the Canadian Food System Policy Process.* Study prepared for the Economic Council of Canada Regulatory Reference (January, 1982).

18. See Slayton and Trebilcock, *op. cit.*

19. See Sandford Borins, *Language of the Sky* (Montreal: McGill-Queen's University Press, 1983).

20. See William Leis, ed., *Ecology Versus Politics in Canada* (Toronto: University of Toronto Press, 1979), G. Bruce Doern, Michael Prince and Garth McNaughton, *Living with Contradictions: Health and Safety Regulation and Implementation in Ontario* (Toronto: Royal Commission

on Matters of Health and Safety Arising from the Use of Asbestos in Ontario).

21. See Liora Salter, *Public Inquiries in Canada* (Ottawa: Science Council of Canada, 1981).

22. See Richard W. Phidd and G. Bruce Doern, *The Politics and Management of Canadian Economic Policy* (Toronto: Macmillan of Canada, 1978), Chapters 12 and 14; and K.J. Rea and J.T. McLeod, eds., *Business and Government in Canada,* Second Edition (Toronto: Methuen, 1976).

23. David Langille, *op. cit.,* p. 105. This section draws on this excellent research study.

24. Quoted in Langille, *op. cit.,* p. 108.

25. Langille, *op. cit.,* p. 124.

26. Interviews by the authors with BCNI members and staff.

27. See Canadian Federation of Independent Business, *A Decade of Action* (Toronto: Canadian Federation of Independent Business, 1979).

28. See Hartle, *op. cit.,* Chapter 3; and Michael Trebilcock, "The Consumer Interest and Regulatory Reform," in G. Bruce Doern, ed., *The Regulatory Process in Canada* (Toronto: Macmillan of Canada, 1978), pp. 94-127.

29. See David Kwavnick, *Organized Labour and Pressure Politics* (Montreal: McGill-Queen's University Press, 1972); David Langille, *op. cit.,* pp. 136-166; and Giles, *op. cit.*

30. David Langille, *op. cit.,* pp. 136-166; and Giles, *op. cit.*

31. See Dodge, *op. cit.;* Phidd and Doern, *op. cit.;* and Douglas Brown and Julia Eastman, *The Limits of Consultation* (Ottawa: Science Council of Canada, 1981).

CHAPTER 4

THE GENERAL POLICY FORMULATION ROUTINE: THE PROBLEMS OF DOING FIRST THINGS FIRST

By looking carefully at the political system and its environment and at ideas, institutions, interests and interest groups, we are now in a position to take two further, but still necessarily general, glimpses into the Canadian public policy system. The first portrait is the routine that characterizes the development and consideration of individual policy proposals within the executive-bureaucratic structures. The second glimpse involves a discussion as to why "routines" and "systems" confront the more complex dynamics, realities and uncertainties of politics and governing, thus revealing why governments have difficulty doing first things first, why notions of a rational policy process have severe limitations, but why, simultaneously, governments still have to try to plan.

The General Policy Formulation Routine

One way to appreciate the general policy formulation routine that occurs within the executive structures of the Cabinet and senior bureaucracy in Ottawa is to first present a simple policy stages model. We then show how this is partly reflected in the formal policy formulation process that lies at the centre of the Canadian public policy system. To do this, however, we must first assume that a policy or a decision is proceeding through the system in an orderly manner, one policy field or proposal at a time. In this sense we will be visualizing, temporarily at least, a rational policy process. In the latter part of the chapter, we examine the obvious limitations of the simple policy stages model. This requires us to examine the general political problems governments have in setting priorities and in managing the several policy *processes* and demands that operate *concurrently* in the real world of making public policy. In Part II of the book we examine in greater detail these concurrent processes and the structures that support them.

A Simple Model of Policy Development Stages

Ideally, and to a certain extent in practice, a policy problem goes through several stages.[1] These stages include:

- identification
- definition
- alternative search
- choice
- implementation, and
- evaluation (feedback and learning)

They encompass the main features of a rational process of thought and action to solve a problem or reach a goal.

The identification of a problem involves the persistent articulation of a concern or issue. It can emerge from an external demand (a general one to "provide jobs" or a particular one to restore railway service in a given locality) or internally, from the executive-bureaucratic arena itself (for example, from a previous study) or from a combination of both external and internal sources.

The definition stage involves a process in which "the problem" is shaped or confined to more practical limits. It is "defined" into what policy makers and advisers believe to be its real meaning. This would involve discussion and elaboration of the ideas inherent in it, of the objectives to be met and of the consequences to be avoided.

Closely tied to the definition stage is the search for, and analysis of, alternative ways of solving the problem. Ideally, all major alternatives would be assessed as to their costs and benefits and likely efficiency and effectiveness. This would involve a search for alternative instruments (exhorting, spending, taxing, regulating) or mixtures of instruments. Theoretically, it could include a consideration of the option of doing nothing and/or of maintaining the status quo.

It is at the definition and search for alternative stages that bureaucratic influence is perhaps at its maximum. The deputy minister, assistant deputy minister and other key senior policy analysts in the sponsoring department and in other departments involved in the problem are engaged in continuous meetings and telephone discussions as they "massage" and analyze the problem. But they do this in concert with their own ministers who are also talking to each other as politicians. Ideas and facts are present in abundance at this stage even though they may be glibly buried in the rhetoric and/or terminology of short-term politics and analysis. Indeed, they meld into what Vickers has called the "appreciative system" of decision makers. These stages are also the point where it is most difficult to separate the myths, realities and perceptions of the relative influence and power of bureaucrats and ministers. This is also a crucial feature of policy formulation.

At the stage when actual choice occurs, the question of resource allocation ceases to be theoretical. Real resources (money, personnel, political goodwill, time, etc.) are committed. The implementation stage follows suit that may or may not involve new legislation by Parliament. Some decisions and policies can be carried out under existing legislative authority or permission and thus are implemented through an order in council, a regulation, a guideline or a rule or an expenditure of funds. Others may require new legislation in the form of an overall new or amended statute or as an expenditure appropriation or tax through the annual passage of the Estimates or Supplementary Estimates or through "ways and means" legislation following a Budget Speech.

As we have seen in earlier chapters, implementation also involves the behaviour of *both* public officials and private citizens. Since it occurs over time, this stage is usually the longest and most permanent. The intent of implementation is to produce results in a reliable, predictable way to meet the ideas and objectives sought.

Finally, it would be both necessary and desirable to evaluate the results to see if the objectives had been met. In the broadest sense it is assumed, ideally, that the policy maker wants to learn and obtain feedback so that corrections can be made.

Even though it is recognized that these stages are not always discrete and watertight but are normally a series of iterative events, it is nonetheless intuitively appealing to visualize the policy routine in this way and to practise policy making according to its precepts. It is in this important sense that the rational model retains its normative but not necessarily its practical appeal.

How the Simple Policy Stages Model Is Reflected in the Policy Formulation Process: Cabinet Papers and the Paper Flow

One of the formal ways in which the policy process in the Government of Canada nominally conforms to the simple policy stages model is in the requirements placed on ministers and officials for the submission of proposals to Cabinet or its committees. The types, content, and paper flow of Cabinet documents partly conforms to a rational model. It must be stressed, of course, that Cabinet documents are only a *written* form of policy advice. They tell us nothing of the perhaps even more crucial *verbal* dimensions of the policy formulation process, let alone much about the dynamics of the process. These aspects are discussed in Chapters 10, 11, 12 and 13. In the meantime, however, it is instructive to review the content of Cabinet papers in relation to the simple policy stages model and as a main element of the general routine of policy formulation.

There are two broad types of Cabinet papers: Cabinet Documents and Other Cabinet Papers. The former includes memoranda to Cabinet, draft bills, agendas and minutes of Cabinet and Cabinet committees, committee reports and records of decisions. These papers are deemed to contain a "confidence of the Queen's Privy Council" and are internal to Cabinet.[2] The papers are secret in order to encourage frank discussion among ministers and to ensure that, once policy is decided, differences among ministers are kept private and Cabinet solidarity is maintained. Other Cabinet papers, such as the Discussion Paper, are not secret documents, though they may be kept confidential as circumstances dictate. Other papers in this category include the annual departmental Five-Year Strategic Overview documents, Multi-Year Operational Plan documents and the Assessment Notes. For the limited purposes of this chapter, we focus briefly on three papers—the Discussion Paper, the Memorandum to Cabinet, and Assessment Notes.

The Memorandum to Cabinet and the Discussion Paper are the main documentary vehicles through which a minister brings an issue to Cabinet. In essence, the Memorandum contains specific recommendations, summarizes the nature of the decisions, and discusses delicate political, including partisan, considerations. It is not supposed to exceed five to ten pages in length but usually does. The Discussion Paper, on the other hand, can be of widely varying lengths. Avoiding a discussion of recommendations and partisan political sensitivities, it provides an extensive discussion of alternatives, background issues and trends suitable for both ministers and officials. Begun in 1977, this dual system was introduced to ensure that ministers "are not burdened with briefing material ... beyond what is necessary for political choice."[3] As we see below, even greater brevity was sought in 1979–80 with the introduction of Assessment Notes. We refer here to the Assessment Notes formally prepared by central agency policy secretariats to brief all ministers on the policy field Cabinet Committee. There are, of course, hundreds, indeed thousands, of other briefing notes prepared for ministers on an individual basis as well.

The main headings for material to be examined in the Discussion Paper are summarized below:[4]

- Object
- Background
- Factors
- Alternatives
- Financial Considerations
- Federal-Provincial Considerations
- Other Considerations
- Interdepartmental Consultation
- Public Information Considerations
- Conclusion

The much shorter Memoranda to Cabinet are decision documents whose headings are:[5]

- Object
- Decision required
- Considerations
  —financial
  —federal-provincial
  —other
  —interdepartmental
  —public information
  —political (caucus consultations, party policy conference)
- Conclusions
- Recommendations

To cite a provincial government example, Ontario cabinet guidelines for policy proposals, legislation and regulation specify headings such as the following:[6]

- Problem
- Background
- Options
- Program priorities
- Liaison with other ministries, Management Board and inter-governmental implications
- Legislative implications

- Economic impact—private sector, public sector (see below)
- Communications plan
- Conclusions
- Recommendations

The economic impact category for Ontario Cabinet proposals is further divided as follows:

Private Sector
- job creation/job loss
- effect on investment capital
- encouragement to the formation of new business
- duplication of the intent and functions of existing organization
- effect on consumer prices
- reduction of the incentive to work
- the cost of compliance

The Public Sector
- effect on the government work force
- expenditure increases

The listing of these headings does not in itself show how decisions are actually made. They convey no sense of whether ministers have time to read documents or to understand them. Moreover, it is important to stress that several provincial governments have only recently adopted guidelines for the submission of Cabinet proposals. Until then, the documentation was often very limited and, in some cases, virtually nonexistent.

The headings in a federal Discussion Paper are fairly straightforward. The "Object" section of the federal Discussion Paper identifies the problem. The "Background" section provides a brief history of the problem, why a decision is now needed, and previous government policies and decisions on the issue. The "Factors" part of the document sets out the characteristics of the problem, including fiscal, legal, economic, social and attitudinal factors and the relationships among them. This is followed by a description and analysis of alternatives, including the status quo.

The remaining sections go into even greater detail. In the section on "Financial Considerations," the question of current and future costs (over five years), revenues and methods of financing are discussed. The sections on "Federal-Provincial Relations" and "Interdepartmental Considerations" describe and deal with the kinds of consultation that have occurred, the jurisdictional interests and sensitivities involved, and related concerns.

Finally, there is a discussion of "Public Information Considerations." This deals with issues of the timing of an announcement, publicity campaigns in the form of ministerial speeches or more elaborate marketing of the policy, program or decisions. It may also contain summaries of recent public opinion polling data on the subject in question. The "Other Considerations" section is a catch-all one and is used to flag other issues such as considerations of Parliamentary tactics, political appointments, political party resolutions and caucus considerations.

These documents contain roughly the same kinds of information and the same sequence of treatment implied in the simple policy stages model. Identification, definition, alternative search and choice are all explicitly present. Implementation and evaluation are less explicitly present, although the documents contain information and analysis of past decisions and programs.

The adequacy of the implementation and evaluation stages of the general policy process raises numerous interesting questions about how evaluations are conducted, who does them, and about the state of social knowledge. We return to these questions. At this elementary stage it is worth stressing, however, that these latter stages have been the object of particular criticism in recent years. The Auditor General of Canada and the Office of the Comptroller General have been extremely critical of the failure, in their view, of the government's overall managerial responsibility to "complete the rational cycle," so to speak—that is, to conduct and utilize formal evaluations of programs to see if past implementation is "efficient and effective" and to change or discard programs and policies if they have not measured up.

It is instructive at this point to take note of the possible headings that do *not* appear on these documents. There is no explicit heading for "effects on the environment" or "scientific and technological factors," or "foreign policy considerations" or "effects on low income Canadians." Some would argue that these headings should be "flagged" as well in an ideal policy process. This is not to suggest that these items do not show up in one form or another under other headings, but they indicate the range of "considerations," that is, processes and ideas that are part of the agenda.

The Cabinet documents outlined briefly above are intended to inform a *collective* Cabinet of the proposals being made to it by one (or more) of its *individual* ministers. It is estimated, however, that there are typically from six to seven hundred Cabinet Memoranda submitted annually to Cabinet and many fewer Discussion Papers. At the same time, there are other kinds of voluminous written material that cross ministers' desks. As a result, there has been a constant concern about both the quantity and quality of ministerial briefing material and how it is prepared.

It is in this context that we should mention the introduction of the Assessment Notes. These are brief three- or four-page notes prepared for Cabinet ministers under the so-called "envelope" system (see Chapters 11 and 12). The notes were deemed to be necessary not only to try to economize on the amount of paper ministers read, but also to ensure that ministers, as Cabinet committee members, were briefed on a *collective* basis rather than only by their own departmental and political staffs. It was argued that in the pre-envelope system in existence before 1979 too much debate occurred over "the facts" and not over the choices to be made. The Assessment Notes are prepared through a process of consultation among ministers, parallel deputy ministerial committees and senior officials to ensure that there is greater prior agreement about the facts, leaving more time, in theory, for real political choice. While such notes can be helpful, they also effectively add to the "paper burden" of ministers and deputy ministers and thus perhaps drive them and require them to place even greater reliance on verbal advice.

An Assessment Note first describes the proposal briefly and then discusses its advantages and disadvantages in relation to such factors as its consistency with the priorities of the envelope/committee, its regional and distributional effects, and its effects on departments other than the one proposing it. The note also contains a firm dollar cost for the current year and the next three years. Assessment Notes do not replace other Cabinet documents but rather are in addition to them. They are used for more particular proposals which may have been given more general approval but have not been examined in an explicit resource allocation sense.

The above documents are not the only ones intended to make the decision process as rational as possible. The envelope process requires the preparation of Five-Year Strategic Overviews by departments as well as Multi-Year Operational Plans. Our intention in discussing these documents briefly here has been to convey some of the formal effort to construct a basic decision process broadly analogous to the rational model. The analysis in Chapters 11, 12 and 13 shows the dynamics and the unintended effects of this effort, particularly in relation to the role of analysis and knowledge and in the context of *both* written and verbal decision processes.

The Limits of the Simple Policy Stages Model

Ministers and senior officials must adhere in a formal way to some kind of a simple policy stages model, primarily because they must attempt to manage, coordinate and control the overall policy and decision process. Most of this book, however, testifies to the inherent limits of the simple policy stages model. This is not because ministers and other politicians are inherently "irrational" while the rest of us make decisions wisely. The limits of the simple policy stages model flow from the unique rationality of politics and government, which in turn is founded on relationships between ideas, structure and process. Thus, to appreciate the limits of the systems and routines enunciated above, we need to return to the basic concepts introduced in earlier chapters.

First, it is essential to stress that public policy is almost never made "one policy field at a time." While there may be periods of time when Cabinet attention is focused on energy policy, medicare, the status of women, or policies for small businesses, political, bureaucratic and economic realities are such that the agenda is almost always filled with several concurrent policy concerns.

This untidy agenda is aided and abetted, indeed ultimately determined, by the persistent presence of the ideologies and dominant ideas discussed in Chapter 2. Normative concern for efficiency, individual liberty, equity, stability, redistribution, national unity and regional sensitivity exist in virtually every major policy field. These concerns are voiced by ministers, political parties, the caucus, as well as by interests, interest groups and other governments in Canada and abroad. This is not to suggest that these dominant ideas are expressed in an even-handed pluralistic way. At various times one or more ideas may have more powerful advocates and friends with greater access to the apex of governmental power. The point is that the dominant ideas are almost always present in some significant way regardless of the effort of government or certain ministers and senior officials to define and control the policy agenda.

The simple policy stages model also fails to take account of the existence of the several processes generated by the basic governing instruments. Thus, the tax process, though related to many substantive policy fields (fiscal, energy, regional and social policies) has, in part, a life of its own, centred in the Department of Finance. A tax community exists which is concerned about the revenue and tax system and the tax process.[7] Moreover, the tax decision process has been dominated by secrecy founded on a normative concern for ensuring that private interests could not gain from prior knowledge of tax measures. In a similar way the regulatory process and the expenditure process constitute separate but obviously related processes with constituencies which are concerned about the overall integrity and the specific benefits and protections these instruments confer, and which advocate regulatory reform or expenditure reform. It is important to stress that these instrument-based processes are not neutral processes. They are normatively valued and are the object of policy dispute, both in aggregate terms and in specific policy situations and fields.

The single policy process concept also breaks down for reasons which theorists of incrementalism have long appreciated. The need to narrow the range of alternatives and to confine the definition of a problem is a product of the political need to obtain a consensus and of an appreciation that only finite resources and information are available.

It is essential to appreciate in this context that there can be "policies without resources" to support them. Resources include money (taxes and spending), personnel, time and political will. Many governments find it necessary to enunciate policy to express their concern about, and support for, a particular constituency or group, since this is usually preferable to expressing no public concern whatsoever. But it does not mean necessarily that the policy will be given full or complete resource support. Thus, only some money may be provided, or only limited enforcement of regulations may be supplied.

The relationship between the policy process and the overall resource allocation process is therefore not necessarily a one-to-one relationship. Chapters 10, 11 and 12 show how the federal *policy process,* prior to the adoption of the envelope system of expenditure management, was once partly separate from the *resource allocation process.*

Even in its present, more integrated form under the envelope system there are often policies without resources.

Another phenomenon which makes the simple policy stages model inappropriate is the frequent emergence of major physical capital intensive *projects* (such as pipelines or airports) on the policy agenda.[8] Canada began its continental existence with such a project, the construction of the Canadian Pacific Railway. Since then, there have been other dominant projects—the St. Lawrence Seaway, the Trans-Canada Pipeline of the mid-1950s, the Olympic Games and the Alaska Pipeline, to name a few. In the early 1980s the concept of "mega projects" emerged as a central part of the federal economic development strategy. Indeed, the strategy envisioned that several dozen such projects would come on stream in the 1980s and 1990s.

Large projects are by definition capital intensive. As events in 1981 and 1982 have shown, they are therefore especially sensitive to financing and capital market problems and conditions including interest rates, inflation rates and medium- and long-term price movements. They induce all parties involved in a project to try to deflect risk as much as possible on others. Because many projects involve joint ventures or consortia, they present different problems for different companies and governments, depending on their particular fiscal position and attitudes to risk. The gradual breakdown of the Alsands consortium in 1982 showed this clearly.

The projects impose on the political system a need to consider a longer-term planning period. In the regular policy process three years is a long time. The realities of obtaining initial approvals and financing and the period of sheer physical construction make some kind of longer-term planning and project management essential. When these temporal and physical attributes are added to the technological novelty and risks of many of the projects, uncertainty is increased and the drive to share or to displace risks on others is overwhelming. Projects such as the Alsands, Cold Lake, Hibernia, Beaufort Sea, Heavy Oil Upgraders, the B.C. Coal Project and the Arctic Pilot Project all involve technological experimentation in the recovery and production process or in transportation and distribution processes.

The first two characteristics combine to produce a third. Large projects involve high political visibility. In the initial decision and construction phase they have a distinct beginning and end. They allow political actors and their private sector partners to experience a visible success, including successful experiments in labour relations, environmental and procurement practices. Or they may suffer a conspicuous failure. Sometimes the same politician can experience both over the same project. Premier Robert Bourassa of Quebec paid a heavy short-term political price over the mammoth James Bay Project but appears to be basking in its glory ten years later. A potential white elephant in the short term becomes an act of courage and foresight in the long term. The reverse can also happen.

The political visibility of a project is not a one-dimensional thing. A substantial portion of large resource development projects are hinterland-based and thus physically remote from national and provincial capitals and other large urban centres. There is high political visibility for the project in urban Canada at the time of decision and perhaps construction, but many of the social effects of the project are in the hinterland and in small surrounding communities. Thus, the effects can be, as it were, "out of sight, out of mind."

A large physical *project* has an even higher probability of triggering concerns and ideas in several policy fields concurrently than does a normal policy initiative. Because each project is partly unique and occurs at different times, it "tests" these policy fields in different ways each time. Although efforts will be made to "be fair" to each project and to treat them equally, there will also be a need to "be reasonable," in short, to strike a new composite policy deal every time. The kinds of policy fields that can be and have been involved concurrently in large projects include energy and resources, economic and fiscal, social and environmental, labour relations and employment practices, regional policy, foreign policy and trade and technology. Each of these are under the custody of different ministers and officials in numerous departments, agencies and boards of several levels of government, federal, provincial, local and foreign.

If several policy fields are involved, it follows that several policy instruments are likely to be involved to ensure that the right, or at the least the acceptable, mix of public and private behaviour occurs in relation to each project and, over time, in relation to all or most projects. Thus, packages of spending grants and subsidies, verbal understandings, procurement activity, taxes or tax breaks, regulations (including administered prices) and direct public investment through Crown or mixed enterprises could be involved. These packages are not easily assembled, partly because there are always disputes (that is, politics) about how much of the carrot and the stick or the iron hand in the velvet glove is necessary to achieve the many purposes of the project. Moreover, the custodian departments and boards must constantly decide when a project arises how much of an exception, if any, the project should be to their normal ongoing policies and policy responsibilities. Such judgements must be made in the context of legal as well as political and financial constraints. These judgements become all the more difficult as more and more mega-projects queue up at the governmental trough. Which ones deserve the most support and on what grounds? Which ones should come on stream first, and why?

For several reasons, then, the simple policy stages model has severe limitations. Our appreciation of these limits is not yet complete, since we also need to relate the above features to the larger priority setting process, the process by which governments try to decide to do first things first.

The Political Imperatives and Problems of Doing First Things First

Governments do attempt to set priorities and to make "the policy process" manageable. On an annual basis these priorities may be formally expressed in the Throne Speech, the Budget Speech and speeches on the tabling of expenditure estimates. Periodically, the prime minister may give special speeches on particular critical issues (for example, the imposition of wage and price controls in 1975 and the three-part talk on the economy in 1982). Thus, there is no shortage of occasions when governments attempt to communicate with the electorate about what things should be done first. Governments do this not only for purposes of internal management, but also to provide reassurance to its supporters and to those who might support it at the next election.

But the task of maintaining and sustaining the priority list over a significant period of time is notoriously difficult because the domestic and international environment is always undergoing change. Once again, we must ask why this is so since it will tell us why there are limits to the simple and orderly policy stages model. Undoubtedly, the strongest incentive against the rational setting of, and adherence to, priorities is found in the inexorable ticking of the electoral clock. A political party without power cannot make policy. Therefore, at best, the ideal political planning cycle extends only to about three years, since electoral preparations are likely to neutralize the fourth year.

There is of course a paradox here because there is inherent in democracy a view that a general form of rational behaviour is occurring. That is, it is assumed that a particular political party is elected with a mandate and that it will "keep" (implement) its major election promises. Even when the public is aware of the inflated bidding war inherent in electoral promises, it seems to expect that at least the major promises and priorities will be implemented.

But this quasi-rational expectation about a government's priorities is confounded by two other equally powerful forces: the need to survive politically and the obligation of the government to *govern,* and hence to reach decisions and set priorities in relation to the host of demands and situations which have impact on it *between* elections. Political survival is a powerful instinct. Most politicians would prefer to be in power rather than in the opposition. The accoutrements of public office—salary, prestige, status, and influence—are valued and coveted. To retain them, political parties in power are often prepared to change priorities to help sustain the coalition of voter support that will preserve them in office. Rarely are these self-interest motivations totally separate from the need to govern and deal with dominant ideas. Thus, self-interest and purposeful *governing* responsibilities are inextricably linked.

Priorities are difficult to sustain because of the inevitable limits of information and knowledge. Many policies fail because we lack theory (that is, a knowledge of causal relations), and we lack knowledge about what is required to change human behaviour in desired ways. Interests do not always want to "behave" properly. Policies rarely fail merely because we lack clear objectives. Because of the limits of knowledge, governments must constantly adjust priorities and policies. In short, they must constantly try to *learn* and adjust to the power of other institutions.

A scarcity of resources also accounts for shifting priorities. Many priority concerns and policy fields have inadequate resources of time, money, personnel and political will. Some have more resources than are needed. There is therefore a constant pressure to change priorities to increase the resource support for neglected areas.

In this context it is also necessary to appreciate the source and intensity of policy initiatives and demands. There are obviously external as well as internal demands and pressures, both for change and to sustain the status quo. External demands can eminate from other countries (foreign policy concerns), from other levels of government in Canada, as well as from interest groups and opposition political parties. Internal demands can come from ministers themselves, political advisors and staff, senior bureaucrats, policy and planning branches, and from line departments equally anxious to expand empires and to do "good things."

The relative predominance of these sources of initiative and demand not only affect and change priorities but also raise normative concern about where the power to initiate *should* rest. Are some outside interests too powerful? Are ministers controlled by bureaucrats? Is the policy and priority setting process a "top-down" one or a "bottom-up" one, the latter implying an inordinate influence by line ministers and departments rather than by the prime minister and central agencies or, alternatively, of excessive influence by bureaucrats over ministers.

To this confusing tug and pull of "interests," institutions and ideas, one must add a point stressed in earlier chapters, namely the largely media-induced tendency of politicians to believe that they must "be seen doing something." The media's attention span *is* short. It does thrive on new announcements and on personalities, and on who is "winning" and "losing." It criticizes priorities but never has to allocate resources. It thrives on the latest reactions to the monthly ritual of unemployment and cost of living statistics and to Gallup polls. This adds a further dimension of pressure to change the priority list or, alternatively, to add to the priority list until it becomes a veritable "wish list" of political goods.

Finally, it must be noted that priorities change in form, but perhaps or..y partly in substance, because of the perceived need to put old priority wine into new bottles. Thus, old priorities may have to be expressed in new ways partly to show that new things are being tried and/or to disassociate current efforts from past failures. Thus, an industrial policy or strategy may become a policy on "economic development," rural development evolves into regional policy, and a war on inflation is repackaged as the pursuit of the "6 percent society." These changes are rarely just "window dressing" because policy circumstances do in fact change over time.

Conclusions

One might be tempted to ask in retrospect why a chapter is devoted to policy development "routines" only to find that it systematically picks apart the very notion that there is a general policy process. One cannot avoid this paradox. The reality is that there are several policy processes operating concurrently. A full understanding of the making of public policy demands that one examine the dynamics of policy making. At the same time the government of the day must manage "the policy process" as a whole and seek to impose order upon it despite the extreme difficulty of doing this successfully. Thus, we have focused initially on the formal Cabinet documentation required and on the vague, often implicit, rational and democratic expectation that the government will implement its major promises—in short, that it will set priorities and do first things first.

NOTES

1. See for example, C.O. Jones, *An Introduction to the Study of Public Policy* (New York: Wadsworth, 1970).
2. See Richard French, "The Privy Council Office: Support for Cabinet Decision Making" in Richard Schultz, O.M. Kruhlak, and J.T. Terry, *The Canadian Political Process* (Toronto: Holt, Rinehart and Winston, 1979), pp. 369-372.
3. *Ibid.*, p. 370.
4. See Canada, Privy Council Office, *Cabinet Paper System* (Ottawa, 1977), Parts I and II.
5. *Ibid.*
6. These and other provincial systems are examined in G. Bruce Doern, "Rationalizing the Regulatory Decision Process." Study prepared for the Economic Council of Canada (Ottawa: 1979), Chapter 2.
7. See David Good, *The Politics of Anticipation: Making Canadian Federal Tax Policy* (Ottawa: School of Public Administration; Carleton University, 1980).
8. See G. Bruce Doern, "Mega Projects and the Normal Policy Process" (Ottawa: School of Public Administration, Carleton University, 1982).

CHAPTER 5

GOVERNING INSTRUMENTS

Another central concept in the study of public policy is governing instruments. Governing instruments are the major ways in which governments seek to ensure compliance, support and implementation of public policy. The main instruments available to governing authorities are:

- exhortation,
- expenditure,
- taxation,
- regulation, and
- public enterprise.

It is usually these instruments that are "summed" to show the outputs of government and to show how government has grown and "intervention" has increased. It has been routinely observed how government spending now consumes a higher proportion of gross national product than it did 30 years ago, how taxes and tax expenditures have increased markedly, how volumes of new regulations grind annually through the machinery of state, how Crown corporations proliferate, and how uncountable studies, royal commissions and reorganizations of government seem to become a substitute for action. Each of these instruments are introduced briefly in this chapter, as are some of the relationships among them and the ideas inherent in them. We examine them again in Chapter 12, showing, in more detail, how they relate to the dynamics of policy within the executive and in the larger political and economic system.

At the outset we must stress one overall conceptual feature that arises from the mere mention of instruments and the growth of government intervention. The aggregate growth patterns shown later in this chapter are the primary prima facie evidence that causality in public policy is interactive and not one way. It flows from the economy and society to government *and* vice versa. Instrument growth is not evidence of a passive state whose leaders are mere receptables for larger social and economic pressures. Causality operates the other way as well in that the realms of private behaviour react to the state, to the decisions of elected politicians and unelected officials and to the perceived cumulative effects of these decisions. The state is neither a leviathan nor a eunuch. Therefore the study of public policy must be based on approaches that understand the dual causal interplay, a point we defend throughout the book.

The mere use of the word "instruments" suggests that they are "devices" or "techniques." In short, they are seemingly the "means" through which the "ends" of political life are achieved. In part, of course, this is what they often are. But to view these basic instruments to be merely matters of technique would be a great mistake. The instruments are also *ends* in themselves. They are the object of political dispute, are embedded with ideas and are valued because they fundamentally affect the *process* and *content* of policy making. In democratic politics, process always matters. Normative content and the choice of governing instruments are always intertwined not only in a "means-ends" chain but also in an "ends-ends" chain of relationships.

Why are instruments also ends? Why are they normatively valued? The first clue to answering this question is to understand the connection between the types of instruments noted above and the degrees of *legitimate coercion* involved in governing.[1] Figure 5.1 displays these characteristics. It shows the instruments arranged, albeit somewhat artificially, along a continuum starting with minimum or almost nonexistent coercion and extending to maximum coercion. Thus, exhortation involves an effort to ensure support and compliance through persuasion, discussion and voluntary approaches. At the other end of the continuum taxation, regulation and public enterprise (especially the nationalization of a firm) are all more coercive because they involve

FIGURE 5.1
THE INSTRUMENTS OF GOVERNING

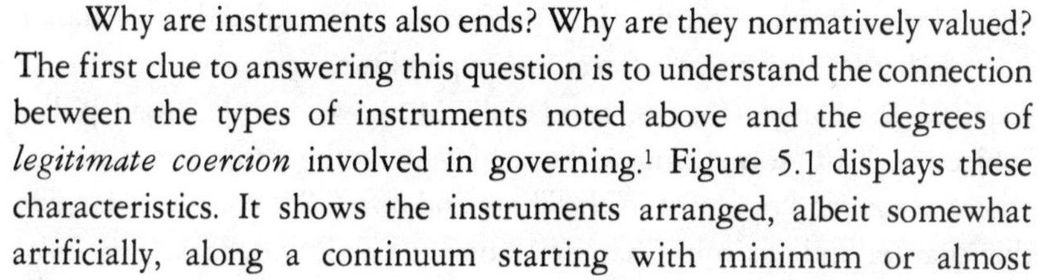

| Self-Regulation (Private Behaviour) | Exhortation | Expenditure | Regulation (including taxation) | Public Ownership |

Minimum   DEGREES OF LEGITIMATE COERCION   Maximum

setting rules of behaviour backed up directly by the sanctions (penalties) of the state. *In theory,* all three of these are "regulatory" in a broad sense in that taxes are rules of behaviour regarding the extraction of income and wealth from private citizens and institutions, and public enterprise involves rules of behaviour regarding the ownership of shares and assets by the state. In practice, of course, we tend to distinguish between these instruments, with public ownership usually being seen as the most coercive and interventionist.

In the middle of the continuum one finds public expenditure. It is only moderately coercive in that governments, when they spend, are distributing the funds as benefits or services (grants, transfer payments, etc.). Actual coercion occurs when the revenue is extracted from the taxpayer but, when it is spent, the coercive edge has disappeared or is at least blurred since the question of who pays and who benefits is not always easily determined.

In policy formulation, the choice of instrument(s) is itself normative precisely because judgements about the degree of coercion and the object of coercion *are* normative. For example, there is probably a liberal democratic presumption that it is preferable to be persuaded to change one's behaviour or to be offered an expenditure incentive than to be required to change (that is, regulated). Moreover, while broad policy "objectives" are something to be achieved in the future, instrument choice is real and operates in the "here and now." We comment later in this chapter and again in Chapter 12 on the particular characteristics of each type of instrument and the dynamics they create, but it is first necessary to deal further with some general issues concerning governing instruments.

Instruments and the Growth of Government

Aggregate data on the main instruments certainly show the growth of government and reveals a snapshot of policy outputs expressed as instruments. Richard Bird's warning about the growth of expenditure data is equally valid about other data on instruments. Bird stressed that

> contrary to popular opinion facts such as these do *not* speak for themselves. Rather they can be understood and interpreted only within some analytical framework, implicit or explicit. The usual simplistic notion that "more" government is somehow "worse" government has insufficient content to tell us anything useful.[2]

Expenditure Growth

The growth of expenditure is the most visible sign of governmental expansion. As a percentage of Gross National Expenditure (GNE) the expenditures of all levels of government have grown from an average of 22.9 percent in 1947 to 1951, to 39.4 percent in 1973 to 1977. In the early 1980s the figure edged over the 40 percent mark since the economic depression caused several automatic social program stabilization expenditures to increase significantly. As measured in the National Accounts, total governmental expenditures rose 73 percent faster than GNE in the 30-year period from 1947 to 1977 and reached over 41 percent of GNE in the late 1970s.[3] Of equal interest is the comparison of expenditures by level of government. It shows that provincial government and local government expenditures have expanded the most rapidly, especially since the mid-1960s. It is important to note, however, that these figures do not convey the degree to which some of the provincial and local increases were triggered by federal fiscal transfers and grants in fields such as health, education and welfare. Also, the overall data on the growth of expenditures do not convey the different claims that different expenditures make on the economy. It is important to note as well that transfer payments (made to individuals who then decide how to spend it) have grown more rapidly than exhaustive expenditures, that is, those which use up goods and services, including labour, directly.

When federal expenditures are looked at by function or broad policy fields, as in Table 5.1, the pattern is fairly clear-cut. Expenditures on health, education and welfare have increased significantly and expenditures on defence have decreased markedly. However, the priority on social programs does not necessarily reflect a full commitment to redistribution as a dominant idea. Debt charges went down slightly, although they do not reflect the burgeoning debt charges of the early 1980s.

As to the more recent pattern of deficits, Table 5.2 presents a composite picture of federal debt and overall total governmental debt. When combined, they reveal that the federal government has had to bear the lion's share of the debt. For some years in the mid and late 1970s, the provincial governments were in a net surplus position. A major factor in the growth of the federal debt in the late 1970s was Ottawa's energy policy decisions to keep energy prices below world levels and to produce fair prices across Canada by subsidizing eastern Canadian refiners who

TABLE 5.1
FEDERAL SPENDING ON SELECTED FUNCTIONS AS A PERCENTAGE OF TOTAL SPENDING

SELECTED YEARS 1954-79
(Financial Management Statistics)
(%)

Year	General Government	Transportation & Communications	Health & Welfare	Education Assistance	Recreation and Culture	Defence	General Purpose Transfers to Other Governments	Debt Charges
1954	4.4	3.2	17.8	0.4	0.3	34.3	7.4	10.6
1957	6.0	4.2	18.3	0.7	0.3	32.2	7.8	10.2
1961	4.0	5.3	24.2	1.0	0.4	25.1	8.6	12.1
1965	3.3	6.5	28.4	2.6	0.6	19.1	4.8	12.8
1967	4.3	6.7	26.0	4.3	0.9	16.6	5.6	11.9
1969	5.4	4.7	28.5	4.7	0.7	14.2	7.3	11.8
1971	6.3	6.6	36.9	5.5	0.7	11.0	8.4	7.8
1973	6.0	6.6	41.4	4.0	1.0	9.1	7.8	7.2
1975	5.5	7.1	40.6	3.4	0.9	7.4	8.2	7.4
1977	5.5	6.6	41.6	3.3	0.9	7.8	8.2	8.1
1979	6.0	6.9	41.0	4.2	0.8	7.7	6.3	8.8

Source: Statistics Canada, *Federal Government Finance*. Reproduced by permission of the Minister of Supply and Services Canada.

TABLE 5.2
FEDERAL GOVERNMENT AND TOTAL GOVERNMENT REVENUE, EXPENDITURE AND NET POSITION
(National Accounts Basis)

	Revenue		Expenditure		Surplus or deficit (−)
Federal Government	(millions of dollars)	(percentage change)	(millions of dollars)	(percentage change)	(millions of dollars)
1974	29,978	31.4	28,869	28.8	1,109
1975	31,703	5.8	35,508	23.0	− 3,805
1976	35,313	11.4	38,704	9.0	− 3,391
1977	36,509	3.4	43,812	13.2	− 7,303
1978	38,325	5.0	48,979	11.8	−10,654
1979	43,361	13.4	52,674	7.5	− 9,213
1980	50,076	15.2	60,773	15.4	−10,697
1981	63,984	27.8	71,488	17.6	− 7,504
Total Government					
1973	46,297	16.3	45,045	13.4	1,252
1974	58,756	26.9	55,961	24.2	2,795
1975	64,239	9.3	68,288	22.0	− 4,049
1976	73,496	14.4	76,718	12.3	− 3,222
1977	81,310	10.6	86,315	12.5	− 5,005
1978	89,567	10.2	96,521	11.8	− 6,954
1979	100,795	12.5	105,486	9.3	− 4,691
1980	114,746	13.8	120,729	14.5	− 5,983
1981	137,224	19.6	139,457	15.5	− 2,233

Source: Statistics Canada, National Income and Expenditure Accounts, quarterly, cat. 13.001. Reproduced by permission of the Minister of Supply and Services Canada.

are more dependent on imported oil. The hefty increases in federal revenue in 1981 reflect new federal energy taxes imposed to redress the fiscal imbalance referred to above. Table 5.2 does not convey the precipitous increase in the federal deficit in 1982. This was forecast late in 1982 to be over 23 billion, a far larger deficit in proportional terms than that of the U.S. government.

Deficits must be linked as well to overall monetary and fiscal policy. Four features of recent Canadian policy must be stressed. First, a monetarist view has influenced policy. The Bank of Canada in the mid-1970s committed itself to a position of gradually reducing the rate of growth of the money supply. This policy has been followed. The federal government has not, however, supported the monetarist view with its fiscal policies. It did, in 1976, commit itself to a policy of ensuring that federal expenditures did not exceed a trend line growth in real GNP (and for a very brief time appeared to succeed), but its overall fiscal stance has not been supportive of its monetary policy. The Budgets of November 1981 and June 1982 seemed to bring the fiscal stance more in line with the management of money supply, but these budgets, as we see below, suffered from their own dilemmas. A second important feature has been the high interest rate policy followed in Canada. This was necessitated by the monetarist stance, but is exacerbated by Canada's perceived need to protect the Canadian dollar and to follow U.S. rates. High interest rates contributed significantly to increased debt servicing costs, as well as to the political misery of the Trudeau Liberals. A final fiscal issue to note is the degree to which the federal government has increased its use of loan guarantees and/or equity debentures to assist beleaguered firms such as Dome Petroleum, Massey Ferguson and Chrysler Canada. Such loan guarantees are not reflected in the above data.

All of the above data are in current prices. When aggregate figures reflect real dollars, the magnitude of growth is less.[4] Thus, the real expansion of total government spending as a proportion of GNE since 1947 is closer to 40 percent than 73 percent. Expenditures on goods and services have hardly grown at all despite almost doubling in nominal current dollars.

There are, of course, other measures of expenditures related to governmental growth. Of special real and symbolic importance is the growth of government as employers. Here again provincial growth has increased more rapidly than federal growth. Recent studies show, however, that the overall proportion of the labour force employed by the public sector has grown very slightly in the 1960s and 1970s, although there was significant growth in the 1950s. Despite this data there has been a remarkably focused political criticism of the growth of bureaucracy, especially in the late 1970s and early 1980s. We will examine this again in Chapters 11 and 12.

Revenue Growth, Taxes and Tax Expenditures

Government revenues and the taxes and charges that produce them have also increased greatly. Total government revenues as a percent of GNE grew 31 percent between 1947 and 1977, most of the growth occurring between the mid-1960s and the mid-1970s. Nontax revenues, especially royalties, have increased quite significantly and were a major factor in the intense energy and resource policy and fiscal struggle between Alberta and the federal government in the late 1970s and early 1980s. Taxes on individual income have increased, while taxes on corporations have declined as a percentage of GNE. As a percentage of total taxes, provincial and local taxes have increased to virtually equal federal taxes. This compares to about a 60-40 split in favour of the federal government in the early 1960s. There has also been an increasing reliance on personal income as opposed to corporate income tax.

Another feature of the growth of the tax system was the debate that emerged about so-called tax expenditures.[5] Tax expenditures arose when the government chose to forego revenue by providing, for some public policy reason, a tax deduction or credit—in short, a tax break to individuals and companies. This issue crystallized in relation to corporate tax breaks in the 1972 election when NDP Leader David Lewis coined the phrase "corporate welfare bums." Later analysis in the 1970s began to show that tax expenditures for individuals and corporations were growing at a faster *rate* of increase than regular expenditures. Moreover, because richer taxpayers were better able to take advantage of these tax breaks, the net effect of this growing use of tax expenditures was to make the tax system less progressive.

Regulatory Growth

Because it is inherently a less quantitative phenomenon and was not a particular concern of social scientists in Canada until the 1970s, the growth of regulation has only recently been assessed.[6] Regulation does involve increases in government spending, but its real impact is on *private* budgets as people and companies spend to comply with regulations set by government. This accounts for its relative lack of visibility *within* government, even though many outside of government were instinctively aware of great regulatory growth. A second aspect of recording the growth is simply one of appreciating the scope of regulation even in the abstract. For example, in the business sector only it is necessary first to appreciate the numerous and varied points in the industrial and commercial production process where governments could (and in most instances) have intervened. They include points very early in the production process where new products or resources are being developed or explored and extend right through to the disposal of waste products. More particularly, the points of intervention include:

- product research and development;
- mineral exploration;
- mining and milling;
- manufacture/processing in workplace;
- transportation;
- consumer use and marketing (domestic and foreign);
- internal environments (public buildings);
- external environments (emissions and effluents);
- insurance requirements; and
- waste disposal (short term and long term) in all stages of production.

A stark presentation of the production cycle suggests why there are numerous federal and provincial departments, boards and agencies, involved in regulation in different industries and why this process is usually bewildering to Canadian citizens and often to public officials as well.

Intervention in any one or all of these points in the production process inevitably raises questions about broad political beliefs, particularly about society's relative preference for using governmental, market, or voluntary "solutions" to solve or rectify problems, real or perceived. But it also brings the key ideas such as efficiency, stability of income, equity and redistribution to the forefront.

The Economic Council's comprehensive study produced the first attempt to measure the growth and scope of regulation.[7] Its stark presentation can be found in Table 5.3 which graphically shows the scope

Table 5.3
The Scope of Regulation in Canada

- **Communications**

  Broadcasting
  Radio (AM, FM)
  Television
  Telecommunications
  Telephone
  Telegraph
  Satellite
  Cable TV

- **Consumer Protection/Information**

  Disclosure (product content labelling, terms of sale, etc.)
  False and Misleading Advertising
  Sales Techniques (merchandising)
  Packaging and Labelling
  Prohibited Transactions, e.g., pyramid sales, referral sales
  Weights and Measures

- **Cultural/Recreational**

  Residency requirements
  Language (bilingualism)
  Canadian content in broadcasting
  Horse Racing
  Gambling (lotteries)
  Sports
  Film, Theatre, Literature, Music, e.g. Canadian content

- **Energy**

  Nuclear
  Natural Gas
  Petroleum
  Hydroelectric
  Coal

- **Environmental Management**

  (a) Pollution Control
      air
      water
      solid waste disposal
  (b) Resource Development
      minerals
      forestry
      water
  (c) Wildlife Protection
      hunting
      fishing
      parks/reserves
      endangered species
  (d) Land Use
      planning/zoning
      development approval
      sub-division
      strata-title
  (e) Weather Modification

- **Financial Markets and Institutions**

  Banks
  Nonbanks
  Trust Companies
  Management Companies
  Finance Companies
  Credit Unions/Caisse Populaires
  Pension Plans
  Securities/Commodities Transactions
  Insurance

- **Food Production and Distribution**

  (a) Agricultural Products
      Marketing
      pricing
      grading
      storage
      distribution
      entry
      supply
  (b) Fisheries (marine, freshwater)
      price
      entry
      quotas
      gear

- **Framework**

  Competition Policy
  Anti-dumping laws
  Foreign Investment Review Act
  Bankruptcy laws
  Corporation laws
  Intellectual and Industrial Property
      copyright
      industrial design
      patents
      trade marks
  Election laws
      contributors
      spending
      reporting

(*Table 5.3 continued*)

- **Health and Safety**

  (a) Occupational Health and Safety

  (b) Products—Use
      explosives
      firearms
      chemicals

  (c) Product-Characteristics
      purity
      wholesomeness
      efficacy
      accident risk

  (d) Building Codes

  (e) Health Services
      nursing homes
      private hospitals
      emergency services

  (f) Animal Health

  (g) Plant Health

- **Human Rights**

  anti-discrimination legislation in respect to hiring, sale of goods or services, etc.
  Protection of privacy, personal information reporting

- **Labour**

  Collective bargaining
  Minimum wage laws
  Hours of work, terms of employment

- **Liquor**

  Characteristics, e.g. alcoholic content
  Distribution and sale

- **Professions/Occupational Licensure**

  Certification/Licensure

  Registration
  Apprenticeship

- **Transportation**

  Airlines (domestic, international)
  Marine (domestic, international)
  Railways
  Intercity Buses
  Taxis
  Pipelines
  Trucking (inter and intraprovincial)
  Urban Public Transit
  Postal Express

- **Other**

  Rent control
  Metrication
  General wage and price controls

FIGURE 5.2

NUMBER OF FEDERAL AND PROVINCIAL REGULATORY STATUTES BY DECADE OF ENACTMENT OR ENACTMENT OF THEIR PREDECESSOR

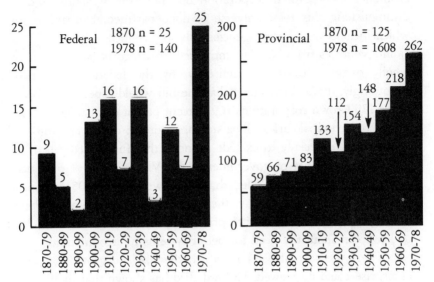

of policy fields and in Figure 5.2 which shows the growth of federal and provincial regulatory statutes by decade. Statutes are, of course, only a crude measure of output, but other measures confirmed the overall growth pattern. These included the growth in the number of statutory instruments and regulations made pursuant to statutes. Despite problems in all these measures of "output" (rather than of outcome or effects) it was evident that the 1970s represented a period of remarkable growth at the federal and provincial levels.

Much of the growth in the 1970s was in the area of so-called social regulation—health, safety and fairness—as opposed to earlier economic regulation.[8] Another area of growth was in agricultural marketing boards as producers sought to stabilize and protect their incomes. We have much more to say about economic versus social regulation later. The point to stress here is simply to note the pattern of growth and the proxy nature of its measurement.

The Growth of Public and Crown Corporations

The effort to chronicle the growth of Crown corporations as a further instrument of policy is also fairly recent and produces mixed results.[9]

Recent federal estimates indicate that there are well over four hundred government-owned or controlled Crown corporations. The Clark government's 1979 Crown corporation bill, however, was premised on distinguishing this total universe of nondepartmental organizations, which included regulatory agencies, advisory councils and "mixed" or "joint" ventures from "true" commercial Crown corporations, that are wholly owned, directly or indirectly, by the federal government. Accordingly, it was envisioned that the bill would especially apply to about 178 Crown corporations (69 percent parent companies and 109 wholly owned subsidiaries). By a similar gradual process of definitional elimination (especially to exclude agencies that functioned much like regular departments of government), the Vining study of provincial Crown corporations concluded that there were about 205 provincial enterprises.[10] Needless to say, there are genuine problems in determining the total number of enterprises. This has been one factor leading to a concern about the need for better systems of accountability.

There are several ways in which the size and growth of public enterprise could be viewed. Richard Bird has shown that in 1961 the recorded *sales* of such enterprises were 30.4 percent of government revenues, but only 21.3 percent in 1975.[11] As a proportion of Gross National Expenditure, public enterprise sales declined from 8.7 to 8.3 percent. Employment trends followed a similar path.

Vining's data compare provincial Crown corporation *assets* along several dimensions.[12] They have fixed assets equal to 36 percent of total corporate assets. The total assets of provincial Crown corporation assets represent 33 percent of federal assets and 49 percent of provincial assets. Vining also compares the growth in the number of provincial Crown corporations with asset growth. He concludes that

> since 1960, 72 percent of all Crown corporations were created. This compares with 3 percent for 1900-1920, 9 percent for 1920-1940, and 16 percent for 1950-1960. . . . Since 1970 we find that 49 percent of all Crown corporations were brought into existence.[13]

In contrast, however, only 11 percent of present total assets were created since 1970.

Analogous federal data have not been assembled. It is known that between 1939 and 1945 a total of 32 Crown corporations were established, most of which were subsequently dissolved after the war.[14]

Federal background papers do refer, however, to the "near geometric growth" in enterprises (especially subsidiaries) in the period since 1968, indicating a strong parallel to the provincial trend described above.

We have no federal data to parallel Vining's 80-year survey of asset growth. However, data on comparative asset growth from 1961 to 1975 show steady rates of growth in both the federal and provincial sectors, but with consistently greater growth rates at the provincial level.[15] This reflects the growing "province building" referred to in Chapter 2 and shows the increasing economic power of provincial governments evident in other expenditure data during this period, and of their willingness to expand the public enterprise sector of their economies relative to federal rates of growth. It is likely, however, that these proportions will significantly change in the 1980s if for no other reason than the federal government's vastly increased investment in Petro-Canada and other energy enterprises, including the takeover of a few of the smaller multinational oil corporations.

Within the federal Crown corporation sector, several points should be noted about absolute size and the relative patterns of growth, whether expressed in assets or employment. The first is to appreciate the obvious differences in absolute size. Canadian National Railways, for example, dwarfs all other Crown corporations in employment (though not in rate of growth in employment), and it is by far the largest of the nonfinancial service Crown corporations in assets. When it comes to asset growth, however, it is clear that the most rapidly expanding Crown corporation sector is in financial services. The Bank of Canada, the Canada Mortgage and Housing Corporation (CMHC), the Export Development Corporation (EDC), the Federal Business Development Bank, and the Farm Credit Corporation have increased their assets, on average, by over 100 percent since 1970. Employment growth rates have also been highest in this sector.

With respect to the origins of provincial Crown corporations, Vining's general conclusion is that ideology is not a significant factor, since right-of-centre provincial political parties create more of them than left-of-centre parties.[16] Given that each party did not have the same opportunity to create such corporations (due to the relative infrequencies of political success by NDP-CCF parties), Vining also examines the ratio of corporations created to years in office. Here, ideology may be shown to be more of a factor, because Vining observes that left-of-centre parties created an average of three corporations for every two years they were in office, compared to one corporation every two years for Liberal and right-of-centre parties.

At the federal level, the sheer dominance in power of the Liberal party makes similar data less useful. The overwhelming majority of federal Crown corporations were created by Liberal governments. Evidence of the absence of ideology is usually cited, however, in the federal case as well, since the Progressive Conservatives, both historically and in the Diefenbaker era, did not find the need to create Crown corporations distasteful. Only in the short-lived Clark government of 1979 did the issue of Crown corporations reach a level of overt ideological opposition. This was reflected in part in the Tory opposition to Petro-Canada and in the Clark government's announced intention to "privatize" several Crown corporations.[17]

Exhortation and Symbolic Outputs

As to exhortation, this is the least studied instrument of all. We have more to say about it in Chapter 12 where we link it to symbolic policies.[18] It is perhaps sufficient to note that exhortation devices have also grown. They include an entire array of ways in which political authorities show concern or respond to demands by making a speech, studying the problem, holding meetings and engaging in consultation, reorganizing agencies, and so on.

To govern by exhortation is to engage in a whole series of potential acts of persuasion and voluntary appeals to the electorate as a whole or to particular parts of it. In this sense many would properly view exhortation as democratic government in its highest and most ideal form. It would be equated with the essence of leadership and of democratic consent, of legitimate government in its most pristine form. The concept would be equated even more broadly to governing based on an appeal to common values. It would be government, in some respects, "without coercion."

There can be little doubt that governing would be impossible, not to mention undemocratic, if there were not a significant element of exhortation defined in this broad way. At the same time there is little doubt that exhortation is not a wholly reliable way to ensure that public policy ideas are implemented in the long run, since human beings respond to other instruments and incentives as well.

The above inventory of instrument growth is important background information. In the aggregate it shows growth without a doubt. But it does not show the myriad interactions among instruments. Arguments about why growth has occurred and whether it is good or bad are the stuff of politics. On this point theory and ideology become hopelessly mixed. Evidence does not necessarily matter. Explanations range from the expansionary habits of bureaucrats, to federal-provincial and party competitions, the phenomenon of rising expectations and the so-called "overload" of governments to the fiscal crisis of the state caused by the internal contradictions of capitalism. These attempts at explanation are best discussed in the context of formal models of public policy discussed in Chapter 6.

Instruments and Ideas

Instruments and ideas are inseparably linked. We can see this in three different illustrative ways: by looking at the social and economic content of the major instruments; by using three brief case studies to give more specific examples. Later, we see the link between ideas and instruments in relation to structure and process.

The first way can be briefly stated. Each of the first four major instruments has been subject to a debate in which the dominant social and economic ideas are central. Thus, the expenditure process involves controversy over social versus economic priorities and over whether certain subsidies are an "investment" or "welfare." The tax system is embroiled in debate about the *equity* of the system among taxpayers at the same income level, the *efficiency* of the system as an aid to investment and growth, and its degree of *progressivity* or *regressivity*. Regulation, as we have seen, has been routinely (and often artificially) divided into economic versus social regulation. Disputes also rage as to the commercial versus public policy and/or social role of Crown corporations.

A second way to relate ideas to instruments is to consider three cases from different policy fields; energy policy, social policy and charitable foundations. The energy policy example concerns the National Energy Policy (NEP). The social policy example concerns means-tested grants versus a tax-based child tax credit, and the example of charitable foundations concerns the tax treatment of such organizations.

Under the National Energy Program (NEP) the federal government changed the energy policy instruments in a major way. Prior to the 1980 NEP, the energy policy "incentives" were conferred primarily through the tax system in the form of deductions and depletion allowances. Companies could take advantage of them if they had a healthy cash flow and were taxpayers. When conferred through the tax system, the incentives were much more in the control of the company, partly because the revenue remained in its hands and partly because tax information is confidential. The NEP shifted most of the incentives from the tax system to direct expenditure grants. The grants are given under guidelines and regulations administered by energy officials in the Department of Energy, Mines and Resources.[19]

The purpose of the change in incentives was related both to energy purposes and to questions of power and control. The energy purposes were reflected in the fact that the grants could be targeted better on Canadian firms, many of which had an inadequate base to take advantage of tax incentives. The grants were also to be applicable to firms that explored in the Canada Lands. In terms of power the grants were *intended* to make the oil and gas industry more visibly dependent upon the federal government—hence the use of visible grants rather than less visible tax breaks. The change in instruments was not a matter of mere technique. It was charged with normative controversy.

The second case illustrates similar issues but in a different policy field. In social policy many programs for low income Canadians are delivered through grants with means-tested conditions of eligibility attached. The recipient must apply for the grant in a visible way with the discretionary decision (within rules) residing with the government official concerned. Contrast this with a social policy formulated to deliver a benefit through the tax system such as the federal child tax credit examined in Chapter 14.[20] Here the benefit can be obtained in the relative privacy of one's home when filling out a confidential tax form. Once again, the different use of instruments is not a matter of mere technique, even though our example has shifted from the oil company to the individual "welfare" recipient.

The third case involves charitable foundations. Charitable foundations greatly prefer to be assisted or encouraged by government through tax exempt status rather than through grants from government. Again, the concern here is with control and power as well as with ideas of charity, gift giving and voluntarism. Policy concerns, therefore, turn not just on the desire to encourage voluntary and philanthropic activity in society but also on where the balance of decision-making power resides.

Numerous other examples could be cited where instrument choice is a critical issue. In research and development policy there are policy conflicts over the grants versus tax breaks issue. Indeed, it can be said that business generally prefers tax breaks to direct grants because of the issue of control and power and the freedom to use resources as it sees fit.

The examples discussed above should also alert us to a problem in dealing with the relationship between coercion and governing instruments, namely the *perception* of coercion and hence of degrees of government intervention in private decision making. It will be recalled that we earlier located expenditure grants in the middle of the continuum and characterized it as only moderately coercive. But the degree of coercion is not a judgement made only by those who govern. It is also a matter of perception by those who are the object of governing.[21] The three cases suggest that grants may involve greater and more visible control by government than benefits conferred by the tax system. These differing *perceptions* of coercion are also an object of further normative dispute, and make policy formulation an even more difficult exercise.

Instruments, Structures and Process

We have stressed that, ideally, the intent of a policy is to obtain or sustain a desired form of human behaviour over a long period of time. The use and choice of instruments over time is intricately connected to the problems of obtaining democratically desired behaviour in the face of an uncertain future. Structure and process are therefore involved. As a policy issue or field evolves over time, it could be expected that governments might need to use all or most instruments. What instruments or mix of instruments will it take? Which ones will yield policy success? Which ones will be acceptable? To whom? Will exhortation and persuasion produce the desired effect? The latter, frequently heard statements are merely metaphorical versions of the problem of instrument choice.

It is useful to inquire into what we know about the use of instruments over time. It is one thing to have a typology or a continuum of instruments, but can research provide any generalization about instrument use over time? The general answer is that no fully satisfactory generalizations exist. By reviewing two or three attempts to generalize, one can show the severe problems of conducting research into such a question and at the same time show why the need to raise such questions is important.

One hypothesis has been suggested by Doern and Wilson. It states that "politicians have a strong tendency to respond to policy issues (any issue) by moving successively from the least coercive governing instruments to the most coercive".[22] Doern and Wilson go on to explain the logic of this proposition:

> Thus they tend to respond first in the least coercive fashion by creating a study, or by creating a new or reorganized unit of government, or merely by uttering a broad statement of intent. The next least coercive governing instrument would be to use a distributive spending approach in which the resources could be handed out to various constituencies in such a way that the least attention is given as to which taxpayers' pockets the resources are being drawn from. At the more coercive end of the continuum of governing instruments would be a larger redistributive program, in which resources would be more visibly extracted from the more advantaged classes and redistributed to the less advantaged classes. Also at the more coercive end of the governing continuum would be direct regulation in which the sanctions or threat of sanctions would have to be directly applied. It is, of course, obvious that once a policy issue has matured and been on the public agenda for many years, all or most of the basic instruments could be utilized.
>
> The above hypothesis seems to make some logical and democratic sense, and is perhaps reinforced by the political requisites of a federal state. This arises because the least coercive instruments can also be utilized with greater constitutional ease and certainty. This applies not only to such obvious examples as creating a study but also to the distributive spending instruments where the federal government's use of the spending power (despite recent talk about constraining its use) has afforded a convenient and frequently used instrument for federal involvement in such policy areas as regional development, youth policy, health care, and even urban policy. The more one moves into outright regulatory areas, the more one requires greater constitutional precision and clarity. Thus, there are other good reasons why the least coercive instruments may be preferred.[23]

This hypothesis is a plausible one, but it would be difficult to satisfactorily test it in the real world. One has to know, for example, when a policy issue is "new," and how long a period of time passes before one sees the continuum of hypothesized behaviour unfold. It is also not easy to deal with the question of whose perception of coercion is involved, the government's or that of the persons, voters, or groups who are the object of policy.

Moreover, one could certainly think of some policy issues where decision makers use regulation first rather than last. Stanbury's analysis suggests that politicians too readily practise the adage that "there ought to be a law" and easily reach for the regulatory political gun first.[24] But here again, one must ask what does "first" mean? What events, decisions and nondecisions *preceded* the decision to regulate? Was regulation really used first?

The reader will recall that in Chapter 3 we cited Hartle's proposition about why, in his view, regulation is a preferred instrument for politicians, especially in relation to the need to satisfy both producer groups and broader public interest groups. Regulation can be promulgated and announced to satisfy the latter reformers in a symbolic way without unduly harming the more cohesive producer groups who will be given elaborate procedural protections and who can afford to participate in them. In this case the proposition assumes that regulations are almost symbolic gestures only, an assumption that has to be explored on a case-by-case basis.

All of the above propositions are undoubtedly too static and unidimensional and too confined to look at instruments in only one policy field at a time. Politics, after all, is a dynamic process and involves exchange relationships between governors and governed across several policy fields. But how does one study a dynamic phenomenon when the policy beast will not stand still? The short answer is that one cannot in any wholly satisfying way.

Consider, for example, the attempt by Trebilcock, Hartle, Prichard and Dewees to construct a broader alternative hypothesis of instrument choice, one which purports to be more dynamic.[25] Their hypothesis (or rather a series of "axioms") is rooted in the premise that all or most political behaviour will be "guided by the calculus of vote maximization."[26] They then conclude (based on this assumption) that instrument choice, interwoven with the choice of actual policy objectives, will be determined by intricate cost-benefit calculations regarding the relationship between marginal swing voters in swing constituencies, and political parties competing for their votes (in the next or most recent election). A hypothesis as such is never stated, but a series of single "axioms" are suggested. For example, one axiom is stated as follows:

> It will be rational for a governing party to choose policy instruments that confer benefits, or perceived benefits, on marginal voters throughout, or at least late into, the current electoral time period, while attempting to defer the real and perceived costs borne by other marginal voters to some point in time beyond the current electoral time period, where causal connections are attenuated. Where this is not possible, instruments may be chosen that impose these costs at the beginning of the current electoral time period rather than at the end, so as to exploit incomplete voter recall. For similar reasons, a governing party will tend to offer policies at election time designed to maximize voter support, while between elections policies may tend to be offered that maximize group support.[27]

This and similar hypotheses or axioms are all intriguing, but they fail to meet the same two tests that Trebilcock et al. suggest are the deficiencies of the Doern-Wilson hypothesis cited above. In criticizing the Doern-Wilson hypothesis, Trebilcock et al. outline the following weaknesses:

> The Doern-Wilson hypothesis that politicians will move successfully from the least coercive to the most coercive instruments is deficient in at least two respects. First, what is meant by coercion is not clearly stated. The most straightforward meaning would simply be an unwanted (or involuntary) cost. With coercion so defined, the Doern-Wilson hypothesis closely resembles Becker's theory of instrument choice. A second deficiency lies in the lack of explanation of the factors that drive politicians along the coercion continuum in their choice of instruments.[28]

In a similar vein the central concept of the marginal voter and vote maximization is not clearly stated, nor is it obvious what factors drive politicians into the several modes of calculus (the many specific axioms). Nor can one specify the conditions where one axiom contradicts another in the same policy field or situation. Above all, the approach appears to reduce all policy making to a series of idea-less strategies.

The point of this brief excursion into the world of research and theory on instrument choice is not to downplay the attempt to grapple with it, but to show how difficult it is to generalize about the use of instruments over time and to show how attempts to theorize about such choices are inevitably couched in the researcher's a priori model of human behaviour. Nonetheless, an understanding of policy formulation will continue to require us to ask questions such as: why and when do governments regulate as opposed to spend? Why and when do governments choose to use public ownership as opposed to taxation? At least the sparse Canadian literature on this subject agrees on one thing, that instruments are not matters of technical efficiency. For example, Doern and Wilson stressed in 1974 that

> The performance of spending or regulatory functions may be viewed by some (such as economists and policy analysts) as being the means of achieving certain objectives or goals (real policy), but to the politician there must be a greater awareness that these very same activities are the essence of this stock-in-trade, namely the application of various forms and degrees of legitimate coercion, which in a democratic state are not merely means or techniques, but ends in themselves.[29]

Trebilcock et al., despite some of their suggested axioms, agree when they state that "in the real world, objectives cannot be determined independently of instruments (and this) reinforces our earlier conceptual point as to the false analytical dichotomy between means and ends."[30]

Despite the problems of generalizing about the choice of instruments, governments have to make the choices all the time. At any given point one instrument could in theory be substituted for another, as was the case in the energy policy and the child tax credit examples cited above. In the seemingly endless search for greater rationality, governments have tried to sharpen their capacity to make wise, efficient and acceptable instrument choices. One of the purposes of the federal expenditure or envelope system is to make ministers more sensitive to instrument choices and to recognize and make better tradeoffs among them. Given policy problem X, should we use the tax system or regulate directly, or perhaps do nothing? Regulatory reform measures have also been premised on a desire to require regulators to think soberly about whether regulation is the best way to achieve a purpose. Despite often elaborate attempts, no applied science of instrument substitution has been developed. Ottawa's envelope system cannot produce such an ideal notion of even-handed instrument tradeoffs. Again, this is because the normative and instrumental aspects of political choice are *both* valued, and decisions about them are interwoven in the fabric of governing and in governmental structure.

Instrument choice is also influenced by ideology, by the nature and source of demands for change, and by constitutional-legal and structural variables. Recent studies of decisions to create Crown corporations show that in nine of the eleven cases examined Crown corporations were created *after* other instruments had been tried and found wanting.[31] They were used as a last resort, a practice that could be viewed as consistent with a liberal ideology. Moreover, as noted above, evidence indicates that NDP governments have a far stronger tendency to create such enterprises than other parties at the provincial level.

That instrument choice is influenced by the nature of the demand for change is also logical. For example, Telesat Canada, a mixed public and private enterprise, became the principal federal satellite policy instrument in the late 1960s as a compromise solution to two types of explicit instrument demands. Private interests were demanding a private corporation, and some federal government departments wanted a full-fledged Crown corporation. A mixed enterprise was the final result, its purpose being to manage a dispute over a new technology and its effects on an old one.[32]

Constitutional, legal and administrative factors are also central to the choice of instruments. Most policy problems do not, in substantive terms, obey the artificial boundaries of federalism. Therefore, there is constant political competition to solve problems, to obtain credit and to deflect blame. But in legal terms, federalism does impose limits on instrument choice. Provincial governments cannot tax by any mode or means. The federal government can. A provincial government may create a Crown corporation in part to avoid federal taxation. The federal and provincial governments must be legally precise and certain when they regulate in a given area because they must have the power to "make laws" in the field concerned. Spending powers, on the other hand, are far less legally constrained, and the federal government has not hesitated to use federal dollars aggressively. Exhortation is, of course, available to either level of government without *legal* constraint.

Legal and jurisdictional factors may also be important among government departments and agencies in the same level of government. For example, statutes may confer the main spending authority on the line department (the Ministry of Transport) but confer major regulatory powers on an independent agency (the Canadian Transport Commission). Tax powers concerning transportation, meanwhile, rest with the

Department of Finance. This legal reality creates problems of policy coordination, and contributes to the inevitable political log-rolling and bargaining among ministers and officials, not only within the transportation policy field but between transportation and other policy fields. These interorganizational features of instrument choice are examined further in Chapters 12, 15 and 16 and in the analysis of how policy is evaluated in Chapter 18.

Finally, it is important to see the connections between instrument choice and the implementation of policy. We have already indirectly spoken of implementation in our earlier reference to the problems of sustaining changes in human behaviour. We now wish to draw attention to two particular features of implementation as they relate to the choice of governing instruments.

The first feature is portrayed in Figure 5.3. It shows a finer breakdown of the main instruments first identified in Figure 5.1. In a very real sense this chart is a portrait of an important part of the world of policy implementation. Implementation involves a series of activities and actions that are derived from the basic instrument list. Thus, the choices can become even more subtle—particular *types* of grants, regulations with varying *degrees* of penalty, different *kinds* of public enterprise, etc.

The figure, however, does not reveal a second equally important connection between policy implementation and instruments. One is tempted to define implementation—getting things done—in relation to the actions of officials and bureaucrats. But implementation also involves *private* behaviour to ensure that things get done in desired ways. Many public policies can only be "implemented" when a governing instrument or combination of instruments produces or induces the appropriate *private* behaviour. Thus, police services are very dependent upon people "calling the cops." Energy policy is dependent on consumers availing themselves of grants to aid them in switching from oil to gas or electricity. And accelerated capital cost allowances are intended to induce greater capital investment and thus "implement" a fiscal policy objective. The willingness of private decision makers to play their implementation role is, however, a function of several normative concerns, including their view of the legitimacy and acceptability of the policy, of the instrument, and of the decision-making power it implies.

This introductory review of the role of governing instruments in

FIGURE 5.3

A SECONDARY CATEGORIZATION OF THE INSTRUMENTS OF GOVERNING:
FINER GRADUATIONS OF CHOICE

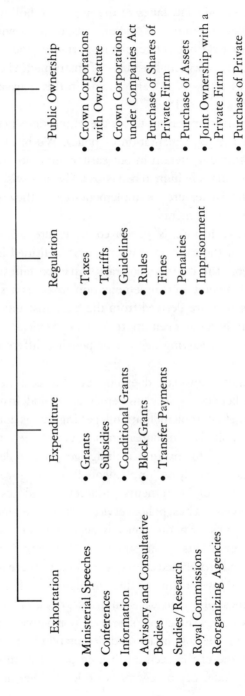

Exhortation

- Ministerial Speeches
- Conferences
- Information
- Advisory and Consultative
  Bodies
- Studies/Research
- Royal Commissions
- Reorganizing Agencies

Expenditure

- Grants
- Subsidies
- Conditional Grants
- Block Grants
- Transfer Payments

Regulation

- Taxes
- Tariffs
- Guidelines
- Rules
- Fines
- Penalties
- Imprisonment

Public Ownership

- Crown Corporations
  with Own Statute
- Crown Corporations
  under Companies Act
- Purchase of Shares of
  Private Firm
- Purchase of Assets
- Joint Ownership with a
  Private Firm
- Purchase of Private
  Firms Output by Long-
  Term Contract

policy formulation has, of necessity, been brief. In Chapter 12 we show more precisely how the basic instruments identified here anchor several important policy processes, processes which have themselves been the subject of attempts at political reform. The expenditure process, the tax process, the regulatory process and the Crown corporation process are all part of the general policy process. These dynamics seemingly lead lives of their own, sometimes separate from the energy policy process, the social policy process or the economic policy process, etc. In the meantime, the issues dealt with to date—the types of instruments, their growth, their relationship to coercion and to ideas, the choice of instruments over time, and the problem of generalizing about such choices, and the links between instrument choice and implementation, federalism and legal mandates among organizations—must be added to one's mental checklist for studying policy formulation in Canada.

NOTES

1. Theodore Lowi, "Four Systems of Policy, Politics and Choice," *Public Administration Review* (July-August, 1972), pp. 298-310.
2. Richard M. Bird, *Financing Canadian Government: A Quantitative Overview* (Toronto: Canadian Tax Foundation, 1979), p. 8.
3. *Ibid.*, pp. 8-9.
4. *Ibid.*, p. 20.
5. Allan Maslove, "Tax Expenditures, Tax Credits and Equity," in G. Bruce Doern, ed., *How Ottawa Spends Your Tax Dollars 1981* (Toronto: James Lorimer Publishers, 1981), Chapter 7.
6. Economic Council of Canada, *Reforming Regulation* (Ottawa: Minister of Supply and Services, 1981), and G. Bruce Doern, ed., *The Regulatory Process in Canada* (Toronto: Macmillan of Canada, 1978).
7. Economic Council of Canada, *op. cit.* and Economic Council of Canada, *Responsible Regulation* (Ottawa: Minister of Supply and Services, 1979) and W.T. Stanbury, ed., *Government Regulation: Scope, Growth, Process* (Montreal: Institute for Research on Public Policy, 1980).
8. See Economic Council of Canada, *Responsible Regulation*, Chapter 2.
9. See Allan Tupper and G. Bruce Doern, eds., *Public Corporations and Public Policy in Canada* (Montreal: Institute for Research on Public Policy, 1981); Marsha Gordon, *Government in Business* (Montreal: C.D. Howe

Research Institute, 1981); R. Pritchard, ed., *Crown Corporations in Canada: The Calculus of Instrument Choice* (Toronto: Butterworths, 1983); and W.T. Stanbury and Fred Thompson, eds., *Managing Public Enterprises* (New York: Praeger, 1982).

10. Aidan R. Vining, "An Overview of the Origins, Growth, Size and Functions of Provincial Crown Corporations." Study prepared for the Institute for Research on Public Policy (Vancouver: University of British Columbia, 1979), p. 18.
11. Bird, *op. cit.*, p. 4.
12. Vining, *op. cit.*, p. 19.
13. *Ibid.*, p. 20.
14. Sandford Borins, "World War Two Crown Corporations: Their Wartime Role and Peacetime Privatization," *Canadian Public Administration*, Vol. 5, No. 2 (Fall, 1982), pp. 380-404.
15. Bird, *op. cit.*, p. 102.
16. Vining, *op. cit.*, p. 22.
17. Tupper and Doern, *op. cit.*, Chapter 1.
18. See Murray Edelman, *The Symbolic Uses of Politics* (Champaign-Urbana: University of Illinois Press, 1967) and Murray Edelman, *Politics as Symbolic Action* (New York: Academic Press, 1971).
19. Canada, *The National Energy Program* (Ottawa: Minister of Supply and Services, 1980). See also G. Bruce Doern and Glen Toner, NEP *and the Politics of Energy* (Toronto: Methuen, 1984).
20. See Rick Van Loon, "Reforming Welfare in Canada," *Public Policy*, Vol. 27, No. 4 (Fall, 1979), pp. 469-504.
21. See G. Bruce Doern and V. Seymour Wilson, eds., *Issues in Canadian Public Policy* (Toronto: Macmillan of Canada, 1974), pp. 337-343; and M. Trebilcock, R.S. Pritchard, D. Hartle and D.N. Dewees, *The Choice of Governing Instruments*, study prepared for the Economic Council of Canada (Ottawa: Minister of Supply and Services, 1982).
22. Doern and Wilson, *op. cit.*, p. 339.
23. *Ibid.*, pp. 339-340.
24. W.T. Stanbury, *op. cit.*, Chapter 1.
25. Trebilcock et al., *op. cit.*
26. *Ibid.*, p. 27.
27. *Ibid.*, p. 33. Reproduced with permission.
28. *Ibid.*, p. 23. Reproduced with permission.
29. Doern and Wilson, *op. cit.*, p. 4.
30. Trebilcock et al., *op. cit.*, p. 27.
31. Tupper and Doern, *op. cit.*, p. 19.
32. Tupper and Doern, *op. cit.*, Chapter 6.

CHAPTER 6

MODELS AND APPROACHES: SIMPLIFYING REALITY

In previous chapters we outlined the basic concepts that are essential to understanding public policy making in Canada. They underpin our approach which focuses on the complex interplay of ideas, structures and processes. All approaches or formal models used by academics, practitioners and policy advocates to study and understand public policy represent simplifications of reality. They shed light on certain attributes of public policy and they blur others. They represent the insights of different academic disciplines and contain within them diverse and conflicting normative assumptions. This is why we have chosen to review other major models or approaches as the *last* element of this section of the book, rather than the first. The strengths and weaknesses of the formal models can only begin to make sense in the larger context portrayed in the previous chapters—especially in relation to the role of ideologies and dominant ideas, structures and processes.

It is important to stress that the four other major approaches or models examined in this chapter—the rational model, incrementalism, public choice and class analysis—are not the product of any single author[1]. They are the product of many streams of thought, rooted in different but related normative concerns, and produced and synthesized by scholars from disciplines and areas of study including economics, political science, public administration and business management and the study of organizations. Our discussion of them is fairly straightforward. We first describe the main features of each of the four models showing the main normative and analytical insights of each one. The reader is invited to consult the other sources cited for more detailed analysis of these approaches. These major insights will be used in illustrative ways in later chapters of the book. We obviously do not use each approach consistently throughout the book, since we regard each as having significant weaknesses and since, in any event, this would be an impossible task. We are concerned, however, with showing how the major approaches directly and indirectly provide an intellectual underpinning for most of the ideas about public policy, for several aspects of our own approach, and for how Canadians judge and evaluate the adequacy of public policies. We have also partially utilized insights from still other broad approaches including systems theory of a simple input-output kind in Chapter 1, interest group pluralism (examined but largely rejected) in Chapter 3 and insights about the importance of nondecisions derived from elite theory and noted in Chapter 1.

The chapter then relates the four approaches to a selection of key analytical issues in the study of public policy. Thus, we relate them briefly to ideologies; to explanations of the growth of government and the role of the state; to their inherent assumptions about the possibility and rate of change; to social versus economic assumptions about what motivates human behaviour; to how each of them treat the concept of coercion; and to their implicit or explicit assumption about social causality, uncertainty and risk.

Finally, we review very briefly a few other selected, somewhat more specific, approaches, each of which contributes other selected insights and poses questions that are important both to the theory and practice of public policy. These include the Lowi typology, the Allison Models, Vickers' concept of the "appreciative system" and input-output systems models which attempt to compare and explain policy outputs by examining several countries, states or provinces on a comparative and usually quantitative basis.

It is essential to keep in mind the ultimate purposes of models and theories and to be aware of the limitations inherent in social science. At a minimum, models exist to classify a phenomenon into manageable chunks of reality and to generate or suggest hypothesized relationships we might not otherwise see. At a more rarified level, models help generate theories that will both explain behaviour and allow us to predict. It is doubtful that any of the models of public policy allow us to do the latter. Certainly, there is nothing even approaching unanimity among scholars nor among practitioners and policy advocates that any one model is fully satisfying or accepted. We should be grateful that this is so. The major contending models are themselves embedded in normative assumptions, and it is the contest between the dominant ideas inherent in each that we should attempt to understand.

The social sciences can undoubtedly contribute to a better under-standing of public policy, but at best the models usually can generate only a healthy form of mental gymnastics. As we stress in several chapters, knowledge is not necessarily power, and both practitioners and theorists of public policy often operate on the basis of very limited knowledge about the possible future effects of current decisions and policies.

The Major Models and Their Underlying Value Assumptions

Four major models are described and reviewed briefly: the rational model, incrementalism, the public choice approach and class analysis.

The Rational Model

There are two streams of thought that influence the content of the rational model. One stream emanates from the hypothesized ideal behaviour of economic man as consumer and decision maker and hence is closely related to the "public choice" approach discussed below. The second stream is broader and embraces a belief in science, the scientific method and, as applied to both public and private decisions, in systematic planning. The first stream of thought is fairly straightforward and is perhaps the best known version of the rational model. Reflected in the numerous standard descriptions of consumer and investor behaviour in economics, the model depicts a decision maker who decides on a course of action to maximize the achievement of an objective (or utility function) or to solve a problem by:

- identifying the problem or objective;
- examining the alternative means, costs and benefits involved in solving the problem;
- selecting and choosing the best way;
- implementing the decision; and
- evaluating the degree of success and then changing one's behaviour to correct errors.

Such a model has been used to describe the ideal and sometimes real behaviour of individual officials making decisions in an organization (the micro level) and to whole organizations and entire governments (the macro level). Both Herbert Simon and Dahl and Lindblom developed basic criticisms of the rational model.[2] Allison's first model (see below) invites the observer to treat the entire government or Cabinet as a single rational purposeful actor.[3] We elaborate later on why Allison's invitation remains an important point to stress in understanding policy formulation.

The second closely related stream of thought in the rational model is a belief in the scientific method.[4] This stream goes well beyond the search for alternatives and the specification of objectives. It embraces a faith in the need to identify causality, to establish "the facts," and to distinguish facts from values. Part of its intellectual baggage is a faith in quantification and scientific management. It should be remembered that the birth of science was hailed by some as the age of reason and the end of utopias, be they religious or ideological.

In recent years it has become fashionable and, in part, valid to reject the rational model. The other approaches examined below all, in part, reject it. After all, it is argued, most decisions and policies are not made that way. It does not explain behaviour. We agree that the rational model does not explain most government policies, but the model remains important since it supplies for many policy actors and organizations a general, albeit often vague, normative standard against which many decisions and policies and the policy process as a whole are tested in a rough-and-ready way, particularly in the rhetoric of debate. It frequently provides a code of language around which political and policy debate is engaged. A few examples will illustrate the continuing importance of the rational model in this normative sense. We refer to these again in later chapters.

At a very macro level the rational model can be said to influence the frequently held view that governments must set and stick to longer-term priorities. This may be accompanied by the view that government must plan and do "first things first." Businessmen often believe, in this sense, that they are more "rational" than politicians. Indeed, for them politics is often viewed as the very opposite of rationality. This does not mean that they support a "planned economy," but that they wish that governments would make decisions more like they think they do. In this regard rationality is also linked to the dominant idea of efficiency, discussed in Chapter 2. The various Trudeau governments were variously held to be influenced by a fascination with rationality, planning and technocratic approaches. This does not mean that this is how policies and decisions were made by successive Trudeau governments, but concepts of rationality are certainly part of the standard against which the Trudeau regimes are assessed, favourably or unfavourably as the case may be.

A second manifestation of the lingering value of the rational model is reflected in the continuous concern expressed by some regarding the adequacy of the search for alternatives for given policies.[5] This shows up in several ways. In the ideal policy process it is expected that Cabinet documents and the verbal advice of officials will produce real alternatives for ministers, and not just strawmen arguments that one can triumphantly dismiss. Even though, as the incremental model teaches us, alternatives are not widely sought or perhaps even wanted by ministers, one of the tests of a good or rational decision process is nonetheless a system which does produce them. In Chapters 11 and 12 we will critically review and show how the demand for more rational and formal "cost-benefit," "environmental assessment" and analogous processes and studies have been advocated, and in some cases implemented, as a part of regulatory, expenditure and tax reform.

A third example which can be cited as an important reflection of the on-going normative importance of the rational model is public policies that involve scientific and technological controversy.[6] Most public decisions and policy fields obviously involve technical and scientific knowledge. Indeed, many policy fields are held to be dominated by experts and technocrats. But some policy areas are of more concern in this regard than others. Controversies arise over policies in such fields as toxic and hazardous substances in the workplace and environment, communications and space policy, and defence policy, where the quality, openness and type of scientific and technological information is in dispute. In this growing realm of public policy, the rational model exercises an explicit and implicit influence in the way many persons, including scientists and technologists, think about such policy problems.

The Incremental Model

The incremental model, or the strategy of disjointed incrementalism (or the science of "muddling through"), is the opposite of the rational model. In its original form the model is the joint product of Dahl and Lindblom, who identified it as but one of society's comprehensive processes or "aids to calculation."[7] The others identified by Dahl and Lindblom were science, calculated risk and utopianism. Though later adapted by Braybrooke and Lindblom and by Lindblom on his own, the essence of the model has not changed.[8] The model purports to describe how decisions are made and should be made. The incremental model suggests that the best predictor of future policy is the recent past. Incrementalism consists of:

- small marginal adjustments to the status quo;
- a restricted consideration of alternatives and of consequences;
- the adjustment of objectives to policies, and;
- the reconstructive and serial treatment of data and analysis.

Incrementalism is a model which places a high normative value on the need for agreement and consensus. The test of a good policy or decision is not just whether it produces good results, but also whether it can command a consensus. The model also appeals to the normal human desire to avoid making large errors. A series of small marginal adjustments helps to avoid large errors and ensures greater control.

The main attributes of the incremental model are derived from a logical and empirical criticism of the rational model. The rational model is weak because it is not adapted to man's limited problem-solving capabilities, the inadequacies of information and costliness of analysis, and to the diverse ways in which policy problems emerge. The rational model takes grossly insufficient account of the close relationships between facts and values and means and ends, a point already stressed repeatedly in earlier chapters.

The incremental model is intuitively persuasive at a commonsense level. Its critics, however, are legion.[9] While many agree that it accurately describes how most decisions are taken most of the time, its critics argue that it does not *explain* much and that it is not the way decisions *should be* made. It is a conservative model. It is the "bête noir" of all those who covet either rational change or radical change.

As shown below both the public choice and the class analysis approaches are dubious about the capacity of incrementalism to explain policy. Some of this criticism is valid, although it is doubtful that either the class or public choice models have any greater claim to credibility. The essential conservatism of the incremental model cannot, however, be denied. Improvement in small doses and broadly pluralistic adjustment seem to be the best that it can offer. And yet there is evidence that this is, indeed, the way that many societies learn and change, in part because political leaders cannot be too far ahead of the political system and society they lead.

The model, moreover, is sometimes difficult to apply. It begs the question "when is a change fundamental as opposed to incremental?" How does one tell? The "evidence" of incrementalism is presumably found in the gradual increases in expenditure, regulation, taxes or tax breaks, and in the growing numbers of agencies, bureaucrats and officials. But was the decision to establish Medicare in 1966 or the establishment of the National Energy Program in 1980 an incremental choice? Were the decisions to build the St. Lawrence Seaway in the 1950s or the Alaska Pipeline in 1978 a marginal adjustment? How does one explain or deal with these apparent quantum jumps in policy or activity? In essence such judgements can only be reached by an examination of the normative content of policy which, in turn, is tested by different groups in society against quite different ideological standards and dominant ideas. For example, class analysis may well lead to a judgement that both Medicare and the NEP are not fundamental changes since they do not fundamentally address the inequalities induced by capitalism. Others may judge the policies as being fundamental in the sense of promoting national identity or a broader view of equity among groups and regions.

The inability of the incremental model to handle these "exceptions," and the acknowledged weaknesses of the rational model, prompted Etzioni to suggest his "mixed-scanning" model.[10] In simple terms this approach suggests that societies do have a capacity to be fairly rational about a very small handful of decisions which they scan and identify, but that they leave the great majority of decisions to the inexorable drift of incrementalism. This observation is of no small importance. We will return to it in our analysis of the priority-setting process in Chapters 10 and 11.

The Public Choice Model

The application of the public choice model to the study of Canadian public policy essentially reflects the growing role of economists in the study of government in areas other than their traditional role in examining macroeconomic policy. Like the other models, it is not a fully coherent body of theory but has received impetus from its vigorous attack in the 1970s on the "public interest" assumptions and failures of liberalism, especially the social programs of the 1960s. It is associated with the emergence of neoconservatism, especially of the Reaganite and Thatcher variety, but also among Canadian Conservatives as well. The model basically involves the application of the assumptions of the self-interest calculating behaviour of individuals to the study of public choice. Individual decision makers are viewed as utility maximizers whose behaviour is best explained, not in terms of their pursuit of the public interest, but rather in terms of their self-interest.

The roots of the public choice approach can be traced to Adam Smith and classical liberal economics. Its more recent lineage begins with Milton Friedman, George Stigler and others in the so-called "Chicago School and Gordon Tullock, James Buchanan and others in the so-called "Virginia School."[11] The approach has been used to study decision processes and institutions as varied as constitutions (society's basic decision rules), political parties and electoral behaviour, bureaucracies, interest groups, public expenditure and regulation.[12]

In Canada the approach has been used by Acheson and Chant to study the behaviour of the Bank of Canada; Edward West on education policy and minimum wage laws, Allan Maslove and Gene Swimmer on the behaviour of the Anti-Inflation Board, Bailey and Hull on revenue dependency and charging for government services, and in a more limited way by Stanbury on competition policy.[13] It is the approach which indirectly informs almost all of the work of the Vancouver-based Fraser Institution. The most comprehensive use of a public choice approach in Canada has been by Albert Breton, who attempted to devise a macro theory of representative government based on it, and by Douglas Hartle writing on his own and with Trebilcock, Pritchard and Dewees.[14] We have already referred in Chapter 5 to the latter work which involved an analysis of the calculus of choosing governing instruments. Breton's work will be referred to later in this chapter.

The basic strengths and weaknesses of the public choice approach can best be illustrated by reviewing some features of the work of Trebilcock, Hartle et al. We refer to other issues raised by the public choice approach in later chapters as well. The basic framework devised by Hartle, in particular, is to view the policy process in Cabinet-Parliamentary government as a series of interlocking games, the special-interest group game, the political game, the bureaucratic game and the media game, with each player's behaviour essentially best understood in relation to the self-interest maximizing behaviour of each sectors' leaders.[15]

It is evident from previous chapters that certain elements of the games played by these actors are obviously an important part of the policy process, and thus reflect the utility of the public choice approach in a general way. It is important to highlight and appreciate many of these essential behavioural attributes. However, we have much greater difficulty in agreeing with what the approach produces in a broader understanding of the Canadian policy process. The specific approach used by Trebilcock et al. lacks a sufficient breadth of appreciation about the broader relations among institutions and among ideas, structures and processes. Most of the other limitations, however, are a direct logical consequence of the assumptions inherent in the public choice model.

Hartle has attempted to deal with the narrowness and purely economic determinism of the public choice model by recognizing the presence of other factors and by recognizing the close interdependence of means and ends (instruments and goals). Indeed, in some of his work the concept of self-interest is extended to such an extent that it becomes virtually everything and hence becomes virtually useless as a model. But in the final analysis, the overall model has to be force-fed into a particular self-interest attribute of each of the main players. Thus, the political game assumes fundamentally that the politician is driven most by electoral calculus and by the need to respond to marginal swing voters. There is no ultimate sense in which one can tell how the four games interact, much less how they relate to broader ideas and processes, especially since the very existence of a "public interest" is summarily dismissed. The approach leads to the product of a number of axioms, or even proverbs. These are statements which are not quite hypotheses nor could most of them ever be isolated for actual study. They are tantalizingly interesting, but one is constantly left with the impression that one is generalizing about the head of a pin.

The fact that the concept of a "public interest" is dismissed by public choice theory is not in itself a fatal flaw in that there is a genuine debate as to what the public interest is. Moreover, it is certainly plausible to argue that self-interest is not necessarily its antithesis. In throwing out the public interest, however, the approach seems to throw out the existence of ideas as well.

The public choice approach cannot be uniquely faulted for failure to satisfactorily explain the public policy beast. It is rooted in profound interdisciplinary and ideological dispute. It raises important questions about the policy process and has led to specific policy prescriptions and reform.

The Class Analysis Model

The use of the class analysis model in the study and interpretation of Canadian public policy began to flourish noticeably in the 1970s, though this view was present much earlier in the work of C.B. McPherson and in Lipset's study of agrarian socialism in Saskatchewan.[16] It also received a general impetus from John Porter's classic book, *The Vertical Mosaic*, one of the first analysis to fundamentally challenge the then (1965) dominant, or so Porter claimed, pluralist or brokerage model of Canadian politics.[17] The brokerage model was, in a sense, the practice of incrementalism at the national political level.

Recent exponents of class analysis such as Panitch have taken the approach well beyond the simpler versions of Marxist class conflict between workers and capitalists with the conspiratorial overtones of the capture of the state by the capitalist class.[18] Modern class analysis recognizes the existence of numerous sectors or fractions of capital and of dynamic relations between an autonomous state and the different classes which emerge from the fundamental conditions of social and economic production. Despite this increased sophistication the approach retains two central tenets as they relate to public policy.

The primary tenet of class analysis is that the relationships of power that exist in liberal capitalist societies are best explained by an understanding of a person's relationship to the means of production or, in short, to "one's ability or inability to dispose of labour—one's own and other's." Panitch stresses that classes are not ordered in a simplistic "higher and lower fashion, as rungs on a ladder, but rather, in terms of peoples' relationship to one another." He explains further that class . . .

> is a multidimensional relationship in that people are dependent on one another (the elements must be brought together in order for production to take place), and yet it is an unequal dependence in that one class appropriates the labour of another. Because the mutual dependence is therefore one of dominance of one class and subjection of another by the appropriation of labour, the social relationship is a contradictory one, entailing the potential of antagonism, of conflict, between the classes. This is not to say that the permanent condition of society is one of strikes, demonstrations, revolts and revolutions. These are but the more explosive outcomes of the contradictory relations in question. But in the sense of an irreconcilable basis of conflict, over how much and under what specific conditions labour will be appropriated from the direct producers, the system is a conflictual one. This has historically been expressed in struggles over control of the labour process, over the length of the working day, over remuneration, over new machines that displace labour and/or require labour to work more intensively. But if these kinds of struggles have

been more common than struggles to "change the system" itself, this reflects the balance of power between the classes. Class analysis is precisely about assessing that balance of power. This does not mean that those who sell their labour to others—the working class in capitalist society—only have power at the moment of social revolution. For it will be seen that what is operating in the relations between classes is never all power to one side and the lack of it on the other. Because the classes are constituted in terms of their mutual, contradictory dependence on one another, both sides always have power. The balance of power may be unequal, and may structurally favour those who own and control the means of production, but depending on given economic, cultural and political conditions, the balance may change. This may alter the terms and conditions of the appropriation of labour, and it may give rise to struggles over changing the historically structured relations between classes themselves. But all of this is the object of inquiry within a class analysis.[19]

The second tenet which is central to a class analysis of public policy is the characterization of the three main functions of the state. The class analysis approach asserts that the state in liberal capitalist economies exists to perform three functions: to foster capital accumulation by capitalists; to foster social harmony through "legitimating" activities; and to coerce or otherwise maintain or impose social order.[20] While it is not always clear which activities of the state are to be lodged in each function, it would appear that examples of capital accumulation activity would be such things as tax breaks for corporations and public investment in infrastructure (roads, railways, etc.). The legitimating function would be represented by what nonclass analysts would call social policy, that is, the whole apparatus of welfare, health and unemployment insurance programs. While liberals would refer to these as major elements of social "reform," a class analysis regards them as legitimating activities, produced out of constant social struggle, but needed to placate the dependent classes in such a way as to ensure the dominance of the capitalist class which owns the basic means of production. The third function of the state, coercion, would be illustrated by the activities of the military, the police and other agents of the state.

The class analysis approach recognizes the relative autonomy of the state because it appreciates that there is often conflict among the different factions of capital (finance, industrial, foreign-owned versus domestic) as well as between capital and labour. This is not, however, a back door rediscovery of interest-group pluralism, because the assertion is that the capitalist state, on balance, is not a neutral referee but rather succeeds over time in sustaining the essential dominance of the capitalist class and the inequalities of power inherent in capitalism. Thus, autonomy exists for the state, but when one probes the approach more closely and asks "how much" autonomy, the answer seems to be "some, but not much." Its essential verdict on all or most public policy made by liberal democratic regimes is that the latter maintains the status quo, albeit a marginally changing status quo. Thus, despite recent acknowledgements of autonomy, the class analysis approach still overwhelmingly sees the direction of causality in public policy flowing from economy to polity.

A class analysis approach is useful in several important respects. First, because of its central tenet, it is an approach which more than any of the others is informed by questions about the inequality of power and income in society. It inherently raises questions about the idea of redistribution both of income and power. At the level of Canada's political parties this is ultimately reflected in the critical role played by left of centre parties such as the Progressives in the 1920s and 1930s, and later the CCF and NDP. While the NDP does not often engage in the rhetoric of class analysis, its ideas are certainly influenced by the redistributive idea inherent in the class analysis approach.

A second useful attribute of class analysis is the view it brings to post-World War II social welfare programs. A class analysis perspective provides a different intepretation of these reforms, as well as of elements of the tax and expediture reform movements. At the same time it shows some of the pitfalls of class analysis. The use of terms such as the legitimating "function" of the state (the category into which all social programs seem to be put) raises important issues about the "purpose" as opposed to function of the state. The post-war reforms seem to be, in the class analysis view, "purposeless" or, at best, a mercilessly calculating set of adjustments conceded by the economic interests of capital. It is portrayed as normatively unredeeming behaviour, and seems to be driven by economic determinism in as mechanistic a way as the public choice approach. For example, it could be equally asserted that the "functions" of a socialist state are also to accumulate capital, to legitimate and to coerce. The capital accumulation would be for the socialist owners of capital. Ideally, according to a socialist view, this would be "democratically" owned, but in practice a wholly socialist state would probably be run by state bureaucrats and, hence, state capitalists. Legitimating activity would be directed at assuaging those who did not agree with such a state, and coercion would be coercion. In this regard Panitch's assertion that "the concept of functions (he uses) need not, if properly employed, give rise to the same problems as are found in other structural-functional approaches" is not at all a convincing one.[21] His model is informed by a class view of political life, and the functions or effects are largely predetermined by it. The class analysis approach does not avoid this inevitable intellectual trap.

A third feature of recent class analysis has been to extend the approach into an analysis of federalism[22] and the structure of government and the bureaucracy. For example, Rianne Mahon's work on the theory of unequal representation raises important questions about how different segments of capital seek and gain representation in different portfolios and departments of government, while labour has difficulty securing such access even in "labour" departments.[23]

Finally, because class analysis has a broad view of capitalism, it is sometimes more inclined than other approaches to raise policy questions about the international dimensions of capitalism and of the division of labour. This has contributed to alternative ideas about Canadian foreign policy, industrial policy and energy policy. In general, then, while it cannot be said that the class analysis approach is the dominant one in Canadian political, bureaucratic or academic life, it has nonetheless emerged to raise important questions about policy ideas, structures and processes. As an aside, it should be noted that it is not an approach often seen in the standard American texts on public policy.[24]

Relationship of the Major Models to Selected Policy Analysis Issues

In addition to the general attributes and insights of the major models, it is important to appreciate how each of them relate to a few selected analytical issues in the study and practice of public policy. Each model does not always explicitly deal with *all* of these issues, but one is entitled to infer certain probable ways in which the logic of the model suggests the issue would be applied. We review these issues in a brief and selective way but refer to them on several occasions in Parts II and III of the book.

Ideologies

It is evident that the models are generally related to, and influenced by, the major ideologies outlined in Chapters 1 and 2. This is most obviously true with respect to class analysis which is, almost by definition, a critique of liberal capitalism (as well as of incremental pluralism and gradualism) and a prescription for some form of future socialism. The market orientation of public choice theory is intricately tied to nineteenth century liberalism and to Reagan and Thatcher styled neoconservatism. Rationalism, in the sense of belief in scientific and technological methods and "progress," is an important strand, originally of liberalism but also of certain elements of planned socialism. Incrementalism can also be tied to a strand of liberalism and conservatism that stresses the need for gradual change and consensus based on compromise and mutual adjustment.

Growth of Government

Directly or indirectly each model, except for the rational model, has generated purported explanations about the growth of government.[25] In Chapter 5 we briefly surveyed the evidence for this growth expressed in each of the main governing instruments. Incrementalism can be said to be consistent with the simple view that present growth is explained by the immediate past and perhaps by a view that there has been a consensus that the state *should* grow. This view could thus capture the overall view inherent in the "overload thesis" advanced in the mid-1970s.[26] According to this view "society" had fostered a consensus of never ending and rising entitlements and "rights" to be supplied by government without adding up the costs and "responsibilities." Thus, government was now overloaded and could no longer satisfy these myriad wants. The "solution," therefore, is somewhat less government and a resort to greater voluntarism and/or a dampening of expectations.

There is a certain sympathy for the overload diagnosis by the public choice and class analysis approaches, but the onus of causality is placed on very different variables by each. The public choice approach tends to place a heavy influence on the self-interest expansionary habits of bureaucrats. At one level this is due to the tendency to oversupply public goods, since there is no market test to determine how much is really wanted nor is there competition.[27] At another level the expansionary habits are said to be attributable to the superior program knowledge of "line" bureaucrats over central agency "controllers," or simply to more Machiavellian power plays by senior bureaucrats.[28] At any rate there is certainly a greater tendency inherent in the public choice approach to explain growth in terms of the "bureaucracy is the problem" school of thought.

The class analysis approach has generally sought to explain growth in terms of the alleged "fiscal crisis" of the state.[29] The state grows because the continuing performance of the capital accumulation function *requires* the state to grow. Growth will occur in all functional sectors, that is, in actions to facilitate capital accumulation per se, in legitimation activities and coercive activities. The "crisis" emerges because increasingly the alleged contradictions of capitalism emerge. Supporting the accumulation function is more and more costly, but legitimation activities cannot keep pace unless capital is prepared to accept much less of the economic pie that it has historically been prepared to accept.

Each of these diagnoses lead to different prescriptions for reform. We return to these reforms when we examine the tax, expenditure, and regulatory process in greater detail in Chapter 12 and in our critique of several policy fields in Part III of the book.

Assumptions About the Possibility and Rate of Change

All policies involve judgements about the relationship between the status quo and change, and thus about how much change is inherently desirable, possible or necessary. The four models vary greatly in the degree to which they explicitly deal with this issue. The rational model assumes that a significant amount of change is both possible and desirable. To say, as many critics of government policy frequently do, that a policy is not rational, is often to imply that much greater change could have and should have been possible. Believers in planning (of the corporate or public sector variety) often make similar assumptions about change.

Incrementalism contains explicit assumptions about the slowness and gradualness of change because of the need to seek and obtain consensus and to avoid conflict and the making of large errors. Class analysis tends to diagnose all liberal democratic policy as mere tinkering designed to preserve the essential power of capital. When it is prescriptive, class analysis implies the need for, and the desirability of, radical or even revolutionary change. It is also more inclined to view conflict as a creative social force rather than as a definition of social and policy failure.

Public choice theory is less explicit about change. When the self-interest maximizing market model is applied to the market itself, the model presumes that change can occur quite quickly. The approach is less sanguine about public sector change, arguing that major public institutions will change only if "proper" incentives are designed to alter behaviour.

The Motivation of Human Beings

Closely related to the four model's assumptions about change are their inherent assumptions regarding the prime motivators of human beings. What makes human beings change? Both class analysis and public choice lean heavily on economic assumptions of human behaviour. "Economic" materialistic man is predominant. Behaviour is reduced in the final analysis to a single economic determinant. Both models are by definition suspicious of claims about the objective existence of a broader "public interest." Self-interest and/or class interests "explain" most of what there is to explain.

The rational and incremental models seem to leave room for other engines of change. What the "other" engines are, however, is not always clear. The stream of thought in the rational model that is rooted in the scientific method seems to leave room for the discovery of some kind of objective truth that could be nobler than mere self-interest. But what it is, other than a belief in progress and a faith in reason, is not clear. The incremental model places normative value on the very need for consensus and agreement. A good policy, or decision, is one that can command a consensus. Thus, the model again leaves normative room for a whole which is greater than the sum of its self-interested parts.

Coercion

How do the major models deal with the issue of coercion? The answer is "in widely varying ways." Coercion is a very important issue in understanding public policy, but one's view of it depends greatly on where one sits. The same applies to the treatment of the subject inherent in each model.

The rational model seems not to recognize coercion at all. Indeed, this is one of the great weaknesses of this model. Since the rational model does not differentiate public from private decisions, it fails to deal with the critical presence of legitimate coercion in the public domain. The rational model implies a kind of blind faith in knowledge as power and in the capacity of the discovered "truth" or of "the facts" to change behaviour in a benign way.

The incremental model is also quite silent about the coercive attributes of public policy. Implicitly, the incremental model rejects coercion by virtue of its normative and descriptive preference for consensus and agreement. Fundamental purposes are not regularly re-examined because this will induce too much conflict.

The public choice and class analysis approaches are more explicit about the role of coercion in public policy. Public choice economists start from the premise that there is no coercion in the market place. The market is for them a place of free and voluntary exchange. In a certain sense this is true, but the noncoerciveness of the market is certainly limited by the assumptions one makes about the distribution of income. A citizen's freedom in the market is certainly restrained by his level of income. The rich are freer than the poor, and the latter are not as likely to view the market as a benignly noncoercive institution.

As we have seen above, public choice economists apply the self-interest maximizing model to public decision makers. Their concern for how such people behave is rooted in the model's assumption that all public policies are by definition coercive—that is, nonvoluntary. More-over, with simple majority decision rules (51 percent of votes) and continuous log-rolling and lobbying, it is possible for minority interests to continuously coerce majorities. But this broad notion of coercion makes it a pretty unwieldly concept. It becomes very quickly a vague synonym for the economist's concept of the desirable "Pareto optimal" decision, one in which everyone wins and nobody loses (or is coerced?). Few public decisions could meet this test. Albert Breton's ambitious framework attempts to define coercion as the net difference for the citizen between the supply of policies he or she receives and the amount demanded. If supply is less, then the citizen is coerced. This is a definition that would be almost impossible to determine in practice.[30]

Thus, in one application of the term, all policy is coercive, while in Breton's view it seems to be a residual category. In Chapter 5, we encountered similar problems in examining the concept of governing instruments and the existence of a continuum of instruments from least coercive to most coercive.

Those who apply class analysis to the study of public policy seem to define coercion in a less inclusive, indeed quite narrow way. The three functions of the state are held to be capital accumulation, legitimation and coercion. Coercion often seems to be equated to physical force (direct military and police action).[31] Coercion is used when "legitimating" activities fail or it is believed that they might fail. The class analysis perspective does not appear to treat as coercion the range of other "regulatory" items examined in Chapter 5 that involves a more subtle range of sanctions such as fines and other penalties.

The above review of coercion is not intended to produce a synthesis of the various models or an agreed view of the role of coercion. Such agreement does not exist. The student of public policy must appreciate the role that coercion plays, but at the same time be aware that it too is a subject of analytical dispute, rooted in the assumptions and core ideas of the various models.

Causality, Uncertainty and Risk

In the study and analysis of public policy, as in the practice of public policy, causality, uncertainty and risk are closely related issues. All the advocates of the various models will make some claims that their preferred model can explain behaviour. In this sense the models aspire to be theories of behaviour. The basis of their respective explanatory claims were outlined in our earlier profile of each model and in our brief comments above on the factors that motivate human behaviour. What we are concerned about in this section is the degree to which the models deal at all with the *connections* between causality, uncertainty and risk.

The nature of public policy and of social relations is such that in most situations an *absence* of causality—that is, of proven causal connections between major policy variables—is likely to be the normal state of affairs. We lack agreed-upon theories of inflation, or unemployment, or regional policy. We do not know how much of policy X will produce a change of behaviour Y. Information and data is imperfect. Therefore, uncertainty in some degree is also the norm. The attitude of decision makers to uncertainty is partly a function of their perception of risks and the degree to which they are risk takers or risk averse. Risk can involve conflict and can result in large errors. Few people like to make big mistakes, let alone be seen making big mistakes.

It must be acknowledged that it is difficult to study in a formal way the nature of risk and uncertainty at the macro public policy level. Political biographers and historians often try to reach such judgements about prime ministers and particular leaders in other spheres of human activity, but it is far more art than science.

Among the four models described above the incremental moc
perhaps the most sensitive to this issue. Incrementalism—the taking of
small discrete steps at the margin—is premised on the desire to avoid
large errors, and on a recognition of the limits of knowledge and
information. The rational model, in contrast, seems to assume either that
every decision maker is a risk taker or that causality is so well established
that one can assume that the expected results will occur. Since the public
choice approach is based on "economic" man as a rational calculator, the
same can be said about it. Class analysis has little formal room for the
concept of risk and uncertainty. It is confident of the direction and
relative certainty of causality often despite the existence of evidence to
the contrary.

It is instructive also to relate ideologies to uncertainty. It is likely
that the more uncertain we are about the causal connection among
variables in a given policy field, the greater is the likelihood that we will
and should rely on ideologies or broad dominant ideas to guide our
behaviour. As one senior economist put it, "whenever we don't know
what to do, we get 'religion'." He was referring to the failure of economic
theory and the increasing reliance on so-called "extreme" ideologies of
the left or right to guide the economy. His view constitutes a very loose
view of ideology, but it does not invalidate the proposition inherent in
the remark. There is a connection between ideologies, dominant ideas
and uncertainty. Ideas are important because they are valued and because
there is almost always uncertainty in public choice.

Other More Specific Policy Approaches:
Selected Insights and Key Questions

We relate the four models of public policy to several aspects of our
analysis in later chapters. They suggest a number of central ideas and
concerns. It is obvious, however, that these are not the only approaches
that can aid our understanding and help raise important questions about
public policy. In this final section we refer briefly to a few other
approaches to highlight particular issues. These approaches are not
described in detail. The reader should again consult the original sources
cited for a detailed account and for other interpretations. The four
approaches are the Lowi typology, Allison's three models, Vickers'
concept of a policy maker's "appreciative system" and of policy as
"governing relations" and comparative studies of policy outputs.

The Lowi Typology

Theodore Lowi has developed a four-part typology of public policy based essentially on the view that policy types vary according to the degree of directness of the exercise of legitimate coercion by the state.[32] The four types of policy Lowi identifies are constituent, distributive, redistributive and regulatory policies. The claim is that each generates a different kind of politics and therefore a different policy process.

Lowi's work is useful in several respects. Inevitably, however, it also has serious limitations.[33] It is useful in providing a classification system which suggests that multiple processes are at work. We have used it in a general way in Chapters 5 and 12, especially to help develop an appreciation of the expenditure and regulatory processes. The Lowi typology breaks down, however, in several other respects. While the effort to distinguish "distributive" from "redistributive" policies is an important one, the boundaries between these dominant ideas are not easily defined or agreed upon. Lowi seems to use distributive policy as a surrogate for efficient allocation, in the sense of horizontal equity (for example, expenditure benefits for this group or that group). His view of redistribution is not well-defined except to say that it involves large amounts of coercion at a macro political level. "Constituent" policies is Lowi's residual "garbage can" category, into which he seems to put his leftovers. It is even less logically defined. We discuss some of the problems of improving this category in Chapter 12 where we examine the role of exhortation as a policy instrument and its relation to symbolic policies.

Lowi does not develop a full-fledged concept of governing instruments such as we develop and criticize in Chapters 5 and 12 and in earlier published work. But his typology has yielded some fertile ground in which one can grow. His use of the concept of coercion is essentially important but also partly flawed. He is right to suggest that there are degrees of coercion in political life, but he is not much clearer than the four major models identified above in defining what coercion is, or in dealing with the problem of how coercion is perceived by various interests and actors.

Allison's Model I, II and III

Graham Allison's book on the Cuban Missile Crisis of 1962 provided another useful typology to assist in the study of public policy.[34] It is essentially a synthesis of other familiar approaches, but Allison endows his models with a level of precision and insight that is both important and helpful. He suggests that one can cut through or dissect a given decision by using each of the models to highlight different concerns. The first model conforms to the rational model and induces the reader to consider the government as a unitary purposeful actor. Model II views policy as an organizational output, and thus requires the reader to deal with conflicting organizational goals and constraints, and the standard operating habits of constituent agencies. Model III views policy as a political resultant. It requires the observer to deal with personalities, stakes and stands, deadlines, channels of action and influence and the detailed calculus of power. There is something essentially "handy" about the Allison Models. They provide a convenient mental checklist. What could be more tidy than Model I, II and III! The reader will undoubtedly be happy to know, however, that they too are flawed.[35]

The most fundamental limitation is that it is ultimately a very narrow approach. The questions it raises are not unimportant for seeking insight into the formulation of policy. Each model, however, successively invites the observer to burrow ever more carefully into the entrails of governments—from government as a whole, to interorganizational conflict, to the "to-ing and fro-ing" of personalities propelled by deadlines, and deadends. Each level of penetration requires data and knowledge on the part of the policy researcher that is increasingly more difficult and costly (in time and resources) to acquire. The Allison approach seems at times to posit the arrival of policy issues on the agenda in a convenient "one issue at a time" pace. None of the Allison models appears to raise explicitly the actual content of the dominant ideas present in political life.

Nonetheless, like all good classifications and typologies, the Allison models suggest insights which are important and which one should look for in the study of the policy process in general and of particular policy fields. For example, an extremely important issue emerges out of the invitation in Model I to view the entire government (in the Canadian case, the Cabinet) as if it were a unitary purposeful actor. This should alert us to asking questions in any policy field such as: Is the Cabinet as a whole united in an entrenched way about its policy? Or, alternatively, does the Cabinet reflect a fragile coalition that could come apart? On which policies or issues is a Cabinet, or prime minister, prepared to stake its power and on which is there room for bargaining.

Sometimes this is difficult to judge. Former Saskatchewan Premier Allan Blakeney candidly spoke of how most government decisions are "60-40 decisions," meaning that the Cabinet is only 60 percent sure that it is right but that its rhetoric will assert that it is 90 percent right. In the life of any government over a five or ten year span, or in the context of a prime minister's tenure in office, only a few issues (priorities) are likely to be entrenched to the degree that Model I assumes, that is, where the Cabinet is functioning as a unitary purposeful actor. Under the Cabinet system, *all* government decisions and policies are nominally and often legally the decision of the Cabinet *as a whole* reinforced by the constitutional norms of Cabinet solidarity and collective responsibility. But this does not make them politically congealed. Some policies and priorities are hard and entrenched while others are soft and politically flabby. We take up this point again in Chapters 10 and 11.

Although it does not require Allison's model to appreciate the importance of interagency goal conflicts, nonetheless, essential features of Allison's Model II will also be used in this book. This will be evident in Part II of the book, where our account of the executive-bureaucratic structures and processes will show the obvious importance of interorganizational accommodation and conflict. Unlike the Allison approach, however, we hope to show how these are also expressions of the dominant ideas prevalent in political life, and show further how the dominant ideas and interests are not necessarily "represented" in an equal way in the bureaucratic arena of Canadian politics.

Vickers' "Appreciative System"—Policy As Governing Relations

Sir Geoffrey Vickers' contributions to understanding public policy present a terrifying prospect to many academic students of public policy—he does not present a tidy typology.[36] He merely forces us to think about policy in a practical way. The low key nature of his insights is reflected in the title of one of his major works, *The Art of Judgement*. Vickers strongly implies that the activity of the policy maker is not one that can easily be assessed in terms of cause-effect analysis. He is far less inclined to view policy as choice. For Vickers, policy is the setting of "governing relations," rather than the making of choices or the setting of "objectives."

Vickers asserts in a commonsense way that policy making begins

with the decision makers appreciation of a situation—in sl
decision maker's "appreciative system." This consists of a
amalgam of judgements about reality and about ideas and valu
and values are judgementally interrelated. Because of this basic ana
intuitively appealing view of policy, Vickers sees policy as a process of
adapting relationships.

Vickers is often too easily dismissed by those who aspire to a science
of public policy and decision making and for whom a distinct means-ends
dichotomy is a cardinal prerequisite. Vickers is not very appealing to
those who seek to reform the decision process by "clarifying" objectives,
and calculating the costs of different "means." Equally, purists of the
public choice and class analysis do not quite know what to do with the
"vagueness" of his insights. Advocates of class analysis, however, will
have some sympathy for his view of policy as a set of relations.

Vickers' concepts of the appreciative system and of policy as
governing relations have important insights to offer. They influence the
importance we attach to the close relations between the overtly
normative content of public policy, the equally normative content of
governing instruments and the interplay of both in structures and
processes. It also raises important questions about the "evaluation" of
policies and about how societies learn and change, both of which are
essential concerns in Part III of the book.

Comparative Policy Input-Output Analysis

A final approach to the study of public policy is the comparative analysis
of policy outputs (usually expressed in expenditures), the objective of
which is to discover the nature and direction of causal relationships
between them and various inputs or environmental factors. This was
part of an empirical quantitative and statistical effort to be more
scientific about studying policy, an effort that required comparison
among countries, or other units (states or provinces).[37] The environmental factors were usually grouped into socioeconomic phenomena
(industrialization, wealth, education, urbanization, etc.) and political
variables (party competition, voter turnout, representation patterns).

While these approaches reach a degree of statistical elegance, they
led to various interpretations that often bordered on the absurd. The
early studies often purported to show that socioeconomic factors were
the key determinants in such cross-country comparisons and that

"politics" (as measured by the specific variables selected) did not seem to matter much. Paradoxically, a 1970 Canadian study of public expenditure growth by economist Richard Bird seemed to argue that broader socioeconomic interpretations did not seem to supply satisfactory explanations and that, therefore, one ought to look at political variables, what he called the "missing link," including the behaviour of bureaucrats.[38]

These broad, quantitative approaches illustrate the on-going debate and assumptions about "economic" versus other "political or social" models of human behaviour which underpin the study of public policy. What they gain in macro comparison they often lose in subtlety and genuine understanding. At the same time it is obviously important to see public policy in comparative terms. It is important, however, not to throw out the comparative baby with the statistical bath water. Studies of a somewhat less ambitious kind can be useful. Two examples of types of comparative study can be cited.

The first example is found in the work of Dale Poel who analyzed on a quantitative basis the degree to which legislative changes are diffused and emulated among provinces in Canada.[39] His work demonstrates in a practical way the degree to which federal systems facilitate collective learning and experimentation when one province initiates change and other provinces then adopt and adapt it later. It is a tidy study that reached plausible conclusions.

A second example is Hugh Heclo's comparative study of the introduction and evolution of social policies in Britain and Sweden.[40] Because only two countries are compared and because the *timing* of the introduction of key social measures differed greatly in two otherwise not dissimilar economies, Heclo was forced to seek out political explanations for why these two countries seemed to learn differently and respond differently, at least in the timing of the response.

As was the case in the four major approaches outlined above and in the other selected perspectives just reviewed, the comparative input-output approach shows the inevitable dilemmas that both social scientists and practitioners face as they try to grapple with the policy beast. The models force us to simplify reality, while our larger intellect and common sense constantly remind us that policy reality is complex and refuses to cooperate with man-made analytical boundaries.

We remind the reader that we have only been able to touch briefly on the four major and the four other more specific approaches discussed above. Other sources should be consulted for a more detailed use and criticism of these approaches. We have attempted to highlight the main features and to analyse their normative assumptions both in a general way and in relation to the selected analytical issues itemized above. We think that the usefulness and the limitation of these models can only be fully appreciated in the broader content of the concepts discussed in Chapters 2, 3, 4 and 5 and in relation to our focus on the interplay between ideas, structures and processes. While we cannot systematically use all of these approaches in all the remaining chapters of the book, neither do we intend to let the models reside in splendid isolation. The ideas embedded in them will re-emerge in later parts of the book. They are absolutely essential mental tools if one is to think carefully and conscientiously about Canadian public policy and if one is to appreciate the strengths and weaknesses of the approach used in this book.

NOTES

1. For other general reviews of approaches to the study of public policy, see W.I. Jenkins, *Policy Analysis* (London: Martin Robertson, 1978); Peter Aucoin, "Public Policy Theory and Analysis" in G. Bruce Doern and Peter Aucoin, eds., *Public Policy in Canada* (Toronto: Macmillan of Canada, 1979), Chapter 1; Richard Simeon, "Studying Public Policy," *Canadian Journal of Political Science,* Vol. 9 (December, 1976), pp. 547-580; and Claus Offe, "The Capitalist State and Policy Formation" in L. Lindberg, et al., eds., *Stress and Contradiction in Modern Capitalism* (New York: Wiley, 1975).
2. Herbert A. Simon, *Administrative Behavior,* Second Edition (New York: Free Press, 1965); and Robert A. Dahl and Charles E. Lindblom, *Politics, Economics and Welfare* (New York: Harper Torch Books, 1953).
3. Graham T. Allison, *The Essence of Decision* (Boston: Little Brown, 1971).
4. See Sanford A. Lakoff, "The Third Culture: Science in Social Thought" in Sandford A. Lakoff, ed., *Knowledge and Power* (New York: Free Press, 1966), Chapter 1.
5. See Aaron Wildavsky, *Speaking Truth to Power: The Art and Craft of Policy Analysis* (Boston: Little Brown, 1979), Chapters 1, 2 and 6.

6. G. Bruce Doern, *The Peripheral Nature of Scientific and Technological Controversy in Federal Policy Formation* (Ottawa: Science Council of Canada, 1981).

7. Dahl and Lindblom, *op. cit.,* Chapter 3.

8. See David Braybrooke and C.E. Lindblom, *A Strategy of Decision* (New York: Free Press, 1963); C.E. Lindblom, *The Policy Making Process* (New York: Prentice-Hall, 1968); and C.E. Lindblom, *Politics and Markets* (New York: Basic Books, 1978).

9. See A. Etzioni, *The Active Society* (New York: Free Press, 1968), Chapters 11 and 12; and Y. Dror, *Design for Policy Sciences* (New York: Elsevier, 1971).

10. Etzioni, *op. cit.,* Chapter 12.

11. See Milton and Rose Friedman, *Free to Choose* (New York: Avon Books, 1979); George J. Stigler, *The Citizen and the State* (Chicago: University of Chicago Press, 1975); Richard B. McKenzie and Gordon Tullock, *Modern Political Economy* (New York: McGraw-Hill, 1978); and James Buchanan, "An Economist's Approach to 'Scientific Politics,'" in M.B. Parsons, ed., *Perspectives in the Study of Politics* (Chicago: Rand McNally, 1968), pp. 77-83.

12. For a general review and criticism see W.I. Jenkins, op. cit., Chapter 4; Douglas Hartle, *A Theory of the Expenditure Budgetary Process* (Toronto: Ontario Economic Council, 1976); and Allan M. Maslove, Review article of the Hartle book in *Canadian Public Administration,* Vol. 21, No. 1, pp. 125-129.

13. See K. Acheson and J.F. Chant, "The Choice of Monetary Instruments and the Theory of Bureaucracy" in J.P. Cairns, H.H. Binhammer and R.W. Boadway, eds., *Canadian Banking and Monetary Policy,* Second Edition (Toronto: McGraw-Hill Ryerson, 1972), pp. 233-252; E.G. West, "The Political Economy of American Public School Legislation," *Journal of Law and Economics,* Vol. 10 (October, 1967), pp. 101-128; Allan M. Maslove and E. Swimmer, *Wage Controls in Canada 1975-78* (Montreal: Institute for Research on Public Policy, 1980); A.R. Bailey and D.G. Hull, *The Way Out: A More Revenue Dependent Public Sector and How It Might Revitalize the Process of Governing* (Montreal: Institute for Research on Public Policy, 1980); and W.T. Stanbury, *Business Interests and the Reform of Canadian Competition Policy 1971-1975* (Toronto: Methuen, 1977).

14. See Albert Breton, *The Economic Theory of Representative Government* (Chicago: University of Chicago Press, 1974); Douglas Hartle, *Public Policy Decision Making and Regulation* (Montreal: Institute for Research on Public Policy, 1979); and M. Trebilcock, R.S. Pritchard, D. Hartle and D. Dewees, *The Choice of Governing Instruments* (Ottawa: Minister of Supply and Services, 1982).

15. Hartle, *Public Policy, Decision Making and Regulation,* Chapter 3.

16. C.B. McPherson, *Democracy in Alberta* (Toronto: University of Toronto Press, 1953) and S.M. Lipset, *Agrarian Socialism* (New York: Anchor Books, Doubleday, 1968).

17. John Porter, *The Vertical Mosaic* (Toronto: University of Toronto Press, 1965), Chapter 12.

18. Leo Panitch, ed., *The Canadian State* (Toronto: University of Toronto Press, 1977).

19. Leo V. Panitch, "Elites, Classes and Power in Canada" in Michael S. Whittington and Glen Williams, eds., *Canadian Politics in the 1980s* (Toronto: Methuen, 1981), pp. 176-177.

20. Panitch, *The Canadian State,* Chapter 1.

21. *Ibid.,* p. 9.

22. See Garth Stevenson, *Unfulfilled Union* (Toronto: Macmillan of Canada, 1979).

23. Rianne Mahon, "Canadian Public Policy: The Unequal Structure of Representation" in Leo Panitch, ed., *The Canadian State,* Chapter 6.

24. For example, it is not one of the major approaches reviewed in Thomas Dye, *Understanding Public Policy,* Third Edition (Englewood Cliffs: Prentice-Hall, 1980), Chapter 1.

25. For a comparative look at the growth of government see Richard Rose and Guy Peters, *Can Government Go Bankrupt?* (New York: Basic Books, 1978).

26. See Richard Simeon, "The 'Overload Thesis' and Canadian Government," *Canadian Public Policy,* Vol. II, No. 4 (Autumn, 1976), pp. 541-552.

27. See Bailey and Hull, *The Way Out, op. cit.,* Chapters 1 and 2.

28. William A. Niskanen Jr., *Bureaucracy and Representative Government* (Chicago: Aldine-Atherton, 1971).

29. James O'Connor, *The Fiscal Crisis of the State* (New York: St. Martin's Press, 1973).

30. See Albert Breton, *op. cit.,* and Douglas Hartle, *A Theory of the Expenditure Budgetary Process,* Chapter 3. See also Andre Blais, "Le Public Choice et la croissance de l'etat," *Canadian Journal of Political Science,* Vol. XIV, No. 4 (December 1982), pp. 783-808.

31. See Panitch, *The Canadian State, op. cit.,* Chapter 1.

32. Theodore Lowi, "Four Systems of Policy, Politics and Choice," *Public Administration Review,* Vol. 32 (1972), pp. 298-310; and Theodore Lowi, "Decision Making Versus Public Policy: Toward an Antidote for Technocracy," *Public Administration Review,* Vol. 30 (1970), pp. 314-325.

33. See W.I. Jenkins, *op. cit.,* Chapter 3.

34. Graham Allison, *op. cit.*

35. See R.J. Art, "Bureaucratic Politics and American Foreign Policy: A Critique," *Policy Sciences,* Vol. 4 (1973), pp. 467-450; W.I. Jenkins, *op. cit.,* Chapter 1; and Michael M. Atkinson and K.R. Nossal, "Bureaucratic Politics and the New Fighter Aircraft Decisions," *Canadian Public Administration,* Vol. 24, No. 4, 1981, pp. 531-562.

36. Sir Geoffrey Vickers, *The Art of Judgement* (New York: Basic Books, 1965); and Sir Geoffrey Vickers, *Value Systems and Social Processes* (London: Tavistock, 1968), Part III.
37. See R.I. Hofferbert, *The Study of Public Policy* (New York: Bobbs Merrill, 1974); Frank P. Scioli Jr. and Thomas J. Cook, *Methodology for Analyzing Public Policies* (New York: D.C. Heath, 1978).
38. Richard Bird, *The Growth of Government Spending in Canada* (Toronto: Canadian Tax Foundation, 1970).
39. Dale Poel, "A Diffusion of Legislation Among the Canadian Provinces." Paper presented to Canadian Political Science Association, Edmonton, June 1975.
40. See Hugh Heclo, *Modern Social Politics in Britain and Sweden* (New Haven, Yale University Press, 1974).

PART II

THE PUBLIC POLICY SYSTEM:

IDEAS IN ACTION THROUGH STRUCTURE AND PROCESS

- Prime Minister, Cabinet and Central Agencies
- Prime Ministers, Political Power and Policy Preferences
- Departments, Agencies, Senior Bureaucrats and Advisors
- Priorities and Priority Setting: In Historical Perspective and in the Trudeau Era
- Public Policy and Resource Allocation
- Governing Instruments, Policy Processes and Resource Allocation
- Knowledge, Information and Public Policy Analysis

CHAPTER 7

THE PRIME MINISTER, THE CABINET AND THE CENTRAL AGENCIES

The main concepts needed to understand Ottawa's decisions and Canadian public policy have now been outlined and examined. However, among the three main elements of our approach, ideas, structures and processes, it is evident that we have given more explicit emphasis to ideas than to structures and processes. An appreciation of how ideas operate through structures and processes and how the latter influence ideas require a more detailed look at the public policy system. In Canada's Cabinet-Parliamentary system this means that one must focus on the executive-bureaucratic arena. In Part II of the book we first explore in Chapters 7, 8 and 9 the key structures involved and the ideas and dynamic processes they evoke. The structures include the prime minister and Cabinet, the central agencies of government, departments and agencies, and senior bureaucrats and advisors. The ideas involved, which must be both added and related to the ideas examined in Part I, include those of responsible government, individual and collective Cabinet responsibility and accountability, centralization and decentralization and the policy-administration dichotomy. They also include the ideas inherent in the agency philosophies or policy mandates of the dozens of government agencies and departments. As we move into Chapters 10, 11, 12 and 13 we are in a position to appreciate in some detail the processes and therefore the dynamics and uncertainties of policy formulation, an appreciation which requires an historical as well as a short-term perspective. Here we are concerned not just with executive structures per se, but with how such structures interact with the institutions surveyed in Part I. Thus, the dynamic processes and uncertainties of priority setting, spending, regulating, taxing and using and abusing knowledge and information involve both executive structures and the structures involved in the work of other institutions as well.

To enter the executive arena of political life is to enter a world of ideas, structures and processes where the men and women involved, as often as not, view themselves as being "caught in the middle" rather than as persons sitting confidently "on top" with a clear, focused eye on the future. They are powerful in a hierarchical sense in that they occupy the highest rungs of the political and bureaucratic ladder. They are often less than powerful in the sense of their individual or collective capacity to persuade, cajole, or even require Canadians to actually change their behaviour in response to the policy cues given. Ministers and senior bureaucrats are at the receiving end of much data and information, written and verbal, numerate and judgemental, but they frequently lack knowledge not only about what to do in the future but also on how they have fared in the past. They must try to pursue a consistent course of action into a future which often refuses to cooperate and in the context of a series of policy contradictions, interdependent ideas and scarce resources, including time.

The executive structures have also been the object of growing political dispute about their growth and power. Particularly since the coming to power of Pierre Trudeau in 1968, there has been a visible and increased concern about the aggrandizement of prime ministerial power, about the unwieldiness of a large Cabinet, and about the degree to which central agencies, their bureaucrats and other senior mandarins in general are held accountable both to ministers and to the broader arrary of political institutions, especially Parliament.[1]

In this chapter we present a general description and analysis of the prime minister and the Cabinet and the central agencies. By focusing on these structures and ideas in some detail, we can begin to add more flesh to the bony skeleton of the general policy process presented in Chapter 4. In Chapter 8 we focus on the power and policy preferences of recent Canadian prime ministers. The role of line departments and agencies and the role of the senior bureaucracy, particularly the deputy minister's role, are examined in Chapter 9.

The Prime Minister and the Cabinet

The prime minister and the Cabinet are the critical centre of the executive arena.[2] They are, in constitutional theory, collectively responsible to an elected Parliament for new policy and for ongoing policies and programs as well. Thus, as we have stressed, policy formulation is affected by Parliament, particularly because the prime minister must anticipate his opposition critics. Institutionally and constitutionally, the

Cabinet-Parliamentary system requires ministers to be both individually and collectively responsible for policy. Although the collective nature of the Cabinet is important, there are obviously inequalities of power among ministers and the organizations they head. This fact is always recognized with respect to the pre-eminent role of the prime minister, but it is less often recognized when considering other characteristics of Cabinet government.

The prime minister's dominant policy role flows from his political power, which in turn is derived from his position as the elected head of a political party which has majority support in the House of Commons. From this he derives his power over his Cabinet colleagues, namely the power to seek dissolution of Parliament at any time of his choosing and the power to hire and fire his ministers. He also has the power to appoint officials by order in council at the deputy ministerial level, as well as their equivalents in the many other agencies and boards. The analysis of prime ministerial policy preferences in Chapter 9 shows how these and other power "assets" must be invested and wielded with great care. Prime ministers, in dealing with both Cabinet colleagues and policy issues, cannot recklessly "spend" their assets. Hence, they rarely win every battle or have their way on every issue, preferring to concentrate their investments on strategically important items.

The importance of the prime minister's power and the constraints placed upon it cannot be overemphasized when discussing the development of policy organizations in the executive arena or when discussing policy making in general. The initial reaction to changes in the late 1960s in prime ministerial philosophy and in organization concentrated on how these changes had enhanced the prime minister's power. The analysis here and in Chapters 8 and 9 show how other elements of the executive arena may also constrain that power and its effects on policy making. The functioning of central policy processes and the evolution of executive organization must also be understood by appreciating the policy and organizational approaches of successive prime ministers. These are also examined in Chapter 8.

The Collective Role of the Cabinet

The Canadian Cabinet is a collective decision-making body in which ministers are both collectively responsible to Parliament for general government policy and individually responsible for their own Cabinet portfolios and departmental programs. While the position of prime minister is obviously pre-eminent, there are strong norms of collective responsibility and hence of the importance of some rough, formal equality of all ministers in the Cabinet. In the Canadian context the imperatives of collectivity are reinforced not only by the growing complexity of government decision making, but also by the fact that the Canadian Cabinet is more than just a decision-making body.

The Canadian Cabinet is also a representative or legitimating institution, notwithstanding the existence of Parliament, in that it is judged not only on what it does but on what it appears to do.[3] The Cabinet has always had not only to represent, but to appear to represent, the diverse regional and ethnic components of the Canadian population. Successive governments have not always been able to actually achieve the optimum representation, but most have been required to make a serious attempt.[4] While it is clear in our later analysis that the prime minister and some ministers and portfolios are obviously more influential than others, it is important to stress at the outset the continuing strength of collective norms in Canadian Cabinet organization and behaviour. These norms are visibly tested and reasserted precisely when, as in recent years, attempts are made to create an inner Cabinet or structure "inner" groups of decision makers such as in the Cabinet Committee on Priorities and Planning, or "inner" groups of advisors such as those in the Prime Minister's Office.

The norms and traditions of collective Cabinet responsibility and solidarity also influence policy making through the strong strictures regarding secrecy and confidentiality in intra-Cabinet and intrabureaucratic decision-making processes. Ministers vigourously debate policy in confidence in Cabinet but are expected to defend all policies in a united way. The dispersal of influence and responsibility among ministers is also a function of the related constitutional practice in Parliamentary systems of assigning responsibility for legislation and programs to individual ministers and departments in order to facilitate Parliamentary accountability. The assignment of individual responsibility is also a function of the sheer complexity of government and of the need to delegate functions to ministers and departments on administrative and technical grounds. The constitutional principles and administrative necessities that generate individual ministerial authority and delegation reinforce the collective nature of the Cabinet in the broad sense of dispersing influence. At the same time they create the need for some inner group to coordinate the Leviathan. Thus, the ideas of decentralization and centralization are in constant tension because both are necessary to manage the government. Ministers (and their deputies) are pulled in two directions at once by their constitutional role—vertically in their line departmental roles where they are individually responsible for policy and decisions, and horizontally in their duties and obligations to all ministers to support government policy on a collective basis.

In recent years many changes have been made to formal Cabinet organization and policy processes.[5] These are examined in detail in Chapter 11. In particular, we focus on the Cabinet committees and their role in resource allocation. While the structure of committees is presented in Figure 7.1, it is essential to stress at this stage of our analysis the practical difficulty of putting policy into watertight compartments. Spillovers abound in the committee process as, for example, when social and economic programs interact or when energy and foreign policies partly conflict. Once again it must be emphasized that this is because the dominant ideas of political life enter the deliberations of all policy committees.

Three other features of Cabinet committees are essential to note at the outset. First, ministers are members of more than one committee and, thus, some policy coordination occurs through this fact alone. But the degree of policy integration that occurs through multiple membership on committees must be qualified by recognizing the time demands

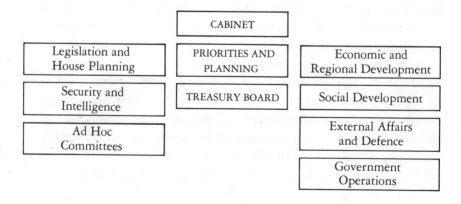

FIGURE 7.1
FEDERAL CABINET COMMITTEE STRUCTURE

CABINET

Legislation and House Planning	PRIORITIES AND PLANNING	Economic and Regional Development
Security and Intelligence	TREASURY BOARD	Social Development
Ad Hoc Committees		External Affairs and Defence
		Government Operations

that committee work places on ministers and by recognizing the widely varying degrees of interest and preparation by individual ministers. Second, there is always tension between Cabinet committees and similar committees at the deputy minister or senior bureaucratic level. For example, in the late 1960s and early 1970s the Cabinet committees were intended to help give more control to ministers and less to senior officials and, indeed, were explicitly intended to replace some senior official level interdepartmental committees. Gradually, however, many ministers complained of burdensome committee duties and of their need to get out of Ottawa and into their constituencies across the country. Consequently, by the late 1970s official-level committees began to be more frequently created, and it was not uncommon for senior officials to participate in Cabinet committee meetings in ways which were virtually indistinguishable from their ministerial superiors. By the early 1980s concern increased again about control by the senior bureaucrats. Thus, when the envelope system described in Chapter 11 was created, care was taken to create parallel committees of officials but with a restricted role. Once again it has led to worry about the misuse of ministerial time and, as we saw in Chapter 4, about the paper burden on ministers and deputies.

Finally, it is important to stress that the committee process has resulted in a considerable amount of decentralization of decision making in that the committees have taken on de facto decision-making roles in areas of decision making which in early periods of Canadian Cabinet government would have been decided by the full Cabinet. Degrees of centralization and decentralization are, however, difficult to gauge and may, however, differ among different prime ministers.[6] Chapters 11 and 12 show these dilemmas in more detail.

Ministerial Skills and Relationships

Central public policy processes ultimately rest on day-to-day, month-to-month relationships between and among individual Cabinet ministers (and senior public servants). These include relationships between those who head the major line spending departments, between the Minister of Finance, President of the Treasury Board, the chairman of the main central policy ministries and the prime minister. They include relationships between various ideological and loyalty groupings within the Cabinet. It is important to explore the general relationships between line ministers and the Finance, and Treasury Board ministers in the general expenditure process and then to explore the narrower but special relations between the prime minister and the Minister of State for Economic and Regional Development, the Minister of State for Social Development, the President of the Treasury Board and the Minister of Finance.

Though ministerial influence is affected by the broader sources of aggregate *organizational* and departmental influence, a minister is ultimately judged by what he or she gets done. His reputation as a fighter for his department and for his own ideas, his intellectual prowess and popularity among voters, his skills as an expenditure combatant and defender of the government in the House of Commons, and the degree to which he is informed and prepared in defending his proposals in Cabinet ultimately determine his real standing in the Cabinet.[7] While there are many Cabinet and minister watchers in the media and in the bureaucracy, it is ultimately the judgement of his or her Cabinet colleagues that determines the current value of a minister's most precious political currency—his or her reputation. In recent years political credit has more easily accrued through spending (though this has not always been the case and may not be so in the future) in that it is the most visible instrument and indicator of political action. This is not to suggest that spending for the sake of spending is the only basic drive. Obviously, spending in the pursuit of certain public policy ideas and objectives is central, but the important value of spending as a governing instrument is that it is an essential grease for the Cabinet wheel.

One should not equate the above point with the notion that reputations as strong ministers are built only by an indiscriminate use of mutual back-scratching. The decision process is sufficiently structured and the norms of Cabinet behaviour are sufficiently well-ingrained that the successful minister must ultimately demonstrate some qualities of moderation as a team player as well. The size of the Canadian Cabinet alone makes formal alliance building a difficult process. Many ministers do not know each other well in the sense of strong social or personal friendship. The minister must be constantly conscious of the fact that he can only infrequently appeal to the court of final ministerial appeal—the prime minister or to the full Cabinet. Frequent appeals in these forums will be indicative of one's inability to carry the day in other arenas such as before the Treasury Board or before other Cabinet committees.

The dynamics of public policy must also be understood in the relationship between the Ministers of State for Economic and Regional Development, and Social Development, the President of the Treasury Board and the Minister of Finance, and the prime minister. These ministers, but especially the Minister of Finance, are dependent on the fairly constant backing of the prime minister. Numerous appeals over the heads of both to the prime minister would be intolerable for all ministers. On a reciprocal basis, the prime minister needs the support of strong Finance and Treasury Board ministers to manage the overall governmental and fiscal policy processes. Thus, there is a considerable political need to leave room in the budgetary and overall resource allocation process for negotiation and trade-offs to occur between the policy minister, the President of the Treasury Board and the departmental ministers.

The breadth and the changing nature of the priorities expressed in the resource allocation process leaves considerable room for intepretation and accommodation. The fact that the budgetary process occurs over several months also facilitates the development of political accommodation and a modicum of political peace and tranquility among ministers.

The relationship between the Minister of Finance and the prime minister is obviously one of the most critical in Cabinet government. The difficulty of the Finance minister's position must be particularly acknowledged by the prime minister.[8] In recent years the special character of this relationship has been formalized by the holding of weekly meetings on the state of the economy. The prime minister and Minister of Finance must also ultimately agree in the critical annual determination and shape of the fiscal framework. Once the basic figures on revenue and on the aggregate sum available for new expenditure— figures largely set by Finance—are determined, there can be only a marginal juggling around them. While relying on the latent and sometimes manifest support of the prime minister, the Minister of Finance's major weapon is taxation. The outer parameters of the politics of the budgetary and fiscal policy process are set by the argument, frequently advanced by Finance portfolios, that either spending must be held down or taxes will have to be increased. This, of course, has always been an important political club. In recent decades the Keynesian clout has been added to this traditional and potent weapon; namely, if expenditure plans are too great and taxes not increased, the economy may be harmed. The importance of this political club holds even though the overall role of the Department of Finance declined in the 1970s and early 1980s.[9]

Ministers who otherwise may be inclined to challenge fiscal policy, even in the face of the above weapons, are likely to be ultimately dissuaded by the fact that they often possess inadequate information to make a successful challenge. This is not to suggest that they do not offer advice, as politicians, to the Minister of Finance at budget time, but they are fully aware that they cannot ordinarily challenge him in the core areas of fiscal and stabilization policy. The specific information gap is reinforced, at least until recently, by the broader practice in Cabinet government in which ministers are briefed by their political staffs and by their senior bureaucrats, primarily to "defend" their own portfolios rather than to be aggressive critics of other portfolios. This is true despite the fact that individual ministers may know something about other portfolios because of their previous Cabinet assignments or because of their work on Cabinet committees. Thus, ministers are in part captured and constrained by the nature of their portfolios and by other political constraints. But within these constraints there is considerable room for individual competence, drive and ability to be the basis of political power.

It is thus essential to understand these special aspects of the key relations among ministers. It should be stressed, however, that these relations are not the only aspects of Cabinet behaviour that have important consequences. They are merely the ones which emerge when one looks at the central policy organizations. Regional and ethnic representational factors are also important.[10] Throughout the Trudeau era, Cabinet representation from Western Canada has been weak, as was Quebec representation in the Clark Cabinet. Chapter 11 shows the problems that arose when the Liberals created a Cabinet Committee on Western Affairs to help overcome their regional weakness. Both historical and journalistic accounts stress, in addition, the importance of personal loyalty by Cabinet ministers, both in and out of the previously labelled inner group of ministers to the prime minister.

Closely related, and often reinforcing such regional and loyalty structures, are ideological structures. Cabinets usually or eventually divide into "liberals" and "conservatives," at least insofar as it becomes possible to discern attitudes towards change. Often these ideological patterns become apparent to Cabinet participants only after a government has been in power for a while and these patterns begin to be clarified and, in part, stereotyped. One of the more interesting examples of how these several patterns can overlap was found in the early Trudeau Cabinet. Two ministers most closely associated with Prime Minister Trudeau on loyalty, ethnic and ideological grounds, Jean Marchand and Gerard Pelletier, were given portfolios related to the prime minister's primary priority areas—regional economic expansion and language and cultural policy, respectively. These ministers were also given wide powers regarding the coordination of their policy areas vis-à-vis other ministers.

Hence, while "functional," "regional," "loyalty" and "ideological" patterns can be abstracted analytically, it is obvious that in general terms, and on any given policy issue (particularly involving a new policy issue), these patterns may be mutually reinforcing or they may be conflicting, or a mixture of both. The particular pattern of forces, events and personalities that affect a particular Cabinet decision on an issue are further complicated by the involvement of the Cabinet minister whose departmental "mission" is most directly affected by Cabinet decisions on his policy area. The involvement of ministers in policy issues (related to Agriculture, Health and Welfare, and so on) is obviously important in such cases, but these ministers will have a more intermittent policy role in the total scheme of things in comparison with the functional ministers who, by virtue of their role, more often have an opportunity to be involved in all issues because of the functional importance of their roles.

None of the earlier suggestions about the dynamics and subsystems of Cabinet behaviour should be taken to imply that no coordination exists. There are obviously centres of power and regular cycles of behaviour that contribute to the coordination of public policy. We see this in the more detailed look at the priority-setting and resource-allocation processes analysed in Chapters 10 and 11.

Central Agencies

The expansion and bureaucratization of the central support agencies of the Cabinet have been influenced by a concern which particularly began to emerge in the mid-1960s about the adequacy of the prime minister's and the Cabinet's ability to plan and to manage the government.[11] This concern was a general one reflected in other western countries, in Ottawa and in provincial capitals as well, and hence cannot be wholly attributed to Prime Minister Trudeau's fascination with rationality. At the federal level the concern was reflected in the development during the Pearson years of the first Cabinet Committee on Priorities and Planning and by the creation of major central advisory councils such as the Economic Council of Canada and the Science Council of Canada.[12] It was emphasized even more under the influence of the rational planning philosophies held by Prime Minister Trudeau and his advisors.

By the 1980s the central agency structures had evolved to produce six recognizable central agencies with perhaps one or two others in the "latent" or contending central agency category. The six major central agencies are the:

- Prime Minister's Office (PMO)
- Privy Council Office (PCO)
- Treasury Board Secretariat (TBS) which includes the Office of the Comptroller General, an official who reports directly to the President of the Treasury Board
- Department of Finance
- Ministry of State for Economic and Regional Development (MSERD)
- Ministry of State for Social Development (MSSD)

In addition, the Federal-Provincial Relations Office, the Department of the Secretary of State for External Affairs and the Department of Justice have some reasonable claim to central agency status, arising out of their roles as federal-provincial, foreign policy and legal advisors, respectively. The mandates of some other ostensibly line departments extend horizontally across the entire government, and thus the notion of what a central agency is is not always clear-cut. This should not be surprising in that when one asks what is central one is asking questions about power and about key ideas at the same time. Mercifully, however, we will confine this initial look at central agencies to the six agencies enumerated above.

The roles of the main central-support organizations are important in three respects. First, they have considerable influence as organizations because of their custody over central cross-cutting activities of government. Second, they must cooperate with each other because their roles continually overlap. For example, the TBS has responsibility for personnel management, but the PCO has a major role in advising the prime minister on the appointment of senior officials. Finally, the organizations afford great personal influence in the policy process to their bureaucratic heads, the Secretary to the Cabinet, the Principal Secretary to the Prime Minister, the Secretary to the Treasury Board, the Deputy Minister of Finance, and the deputy ministers of state in the economic and social policy fields. Thus, senior officials such as Gordon Robertson, Michael Pitfield, Gordon Osbaldeston, Robert Bryce and others are important actors in policy development and in advising on the appointment of others who, in turn, will also exercise influence.

In a general sense the roles of the PCO, PMO, TBS and the Department of Finance have always existed. The roles of strategic governmental coordinator, partisan political advisor, general manager, fiscal-policy advisor are present in government in one form or another. The two economic and social ministries of state are in a formal sense a newer coordinative phenomenon, but they have also existed in some previous form as well. In the 1960s these central agency roles in the Government of Canada underwent a transformation in that the roles became more organizationally differentiated, less personalized, more bureaucratic, and more active.[13] The organizational differentiation occurred with the separation of the Treasury Board from the Finance department in 1966 and with the clearer identification of a Prime Minister's Office in the 1960s. The roles were further complicated by the establishment in 1978 of the Office of the Comptroller General who reports to the President of the Treasury Board. Roles previously played by key officials supported by very small organizational staff became less personalized precisely because of the bureaucratization and growth of the support organizations around them. This bureaucratization was perhaps most visibly reflected by the development in the late 1960s and early 1970s of "planning" units or branches in each of the central organizations.

It was precisely because of the differentiation and bureaucratization that the key roles were given more time and capacity and, hence, could be carried out in a more active and aggressive manner. This activeness has undoubtedly made it possible for more aggressive initiatives to emerge from the central agencies. With regard to the PCO and the PMO in particular, we have witnessed far more concern about both the degree of influence and the legitimacy of the influence of these agencies and their key personalities. They create and foster concern about "super groups" of unelected advisors usurping the legitimate roles of the elected politicians.[14]

Evidence about the exact nature of central agency influence is mixed. An empirical survey of the attitudes and characteristics of central agency officials by Campbell and Szablowski shows that, on the one hand, these officials tend to come from a broader socioeconomic strata of Canadian society than regular-line departmental officials.[15] On the other hand, it indicates that they were attracted to the central agencies by an explicitly expressed desire to have and to exercise influence. But this kind of analysis does not necessarily tell us very much because it does not deal with policy fields or actual decisions, only with the perceptions of officials.

An analysis of social security policy in the 1970s attributes a major and growing influence to the central agencies.[16] We explore this more completely in Chapter 14. This central agency influence may be especially strong when highly visible and potentially redistributive issues are at stake. Possible changes then being considered in income security and supplementation programs, including the Family Allowances program, involved a potential visible shift of resources from broadly middle-class to lower income recipients. In the early stages one major initiative by the Department of Health and Welfare was successfully rebuffed by the Department of Finance, but a smaller package involving a child tax credit was successfully reintroduced on the initiative of the PMO, supported by the health and welfare minister. On the other hand, a study of the making of the federal "Make or Buy" science policy in 1971-72 shows critical influence resting more with a line department.[17] Again, this may be because the policy at stake in this case was somewhat more distributive, that is, oriented, towards a particular constituency. It was, by definition, a much lower profile issue than social security policy.

Richard French's analysis of the making of industrial policy portrays the central agency and priority-setting process as a debilitating struggle among three contending views of planning held by the PCO, Treasury Boad and Department of Finance, respectively.[18] The PCO's view was diffuse and interdisciplinary and was linked to the influence of Michael Pitfield. Based on the "softer" noneconomic social sciences, "planning" emerged here as a procedural necessity to achieve better short- and medium-term coordination. The Treasury Board's view was centred in microeconomics, efficiency oriented cost-benefit analysis and program evaluation on a planned cyclical basis. Though led initially by Douglas Hartle, this "planning as evaluation" school did not triumph in the Treasury Board. It has re-emerged, however, in the Office of the Comptroller General and especially in the Ministries of State, particularly the MSERD (see Chapter 11). The Department of Finance's view of planning was the oldest of the three and, in French's view, centred on Keynesian economics and short-term demand management.

French is right to stress that the three central agencies had different perspectives on the world. He exaggerates reality, however, when he describes them all as "planning systems." The term implies a coherence of thought which a broader view of the policy process and of economic management does not support.[19] First, the PCO's view was too wooly to be deemed planning. There was in the PCO an earnest search for, and even belief in, rationality and orderliness but it could hardly be called planning. The Department of Finance's Keynesian view of the world was certainly part of an effort to manage the economy, but it was almost never referred to by senior Finance officials as a planning system. Finally, the concept of planning as evaluation was not the dominant view of the Treasury Board, whose role in most of the 1970s was centred in the general management of the expediture process. The idea of planning was centred only in the Board's planning branch, not its program branch.

Sandy Borin's analysis of the early years of the two Ministries of State, MSERD and MSSD, suggests that MSERD became the new home for some of the Hartle-inspired Treasury Board microeconomics graduates.[20] As we see in Chapters 11 and 12, they began to influence the way economic development was viewed, analysed and presented to ministers in the Cabinet Committee on Economic and Regional Development. Both their ideas and the closer access they enjoy as an analytical central agency are important, but their influence is by no means uniform or unidimensional since other factors also determine industrial policy. We also explore Borin's observations about the MSSD. He finds that the social policy advisors in MSSD come from the softer social sciences and contain more "proactive types" interested in social intervention.

What may be just as important as hard "case" study evidence or more general studies about central agency influence are the beliefs or perceptions of such influence. In short, the central agencies are *believed* to have a growing and perhaps disproportionate influence. There is evidence that the governing Liberal party caucus believed this, especially in relation to the role of the PMO in the 1970-72 period and in the early 1980s.[21] A paper by A.W. Johnson, a senior public servant with both line department and central agency experience, expresses a similar belief. Johnson disguises his verdict under a general veiled discussion of various ways to enhance "creativity" in policy making, but it is clearly a critique of how Ottawa's coordinators were stalemating the "doers."[22]

The above concerns and beliefs about central agency power are normal and important, but their real import can be easily exaggerated, especially in the long run when one considers the other interplay of forces and ideas reflected in the Cabinet committees and in the regular departments of government.

The transformation from a fused, personalized and passive relationship to a more differentiated, bureaucratized and active one is clearly a relative change. The new pattern does not totally replace the old. Recent changes, in fact, reflect the constant contradictory demands of governmental and policy structure. When differentiation occurred, it raised, in a renewed way, the need for new elements of coordination and integration. When significant bureaucratization occurred, it did not replace the personalized and often verbal nature which characterized the way policy information and advice is exchanged between policy actors. Indeed, it creates a new need to insure that the bureaucratized units do not take on roles, or interpretation of roles, that distort the complementarity of policy roles that the key actors in the PCO, PMO, Treasury Board, the policy ministries and Finance department must understand. And, finally, when activism becomes more possible, it is important to stress that it too will only be a relative change, because no matter how differentiated and bureaucratized the main roles become, they will always be severely constrained by the greater volume of incoming demands of the even larger organizations which surround them.

The essence of the central roles is still complementary in nature. The provision of strategic political advice, including the ideas and priorities of the political system, are fed to the prime minister and Cabinet by the PMO and in part by the PCO (as well as, of course, by a host of other channels of political communication including the policy ministries, the minister's staff, the caucus, Parliament and the press). The PCO tends to be the main source of overall governmental and strategic organizational advice. The PCO provides the basic record-keeping support to the Cabinet and to all of the Cabinet committees except the Treasury Board. It ensures, with the policy ministries, that adequate analysis and coordination of policies and policy proposals are carried out. The main source of advice regarding the broad economic and fiscal impact of government activity is the Department of Finance, and the main source of advice on the general expenditure, administrative and managerial implications of both new and existing programs (and of the relationships between the two) is the Treasury Board and its staff and that of the policy ministries.

An analysis of the basic roles played by the prime minister, the Cabinet and the central agencies alerts us to the importance and continuing presence of inner centres of Cabinet power. Certain Cabinet roles are obviously inherently more important than others. At the same time, the Canadian Cabinet and the *idea* of responsible Cabinet-Parliamentary government pulls ministers in two directions at once, as persons who are both collectively and individually responsible. Cabinet life is reinforced by the need to delegate, to specialize and to deal with the diverse reality of public policy. The analysis in Chapter 8 and 9 elaborates further on these contradictory tendencies inherent in Cabinet-Parliamentary government.

NOTES

1. See G. Bruce Doern and Peter Aucoin, eds., *Public Policy in Canada* (Toronto: Macmillan of Canada, 1979), Chapters 2 and 3; Richard French, *How Ottawa Decides* (Toronto: James Lorimer Publishers, 1980); and A.D. Doerr, *The Machinery of Government in Canada* (Toronto: Methuen, 1981).

2. See Thomas Hockin, ed., *Apex of Power,* Second Edition (Toronto: Prentice-Hall, 1977) and W.A. Matheson, *The Prime Minister and the Cabinet* (Toronto: Methuen, 1976).

3. R. Van Loon and M. Whittington, *The Canadian Political System,* Third Edition (Toronto: McGraw-Hill Ryerson, 1981), Chapter 14.

4. *Ibid.,* Chapter 14.

5. See Doern and Aucoin, *op. cit.,* Chapters 2 and 3. See also Andrew Johnson, "The Structure of the Canadian Cabinet." Unpublished Doctoral Thesis, University of Oxford, England, 1980.

6. See Johnson, *op. cit.* for a detailed comparison of the Diefenbaker and St. Laurent eras.

7. For a comparative view see Hugh Heclo and Aaron Wildavsky, *The Private Government of Public Money* (London: Macmillan, 1973).

8. See David Good, *The Politics of Anticipation: Making Canadian Federal Tax Policy* (Ottawa: School of Public Administration, 1980); and Douglas Hartle, *The Revenue Budget Process of the Government of Canada* (Toronto: Canadian Tax Foundation, 1982).

9. On the decline of the Department of Finance, see Richard W. Phidd and G. Bruce Doern, *The Politics and Management of Canadian Economic Policy* (Toronto: Macmillan of Canada, 1978), Chapter 14; and Hartle, *op. cit.*, Chapter 5.

10. Van Loon and Whittington, *op. cit.*, Chapter 14.

11. See Colin Campbell and George Szablowski, *The Superbureaucrats* (Toronto: Macmillan of Canada, 1979); French, *op. cit.*; Doern and Aucoin, *op. cit.*, Chapters 2 and 3; and V. Seymour Wilson, *Canadian Public Policy and Public Administration* (Toronto: McGraw-Hill Ryerson, 1981), Chapter 9.

12. See chapters by R.W. Phidd and G. Bruce Doern on the Economic and Science Councils, respectively, in G. Bruce Doern and Peter Aucoin, eds., *The Structures of Policy Making in Canada* (Toronto: Macmillan of Canada, 1972), Chapters 8 and 9.

13. See Doern and Aucoin, *Public Policy in Canada*, Chapter 2.

14. See Campbell and Szablowski, *op. cit.*, Chapter 7. The tendency to attribute virtually all such relations to the personal influence of key advisors as opposed to structures is especially strong among journalists. See Christina McCall-Newman, "Michael Pitfield and the Politics of Mismanagement," *Saturday Night*, October 1982, pp. 4-44. See also her book *Grits* (Toronto: Macmillan of Canada, 1982).

15. Campbell and Szablowski, *op. cit.*, Chapters 4 and 5.

16. Rick Van Loon, "Reforming Welfare in Canada," *Public Policy*, Volume 27, No. 4 (Fall, 1979), pp. 469-504.

17. M. Skinner, "The Federal Make or Buy Policy: A Preliminary Evaluation of Policy and Implementation." Unpublished M.A. Thesis, School of Public Administration, Carleton University, Ottawa, 1978.

18. French, *op. cit.*, Chapters 1 and 2.

19. Phidd and Doern, *op. cit.*, Chapters 12, 13 and 14.

20. Sandford F. Borins, "Ottawa's Envelopes: Workable Rationality at Last?", in G. Bruce Doern, ed., *How Ottawa Spends Your Tax Dollars 1982* (Toronto: James Lorimer Publishers, 1982), Chapter 3.

21. See McCall-Newman, *Grits*, Chapter 3 and Richard Gwyn, *The Northern Magus* (Markham, Ontario: Paperjacks Ltd., 1980), Chapter 5.

22. A.W. Johnson, "Public Policy: Creativity and Bureaucracy," *Canadian Public Administration*, Volume 21, No. 1 (Spring, 1978), pp. 1-15.

CHAPTER 8

PRIME MINISTERS, POLITICAL POWER AND POLICY PREFERENCES

It is often said that in modern media-based politics, political leadership is everything and that personality triumphs over policy. Many point to how much better things would be if Canadians would debate issues instead of leadership. Yet it is evident that policies, ideas and leaders are inseparably linked in at least two ways. Prime ministers do have policy preferences and ideas and have the power to act on them, certainly more often than any other minister. At the same time, in many areas, the prime minister lacks power in the sense of having only a limited ability to actually solve problems if broader policy circumstances, including the power of other leaders, interests and countries, conspire against him. He may also decline to invest his power in policy fields that simply do not interest or concern him as much as other fields do.

In this chapter we survey the key policy preferences of several recent Canadian prime ministers from Pierre Trudeau to John Diefenbaker.[1] Where such views can be discerned, we also survey their views about the general policy process and the management of the policy process within government. In comparing political leaders in this way, we are obviously spanning a broad historical period with different social, political and economic circumstances. In short, we are to a considerable extent comparing "apples and oranges." This makes comparison difficult but not uninstructive, particularly if the comparisons attempted here are not viewed in isolation. They must be seen in relation to the enduring major ideas of Canadian political life, to the general pattern of relations among ministers, examined in Chapter 7, and to the analysis of actual policy priorities in Chapter 10. Before proceeding to our brief profiles of the policy preferences of Prime Ministers Trudeau, Clark, Pearson and Diefenbaker, we need to understand some of the problems in evaluating prime ministerial power and policy preferences.

Problems in Evaluating Prime Ministerial
Power and Policy Preferences

Several characteristics and problems arise in assessing a prime minister's policy preferences and his infuence in the policy process. The major ones examined here are: the concept of fixed versus variable power; the relationship between longevity in power and the rhetorical labelling of regimes; the personal and career background of prime ministers; the prime minister's control of the Cabinet agenda; and the power to appoint ministers and senior officials.

Fixed or Variable Sums of Power?

There has always been an implicit controversy over the kind of power a prime minister possesses. Is his power a kind of fixed sum which he "acquires" on election and which he then dissipates, spends, or invests (but which invariably reduces over time), or is it a sum which he can augment and replenish? According to the former notion, a prime minister's power is at its maximum in the first year or two of his mandate and, hence, this is the optimum time to act and to change the policies he most wanted to change. If he did not act early, the pressures, accumulated grievances and challenges to his personal authority would invariably mount and his failures would increasingly become part of political memory. The contrary view is that a prime minister's power can be replenished most obviously through re-election (especially with a majority), through the successful handling of a crisis situation or simply through strong leadership and successful policies.

It is not difficult to see that these differing views of the kind of power possessed by a political leader are difficult to analyze and agree upon. One obvious and blunt indicator is shear longevity in power and electoral success. But the importance of investing and spending power also affects the conduct of public policy and priority setting in other ways. For example, Prime Minister Pearson's "60 days of decision" concept in 1963 could be viewed as being based on an explicit strategy corresponding to the "fixed sum of power" concept. Major initiatives were to be taken early by a new government with a fresh, albeit minority, government mandate. In contrast, the first Trudeau government from 1968 to 1972 seemed to operate from the opposite premise. The strategy in part seemed to be to think carefully and plan a course of action in the first year, take action in the second and third year, explain one's actions in the fourth year, get re-elected, and repeat the cycle again.

Alas, political strategies are based on more than just the notion of fixed or expandable concepts of power. Pearson's "60 days of decision" approach was also motivated by the Liberals' desire to contrast his governmnent's decisiveness with the previous Diefenbaker government's alleged indecisiveness.[2] Similarly, the new Trudeau government of 1968 wanted to display its rational planned orderliness as a contrast to the perceived chaotic untidiness of the last years of the Pearson government.[3]

Despite the limitations of the sum of power concept, it is nonetheless true that all prime ministers and their closest advisers must consider the concept in some strategic way, even if they cannot always control events or carry out the strategy. In addition, the concept of the sum of power enters into a prime minister's judgement about the key policy issues in which he will "stand or fall," so to speak. As we show in this chapter, every prime minister stakes out a certain policy terrain in which he is prepared to invest all or most of his power and influence and which others dare not challenge.

Longevity and the Perception of Regimes
It is elementary to observe that longevity in power affects a prime minister's approach to policy. His regime begins to collect political baggage, an amalgam of credits and debits and friends and enemies that form the political record. Prime ministers become entrenched defenders of what they and others view as their chief policy successes. They try to distance themselves from their past failures, hoping as always that the electorate has a bad memory and short attention span. Above all, longevity produces the inevitable labelling of regimes, the application of an overall brand name by journalists, opposition parties and others as a codeword to sum up the regime's successes or failures. These labels do not always coincide with policy fields per se, but rather convey views about the prime minister's overall approach and/or personality. Thus, Trudeau governments have earned the epitaph of being technocratic and arrogant. The Diefenbaker regime was characterized as being both intuitively humane and then indecisive and insecure, with Diefenbaker himself labelled a "renegade in power." The Pearson regime was first viewed as being innovative and decisive but later characterized as almost hopelessly disorganized. These labels are not always wholly accurate or

even fair, but the reality is that they stick and prime ministers have to live with them.

Regimes also acquire labels expressed in terms of policy fields as well. We see this in greater detail in the next section of this chapter. One interesting illustration of this kind of perception was the persistent view that Prime Minister Trudeau was simply not interested in the economy. Language policy and the Charter of Rights were his chief interests, while economic policy assumed a distant second place. While the evidence in Chapter 10 does not fully support that view of the Trudeau regime, the more general point to be made in relation to prime ministerial policy preferences is that virtually all recent occupants of the office lean to the social policy side of the policy continuum. This is partly because party leadership conventions seem to prefer leaders who display or are perceived to have a preference for the "softer" human issues on the not unrealistic expectations that this is where the "votes" are.

Career Experience and Personal Leadership Style

The tautalogical adage that people "are what they have been" or, alternatively, that a leopard "cannot change its spots" obviously has some relevance to understanding how prime ministers behave, their policy preferences, and the strengths and limitations of the skills they bring to high office. These behaviour traits also become bound up in judgements about how charismatic a leader is. In this context the media plays a decisive role. Prime ministers in the television age face a two-edged sword in this regard. Easy access to, and manipulation of, the media can be a decisive attribute of the exercise of leadership by a prime minister. At the same time constant *daily* visual exposure can also breed familiarity and contempt as prime ministers utter the "same old line" or "yesterday's speech."

It is evident and natural that career experience influences a prime minister's policy preferences, views of political power, and at the same time limits his skills in some ways. Prime Minister Trudeau came to political power almost directly from an academic career. He had written about government, about political philosophy, and his views were known on such topics as nationalism and federalism, human rights and French-English relations in Canada.[4] He had limited Parliamentary experience, nor had he worked in a large organizational setting or acquired managerial experience.

In sharp contrast Prime Minister Clark was a product of party politics and was familiar with the entrails of party machinery, local constituency politics and the frustrations of Parliamentary life on the opposite side.[5] Clark also lacked any significant experience in managing a large organization. Moreover, he did not have the intellectual range or communication skills of Trudeau. Clark was utterly victimized in the 1979-80 period by the so-called "wimp factor," a combination of media exaggeration of his alleged physical gangliness, periodic nervous speech habits and general youth and inexperience.[6]

Prime Minister Diefenbaker was also a political outsider and, in addition, a proverbial lone wolf. A small-town prairie lawyer and a non-Anglophone, Diefenbaker had suffered numerous political defeats and saw himself as constantly battling his political enemies, whether they were Eastern Bay Street financiers or leadership threats from within his own Cabinet. Long years in Parliamentary opposition had ensured that Diefenbaker would never be an "organization man" interested in or concerned about the machinery of government.[7]

In contrast to all of the above, Prime Minister Pearson had considerable experience in Ottawa as a deputy minister, minister and diplomat. He was not a constituency politician. As a historian by education and a diplomat by experience, he was not, however, embued with a fascination with bureaucracy.[8] Possessed of an infectious amiability and legendary diplomatic skills, Pearson was both liked and at the same time often viewed as the consummate incrementalist who "muddled through" to a satisfactory, if temporary, consensus. He lacked the charisma and overall leadership skills of either Diefenbaker or Trudeau.

The regional origins and political base of a prime minister is of critical importance in defining his policy ideas and preferences. Pierre Trudeau is a Quebecer and was concerned about Quebec's place in confederation. John Diefenbaker and Joe Clark had their political base in Western Canada, and it affected their emphasis on regional, agricultural, resource and energy policy. Lester Pearson was from Ontario and brought a special concern about English-Canada's relation to French Canada.

Prime ministers are obviously not totally imprisoned by their past accumulated traits. There is obviously a certain amount of "on the job" training and learning as experience is gained, crises are surmounted, and failures and mistakes are absorbed and stored in some corner of the political brain. Sooner or later, however, a prime minister must learn to manage the governmental and political leviathan he heads. He is never fully trained for the job in advance, but must survive in an environment where ideas are in conflict, the guideposts are vague, the advisors and the advice numerous and contradictory, and the future never as clear as his many critics believe it to be.

Controlling the Agenda and the Power of Appointment

Within the Cabinet and executive-bureaucratic arena itself two of the major levers and/or points of prime ministerial control over policy are the Cabinet agenda itself (including the agenda of the Priorities and Planning Committee of Cabinet) and the power of appointment of ministers and senior officials. These powers are an amalgam of legal, constitutional and prerogative powers, and are backed ultimately by the prime minister's power to dissolve Parliament and call an election. This latter power cannot be used or threatened very frequently, but then again it may not have to be because ministers and others are aware of its potential use.

The prime minister (and his key advisors) try to exert as much control as possible over the Cabinet agenda, namely the issues to be considered, the order of consideration, and the relegation of lower order problems for "further study." Such control is never fully exercised. In the past there has always been concern about the capacity of other ministers to conduct what, in football parlance, was called the "end run," that is, the tactic of disobeying the agenda-setting rules to bring a pet project or even an urgent project directly to Cabinet without "proper" prior assessment. In the simpler Cabinet committee and central agency days of the 1940s, 1950s and early 1960s it was often believed that "end runs" were too frequent. In part, of course, end runs were simply evidence of the influence of other line ministers who in those days did not have to run the minefield of the more elaborate central agency and Cabinet committee system constructed in the late 1960s and early 1970s.

The issue of Cabinet "end runs" and agenda control raises some interesting paradoxes when one attempts to assess the power of a particular prime minister or of different prime ministers at different times. Consider, for example, a comparison between Prime Minister

Trudeau and Prime Minister MacKenzie King. It is probable that most people would argue that Trudeau was more powerful than King due to his greater command of the media and the centralization of power in central agencies, including the PMO. When one considers the agenda-setting process in the two eras, however, one may be inclined to reach a different conclusion. In King's day the Cabinet agenda and the central machinery was a more fluid and uncertain affair.[9] King's fellow ministers did not necessarily know what the agenda was. Where there is uncertainty in a relationship, there is a greater opportunity for the exercise of power, in this case by MacKenzie King who controlled the process. In contrast, in the Trudeau era the agenda-setting process and the Cabinet committee apparatus had become heavily bureaucratized, that is, the relations between ministers and the prime minister had been made more rule-ridden and *predictable.* The more predictable the process, the less room there is for arbitrary discretion. In this sense Trudeau may have had less power than often thought because he also had to obey the rules of the policy game he wanted his ministers to obey.

Once again, it is important to stress that this power-uncertainty variable is only one of many attributes that influence a prime minister's role in policy formulation. It must also be stressed in the case of the Trudeau era, or any other leader's regime, that the prime minister, more than any other person, can disobey whatever rules of procedure he puts in place and design others to suit his needs.

The power of appointment is also a crucial basis for a prime minister's influence on policy and reflects his central role as the bridge between the Cabinet and the public service as a whole. It is also closely tied to his power to reorganize departments and the overall machinery of government. The appointment of ministers and senior public servants is a prerogative which most leaders protect carefully. Peter Aucoin has developed the concept of positional policy, a concept which alerts us to the fact that overall policy for a given period of time in a given department or agency is set, not just by what the head of the agency does or says, but by the prior choice by the prime minister of the person whom he appoints and the organizational restructuring that may, on occasion, accompany such appointments.[10] This is perhaps the most human interpersonal dimension of politics and public policy, since it involves the complex calculus and chemistry of friendships and loyalties, competence and representativeness, patronage and purpose, and vanity and pride. Prime Minister Lester B. Pearson put the dilemma in human terms.

> Politics is more than differing opinions over issues and ideas, of how best to serve the public interest. Politics also embraces power and position. Hence in politics pride is often stronger than tolerance, and prejudice more current than understanding. Conceit, even arrogance, to which the successful politician is exposed, can be a danger to those who gave him the power on which his conceit is based.[11]

There is little science to the appointment process.[12] It is the art of judgement personified. Prime ministers face a welter of often contradictory principles and must face up to their own knowledge, toughness, and/or weaknesses in dealing with friends, enemies, and with many people they do not know well. Louis St. Laurent was known to keep his own counsel on appointment matters and made them expeditiously. John Diefenbaker discussed them with colleagues and had difficulty making up his mind.[13]

The potential conflicting principles and ideas inherent in appointment criteria are numerous. At the Cabinet level there are the issues of regional representativeness, competence, knowledge and experience, and the need to choose from the often limited personnel produced somewhat capriciously by the electoral and party process. At the senior official level there is the need to maintain some sense of a career public service, while at the same time ensuring that public service and agency appointees are sensitive to, and supportive of, the government's preferences in the policy field concerned. At both levels there are needs to balance the concept of turnover versus tenure.[14] By increasing the turnover of ministers, the prime minister may enhance his power over his colleagues simply by a visible exercise of his appointment power. It can also enable him to weed out weaker ministers and put a new public face to his government. It allows him to put a minister in place with specific instructions about what he, the prime minister, wants done. On the other hand, increased tenure can augment a minister's knowledge of his responsibilities, enhance his familiarity with a powerful clientele or region of the country, or even ensure that a Cabinet enemy is isolated and preserved in a safe place. By increasing the tenure of ministers and simultaneously increasing the turnover of deputy ministers, the prime minister may feel he can enhance political control of the public service.

Correspondingly, a deputy kept in a department while several ministers rotate in and out may also enhance a political leader's policy purpose.

Not surprisingly, in the face of this array of principles practice varies in infinite ways both in the same prime minister's tenure in office and among prime ministerial regimes. For example, in the Trudeau era agricultural policy has enjoyed considerable success. It is both a cause and an effect of the long tenure of Eugene Whelan as Minister of Agriculture and relative stability at the deputy minister level as well. At another extreme, there have been several ministers of consumer and corporate affairs reflecting an unwillingness to proceed further in the 1970s with changes to competition policy that were strongly opposed by the business community.[15] In this instance the several ministers were offered as veritable sacrificial lambs while they maintained a holding operation for a year or two. Between these extremes are a host of other permutations and combinations of "policy making by appointment."

It is evident, of course, that not all appointees perform as expected in ministerial or other realms. For example, it is doubtful that the Diefenbaker government's appointment of Mr. Justice Hall in the early 1960s was premised on the assumption that he would produce a report that was enthusiastically supportive of compulsory medicare. Nor was the appointment of Justice Berger by the Trudeau government expected to yield the controversies resulting from his later report on energy and the northern environment.

Appointments also raise issues, especially at the ministerial level, but at other levels as well, about how to deal with political deadwood or incompetence, or simply with persons who, for many reasons, are no longer suited to their current tasks. As human beings, prime ministers are reluctant to deal ruthlessly with fellow partisans and politicians. They have an appreciation of how hard it is to get good people to commit themselves to the risks of a political career. This is why the Senate and other agency appointments assume an importance out of all proportion to the role of these institutions per se. Prime ministers search inevitably for substitutes for the ignominy of the political firing.

All of the above elements affect the prime minister's efforts to formulate policy, set priorities, maintain power and manage the policy process within government and in the country at large. It is in this context that our survey of prime ministerial policy preferences must be viewed.

The Policy Preferences of Prime Ministers

The profiles presented here are brief. They are intended to illuminate the importance of the general preferences of Prime Ministers Trudeau, Clark, Pearson and Diefenbaker, both on policy issues and, where it can be discerned, on policy structures and processes. It is essential to stress again the difficulties of making these comparisons due to factors such as the widely varying periods of tenure in office. It must also be emphasized that no political leader is fully consistent in the application of the principles or ideas he most cherishes. Often, he is also reacting to the perceived excesses or weaknesses of his predecessor in office or of the leaders of the opposition political parties.

Prime Minister Trudeau

Prime Minister Pierre Elliott Trudeau is unique among the four prime ministers surveyed not only because of a much longer tenure in office, but also because prior to entering politics he wrote extensively about his philosophy of politics. We will summarize his key policy preferences with particular brevity in this chapter because in many ways several other chapters in the book deal with the Trudeau era in much more detail than with any of the other recent prime ministers. Four basic philosophical premises anchor the Trudeau view of public policy in general and which, in turn, have had an impact on his policy preferences. These are an opposition to narrow nationalism, a belief in the view that governments exist to support and defend individual rights, a belief in the need to countervail powerful policy tendencies, and a belief in rationality as opposed to emotion as a guide to human behaviour.

Trudeau's famous articles on nationalism and French Canadians clearly reflect his opposition to what he viewed as narrow cultural nationalism.[16] Trudeau did not oppose a broader nationalism but strongly criticized one whose boundaries reinforced a purely cultural definition of such nationalist sentiment. This view not only propelled Trudeau into federal politics but strongly influenced the view of Canada he espoused and enshrined both in the Official Languages Act which institutionalized bilingualism and later in the Charter of Rights and constitutional reform passed in 1982. He stoutly rejected the two-nation view of Canada and sought to ensure that French Canadians would feel at home in any province and not just in Quebec.

Trudeau's belief in the freedom of the individual as the ultimate purpose which the state exists to serve was expressed by his very early proposal for a Charter of Rights. The Charter itself was not achieved until 1982 after Trudeau's unforseen return to power, but there can be little doubt that it will profoundly affect both the nature of government and public policy.[17] There are, of course, contradictions between Trudeau's first two premises and the third, his devotion to the theory of counterweights in which government would shift its weight and direction to counteract evolving excesses, be it in centralized federalism, market power or dependence on other states. Trudeau observed that:

> the theory of checks and balances, so acutely analysed by [Montesquieu and de Tocqueville], has always had my full support. It translates into practical terms the concept of equilibrium that is inseparable from freedom in the realm of ideas. It incorporates a corrective for abuses and excesses into the very functioning of political institutions. My political action, or my theory—insomuch as I can be said to have one—can be expressed very simply: create counterweights.[18]

While the notion of counterweights can be a philosophical premise of a decidedly wooly nature, it appears to have guided his thinking in the decision to impose wage and price controls in 1975 and in the new nationalism directed against the provinces in 1980 and 1981.[19] Both of these are examined in Chapter 10. It also influenced his thinking in the foreign policy field reviewed in Chapter 14.

Finally, there is the Trudeau preference for rationality. Trudeau's view of rationality only partly converges with the concept of a rational model outlined in Chapter 6. Radwansky characterizes Trudeau's views as follows.

> The emphasis on rationality introduces an element of intolerance into a system which otherwise is designed to encourage diversity. Trudeau doesn't really acknowledge the individual's right to choose to be irrational, to put more weight on emotion or instinct than on intellect. He assumes that other minds function like his—and, indeed, have comparable intelligence—and shuns any other approach as a failure to meet the standard of acceptable human behaviour.
>
> The second consequence is his insistence on "cold, unemotional rationality" in politics: "If not a pure product of reason, the political tools of the future will be designed and appraised by the more rational standards than anything we are currently using." That is the essence of Trudeau's idea of "functional politics," a concept whose lasting

importance to him may be deduced from the fact that it was the title and theme both of the first article he wrote for *Cite Libre* in 1950 and of the manifesto he wrote with Marc Lalonde and several others in 1964. His "functionalism" is not so much a theory as a state of mind: a pragmatic willingness to tackle each problem on its own merits, without reference to dogma or ideology. He abhors ideologies, considering them irrational in that they dictate approaches without reference to the particular facts of each situation: "I early realized that ideological systems are the true enemies of freedom. ... I am a pragmatist. I try to find the solution to each problem as it comes up in order that it be the best possible solution for the present situation, and I do not feel myself bound by any doctrines or any rigid approaches to any of these problems.[20]

Trudeau did strive to make the policy process within the Cabinet and executive structures more rational. Indeed, if there is one overall perception of his era in power, it is that of a technocratic government. That he was not very successful in being rational should not be surprising, but we will reserve further judgement on this question until Chapters 10 and 11. It is useful to note, however, the apparent contrast between Trudeau's fascination with rational structures and his often dogmatic and argumentative public persona and the accounts of his actual conduct of Cabinet meetings. Several ministers publicly and privately attest to his fair minded, almost socratic and consultative behaviour in guiding Cabinet meetings.[21]

Prime Minister Clark

The contrast between Prime Minister Joe Clark and Prime Minister Trudeau is stark in almost every respect: regional origins, length of tenure in office, career background, personality and the degree to which he openly expressed a political philosophy. Many of Clark's views were also forged in direct opposition to what he saw as the excesses and weaknesses of Trudeau's philosophy, policy record and approach. As a slightly left-of-centre Conservative from Western Canada whose political experience had been in the Opposition, Clark's policy preferences were expressed in very general ways.[22] He brought with him to office a far greater concern, although by no means a strident one, about the excesses of government and bureaucracy. His initial opposition to Petro-Canada, which were clearly against the general trend in public opinion and proved to be a political mistake, were partly based on his view that government needed to be trimmed. He believed that his opposition to Petro-Canada would symbolize his support for the private sector and for the builders and doers of Western Canada in particular. He did not appear to see the issue in energy policy terms per se.

A second view that emerged fairly early was Clark's "community of communities" view of Canada and of federal provincial relations. This was both a philosophical preference and a political necessity. Clark's preference was to deal cooperatively with the provinces, a view which was later badly bruised but not totally destroyed by his own difficult experience in bargaining over energy matters with Alberta. It was also a practical necessity in that, despite being the federal leader of the Progressive Conservative party, he was perceived as being new and inexperienced by several of his Tory colleagues who were veteran premiers in several provinces. The "community of communities" thesis was intended to capture this political and policy preference.

As to the organization of government and the conduct of policy within the Cabinet, Clark's views were also in evidence. One of Clark's earliest speeches in the House of Commons was devoted to a focused attack on the growth of the Prime Minister's Office and the affect this and other Trudeau changes were having on Parliamentary government. He spoke far more frequently than most on the need for Parliamentary reform and for Freedom of Information legislation, proposals on which were introduced but not passed during his brief nine-month term in office. Somewhat paradoxically, however, Clark succumbed to his own version of a belief in formal rationality, albeit expressed more in terms of the need for efficiency in government. This was reflected in his adoption of a formal Inner and Outer Cabinet. The visibility and fanfare given to this reform went beyond the bounds of the collective norms inherent in Cabinet government. If one was not in the inner group, one did not count for much. The system resulted in a virtual abandonment of full Cabinet meetings and led to numerous problems in the perceived legitimacy of the Cabinet's inner group.[23]

Clark also gave full support to the envelope system, examined in Chapter 11, which he introduced. His government, however, advertised it as a system for expenditure management and *control*, rather than as an elegant *policy* management system, the view conveyed by the Liberals on their return to power in 1980. Thus, again Clark saw it more in terms of efficiency in government.

A final issue of no small importance to the Clark regime was the prime minister's view of relations with the senior public service. Here, Clark was on the horns of a dilemma not entirely of his own making. The Clark government had in part compaigned on an anti-government and anti-bureaucracy ticket. Leading Conservatives were conscious of the fact that the earlier Diefenbaker government in 1957 had not engaged in the practice of removing key senior public servants identified with the "Liberal" bureaucracy because of the dominance of the Liberals in power. At the same time Clark was aware of the need to rely on experienced public servants, a view borne out of necessity due to the lack of expertise available to Opposition parties, *especially* those long out of power. He was also a traditionalist and supporter of Parliamentary government and hence believed in the *idea* of a loyal, neutral public service. The main source of alternative governmental expertise would have been from provincial governments run by the Tories. Even here, however, there was some concern about their loyalty to a federal Conservative government. There was also questions whether some would actually come to Ottawa when Clark headed only a tenuous minority government.

The net effect was that Clark made only two or three major changes at the senior level. He assiduously cultivated the loyalty of the senior mandarins and carefully explained to them the government's priorities. On balance he opted to rely on the established personnel. Although the short-lived nature of the Clark government of 1979 makes judgements of these and other issues difficult, to say the least, the Clark experience shows the dilemmas of overall structural choice when several policy, political and institutional needs intersect. In one field at least, energy policy, there is evidence to suggest that the Clark government's preferences and those of senior bureaucrats did not coincide.[24]

Prime Minister Pearson
Prime Minister Lester B. Pearson presided over five years of minority government, but this difficult political liability was compensated by the opportunity to govern during a period of economic buoyancy.[25] He also had to respond to and manage extremely delicate changes in the relations between English and French Canadians, as the national impact of Quebec's quiet revolution began to be felt for the first time. As it is with every Canadian political leader, Pearson's policy preferences and ideas

were partly his own and partly the product of the times and of the views of the political party he headed. Although political party platforms per se usually only bear a tenuous resemblance to what governing parties actually do, the early 1960s were an exception. The Liberal's 1960 Kingston policy conference had clearly helped set the Pearson agenda, particularly in the social policy field.

Pearson himself was best known for his views and skills in foreign policy, where he had won a Nobel Prize. His two governments, however, were most identified with the major initiatives they took in the social policy field, including the Canada Pension Plan, Medicare, a major expansion of federal financing for higher education and major initiatives in manpower training. His government also introduced collective bargaining in the federal public service. In addition, the Pearson government forged ahead with the establishment of the Maple Leaf as Canada's flag. In the delicate area of relations between English and French Canadians, the Pearson regime enunciated the concept of "cooperative federalism," witnessed the work of the Royal Commission on Bilingualism and Biculturalism, and saw the passage of legislation to allow Quebec to opt out of certain joint programs in exchange for tax points.

It is clear that Pearson strongly supported and preferred these largely social policy initiatives. Though not Kennedy-like in style or manner, he was influenced by the social buoyancy of the Kennedy era in the United States. This was perhaps best symbolized by his support for the creation of the Company of Young Canadians. One cannot underestimate, however, the degree to which Liberal policy thinkers, including Walter Gordon, Pearson's first Minister of Finance, forged their social views on the assumption and belief that the economy would be a buoyant one and that the social programs were affordable without the need to impose overly burdensome new taxes. The economy was in a sense taken for granted by Pearson. This was partly reflected in the lack of attention he personally gave economic uses and the difficulties his government encountered over selected economic issues such as in labour relations and strikes and foreign investment issues, especially in the first Walter Gordon Budget Speech.[26]

As to structure and process, the Pearson views and record present a mixed package. We have already referred earlier in this chapter to Pearson's quixotic "60 days of decision" approach, his antidote to

Diefenbaker's indecisiveness. As a man with extensive Ottawa experience, Pearson was not especially enamoured of the need to reorganize the Cabinet, at least not until near the end of his tenure in office when he established the Cabinet Committee on Priorities and Planning. He did support the vague "planning" notions inherent in the establishment of the Economic Council of Canada and the Science Council of Canada, but these bodies were attributable much more to the views of advisors and ministers such as Maurice Lamontagne, who saw them, equally vaguely, as hybrid Canadian versions of French-style "indicative planning."

Matheson's analysis of the Pearson habits in the actual conduct of Cabinet stresses the looseness of the prime minister's approach, something which later appalled Prime Minister Trudeau when he was Minister of Justice in the Pearson Cabinet. Matheson concludes:

> He was not a disciplinarian, as were most of his predecessors. "My style of conducting Cabinet meetings was relaxed, and informal. . . . Mackenzie King never allowed anyone to smoke in Cabinet or have a coffee or any other kind of break. He was the headmaster! Mr. St. Laurent's Cabinet was more formal than were mine. . . ." Possibly because of this informal atmosphere some of his ministers often revealed what was going on in Cabinet in spite of admonitions from the prime minister. Divisions within the Cabinet became public knowledge and caused dissatisfaction in the country. Cabinet disagreements are not uncommon in Canadian government, but usually the public is unaware of them until they become history. This was not the case, however, in the Pearson era and Mr. Pearson did not impose his will on his ministers in the way Mr. King or Mr. Diefenbaker could.[27]

While an easy-going amiability is perhaps congruent with Pearson's personality and diplomatic habits, it is nonetheless important to recall again the perpetual minority government status of his five years in power, a political condition even less conducive to orderliness and discipline, assuming such a condition can ever exist in any Cabinet.

Prime Minister Diefenbaker

Prime Minister John Diefenbaker was a Western Canadian populist and a charismatic leader. He and the Progessive Conservatives came to power in 1957 and formed a minority government after 22 years of Liberal rule. In a very real sense Diefenbaker arrived as the embodiment of an eclectic set of grievances held by those who had not fully shared in the heady prosperity of the post-war years. He had successfully labelled the tired St. Laurent–C.D. Howe Liberals as an arrogant, smug and uncaring government. Diefenbaker's minority regime of 1957-58 was therefore characterized by a spate of what were essentially a diffuse set of social, often regionally defined, measures.[28] Thus, changes in old age security benefits, support for hospital construction, improved equalization payments for poorer provinces, increased agricultural support payments and special rural development initiatives were begun, the latter being the precursor of Canada's later explicit "regional development" policies.

Some of this social energy was also later reflected in the early years of the massive Diefenbaker majority government elected in 1958. By then Diefenbaker had spoken passionately of his views of "One Canada" and his "northern vision," including a "roads to resources" program. The former was symbolized in the federal Bill of Rights passed in 1960 which defined Diefenbaker's view of the unhyphenated Canadian. The northern vision never materialized, partly because it was never clear what it meant. Diefenbaker embodied ideas but had little intellectual discipline or inclination to think them through.

Diefenbaker's strong views about "One Canada" undoubtedly adversely affected his ability to deal effectively with French Canada, including the large contingent of Quebec M.P.'s in his own caucus. It was an idea which screened out other possible forms of accommodation. This prospect was not aided by another aspect of his vision, his foreign and trade policy view that Canada could reduce its excessive dependence on the United States by diverting a higher portion of its trade to Britain, the mother country.

The persistence of Diefenbaker's nationalism was also reflected in his view of whether Canada should accept nuclear warheads as part of its BOMARC missile bases, as the American's were pressuring his government to do.[29] This issue ultimately brought down his government. Though Diefenbaker's indecision on this matter was a product of many factors, there is little doubt a major one was his ingrained instincts not to be, and not to be *seen* to be, catering to American pressure. But his nationalism and latent anti-Americanism, not surprisingly, were exercised in a selective way. For example, despite the symbolism of the historic 1956 "Pipeline Debate," a debate which forged Diefenbaker's public persona, there was little reluctance in 1961 to devise a National

Oil Policy, which was strongly supported by the American government. This was the policy which divided the Canadian oil market at the Ottawa valley, with points west served by Canadian sources of supply and points east by foreign U.S. multinational sources of supply.[30]

Diefenbaker's views were also influenced by his perpetual concern over the loyalty of his colleagues and his lack of knowledge or interest in certain policy fields. His views of the serious dispute between his government and James Coyne, the governor of the Bank of Canada, were in part due to a simple lack of interest in monetary affairs and in part because of Diefenbaker's mistrust of his own Minister of Finance, Donald Fleming. Fleming had finished second to him in the Tory leadership race and had close connections with the Toronto business and financial community, which Diefenbaker also suspected.

Prime Minister Diefenbaker's overall conduct of the Cabinet was also reflected by a frequent lack of trust of his colleagues. Andrew Johnson's extensive study of the Diefenbaker Cabinet, in comparison with the previous St. Laurent Cabinet, draws out the different features of each period and hence of the two prime ministers. He characterizes the Diefenbaker regime as "collegial" in the extreme, while St. Laurent fostered a "pluralistic" Cabinet in which he trusted ministers to take initiatives. While these differences cannot all be attributed to personality, they are certainly partly due to this reality. Johnson's overall conclusions are worth quoting at some length.

> Individual ministerial responsibilities were emphasized much less under Diefenbaker than under St. Laurent. The primary emphasis became collective decision taking; the approach was fundamentally collegial though the machinery was not reorganized accordingly. The Cabinet was treated more as exemplifying "government by committee" and less as a plural executive. Individual responsibilities were not disregarded or consistently interfered with—"the general operation of a department was left to the minister himself"—but they were regarded differently than under St. Laurent. Diefenbaker took pains to uphold the view that no one minister "is senior and another junior in the relations of a prime minister and the members of his Cabinet," but the conclusion drawn was not (as it had been under St. Laurent) that individual responsibilities should be emphasized and decentralization maximized, but rather that as far as possible all ministers should be involved together in making policy. Ministers' independence was checked and their motivation to use their responsibilities imaginatively was gradually constrained by the focus upon Cabinet decision

making and by Diefenbaker's own methods of controlling ministers. Ministers had scope for initiative—as witness Alvin Hamilton's career—but it was too often blocked from final fulfillment by Cabinet busy-ness. . . .

Individual responsibility was diffused not only by the greater collective emphasis but also by the several cross-cutting divisions which tended to encourage ministers' concern with their colleagues' activities. The regional roles of ministers, in particular, became more important: more regional understanding was indeed needed, but its great salience under Diefenbaker made government harder too. Individual responsibility was also weakened by ministers' inexperience, by weaker ministers who could not or would not fulfill their responsibilities effectually, and (perhaps more importantly) by misjudged ministerial appointments. Fleming, for example, carried his central agency responsibilities as Minister of Finance too far and too persistently when he could only irritate other ministers; the response—seemingly supported by Diefenbaker—was for other ministers to disrespect his responsibilities in return. Thus the bases did not exist under Diefenbaker for the dispersal of individual responsibility which prevailed under St. Laurent.

The new collegial emphasis recognized some of the real needs of this or any government, but it failed to recognize others and was not implemented successfully. Cabinet solidarity around collective decisions was re-emphasized. Indeed, Harkness resigned on this principle. But the emphasis was taken to almost self-defeating ends when Diefenbaker was so offended by leaks that he ended the circulation of Cabinet conclusions—a symbolic denial of the importance for collective decision taking of internal openness.

The Diefenbaker collegial emphasis reflected a view that collective decision taking meant not merely the reaching of decisions all could accept, but the reaching of decisions all had taken together, at least by actively signifying a consensus and preferably by actually participating in the formulation of the decision.[31]

As we noted earlier in the chapter, Diefenbaker was not an "organization man." He was a small-town prairie lawyer who had defended society's outcasts in court. He was a politician used to years of opposition politics. Structure did not interest him greatly. He was concerned enough about a perceived "Liberal dominated" public service to "consider" wholesale changes at the deputy minister level but did not act on this concern. He appointed businessman J. Grant Glassco to head a Royal Commission on Government Organization, but its results were left to the Pearson government to deal with.

Concluding Observations

This and the previous chapter must be viewed together. Prime ministers are different. They do have more power than their colleagues. They do have different policy preferences, career experiences and definitions of Canada's future as they see it. They possess the normal range of human strengths and weaknesses. They reflect different attitudes to knowledge and analysis—from the intellectual and cerebral Trudeau to the gut political instincts of Diefenbaker. At the same time they are propelled by ideas and conditions not wholly within their power to change. Like their ministers, they are pulled by the idea of Cabinet government in two directions at once, the need for collective legitimacy and coordination and the need to delegate and allow for the individual decisiveness of other persons, some of whom are often as ambitious and skilled, as well as flawed, as they are.

NOTES

1. For other general reviews see W. Matheson, *The Prime Minister and the Cabinet* (Toronto: Methuen, 1976), Chapters 6, 7 and 8; T. Hockin, ed., *Apex of Power,* Second Edition (Toronto: Prentice-Hall, 1977), Chapter 21, 23 and 24; and Andrew Johnson, "The Structure of the Canadian Cabinet." Unpublished Doctoral Thesis, University of Oxford, England, 1980.
2. See Peter C. Newman, *The Distemper of Our Times* (Toronto: McClelland and Stewart, 1968), Chapter 2. See also Denis Smith, *Gentle Patriot: A Political Biography of Walter Gordon* (Edmonton: Hurtig, 1973), Chapters 7, 8 and 9; and Lester B. Pearson, *Mike* (Toronto: Signet, 1976), Chapter 4.
3. See George Radwanski, *Trudeau* (Toronto: Macmillan of Canada, 1978), Chapters 3 and 8; and Doern and Aucoin, *The Structures of Policy Making in Canada* (Toronto: Macmillan of Canada, 1972) Chapter 2.
4. See Radwanski, *op. cit.* and Richard Gwyn, *The Northern Magus* (Markham, Ontario: Paperjacks Ltd., 1980), and Pierre Elliott Trudeau, *Federalism and the French Canadians* (Toronto: Macmillan of Canada, 1968).

5. See Jeffrey Simpson, *Discipline of Power* (Toronto: Personal Library, 1981) and David Humphreys, *Joe Clark: A Portrait* (Ottawa: Deneau and Greenberg, 1978).

6. Simpson, *op. cit.,* Chapter 3.

7. On Diefenbaker, see Peter C. Newman, *Renegade in Power* (Toronto: McClelland and Stewart, 1963); John G. Diefenbaker, *One Canada* (Toronto: Macmillan of Canada, 1975); and George Grant, *Lament for a Nation* (Toronto: McClelland and Stewart, 1965).

8. Peter C. Newman, *Distemper of Our Times,* Chapters 3, 4 and 5; and Lester B. Pearson, *op. cit.,* Chapters 4 and 8.

9. Johnson, *op. cit.,* Chapter 2 and J.W. Pickersgill, *The Mackenzie King Record,* Vol. I, 1939-1944 (Toronto: University of Toronto Press, 1960), pp. 6-8.

10. On the excesses of reorganization, see Doern and Aucoin, *Public Policy in Canada* (Toronto: Macmillan of Canada, 1979), Chapters 3, 8 and 11.

11. Quoted in *Mike,* Vol. III. The Memoirs of the Rt. Hon. Lester B. Pearson, 1957-68 (University of Toronto Press, 1975), p. 186. Reprinted with permission.

12. Pearson, *op. cit.,* Chapter 8.

13. Johnson, *op. cit.,* Chapter 4; and Matheson, *op. cit.,* Chapter 8.

14. The 1979 Lambert Royal Commission focused on this point but treated it in a very narrow and unsatisfactory way since it applied only managerial criteria to it and not political criteria. See Royal Commission on Financial Management and Accountability, *Final Report* (Ottawa: Minister of Supply and Services, 1979), Chapter 10.

15. See W.T. Stanbury, "Consumer and Corporate Affairs: Portrait of a Regulatory Department" in G. Bruce Doern, ed., *How Ottawa Spends Your Tax Dollars 1982* (Toronto: James Lorimer, 1982), Chapter 8.

16. Trudeau, *op. cit.*

17. See Robert Sheppard and Michael Valpy, *The National Deal* (Toronto: 1982) and Peter H. Russell, "The Effect of a Charter of Rights on the Policy Making Role of Canadian Courts," *Canadian Public Administration,* Vol. 25, No. 1 (Spring, 1982), pp. 1-33.

18. Quoted in Radwansky, *op. cit.,* pp. 136-137.

19. See Radwansky, *op. cit.,* Chapter 7; and G. Bruce Doern, ed., "Liberal Priorities 1982: the Limits of Scheming Virtuously," in G. Bruce Doern, ed., *How Ottawa Spends Your Tax Dollars 1982* (Toronto: James Lorimer, 1982), Chapter 1.

20. Radwansky, *op. cit.,* pp. 121-122. Reproduced by permission.

21. *Ibid.,* pp. 141-143.

22. Simpson, *op. cit.,* Chapter 2. See also George Perlin, *The Tory Syndrome* (Montreal: McGill-Queen's University Press, 1980).

23. Interviews. See also Simpson, *op. cit.,* Chapters 5 and 8.

24. See G. Bruce Doern and Glen Toner, NEP *and the Politics of Energy* (Toronto: Methuen, 1984). Chapter 3.

25. See Peter C. Newman, *Distemper of Our Times;* and Robert Bothwell, Ian

Drummond, John English, *Canada Since 1945* (Toronto: University of Toronto Press, 1981), Chapters 26, 27 and 28.

26. See Denis Smith, *op. cit.,* Chapters 8 and 9.

27. Matheson, *op. cit.,* p. 167.

28. See Peter C. Newman, *Renegade in Power,* Chapters 4 and 5; and Bothwell et al., *op. cit.,* Chapters 21 to 25.

29. See Peyton V. Lyon, *Canada in World Affairs 1961-1963* (Toronto: Oxford University Press, 1968).

30. See John N. McDougall, *Fuels and the National Policy* (Toronto: Butterworths, 1982), Chapters 5 and 6.

31. Johnson, *op. cit.,* pp. 371-376.

CHAPTER 9

DEPARTMENTS, AGENCIES, BUREAUCRATS AND ADVISORS

There can be no doubt that the central agencies of government have grown in visible ways. A large layer of bureaucracy and officialdom has been inserted between the line departments, their ministers and deputy ministers, and the nominal fount of decision making, the Cabinet and prime minister. The political distance between outside interests and access to the political centre must therefore seem to many outside interest groups to be all the greater, as these groups contemplate and attempt to traverse the governmental maze. The central agencies, however, are by no means all there is to the bureaucratic elements of the policy process.

This chapter focuses on an even larger bureaucratic dimension, the role of the line departments and agencies and the role of deputy ministers and other senior advisors in policy formulation. Once again we must inevitably deal with ideas that are separately justifiable but that in combination and in reality often conflict. One central idea is that ministers should make policy and that bureaucrats implement it. But this must be done in the face of the idea of individual ministerial and collective Cabinet responsibility and in light of the idea that bureaucrats have a duty to obey current laws and tender the best advice they can.

Another point to stress is that the number of line departments and independent agencies has also grown as new departments, regulatory and advisory agencies, and Crown enterprises have been created. The policy process is obviously influenced by the sheer proliferation of these units of government, as well as by their individual legal and practical roles and interrelationships. These departments and agencies exercise influence in the policy process in different permutations and combinations depending upon the policy field in question, be it agricultural policy, harbours, energy, education or foreign aid. To understand the policy process and how it is organized, we first need to understand something more about the aggregate features of line departments and agencies.

These features will not tell us precisely who has power over whom in specific policy fields and circumstances, but they will alert us to how organizational structures and processes interact with and embody ideas, and thus help explain why some policies may proceed while others are stalemated or watered down. In one sense we are entering the terrain encompassed by Allison's Model II, except that we are examining interorganizational relations in a total governmental sense rather than, as Allison did, in the context of a specific case study.

Horizontal Versus Vertical Departments

It is essential to remember that government departments can be viewed in different ways. One important perspective is a historical one. For example, J.E. Hodgetts has shown how Ottawa's departmental structure has evolved over the last century in relation to the imperatives of governing Canada and in relation to the changing view of the functions of the state. Thus, government organization initially reflected the imperatives of territorial defence and physical security, communications, transportation, natural resources and human resources, the latter evolving later into a broader notion of the welfare state.[1]

Another way, and the one on which we focus in this section of the chapter, is to identify the vertical versus horizontal roles of the 30 or more federal departments that exist in the 1980s and that are headed by Cabinet ministers. One instinctively thinks of government in terms of a hierarchy. The prime minister and Cabinet are poised on top and the line departments reside below, their functions extending out vertically to serve particular constituencies, regions and groups with suitable policies, goods and services. Observers point with some fondness to the 1940s and 1950s when powerful line ministers such as C.D. Howe and Jimmy Gardiner and their deputies held sway. Central agencies were "lean and thin" and there was a clear track to the full Cabinet to gain approval for proposals. The problems of horizontal coordination were taken care of by the small personal network of highly educated super-generalist mandarins and their political bosses.[2]

The evolution of departmental mandates and central agencies since the mid-1960s has produced a system where such a simple hierarchical organization chart creates a decidedly distorted view of reality. The federal government might be better portrayed as a matrix, in which almost half of the departments exist to coordinate the other half.[3] In short, there has been a significant increase in the number of departments and ministries whose mandates extend horizontally across the government to coordinate some particular cross-cutting normative idea or purpose. Each of these ideas or purposes, individually and separately, are quite desirable. The key question which arises is what effect the horizontal-vertical maze has on the total prospect of governing in a coordinated and democratic way.

The most recognizable departments are the traditional central agencies already identified in Chapter 7. Thus, the prime minister, the President of the Privy Council, the Minister of Finance, the President of the Treasury Board, the Minister of Justice and the Secretary of State for External Affairs all deal with broad horizontal responsibilities and values. With the exception of the Finance department these portfolios do not directly possess large operating budgets. They have inherently high policy influence because of the formal authority they possess and because they afford their occupants the highest number of strategic opportunities to intervene in almost any policy issue if the occupant wishes. They deal with the traditionally most basic horizontal or cross-cutting dimensions of government policy, namely, overall political leadership and strategy, foreign policy and the foreign implications of domestic policy fields, aggregate economic and fiscal policy, the basic legal and judicial concepts and values of society, and the overall management of government spending programs and personnel.

To these traditional horizontal coordinative portfolios have been added in the 1970s and 1980s a series of newer hybrid horizontal ministries. The first two were the Ministry of State for Science and Technology (MOSST) and the Ministry of State for Urban Affairs (MSUA, now abolished) whose mandates nominally cut across all other departments.[4] Science and Technology was a horizontal dimension to the extent that it is, more or less, an input in all policy fields. Urban Affairs sought to define a policy field in terms of a spatial concept—the city— and dealt on a cross-governmental basis as well. The influence of these portfolios was supposed to be based almost totally on knowledge and research. They were to "persuade" other departments by the quality of their advice on these subjects. Reliance on this base of influence has proved to be insufficient since knowledge is *not* power.

Other hybrid ministries have been created as well, albeit none with the innocent "knowledge is power" basis for their existence that MOSST and MSUA had. Thus, ministers of state for federal provincial relations and for small business were created. The experiment with coordinative policy ministries reached a new and more significant plateau with the establishment of the ministers of state for economic development and social development to support Cabinet committees of the same name. These are discussed in detail in Chapters 11 and 12.

There is a third type of department with a horizontal mandate, which might at first glance escape our attention but should not. These administrative coordinative departments include National Revenue, Public Works and Supply and Services. The Public Service Commission would ordinarily be mentioned here as well, except that it is not headed by a minister.[5] It has an overall role to preserve, on Parliament's behalf, the merit principle in government recruitment, hiring and promotions. The above-mentioned portfolios are usually perceived to be among the least influential of Cabinet positions. They are more likely to be perceived as administrative "nuts and bolts" departments needed to keep government operating. In recent years their functions have been viewed more and more by some as "common service" agencies. This implies a nonpolicy function, although frequently the occupant of these portfolios will quite appropriately refuse to accept such a designation. The portfolios deal with budgets that are quite modest, but the mere fact that they deal with the means of government, for instance, buildings, real estate, supplies, tax and revenue collection, implies a latent and sometimes manifest coordinative role, especially when it is suggested that the government use its procurement powers as a lever in industrial and regional policies. These activities are also closely related to traditional but nonetheless important ideas such as probity, fairness and honesty in government in the acquisition of such goods, services and resources.[6]

We have already accumulated almost fifteen ministers whose departmental mandates are broadly horizontal in nature. This leaves some fifteen to twenty vertical constituency departments (for example, agriculture, fisheries, environment, corrections, regional and industrial development). Alas, even some of these (for example, environmental and regional) have aspired to play horizontal coordinative roles as well.[7] Generally speaking, however, this group includes the portfolios that normally have the largest budgets and represent the "vertical" dimension of government in that they tend to extend outward to deliver programs to their respective constituencies, including many of the interest groups discussed in Chapter 3. In recent years this cluster has come to include a second type of smaller ministry of state, namely those created to assist other ministers, with program and/or policy responsibilities. These include Fitness and Amateur Sport, Mines, and Multiculturalism. Within this cluster are the group of portfolios which, generally speaking, are second in order of general influence, ranking behind the traditional horizontal coordinative portfolios identified earlier. The largest part of the budgets of these portfolios represent existing on-going programs, but within these programs there are often large but varying amounts of discretionary spending. The occupants of these portfolios therefore possess a fairly strong constant base of influence. This base can be augmented or reduced when the policy field in their portfolio becomes the object of political review, criticism or controversy. Occupants of these portfolios likely have mathematically fewer opportunities to intervene in another policy field or portfolio, at least in comparison with the traditional and perhaps even with the new horizontal coordinating portfolios. Ministers obviously possess some opportunities to intervene because of their Cabinet committee memberships, but even under the envelope system these occasions are still less frequent, generally speaking, than the traditional coordinative portfolios.

Coordination and Dominant Ideas

The classification of portfolios presented above captures in a stark way the genuine problems of coordination among line departments. To state that half the portfolios exist to coordinate the other half is to suggest that the system may well only produce a form of acute policy and organizational constipation. The ministry structure, it could be argued, is mesmerized by the relationship of everything to everything else. There are too many coordinators and not enough "doers."[8]

Here again we also have evidence, this time in organizational form, of the absence of a tidy "means-ends" chain in political life. Each horizontal *and* vertical mandate is purposeful and can be defended separately. Cumulatively, however, the purposeful mandates may intersect to produce an unmanageable state.

It is possible that policy and departmental organization has evolved in recent decades so as to replace one weakness of government with another. We have moved from the heyday of the line ministerial czar when the vertical dimensions were dominant to the heyday of the grand coordinators. Remember that Cabinet government, by definition, always pulls ministers in both a horizontal and vertical direction. The trick is to devise some reasonable balance and to know when one has achieved it. This daunting task is clearly an art and not a science.

Another feature which emerges out of a serious look at Cabinet portfolios is the degree to which departments are the custodians of dominant ideas. The reader will recall that in Chapter 2 when we discussed the dominant ideas of Canadian political life we suggested that one could, in the abstract, envisage a simple political system in which there would be separate departments of efficiency, equity, redistribution, income stability, national unity and regional sensitivity. In effect the classification of departments analysed in this chapter carries this notion forward, albeit in a much more complex way. Obviously, departments are the custodians of certain policy ideas. These include not only the dominant ideas listed above but numerous other ideas as well, such as honesty and probity in financial transactions, environmental well-being, and law and order.

While there are certain insights to be gained from the identification of ideas with organizational units, in either the simple or complex version, there are obviously dangers in using these typologies. First, there is a sense in which the typologies imply that all the dominant ideas and public policy fields are reflected in an even-handed "pluralistic" way, or that government departments are a fully accurate microcosm of Canadian society. We have already suggested in previous chapters that the concern for redistribution is not well or persistently "represented" in the organization of government. This is true when expressed at the level of the dominant ideas examined in Chapter 2. It is also reflected in more particular terms when one looks at individual departmental mandates. For example, there are many more departments whose overt mandate is to look after particular industries and producer groups (DREE, EMR, Fisheries, Agriculture) than to look after labour. Indeed, even the Department of Labour does not generally regard itself as a pro-labour agency.[9] It tends to see itself as a defender of a system of labour-management *relations*, and hence as a neutral referee overseeing the collective bargaining process. Thus, it is clear that there is a structure of power within the Cabinet and its organizational units that goes beyond the simple pecking order of vertical and horizontal Cabinet portfolios described above.

The typology of portfolios should not be used to reach the conclusion that no coordination exists or that the horizontal-vertical maze is a portrait of perpetual stalemate. Policies *are* enunciated. Resources *are* allocated which favour some groups, classes and regions over others. In short, some coordination occurs because *power* is exercised by some ministers, officials, organizations and interests over others. In a host of other situations a more episodic but incrementally stable form of coordination occurs through numerous bargains, accommodations and compromises where ministers, officials and interests satisfy themselves with small victories, while they prepare to struggle through the next round of adjustments.

Policy Field Departments and Portfolios:
The Paradoxes of Delegation and Initiation

The policy process is profoundly influenced by a simple human organizational need—the need to delegate and to specialize—in short, to chop policy into chewable organizational and analytical chunks. This need is aided by a political desire to disperse political power or to avoid an excessive concentration of power. We have already spoken of two ways in which this delegation is reflected at the macro governmental level. The first way is through the delegation of tasks to ministers grouped in Cabinet committees and in the mandates assigned to the departments which they head. The second way is the delegation of tasks to a host of quasi-independent agencies, boards, commissions, and Crown corporations. Thus, at the macro level, a prime minister must not only manage his ministers but also the huge amalgam of quasi-independent units. The same problem exists for the individual minister at the micro departmental and portfolio level, where the minister's domain may consist not only of his own department, but of a stable of other agencies as well. An appreciation of policy formulation requires an understanding of the constraint this places on both ministers and on those interests that are advocating change or otherwise seeking to influence policy outcomes.[10]

The most important constraint is that ministers may not be in a legal position to order the quasi-autonomous agency to change policy or to do some specific act without gaining further Parliamentary authority. Regulatory agencies and Crown corporations have defined legal spheres of competence. Though the minister may try to persuade such a board or agency to behave according to his or the government's wishes, it is not always legally or politically easy to take back what has been delegated. All public policy proposals must traverse a minefield of existing statutes. The rule of law implies that governments must obey present laws even while they may be trying to change them.

There is also a profoundly human element which reinforces the legal spheres of influence, namely the morale and esprit de corps of the quasi-independent unit. They have been given tasks to do and possess the expertise to do them. There is an inevitable price to be paid when ministers too frequently take back the authority delegated to these bodies. It is to be remembered, of course, that ministers in their relations with such agencies are pulled in two directions at once. They are likely to be blamed by the opposition parties and the media for decisions that go awry regardless of whether the regulatory board or the Crown corporation made them or not. They are expected to "manage" their portfolio, not just their department. They are potentially damned if they do and damned if they do not.

Obviously, the situation in this regard can vary greatly among ministers. For example, the Minister of Transport and the Minister of Energy Mines and Resources have a large stable of units within their ministerial bailiwick.[11] The former includes not only the Department of Transport, but bodies such as the Canadian Transport Commission (CTC), the Canadian National Railway (CNR), Via Rail and the St. Lawrence Seaway Authority. The latter's domain encompasses the National Energy Board, the Atomic Energy Control Board, Petro-Canada and Atomic Energy of Canada Ltd. Other ministers such as Consumer and Corporate Affairs or Supply and Services have less complicated organizational entities to manage.

Despite these organizational and policy complexities, the main ministerial departments have an important initiating role in the policy process. Aided by their own policy and planning branches, by their own reviews of the adequacy of existing programs, by the pressure of "their" constituency interest groups, and by normal bureaucratic self-interest, the line departments press for new or changed policy and for more resources. They also press for the status quo and against some of the proposals that emanate from other departments. It should not be assumed, however, that line departments are an automatic or easy conduit for the needs and "wants" of the interest groups most interested in their activities. As we stressed in Chapter 3, much time is spent by ministers and deputy ministers listening to such groups, to keep relations in good repair, to obtain information and intelligence and to find out what they oppose and will not tolerate. But these demands and concerns must clearly be juxtaposed by the department against the horizontal pressures emanating from other parts of the government and from other interests and jurisdictions, including the provinces and other countries.

There is no satisfactory way to generalize about the balance or the lack thereof between the "bottom-up" versus "top-down" sources of policy initiation, since these are governed by both perception and by evidence. The emergence of central agency bureaucrats in large numbers suggests that the days of line department hegemony are over. Innovations such as the Child Tax Credit are said to have been spawned by the central agencies and not by the Department of National Health and Welfare. The influence of the Department of Consumer and Corporate Affairs is shown to have declined, at least in terms of legislation passed. On the other hand, the Department of Agriculture has successfully seen to fruition several initiatives that resulted in new marketing boards to protect particular commodity producers. The National Energy Program was a departmental initiative of EMR, but one which coincided with a receptive political climate among influential Liberal ministers in 1980.[12]

As always, this kind of evidence is mixed, both as to the period being considered (1950s and 1960s versus the 1980s) and in relation to different policy fields. It is nonetheless safe to say that departments, their ministers and senior officials are important players in the policy process, sometimes confidently in charge while in other cases, like their central agency compatriots, uncomfortably in the middle.

The Senior Bureaucracy:
The Policy-Administration Dichotomy

The role of the senior bureaucracy (deputy ministers, heads of boards and Crown corporations, and central agency advisors) in the policy process has never been more controversial nor more difficult to sort out. An understanding of bureaucratic influence is made difficult by the need to differentiate the reality of the roles from perceptions not only of senior public servants per se but of big bureaucracy in general.

The starting point for dealing with the bureaucrats' role is the idea of the policy-administration dichotomy. This concept must be examined both as an idea and as a description of reality. As an idea, indeed as a constitutional principle, the implications of the policy-administration dichotomy are clear: elected ministers should make policy and public servants should implement it loyally, efficiently and effectively. It evokes a sharp distinction between ends and means. While there is much evidence to suggest that senior bureaucrats do more than just implement, there can be little doubt, as Vince Wilson has forcefully reminded us, that the belief in the policy-administration idea is an essential and powerful normative standard against which we judge the democratic policy process.[13]

Many governments at the federal and provincial levels have been concerned about how best to ensure that the policy-administration dichotomy is not only preached but practised. Both the Diefenbaker and Clark Conservative governments were exercised by this question when they assumed power after many years of Liberal dominance.[14] In general, however, they did not act forthrightly on their concerns, preferring instead to rely on the entrenched officials. The early Trudeau governments were also concerned. At the provincial level the emergence of NDP governments in Saskatchewan, Manitoba and British Columbia and their alteration in power with Conservative and Social Credit regimes has raised concerns about the loyalty of the civil service. The Conservative government of Premier Devine carried out an extensive removal of senior officials in Saskatchewan believed to be sympathetic to the NDP.

The above concerns reflect the policy-administration debate at a general macro governmental level. But the heart of the practical concern resides also in the day-to-day relations between a minister and his deputy minister. Ministers must ultimately allocate their time, energy and preferences among several aspects of their role. These include such aspects as their role

- in general policy development,
- in defending themselves and the government in the House of Commons, especially in Question Period,
- in cultivating media relations,
- as a special regional minister,
- in developing relationships with the caucus and the party,
- as M.P. for his or her own constituency,
- in Cabinet and in several Cabinet committees, and

- as titular manager of his department where sometimes little things can get him into as much trouble as matters of "high policy."

The specific allocation of time and energy vary greatly according to the personality and abilities of the minister, his policy interests, electoral status (a safe or unsafe seat) and the type and size of the department he heads. He or she is assisted by a personal political staff who are concerned not only about how well he does in real terms, but also about his image and future political prospects. Some ministers are more interested in their next Cabinet portfolio than in their current one.

Into this world of ministerial politics enters the deputy minister (and, to a significant extent, other senior bureaucratic and political advisors, especially in the central agencies). The deputy is usually someone the minister did not have a hand in choosing, but he or she must nonetheless become an alter ego to the minister. The deputy is responsible for the general management of the department, but must also serve as policy advisor, sensitive to, and fully cognizant of, the political constraints and concerns of the minister. The deputy has a constitutional duty to warn and to advise the minister. There are also obligations to serve the rest of the government in a collective sense, just as the minister must. The mirror committees of deputies place other burdens on deputies, not only in terms of meetings, but also in briefing their minister on proposals and decisions of *other* departments being considered by Cabinet or its committees.

Several other important points about modern ministerial-deputy ministerial relations should be emphasized. First, it has become increasingly difficult to speak to an integrated Cabinet with full governing responsibility. While most departments, agencies and Crown corporations nominally report to or through ministers, there are different kinds of reporting relationships and hence different degrees to which ministers feel themselves to be responsible and deputies consider themselves to be accountable.

Second, because many ministers often prefer to allocate their time to their policy and political party duties and many have a distaste for administrative and managerial matters, administrative matters are increasingly the concern of deputy ministers. The evolving relationship between ministers and their deputies is often less of a superior to a subordinate, but much more a matter of mutual dependence.

A third point raised in recent years concerns the consequences of the turnover of both ministers and deputy ministers. The general argument in the late 1960s was that a higher turnover rate and shuffling of deputy ministers would enhance control of the senior public service by the Cabinet because deputies would be less entrenched. However, any potential benefits were largely obviated as Prime Minister Trudeau at the same time shuffled Cabinet ministers with increasing frequency. Many senior public servants argue that this "musical chairs" approach had a negative impact on management and, moreover, had caused both ministers and deputy ministers to adopt a "low profile-low risk" approach to their responsibilities to ensure their own survival. These patterns were exacerbated by numerous reorganizations of existing portfolios and the creation of others, each making it more difficult to pinpoint accountability and easier to evade responsibility.

Finally, it is essential to point out that deputy ministers must in some respects cater to at least three masters: their minister, the prime minister by whom they are appointed (on the advice of the Secretary to the Cabinet), and the Treasury Board and Cabinet committees which exercise general managerial and expenditure authority. They must also pay heed to the activities of agents of Parliament such as the Federal Human Rights Commission, the Official Languages Commissioner and the Auditor General.

Deputy ministers thus face extraordinary and sometimes conflicting pressures.[15] In addition to their normal roles as policy advisors and general managers, they have been deluged in the last decade with a seemingly endless stream of reforms and directives, each of which separately may have been desirable, but which cumulatively have often distracted them from their primary departmental responsibilities. These reforms include the introduction of collective bargaining and new budgetary systems.

Deputy ministers properly point out that as long as they are subject to conflicting and/or vague instructions from ministers, the Cabinet, the central agencies, the special agencies of Parliament, and the many statutes they must administer, there can be no simple concept of accountability.

Views about the influence of bureaucrats on public policy are also affected by the broader and increasingly unfavourable perceptions of bureaucracy in general and of the public service in general. A study of the image of the public service in Canada concluded that over the decade of the 1970s the perception of Canadians regarding the fairness and promptness of government has improved, although the public service is still viewed as less able than the private sector to carry out its responsibilities.[16] It also concluded that increased contact with specific parts of the public service, even when favourable, does not spill over into a favourable overall view of the public service. A public opinion poll conducted in the midst of the deep 1982 recession concluded that there was a desire to see some measure of punishment of the civil service, and public service unions, because they are not giving the public what Canadians consider to be value for their money.[17] The June 28, 1982 Budget that imposed wage controls on federal public servants and virtually eliminated collective bargaining for two years reflected political action taken partly on the basis of the perceived popularity of this view.

It must be remembered that in the 1960s and 1970s the bureaucracy itself increasingly became the *object* of public policy. This was true not only with regard to wage controls (1975 to 1977 and 1982) and macro fiscal policy, but also in the introduction of collective bargaining, language policy, human rights legislation, freedom of information laws, "value for money" auditing, and the decentralization and relocation of government agencies. Problems and controversies regarding these policies in the face of growing economic malaise have helped alter the once more favourable or at least more neutral perception of the public service.

It should also be emphasized that the growth of public service unions and militancy has been a significant force in the last decade. Unions such as the postal workers and the Canadian Union of Public Employees (particularly in provincial and local government levels) became the most radical part of the general labour movement in Canada and assumed an even larger proportion of the membership of the Canadian Labour Congress.[18] Quebec's public service unions became very powerful with close alliances to the state, especially under the Parti Quebecois. Many of these unions associated themselves closely with the fate of certain public policy fields—especially social programs in education, pensions and health, and in the transportation services. Thus, despite prohibitions against the right to bargain about matters of public policy, the collective bargaining process inevitably embraced public policy concerns in these fields.

Senior Bureaucrats and Advisors As Policy Initiators, "Massagers" and Obstacles

Perhaps the nub of the concern about the role of senior public servants and senior advisors in policy formulation centres on their role in initiating policy ideas and proposals, analyzing and "massaging" policy proposals and in blocking or frustrating the plans or ideas of elected ministers or political parties. As was the case above, when we examined the role of central agencies, the evidence is both mixed and hard to come by. Moreover, it is assessed against sometimes contradictory standards regarding how the senior bureaucrat *should* behave. Let us explore several kinds of evidence, some general and some specific.

It is evident that bureaucrats have a considerable capacity to initiate policy. In part the political system expects them and encourages them to do so when it berates them on those occasions when they have failed to plan, to adequately estimate costs and effects, and when legislators leave wide discretionary powers in their hands or assign such powers to separate boards and agencies.

The reality of decision making in a complex Cabinet-bureaucratic structure is that policies are not always clear, frequently conflict with each other, and must be constantly reinterpreted as they are applied to single cases or projects. It is not always clear whether the dominant policy is found only in the statute(s) that govern a program or department, the Cabinet's latest directive, a minister's speech made over the weekend or a combination of all of these. Analysts and advisors at and below the deputy minister level are constantly meeting in departmental, interdepartmental and federal-provincial settings to determine what ministers want or what "my" minister's preference is. As Cabinet documents and memoranda are drafted, advisors attempt to add the right nuance of meaning to particular features of a proposal. Data and estimates may be challenged or questioned. Interdepartmental concerns are raised. Questions of timing and cost are identified. All of this is done with advisors engaged in constant discussions "up the line" to the minister through his deputy minister and across departmental lines through other ministers, departmental officials, political aids and central agency officials. Frequently, there is also contact with outside interests and with provincial governments. Though senior advisors may see the end product of this iterative process as a polished Cabinet document, the reality is a mixture of a verbal and written exchange of views. The volume of written documentation, however, is beyond the human bounds of any minister or deputy to fully digest, and thus a premium is increasingly placed on verbal advice.

The degree and extent of this analysis and massaging varies greatly of course, but the paradoxes of the process must be appreciated when judging the bureaucrats' overall policy role, both normatively and descriptively. A specific example may help illustrate the problem of why policies interact and are subject to reinterpretation, why bureaucrats are expected to have influence and why they frequently initiate the need for decisions. Under the National Energy Program (NEP) devised in 1980, the overall policy was reflected in the goals of energy security, fairness and Canadianization. Within the NEP, however, there were a myriad of other particular initiatives which involved other policy decisions, including nonenergy policy concerns. One of these was a commitment to create a new, renewable energy Crown Corporation, later called Canertech. The creation of a company was also a policy, but it was established partly as a symbolic gesture to the renewable energy field which was otherwise not a central focus of the NEP. Since there was ministerial pressure for the company to be located in Winnipeg, it was visualized as part of the then emerging Liberal strategy in Western Canada. Policy decisions at this level were taken by ministers. Later, when the company's plans were presented, bureaucrats in EMR and in the central agencies raised concerns and pressed them hard in response to other concurrent government policies, which were as much "policies" as was the NEP itself and the decision to create Canertech. Thus, there were industrial policy concerns about whether the company was to compete with private sector firms or other sources of venture capital, whether it should focus on solar technologies or on conservation technologies, whether its approach violated government policies on loan guarantees, and whether the regional distribution of its initial investments would be appropriate and sufficiently visible.

It would be easy for some group to interpret the latter reviews as excessive bureaucratic influence, perhaps even leading to fundamental changes in the nature of the company and the policy rationales behind it. But the rationales are not necessarily clear. Are they the same in 1980 as in 1982 when energy and overall budgetary dollars became much more scarce? Morever, what is the alternative to bureaucratic influence of this kind? Appointing more junior ministers to follow these issues more closely? Appointing advisors who are more politically trustworthy, in a partisan sense, below the deputy minister level? There are difficulties with all these ideas because in the final analysis one must confront a very large grey area in the policy process, where "bureaucrats" of some stripe must and will exercise policy influence as specific and, by no means, small decisions run the gauntlet of many, indeed dozens, of "policies" devised by the Cabinet and individual ministers, including those enshrined by a Parliamentary and statutory blessing.

Beyond individual examples one must appreciate the sheer volume of decisions which continuously test the policy maze. Decisions confront not only energy policy dictates but also other cross-cutting policy concerns such as policies for expenditure restraint, the "6 and 5" percent wage and price guidelines, the new job creation initiative, make or buy contracting provisions, policies to encourage the private sector, bilingualism policies and so on.

It should not be surprising, then, that virtually every minister privately and sometimes publicly displays his or her anecdotal saga about the great idea that was sabotaged by the senior bureaucracy or by the P.M.'s henchmen. In each of these it is difficult, if not impossible, to sort out why a given ministerial initiative or pet project may have been changed or stalemated. Was there a difference in values and priorities whereby a deputy was able, by a process of wearing down his minister, to impose a decision on him? Was the deputy, on the contrary, merely playing his proper constitutional role in warning the minister of the pitfalls of the proposal or the possible contradictions between it and the law? Was the proposal in reality shot down not by the minister's bureaucracy, but by other ministers whose concerns and priorities were different?

Flora MacDonald's brief account of her nine-month ministerial experience as Secretary of State for External Affairs shows the empirical wooliness of the bureaucratic influence question.[19] Her article describes the many ways in which bureaucrats furnish "entrapment devices" for ministers (for example, delayed recommendations, multiple deputy ministerial committees, bogus "options"). It describes the difficulties she had in establishing alternative advisory networks of academics and of her personal political staff. She is careful to say that the problem does not arise from the overt partisanship of senior public servants, but rather from the fact that public servants regard themselves to be above the partisan battle. She quotes approvingly other experienced politicians on this score, from Tony Benn to Henry Kissinger. But nowhere in her account is there a specific example of a policy blocked or an initiative frustrated. The impression one is left with is that there is a feeling that there is a problem. This should not be surprising, since both perception and reality have real effects on behaviour and on the views expressed on this kind of complex subject.

A particular manifestation of the larger issue of the relations between elected and appointed officials is the often fine line needed to distinguish partisan political advisors from senior bureaucrats who are also known personal confidants of the prime minister or other key ministers. No political system can avoid the presence of relationships of personal trust, loyalty and confidence. Those who enjoy such confidence are almost by definition influential and have frequent access to key ministers. Overall strategic approaches to policy are not forged by a simultaneous discovery of the approach by over 30 ministers. Leadership of a strategic kind is the catalyst, and senior partisan and bureaucratic advisors are positioned to be a part of that leadership.

We have already referred to concerns which arose in the Trudeau era about many of his key PMO, bureaucratic and party advisors. These have included at various times Marc Lalonde (who later became a powerful minister), Martin O'Connell, Jim Coutts, Tom Axworthy, Keith Davey, Michael Kirby and Michael Pitfield, as well as others such as Pierre Juneau, Joel Bell and Jack Austin (who, as a senator, also became a senior minister in the early 1980s). The first five had especially strong ties to the Liberal party per se and, with the exception of Connell, exercised great influence. Lalonde, as head of the PMO, shared many of Trudeau's overall views about the place of Quebec and French Canadians in Canadian federalism and was his intellectual equal. Coutts and Axworthy are both left-of-centre Western Liberals who revel in short-run political tactics and share an exuberant 1960s view of progressive Liberalism. They were influential in the several abortive attempts to construct an approach to win greater support for the Liberals in Western Canada and were ardent advocates of the aggressive National Energy Program. Keith Davey, while never a PMO official, has been, since the Pearson era, the key Liberal party electoral strategist. He has also exercised influence in specific areas such as in the design and selling of the 1982 "6 and 5" anti-inflation package.

The next five advisors mentioned above take us into a somewhat muddier mixture in that overt partisan associations are somewhat less in evidence and bureaucratic careers are partly entwined, thus raising, especially in the case of Michael Pitfield, the issue of politicizing, in a partisan sense, the senior public service. For example, Michael Kirby had been a key advisor to Nova Scotia Premier Gerald Reagan before Kirby joined the PMO. He later became Principal Secretary for Federal-Provincial Relations, nominally a public service position, but in this capacity was a key strategist in the constitutional negotiations of 1980 and 1981 and an architect of the overall Liberal strategy to battle the provinces on the issue of visibility, referred to as the "new nationalism" in our analysis in Chapter 10. He later headed a study of the fishing industry in the Maritime provinces, and after that became a vice president of CNR, partly to politically oversee the implementation of key elements of the Crows Nest reform package which was to facilitate expanded railway investments. Pierre Juneau was first a respected head of the Canadian Radio and Telecommunications Commission (CRTC) charged with implementing the Canadian content provisions of the then new broadcasting legislation. Later, he was Deputy Minister of Communications and still later President of the Canadian Broadcasting Corporation. Between these postings he was an unsuccessful Liberal candidate in Quebec and, for a time, Minister of Communications. There can be little doubt therefore that Juneau influenced Canadian cultural and broadcasting policy, enjoyed the confidence of the prime minister, and built a mixed public servant-partisan career.

Joel Bell occupied several strategic roles in the energy and industrial policy spheres. He helped author the Gray report on foreign investment in the early 1970s which led to the establishment of the Foreign Investment Review Agency (FIRA). He later became vice president of Petro-Canada, and hence was strategically placed to relate Ottawa's wishes to Petro-Canada, and vice versa. In 1982 he was appointed to head a new Canada Industrial Development Corporation to manage and perhaps divest the assets of several Crown corporations. Bell had perhaps the least overt party connections of the persons we are discussing, but partly because he was associated with interventionist initiatives, he also took on a Liberal tinge, especially in the eyes of Conservative opposition critics.

One can also cite the case of Senator Jack Austin. He had been a businessman and Deputy Minister of Energy, Mines and Resources. Later he became head of PMO and eventually a senator and then Minister of State for Social Development at a time when social programs were under attack in the midst of a depressed economy and at a time of enormous budgetary deficits.

Finally, there is Michael Pitfield, without doubt the official who most elicited concern about the public service-partisan dilemmas. Pitfield was a senior advisor who encouraged Trudeau to seek the prime minister's office, agreed with and helped shape Trudeau's view that government had to be more rational, and fostered the Trudeau era's fascination with systems and reorganization. He served as a Deputy Secretary in the PCO, Deputy Minister of Consumer and Corporate Affairs, and then at an unprecedentedly young age, Clerk of the Privy Council, Ottawa's pre-eminent public service position. Pitfield genuinely strived for an improved Cabinet system and was one of the few to operate as Trudeau's intellectual equal, but he was often rightly perceived as being excessively preoccupied with process. This does not mean that he did not influence the substance of policy as well. For example, Pitfield eventually became a strong advocate of the wage and price controls program launched in 1975. He also helped foster a group of Pitfield PCO graduates who have since gone on to become deputy ministers and assistant deputy ministers of various departments in Ottawa.

There is a certain inevitability to the existence in any prime ministerial regime of a small cadre of quasi-civil service, quasi-partisan, key advisors who exercise influence and upset the pure models of either a neutral public service marching to the beat of the policy-administration dichotomy, or ministers operating in spendid isolation without the occasional whiff of the Machiavellian interloper. In the Pearson era, for example, it is possible to argue that Tom Kent, Pearson's chief advisor in the PMO, exercised an even more profound influence than his Trudeau era successors ever dreamed of. Kent had been a major idea man at the Liberals' 1960 Kingston Conference which set the agenda for the major Pearson social welfare reforms of the mid-1960s. While his influence later waned, he also became Deputy Minister of Regional Economic Expansion and later head of the Cape Breton Development Corporation. The Pearson Cabinet also included several former senior public servants including Mitchell Sharp, Maurice Lamontagne and Pearson himself.

None of the above is intended to argue that there are no problems regarding the power of bureaucrats and key advisors. It is a perpetual and genuine democratic concern. Part of the problem at the federal level undoubtedly arises out of the sheer fact of Liberal party dominance. But beyond a certain point there are limits as to whether any permanent solutions exist, since each reform suggested to solve the problem has its disadvantages as well and a capacity to produce its own excesses. Americans complain as much about bureaucratic Washington despite the power of the American president to appoint officials well below the deputy minister or equivalent level.

To generalize about the respective kinds of influence that ministers, deputies and key senior advisors exercise, one needs to discuss evidence in a large number of particular policy fields, and one needs to characterize the relationships more precisely, taking into account the factors outlined above.[20] An article by Andrew F. Johnson conveys something of what is required. He reviews the development of unemployment insurance in the 1970s. He characterizes the role of Bryce Mackasey, the minister responsible for introducing a new scheme of unemployment insurance in 1971, as that of a major change agent, particularly in carrying out what Johnson calls the "surveillance" and "legitimation" functions necessary for major policy reforms. His successors, Robert Andras and Bud Cullen, began to routinize the program, and thus their legitimation and surveillance skills became increasingly unnecessary and inconspicuous. The role of bureaucratic experts was correspondingly minor in the first phase of reform and larger in the second phase. The overall relationship was essentially one of mutual dependence.

What is not adequately reflected in the Johnson analysis is the even more powerful influence of dominant ideas and the economic climate. In the prosperous climate of the early 1970s, unemployment insurance was viewed more as a social policy than as economic "insurance." Mackasey articulated that view. By the mid-1970s the view was emerging that resources were scarce and insurance principles would lead to a tightening of the unemployment insurance program. This was aided by strong support for the work ethic and the emergence of a growing *perception* that there were many cheaters and free loaders on the unemployment insurance rolls. Economic analysts argued, moreover, that generous benefits were a growing barrier to labour mobility.

There are other snipets of evidence in other policy fields that show the interdependence of minister and deputy, but that led to contradictory interpretations of the policy balance between them. Studies of wage and price controls, Indian policy, energy policy and science policy point to the same *empirical* and *normative* dilemmas outlined in the discussion above.[21] We see them again in our more detailed look at the broad evolution of foreign, social and economic policies in Chapter 14.

Conclusions

We have by no means identified all the dimensions of the role of the senior bureaucracy in policy formulation. For example, the deputy interacts with interest group leaders on a regular basis as well as with provincial bureaucrats. Several senior public servants have left the public service to head interest group secretariats or to form consulting firms engaged in both lobbying and policy analysis. We have more to say about bureaucratic roles in later chapters, but the point to be stressed is that the senior public servant's role, like that of other institutions, is rooted in a normative concept of government, the policy-administration dichotomy, around which swirl some contradictory patterns of behaviour and evidence. The analysis counsels us to be less glib than we sometimes are about the sins of commission and omission committed by or attributed to Canada's senior bureaucrats. Bureaucrats have undoubtedly scuttled some good policy initiatives. They have also undoubtedly saved Canadians from some hare-brained schemes as well.

The intent of this chapter and of the previous two as a whole has been to provide a broad analysis of what the executive is and what it does. The prime minister and the Cabinet, central agencies and line departments, ministers and senior bureaucrats and advisors must march to the sound of many drums. They find themselves having to meet many interlocking and sometimes contradictory organizational needs, principles and policy ideas, while at the same time attempting to steer the ship of state into an often foggy future.

NOTES

1. J.E. Hodgetts, *The Canadian Public Service* (Toronto: University of Toronto Press, 1973), Chapters 5 and 6. See also O.P. Dwividi, ed., *The Administrative State in Canada* (Toronto: University of Toronto Press, 1982); and V. Seymour Wilson, *Canadian Public Policy and Administration* (Toronto: McGraw-Hill Ryerson, 1981), Chapters 9, 10 and 11.

2. See J.L. Granatstein, *The Ottawa Men: The Civil Service Mandarins 1935-1957* (Toronto: Oxford University Press, 1982).

3. See G. Bruce Doern, "Horizontal and Vertical Portfolios in Government" in G. Bruce Doern and V.S. Wilson, *Issues in Canadian Public Policy* (Toronto: Macmillan of Canada, 1974), Chapter 12.

4. See Peter Aucoin and Richard French, *Knowledge, Power and Public Policy* (Ottawa: Science Council of Canada, 1974).

5. W.D.K. Kernaghan, ed., *Public Administration in Canada,* Fourth Edition (Toronto: Methuen, 1982), Chapter 5; and Hodgetts, *op. cit.,* Chapter 12.

6. See Douglas J. McCready, "The Department of Supply and Services: Efficiency Canada?" in G. Bruce Doern, ed., *How Ottawa Spends Your Tax Dollars 1982* (Toronto: James Lorimer Publishers, 1982), Chapter 9.

7. Doern, *op. cit.*

8. See H.L. Laframboise, "Here Come the Program-Benders," *Optimum,* Vol. 7, No. 1 (1976), pp. 40-48.

9. See Eugene Swimmer, "Labour Canada: A Department 'Of' Labour or 'For' Labour" in G. Bruce Doern, ed., *How Ottawa Spends Your Tax Dollars 1981* (Toronto: James Lorimer Publishers, 1981), Chapter 5.

10. See John Langford, *Transport in Transition* (Montreal: McGill-Queen's University Press, 1970); and Peter Aucoin, "Portfolio Structures and Policy Coordination" in G. Bruce Doern and Peter Aucoin, eds., *Public Policy in Canada* (Toronto: Macmillan of Canada, 1979), Chapter 8.

11. See Langford, *op. cit.* and G. Bruce Doern, "Energy, Mines and Resources and the National Energy Program," in G. Bruce Doern, ed., *How Ottawa Spends Your Tax Dollars 1981, op. cit.,* Chapter 2.

12. G. Bruce Doern and Glen Toner, *The NEP and the Politics of Energy* (Toronto: Methuen, 1984). Chapter 3.

13. See Wilson, *op. cit.,* Chapter 4; and K. Kernaghan, "Politics, policy and public servants: political neutrality revisited," *Canadian Public Administration,* Vol. 19, No. 3 (Fall, 1976), pp. 431-456.

14. On the Clark government's concerns, see Jeffrey Simpson, *Discipline of Power* (Toronto: Personal Library, 1981), Chapter 5.

15. On the role of the deputy minister, see Royal Commission on Financial Management and Accountability, *Final Report* (Ottawa: Minister of Supply and Services, 1979), Chapters 9 and 10; and A.W. Johnson, "The Role of the Deputy Minister," *Canadian Public Administration,* Vol. 4, No. 4 (December, 1961), pp. 363-369.

16. David Zussman, "The Image of the Public Service in Canada," *Canadian Public Administration,* Volume 25, No. 1 (Spring, 1982), pp. 63-80.
17. Reported in *The Globe and Mail,* July 15, 1982, p. 1.
18. See E. Swimmer and M. Thompson, eds., *Public Sector Industrial Relations in Canada* (Montreal: Institute for Research on Public Policy, 1983).
19. Flora MacDonald, "The Minister and the Mandarins," *Policy Options,* Vol. 1, No. 3 (September/October, 1980), pp. 29-31. See also Mitchell Sharp's critique of the MacDonald article in Paul W. Fox, ed., *Politics Canada,* Fifth Edition (Toronto: McGraw-Hill Ryerson, 1982), pp. 476-479.
20. Andrew F. Johnson, "A minister as an agent of policy change: the case of unemployment insurance in the seventies," *Canadian Public Administration,* Vol. 24, No. 4 (Winter, 1981), pp. 612-633.
21. See Allan Maslove and Eugene Swimmer, *Wage Controls in Canada* (Montreal: Institute for Research on Public Policy, 1980), Chapter 2; Sally Weaver, *Making Canadian Indian Policy* (Toronto: University of Toronto Press, 1981), Chapter 2 and 5; Doern and Toner, *op. cit.,* Chapter 3; and G. Bruce Doern, *Science and Politics in Canada* (Montreal: McGill-Queen's University Press, 1972), Chapter 6.

CHAPTER 10

PRIORITIES AND PRIORITY SETTING: IN HISTORICAL PERSPECTIVE AND IN THE TRUDEAU ERA

We have already reviewed a number of fundamental political factors that have made it difficult for governments to do first things first and to take a long-term concerted view of their priorities. These include the ebb and flow of dominant ideas and beliefs, the inexorable ticking of the electoral clock and the partisan political survival instincts it encourages, the constant demands from agencies, groups, classes and regions dissatisfied with the status quo or the current view of priorities, the limits of resources and knowledge, the partly media-induced need to be constantly seen doing something, the increasing incidence of large physical projects that trigger policy concerns in several policy fields concurrently, and the practical need to put old policy wine in new bottles.

Despite these difficulties, governments and political leaders must attempt to set priorities. These priorities, even when short term or medium term in nature, affect the fate of particular individual policy fields. It therefore follows that one cannot understand or explain the drift or evolution of a single policy field except in relation to the broader cluster of priorities present in any given time period. Some policy fields are persistently high on the priority list (for example, inflation, unemployment) while others bob up and down like pistons on an engine (for example, policies for research and development). Still others manage to squeeze their way on to the agenda but only to its outer fringes (for example, occupational health or policies for native peoples).

Federal and provincial Cabinets have several major occasions during the year when they attempt to inform Canadian citizens about priorities and about what they stand for. These include Speeches from the Throne, Budget Speeches, speeches on the tabling of expenditure estimates, and crisis speeches by the prime minister or premier. From time to time political party conventions and the electoral hustings provide additional vehicles for this essential act of political communication and policy making.

The purpose of this chapter is to critically review priorities and priority setting in greater detail. This is done by taking two portraits of priorities over two time periods. The first portrait is historical and encompasses Canada's history since 1867. The second view focuses on a shorter period, the Trudeau era from 1968 to the early 1980s and includes an analysis of the formal expression of priorities in Throne Speeches and Budget Speeches. This will help set the scene for our analysis in Chapter 11 of the formal annual priority setting and resource allocation process. The even more detailed subsidiary economic-social, and foreign-domestic policy processes and the priorities they reveal are examined in Chapters 11, 12 and 14.

An Historical Review of Priorities

Priorities always look clearer in the past than in the future. Hindsight has its much advertised advantages. The main reason for reviewing priorities in an historical perspective is that political systems have memories. Both policy successes and failures become a part of political institutions, partisan allegiances, regional identities, and the overall collective political and social composition of Canada. While certain decades may have been dominated by one or more overall priority concerns, they also communally produce an historical list of grievances and perceptions of grievances that affect the priorities of subsequent decades. Some of these unresolved grievances persist to the present day. These concerns were initially reflected in our review in Chapter 1 of the main characteristics of the Canadian political system and in Chapter 2 of the dominant ideas of Canadian political life. In this section we briefly review national priorities in six time periods, 1867 to 1914, 1914 to 1929, 1930 to 1945, 1945 to 1957, 1957 to 1970, and 1970 to the 1980s. Needless to say, these dates are somewhat arbitrary since history can rarely be chopped up quite this conveniently. For our limited purposes, however, the periods help us highlight major events and trends.

1867 to 1914: The National Policy

This period can be characterized as being dominated by Sir John A. Macdonald's National Policy.[1] The National Policy was, in fact, an array of policies intended to create an industrial base in Ontario and Quebec under a protective tariff, unite the country from sea to sea by building the

Canadian Pacific Railway, and settle the West to develop its resources and to supply the Eastern industrial heartland, and also to head off encroaching American interests anxious to exploit the Canadian frontier. The National Policy was national and regional policy rolled into one. It was an act of defiance against the "efficiency" of the north-south axis of North America. It embraced tariff policy, transportation policy and immigration policy. It was achieved through an English-French Canadian political alliance within the Conservative party that survived, initially at least, both financial scandal and the hanging of Louis Riel.

Though challenged by the Laurier government and a brief flirtation with free trade, the National Policy essentially survived intact. It helped create the modern Canadian industrial structure, centred in Ontario and Quebec, but truncated in shape in the sense of having to serve a small Canadian market with limited export potential for manufactured goods. It was also a resource-based policy dependent on the resources of the hinterland, both to serve the industrial heartland and to export abroad.

1914 to 1929: The Attack on the National Policy

Those Canadians who increasingly saw themselves regionally, and even in terms of economic classes, as the victims of the National Policy, made some political headway in the 1914 to 1929 period. The period can therefore be seen as a period of attack against the National Policy. Aided by the massive changes induced by World War I, including the Conscription crisis and the continuing rapid settlement of the West, the period produced major challenges to the previous national consensus.[2] Prairie populism rose in opposition to Eastern financial and industrial power. Provincial governments, thought initially to be minor appendages to a centralized federal government, began to exercise influence because of the need to build and finance the social, economic and educational infrastructure of an increasingly industrialized, urbanized and less agricultural and rural population. Hydro facilities, schools and highways had to be built, and minimum social insurance programs had to be created to assist those who were the casualties of the market. Increased labour militancy resulted as well from a struggle for basic recognition of labour's rights—rights which were, in the main, not achieved until World War II.

1930 to 1945: Depression and War

Depression and World War II traumatized this period of Canadian and global political life. It emblazoned on the consciousness of post-World

War II political leaders a desire to avoid future wars and depressions, but did not produce results in the specific period between 1930 to 1945. It was essentially war itself that ended the depression and put labour, capital and land back to productive use.[3] Though made infinitely worse by the depression, the period was nonetheless initially a continuation of the pattern of challenge to the National Policy by those who were not its beneficiaries. It produced yet another wave of prairie populism and eventually yielded the agrarian and labour alliance that later became the Cooperative Commonwealth Federation (CCF), the predecessor to the social democratic NDP party. In the midst of World War II, the political left enjoyed its greatest electoral success until that time, forming a government in Saskatchewan and the official opposition in Ontario.

Despite the growing protest against the status quo there was, in the 1930s, no equivalent level of national leadership or reformist social philosophy in Canada to that of Roosevelt's New Deal in the United States. Canada's national politics continued to be influenced by the inevitable delicacy of French-English relations, relations which soured badly in the midst of another conscription crisis in World War II.

World War II resurrected and greatly expanded Canada's industrial base, but left it centred in Ontario and Quebec. Canada's natural resources again became valuable to a Western alliance desperately in need of an expanded and secure resource supply base. Since the cooperation of labour would be essential to the war production effort, the period saw the first extensive national recognition of labour's right to bargain collectively and to strike.

1945 to 1957: Keynesianism and the Second National Policy

This period is often viewed to be one in which a Second National Policy was assembled to dominate federal priorities in the post-war decade. Such a policy was forged, it is often suggested, by the Keynesian doctrine, which created an acceptable economic and social rationale in a capitalist economy for increased intervention by the state.[4] Thus, governments had to construct both a permanent infrastructure of programs that would stabilize the economy in the post-war era, and also strategically alter aggregate taxing and spending activities to ensure that economic investment and consumer demand was maintained. While Keynesianism helped legitimize the idea of this kind of macro intervention, it was not the only normative basis for intervention in Canada. The post-World War II reconstruction program was also influenced by the strength of populist and left-wing political pressure, by the pre-war and wartime use of public enterprises, and by the general social welfare concepts articulated in the United Kingdom by the Beveridge Report and its Canadian equivalents.

It is probably fair to characterize this period in terms of the emergence of a Second National Policy, but it is an error to associate it fully with Keynesian economics. Keynesian fiscal policy has never been fully practised in Canada, and certainly not in this period. Moreover, other than the new array of social welfare programs launched in the post-World War II period (family allowances, expanded old age security programs, etc.), the core of Canada's economic policies during this period were not forged by a Keynesian Department of Finance but rather by a Department of Reconstruction, Defence Production, and later Trade and Commerce headed by C.D. Howe.[5] Howe's policies were essentially to use tariff and tax policies to encourage foreign equity investment in Canada. The result was to produce continued prosperity until the late 1950s but also to reinforce the age-old pattern of Canada's truncated industrial structure first put in place by Macdonald's National Policy.[6] But by the end of the 1950s it was dominated by foreign ownership.

The period was also characterized by Liberal party dominance and by the dominance of the federal government over the provincial governments.[7] The latter was reflected in the tight post-war tax agreements which centralized fiscal control in Ottawa. Liberal party dominance was assured by the renewed English-French accommodation, evident in the King-Lapointe, King-St. Laurent, and St. Laurent-Howe-Pearson leadership alliances within successive Liberal Cabinets, and by the Liberal's successful portrayal of the Tories as the anti-Quebec party.

1957 to 1970: The Heyday of Social Programs

We have already examined key features of this period in Chapter 8 when we surveyed the Diefenbaker and Pearson regimes. We will also examine in some detail the priorities of the latter part of this period, in the early Trudeau years, in the next section of this chapter. It is essential to highlight certain general attributes of this period as a whole. In general we characterize it as the heyday of social policy. This was first reflected in the regional definition of social policy and other grievances which led to the election of the Diefenbaker government. The quasi-populist basis of the Diefenbaker appeal was reflected in the spurt of reforms in 1957 and

1958, which included agricultural and rural development programs, hospitalization grants, and old age pension increases. It was evident in the loosening of the federal fiscal reigns through more generous tax agreements with, and equalization payments to, the provinces.[8]

The second round of change occurred in the mid-1960s when the Pearson government launched several major social policy initiatives, including the Canada Pension Plan, Medicare, further old age security increases, the Canada Assistance Plan, and federal assistance to higher education and manpower training.[9] Much of this was accompanied by buoyant expectations about a growing economy. The economy was buoyed by the expansionary consumer demand of the post-war baby boom, as well as extensive immigration in the 1950s and 1960s. The growing economy would produce increased revenues even without the need for massive tax increases, and hence the social programs were affordable, both those launched by Ottawa and still others launched by increasingly expansionary and aggressive provincial governments.

The early Trudeau years promised more of the same, albeit sold under the label of "the Just Society." Where the Pearson Liberals offered a quantum jump in social welfare, Trudeau offered a qualitative leap, promising a renewed effort to reduce regional disparities and to improve linguistic, cultural, environmental and individual rights.[10]

1970 to the 1980s: The Slow Rediscovery of Scarcity

The period from the early 1970s to the present is perhaps best characterized as one in which there was a grudging and belated rediscovery of scarcity. As declining economic growth and high inflation rates exerted their deadly double influence, politics, policy and the allocation of resources became increasingly a zero sum game. Gains for one group, region or class increasingly became a visible loss for another group, region or class. The OPEC oil crisis and the continuing pressure of the environmental movement initially taught Canadians more about scarcity in its even broader ecological dimensions. By the early 1980s social policy programs were under attack as beleagured debt-ridden governments sought to redeploy scarce tax dollars to shore up the industrial base of the economy or to reduce huge deficits.

We will have much more to say later about the specific priorities of the last two periods, especially in the Trudeau era, and thus we have treated them briefly here. In terms of the six periods, however, it is possible to see the dominant concerns of each era. Depending upon one's metaphorical preference, they show a different ebb and flow, or a different phase in the swing of the pendulum between different aspects of public policy, politics and ideas: in short, between creating economic wealth and redistributing it regionally and among income groups, between economic policy and social policy, between national policy and regional equity and sensitivity, between the centralization and decentralization of federalism, and between those who benefit from technological and other kinds of change and those who attempt to stabilize and protect their lives from the adverse effects of such changes.

Hindsight allows us to see priorities with greater clarity. But the priorities of the past have also been forged in vastly different political times. For example, the role of mass communication, especially television, is only a recent phenomenon. The early decades were not characterized by democratic mass suffrage and by democratic methods of choosing leaders. For these and other reasons, not the least of which is that it is part of Canada's more recent political memory, we need to have a second portrait of priorities, one in which all of the general modern conditions of democratic politics are present.

Priorities in the Trudeau Era: A More Detailed Look

The priorities of the several Trudeau governments should be ultimately viewed in the context of the broad historical priorities sketched above. But they are also noteworthy because they were devised by governments headed by a prime minister who, as we have seen in Chapter 8, had openly enunciated a philosophy whose intent was to make public policy processes more rational. When he first came to power, Trudeau was very critical of what he perceived to be the disorganized nature of the previous Pearson government. The Trudeau philosophy was not always internally coherent or logical, but it was quite clearly pronounced and even given considerable fanfare. That the philosophy and subsequent practice have not been the same is quite evident, a fact which happily lends credence to the view that politics has a rationality of its own and that it is consequently difficult to take the "politics" out of politics. Nonetheless, the Trudeau era in Canada, in concert with parallel developments in other countries, witnessed the most exhaustive and serious attempt to rationalize and manage policy processes.

We review the Trudeau priorities and the priority-setting process in a dual way. We survey them chronologically in each of his periods in office, but in each period we will also compare selected Throne Speeches and Budget Speeches, particularly to illustrate the continuous difficulty in meshing general priorities with economic priorities. Even though we have properly referred to the period since 1968 as the Trudeau era, we will also refer to the Clark government's priorities and priority-setting machinery.[11]

When comparing the general internal documents on priorities with Throne Speeches and Budget Speeches, it is essential to remember that we are not comparing totally analogous documents or policy occasions. They each deal with different time periods. The internal priorities exercise and the documents it produces is centred in the Priorities and Planning Committee of the Cabinet, chaired by the prime minister. It is intended to drive the *internal* decision and resource allocation process and operates annually. The Speech from the Throne is a *public* document intended to convey the government's overall legislative and policy plans to Parliament as well as to communicate a general view of priorities to Canadians. Throne Speeches are not necessarily given on an annual basis but rather to open a new session of Parliament. The Budget Speech presents the Minister of Finance's (and the government's) view of the state of the economy and the fiscal and other policy measures needed to manage the economy effectively. Budget Speeches are prepared in relative secrecy even within the Cabinet. They usually occur annually, but in some years there have been two Budget Speeches per year. We will defer until the next chapter the detailed analysis of the machinery of priority setting and resource allocation and will refer here only to selected major developments since 1968. It is sufficient to stress, however, that our brief chronological review of the Trudeau years shows the difficulty of coordinating the priorities reflected in these several priority-setting documents and time frames.

1968 to 1972

In 1968-69 and 1969-70 the internal priority-setting exercise was characterized by the development of a short list of general but tough priorities, including language policies and the removal of regional disparities. Most other programs were held constant in budgetary terms. The priorities reflected the initial flowering of the Trudeau "rational" priority-setting process, and were aided by the newness and hence the power of the 1968 Trudeau mandate. The toughness and shortness of the priority list were aided by the 1969 fight against inflation which included an effort to curtail government-expenditure growth. The 1968-69 effort included, among other things, the development of an X budget of so-called expendable programs, and resulted in the cancellation of programs such as the Winter Works employment scheme (albeit soon to be resurrected in a new form a few years later when unemployment was perceived as the main problem).[12]

By 1970, however, both the general political environment and the pressure of ministers and bureaucratic departments made the priority exercise less formally "rational" in the abstract sense of that word, but quite politically rational. Thus, the October Crisis of 1970 converted the internal priority-setting exercise into a vague search for programs that would aid "national unity." In addition, the pressure from ministers and departments that had been "ranked" low for two or three years in a row increased greatly. They increasingly demanded fairer treatment and equity in the budgetary and the priority-setting process. These internal arguments and the need to maintain bureaucratic and ministerial peace and tranquility were aided by, and reflected in, the declining political strength of the Trudeau government in 1971 and 1972 and by growing unemployment. By the 1972 election the priority-setting process generated a veritable "wish-list" of priorities.

In terms of substantive content, as expressed publicly in Throne Speeches, Table 10.1 illustrates the evolution of the priorities. In 1968 the priorities were packaged as "the Just Society" and corresponded to the internal list enunciated above. Given expenditure restraint, many of the key priorities did not, at the outset at least, involve heavy expenditure commitments. By 1970, in a Throne Speech which predated the Quebec October Crisis, the priorities were expressed in terms of the "new age of the 1970s." The major priorities were generally social in nature. By 1972, as Table 10.1 shows, the priority list had become decidedly economic in emphasis, with the more social issues relegated to a low priority status. The 1972 pre-election Throne Speech was couched, nonetheless, in the somewhat vague theme of the need to "remove the barriers that create isolation."

Selected Budget Speeches during this period, as shown in Table 10.2, highlight the initial effort at securing expenditure restraint in 1968-69 as a major part of the priority concern about inflation. The 1968

TABLE 10.1

TRUDEAU GOVERNMENT PRIORITIES AS REFLECTED IN THRONE SPEECHES IN SELECTED YEARS

Year	Main Theme (if any)	Major Priorities Stressed	Lower Priority Items Mentioned
1968 (Sept. 12)	—"The Just Society"	—Foreign policy and Defence —Constitutional Reform —Official Languages Act —Expenditure Restraint —Parliamentary Reform —Regional needs and opportunities	—"Careful planning and hard Reviews" —Information Services to be Improved (Information Canada) —National Parks & Monuments —International Development Centre
1970 (Oct. 8)	—No major theme —Opened with views of "New Age of the 1970s," and Canada on the "Threshold of Greatness"	—Urban problems —Law reform (debate on abortion and nonmedical use of drugs) —Improved unemployment Benefits —Tax reform —Pollution control	—Grain export sales —Adjustment of textile industry —Inflation —Unemployment in some regions
1972 (Feb. 17)	—"The need to remove the barriers that create isolation"	—Unemployment and economic security —Industrial strategy and science and technology —Trade policy —Competition policy —Farmers and fishermen income and price stabilization	—New Canada Labour Code —Equality of women —Family Income Security Plan —Nonmedical use of drugs —Protection of privacy —Extension of CBC services to cover 98% of Canadians
1973 (Jan. 4)	—No overall theme but stress on priority for economic and social policy	—Strengthening trade ties with Europe —Job creation	—Competition policy —Airport security —Fitness and amateur sport

(*Table 10.1 continued*)

	—Reformed social security system —Housing and urban assistance		—Tightening immigration rules —Conference on Western Economic Opportunities

1974 (Sept. 30)	—Serious international economic situation	—Inflation
		  —Increase the supply of goods and services
		  —Protect those least able to protect themselves
		  —Soften the impact of soaring oil prices
		  —Expenditure restraint
			—Consultative processes with business, labour, provinces, professions and farmers
			—Transportation services to improve economic supply
			—Preventative health care
			—Social security review
			—Equal status of women

1976 (Oct. 12)	—No overall theme	—National unity
		  • Language policy
		—Equality of opportunity
		  • Inflation
		  • Fiscal restraint
		  • Reduction in public service
		  • Small business incentives
		  • Job creation targeted to areas of high unemployment
		  • Less adversarial labour relations
		—Individual freedom
		  • Freedom of information legislation
		  • Human rights
			—Competition policy
			—Oil and gas conservation
			—200-mile limit over waters
			—Resume indexing of family allowances

—Role of Governments
- A middle road between laissez faire and growing intervention

1978 (Oct. 1)	—Strengthening the economy and the renewal of the federation	—Expenditure restraint ($2 billion reduction in projected spending)
		—Wage restraint in public sector
		—Transfer dollars to:
		  • Industrial expansion
		  • Job creation
		  • Assistance to the needy
		—Revised Constitution Bill
		—Publication of "A Time for Action" proposal for constitutional renewal
			—Increased training for young people
			—Reduce costs of unemployment insurance
			—Child benefits system
			—Make Post Office a Crown Corp.
			—Consultation with business, labour and other groups

1980 (Apr. 14)	—Canadians want more effective government not less government	—Expand Petro-Canada —50% ownership of petroleum industry —Mandatory fuel efficiency standards —Strengthening of Foreign Investment Review Agency —$35 per month increase in Guaranteed Income Supplement	—National Trading Company —Employment programs for women —Efficiency in government

Source: Throne Speeches. Various Years.

TABLE 10.2

TRUDEAU GOVERNMENT PRIORITIES AS REFLECTED IN BUDGET SPEECHES IN SELECTED YEARS

Year	Main Theme (if any)	Major Priorities Stressed	Major Tax Changes
1968 (Oct. 22)	—Prosperity with problems	—Control of public expenditures, especially federal-provincial social programs —Resisting inflation —Tax reform consultative process to discuss Carter Commission reforms	—Exemptions for estate & gift taxes —Changes in tax on life insurance companies —2% Social Development Tax to maximum of $120.
1970 (Mar. 12)	—Need to fight entrenched inflation	—Fight inflation —Ameliorating the regional impacts of macro fiscal and monetary policies —Expenditure restraint —Credit control powers —Measures to control inflation in construction industry	—None
1972 (May)	—Economic expansion to reduce unemployment	—Promote greater social justice by easing financial burden borne by pensioners, blind, disabled, veterans & students —Reinforce competitive position of manufacturing and processing industries, especially in light of uncertainty created by recent international monetary crisis	—Two year capital cost allowance provision

1973 (Feb. 19)	—Reduction of unemployment	—Reduce unemployment —Increase old age pensions —Reduce inflation without controls	—Two year capital cost allowance provision to be accompanied by review mechanism to insure jobs are created —Indexation of tax system to begin in 1974 —Reduction of basic federal tax by 5%
1974 (May 6) (Pre-election Turner Budget defeated) Basically reintroduced in Nov. 18, 1974 Budget after Liberal majority restored	—Attack inflation by encouraging increased supply of goods & services —Inflation traceable primarily to international forces including high energy & food prices	—Encourage supply —Act directly against high prices where practical —Alleviate adverse impact of rising prices, particularly low income Canadians —Reduction of budgetary deficit compared to previous year (from $1 billion to $450 million) —In reintroduced Budget of Nov. 18, 1974, emphasis placed on cooperative consultative effort to achieve consensus to slow price increase	—Nondeductibility of provincial royalties & taxes on mining & petroleum corporations —10% surtax on corporate income tax —Increased excise taxes on high energy consuming vehicles —12% federal sales tax removed on clothing & footwear —Registered Home Ownership Savings Plan introduced

(Table 10.2 continued)

1976 (May 25)	—Anti-inflation, but need to attack the underlying structural problems of economy in consultation with major groups	—Reinforced the priority for wage & price controls introduced Oct. 15, 1975
		—Structural policies
		  • Conserving energy
		  • More efficient pricing of govt. services through user fees
		  • Productivity
		  • Employment & labour force
		  • Expenditures to be kept to no higher than trend in GNP
		  • Gradually lower rate of monetary expansion
			—Two year tax write-off on equipment enabling companies to use industrial waste as fuel source
			—Increased small business tax incentives
			—Doubling of deductions for expenses of child care

1978 (Nov. 16)	—Laying the basis for future growth	—Gradually reduced rate of monetary expansion —Expenditures to be kept below rate of growth of GNP —Reduced rate of growth in transfers to provinces —Need for improved consultation but "skeptical about the search for a single grand industrial strategy" —Reallocation of $300 million to assist industry	—Reduction in UIC payments by employees & employers —Doubling of employment expense deduction —Refundable child tax credit —Increase investment tax credit with higher rates for depressed regions —Doubling of R&D investment tax credit

1980 (Oct. 28)	—The National Energy Program	—Major new energy revenue taxes & charges —8% surtax on net oil & gas production —Natural gas & gas liquids tax —Petroleum compensation charge levied on refineries to produce blended price of oil —Elimination of oil & gas depletion allowances
	—Energy self-sufficiency, opportunities for Canadians & fairness in pricing —Need to reduce the deficit —Monetary restraint —Major shift of energy incentives from tax incentives to direct grants —Western Canada Fund	
1982 (June 28)	—How to get the economy growing again by bringing down inflation & increasing productivity; "The Six Percent Society"	—Proposal for creation of new investment instruments to tax only real investment income & capital gains —Postponement & alteration of controversial Nov. 1981 Budget effort to close off tax loopholes
	—Controls on federal Public Service wages to 6% in 1983 and 5% in 1984, & —"temporary" elimination of collective bargaining —Limitation of federal administered prices to 6 & 5% objectives —Limitation of indexation of taxes and selected social benefits to 6% and 5% rather than at full inflation rate —$300 million housing incentive; $3,000 grant to purchasers of new houses —Relaxation of FIRA foreign investment rules	

Source: Budget Speeches. Various Years.

Budget Speech also highlighted the promised post-Carter Commission tax reform process. The Commission had focused on the need for a simpler, more egalitarian tax system based on the concept that a "dollar is a dollar" and that all forms of income should be taxed on a fair progressive basis. Meanwhile, the 1968 Budget and subsequent budgets continued to tax and confer tax benefits on an incremental basis in response to ongoing political and fiscal needs. The 1970 Budget Speech continued to stress the need to fight inflation with specific targeted measures but also revealed the need to ameliorate the regional impacts of the otherwise blunt macro fiscal and monetary policy levers.

The pre-election Budget of May 1972 and the post-election Budget of February 1973 saw priorities shift to a concern for unemployment and social justice. This represented a response to genuine problems, plus the electoral imperatives of a government in political trouble. In addition, the international monetary crisis and the Nixon economic shocks of 1971 prompted the government to offer a new round of special capital cost allowances to enable Canadian manufacturers to compete and create jobs.[13] The 1972 election campaign was highlighted by NDP Leader David Lewis's campaign against "corporate welfare bums." This led the minority Trudeau government in the 1973 Budget Speech to promise a published review of the capital cost allowance program to ensure that it was producing the economic benefits claimed by the government.

1972 to 1974

Between 1972 and the election of 1974, during a time of minority government, the internal priority-setting process, all efforts to the contrary notwithstanding, was virtually indistinguishable from the processes of Parliamentary survival. Thus, during this time the Priorities and Planning Committee and the Legislation and House Planning Committee of the Cabinet had to work closely together. Despite the changed political circumstances and the criticism by the Liberal caucus of the growing power of the central agencies, the formal internal priorities exercises continued to be processed by the Privy Council Office in much the same way as before 1972. The terminology to describe the process changed, however. Thus, priorities were expressed as "major objectives" and "policy thrusts." The process also changed through the initiation of "Cabinet planning studies." This was a new name given to what in the early period had been referred to as the identification of "priority problems." These were not the same as the priorities themselves, but rather were issues requiring analysis and possible future action. By 1974 there were studies underway in a host of areas including mineral policy, demographic objectives, decentralization of the public service and education, to name only a few. As Richard French points out, the net effect of these cosmetic changes was that the paper flow did not fundamentally change.[14] The sobering results of the 1972 election did, however, lead central agency officials to ponder why the line departments were not responding to the policy signals emanating from the apex of power. In short, there was concern that the troops were not marching on cue and that the government's priorities were not well understood by the Canadian people.

The substantive priorities in this period articulated in the Throne Speech of 1973 displayed a more balanced economic and social list. This is perhaps indicative of the government's tactical effort to secure the support of the NDP in the minority House of Commons situation, through an emphasis on direct job creation and a reformed social security system. It is important to note that the 1973 Throne Speech pre-dates and thus does not even mention the OPEC oil crisis or energy policy. This crisis, coupled with Tory and NDP criticism of energy policy, resulted in Prime Minister Trudeau's speech in December 1973 outlining federal energy policy.[15] It included a commitment to cushion oil prices for Eastern consumers and to establish Petro-Canada as a state-owned company.

The Budget Speeches in this minority government era revealed a primary concern, first for unemployment in the second Turner Budget of February 1973 and then inflation in 1974. The basic provisions of the 1973 Budget were described above. Of particular interest was the introduction of indexation of the tax system and of selected social programs. This was a direct response to Conservative Opposition Leader Robert Stanfield's criticism of the way in which the government was profiting from inflation, from increased revenue which it was able to collect without having to impose increased taxes.

The May 6, 1974 Budget Speech, which was defeated in the House of Commons, gave clear emphasis to anti-inflation measures. The government traced the main cause of inflation to international factors, including the OPEC oil cartel's price increase. The Budget stressed the need to increase the supply of goods and services. The Budget was the first in the 1970s to bring energy policy and federal-provincial conflict over resource control and resource revenue shares to a head. This arose when the Turner Budget made provincial royalties and taxes on mining and petroleum companies nondeductible for federal tax purposes.

1974 to 1979

As with most experiments in human organization, people charged with responsibility for the priority-setting process tried to learn from their early experience. Following the return to a majority Trudeau government in 1974, efforts were made to enhance both the legitimacy of the priority-setting process among ministers and their officials, and the follow-up exercise. This included more elaborate ministerial meetings, as well as the submission from departments of their plans regarding how they would contribute to and implement the priorities. An effort was also made in the mid-1970s to make the priority list more explicit and detailed.

The crux of the problem was highlighted in an internal Cabinet report dated January 30, 1975. It noted that

> Over the past few years, the government has established a set of priorities which were meant to guide government activities and the allocation of resources—not only resources in terms of dollars and man years but also resources in terms of the time of the House of Commons, the Cabinet, and policy analysts. In the past two years this statement of government priorities has taken the form of a set of policy thrusts and major objectives. The process has been useful and has resulted in significant progress being made in many areas. However, the process has not been too successful in bringing a concerted effort to bear on the achievement of the government's priorities, nor have the priorities been related to the bulk of the ongoing activities of the government. One of the main problems with the priorities as stated in the past is that they have led to consideration of only new government activities and of the need for new resources, with little attention being paid to possible shifts in the resources already deployed throughout the government. This problem should be substantially overcome by Cabinet's decision to carry the process one step further by requiring responses to the Government's Priorities from each department and certain agencies.[16]

As a result, the new priority exercise of 1974-75 involved a small group of PCO and PMO officials interviewing each minister. As Richard French points out, these interviews revolved around two questions posed to each minister in the newly elected Cabinet: "What does the government have to do during its mandate to win the next election?" and "What do you want to be remembered for having done, should the government lose the next election?"[17] This produced a list of priorities. Departments were then asked to indicate how they could contribute to these priorities. After each area on the list was discussed in detail with departmental officials, an overall memorandum was prepared and discussed at the Cabinet's Meach Lake retreat. This document identified five themes and sixteen priority policy areas as follows:

I. A more just, tolerant, Canadian society including:
—social security
—native rights
—law reform
—bilingualism
—labour-management relations

II. With a greater balance in the distribution of people and the creation and distribution of wealth between and within regions including:
—demographic and growth patterns
—transportation
—national industrial and regional development

III. Which makes more rational use of resources and is sensitive to the natural and human environment including:
—conserving our natural resources, particularly energy resources
—maximizing the use of Canada's agricultural and fisheries resources
—diversity of lifestyles and mental and physical health

IV. Accepting new international responsibilities, particularly with regard to assisting developing countries, including:
—sharing of resources
—alleviating international crises

V. With an evolving federal state capable of effective national policy as well as sensitive, responsive and competent government at all levels including:
—federal-provincial relations
—communications
—Parliamentary reform[18]

It is instructive to note that nowhere in this document was the growing concern for inflation and unemployment reflected. By the fall of

1975 the priority exercise had disintegrated, replaced by the wage and price control program and a "law and order" package devised by a handful of officials and ministers in Finance, the PCO and the PMO. Richard French supplies a succinct epitaph for the burial of the exercise.

> At the moment which should have been its greatest triumph, the Cabinet Planning System was at the point of collapse. The disparity between the nature of the political pressures bearing upon the government in the House of Commons, in the media and elsewhere, on the one hand, and the abstractions-like "lifestyles" or "demographic patterns"—typical of the Priorities Exercise—on the other, robbed the Exercise of its relevance and credibility. Economic and political events had evolved beyond it. The wage-price spiral continued unabated, John Turner pondered his political options and the Prime Minister's Office, intimately involved in the Priorities Exercise from the beginning, smelled disaster. The PMO commissioned a public opinion survey of the concerns of Canadians. To no one's surprise, inflation and the state of the economy constituted the issue of greatest concern, while violent crime and firearm tragedies were a distant second. In the end, the few thousand dollars invested with the Liberal party's house pollster to confirm the instincts of political insiders was to have a far greater influence on the government's priorities than the thousands of bureaucratic manhours invested in the Priorities Exercise.
>
> The second Meach Lake Cabinet meeting, which took place in mid-September 1975, was far different from its predecessor ten months earlier. The resignation of John Turner, the conversion of the Department of Finance to a policy of wage and price controls, and the PMO's polling results gave the Meach Lake meeting a tangible focus and a sense of urgency. The Memorandum to Cabinet consolidating the results of the Priorities Exercise was ignored. The Cabinet adopted the Economy and "Law and Order" (later to become "Peace and Security") as its two priorities. The Economy priority was composed of the program of wage and price controls, to be instituted immediately on announcement in the forthcoming Speech from the Throne. Relevant sectors of the bureaucracy were galvanized into action with urgency unknown since the October Crisis of 1970. The Law and Order package was to be unveiled in the spring of 1976, to coincide with the Progressive Conservative leadership convention. It was to be a potpourri including gun control, abolition of capital punishment and other measures which were to be marked under a "lock 'em up and throw away the key" theme, since this was what the poll indicated Canadians wanted. (The package later become unravelled when the abolition of capital punishment was rejected by the man on the street, overshadowing the other initiatives entirely, and

became a substantial political disadvantage.)

By 1976 a further apparatus, the committee of ten deputy ministers known as "DM 10," had been added to help ministers generate priorities and options for the post-income-controls program. By the late 1970s, ministers were increasingly skeptical of the process of generating abstract priorities which left the important "details" to be worked out by the bureaucracy. In a period of increasing criticism of expenditure growth, ministers wanted to be in on the details.[19]

The content and process of the 1975 priority setting exercise is all the more remarkable because the previous Throne Speech of September 30, 1974 did stress the serious international economic situation. As Table 10.1 shows, the priorities were inflation and restraint, ameliorated by the need to soften the impact of soaring oil prices.

While the income control program was being put in place late in 1975 and early in 1976, priorities lurched in yet another direction. By the October 12, 1976 Throne Speech, the priority item was national unity and language policy, a priority precipitated by the air traffic control strike and the bitter dispute over language policy and air safety.[20] The dispute resulted in Prime Minister Trudeau's national television address prior to the Olympic Games, which described the crisis as being equal to the Conscription Crisis of World War II.

The 1976 Throne Speech also reflected the growing influence of neoconservative criticism of the growth of government. While leaning to the right, the Liberals portrayed themselves as having a middle-of-the-road view of the role of government. This was also reflected in the publication of two philosophical position papers, *The Way Ahead*, and *Agenda For Cooperation*, both of which addressed issues regarding the "post-incomes control" society, and the need to fundamentally restructure the economy.[21]

By the fall of 1978 and the new Throne Speech of October 1st, the major themes of the 1976 Speech were even more entrenched. The election of the separatist Parti Quebecois government in Quebec resulted in a new round of proposals for constitutional renewal. The growing popularity of the Progressive Conservatives under Joe Clark, expressed in both polls and by-elections, strengthened the neoconservative emphasis in Liberal priorities (for example, expenditure restraint, public sector wage restraint and industrial expansion). This included a sudden "two billion dollar expenditure cut" exercise ordered by Trudeau in

August 1978.[22] This exercise was carried out through processes entirely separate from the "normal" priority-setting routine. It was a prime ministerial "lightning bolt" which hit while most ministers were on their August vacations.

The economic policy emphasis on anti-inflation policy is evident in the two 1974 Budgets of John Turner and the 1976 Budget of Donald Macdonald. The content, however, is quite different. Turner opposed controls and promoted priorities and policies that would encourage the supply of new goods and services. Following the 1974 election which returned the Liberals on an anti-controls mandate, Turner attempted an elaborate but unsuccessful consultative process with business and labour to bring down prices.[23] When the Macdonald Budget was brought down following Turner's resignation, wage and price controls were a fait accompli. The Macdonald Budget focused on the need for major underlying structural policies including energy conservation, expenditure growth not to exceed the growth of the GNP, and gradual reductions in the rate of monetary expansion.

The Chretien Budget of November 1978, the last Budget prior to the 1979 election that saw the defeat of the Liberals, witnessed a continuation of the 1976 themes about structural reform of the economy but couched the budgetary priorities in terms of "laying the basis for future growth." It contained a pre-election mixture of neoconservative restraint with social measures such as the Child Tax Credit, as well as investment tax credits with higher rates earmarked for economically depressed regions. Even though the Budget Speech had been preceded by the August budget cuts exercise and the formation of the Board of Economic Development Ministers to coordinate and devise an industrial strategy, Mr. Chretien pointedly expressed his skepticism in the Budget Speech about the search for a single, grand industrial strategy.

The 1980s

The Liberal Throne Speech of April 1980 gave testimony to the Liberals' new aggressive post-election position. Reacting against the Clark government's "community of communities" and neoconservative view of Canada, the Liberal Throne Speech asserted that Canadians wanted more effective government not less government and that they wanted someone to speak for Canada. It promised constitutional renewal, an expanded Petro-Canada, steps to achieve 50 percent ownership of the petroleum industry and a strengthened mandate to enable FIRA to review foreign investment more vigorously.

The 1980 Throne Speech did not, however, reveal the degree of aggressiveness and initial coherence of the overall *internal* strategy devised by senior ministers, advisors and officials.[24] The basis of the strategy can be summarized briefly.

- There was a fundamental belief among senior Liberals that the national government could not restrict itself to acting merely as a referee between competing interests of the Canadian "communities." They profoundly rejected the short-lived Clark government's "community of communities" concept of Canada.
- The Trudeau Liberals concluded that their plans and policies had to be designed, wherever feasible, to reassert federal presence and visibility. Such a presence and identity was to be fostered by actions and decisions in which the federal government dealt *directly* with individual persons, businesses, and other social institutions rather than channelling its support *through* the provincial governments.
- Federal ministers were increasingly tired of reacting to the initiatives of provincial governments and of being perceived as a mismanaged, debt-ridden and remote government, while the provincial governments basked for most of the 1970s in the political glory of balanced budgets, perceived competence, and sensitivity and closeness to "their" people.
- With the Quebec referendum "settled," the Liberals turned their attention westward to try to forge some kind of a new political coalition that would strengthen their representation, legitimacy and power in the West. This search was premised on a strategic political view that they would have their best electoral prospects if they tried to woo the left-of-centre NDP voter. They would also have to latch on to the western resource boom, influence its direction, and be *seen* to be influencing it in significant ways.

The federal identity approach or the "new nationalism" was centred in the Constitution with its Charter of Rights and the National Energy Program. In addition to these high risk initiatives, the 1980 plan envisioned three other large aggressive initiatives—an industrial strategy, a Western Canada Fund to help build Liberal support in the otherwise barren Liberal electoral territory, and major changes in social programs, especially the federal-provincial arrangements for financing health and education. The nationalism and federal identity focus, carried out on several policy fronts concurrently, was intended to be conflict-oriented and to assert federal jurisdiction.

In terms of resource allocation the Liberal expenditure plans gave a clear indication, if carried out, that economic development and energy expenditures would receive the top priority, and social expenditures would be given a low priority. The Trudeau Liberals retained the full-scale envelope system begun by the Clark government, including the publication of five-year expenditure plans. This system was intended to bring the priority-setting machinery closer to a possible resolution of the problems identified earlier in the 1970s, namely, the need to link policy choices directly to resource allocation and the need to link new expenditures to on-going or "A-base" expenditures. The prime minister, however, abandoned the Clark experiment with an Inner Cabinet because of the obvious tensions it had created among Clark ministers excluded from the inner group.

The Budget Speeches of the early 1980s reflected the usual range of coherence and incoherence with overall priorities. Finance Minister Allan MacEachen's first Budget in the fall of 1980 was the NEP Budget. It contained radical changes to the structure of oil and gas industry incentives, from tax incentives to direct grants favouring Canadian firms. The second MacEachen Budget of November 1981 diverged from overall priorities in some respects. On the one hand it asserted the need to fight inflation, reduce the deficit and to stick to a tough monetary policy and high interest rates. On the other hand, it experimented with a quasi-social policy of closing off loopholes or tax expenditures and reducing the highest marginal tax rates. As we saw in Chapter 5, tax expenditures increasingly favoured the rich. The 1981 Budget, however, did not redistribute the additional revenues obtained to low income Canadians, but rather shuffled them around to other middle and higher income Canadians. The Budget produced a political disaster in an economy sinking into depression. It was widely perceived to be one which produced neither good economic or social policy.[25]

The June 1982 Budget was designed to recover from the previous budgetary debacle. It was produced by yet another aberration from the overall priority setting process, a small ad hoc group of ministers. The Budget produced the plan for the "Six Percent Society." The focus was on an anti-inflation attack anchored on a policy of statutory control of public service wages. All three MacEachen Budgets contained some underlying continuity of concerns over inflation and the deficit, but in other respects they revealed the normal political need to respond to often contradictory short- and medium-term realities and perceptions of realities.

Observations on Priority Setting

We have taken two portraits of priorities, one capturing a 115-year period and the other a decade and a half of the Trudeau regime. When looking at whole decades in the distant past, priorities seem clearer. When priorities deal with the future, politics and uncertainty are the constant companions. Governments are caught between a rock and a hard place. If they try to stick to a medium-term view, they may be guilty of arrogant rigidity and of being insensitive to present needs. If they engage in too many ad hoc short-term responses, they are accused of failing to plan or failing to create a "climate for investment." Neither rationality nor incrementalism is good enough.

In our account of the Trudeau priorities and priority-setting processes we have paid little attention to the actual achievement of goals and to the real pattern of resource allocation. We have noted some of the major trends in Chapter 5, but we otherwise reserve this larger task to later parts of the book. At this point we wish to draw concluding attention to several general features of priority setting, all of which support the general thesis developed in Chapter 4 that there are severe political constraints on "doing first things first."

Throne Speeches in the Trudeau era have evolved from quite philosophical documents in the early years to somewhat more prosaic ones in the later period. All, however, contain the veritable wish list of "priorities" for different constituencies and regions, an act of essential political communication. The trends in substantive priorities show the Liberal tendency for continuous movement across the middle of the political stage, a "to-ing and fro-ing" between a relative focus on social priorities (1968, 1970) and economic priorities (1972, 1974) between left (1980) and right (1978). Despite this tendency, certain subjects are persistently at or near the top of the priority list (inflation, national unity), while others move on and off the list (competition policy, immigration, women's issues) on the fringes of politics.

The expression of general public priorities is partly an act of political theatre. This does not necessarily make it unreal or a meaningless charade. We have seen, however, how public priorities expressed in Throne Speeches do not usually equate well with internal resource allocation processes, including those expressed in Budget Speeches. The chapter shows how the machinery had to be constantly changed to get a better fit between internally expressed priorities and actual resource decisions. Various ways have been tried, including the special exercises of 1974, the creation of BEDM in 1978 and the envelope system of 1979. Indeed, there have been several occasions where the prime minister and his senior advisors deemed it necessary to concoct special priority-setting devices. The October Crisis of 1970, the wage and price controls priority of 1975, the August Budget Cuts of 1978, the National Energy Policy of 1980, and the "Six Percent Society" initiatives early in 1982, all emerged from special machinery which disobeyed the normal priority-setting rules. Indeed, it can be said that there are as many abnormal priority-setting procedures as normal ones in the Trudeau era.

Budget Speeches also reveal the varied and episodic links between nominally economic priorities and the broader Throne Speeches. They raise the oldest "chicken versus the egg" question about priorities. Should the economic framework and fiscal posture largely set the scene for overall political priorities or should it be vice versa? A review of several Budget Speeches shows the obvious economic tone of Budget Speeches but reveals them to be profoundly political documents as well. As is the case with several of the themes raised in this chapter, we examine these concerns in greater detail in Chapter 11 and in our detailed analysis of policy fields in Part III.

NOTES

1. See Donald Creighton, *John A. Macdonald: The Old Chieftain* (Toronto: Macmillan of Canada, 1955), Chapter 6; W.L. Morton, *The Kingdom of Canada* (Toronto: McClelland and Stewart, 1963), Chapters 18 and 19; and Vernon Fowke, *The National Policy and the Wheat Economy* (Toronto: University of Toronto, 1957).

2. See Donald Smiley, "Canada and the Quest for a New National Policy," *Canadian Journal of Political Science,* Vol. 8 (March, 1975), pp. 40-62; W.L. Morton, *The Progressive Party in Canada* (Toronto: University of Toronto, 1950; and M. Janine Brodie, *Crisis, Challenge and Change: Party and Class in Canada* (Toronto: Methuen, 1980), Chapters 4 and 5.

3. See Blair Neatby, *The Politics of Chaos: Canada in the Thirties* (Toronto: Macmillan of Canada, 1972); David Lewis, *The Good Fight* (Toronto: Macmillan of Canada, 1981), Chapters 6, 7 and 8; and Reginald Whitaker, *The Government Party* (Toronto: University of Toronto Press, 1977), Chapters 1 and 14.

4. Robert Campbell, *Grand Illusions: The Keynesian Experience in Canada* (Manuscript—in press); A. Armitage, *Social Welfare in Canada* (Toronto: McClelland and Stewart, 1975); and L. Marsh, *Report on Social Security for Canada—1943* (Toronto: University of Toronto Press, 1975); and Robert Bothwell, Ian Drummond and John English, *Canada Since 1945* (Toronto: University of Toronto Press, 1981), Chapters 9, 15 and 17.

5. Richard W. Phidd and G. Bruce Doern, *The Politics and Management of Canadian Economic Policy* (Toronto: Macmillan of Canada, 1978), Chapters 7 and 8; and Bothwell et al., *op. cit.,* Chapter 7.

6. Glen Williams, "The National Tariffs: Industrial Underdevelopment Through Import Substitution," *Canadian Journal of Political Science,* Vol. 12, 1979, pp. 333-368.

7. See Whitaker, *op. cit.,* Chapter 5; and Donald V. Smiley, *Canada in Question,* Third Edition (Toronto: McGraw-Hill Ryerson, 1981), Chapter 6.

8. See Bothwell et. al., *op. cit.,* Chapter 27; Peter C. Newman, *Renegade in Power* (Toronto: McClelland and Stewart, 1963). See also our survey of this period in Chapter 8.

9. See Richard Simeon, *Federal-Provincial Diplomacy: The Making of Recent Policy in Canada* (Toronto: University of Toronto Press, 1982); Kenneth Bryden, *Old Age Pensions and Policy Making in Canada* (Montreal: McGill-Queen's University Press, 1974), Chapter 8; and Malcolm Taylor, *Health Insurance and Canadian Public Policy* (Montreal: McGill-Queen's University Press, 1978).

10. See Bothwell et. al., *op. cit.,* Chapters 31 and 32; and George Radwansky, *Trudeau* (Toronto: Macmillan of Canada, 1978). See our review in Chapter 8.

11. Jeffrey Simpson, *Discipline of Power* (Toronto: Personal Library, 1981).

12. R.M. Burns and L. Close, *The Winter Works Program* (Toronto: Canadian Tax Foundation, 1971).

13. Michael Tucker, *Canadian Foreign Policy* (Toronto: McGraw-Hill Ryerson, 1980), Chapter 2.

14. Richard French, *How Ottawa Decides* (Ottawa: Canadian Institute for Economic Policy, 1980), pp. 50-54.

15. See David Crane, *Controlling Interest* (Toronto: McClelland and Stewart, 1982), pp. 68-70.

16. "Responses to the Government's Priorities," Unpublished Cabinet Discussion Paper (Ottawa: January 30, 1975), p. 1.

17. French, *op. cit.,* p. 77.

18. Quoted in French, *op. cit.,* pp. 79-80.

19. French, *op. cit.,* pp. 83-84.

20. See Sandford F. Borins, *Language of the Sky* (Montreal: McGill-Queen's University Press, 1983).

21. See Canada, *The Way Ahead: A Framework for Discussion* (Ottawa: Minister of Supply and Services, 1976); and Canada, *Agenda for Cooperation* (Ottawa, Minister of Supply and Services, 1977).

22. French, *op. cit.,* Chapter 6; and G. Bruce Doern and Richard W. Phidd, "Economic Management in the Government of Canada: Some Implications of the Board of Economic Development Ministers and the Lambert Report." Paper presented to Canadian Political Science Association; Saskatoon, May 1979.

23. See Allan Maslove and Eugene Swimmer, *Wage Controls in Canada* (Montreal: Institute for Research on Public Policy, 1980), Chapter 1.

24. See G. Bruce Doern, ed., *How Ottawa Spends Your Tax Dollars 1981* (Toronto: James Lorimer Publishers, 1981), Chapter 1.

25. See G. Bruce Doern, ed., *How Ottawa Spends Your Tax Dollars 1982* (Toronto: James Lorimer Publishers, 1982), Chapters 1 and 2.

CHAPTER 11

PUBLIC POLICY AND RESOURCE ALLOCATION

Since governments must both lead society and at the same time be responsive to at least some of the democratic demands placed upon them, it should not be surprising that priority setting is at best an episodic affair. The previous chapter showed this in graphic detail. Despite these difficulties every government is obliged, on an annual basis and over longer periods of time, to relate its policies to the available resources. In short, it must deal with scarcity, and it must choose from among several competing public demands, programs, ideas and activities the level and the form of the resources it will devote at any given time. Choices must also be made between longer-term capital development and current consumption and hence involve decisions affecting future generations of Canadians regarding who will pay and who will benefit. Resources include not just expenditures and taxation but decisions to regulate, since the latter impose costs on private citizens and corporations. Resource allocation involves decisions to borrow and loan funds or to guarantee loans. It includes decisions about personnel and thus must address questions such as: How many inspectors? What kind of expertise? How "representative" should the person who heads an agency be or should the members of a commission or tribunal be? Last, but certainly not least, it involves commitments of time and political energy and goodwill both in leadership and in selling, and communicating the policy. Given the tasks and complexity of modern government and the ideas inherent in Cabinet government, this involves the need to coordinate the overall resource-allocation process and simultaneously to delegate resource allocation to Cabinet committees and the myriad of agencies examined in Chapter 9.

It is necessary to examine in two stages the dynamics and processes of resource allocation and the ideas and structures involved. The most traditional and familiar way is to focus first on the overall central revenue-expenditure dynamics, including the main policy field categories of expenditure. At the risk of some inevitable repetition, it is necessary then to view resource allocation in an even broader and somewhat less familiar way by encompassing regulation, public enterprise and exhortation, as well as taxing and spending.

The overall focus of this chapter is on the first stage, namely the central resource allocation process and on the economic and social resource-allocation dynamics and processes of the Cabinet committees in these major policy fields. In Chapter 12 we deal with the second stage by examining in greater detail resource allocation processes defined by the larger expenditure, tax, regulatory, public enterprise and exhortation instruments of governing, rather than by policy fields per se. Though the two are treated into two chapters, these processes are in reality closely connected.

In this chapter we first examine the overall resource-allocation process and the evolving criticisms of it. The second section of the chapter describes the so-called policy and expenditure management, or "envelope" system, adopted in 1979. The latter half of the chapter then highlights central features of the allocation process in the economic, social and energy policy fields, as well as in the special case of a regional policy dilemma, policies for Western Canada. The detailed substantive content of these policy fields is examined further in Part III of the book.

Main Features of the Overall Annual Resource Allocation Process

What does the overall resource allocation system look like? It is helpful to view two general portraits of it. The first is portrayed in Figure 11.1 and shows in simple terms the elementary parts of the revenue and expenditure halves of the resource-allocation system. The revenue inputs include taxes, tariffs, royalties and user fees and charges. The ideas which govern the revenue-generation process include the by now familiar ones of efficiency (will the tax system promote initiative and risk taking?), equity (will taxpayers at similar income levels be treated equally?), stability (will the tax system produce a "climate for investment?") and redistribution (will the system redistribute income from rich to poor?). The revenue side also raises concerns about the adequacy of the total revenues to meet the government's needs, the size of deficits and surpluses, and the simplicity and ease of revenue collection. On the output side, taxes reappear in the form of tax expenditures that serve as policy incentives, as we discussed in Chapter 5. Expenditures of many

FIGURE 11.1
**THE REVENUE-EXPENDITURE COMPONENTS
OF THE RESOURCE-ALLOCATION SYSTEM**

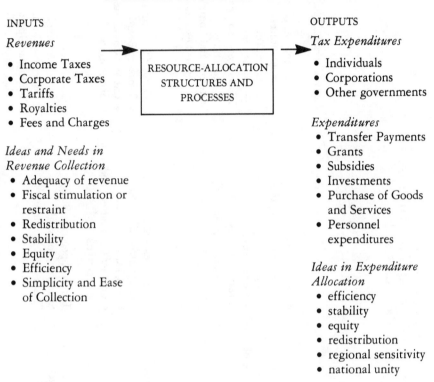

INPUTS

Revenues

- Income Taxes
- Corporate Taxes
- Tariffs
- Royalties
- Fees and Charges

*Ideas and Needs in
Revenue Collection*
- Adequacy of revenue
- Fiscal stimulation or
  restraint
- Redistribution
- Stability
- Equity
- Efficiency
- Simplicity and Ease
  of Collection

RESOURCE-ALLOCATION
STRUCTURES AND
PROCESSES

OUTPUTS

Tax Expenditures

- Individuals
- Corporations
- Other governments

Expenditures
- Transfer Payments
- Grants
- Subsidies
- Investments
- Purchase of Goods
  and Services
- Personnel
  expenditures

*Ideas in Expenditure
Allocation*
- efficiency
- stability
- equity
- redistribution
- regional sensitivity
- national unity

kinds are generated, including transfers to individuals, grants (conditional or unconditional), subsidies, investments, and the purchase of goods, services and personnel. The contending ideas inherent in the expenditure and tax expenditure outputs are the same, as we have stressed throughout the book.

If one was to portray an even more realistic chart of a resource-allocation system, one would have to add to the output side items such as regulation, public enterprise and exhortation. But let us take first things first and concentrate on the overall revenue-expenditure aspects of the resource-allocation process.

Figure 11.2 therefore presents a second somewhat different snapshot of its most recognizable features, the overall priority setting mechanisms, the fiscal framework and the expenditure process.[1] The

Figure 11.2

A Simplified View of the Overall Internal Federal Resource-Allocation System

Fiscal Framework and Revenue Budget ⟷ Overall Priorities ⟷ Expenditure Budget

	Fiscal Framework and Revenue Budget	Overall Priorities	Expenditure Budget
Components	Fiscal stimulus or restraint; short versus medium term based on judgement about state of the economy	• overall social/economic priorities and political judgement • short-term responsiveness versus long-term "planning"	"A" Budget (on-going expenditures) "B" Budget (new initiatives) "X" Budget (cancellation or reduction) Statutory and Controlled versus Discretionary spending
Primary Units Involved	Department of Finance	• Priorities and Planning Committee of Cabinet • PCO, PMO • Cabinet Committees and Secretariats	• Cabinet Committees • Treasury Board • Cabinet Committee Secretariats
Kinds of Documents or Policy Occasions	Fiscal Outlook Paper Medium-Term Track Documents Budget Speeches	Throne Speeches, Budget Speeches, Internal "Priorities" Documents	• Estimates • 5-Year Strategic Overview Documents • Multiyear Operational Plan Documents

latter two in particular combine to form some kind of desired balance or relationship between revenues and expenditures. Until the late 1970s the overall resource allocation operated on about an eighteen-month time frame, that is, about eighteen months prior to the start of the federal governments fiscal year (April 1st). Thereafter an attempt was made to extend the time frame to a four- or five-year period, but in reality, as we see in this chapter, it is a series of annual rolling resource-allocation exercises. The system functions through the Cabinet committee system. Each of the above features are described in order.

Overall Priorities

Chapter 10 shows that there are several mechanisms that help produce or express priorities, including Throne Speeches and Budget Speeches. These are not necessarily annual in nature. The prime minister and the Cabinet must, however, have some annual mechanism to help guide the allocation process and to express the ultimate political judgement of the government. In Ottawa this has centred on the Cabinet Committee on Priorities and Planning, chaired by the prime minister and advised primarily, though certainly not exclusively, by the PMO and PCO.

The Fiscal Framework

Priorities must be forged in the context of some judgement about the fiscal position and revenue needs and capacity of the government and the economy. The Department of Finance has historically been the lead agency in carrying out this difficult task.[2] The setting of the fiscal framework has involved the development of a formal economic outlook document setting out the government's view of the current and likely future state of the economy. It sets out the Keynesian judgement about the fiscal balance, namely the degree to which the fiscal position should help stimulate the economy (with deficits), restrain it (with surpluses), or be in some generally balanced position. This kind of annual to eighteen-months Keynesian fine tuning has grown into considerable disrepute due to the evidence of a declining economy and criticism from monetarists and others.[3] It is viewed by these critics to be more a part of the problem than the solution. In the late 1970s and early 1980s an effort was made to extend the fiscal framework into a slightly longer time frame, into a document setting out the "medium-term track" of the economy. Needless to say, the fiscal framework is judgementally and normatively loaded. There are significant problems in the art of forecasting the Canadian and world economy, the behaviour of investors and consumers and other governments' revenue and expenditure decisions.

The Expenditure Budget

The development of an annual expenditure budget, to be presented to Parliament as the Estimates, is both a product of, and a contributing factor in, the overall priority-setting process and the fiscal framework.[4] The dual relationship is shown by the inevitable existence of a so-called "A" and "B" Budget and of the different legal and political constraints involved in the control and discretion of budgetary expenditures. The "A" Budget refers to those expenditures of an on-going nature needed to maintain existing programs or to fund them at new levels caused by changes such as population growth. The "B" Budget refers to expenditures on new initiatives or programs. Sometimes the level of scarcity is such that an "X" Budget must be created, one which identifies items in the "A" base that can be or should be eliminated in whole or in part either to achieve restraint or, more typically, to be reallocated to some new "B" Budget initiative.

The issues of what is on-going and new, and desirable and expendable, are political by their very nature.[5] The political past and the possible future are closely linked. The expenditure process is therefore a central and visible part of policy formulation. Many expenditures are statutory, fixed for a period of years, or without a time limit. These include large social programs involving federal-provincial transfers, conditional grants and tax agreements. On an annual basis, significant change is difficult, legally and politically. Some basic kind of certainty and level of past commitments must be maintained. At the same time circumstances change and so must budgets.

Decisions about the expenditure budget are made by several Cabinet committees. The Priorities and Planning Committee sets out the general allocations. Individual Cabinet committees (see below) can influence or actually determine allocations within their policy field. The Treasury Board and other agencies exercise influence through their roles in approving "A-base" expenditures and advising on issues of efficiency, controlling personnel establishments (person-years), collective bargaining, administrative policy (for example, on contracts) and evaluations. Bargaining, log-rolling and mutual backscratching are central to the budget process. This is why it has been characterized as being essentially incremental in nature and why it is always the target for "rational" reform.

The above features are not the only aspects of resource allocation. They are merely the most visible and recognizable. The regulatory and tax processes also allocate resources in less visible ways, as we see in Chapter 12.

Evolution and Criticisms of the Overall Resource Allocation System

It is not difficult to see why the overall resource allocation system is subject to diverse and continuous criticism. The system has evolved in response to changing ideas about politics and economics and to different rankings of the institutional, substantive and procedural ideas that should be maximized at any given time. Some of these changes can be linked, especially in retrospect, with changes in structure. For example, prior to the Glassco Commission on Government Organization in the early 1960s, the Treasury Board functioned virtually as a staff arm of the Department of Finance. This symbolized a view that the revenue and expenditure process should be intricately and closely coordinated "under one roof," so to speak. Following Glassco, the Treasury Board was separated from the Finance Department, not because of problems with fiscal policy per se, but because of the Glassco Commission's concern about the better "management of government," the need it expressed to let departmental managers "manage."[6] This symbolized the greater separation of the expenditure process from the fiscal process and framework. Other developments also contributed to this process, including the other changes in the Cabinet and the central agencies examined in Chapter 7, and the changing ideas and conflicts inherent in economic policy and economic management.

By the late 1970s the system was judged by some to have resulted in too great a separation of the revenue and expenditure elements. There was a need to link more explicitly and carefully the policy decisions of the Cabinet with its resource allocation decisions.[7] This led to the envelope system. Before examining it, however, one must appreciate in greater detail the general criticisms and the partial contradictions among these criticisms, of the overall resource allocation system as it had evolved until the late 1970s. This is especially important because no "system" is permanent or cast in stone. The underlying ideas in conflict are, however, fairly constant and recurring. They reappear in different permutations and combinations as ideas about "process" and about policy fields and values are ranked differently at different times by the same government or political party or by different governments. The main criticisms are centred on a normative concern for imposing greater coordination and discipline between policy ideas and the availability of resources; increasing ministerial control over bureaucrats in the policy and decision process; and increasing the time frame of decisions and the capacity to plan. Contained within these concerns are other particular problems, including the need to improve the capacity to estimate revenues, the need to evaluate programs, especially the seemingly sacrosanct "A-base" of expenditures, and the need to provide ministers with better analytical support and policy analysis in a timely, economical way.[8] Each of these concerns are analyzed briefly below.

The Integration of Policy and Resource Allocation

The overriding criticism of the system as it had evolved in the 1970s was that policy determination and resource allocation were not adequately linked. A new system was needed so that ministers in the various Cabinet committees would directly have to face the fiscal consequences of their own decisions. Under the pre-envelope system, Cabinet committees could all too easily approve policy ideas, leaving the resource implications to be dealt with primarily by the President of the Treasury Board and/or the Minister of Finance. Thus, only two ministers had an institutional responsibility to say "no." This reinforced the pro-spending instincts of ministers, especially in the early 1970s when there was economic prosperity and a decided lack of concern about costs. The analysis of priorities in Chapter 10 shows how concern about coordination began to appear. The ill-fated priorities exercise of 1974-75 was premised on a need to solve this problem.

The failure to relate policies to resources in a concerted way was evident in other particular problems as well. One was revenue estimation and the phenomenon of "March" spending. It was felt that the system contained a strong bias to underestimate tax revenues. When the "unexpected" extra revenues materialized near the end of the fiscal year in March there was an unseemly March rush to spend them. March spending was further exacerbated by the availability of any other unspent funds originally approved. In the late 1960s and early 1970s the excess revenue was increased by the fact that the tax system was not indexed for inflation. Thus, the government gained additional "easy" revenue as peoples' inflated incomes pushed them into higher marginal tax brackets.

There can be little doubt that the system or structure helped bias decisions in this way. It is important to stress, however, that structure is inextricably linked with ideas and changing normative concern. In this instance the ideas were reflected in the growing neoconservative belief that government lacked discipline, that expenditures were out of control, and that excess spending was itself the major cause of inflation and the growing economic malaise of the late 1970s and early 1980s. Closely related to this was the concern about the apparent political sanctity of the "A" Budget expenditures and the failure to evaluate on-going programs.[9] All of these themes were stressed in the Auditor General's criticisms in the early 1970s, by the Lambert Royal Commission on Financial Accountability in 1977 and by the Clark Progressive Conservative party, both when in Opposition and when it formed a government in 1979.

The Need for Greater Ministerial Control

The need for greater control of decisions by ministers was inherent in the concern for coordinating policy with resource allocation. However, greater ministerial control can mean different things. It means in part greater control over bureaucrats, but it also implies a desire to make ministers more accountable to each other collectively. Once again the Cabinet system pulls ministers in two directions. Ministers are expected to be held individually responsible, but by having ministers more involved in the resource trade-offs of all departments in their committee-envelope, they are in fact less and less in individual control of their own department.

Nonetheless, on balance, the evolving criticism focused on the need to decentralize decisions in the policy Cabinet committees in recognition of the need to delegate and the need to leave the Cabinet Committee on Priorities and Planning to focus on major strategic issues or overall priorities and on a longer-term view of policy and resource allocation. A necessary corollary to the new system would have to be changes in the analytical support for the Cabinet committees *as a collectivity*. Chapters 4 and 7 have shown how central agencies had evolved to support the prime minister and other key ministers. But other individual ministers were still briefed primarily by their own departments and political staff. The new system would attempt to brief them in a common way, as members of a committee. This led, in combination with the perpetual concerns about the growing paper burden faced by ministers, to the institution of the brief "assessment notes" referred to in Chapter 4.

Lengthening the Time Frame of Decisions

If policy was to be better linked to resources, and if ministers were to exercise control, it followed that neither could happen unless a longer-term "planning" period was envisioned. One immediate problem of the pre-envelope system was to ensure that ministers *collectively* (as opposed to just the Treasury Board) were constantly aware of how their *current* decisions were going to affect the availability of resources in the medium-term *future* (about three to five years). They also had to have better cost estimates and projections, especially for large capital projects. The dilemma here, as we have seen in the analysis of priority setting in Chapter 10 and of policy analysis models in Chapter 6, is that political-electoral incentives conspire to create a "short-term" game, while allocative realities are such that longer-term consequences are inevitable, not only because of scarcity itself, but also because of the need to make choices between expenditures on current consumption and on longer-term capital development.

Ottawa's "Envelopes": The Policy and Expenditure Management System

The policy and expenditure management system (the envelope system) was introduced by the Clark Conservative government in 1979 and was maintained by the Trudeau Liberals on their return to power in 1980. The system assigned nine blocks of expenditure (envelopes) to different Cabinet committees (see Figure 11.3 and Appendix A). By 1981 the stated principles of the system reflected the criticisms discussed above. The principles are:

- the integration of policy and expenditure decision making to ensure that policy decisions are taken in the context of expenditure limits with full consideration of the cost implications and that, in turn, expenditure decisions are taken with an understanding of and responsibility for the policies and priorities of ministers.

FIGURE 11.3
CABINET COMMITTEES AND THEIR RESOURCE ENVELOPES

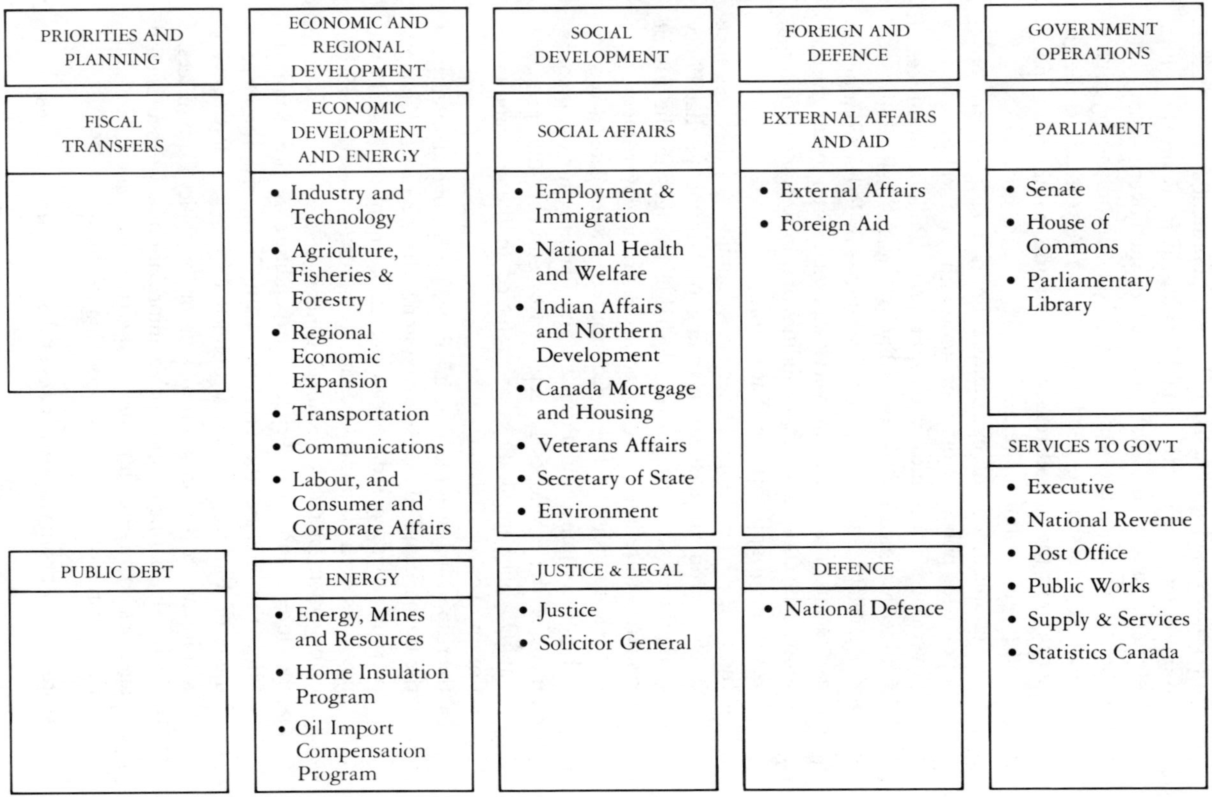

PRIORITIES AND PLANNING	ECONOMIC AND REGIONAL DEVELOPMENT	SOCIAL DEVELOPMENT	FOREIGN AND DEFENCE	GOVERNMENT OPERATIONS
FISCAL TRANSFERS	**ECONOMIC DEVELOPMENT AND ENERGY** • Industry and Technology • Agriculture, Fisheries & Forestry • Regional Economic Expansion • Transportation • Communications • Labour, and Consumer and Corporate Affairs	**SOCIAL AFFAIRS** • Employment & Immigration • National Health and Welfare • Indian Affairs and Northern Development • Canada Mortgage and Housing • Veterans Affairs • Secretary of State • Environment	**EXTERNAL AFFAIRS AND AID** • External Affairs • Foreign Aid	**PARLIAMENT** • Senate • House of Commons • Parliamentary Library
	ENERGY • Energy, Mines and Resources • Home Insulation Program • Oil Import Compensation Program	**JUSTICE & LEGAL** • Justice • Solicitor General	**DEFENCE** • National Defence	**SERVICES TO GOV'T** • Executive • National Revenue • Post Office • Public Works • Supply & Services • Statistics Canada
PUBLIC DEBT				

- the decentralization of decision-making authority to Policy Committees of Cabinet in recognition of the increasing range and complexity of government responsibilities, the interrelationships of policies and programs, and the requirement for the Cabinet Committee on Priorities and Planning to focus on the central strategic issues and overall priorities of the government.
- the publication of a longer-term fiscal plan encompassing government revenues and expenditures over a five-year period thereby setting out the overall resource constraints within which policy and program choices are made.
- the establishment of expenditure limits (i.e., "resource envelopes") for policy sectors consistent with the fiscal plan and the government's priorities, with appropriate Policy Committees of Cabinet assigned the responsibility to manage their envelopes.
- the development of policy sector strategies by Policy Committees as a means of providing an overview of their sector to integrate the individual actions and responsibilities of ministers into a common government approach for that sector.
- the review of existing policies and programs and their resource levels within an adequate planning time-frame so that Policy Committees can bring about desirable changes in the use of resources to reflect changing priorities of the government.
- the responsibility of Policy Committees as delegated from the Cabinet Committee on Priorities and Planning for the management of the envelopes be achieved by ensuring that proposals having policy implications are referred to the relevant Policy Committees for decision.
- the responsibility of the Treasury Board for the overall integrity of the financial and other resource systems, the accuracy of costing of present and proposed policies put before ministers and Parliament, as well as timely advice to ministers on the efficient management of public resources generally.
- the integration of policy and expenditure advice from the Ministries of State, the Treasury Board, Secretariat, the Department of Finance, the Privy Council Office, and departments, within the locus of decision making of the Policy Committees.
- the timely sharing of appropriate information between all central agencies in discharging their respective and joint responsibilities towards the effective functioning of the system.[10]

The system also brought with it several important features:

- a strengthening of the role of Cabinet policy committee chairmen.
- inclusion in the expenditure envelopes of both direct expenditures and tax expenditures.

- a major strengthening and expansion of the bureaucratic support staff of Cabinet committees (especially the economic development and social development committees).
- an increased role for parallel envelope committees of deputy ministers to support the Cabinet committee, especially to increase agreement among departments, ministers and officials about what the information base or "the facts" were in a particular problem.

A further central concept in the system is found in the composition of the envelope and its handling of the age-old issue of "A" and "B" Budgets. Each envelope is composed of an operational planning level and a policy reserve. The former consists of:

- the forecast cost of existing programs outlined in the approved departmental Operational Plans; and
- an Operating Reserve established to meet the cost of any overruns associated with the programs in the approved Operational Plans. The amount required for the Operating Reserve is determined in advance for each envelope by the Treasury Board, which controls allocations from the Reserve through the course of the year and identifies program management savings on existing programs with a view to avoiding a net overrun of the Operating Reserves. Policy Committees do not have access to the Operating Reserve to finance new or enriched programs.[11]

The policy reserve can be positive or negative.

During the annual review of the fiscal plan, Policy Reserves may be provided within an envelope to allow for the financing of new or enriched programs. In other instances it may be that no such reserve is provided, but rather certain reductions are to be achieved through changes to existing programs or policies in the level of commitments in the Operational Plan. The Policy Committees control allocations from the Policy Reserve for new or enriched programs, and can supplement the Reserve initially provided in the fiscal plan through policy decisions to reduce or eliminate existing programs.

An essential responsibility of Policy Committees is to ensure that the base of existing programs reflects the priorities, direction and strategy for their sector. The on-going review of existing programs by Policy Committees within the context of their sector's priorities and envelope resource levels will provide an important means to reduce or eliminate certain programs, thereby freeing up resources for reallocation to other priorities. Expenditure savings resulting from policy and program decisions by the Committee to reduce or eliminate existing programs accrue to the policy reserve for use by the Committee.[12]

Ottawa's Envelopes in Practice

Beneath the numbing prose of the official description of the envelope system are important *ideas*, even theories, about both the content and the process of public policy making. This is why we have stressed that while envelopes are a fairly recent structural change, they are only the latest "system" designed to deal with old problems and contradictions: How to plan and be rational while at the same time being sensitive and responsive to democratic demands and needs?; How to ensure reliability and predictability, essential to political power and control, and yet how to ensure acceptable and legitimate social and economic change, also an essential ingredient in political power and control?; How to survive the present without bankrupting future generations of Canadians?; How to distribute resources fairly among regions, income classes, groups, governments and individual Canadians?; How to "manage" the economy and yet at the same time manage the government to ensure the re-election of one's own political party?; How to explain complex policies in simple media related ways?; How to produce policies and allocate resources and instruments so that behaviour is *actually* changed in desired ways?; How to make ministers responsible individually and collectively for decisions while accommodating ministerial ambitions and egos?

These are what "envelopes" are really all about. How do they therefore work in practice? In our analysis below we deal with experience in the early 1980s in the economic, social and energy policy fields. But understanding how these general subsidiary policy and resource-allocation processes work does not require a focus only in the 1980s. Previous governments have tried to grapple with similar problems, and so we refer to earlier efforts as well, both here and, in greater detail, in Part III of the book.

In the context of Ottawa's envelopes we present a view of four capsule case studies in four envelope areas: economic development, social development, energy and Western Canada. The last of these represents a case study of how "special" or unofficial envelopes can be and indeed are always likely to be created. First, however, it is essential to understand one further feature of the content of envelopes, namely, the degree to which the envelopes vary in the *types* of expenditure they contain. Among the two major economic and social envelopes, for example, there is much more discretionary expenditure available in the former than in the latter. Expenditures in these envelopes are primarily in the form of grants, transfers and subsidies. In the foreign, defence, government services and justice and legal envelopes expenditures are much more personnel-oriented and (especially in defence) capital intensive in nature. This imposes quite different constraints on ministers and produces different political relations and problems. People are hard to hire and fire in a civil service setting, and capital projects (for example, weapons systems) require long lead times to plan.

Overall Expenditure Priorities

In this section we generally deal with an example of *future* priorities expressed in 1981-82 according to the broad envelope categories. It is useful, however, to relate these to *past* expenditure trends and categories, even though the categories are not fully comparable. Governments have for some time kept statistics on spending in different policy fields. They have been aware of the trends as they made their on-going choices. The difference between these past categories and the envelopes of the 1980s is that the former were not as closely linked or as visibly evident in the actual Cabinet committee and annual resource-allocation process.

It will be recalled that in Chapter 5 (Figure 5.1) we surveyed expenditure trends over a 25-year period. We showed that spending on health and welfare and on education assistance had more than doubled as a percentage of total spending since the mid-1950s. Spending on defence had shown by far the greatest percentage decline. The cost of financing the debt declined slightly over the entire period. Table 11.1 covers the period from 1970 to 1980, but its functional (policy field) categories are broken down somewhat more finely than the data presented in Chapter 5. It shows that health and welfare and education assistance increased its share over the decade and that defence declined. Expenditures on economic development declined over the decade. The servicing costs of the national debt increased significantly.

It must be remembered that these are only the priorities expressed in terms of *expenditures*. The tables tell us nothing about priorities expressed through taxation or through regulation. Nonetheless the ex post expenditure data provides an accurate context for the a priori priorities expressed in 1981 and examined below.

Table 11.2 presents the federal five-year expenditure plan by envelope presented by the Trudeau Liberals in November 1981.[13] We

TABLE 11.1
**BUDGETARY* EXPENDITURES BY FUNCTION AS A
PERCENTAGE OF TOTAL SPENDING**, 1969-70,** 1979-80

Function	1969-70	Fiscal Year 1979-80
Health and Welfare**	29.6	35.5
Public Debt	12.6	16.5
Economic Development and Support	13.0	10.9
Defence	16.2	10.5
Transportation and Communications	6.5	5.9
Fiscal Transfers to Provinces	6.8	5.5
General Government Services	3.8	4.4
Education Assistance	2.3	3.7
Internal Overhead Expense	4.7	3.1
Foreign Affairs	2.7	2.0
Culture and Recreation	1.8	2.0

Source: Treasury Board Canada, *Federal Expenditure Plan 1979-80*, p. 65, and News Release, Estimates Fact Sheet.
*Does not include nonbudgetary expenditure such as capital loans.
**This is a larger expenditure category than the Department of National Health and Welfare and should not be confused with it.

will use it as an example of the resource-allocation process at work. The practice of publicly presenting five-year expenditure plans began with the Clark government in 1979. The envelope limits are set by the Priorities and Planning Committees with input from the Department of Finance, the policy field committees and the Treasury Board.

Priority allocations at this level of aggregation are an act of overall political judgement, combining realities that must be faced and future directions to be taken. In terms of general priorities, the cost of servicing the federal debt is increasing at the highest rate. This is, in some ways, an involuntary "priority." Among the three major envelopes examined, the highest priority over the five-year period is to be given to energy and economic development. Social policy is a much lower priority, losing not only relatively but even absolutely. The percentage increases are not projected to keep pace with forecasted rates of inflation. In the more immediate context of the next two years the highest percentage increases actually accrue to the Defence and External Affairs envelopes. These increases arise from past commitments to increase defence spending in

TABLE 11.2
THE FEDERAL EXPENDITURE PLAN BY ENVELOPE

	1980-81	1981-82	1982-83	1983-84	1984-85	1985-86
Economic Development						
Millions of dollars	5,183	6,767	7,559	8,644	9,576	10,622
Percentage change	-3.5	30.6	11.7	14.4	10.8	10.9
Percentage of total	8.8	9.9	9.9	10.2	10.2	10.3
Energy						
Millions of dollars	3,624	2,672	3,039	3,602	4,115	4,779
Percentage change	53.4	-26.3	13.8	18.5	14.2	16.1
Percentage of total	6.2	3.9	4.0	4.2	4.4	4.6
Social Affairs						
Millions of dollars	24,633	27,693	30,150	33,795	37,571	41,683
Percentage change	8.6	12.4	8.9	12.1	11.2	10.9
Percentage of total	42.0	40.5	39.5	39.7	40.0	40.4
Justice and Legal						
Millions of dollars	1,213	1,399	1,541	1,750	1,930	2,133
Percentage change	17.0	15.3	10.2	13.6	10.3	10.5
Percentage of total	2.1	2.0	2.0	2.1	2.1	2.1
Services to Government						
Millions of dollars	2,732	3,350	3,448	3,676	3,852	4,213
Percentage change	17.0	22.6	2.9	6.6	4.8	9.4
Percentage of total	4.7	4.9	4.5	4.3	4.1	4.1
Parliament						
Millions of dollars	130	140	156	174	192	209
Percentage change	31.3	7.7	11.4	11.5	10.2	8.9
Percentage of total	0.2	0.2	0.2	0.2	0.2	0.2
Defence						
Millions of dollars	5,058	5,915	7,000	8,000	8,850	9,800
Percentage change	15.2	16.9	18.2	14.2	10.6	10.7
Percentage of total	8.6	8.7	9.2	9.4	9.4	9.5
External Affairs						
Millions of dollars	1,421	1,728	2,167	2,508	2,819	3,329
Percentage change	1.2	21.6	25.4	15.7	12.3	18.1
Percentage of total	2.4	2.5	2.8	2.9	3.0	3.2
Fiscal Arrangements						
Millions of dollars	3,908	4,477	4,971	5,610	6,242	6,901
Percentage change	7.5	14.6	11.0	12.9	11.2	10.6
Percentage of total	6.7	6.6	6.5	6.6	6.6	6.7

(Table 11.2 continued)

Central Reserve	0	500	800	900	1,050	1,150
Percentage change	—	—	60.0	12.5	16.7	9.5
Percentage of total	0	0.7	1.0	1.1	1.1	1.1
Lapse						
Millions of dollars	0	−1,035	−1,196	−1,424	−1,557	−1,694
Percentage of change	—	—	15.6	19.1	9.3	8.8
Percentage of total	0	−1.5	−1.6	−1.7	−1.7	−1.6
General overhead reduction						
Millions of dollars	—	—	−100	−100	−100	−100
Total outlays (excluding public debt charges)						
Millions of dollars	47,902	53,605	59,535	67,135	74,540	83,025
Percentage of change	10.6	11.9	11.1	12.8	11.0	11.4
Percentage of total	81.8	78.5	78.0	78.8	79.4	80.4
Public debt charges						
Millions of dollars	10,687	14,695	16,765	18,015	19,360	20,275
Percentage change	25.4	37.5	14.1	7.5	7.5	4.7
Percentage of total	18.1	21.5	22.0	21.2	20.6	19.6
Total outlays						
Millions of dollars	58,589	68,300	76,300	85,150	93,900	103,300
Percentage change	13.0	16.6	11.7	11.6	10.3	10.0
Percentage of total	100.0	100.0	100.0	100.0	100.0	100.0

Source: Canada. *The Budget in More Detail* (Ottawa: November 12, 1981).

real terms by 3 percent per year and to increase Third World development assistance to 0.5 percent of GNP by the mid-1980s.

While overall priorities are expressed in this way, they do not necessarily tell the envelope committees how they should behave or what *they* should do. What should the priorities be *within* the economic development envelope and the social envelope? What criteria should govern resource allocation? Ten or so ministers, including the policy committee chairman, must somehow decide what to do. How much of the current "A" base should continue? What new initiatives are needed? What can we afford? How will it affect our political support and standing in the country? What *is* social policy? What do we mean by economic development?

A closer look at the ideas inherent in the criteria for allocating funds prescribed by the major envelope committees, and at the envelope expenditure decision process itself, will show that there is some consistency with the stated priorities. There are, however, some quite fundamental contradictions among the ideas, which can only be resolved by political judgement and compromise and, above all, by political *power* (someone "winning" and others "losing"). We will look at three of the major envelopes as well as one special unofficial envelope, the Western Development Fund, to highlight trends and problems, and to suggest questions that are raised. Each envelope committee is a unique structure and has its own dynamics as it relates to the pressures and ideas inherent in its policy domain.

Resource Allocation in Economic Development

The Cabinet Committee on Economic Development and its supporting Ministry of State for Economic Development (MSED) had in 1981 inherited all the trials and tribulations of Canada's never ending effort to construct an industrial strategy[14] (see Chapter 15). The policy and allocative dilemmas in industrial policy are numerous. What industries should be supported? Which ones should be phased out? In what regions of the country? Should certain Crown corporations be favoured over private firms? Its envelope included numerous economic departments and agencies and an array of grants, incentives, subsidies and regulations. Key participants in the committee and in MSED were aware of previous, usually frustrating, efforts to develop industrial policy. These past efforts are briefly surveyed to show how different ideas emerged, how structures were altered to try to achieve policy results, and to show the importance of political memory, the need to try "something" different when the past produces failure or unsatisfactory results.

For the purposes of this chapter, we identify two phases in the attempt to devise an industrial policy and then to allocate resources accordingly. (Chapter 15 examines these phases in greater detail.) The first phase from the early 1960s to the early 1970s involved a patchwork of industry-by-industry and some across-the-board incentives and programs produced without much systematic consultation with business and labour. These programs were devised and implemented with only the most tenuous kind of coordination within the federal government. This phase coincided with relative economic prosperity. For those regions that wanted industry but did not have it, the federal government offered the Department of Regional Economic Expansion (DREE). For Atlantic Canada and even Eastern Quebec, DREE came to be increasingly viewed as *their* department.

The second phase, from the early 1970s until 1978, was ostensibly focused on industry but was different in that it involved a somewhat more concerted attempt by the federal government to consult business and labour organizations. The period of wage and price controls from 1975 to 1978 was a particularly important catalyst in pressuring the government to consult these major interests or, at the very least, to be *seen* consulting them.[15] Even though it was thought to be necessary, the consultations with major business and labour interest groups were not particularly successful. However, a somewhat different effort in 1978 involved 23 industry sector task forces composed of business and labour representatives. These task forces produced specific suggestions for each sector, many in the form of a veritable flood of requests for tax benefits. A "tier-two" group also produced general recommendations concerning such questions as manpower skill shortages, research and development and the need to encourage capital investment to avoid the further "de-industrialization" of Canada.

This second phase was also characterized by a more serious attempt to coordinate the federal government's own initiatives. The attempt was first reflected in the formation of "DM-10," a group of economic deputy ministers during the controls program. This in turn was part of the catalyst that lead to the formation in 1978 of the Board of Economic Development Ministers (BEDM). This became the Cabinet Committee on Economic Development, later renamed the Cabinet Committee on Economic and Regional Development.

It should not be surprising to note that the instinct of practical politicians is to think of the decisions they make in terms of benefits and support for particular industries in their regions and constituencies. It is not easy or even comfortable for them to think in terms of longer-term economic *development* needs. Officials in the MSED, however, began to try to persuade ministers to think (and, they hoped, act) differently on the subject. This effort, plus the obvious evidence of economic malaise in the late 1970s, resulted in the announcement in 1980 of an eight point agenda by Senator Bud Olson, the Minister of State for Economic Development. The agenda was expressed in terms of the factors or elements that contribute to economic development rather than in terms of particular industries. The "industry" focus of the earlier phase was broken, at least symbolically. The Olson agenda stressed the eight factors involved in development, namely, human resource development, capital investment, energy development, natural resources, technology, infra-structure, institutions and market development. The general thrust was to support capital development and to de-emphasize current consump-tion and "uneconomic" subsidies. The former would support efficiency, while the latter was viewed as a form of welfare. This focus was later reflected in such decisions as the reduction of VIA Rail subsidies, and on the Crow's Nest freight rate issue (see below).

This basic example by no means captures all of the political reality of economic development. It is a mere snapshot in time. But it shows some of the ideas in conflict and the tension between political instincts, an agenda that refuses to stand still, and the time-frame of decisions. A closely related example of resource-allocation expenditures in Western Canada also shows the dilemmas and, moreover, demonstrates the constant need not only for regional sensitivity but also for "special" allocative procedures and structures to handle special political problems, a tendency we saw in abundance in Chapter 10.

The Western Development Fund: Handling "Special" Resource Allocation Problems

The Trudeau Liberals' early 1980s strategy to woo voters in Western Canada and to enhance economic development in the West was tied symbolically to a Western Development Fund. Announced initially as a $4 billion dollar fund with $2 billion to be spent in the 1981-82 to 1983-84 period, the fund shrank in the revised plan announced in 1981. The commitment then was for $148 million to be spent in 1981-82, $182 million in 1982-83 and $375 million in 1983-84. For 1984-85 and 1985-86 a further $415 million and $400 million, respectively, was to be allocated to the fund. The reason for the shrinkage is that the original sums were pulled from the air, since no one knew what revenue flows would arise from the energy agreement with Alberta being negotiated in 1980. The Liberals were on the horns of a dilemma. The idea of the fund was a political move to help symbolize their Western strategy. In fact, however, sums of money much larger than the Western Development Fund would be spent in Western Canada. For example, large amounts of the Energy envelope (see below) would be spent there.

While the initial development of the fund was characterized by political confusion, the subsequent decision in 1982 to focus the bulk of the fund on one major issue, Western transportation and the historic Crow's Nest controversy, reflected an occasion when a longer-term view was taken. A much smaller but not unimportant sum of money from the Western Development Fund was also allocated to the Social Affairs envelope (see below) to deal with the social and economic needs of native people.

The chances were high when the Western Development Fund was first announced that the moneys would be distributed "pork barrel" style into dozens of small projects "liberally" sprinkled into numerous communities, especially those deemed potentially "winnable" by Liberal strategists. The fund was a part of the economic development envelope and hence of its Cabinet committee. But the decisions were influenced by the special Cabinet Committee on Western Affairs, a committee needed to compensate for the lack of Western representation in the Liberal Cabinet. The Liberals, however, decided to take a longer-term approach. The decision to focus on the Crow transportation question was strongly influenced by the "discipline" of the envelope decision process, and reflects one area of coherence with the priorities of the Economic Development Committee and MSED outlined above. The Crow's Nest decision sought to induce capital and infrastructure investment by the railways, reduce "uneconomic" subsidies, and promote resource development and spin-off manufacturing benefits in the West.[16]

The Liberals decided that they would hit the Crow issue head on. The statutory Crow's Nest rates for shipping grain can be traced to a historic pact in 1897 among farmers, the railways and the federal government. It has resulted in heavily subsidized transportation costs for shipping grain. In 1982 grain accounted for about 20 percent of the railways freight business but garnered only 3.5 percent of revenues. The railways have been reluctant to invest in new transportation infrastructure needed not only for expanded grain exports but, even more importantly, for other resources in the expected resource boom. To break the log jam one had to deal with the Crow rates.

The Minister of Transport, Jean-Luc Pepin, announced the broad outline of the Liberal decision on February 8, 1982. The Liberals would spend $1.3 billion over the next four years on top of $1.85 billion previously committed for railway transportation.[17] Farmers were assured that there would still be a statutory rate, but one that would have a built-in escalation formula to deal with increasing costs. The increased amount that farmers would have to pay would be set after a period of negotiations. The railways would be required to produce performance guarantees. These would include some guarantee that a very high percentage of the spin-off procurement and development would occur in the West.

The politics and economics of the Crow decision on resource allocation is both complex and interesting and raises questions about the meaning of budgetary language and its relationship to dominant ideas. The then existing statutory "subsidies" to farmers were viewed by the NDP and some prairie farm organizations, especially in Saskatchewan, as a social pact, a "Magna Carta" of Confederation. It promoted stability and equity for farmers, as well as a partial redress of Western grievances against Eastern Canada. In their view it was the villainous CPR that was "subsidized" in the first instance by a generous grant of federal lands and the resources that went with them. The question of what constitutes capital development as opposed to social welfare is indeed often a moot point. Was the economic committee making a social policy decision? In part, it was.

It must be stressed that there was no ringing cry in 1981 emanating from Western indigenous interest groups to solve the Crow issue. While some farm groups did recognize that the current level of subsidies for farmers could not continue, they were not clamouring for change. To gain a Western-based constituency interested in changing the Crow, the Liberals had to create one, or at least encourage it to come out of the political underbrush. This was in line with the general Liberal strategy in 1981 to build direct bridges with indigenous Western groups and to skirt provincial governments. The principal constituency that helped carry the Liberal message was a broad umbrella of about 60 resource-based companies, including companies in the agri-food industry which would benefit most from a breakthrough in the Crow issue. To this coalition was added some farm groups. These groups in total would benefit because the resolved Crow issue would enable the transportation system to be modernized and would allow several resources (grain, coal, sulphur, potash, etc.) to be developed with potentially higher Canadian and Western Canadian "value added" economic benefits.

The Western transportation system was a genuine obstacle to

future economic development. Moreover, it is largely a matter of federal jurisdiction. The Crow's Nest issue was also tackled by the Liberals on the assumption that Ottawa could play a divide and conquer strategy against the four Western provincial governments. Each province has a different stake in the issue depending upon the nature of its economy and its own political strategy. British Columbia and Alberta interests tend to gain from the resolution of the issue because it could potentially benefit their resource-based economies and their historical desire for economic diversification. Saskatchewan opposed it strongly because the elimination of the then existing statutory subsidies threatened the continued existence of many small prairie towns. Saskatchewan, moreover, would benefit much less from resource spin-offs. The then new NDP government of Manitoba had initially aligned itself with Saskatchewan. But in the longer term, the Manitoba-Saskatchewan alliance was a fragile one. This was because the more diversified but still depressed Manitoba economy stood to benefit from the spin-offs of the Crow changes, especially in agri-business. Moreover, the Pauley government had promised to cooperate with Ottawa because it believed that the political pugilism of the previous Tory government of Sterling Lyon hurt Manitoba badly.

In political and electoral terms, the Liberals calculated at the time that some seats were winnable in Manitoba and British Columbia, but not elsewhere. But nothing was guaranteed. In the medium term the Crow issue could also lose the Liberals political support in Ontario and Quebec where industries could eventually be adversely affected by breaking the Crow-based economic logjam. Political risks existed for the federal Tories and the NDP as well. The NDP's opposition to the changes in the Crow rates easily led to their being portrayed as a group opposed to major change, indeed of being defenders of the nineteenth century. Meanwhile, the federal Tories faced problems with their powerful Alberta wing if they opposed the Crow changes too strongly.

Finally, the Crow issue raised a recurring central economic development dilemma, the balance between resources and manufacturing. Did the breaking of the transportation logjam merely increase the speed at which Canada sold its resources? It also raised questions about how the federal government maintains political leverage on the economic decision makers to ensure that both Canadian content *and* Western content benefits accrue *over time*? In the first stage, this involved the need to obtain leverage primarily over the CPR and CNR to ensure that performance criteria were met as the new transportation facilities are built. In the second stage, this involved quite different problems of obtaining leverage over 60 or 70 resource-based companies (government-owned and private) which benefited from the transportation infrastructure that was built.

Resource Allocation for Social Development

The Social Affairs envelope consists primarily of transfer payments such as old age security, the guaranteed income supplement and the Canada Assistance Plan.[18] The social development committee is also concerned about the so-called Established Programs Financing (EPF) arrangements with the provinces for the support of education and health care, but the EPF negotiations are controlled by the Priorities and Planning Committee. In addition, the envelope contains expenditures on labour markets and training, cultural programs, environment, housing, fitness and amateur sport and programs for Native Canadians. Many of these programs are statutory and thus not easily changed. In 1981, however, the EPF programs were being renegotiated. This imposed an immediate reality of power on the Cabinet Committee on Social Development, namely that negotiations were in the hands of the Minister of Finance, who wanted to reduce federal commitments from their projected levels if the existing EPF agreement had continued.

In viewing the Social Affairs envelope, one must always keep in mind the three dimensions that have characterized Canadian social policy over the years. Social policy embraces the idea of redistribution of income to low income Canadians as well as the idea of equity through universal programs. It also includes vague "quality of life" ideas. The latter can include culture, health care and ideas as ill-defined as national unity and national identity. The increasing challenge has been to find ways to support these disparate purposes within the context of shrinking dollars. One must also keep in mind that the boundary between social and economic policy is extremely blurred, regardless of how the government and academic disciplines try to carve society into sectors.

Table 11.2 shows that in 1981 the Social Affairs envelope was by far the largest of the expenditure categories, but would grow the least rapidly of the major envelopes over the next several years. The envelope, moreover, was not given a policy reserve for new initiatives. Any room for new policy initiatives had to come primarily from within the envelope through savings from existing programs. But the projected rates of growth set out in the November 1981 Budget were significantly better than those set out in the October 1980 Budget. These increases were due to the growing social pressure caused by a stagnant economy and high inflation, the inevitable internal pressure from ministers and officials who wanted social policy initiatives to increase, especially in anticipation of the next election, and the increased capacity of the Cabinet Committee on Social Development and its secretariat in the Ministry of State for Social Development (MSSD) to play the envelope game with greater ingenuity.

In 1980 the Cabinet Committee on Social Development and MSSD, then in its first year of existence, tried to guide its decisions by identifying four very broad goals: the improvement of the quality of life; the reduction of poverty; the assurance of "social justice"; and the enhancement of a sense of national identity. In addition, visible target groups were identified, namely, the elderly, the handicapped, native people, women and young people. There was a connection between these target groups and the federal initiative to entrench a Charter of Rights, eventually passed into law in 1982.

In 1981 the Social Development ministers, while maintaining these objectives and target groups, chose to redefine their approach to give it a slightly harder economic edge, a line of argument more conducive to appealing to the economic priorities of the majority of the Trudeau Cabinet. They began to couch social initiatives in the context of the obvious social effects of the high rates of inflation rampant in 1981. This view was reflected in the measures announced in the Budget Speech of November 1981 to assist those having difficulties meeting mortgage payments due to high interest rates. In a more general way the Social Affairs ministers tried to stress that inflation's greatest effects were on the elderly, and on low income families, the majority of which were headed by single women. This general line of argument and pressure was designed to help pave the way for any one or all of three social initiatives which ministers thought would have a significant electoral impact in 1984-85:

- A further increase in the Guaranteed Income Supplement (GIS) especially to bring elderly single women and men above the

poverty line. This could cost about 600 million dollars annually.
- A greatly expanded child tax credit financed by eliminating the child tax exemptions in the income tax system and by altering the system of family allowance payments. This could redistribute income to low income Canadians in a significant way.
- The reform of pensions, particularly by trying to force improvements in private pension plans or, if necessary, in the Canada Pension Plan.

There is always a mixture of high and low political calculus involved in deciding how much redistribution is enough—enough to help in human terms, and enough to secure electoral victory by not alienating the majority middle-class voter.

A second social policy tune increasingly strummed by the Social Development ministers was that of ensuring that the adjustments needed by thousands of individual Canadians (including those in the targeted groups identified above) who were the objects or victims of the federal economic development strategy were treated in an individual human context. Economic ministers were being reminded by their social counterparts that social adjustment is a necessary corollary or even prerequisite to economic development. In this vein, the Social Development Committee successfully claimed and acquired custody of $345 million from the Western Development Fund to be directed towards native peoples, including nonstatus Indians and Metis located in the inner cities, particularly in Western Canada.

In a similar way, funds for manpower training and higher education were being viewed as social expenditures with economic policy clout.[19] The federal proposals for manpower training tabled in 1981 by the Minister of Employment and Immigration envisioned a direct federal role in identifying and funding certain critical national occupational/skill needs that are deemed essential for economic development. Another significant feature of the proposals was that women would be needed in large numbers to fill many of the jobs. Labour force demands were expected to be so far in excess of the available male population that women would be needed in large numbers. Thus, women's issues increasingly could take on the hue of being an economic necessity rather than a social frill, as they had often been perceived by conservatives in the past.

The overall reality, however, was that the Social Affairs envelope did not contain much room for manoeuvre in the short term. But pressure was building up within it. The pressure increased as an election drew closer. The new social policy initiatives emerging within the envelope would exceed three billion dollars in 1985-86, about a 7 percent increase in the Social Affairs envelope. It was highly unlikely, however, that all of these initiatives could be implemented.

This internal agenda within the Cabinet Committee on Social Development added even more impetus to the Liberal's need in 1981 and 1982 to settle the EPF and equalization financial arrangements then being negotiated with the provinces.[20] The "savings" from these arrangements would create only a small part of the expenditure reserve for new initiatives such as pensions, the expanded child tax credit, and the guaranteed income supplement. Each of these initiatives would, in addition, be dependent upon different financial arrangements. Pension costs could be forced on the private sector, although it could also cost the government tax expenditure dollars. The child tax credit could be financed by rearranging existing child benefit programs. The guaranteed income supplement would require new funds from outside the Social Affairs envelope.

The envelope system has not been the only mechanism created to coordinate social programs. At one stage the Department of Health and Welfare, despite its large operational role, was virtually a central agency for social policy purposes. In the mid-1960s, in the midst of the burgeoning social policy initiatives of the Pearson government, a special planning secretariat was created in the PCO to review Canada's "war on poverty." In the early 1970s a special social security policy review was launched involving the Department of Health and Welfare and the Privy Council Office. It is examined in detail in Chapter 14. These efforts were more episodic than the envelope system and were not tied as closely to the actual resource allocation process.

Resource Allocation in Energy Policy

Energy policy is the final policy field whose 1981-82 envelope resource allocation experience we review as a case study. (Chapter 16 deals with energy policy in greater detail and in a broader historical context.) The energy envelope in 1981 had its special characteristics, not the least of which was that it was the primary vehicle for making decisions to implement the 1980 National Energy Program, the priority issue on which the Liberals staked their greatest political prestige during this period.

The Energy envelope was established as a separate new expenditure envelope in 1980 to ensure that the goals of the National Energy Program (NEP) were adopted. Decisions about expenditures were made by the Cabinet Committee on Economic Development. For energy decisions, however, the parallel group of deputy ministers was not the economic deputies, but rather a much smaller group of energy deputies.[21] The Energy envelope was effectively controlled by Energy Minister, Marc Lalonde, and senior officials in the Department of Energy, Mines and Resources (EMR).

Among the three major envelopes, the Energy envelope was projected in 1981 to have the highest overall rate of growth between then and 1985-86. Table 11.2 shows growth rates of 13.8, 18.5, 14.2 and 16.1 percent for each year, respectively. These energy figures, however, were only the visible part of the energy expenditure iceberg. They did not include expenditures from the Canadian Ownership Account. This account contains the revenues collected through the special Canadian Ownership Charge imposed on oil and gas consumers in Canada to be used to acquire one or more privately owned oil companies. Several billions were being raised through these charges. Petro-Canada's $1.4 billion acquisition of Petrofina in 1981 was financed through this account. The management of the Canadian Ownership Account was even more closely controlled than the Energy envelope. Because of the sensitivity of these takeover decisions, control rested with the Priorities and Planning Committee of Cabinet and a handful of EMR and Finance officials.

The criteria applied to the energy allocations emanated from the stated purposes of the NEP: security of supply; opportunity for Canadians to participate; and fairness regarding pricing and revenue sharing. In short, the NEP was to promote stability (in the sense of easing the threat of disruptions of imported oil), equity (among regions) and national identity (through Canadianization of the industry). However, the reality of expenditure politics and of governing Canada made it difficult to confine the energy allocations to these criteria and these ideas alone.

Table 11.3 shows the then projected Energy envelope expenditures until 1985-86. The first item to note is the sharp decline in petroleum compensation payments, the program created in the early 1970s to

TABLE 11.3
SUMMARY OF ENERGY ENVELOPE EXPENDITURES
(millions of dollars)

	1980-81	1981-82	1982-83	1983-84	1984-85	1985-86
Net petroleum compensation payments	2,684	120	—	—	—	—
Federal share of costs for the petroleum incentive program	—	940	1,040	1,150	1,480	1,850
Other energy expenditures	940	1,611	1,999	2,452	2,635	2,929
TOTAL	3,624	2,671	3,039	3,602	4,115	4,779

Source: Canada, *The Budget in More Detail*, November 12, 1981, p. 21.

compensate Eastern Canadian refiners dependent upon more expensive foreign oil. This budgetary decline is in part a product of fiscal sleight of hand, since the scheme has been replaced by new charges to Canadians under the Petroleum Compensation Charge. Thus, Canadian "consumers" were then paying the cost rather than Canadian "taxpayers," a distinction without much of a difference to most Canadians, though of great importance to persons concerned with the appearance of public expenditures and embarrassing deficits. The change in the base of payment could also have different distributional effects.

From 1982-83 on, the Energy envelope is shown to contain two types of expenditures, those on the petroleum incentives program for industry and those on the other energy activities contained in the NEP. The incentives program for industry included the new system of exploration grants to Canadian-owned firms. Included in the "other" category in Table 11.3 are the incentives to Canadians to switch off oil. Both of the incentive programs were difficult to estimate. This is because they are essentially demand-driven programs, dependent on the willingness of Canadians to accept the incentives and switch off oil and on the speed with which the energy industry can "Canadianize" to take up the grants. Demand for the incentives is in turn a function of general energy prices as well as of the reliability of information about which nonoil energy source (gas or electricity) one should use. The signals to consumers on the alternatives are ambiguous at best and vary by region. For example, there were indications in 1981 that Ottawa would like Quebec residents to switch to electricity, but the deficit-ridden Quebec government discouraged this directly or indirectly by taxing electricity to produce more revenue, thus discouraging demand. These types of "demand-driven" programs are an especially good example of the role of private behaviour in the implementation of policy, a point stressed in Chapters 1, 5 and 6.

As for other energy expenditures in the envelope, there are also analogous problems which produced a large amount of unspent ("lapsed") funds because programs could not possibly be geared up as rapidly as NEP enthusiasts initially envisioned. For example, the funds for Petro-Canada International, the Third World arm of Petro-Canada, were not spent as quickly as first thought. Energy expenditures on research and development depended on the availability of competent researchers as much as they did on hard cash. Similarly, funds required for mega-projects such as the giant Alsands project were subject to bargaining and delays. Later, in 1982, the Alsands project was cancelled.

The largest single energy expenditure of 1981-82 was the Petro-Canada acquisition of Petrofina, noted above. As mentioned, this does not appear in the Energy envelope per se. It was but one of the takeovers triggered by the NEP. Most were private takeovers, but two of the three largest, the Petro-Canada takeover and the Canada Development Corporation's acquisition of Aquitaine, were strongly mandated or encouraged by the federal government. The total result of the acqusitions were to increase Canadian ownership by about 6 percent and Canadian control by about 10 percent. The overall pace of acquisitions, however, had been slowed by the related effects of an unprecedented outflow of Canadian capital in 1980-81. This outflow was caused only partly by the NEP.[22] It was also caused by other related issues which affected the climate of investment in 1981, including high interest rates, the threatened changes in the Foreign Investment Review Agency (FIRA), and the pro-business views of the Reagan government in the United States which made investment south of the border more attractive. The energy envelope did not fully reflect energy expenditures because it did not include most of Petro-Canada's investment and expenditure activity.

There is one further overall feature of the Energy envelope in 1981 which deserves emphasis. The envelope appears from the projections in

Table 11.2 to have been a prosperous one in 1981, but this was, in part, misleading. The envelope was tightly controlled in the sense that only a small handful of ministers and officials made the decisions. At the same time, however, there was a sense in which the Energy envelope and energy expenditures in general were out of control. The lack of control was caused not just by the demand-driven nature of the incentive programs referred to earlier or by the newness of the NEP, but also because the NEP made numerous public commitments for expenditures which energy decision makers knew could not be met. The energy expenditure reserves were evaporating, the victims of a future which refused to cooperate with the fragile projections on which NEP expenditures, prices and revenues were based. However, because so much political prestige had been invested by the Liberals on the NEP, the commitments were made, nonetheless.

It is instructive to point out that prior to the late 1970s and the establishment of the Energy envelope in 1980, energy policy, while important, did not enjoy a quasi or real central agency status. Nor will it necessarily remain as a separate envelope in the future. The central policy categories change as political circumstances change. For example, defence expenditures, though still large, were even more dominant in the World War II and postwar periods. During this period the Defence Department and the Department of Defence Production functioned much like a central agency in de facto political and resource allocation terms.

Conclusions

In this chapter we have not covered all of the dimensions or subordinate policy fields reflected either by the titles of Cabinet committees or by the composition of expenditure categories and envelopes. More attributes of resource allocation, especially in the tax and regulatory processes, are examined in Chapter 12. It is there that we attempt an overall assessment of Ottawa's envelopes and of systems that might replace the envelope concept. In short, we raise questions about how one would go about devising criteria to judge the ideal or successful resource-allocation system. A more complete appreciation of the role of ministers and deputies in resource allocation must await the examination of knowledge and information in Chapter 13. Other major substantive policy fields, such as foreign and defence policy, are examined in Chapter 14.

All that we have been able to present in this chapter is a broad look at the general processes and dynamics of policy making and resource allocation and at the evolving criticism of these processes. We have also seen glimpses of some of the continuity and discontinuity of the ideas, structures and processes reflected in resource allocation in the economic development, social policy and energy policy fields, as well as in the effort to coordinate regionally defined policies for Western Canada. Though we have used examples from the 1981-82 period as brief case studies, and though machinery may change, the underlying ideas and dilemmas do not change very much. The capsule glimpses invariably show the slippery boundaries between policy fields as different ideas and organizing concepts are tried, discarded or recombined. When combined with the analysis of priorities and priority setting in Chapter 10, they convey some sense of the tasks of governing where the past, the present and several views of the preferred but uncertain future clash in a maddeningly untidy way.

NOTES

1. See Douglas Hartle, *The Expenditure Budget Process in the Government of Canada* (Toronto: Canadian Tax Foundation, 1978); Royal Commission on Financial Management and Accountability, *Final Report* (Ottawa: Minister of Supply and Services, 1979); Douglas Hartle, *The Revenue Budget Process of the Government of Canada* (Toronto: Canadian Tax Foundation, 1982) and David Good, *The Politics of Anticipation: Making Canadian Federal Tax Policy* (Ottawa: School of Public Administration, Carleton University, 1980).
2. The fiscal role of the Department of Finance must be distinguished from its broader and declining role in economic management. See Richard W. Phidd and G. Bruce Doern, *The Politics and Management of Canadian Economic Policy* (Toronto: Macmillan of Canada, 1978), Chapters 1, 7, 13 and 14.
3. See Thomas J. Courchene, *The Strategy of Gradualism* (Montreal: C.D. Howe Research Institute, 1978); and Arthur W. Donner and Douglas D. Peters, *Monetarist Counter-Revolution* (Ottawa: Canadian Institute for Economic Policy, 1979).

4. See Hartle, *The Expenditure Process, op. cit.,* Chapter 2.

5. The classic reference is still Aaron Wildavsky, *The Politics of the Budgetary Process,* Third Edition, (Boston: Little Brown, 1979).

6. See Phidd and Doern, *op. cit.,* Chapter 1.

7. Hartle, *The Expenditure Budget Process, op. cit.,* Chapter 5; Royal Commission on Financial Management and Accountability, *op. cit.,* Chapter 5; and G. Bruce Doern and Allan Maslove, *The Public Evaluation of Government Spending* (Montreal: Institute for Research on Public Policy, 1979), Chapter 1.

8. On the needs and dilemmas of evaluation, see Rodney Dobell and David Zussman, "An evaluation system for government: if politics is theatre, then evaluation is (mostly) art," *Canadian Public Administration,* Vol. 24, No. 3, pp. 404-427.

9. See Sharon L. Sutherland, "The Office of the Auditor General of Canada: Watching the Watchdog," in G. Bruce Doern, ed., *How Ottawa Spends Your Tax Dollars 1981* (Toronto: James Lorimer Publishers, 1981), Chapter 6.

10. Treasury Board, "Policy and Expenditure Management System: Envelope Procedures and Rules." (Mimeo copy, dated July 1, 1981), pp. 1-2.

11. *Ibid.,* p. 3.

12. *Ibid.,* pp. 3-4.

13. See G. Bruce Doern, ed., *How Ottawa Spends Your Tax Dollars 1982* (Toronto: James Lorimer Publishers, 1982), Chapter 1. For ongoing annual reviews of Ottawa's main expenditure categories on which this chapter is partly based, see the School of Public Administration's annual publication cited above.

14. See Richard French, *How Ottawa Decides* (Toronto: James Lorimer Publishers, 1980), Chapter 5.

15. David I. Langille, "From Consultation to Corporatism," M.A. Research Essay, Department of Political Science, Carleton University, 1982.

16. For the transportation context of these decisions, see John W. Langford, "Transport Canada and the Transport Ministry: the Attempt to Retreat to Basics" in G. Bruce Doern, ed., *How Ottawa Spends Your Tax Dollars 1982, op. cit.,* Chapter 7.

17. Minister of Transport, "Policy Statement on Western Rail Transportation," Ottawa, February 8, 1982. For other background on the Crow see David R. Harvey, *Christmas Turkey or Prairie Vulture?* (Montreal: Institute for Research on Public Policy, 1980) and Howard Darling, *The Politics of Freight Rates* (Toronto: McClelland and Stewart, 1980).

18. On social programs in general, see James Rice and Michael Prince, *Social Policy and Social Administration in Canada* (Manuscript in press); Economic Council of Canada, *Financing Confederation* (Ottawa: Minister of Supply and Services, 1982), Chapter 6 and 7; and Keith G. Banting, *The*

Welfare State and Canadian Federation (Montreal: McGill-Queen's University Press, 1982). See also Chapter 14.

19. See Employment and Immigration Canada, *Labour Market Development in the 1980s* (Ottawa: Minister of Supply and Services, 1980).
20. Economic Council of Canada, *op. cit.,* Chapter 6.
21. See G. Bruce Doern and Glen Toner, *The NEP and the Politics of Energy* (Toronto: Methuen, 1984). Chapter 9.
22. See Stephen Clarkson, *Canada and the Reagan Challenge* (Ottawa: Canadian Institute for Economic Policy 1982), Chapter 7.

CHAPTER 12

GOVERNING INSTRUMENTS, POLICY PROCESSES AND RESOURCE ALLOCATION

In this chapter we look even further and more comprehensively into the dynamics of resource allocation. This time our focus is on the major governing instruments and on the ideas, structures and processes they embrace. In Chapter 11 we focused on the most familiar aspects of resource allocation, the general revenue-expenditure process and on the major policy fields. These are processsses which operate in part with lives of their own and in part in relation to each other. The same is true for the dynamics defined by basic governing instruments. There is an expenditure process, a tax process, a regulatory process, and so on. At the same time we know that governments have to coordinate, bring together, or make some aggregate sense of all of these instrument processes and choices as they operate in numerous policy fields *concurrently*.

In Chapter 5 we surveyed the basic characteristics of the main instruments—exhortation, expenditure, taxation, regulation and public ownership. This survey included an account of their growth and the several ideological explanations of that growth, their relationship to the coercive powers of the state, the connection between instruments, ideas and the means-ends dilemma of democratic political life, and the relationship between instruments, structures and processes. The last of these topics, in turn, enabled us to relate governing instruments to such issues as the substitution of one instrument for another (for example, taxing for spending), legal and jurisdictional constraints on instrument use, and the relationship of instrument choice to the implementation of policy, including the inducement of changes in private behaviour.

We have also used the concept of governing instruments in our analysis of interest groups in Chapter 4, relating it to consultative processes. Consultation could be either a prelude to or a substitute for other more concrete action (that is, decisions to tax, spend or regulate). We also stressed the problem of what happens when the modern political climate, including media politics, creates pressure to such an extent that governing politicians do not seem to have the option of "doing nothing." They must, at a minimum, *be seen* doing *something*. We advanced the proposition that in any political setting, politicians trade in a market of governing instruments. If the availability of spending is reduced, politicians will regulate more or tax more or do something "for show," including the genuine need to show concern. Government is therefore like a balloon. If you squeeze it in one place, it bulges somewhere else. The concept of governing instruments also helps us see why it is possible, indeed inevitable, that there will be policies with varying resource commitments, including policies without concrete resources. Some policies may merely be expressions of concern. Others may include overtly tough regulations but backed by only limited enforcement. Still others may be backed by full resource support (taxing, spending, regulating and other instruments). The same policy, more-over, may be given different degrees of resource support at different times, as the policy evolves or as its place in the priority list changes.

As was the case in Chapter 11, it is best to digest these important features of public policy in small doses. Figure 12.1 is intended to help guide the way. It is a slightly more complex version of the figure used to introduce Chapter 11. It shows the full array of outputs, not just expenditures and taxation, by adding regulation, public enterprise and exhortation, but it contains the same ideas through which these

FIGURE 12.1
RESOURCE ALLOCATION AND GOVERNING INSTRUMENTS

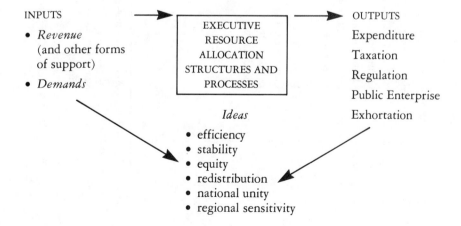

TABLE 12.1
INSTRUMENTS AND POLICY PROCESSES: A PROFILE OF CHARACTERISTICS AND REFORM IDEAS

	Expenditure	Taxation	Regulation	Public Enterprise	Exhortation
Basic Characteristics	• Quantified • Multi-minister and departmental participation and bargaining • Recognized Central Agency point(s) of coordination	• Partially quantified • Focused Ministerial Power (Finance) • Limited bargainings due to secrecy and limits on ability to consult private interests • Recognized central agency	• Limited quantification • Multi-minister and departmental agency-participation • Limited bargaining over content of regulations but considerable over severity of enforcement • No easily recognized central agency	• Limited quantification • Multi-minister and agency involvement • Independent sources of revenue • No easily recognized central agency	• Nonquantified • Multi-minister "leadership" and involvement • Numerous discrete acts of persuasion and information • Production of Policies "for show" or to express symbolic concern • No recognized central agency
Reform Ideas and Events Since 1970	• Auditor General's call for value for Money Practices • Lambert Report	• Carter Commission "A Dollar is a Dollar" • 1972 "Corporate Welfare Bums" Tax	• Increased Public Participation and Hearings • Socioeconomic Impact Statements	• PCO Blue Report of 1976 • Lambert Report • Privatization • Single Window Concept	• Information Canada • Growth of monitoring and advisory agencies • Advocacy Advertising

• Call for program evaluation • Indexing of social expenditures • Spending growth limits to trend line GNP increases • Reduce size of civil service • Charging for services • The Envelope System	• Debate • Indexation of tax system • Tax Expenditure Debate • Budget Consultation • Lower Marginal Rates • The Deficit • Simplify the Tax System • The Envelope System	• Deregulation • Reducing the Paper Burden • A Guidelines approach • Economic Council of Canada reports • The Envelope System	• Expansion of Public Enterprise • Open Policy Subsidization • Clark and Trudeau Draft Bills on Crown Corporations	• More studies and royal commissions and less as well • New consultative exercises
Basic Informational Documents (Existing or Proposed) • Blue Book (Estimates) • Public Accounts • 5-Year Fiscal Plan • Strategic Overviews • Multi-Year Operations	• Budget Speech and Papers • Tax Expenditure Account	• *Canada Gazette* • Proposed Regulatory Calendar (a regulatory "Blue Book") • A regulatory budget	• Annual Reports • Five Year Corporate Plans and annual Capital Budgets	• Speeches • Press Releases • Advertisement

instruments are ultimately judged and debated. Table 12.1 takes us into a more detailed look, not only in a static way but also with reference to the influence of the reform ideas advanced since about 1970 for each of the main instruments. We refer to this table continuously throughout the chapter. It shows that the chapter focuses on three ways of analyzing the ideas, structures and processes.

First, we characterize the basic dynamics of each instrument. Then we show how each instrument process, separately, has been the subject of pressures for reform in the 1970s and 1980s. The ideas advocated through such pressure embrace a broad ideological spectrum of political debate. We then show at the end of the chapter how each process produces its own array of key information documents. The latter information helps pave the way for our analysis of the role of knowledge and information in Chapter 13. Finally, we bring these disaggregated processes back together. Since the envelope system analyzed in Chapter 11 also aspired to integrate instrument choice as well as policy fields, this final section in the chapter will allow us to understand the overall resource allocation process in a more complete way.

The Expenditure Process

Since we have already dealt at some length with the expenditure process in Chapter 11, our analysis here can be more succinct than for the other processes discussed below. Three basic characteristics of the expenditure process deserve emphasis. First, it is a highly quantified process. The ideas and priorities of political life can be translated into the common denominator of dollars. This produces at least some kind of comparability, much more so, as we will see, than occurs, for example, in the regulatory process. Quantification does not itself eliminate policy controversy, but it helps to bring the process to somewhat more manageable proportions.

The expenditure process is also characterized by the active participation, bargaining and log-rolling of numerous ministers and officials. The bargaining is somewhat more peaceful and politically enjoyable if the participants are bargaining over a growing expenditure pie, as was the case in the 1960s and early 1970s. In conditions of severe restraint where there are "X budgets" to be carved from the expenditure base, the expenditure process is almost by definition more conflict-oriented. The fact that expenditure bargaining, at least over details, goes on over several months in a typical year is also important politically since it allows ministers and officials "to win some" and "lose some" and thus generate some sense of political peace and fair play. In a large unwieldy Cabinet and bureaucracy this is a by-product of no small importance.

Compared to some of the other processes discussed below, the expenditure process has a highly visible and well-recognized point of central agency coordination. Historically, this has been the Treasury Board. Since 1979 the central point of coordination has been the policy sector Cabinet committees and the Treasury Board.

Table 12.1 shows the events and ideas that have been part of the continuous effort to reform the expenditure process and other processes as well. These ideas emerge from both the political left and the political right, with the latter gaining greater support as the 1970s ended and the 1980s began. The left of centre political ideas were reflected in the advocacy of increased expenditures, especially in social programs and in a reluctance to support measures to promote better program evaluation. Critics on the left were aware of, and even concerned about, some expenditure waste but were unwilling to be a part of a general attack on government expenditures or processes. They were also unwilling to support any general attack on universal social programs, raising the age-old question of the unfairness and regressivity of means tests and deterrent or user fees to low income Canadians. They did support measures such as the indexation of some social programs such as old age security payments as a protection against inflation.

The right of centre political criticism of the expenditure process took many forms, and had many specific targets. The most persistent since 1970 has been the criticism of the Auditor General, Parliament's expenditure watchdog.[1] James Macdonell, the Auditor General from 1973 to 1981, was particularly skillfull in using the media to help build a political constituency critical of spending itself and of the expenditure process. Macdonell sold the concept of "value for money" auditing and secured new powers for his office. Instead of just auditing for control purposes to detect illegal and improper expenditures, the Auditor General's office would audit to see if government departments had the proper "system" in place to evaluate programs so that value for money could be determined. In short, it was believed by some that the proposed system would lead to the discovery of the government's "bottom line," the equivalent to business profit measures and calculations of return on investment.

Much of the Auditor General's simple line of argument was echoed by the Lambert Royal Commission on Financial Management created in 1976 in response to the Auditor General's criticisms.[2] To a somewhat lesser extent they were also reflected in the early work of the Comptroller General of Canada, a deputy minister level official who reports directly to the president of the Treasury Board. His task is to ensure that departments have the systems in place and that they actually carry out program evaluations.

All of the above was a nominally apolitical development clothed in the soothing ethos and language of rational managerial reform and couched in the need to allow Parliament to be "restored" to its alleged former heights as controller of the public purse. In reality the ideas were anything but apolitical. They reflected small "c" conservative ideas about, and criticisms of, the growth of government expenditure and the perceived expansionary appetites of bureaucrats and their alleged inability to manage properly.

Some of this line of criticism was undoubtedly valid. For example, there is little doubt that there were serious problems and inadequacies in the federal system for estimating and managing large capital projects and for managing the government's cash flow. Beyond these genuine problems, however, there was a deceiving and far from politically neutral simplicity to the argument. It was that, underlying the call for rational evaluation studies and better management, there was a discoverable bottom line to government activities, analogous to and as quantitatively endowed as the profit motive was to the private sector. There was little inclination among such reformers to acknowledge the multi-valued and therefore "multi-bottom" line nature of political life and of public programs. Reform lay in "getting the systems right."

The professional conservative reformers of the expenditure process had a natural ideological constituency in the broader political system. The Progressive Conservative party, both federally and in several provinces, supported the expenditure reform concepts. The larger political debate of these issues was also joined to the popularity of "bureaucracy bashing." Growing expenditures, coupled with media exposure of a few expenditure boondoggles, unpopular public service strikes in high visibility industries (for example, postal workers and air traffic controllers) and the perceived insensitivity of distant Ottawa "bureaucrats" created an easy political target. Expenditure reform became allied with proposals and promises to either cut or freeze the growth in the public service, and to eliminate or reduce the scope of collective bargaining. The June 1982 MacEachen Budget, which imposed the "6 and 5" two-year ceiling on federal public service wages and on federal administered prices virtually eliminated collective bargaining for a two-year period. It showed the political strength of this constituency of interests and ideas.[3]

Also important during this period was the link between monetarism and criticisms of expenditure growth. These ideas, as we saw in Chapter 10, were reflected in Budget Speeches in 1976 and included the government's commitment to hold federal expenditure increases to the trend line rate of increase in real GNP. This resulted in an immediate reduction in the rate of expenditure increase but not in the actual achievement of the overall commitment.

Linked to these developments, but a much more subtle reflection of them, were reform proposals to increase the use of user fees and charges and to increase revenue dependency. The central concept was simple— make citizens who use particular services pay more for them.[4] These ideas were influenced in part by the application of public choice theory to the behaviour of bureaucrats. Rational bureaucrats, it is argued, have a natural tendency to expand and oversupply goods and services or to produce output inefficiently because they are not subject to market discipline and competition.[5] By charging for services and/or making departments more dependent on their own revenue sources (that is, rather than on the revenues provided by the broader tax base and "given" to them by central budget agencies), bureaucrats would be more sensitive to consumer needs and demands, and to input costs. The idea of user fees was also revived because of the sheer need for more revenue in the face of growing deficits. Fees became a new way to "tax" without calling it taxation and sometimes without having to go through the more visible political pain of a tax change, including a formal Budget Speech.

User fees also tended to be paraded in a very misleading way as a neutral managerial tool. It is evident, however, that such fees are politically and normatively loaded. They embrace not just the nuts and bolts problems of airport fees, highway tolls, and charges for passports, but include deterrent fees for visits to doctors and hospitals, higher tuition fees, and special charges on oil consumers. Because they are often flat charges regardless of the income of the payer, they become a vehicle of reverse redistribution and therefore a tool of social policy.

Finally, we note the envelope system itself as a reform idea. It was a response to the weaknesses of the resource allocation system discussed in Chapter 11 and to the broader expenditure reform constituency identified above. We return to an analysis of its implications in the last part of this chapter.

The Tax Process

We have dealt with the tax process in a general way in Chapter 11 as the revenue half of the overall resource allocation process. In Chapter 5 we surveyed briefly the growth of taxation and the growth of tax expenditures especially since 1970, stressing that the latter had significantly reduced the progressivity of the tax system since higher income Canadians could better avail themselves of the tax "loopholes," "breaks" or "expenditures," as these benefits were variously referred to. We also stressed that the very concept of a tax expenditure, as revenue that a government chooses not to collect, is subject to intense dispute about the very purpose of government. Conservative and business opinion generally holds that such "expenditures" are not revenues that the government deigns not to collect, but is the money of ordinary Canadians that is *theirs* until it is duly and legitimately taxed.

It can be readily seen that the tax process is itself replete with its own mix of contending ideas.[6] Four of them are inherent in the purposes that the tax system has acquired over time. The tax system must produce sufficient revenue to enable the government to carry out its functions. It must acquire that revenue fairly as between taxpayers in similar income levels. Hence, the idea of horizontal equity is central to tax decisions. It must tax income according to the general principle of ability to pay and thereby contribute to the redistribution of wealth and income. Finally, it must perform all the other special public policy purposes that governments have increasingly conferred as tax expenditures through the tax system—housing, job creation, job displacement, research and development, health care, and so on.

The basic characteristics of the tax process within government can be readily identified.[7] It is a partially quantitative process, not in an across-the-board sense that the expenditure process is, but certainly in the sense that tax-revenue decisions are based on some well-established but by no means wholly accurate bases of calculation, estimation and analysis. In sharp contrast to the expenditure process, however, the tax process has a focused centre of ministerial power and very limited room for interministerial bargaining. In part this is due to the convention of Budget secrecy, a norm devised in the late nineteenth century to prevent persons from benefiting personally through advance knowledge of tax (then, usually, tariff) changes. Around the concept of Budget secrecy has been built a subtle fortress which has preserved the powers of taxation in a remarkably centralized way. Until the early 1980s only the Minister of Finance, and in the very last stages, the prime minister were privy to the Budget's content.

Two aspects of the tax process deserve particular comment, the power of the Department of Finance and the issue of the extent of tax bargaining. First the focused power of the Department of Finance over on-going *tax* decisions remains undiminished since 1970. This is not, however, the case in the department's overall role in *economic management*.[8] The latter activity, by definition, embraces policy fields departments and instruments which Finance does not control. In this broader realm there is considerable agreement that the department's role has declined. Whether this is good or bad depends upon one's criteria of evaluation, which in turn is partly a product of where one stands on the ideological spectrum.

As to the extent of tax bargaining, the conclusions vary somewhat. David Good's analysis of the tax process characterizes it broadly as the "politics of anticipation."[9] He refers here particularly to the relations between the minister (and senior tax officials) and outside groups. Secrecy and other related norms prevent the former from actually bargaining with affected interests and hence tax policy makers rely more on intelligent "anticipation." To a certain extent this is a reasonable characterization, especially when contrasted with the expenditure process. Douglas Hartle's analysis of the revenue budget process criticizes the politics of anticipation concept devised by Good.[10] In part his criticism is misplaced because he argues that Good applies his concept to relations *among* advisors within the Finance Department. In fact, Good relates his concept to Finance's external relations, that is, outside of government, where it is quite a reasonable characterization of the tax process. On the other hand, one has to be careful in utilizing the concept of anticipation in too general a way since anticipating other actors in the policy process is an inevitable part, in *some* degree, of all decision making. It will be recalled that we have used this concept in Chapters 1, 4,

7 and 10 to highlight the policy role of Parliament vis-à-vis the executive. Some limited bargaining occurs in the executive-legislative relationship, but a great deal more occurs "by anticipation."

Despite these controversies in characterization it can be said with considerable emphasis that the tax process differs from the expenditure process in significant ways and to a significant degree. Not unexpectedly, then, it has become the *object* of debate to reform it. Undoubtedly, the most sweeping event was the debate which ensued late in the 1960s and early in the 1970s in the wake of the Carter Royal Commission on Taxation. One tax expert has succinctly observed that the tax system is "anything but systematic."[11] The work of the Carter Commission in the late 1960s was the first major effort to examine the tax system in any coherent way. Its clarion call was that in a fair tax system a "dollar is a dollar" and, therefore, income and wealth should be defined broadly. Carter also supported the need to reassert "ability to pay" as a cardinal principle of a progressive tax system and suggested ways to simplify the system, eliminate loopholes, and therefore enable the reduction of marginal rates.[12]

An elaborate "White Paper" process followed the Carter report involving extensive consultation with interest groups. While some changes, such as the taxation of capital gains, followed in the wake of the White Paper, the White Paper process itself showed the power of specific interests with a vested interest in the status quo to wear down the decision process. As a result the Carter impetus quickly faded. The tax reform agenda, however, basically has not changed since the late 1960s.

Tax content and the tax process were simultaneously the object of political attack from the political left and the political right. The 1972 election which produced a minority Liberal government was noteworthy primarily because of the campaign by NDP leader, David Lewis, against "corporate welfare bums."[13] This was the precursor to the larger tax expenditure debate of the mid and late 1970s. The debate not only asserted the concept of corporate welfare and the use of tax breaks by corporations, but also painted a portrait of the declining share of the tax burden borne by corporations. The debate was successful enough that Finance Minister John Turner, when offering a new capital cost allowance to corporations, coupled it with a promise to report back to Parliament on whether corporations had actually used the tax break to help generate more jobs and/or had used it for other purposes.

Another reform concept, one embracing support from the political left and right, was indexation of the tax system against inflation. Conservative opposition leader Robert Stanfield pressured the government into adopting indexation in 1973 by appealing to the unfairness and lack of fiscal integrity caused by the "painless" infusion of new revenue into government coffers. The extra revenue flowed in because inflation was pushing taxpayers into higher income brackets with higher marginal tax rates. The government, Stanfield argued, was profiting from inflation without having to endure the political discipline of increasing taxation in an open Parliamentary way. The indexation issue was itself used in other ways in the on-going debate about taxes and economic management. Thus, when Canadian Conservatives urged the Trudeau Liberals in 1981 to emulate the initial large Reagan tax cuts in the United States to promote supply side economic growth, the Liberals argued that this was unnecessary in Canada because indexation since 1974 had resulted in tax cuts every year. The Americans had not indexed their tax system against inflation. Similarly, indexation was viewed in Canada as a way to provide automatic benefits so that weaker groups in society such as the aged were not held hostage to unseemly short-term partisan politics, having to "beg" annually for protection from inflation. This did not, however, prevent the government from capping the indexation percentage in 1982 as part of its campaign to keep inflation to 6 percent in 1982-83 and 5 percent in 1983-84 and to save money in the face of ballooning deficits.

Tax reform and the reform of the tax process gradually broadened in the mid and late 1970s to embrace virtually all of the Carter issues. Increasingly, however, they were debated at a time of serious and evident economic malaise. One manifestation was the formal debate about tax expenditures.[14] The Americans had begun in 1976 to publish an annual report on tax expenditures showing the cost of new tax benefits granted. Increased research in Canada, as we saw in Chapter 5, began to show the sharply growing use of tax expenditures, its regressive effects and the growing complexity and costliness of the tax system that resulted. In 1979, Conservative Finance Minister John Crosbie published the first tax expenditure account with his Budget. He justified the reform on the need to open the tax process and to broaden political scrutiny. The information in the tax expenditure account is very general in nature and is not tied to corresponding spending programs. Its publication, however, shows the evolution of an idea that ultimately can be traced to the Carter Commission and the "Corporate welfare bums" debate of 1972.

The degree to which the tax process was subject to a tax expenditure debate was further revealed in 1981. In his November 1981 Budget, Finance Minister Allan MacEachen unexpectedly announced that he would be closing off several tax "loopholes" on the grounds that they favoured the wealthy. He coupled these changes with a general lowering of marginal rates at the upper income levels, thus favouring those who wanted a somewhat more simplified tax system without high rates which sapped initiative and risk taking. While the Budget was virtually replaced six months later and suffered from many problems, it showed again the political staying power of those who benefited from the current tax system. Ideas clashed. A supposedly egalitarian "cut out the loopholes" Budget was charged, among other things, with being an attack on enterprise and initiative, in short, on efficiency. In addition, suddenly there were concerns, mainly from the business community, that the Budget process had broken down and had to be reformed. More and better consultation was needed to ensure that the Finance Department did not lose touch with reality again. It was argued by some that the norms of secrecy were too pervasive and Finance had become too "academic."[15]

The need to reduce Budget secrecy and improve consultation had arisen before 1981 but never as vociferously.[16] The 1981 Budget was perceived by business interests to be anti-business and therefore the process was wrong. The contrast between the 1981 experience and the Carter and post-Carter tax process is instructive. In the Carter-White Paper process there was much consultation. Concern was expressed by business interests that the process would create uncertainty. In the end, however, only business interests could afford to participate in the elongated consultative process. In the 1981 debate over the MacEachen Budget the tax reform process was too swift. Finance had acted irresponsibly. After the Budget, business interests marshalled their resources and through intensive lobbying succeeded in having the Budget proposals watered down. In this case Finance had acted first and consulted later. In the Carter exercise it had consulted first and acted later. The result was not noticeably different in either case.

Growing deficits and the need to restore basic fiscal balance and integrity were as much a part of the debate to reform the tax process as it had been of the expenditure process. The Lambert Commission, for example, opened its report with a stinging denunciation of the federal deficit and linked it to the need to relate revenue closely with expenditure.[17] At no point, however, did the Lambert Report attempt to explain the causes of the growing deficit. It seemed to equate it with the absence of proper systems. Despite purporting to write a report on financial accountability, scarcely any of the tax reform issues discussed above entered the pages of of the Lambert Report. As a result it offered only a narrow view of barely one half of financial and political reality. The tax process was part of the problem but was ignored. Lambert did address other important issues, including the envelope system and other reforms already discussed in Chapter 11. We make some further observations about the handling of taxes in the envelope system later in this chapter.

The Regulatory Process

In Chapter 5 we traced the growth of regulation, including the attempt to differentiate between economic regulation and social regulation. We noted the numerous points of intervention that exist along the production cycle where governments have regulated or are contemplating regulation. We stressed the large number of line departments and special quasi-independent agencies and boards involved in regulation. When viewed in this way, regulation is both visible and omnipresent.

Within the confines of government, however, the regulatory process has been a much less visible and focused activity than either the tax or expenditure processes.[18] This is partly due to the fact that the regulatory process in general has been far less quantitative in nature than either taxes or spending. Regulations obviously result in the allocation of resources, but these are, in the main, private resources, not governmental resources, though the latter are affected as well. Regulations are a form of tax. These allocations are therefore hidden, at least in the eyes of regulators and ministers. Moreover, annual regulations are not aggregated into a kind of "regulatory budget" of public *and* private resources and reviewed by a super central agency. It is argued by some that this hidden nature, and the unequal scrutiny of regulation, compared to other instruments is a major reason why it is used frequently. The burden of many proposals for regulatory reform, as we see below, is to alter this state of affairs by requiring more prior quantitative analysis and review of proposed regulations.

The regulatory process is not totally devoid of quantitative assessment and central review. Quasi-independent boards such as the Canadian Transport Commission, the National Energy Board and the Canadian Radio and Telecommunications Commission have elaborate processes for prior analysis, including formal hearings.[19] A form of central review occurs because both the federal and provincial governments have regulation or statutory instrument statutes.[20] These acts typically require that all formal regulations (subordinate legislation), but not necessarily all "guidelines," be vetted by a registrar or similar official. These assessments are based on such tests as whether the regulation flows properly from the enabling powers of the parent statute; whether it contravenes a bill of rights; whether it imposes a tax, and other similar concerns. One should not lose sight of the fact that the normal informal processes of Cabinet discussion, ministerial and official telephone calls, and behind-the-scenes communication are also a part of the regulatory decision process.

In general, however, regulation is an activity carried out in a disaggregated decentralized way by many ministers and officials and special agencies. In this way the process is similar to the expenditure process but not the tax process. The regulatory process is in a sense even more decentralized than the expenditure process because *within* line departments, as well as at the central governmental level, there is often no single point of on-going regulatory review by the Minister and his deputy as there is with expenditures.

The problem of securing greater review both by the central agencies of the government and of the departments is not just a product of its hidden nature or lack of quantification. It is also due to the persistent problems of knowing what a regulation is as distinct from a standard or a guideline.

For example, in Chapter 5 we defined regulation in a somewhat narrow way as rules of behaviour backed by the direct sanctions and penalties of the state. Thus, regulation occurs when the more coercive powers of the state are used to back up norms of conduct. In this political sense both statutes or legislation as well as so-called subordinate legislation would be regulatory in nature and would be distinguishable from other instruments of governing such as spending, taxation or exhortation.

Government officials, however, will often use regulation to denote only subordinate legislation, that is, "regulations" which are made pursuant to a parent statute and which go through legally prescribed steps including publication in the federal or provincial *Gazette*. Similarly, "standards" in fields such as health and safety regulation are usually viewed by officials as statements arising as subordinate legislation, setting out upper or lower health and safety limits or setting out procedures that must be followed. In this sense they are rules of behaviour backed up by sanctions that apply if the standards are not met.

But these are not necessarily the same as guidelines. In the health and safety field, for example, guidelines are often viewed to exist because of the presence of greater scientific uncertainty or because it is agreed that there is no safe threshold limit; that is, a point of measurement within which something is "safe" and beyond which something is "unsafe."[21] But regulation defined as "guidelines" does not occur purely because of differences in scientific and technical precision. Guidelines also have political qualities and embody ideas that many groups prefer.

Strict regulations (rules of behaviour) and standards carry with them the notion of equality of treatment and equality before the law, a powerful and important idea in Canada and in other Western societies. Guidelines, on the other hand, suggest flexibility and a capacity to recognize that circumstances and situations are different or unique. Both of these combine to suggest a defence of fairness and equity, also powerful and important ideas, as Chapter 2 has shown.

As if these distinctions were not confusing enough to the layman, they do not complete the picture. The fact is that "standards" are often in reality applied flexibly, and "guidelines" are often obeyed as if they were standards.

As in so many other aspects of political life, language and the use of words, though rarely clear, matter a great deal. In the words "regulation," "standard" and "guidelines," we have code words for two closely linked but overriding ideas of democratic society. Governments are enjoined simultaneously to treat people in equivalent situations equally and to treat people who are not in equivalent situations unequally (that is, to be fair and reasonable). Both of these ideas are equally desirable and, in a broad sense, form a consistent philosophical and democratic concept. In practice, however, they are often in conflict.

The regulatory process is therefore, for several reasons, not nearly as uniform or ritualistic a process as the expenditure or tax process. It has, however, been the object of reform pressures. Again, the ideas for reform reflect both the left and right of the political spectrum. To appreciate the nature of the reform ideas listed in Table 12.1, however, one must understand in greater detail the attempt to differentiate social regulation from economic regulation.[22]

Economic regulation is the older familiar form of regulation. It tends to be specific to a particular industry (for example, communications, transportation, energy) and focuses on regulating entry to the industry, ownership, rates of return and, sometimes, prices. It is "economic" because government intervention was, in part at least, premised on the need to overcome market imperfections such as monopoly and oligopoly. It was originally the product of the criticism of capitalism by liberal progressives early in this century and of a desire to "restore" competitive forces and efficiency, or at least prevent things from getting worse. In Canada such regulation was also based on a desire to prevent incursions from the American giant and therefore embodied nationalism. Regulators in these sectors were later usually accused of being captured by the industries they were intended to regulate.

Social regulation, on the other hand, is a more recent phenomenon, primarily a product of another phase of liberal criticism of capitalism in the 1960s and early 1970s during a period of economic prosperity.[23] Social regulation cuts across industries and deals with "health, safety, and fairness." Thus, it intervenes even more directly in the production technology and processes of firms and in their marketing practices. As we saw in Chapter 5, the volume of environmental, occupational health, and consumer product regulations increased markedly in the 1970s. In terms of economic theory the state is supposedly intervening in social regulation because of the need to deal with "externalities" or the effects of market transactions on third parties. Social regulators, it was argued by some, tended not to be as easily "captured," since there were several industries among their industrial clientele. Moreover, particularly in the United States, they seemed to pursue their regulatory tasks with considerable missionary zeal.

Since the mid-1970s, during a period of economic malaise, social regulation in particular has become a target of conservative political interests in both the United States and Canada. In this respect it became merely one of many targets, as interests and experts sought to discover the causes (and perhaps the villains) of high inflation and sluggish economic growth. To trace the evolution of this criticism and its effects on regulatory reform, it is necessary to appreciate the existence of two broad phases of social regulation in the 1970s.

During the first phase, social regulations required private firms (especially in the environmental and occupational health fields) to undertake major capital-intensive investments and expenditures. In general, (although even here there is dispute) this first regulatory wave produced a quantum jump in environmental improvements. However, as the second phase of regulation-mandated capital investments were being proposed in the mid-1970s, circumstances were different. First, economic times were much more difficult but, equally important, the second wave of capital-intensive regulation could only produce, so it was argued, much smaller marginal gains in health and safety. Critics argued that social regulators were being unreasonable, unfair and inefficient. Regulators reached for the heavy regulatory guns when other solutions might be more useful and more cost-effective as well.

The issue which perhaps best symbolized this line of argument was the frequent dispute over the use of masks in occupational health situations. Masks were much less expensive than installing new production processes and were preferred by employers. Regulators, pressured by labour unions, argued that by focusing on masks the responsibility for the hazard was being placed on the worker. Besides, they argued, it was impossible to implement such a control program. There were thousands of workers and enforcement was impossible. There are many fewer firms; therefore one could monitor them more easily for compliance purposes. In short, it was more appropriate to change production technologies. Nothing illustrates more distinctly the close connection between political ideas, economic costs, assumptions of human behaviour and the real world of regulatory implementation than the case of the dispute over workers' masks.

As the search for solutions to the economic malaise continued in the late 1970s, social regulation became more intensely scrutinized. This began first in the United States where regulators were required in 1975 to prepare "inflation impact statements" for proposed regulations.[24] Studies also began to appear outlining the annual and aggregate private sector costs imposed by social regulation and its effects in lost production and jobs. An anti-regulation movement became a part of the larger anti-government ethos, which culminated in the election of the Reagan administration, a regime bent on reducing spending, taxes, and regulations—in short, on having less government.

The Canadian version of this general line of argument followed somewhat later and in more muted tones, but it occurred nonetheless.[25] During the period of wage and price controls, between 1975 and 1978, the committee of ten federal deputy ministers (DM 10) launched the initial trial studies which led to the adoption of the federal Socio-Economic Impact Assessment (SEIA) process in 1978. The Progressive Conservative premier of Manitoba, Sterling Lyon, easily persuaded the First Ministers' Conference of 1978 to launch a major study by the Economic Council of Canada into regulation (social and economic). In 1979 the Ontario and British Columbia governments began their own deregulation and regulatory review programs. In 1980 and 1981 a special Parliamentary Task Force on Regulatory Reform held meetings and issued its report. The politically weaker nature of the Canadian regulatory reform process compared to that in the United States can be seen by the fact that the Economic Council's study generally advocated a form of deregulation in several sectors but advocated *stronger* regulatory action in social regulation fields.

In terms of regulatory decision making within government, the regulatory reform debate has produced some differences in the formal decision process. The federal SEIA process was launched by Cabinet directive in August 1978.[26] It applies to "major" new proposed regulations in the health, safety and fairness field under sixteen specific federal statutes. "Major" regulations are understood to be those which are likely to impose private sector costs in excess of ten million dollars. Proposed regulations imposing lower costs are exempt from the SEIA process.

Under the SEIA process federal departments are required to prepare and publish, for comment by affected interests, a socioeconomic impact statement on the likely costs and benefits of the proposed regulation. There is no requirement, if costs exceed benefits, that the regulation cannot proceed. Rather, the intent is to produce more systematic "second sober thoughts" and to consult interests more formally and deliberately. Only a few proposed regulations have gone through a full SEIA cycle since 1978, and thus experience with the process is very limited.

While the formal prior evaluations are fairly new, they do raise in explicit ways the controversy over regulatory ideas in the health and safety fields. First, they apply formally only to social regulation and thus reflect the growing influence of conservative ideas in the late 1970s. They raise questions about the use of cost-benefit and other economic ideas about efficiency in the health and safety field. Labour unions argue that health criteria should be the only criteria recognized.

It should be noted that earlier in the 1970s regulatory reform was influenced more by the political left, which pressed for greater public participation in the regulatory process. This usually meant participation by public interest groups, some of which received, and still receive, public funds to enable them to participate on a reasonable financial footing. As stressed in Chapter 3, such groups clearly suffered from the "free-rider" problem and became dependent on the state for funds.

Certain producer interest groups, on the other hand, practised their own brand of regulatory reform. Agricultural producer groups succeeded in creating more marketing boards to stabilize their incomes.[27] This was possible in part because the highly decentralized regulatory process allowed agriculture departments to agree with their producer clientele groups without much worry about central agency intervention. The continuing influence of agricultural producer interests was reflected in the reaction to the Economic Council of Canada's regulation studies. The Council was extremely critical of the inflationary impact of marketing boards and suggested a form of deregulation. Agricultural interests and the Minister of Agriculture, Eugene Whelan, dismissed the report with contempt, and there seemed little doubt that no one was prepared to risk angering the agricultural lobby.

In other respects as well the call for deregulation did not take hold in Canada.[28] There was no equivalent in Canada to the swift deregulation of the American airline industry, though some loosening of regulation occurred in the Canadian airline industry. There were several calls among business interest groups for a "guidelines approach" but to little avail. Governments did try to respond to the call to reduce the paper burden of government (the excessive number of forms, surveys, etc.) since this was a particular concern of the small business lobby. As noted in Chapter 3, the emergence of an aggressive small business lobby was a particularly noteworthy development in the 1970s in the overall structure of business interest groups.

The Public Enterprise Process

It is awkward to even speak of a public enterprise process. A process of a sort exists, but it is not one that is as well-recognized by outsiders or practitioners as the tax, expenditure or even regulatory process. Chapter 5 has shown that there are certainly a large number of Crown corporations and mixed or hybrid enterprises. The public enterprise process, in fact, shares many of the features of the regulatory process. It is highly disaggregated and involves many ministers and officials. It is not a very quantitative process, at least at the centre of government, nor is it characterized by focused central agency review.

There are two aspects in identifying a public enterprise process: the process leading to their creation and the subsequent process which accompanies decisions about their investments and operations. The first aspect is to discover whether there is a process about which one can generalize governing the *initial establishment* of a public corporation; that is, the choice of the public ownership instrument itself. How are new enterprises created? There is no easy answer to this aspect of identification. In a review of the origins of a dozen federal and provincial Crown and mixed corporations, Tupper and Doern conclude that ownership was selected in all but two cases as a last resort, after other instruments had been tried and found inadequate in some way.[29] But this finding does not allow us to pin down a recognizable process, particularly since the time frames involved varied considerably.

Reformers from the political right have, however, been concerned about the need to control the proliferation of new Crown corporations and to ensure that they have been given Parliamentary scrutiny. This view was of little avail, however. For example, in the energy bills passed in the wake of the National Energy Program in 1982, there were virtual carte blanche powers given to the Cabinet to create such enterprises at will.

The second aspect of the public enterprise process concerns the actual operations of such companies, including their capital investment decisions. A further characteristic of the operations process is that those enterprises with a commercial function (for example, Air Canada, Canadian National Railways) have their own sources of revenue. Though reformers in the late 1970s and early 1980s sought to secure some greater overall process of coordination and accountability of the total stable of public corporations, especially the large commercial ones, this effort has numerous inherent limitations. The reality is that there are a plurality of processes in which public corporations must interact. We will highlight only three of them, since much of the basis for the existence of these diverse processes flows logically from the analysis in previous chapters. The three related processes are the public corporation's "home" policy portfolio or ministry, the regulatory process, and the process of economic management.

While all Crown corporations are influenced by the general state of the economy and the nature of the general political agenda, they are ultimately domiciled in a "home" policy field or ministry. Thus, they respond to, and attempt to influence, the nature of energy, transportation or communications policy, as the case may be. They are also under pressure, however, not only from central agencies of government but from other closely adjacent policy ministries. For example, environment departments have sought to influence the way decisions are made about the location of major projects planned by public corporations. Eldorado Nuclear Ltd.'s proposed refinery site near Saskatoon was abandoned following an unfavourable environmental assessment panel report. The CBC has been under interdepartmental as well as community pressure regarding advertising directed at children.

Even within its own home ministry, a public corporation, especially at the federal level, may be only one of a small stable of Crown corporations competing for funds, capital and ministerial attention. The energy, transportation and communications ministries are characterized by the presence of a stable of enterprises. From the point of view of the senior management of any particular Crown corporation at any one particular time, the crowded stable can be either a curse or a blessing. A minister preoccupied with other concerns can be a distinct asset, since the corporation may well be then left alone to do its job. In other circumstances the lack of ministerial time and attention may prevent desired actions or funding from being achieved.

Crown corporations are always involved, in part at least, in an interdepartmental and ministerial tug of war. If a Crown corporation is in political trouble, its minister will bear the brunt of Parliamentary and media criticism regardless of the formal arms-length reporting relationship. Controversy over whether a minister or the Cabinet as a whole should have the powers to issue directives to Crown corporations is a reflection of this political reality. Regardless of their stated mandate,

Crown corporations are increasingly subject to the vagueness of their own minister's priorities as well as to the pressure to have the Crown corporation, often at the behest of other ministries, function as the model public corporate citizen. In the latter role it is expected to be sensitive to the need to favour Canadian suppliers, support regional policies, practise proper language policies, adopt progressive environmental and occupational/labour relations practices, adopt federal wage guidelines, and so on.

The role of Crown corporations in the regulatory process involves many of the same issues enunciated above, since in practical terms regulation is merely one other way in which benefits/subsidies can be secured for oneself or sanctions imposed on others. Canadian regulatory bodies under the Cabinet-Parliamentary system have never been as "independent" as their American counterparts. Moreover, regulatory bodies are not always viewed by their own members as being purely regulatory in nature, since some of them engage in the use of other instruments. Regulators cannot help but take into account the fact that they are merely one part of an array of public institutions created to politically/governmentally "manage" an industry or policy field. They are often part of the same stable of agencies reporting to their minister as is the Crown corporation they are regulating.

A question arises, therefore, about whether Crown corporations get special regulatory treatment in comparison with their private sector competitors. Nominally, in a strict legal and procedural sense they do not. In a practical political sense, however, they are intended to get a special deal, but the degree of discriminating treatment varies greatly, is partly a function of the eye of the beholder, and is the product of widely varying degrees of discretion exercised by regulators, the Cabinet, the courts, or all three. For example, Atomic Energy of Canada's nuclear facilities were, until recently, not formally licensed by the Atomic Energy Control Board, a special deal of no small initial advantage to the company, but now an indirect source of its malaise in the public eye. Similarly, Air Canada has been perceived to be and has been the Canadian Transport Commission's (CTC) favoured child among the airlines, as mandated by public policy and successive Cabinets.

Crown corporations are a central element of general federal and provincial economic management policies and processes. They have been established in part to create jobs, or save jobs, to increase resource trade and domestic "value-added," to promote Canadianization, and to resist foreign capital, especially from south of the boarder. Crown corporation decisions that have an impact on these areas are, of course, in one sense "evaluated" all the time within the company and policy-field ministries and departments. There are, however, grounds for concern about the degree to which some of the aggregate investment impacts, especially of the largest public corporations, are incorporated into the central processes of economic management. Obviously, the Department of Finance and the Treasury Board Secretariat have some notion of the annual capital demands of major federal corporations (and some major provincial ones), but there are only the most haphazard mechanisms in place to determine, with sufficient advance knowledge, the capital and other economic plans of these major enterprises on a longer-term basis.

This invariably raises the question of economic planning and industrial policy in a liberal federal state. Crown corporations merely provide another prism through which the importance of the planning issue emerges. The domestic and foreign borrowings and capital requirements of these firms, the proposals and practices to endow them with Canadian sourcing mandates, the pricing, subsidizing, and regulatory preferences accorded them, and the effort to utilize them as opportunities to develop indigenous technology, when added together constitute important dimensions of central economic management.

All of the above concerns about the unwieldy world of Crown corporations has led to numerous reform proposals, again reflecting different political ideas.[30] An initial Privy Council Office study, and later the Lambert Report, focused on elaborate ways to classify enterprises, subjecting each type to different regimes of accountability. There were also proposals to improve the appointment process of members of boards of directors; to adopt a "single window" concept where budgets (especially capital budgets) would be criticized by a special central group; and to enable ministers to issue public directives to Crown corporations. An interesting example of different ideological views occurred on the issue of whether Crown corporations directed by their minister to perform a public policy goal should be financially compensated. The Clark Conservatives favoured the principle of open compensation, while the Liberals left it as a discretionary decision on the grounds that Crown corporations were set up to carry out social or public policy functions and should not have to be "bribed" to carry out their duties.

There were, of course, even broader manifestations of ideological views of reform than the above example. The NDP have continued to favour public enterprises but do not parade their view in terms of strident proposals for nationalization. The Conservatives under Joe Clark, on the other hand, actively promoted the concept of privatization. The Clark Conservatives adopted a privatization policy because ministers, led by Sinclair Stevens, genuinely believed that there should be less government and that selling some Crown corporations to private buyers would signal in a concrete way their philosophical preferences. Following a study of several possible candidates for sale, the government announced its willingness to privatize Eldorado Nuclear, Canadair, de Havilland, Teleglobe Canada and Petro-Canada. When the Liberals returned to power in 1980, they did not totally abandon the idea of privatization, but did put the question much lower on their political priority list. Indeed, the 1980 Liberal National Energy Program led to the creation of several new Crown corporations, as well as joint ventures between Petro-Canada and the prairie cooperative enterprises.

Privatization in the sense of selling to private buyers proved to be a more intractable problem. The first problem is to find an appropriate buyer. Presumably the intention is not to sell to foreign buyers. If the Crown corporation is very profitable and hence marketable, then the government itself is reluctant to lose this source of revenue. If the agency is only modestly profitable or a losing proposition, then no one will want to buy it. There are also questions of whether one sells its shares, its assets, or part of its shares and assets.

The privatization issue was complicated by the fact that the concept was also defined by some to include the selling or giving of shares to Canadian citizens. The British Columbia Resources Investment Corporation (BCRIC) and the debate over selling Petro-Canada raised this citizens' "public" ownership to a high level of visibility in 1979 and 1980. The British Columbia Social Credit government offered free 80 percent of its fifteen million BCRIC shares to eligible citizens of British Columbia who applied for them to a limit of five per individual. It also raised extraordinary sums of capital through additional sales to B.C. citizens and other Canadians. At the outset, this was hailed as the triumph of people's capitalism. "Public" ownership meant ownership by the "people" rather than by their government. Later the BCRIC bonanza fell from public favour when the company's share prices declined and when controversy arose over some questionable investments and takeovers.

For a time at least there was some consideration given in Clark government circles to dealing with Petro-Canada in a similar way.[31] In the end the Tories took refuge in a more muted and emasculated concept of privatizing Petro-Canada. They resolved simply not to let it expand very much. In the climate of the 1979 and 1980 elections, the Conservatives badly misjudged the public mood about Petro-Canada in particular, though not necessarily about government intervention in general.

Exhortation and Symbolic Politics and Policy

If the notion of a public enterprise process is an uncomfortable one, then the designation of an "exhortation process" may seem grotesque, both conceptually and grammatically. It is the element of the larger public policy process that is perhaps the least analyzed in any systematic way. We have placed it last in our analysis of instrument-based subsidiary policy processes not because it is the least important—the reverse may well be true—but because it seems to become a residual category into which one puts everything that does not quite fit into the other processes examined above. We have combined the notion of governing by exhortation with the notion of symbolic politics both to reflect the breadth of this category and to demonstrate the analytical problems inherent in it.[32] These two concepts must first be discussed before attempting to define the overall process.

To govern by exhortation is to engage in a whole series of potential acts of persuasion and voluntary appeals to the electorate as a whole or to particular parts of it. In this sense many would view exhortation as democratic government in its highest and most ideal form. It would be equated with the essence of leadership and of democratic consent, of legitimate government in its most pristine form. The concept could be equated even more broadly to governing based on an appeal to common values. It would be government without coercion.

There can be little doubt that governing would be impossible, not to mention undemocratic, if there were not a significant element of exhortation defined in this broad way. At the same time there is little doubt that exhortation is not a wholly reliable way to ensure that public policy goals are achieved in the long run, since several main ideas compete for attention and since human beings respond to other instruments and incentives as well.

The notion of symbolic policies or politics must be added to the concept of governing by exhortation because it adds the additional dimension of perception.[33] Symbolic politics does not just embrace an appeal to national symbols such as a flag or the national anthem; it implies an array of ways in which governments express symbolic concern. Such concern is often expressed because to show no concern at all may be both uncaring and inhuman or, somewhat more basely, politically unwise. Moreover, symbolic concern may be expressed because there is genuinely no solution to the problem at hand. Thus, concern can be shown symbolically, as opposed to taking more concrete actions, by making a speech expressing concern, by studying the problem, by holding meetings and discussions and consulting interests, by reorganizing a department or creating a new one such as the Ministry of State for Small Business, or by making available certain kinds of information so that people affected are better able to take their own action as individuals or in collective groups and associations.

Symbolic actions may also be needed to assuage and placate those with concerns that, for any number of valid or invalid reasons, are simply ranked at the lower end of the government's priority list. It is in this sense that action which we might otherwise wish to classify under one of the other instrument lists may at times be *perceived* to be a symbolic act, that is, an act perceived by the interest concerned to be an *insufficient* response or an act designed merely to buy time. Thus, groups that wanted action may get a royal commission instead. Or, alternatively, those that said "there ought to be a law" get their regulation passed, but it is then only feebly enforced.

It is not difficult to see that the excessive use of symbolic politics and of exhortation can easily lead to the alienation of citizens from the state and from democratic government. It can bring government and politicians into disrepute. Not all of this dissatisfaction is necessarily directed against "the system." Some may well be channelled as support for opposition political parties, which collect and marshall these grievances.

There is already some considerable evidence that symbolic politics has already reached an epidemic proportion. We have suggested this in earlier chapters when we linked the role of the media to the increasing need for politicians to be *seen* doing *something*. This has resulted in an even greater need for policies "for show" or for an increased series of symbolic acts. These may well increase even further in direct proportion to the increased scarcity of *real* expenditure, tax and regulatory resources.

The concept of governing by exhortation and symbolic politics is also directly related to ideological and other ideas. At one level it is an essential and desirable feature of democratic politics. People probably prefer to be consulted and persuaded rather than coerced, legitimately or otherwise. At the same time small "c" conservatives see the symbolic malaise as simply further evidence of the inherent limits of state activity and of the need to appreciate that government cannot and should not do everything, since it creates a virtually immoral dependence on the state rather than on individual responsibility or community initiatives. In many respects sections of the political left agree with this critique of modern government, even while simultaneously advocating such things as more state enterprise.

With these explanations and issues in mind it should now be possible to characterize the exhortation process, at least to some degree, again with the aid of Table 12.1. The first point to note is that it is the least quantitatively based process of all those identified in this chapter. Second, it involves virtually all ministers and senior officials engaged in a series of numerous acts of persuasion, consultation, speeches, and the like. It involves, accordingly, policies "for show" as well as activity that is the epitomy of democratic leadership and democratic consent. Finally, it is evident that the exhortation process is not visibly anchored in any one central agency. The creation in the early 1980s of a Cabinet Committee on Communications may be a step in this direction, but even it has only a limited role in relation to the way exhortation is defined here. It was established not only to improve the communication of federal policies but to support the campaign to ensure the visibility of federal initiatives vis-à-vis the provinces.

Table 12.1 shows a sampling of the reform ideas that can be broadly viewed to be a part of this process. All have been subject to dispute and criticism, and each demonstrates the fine line between a reform idea that is viewed as the epitomy of democratic virtue by some, and, at the same time as the quintessential example of democratic vice by others. For example, Information Canada was created in the early Trudeau years. It was heralded with metaphorical fanfare as an example of the new cybernetic view of government. Government needed good information about citizen preferences coming "in" and good information about public policies going "out." It quickly became perceived as a propaganda agency. This same issue was revived in the early 1980s when the Trudeau Liberals engaged in aggressive advocacy advertising of their policies in the print and television media. The latter were intended to "inform" people and to show federal visibility, since it was felt by some that the provinces and the media would not adequately and fairly report on and communicate these policies.[34] For the Liberals it was the consummate act of political communication. For many others it was blatant partisan propaganda at public expense.

Another example of governing by exhortation was the emergence of monitoring and policy advisory agencies. They included bodies like the Petroleum Monitoring Agency and the Food Prices Review Board. They were established to produce information of a more independent kind. The logic of both was that exposure to this information would exert pressure on the industries concerned and help improve public understanding. We comment further on this kind of information in Chapter 13.

Finally, Table 12.1 contains an old Canadian friend, the royal commission or other analogous studies and task force inquiries.[35] Such acts of exhortation or symbolic politics can be both an input to policy and a policy output, a device to buy time. Again they can be, and have been viewed, as essential acts of democratic life and as a bane to democracy. Other acts and forums of consultation and advice could just as easily be noted here as well. Some of these have already been analyzed in Chapter 3 and are examined further in Chapter 18.

It is evident that we have not yet commented on the list of basic information documents presented at the bottom of Table 12.1. We have included this merely to show how each instrument generates its own basic type of written documentation, albeit of very uneven quality and utility. For the expenditure process there is the Estimates Blue Book (now published in three parts) which sets out the annual expenditure requests of the government to Parliament and the Public Accounts which presents an audit of actual spending.[37] There is also the five year fiscal plan by envelope which is included in the Budget Speech and Papers. Documents that are not in the public domain but are important in the internal federal process are the departments' five year Strategic

Overview documents and the Multi-Year Operational Plan documents. The basic tax process documents include the Budget Speech itself and the Budget Papers. Since 1979 a Tax Expenditure Account has also been published.

The hidden nature of the regulatory process is perhaps symbolized by the absence of analogous public documents. While the *Canada Gazette* contains regulations as they are proposed *ad seriatum*, there is no equivalent for regulation of the expenditure Blue Book, that is, an annual indication of planned regulation for the next year. The Economic Council of Canada has proposed that the government publish such a "regulatory calendar," but none has been published at the time of writing this book. Another reform that has been suggested in the United States, but is much more difficult to adopt, is the publication of a regulatory "budget." This did not refer to the publication in a single place of the budgets of regulatory agencies. Instead, it envisioned a process whereby each agency with a regulatory role would be assigned a fixed account, setting an annual limit on *private* sector resources that it could consume or allocate *through regulation*. This would be a direct parallel to the expenditure budget. The problem of determining what that limit should be disuaded reformers, but this idea is indicative of the regulatory reform movement's search for "solutions."

The public documents for the public enterprise process are equally sparse and uninformative. Annual reports are available for some campanies, but there is little aggregate information. The exhortation process, of course, consists of volumes of speeches, reports, press releases and advertisements, all of which is almost by definition difficult to aggregate.

Instrument Processes and Ottawa's Envelopes

In this chapter we have examined each instrument-based process, drawing attention to the similarities and differences in their main characteristics but generally making the case that each, to a certain extent, has a life of its own. This has been evident in the degree to which each process has been subject to pressure for reform, sometimes on a one-instrument-at-a-time basis, and sometimes in a more concerted ideological view of all of the instruments of governing. The review of reform ideas has served a twofold purpose. The first purpose is to reinforce the point stressed in Chapter 5 and elsewhere, that instruments are not matters of mere technique but are the object of normative dispute and are inextricably linked to structure and process. They are valued in and for themselves, as well as in relation to whether they produce better social policy, energy policy, economic policy, etc. The second is to develop a further appreciation of the historical evolution of these debates. Debates rarely begin *de novo*. They are a cumulative product of previous debate on issues and ideas which have endured for decades.

Our disaggregation of the instrument processes also allows us to see other features of the resource allocation process, including Ottawa's envelope system, which do not emerge automatically in Chapter 11's more general analysis. Ideally, the envelope process is supposed to be one where two kinds of trade-offs can be made, trade-offs among policy fields and programs, and among instruments. On the latter point, the stated purpose of the envelope accounting system is to "avoid biasing a committee's deliberations on the choice of the proper policy instrument."[36] Ideally, according to this notion, the envelope should be like a supermarket of instruments. Ministers pick the best one or combination of instruments to do the policy job at hand.

Alas, it is evident from a careful look at instruments processes and the ideas embodied in them, not to mention other Cabinet realities, that instrument choice is and probably must be decidedly biased. Consider, for example, three illustrative issues in the envelope process: the so-called "queing" problem, the treatment of tax expenditures and the issue of financing Crown corporations.

The "queing" problem is one that no system of resource allocation can avoid, namely, how to handle the temporal sequence of decisions. Decisions occur over time and proposals pour into the envelope committees. How then does one avoid having resource allocation dominated by the principle of "he who gets there first, gets the most" rather than on the basis of ranking ideas or priorities? How does the Cabinet know in an on-going way that the decisions it is making *ad seriatum* add up to the achievement of its previously endorsed priorities. We saw this problem at the aggregate level in Chapter 10, but the envelope Cabinet committees have had to deal with it at an on-going micro level as well. Indeed, that was one of the claimed benefits of the envelope system.

The two major committees, economic and social development, have instituted "auction" or "banking" days, respectively.[37] These are periodic meetings held to review decisions previously approved "one at a time," to see that they still conform to the overall view of things, to ensure that there are still funds in the envelope now and in future years to pay for them, and that there is still room in the envelope for future items that are "queing" up but have not yet been approved. In this respect it is noteworthy to stress several things. First, "auctions" in the economic envelope are somewhat more meaningful than in the social envelope because, as we stressed in Chapter 11, there is more discretionary spending in the former. Second, "auctions" refer primarily to spending allocations and essentially leave out regulatory allocations. The latter are still somehow ranked but not in a visible "auction" day format. Finally, though envelope auctions involve formal envelope days for the committees, it is almost inevitable that much of the real auctioning occurs behind the scenes as senior ministers and their deputies bargain.

A second illustrative issue concerns the treatment of tax expenditures in the envelopes. At a theoretical level the inclusion of tax expenditures makes sense since they, along with regulation, are the major alternative instruments available to achieve policy results. The process works, however, only in a one-way direction. If a department proposes (and the Minister of Finance agrees to) a new tax expenditure, the revenue lost to the government is charged against the envelope and reduces the amount remaining in the envelope for other programs. On the other hand, if a department succeeds (again with the agreement of the Minister of Finance) in reducing a tax expenditure, the increased revenues do not accrue to the envelope. They accrue to the general Consolidation Revenue Fund. The envelope system was intended to encourage a more thorough analysis of alternative instruments such as taxing and spending, but the incentives to do so are only partially present. The key factor in the case of tax expenditures is the need to preserve the power and prerogatives of the Minister of Finance in the tax and fiscal policy process.

Some analogous problems have arisen with respect to Crown corporations. The envelope system was initially designed with little thought given to the various ways of financing Crown corporations. The government can finance them with advances, loans or equity. The question arises as to whether market interest rates should be charged against the envelope. If equity financing is used should the envelope be charged a shadow interest rate so as not to skew the incentives to favour more equity financing? Similarly, when Crown corporations pay dividends should they accrue to the envelope? Given the large size of the Crown corporation sector, these are not unimportant questions.

Regulatory proposals do not appear to be an integrated part of the envelope concept. Some regulatory proposals reach Cabinet committees, but many do not. Even where they do there is no system of information or analysis that would enable the "regulatory versus tax versus expenditure" trade-offs to be examined. Nor would there be adequate ministerial time or patience to allow such a process to occur. All past agreements cannot be resurrected or challenged every year. Instruments are the object of control and political power. They are not merely tidy "means" mobilized at will to produce better policy.

Conclusions

Chapters 11 and 12 allow us to see the policy and resource allocation process in some detail, and with greater realism than our initial portrait in Chapter 5 or even our historical review of priorities in Chapter 10. They show concretely the connections and mutual influence of ideas, structures and processes. They allow us to see why it is virtually impossible to secure any lasting agreement on what constitutes the ideal policy structure and resource allocation system. In the early 1980s Ottawa had its envelopes, but in the 1990s, if not sooner, it is likely to call the system something different. Specific structural titles may change, but the underlying imperatives do not. How to deal with contending ideas. How to plan without calling it planning. How to be responsive but not spend recklessly. How to centralize, delegate and decentralize at the same time. How to keep bureaucrats under control but at the same time get better analysis and advice. How to insure both individual and collective ministerial responsibility while catering to powerul individual egos and personalities. How to link social, economic and foreign policies and actually change private behaviour in a democratic way.

Our understanding is not yet complete, however. Policy formulation is also affected by the way knowledge and information are handled and transmitted both within government and between government and society. This is the subject to which Chapter 13 is devoted.

NOTES

1. See Sonja Sinclair, *Cordial But Not Cosy: A History of the Office of the Auditor General* (Toronto: McClelland and Stewart, 1979). For a more critical review, see Sharon L. Sutherland, "The Office of the Auditor General of Canada: Watching the Watchdog," in G. Bruce Doern, ed., *How Ottawa Spends Your Tax Dollars* (Toronto: James Lorimer, 1981), Chapter 6.

2. Royal Commission on Financial Management and Accountability, *Final Report* (Ottawa: Minister of Supply and Services, 1979).

3. See Eugene Swimmer and M. Thompson, eds., *Public Sector Industrial Relations in Canada* (Montreal: Institute for Research on Public Policy, 1983), Chapter 1.

4. See A.R. Bailey and D.G. Hull, *The Way Out: A More Revenue Dependent Public Sector and How It Might Revitalize the Process of Governing* (Montreal: Institute for Research on Public Policy, 1980).

5. *Ibid.*, Chapters 1 and 2.

6. See Robin W. Boadway and Harry M. Kitchen, *Canadian Tax Policy* (Toronto: Canadian Tax Foundation, 1980); and David Good, *The Politics of Anticipation: Making Canadian Federal Tax Policy* (Ottawa: School of Public Administration, Carleton University, 1980).

7. See Good, *op. cit.*, and Douglas Hartle, *The Revenue Budget Process of the Government of Canada* (Toronto: Canadian Tax Foundation, 1982).

8. Richard W. Phidd and G. Bruce Doern, *The Politics and Management of Canadian Economic Policy* (Toronto: Macmillan of Canada, 1978), Chapters 7, 12, 13 and 14.

9. Good, *op. cit.*, Chapter 2.

10. Hartle, *op. cit.*, Chapter 5.

11. See John Bossons, "The Analysis of Tax Reform" in L.H. Officer and Lawrence B. Smith, eds., *Issues in Canadian Economics* (Toronto: McGraw-Hill Ryerson, 1974), p. 303.

12. On the general aspects of tax reform, including the Carter reforms, see Irwin Gillespie, "Tax Reform: The Battlefield, the Strategies, the Spoils." Paper presented to Conference on "The Limits of Government Intervention," School of Public Administration, Carleton University, Ottawa, October 1982; and Audrey Doerr, "The Role of the White Papers," in G. Bruce Doern and Peter Aucoin, eds., *The Structures of Policy-Making in Canada* (Toronto: Macmillan of Canada, 1971), Chapter 7.

13. Richard Gwyn, *The Northern Magus* (Markham, Ontario: Paperjacks Ltd., 1981), Chapter 6.

14. See Allan Maslove, "Tax Expenditures, Tax Credits and Equity" in G. Bruce Doern, ed., *How Ottawa Spends Your Tax Dollars 1981, op. cit.*, Chapter 7.

15. See G. Bruce Doern, ed., *How Ottawa Spends Your Tax Dollars 1982* (Toronto: James Lorimer Publishers, 1982), Chapter 1.

16. See Canada, *The Budget Process* (Ottawa: Minister of Finance, April 1982) and Hartle, *op. cit.*, Chapters 4 and 5.
17. Royal Commission on Financial Management and Accountability, *op. cit.*, Chapter 1, pp. 13-15.
18. See Economic Council of Canada, *Responsible Regulation* (Ottawa: Minister of Supply and Services, 1979).
19. See G. Bruce Doern, ed., *The Regulatory Process in Canada* (Toronto: Macmillan of Canada, 1978).
20. See Robert D. Anderson, "The Federal Regulation-Making Process and Regulatory Reform, 1969-1979" in W.T. Stanbury, ed., *Government Regulation: Scope, Growth, Process* (Montreal: Institute for Research on Public Policy, 1980), Chapter 4.
21. See G. Bruce Doern, Michael Prince and Garth McNaughton, *Living with Contradictions: Health and Safety Regulation and Implementation in Ontario"* (Toronto: Royal Commission on Matters of Health and Safety Arising from the Use of Asbestos in Ontario, 1982), Chapter 1.
22. Economic Council of Canada, *op. cit.*, Chapter 4.
23. See Paul H. Weaver, "Regulation, Social Policy and Class Conflict," *The Public Interest*, Vol. 50 (Winter 1978), pp. 45-64; and Doern et al., *op. cit.*, Chapter 1.
24. See Fred Thompson, "Regulatory Reform and Deregulation in the United States" in W.T. Stanbury, *op. cit.*, Chapter 5.
25. See W.T. Stanbury and Fred Thompson, *Regulatory Reform in Canada* (Montreal: Institute for Research on Public Policy, 1982).
26. See Anderson, *op. cit.*, pp. 176-178.
27. See J.D. Forbes, R.D. Hughes and T.K. Warley, *Economic Intervention and Regulation in Canadian Agriculture* (Ottawa: Economic Council of Canada and Institute for Research on Public Policy, 1982).
28. See Stanbury and Thompson, *op. cit.*, Chapter 3.
29. Allan Tupper and G. Bruce Doern, eds., *Public Corporations and Public Policy in Canada* (Montreal: Institute for Research on Public Policy, 1981), Chapter 1. See also Marsha Gordon, *Government in Business* (Montreal: C.D. Howe Research Institute, 1980).
30. See John Langford, "The Identification and Classification of Federal Public Corporations: A Preface to Regime Building," *Canadian Public Administration*, Vol. 23 (Spring 1980), pp. 76-104; and Tupper and Doern, *op. cit.*, Chapter 1.
31. See Jeffrey Simpson, *The Discipline of Power* (Toronto: Personal Library, 1981), Chapter 6.
32. See Murray Edelman, *The Symbolic Uses of Politics* (Champaign-Urbana: University of Illinois Press, 1967).
33. See Douglas Hartle, *Public Policy, Decision Making and Regulation* (Montreal: Institute for Research on Public Policy, 1979), pp. 33-35.

34. See W.T. Stanbury, "Government Expenditures: The Critical .001 Percent Advertising:" in G. Bruce Doern, ed., *How Ottawa Spends Your Tax Dollars 1983* (Toronto: James Lorimer Publishers, 1983), Chapter 5.

35. See V. Seymour Wilson, "The Role of Royal Commissions and Task Forces," in G. Bruce Doern and Peter Aucoin, eds., *The Structures of Policy Making in Canada* (Toronto: Macmillan of Canada, 1971), Chapter 4; and Liora Salter and Debra Slaco, *Public Inquiries in Canada* (Ottawa: Science Council of Canada, 1982).

36. Treasury Board, "Policy and Expenditure Management System: Envelope Procedures and Rules" (Mimeo copy, dated July 1981), p. 3.

37. See Sandford F. Borins, "Ottawa's Envelopes: Workable Rationality at Last?," in G. Bruce Doern, ed., *How Ottawa Spends Your Tax Dollars 1982* (Toronto: James Lorimer Publishers, 1982), Chapter 3. See also Rick Van Loon, "Stop the Music: The Current Policy and Expenditure Management System in Ottawa," *Canadian Public Administration,* Volume 24 (Summer, 1981), pp. 175-199.

CHAPTER 13

KNOWLEDGE, INFORMATION AND PUBLIC POLICY

Knowledge is not necessarily power. It is only one type or basis on which influence might be exercised or power exerted. Like so many other axioms the commonly heard "knowledge is power" thesis needs examination and qualification. Knowledge is an amalgam of facts and values produced both by intellectual-analytical processes and by social interaction among decision makers, their "advisors" and interests in and out of government. It involves ideas about knowledge and about the language and rhetoric of public debate. It involves numerous types and sources of information. Information, moreover, is both an output of policy and an input to policy development. The policy formulation process is characterized by both an active trade in information and knowledge and by strategies for strenuously withholding information and knowledge. In some areas of policy there is too much information and knowledge, and in many other areas of policy there is a great scarcity. In this chapter we take the examination of policy formulation into the world of knowledge and information, a world which is both difficult to generalize about but absolutely essential to understand.

In the first part of the chapter we examine different types of knowledge and information, focusing in particular on several pairs of dichotomous categories; written versus verbal information, facts versus values, voluntary versus compulsory information, causal knowledge versus uncertainty; and input versus output information and knowledge. In the second part we examine different sources of knowledge and information from the so-called "hard" statistics collected by agencies like Statistics Canada to softer kinds of data that come in the form of political intelligence and "street smarts" supplied by sources such as members of Parliament, party officials or local radio hotline shows. Finally, we conclude with some observations about why knowledge is not necessarily power, and why more research and analysis, though often desirable, does not necessarily produce better policy.

Types of Knowledge and Information
Verbal Versus Written

The first type of distinction to make about information and knowledge in the policy process is that between written and verbal. Ministers and senior officials are beseiged by a constant flow of paper, memoranda, statistical data and reports. Bureaucracies thrive on the written word. We drew particular attention in Chapter 4 to the importance of Cabinet background papers, Memoranda to Cabinet, and the brief Assessment Notes begun under the envelope system. The volume of written information has developed to the point where no minister can read, let alone digest, all the material. The federal envelope system increases this load on both ministers and deputy ministers because there are greater obligations to be prepared to deal with the proposals of other departments, as well as one's own.

The increasing paper flow and the need to interact with more central agencies have placed an even greater premium on the verbal transmittal of advice, knowledge and information. Verbal person-to-person communication via meetings, telephone calls and the luncheon circuit has perhaps always been the central human dimension of politics. It therefore places a premium on who has access to ministers and who controls their schedule. For the prime minister this may be a handful of senior officials and advisors who meet him every day. For individual ministers it is the deputy minister and his or her senior political staff. Indeed, there is nearly always some tension between the minister's partisan political and bureaucratic advisers in the kind of access and expertise they each possess.

Facts Versus Values

The crucial relationships between advisors and decision makers raise a very old concern regarding knowledge and information, namely the alleged facts versus values dichotomy.[1] Some scholars of decision making have tried to distinguish between advising on facts and on values. Indeed, a "policy and decision science," for many of its advocates, is premised on the clear possibility of separating the two.[2] Others, such as Sir Geoffrey Vickers, whose work we referred to in Chapter 6, argue that no such distinction can ultimately be made. He refers to the "appreciative system" of decision makers and advisors, in effect an amalgam of values and facts, preferences and experience.[3] Similar conclusions are reached by other students of policy making.[4] The concept of incrementalism is basically in agreement with this view in that small adjustments are the norm because knowledge is limited and ends may not be seriously reviewed lest such a debate ruins the chance for consensus. This view also suggests that there is an inevitable link between policy analysis and policy advocacy, a point we stressed both in Chapter 1 and in Chapter 9 on bureaucratic advisors.

There is no easy guide through the maze of relationships, concepts, and ways of viewing the advisor-advisee relationship and the facts-value controversy. Consider, for example, the debate about what policy analysis is or should be and about what policy analysts in government do. Wildavsky distinguishes between intellect versus interaction as forms of analysis.[5] The former involves "cerebral cogitation" and calls for the need for causal knowledge, "theories of society to predict the paths of the complex sequences of desired action and power to sustain this effort."[6] Such knowledge is by definition limited. Social interaction in markets and in other social forums is also a form of analysis. Social interaction among decision makers and others "gives analysis a historical outlook made up of the past pattern of agreements, including agreements to disagree until next time."[7] Policy analysis consists of enabling the "recognition, reformulation and resolution of problems."[8]

When policy advisors and analysts describe what they do, the picture is never very clear. The task involves partly facts and partly values. It involves partly the application of pet theories and partly "seat of the pants" experience.[9] It embraces an amalgam of analysis and advocacy. Often the process is characterized as "fire fighting," merely surviving to deal with the same old policy problem over and over again. Analyses of Canadian decisions and decision maker-advisor relations are often not very helpful. This is partly because few studies have been carried out, but even where they exist it is clear that it is an extremely difficult area to study. We noted similar problems in Chapter 9 when commenting on the role of deputy ministers. To obtain a sufficient subtlety in understanding the advisory role, one needs detailed case studies. But unique case studies do not allow for much generalization. If on the other hand one attempts broad-based surveys of decision-maker's attitudes, one obtains questionable generalizations because the studies lack the subtlety that everyone knows exists in real decision-making situations.[10]

In the final analysis we are left with a limited number of illustrative

Canadian glimpses of the facts-values relationships in different public policy fields. We will note two of these in quite diverse fields. The first concerns the role of economists as advisors and the second concerns scientists, and brings us into the realm of professional knowledge interests.

While one is tempted to stereotype all economists, this is not always very helpful. It is possible to show the influence of different economists who adhere to different basic schools of thought, policy paradigms or policy ideas. Economists are recruited in increasing numbers to the upper echelons of government, but it is their adherence to particular schools of thought that shows up in advice and in some, but certainly not all, policies and decisions. For example, Sandford Borins has stressed that the team of analysts working in the federal Ministry of State for Economic and Regional Development (MSERD) in the early 1980s were primarily economists with a basic microeconomic view of the world and of what constitutes economic development.[11] They are suspicious of intervention and enthusiasts for the need for cost-benefit analysis. In Chapter 11 in our review of the economic development envelope we noted that these views, particularly on economic development, gained some momentum and were reflected in decisions to eliminate subsidies that were viewed by the MSERD economists as being a form of social welfare. The question which one has to ask, however, is whether it is their ideas which are having an effect or whether it is the broader flow of events and ideas and the lessons of the previous decade of experience that are producing some change? And what of the previous decade? Industry, Trade and Commerce and DREE were also well-populated with micro-economists during the 1970s, many of whom advocated similar views, but often to little or no avail.

In a similar way one can analyze the role of Keynesian economists and monetarists.[12] The former held sway in the Department of Finance for much of the 1950s and 1960s, and the latter began to exercise influence at the Bank of Canada in the mid and late 1970s. Even in the heyday of a Keynesian finance department, however, it cannot be said that a Keynesian policy was followed. Keynesianism was nonetheless the dominant paradigm or prism through which fiscal policy was viewed, and its transmitters were economists. The rise of monetarist thought was also transmitted by economists who enjoyed their moments in the economic policy sun.

The complexity of the fact-value interplay as revealed in economic advice is also reflected in the debate on a policy field that is much less frequently in the policy limelight, agricultural policy.[13] In Chapter 12 we referred to the Economic Council of Canada's efforts to criticize agricultural marketing boards. Such income stabilization measures run counter to a microeconomist's alleged view of economic efficiency. But farm producer groups have succeeded politically in sustaining support for the idea of stabilizing producer incomes by appealing to the existence of market and climatic vagaries and uncertainties in man's most essential need, his food basket. Indeed, their views were often supported by agricultural economists, a group often reared in different concerns and traditions than mainline economists.

The role of scientists in policy formulation shows a similar variety of possible professional relationships in the facts-values and advisor-decision maker web.[14] Scientists are even more likely to be viewed as experts than are economists, partly because scientific theories are perceived to be harder edged and more technical. Hence, there may be a greater tendency to defer to scientific opinions. On the other hand, even though scientific advice is an important part of many policy fields, scientists are generally not deputy ministers or central agency advisors. Thus, they are often one step removed from access to decision makers. Moreover, because of their training in scientific methods and in rational calculation, scientists often view themselves to be apolitical. Things that are not technical are viewed by them to be emotional or irrational, a defiance of "the facts." These labels have certainly characterized the debate and interaction between scientists and others engaged in policy fields such as nuclear power and environmental and occupational health and safety.[15]

Scientists are, of course, not a monolithic group either. They are divided by different interests in basic versus applied research, and they operate in different disciplines and fields, from physics, biology and geology to engineering. They are as prone as economists or any other knowledge group to speak "ex-cathedra," that is, advising about a subject that is not in their area of technical expertise but rather is in the realm of broader values and ideas.

The fact-value dimensions of knowledge and information must also be related to the issue of the presentation of alternatives. The classic rationally ideal model of the advisor, indeed of the ministerial-civil servant relationship, is that the advisor's obligation is to generate and suggest alternative means to meet a given policy purpose or goal. Many advisors conscientiously try to supply alternatives. Many, however, do not. Indeed, the processes of interagency "massaging" of ideas and the constant meetings prior to a formal decision being made often induce the advisor to produce a consensus. If alternatives are presented, they are often of necessity "strawmen" alternatives which can be triumphantly knocked down on the way to the previously arranged consensus. Moreover, ministers are not always interested in having alternatives since it may imply a need to decide and take risks, something not all ministers are willing to do, or often are allowed to do, by their Cabinet colleagues.

Causal Knowledge Versus Uncertainty

We have stressed in Chapters 1 and 2 that the essence of public policy is to change or sustain desired behaviour in reliable predictable ways. It therefore often requires a capacity to change private behaviour. It must deal with causality—in short, with theory. But there is only a limited supply of causal knowledge in the sphere of social relations and even it is in considerable dispute. People do not always behave in expected ways. Interests can often resist change and act in opposition to "the facts." There is usually considerable uncertainty not only about results in a single policy field but even more so when policy fields intersect, as they invariably do. Thus the policy process must be thought of in relation to the existence and limits of causal knowledge.[16] It is in this sense that it can be said "if there is no theory, there is unlikely to be successful practice."

The issue of causal knowledge must be linked to the limits of evaluation, as we show in greater detail in Chapter 18. Full blown program evaluations imply a capacity to link observed actions with discrete effects and results. Few program evaluations can meet this ultimate test. Results, moreover, are time related. Is the program to be judged over one year or over five or ten years? Information and program evaluation studies will be and should be viewed with suspicion. The political system learns, that is, "evaluates," in many ways. Formal evaluation studies are only one form of knowledge.

At the same time it is evident that policy makers should not ignore the packages of partial causal knowledge that do exist. For example, even though there is no agreed theory of accident causation in the health and safety field, governments have constructed policies based on partial theories and ideas about what will work.[17] The basic theory of Keynesian policy was adopted in general though not practised in detail or consistently. The assertion of different theories of inflation, such as "cost-push" versus "demand-pull," have partly influenced anti-inflation policies.[18] Contending theories and models of penal reform in the corrections field have been tried and usually found to be wanting as ideas, and public opinion, ebbed and flowed between tough law-and-order measures to reformist self-help and humanitarian measures.[19] This notion of partial causal knowledge should be linked to our discussion in Chapter 2 of the role of policy paradigms. These are ways of viewing and acting on policy problems which are often entrenched in the education of professionals in different policy fields.

Uncertainty in the use of information is also evident in the constant need to forecast future events based on past data and on hypothesized relationships among variables. This need is unavoidable, and yet the perils are evident. Transportation policy must be based on estimates of future traffic patterns and use preferences whose estimation is in turn based on a host of other economic and social variables. Energy policy is dependent upon calculations of future oil and gas reserves and consumer behaviour in the use of different energy forms. Pension policy, education policy and other policy fields are dependent upon demographic projections.

Mervin Daub's analysis shows that the use of formal forecasting and econometric models is a very recent phenomenon in the federal government.[20] Though some basic survey activities were begun in the 1940s, other models were not developed until the late 1960s and early 1970s. Controversy surrounds major models such as the CANDIDE model. Although there are now several private sector modelling efforts on the economy, it is a matter of no small importance to stress that *within* the federal government there has never been a process, through formal modelling or otherwise, to generate an agreed portrait among the central agencies of what the medium-term, three-to-five year state of the Canadian economy was likely to be. Some degree of progress in this state of affairs was made in the early 1980s and coincided with the emergence of the Ministry of State for Economic and Regional Development. An annual "medium-term track" document began to be prepared that supposedly represented a consensus of views. But, as we see in Chapter 15, it is a very shaky consensus indeed.

This does not mean, however, that such a consensus forecast portrait will govern all or even most policy decisions. The macro realities and the micro pressures are always in a state of tension. For example, the National Energy Program of 1980 was based in part on an EMR economic model that projected a more optimistic future price scenario than either Finance or MSERD.

Voluntary Versus Compulsory Information

The acquisition and use of information and knowledge in the policy process frequently involves sharp controversy over the idea of whose privacy will be invaded to obtain and use the information. The evolution of several policy fields show a history of the increasingly compulsory nature of information acquisition. Initially, policy may be based on voluntarily supplied data, but gradually data becomes statutorily required. Not surprisingly, many object on ideological grounds to this growing compulsion and state involvement. In some cases special monitoring agencies have been created to collect, publish and interpret the data. Several examples can be cited to show the importance of the voluntary versus compulsory controversy. They have arisen in energy policy, education, environmental regulation and occupational health, to name only a few.

In energy policy a major controversy in the 1970s arose over the degree to which the federal government depended upon the oil and gas industry for information both on oil and gas reserves in the ground and on industry financing. The response to the former problem was in part to strengthen EMR's forecasting abilities and in part to create Petro-Canada as a so-called "window on the industry." As to industry finances, the powers of the Petroleum Monitoring Agency compelled the production of information which could not otherwise be gleaned, let alone legally published, from corporate tax returns.

A second example can be found in education policy. The federal government transfers billions annually to the provinces, both in grants and tax points, as part of the Established Programs Financing Arrangements. In 1981 and 1982 when these arrangements were being renegotiated, the federal government concluded that several provinces were diverting money to other noneducational areas. They indicated they were no longer prepared to tolerate this and wanted a new system of compulsory information and reporting to ensure it would not happen in the future. Provincial governments opposed this concept on the grounds that it violated their jurisdiction over education.

Similar sensitivities have occurred regarding the compulsory testing data on chemicals that companies are required to submit under the federal Environmental Contaminants Act for new chemical products.[21] In this instance companies raised the principle of protecting commercial secrets or commercial privilege from competitors. In an analagous way many workers and unions have objected in principle to the publication and use of employee medical records as a way of learning more about, and hopefully combatting, occupational health problems. In this case individual privacy was the principle asserted to be balanced against a broader concept of public good.

Information and Knowledge as Input and Output

It is evident from the above examples that information and knowledge are both an input to the policy process and an output. We have more to say in the next section about the sources of information, but it is essential to stress its obvious presence on both sides of the policy system. Information and knowledge are necessary to identify and characterize a particular state of affairs. It is "analyzed" in both of the ways to which Wildavsky alludes, that is, by intellectual cogitation and by social interaction.

Information is also an output. As our discussion in Chapter 12 of the issue of symbolic politics and exhortation showed, information and knowledge are produced so as to help influence private behaviour in certain desired ways and to show concern. Economists refer to the high "transaction costs" that face many groups and individuals in making decisions.[22] A justification for government involvement is provided where government-supplied information becomes a public good to help overcome these costs. Thus, information is compelled or otherwise produced in fields such as consumer protection and securities to enable decision makers to make more informed market choices.

We also saw in Chapter 12 that information output can become propaganda as governments use resources for advocacy advertising and partisan advantage. It is necessary to add that some of the input information coming to government from interest groups can also be characterized as a form of propaganda or advocacy, depending upon the adjective applied.

The different characterizations of information and knowledge and the ideas they invoke on both the input and output sides are one of the reasons why freedom of information legislation presents problems that go well beyond the motherhood concepts inherent in such legislation. The federal legislation passed in 1982 endorses the principle of freedom of information but also creates other major exceptions where the legislation will not apply. These exceptions are widely defined and include information for federal-provincial relations, for the scientific testing of data that might be subject to misleading interpretations, for matters of commercial privilege, for foreign policy relations and national security, and for information involved in Cabinet deliberations and policy development.[23] In each case a counter idea is marshalled to sustain the need for an exception to the idea of freedom of information.

Major Sources of Information

One way of looking at the sources of information and knowledge is to range them along a continuum from "hard" to "soft." The former suggests official statistical, quantitative and scientific data, perhaps including public opinion polls. At the soft end of the continuum there exists many kinds of political intelligence, usually much less quantitative and much more judgemental and interactive, emanating from ministers, their political staff, the party caucus, party professionals, the media, individual citizens and opinion leaders. This way of viewing information and knowledge would be quite valid were it not for the frequent implications that "hard" means quantitative and therefore good data, while "soft" means nonquantitative and therefore less than good data. The fact is that democratic policy making must have both *hard* (that is, good) quantitative and statistical data, and *hard* (that is, good) political intelligence. This necessity should be kept in mind as we review the major sources of information and knowledge.

The purpose of the brief profiles of these sources is a simple one, to make the student of policy formulation aware of their existence and of some of the issues and characteristics involved in their use. In fact, we have already begun this process in the previous chapter when we noted the public documentation emanating from each of the tax, expenditure and regulatory processes.

Official Statistics

Public policy is influenced by both the content and the timing of the release of statistical and other data on major economic and political aspects of Canadian society, much of it collected by Statistics Canada. On the question of timing it is of no small importance to note the effect of the release of the monthly data on the Consumer Price Index and unemployment levels. Their release induces a political ritual equivalent to the proverbial dance of the seven veils. The government is routinely raked over the coals by the opposition political parties in the media and in the House of Commons and urged to do "something" about inflation or unemployment or both. The government routinely defends its economic wisdom while privately confessing to itself that it will have to do "something" more "soon." It can be easily argued that the mere release of this data contributes pressure to further "fine tune" the economy or to produce policies "for show" as we have previously put it. This is not necessarily an argument against publishing such data (the Rhinoceros party once advocated eliminating unemployment by abolishing Stats Canada!), but it does illustrate the connection between information, the media, and Parliamentary politics.

The content of these official major statistics (and others like them) also deserve understanding since beneath the data are disputes both about methodological issues and ideas. Consider first the Consumer Price Index (CPI). The CPI is considered by many to be a "cost-of-living" index.[24] It has important resource allocation implications since it is tied to an increasing number of collective wage agreements through "COLA" clauses, to the indexation of some pension and social program benefits and to the indexation of the tax system. But the CPI is not a totally reliable measure of changes in living costs. It is in fact an index of retail prices. Statistics Canada publishes other price indices, the most important of which is the gross national expenditure (GNE) implicit price deflator, which includes price changes for all goods and services traded in the economy and counted in the National Accounts. But the CPI clearly gets the lion's share of the political and media attention.

The CPI, in fact, measures the changes in prices for a basket of four hundred goods and services purchased by individuals and families living in large cities with a population of more than thirty thousand. In the index several prices are grouped together and weighted in their importance relative to the proportion of family income spent on the various goods and services in the basket. The weights stay the same for a decade or so at a time. Food prices are also shown separately, as well as included in part of the overall CPI. Cheveldayoff has highlighted the major weakness of the CPI as a cost-of-living indicator as follows:

> A major weakness is that it reflects a very broad average of price movements, and an individual could experience faster or slower rising costs than the CPI indicates. The spending weight for food, for example, is set at 22 percent of the family budget; while housing is set at 34 percent; clothing, 10 percent; transportation, 16 percent; health and personal care, 4 percent; recreation, reading and education, 8 percent; and tobacco and alcohol, 6 percent. If food costs are rising twice as fast as the rate for other goods and if a family spends substantially more than 22 percent of its budget on food, then the average cost of living for that family is actually rising faster than the CPI would show.
>
> At the same time, however, the food costs to another family could be rising much more slowly than the CPI indicates because it has chosen to substitute cheaper products for the ones it normally buys—such as artificial sweetener for sugar, bologna for steak, or vinegar for expensive cleaning fluids. This kind of substitution is not taken into account because the commodities surveyed and the spending weights stay the same, despite the effectiveness or enjoyment. As a result, the CPI could substantially overestimate the actual cost-of-living increase for some families. . . .
>
> The pensioner or wage-earner whose income is tied to the CPI is open to the danger that the index may not fully reflect the increases in the cost of living. If so, an individual's real income can drop, and this reduction would result in a reduction in the standard of living—assuming the person has no saving to fill the gap. The impact of an underestimation of just one percentage point in the annual rise in living costs, showing, for example, a 6 percent gain for the CPI while actual living costs go up 7 percent, would amount to hundreds of millions of dollars a year in total losses to Canadians whose income levels are tied to the CPI.[25]

Statistical data on the unemployment rate present similar methodological and policy dilemmas, as well as problems of political visibility. Some of these are referred to again in Chapter 17 when we review the evolution of labour market and employment policy. Problems arise because the composition of the labour market, and of the unemployed, have changed dramatically in the 1960s and 1970s.[26] Moreover, Canada has experienced labour market changes that have been markedly different than other countries. This was especially the case in the higher level of growth in the labour market and in higher levels of unemployment due to seasonal/climatic factors. These issues in turn affect the vague and highly politicized debate about what constitutes a reasonable measure of full employment.

Statistics Canada does not, as some countries do, estimate the number of unemployed by looking at the number receiving unemployment benefits. It conducts a monthly survey of about fifty-five thousand Canadian households. There are continuous disputes, certainly in the realm of political rhetoric, about the failure of this measurement approach to capture the hidden unemployed. This is further exacerbated by the fact that there is often more than one worker in a family or household. The increased number of employed women or wives looking for work leads to different political interpretations of how serious the unemployment is, especially as a measure of hardship. Cheveldayoff summarizes the range of views:

> Two decades ago, the unemployment rate was a better indicator of hardship than it is today. The improvement over the years in welfare and unemployment insurance are sufficient to prevent widespread destitution in the ranks of the unemployed.
>
> As well, the shifting composition of the labour force means that a lower proportion of the unemployed are male breadwinners with families to feed. Indeed, around 40 percent of the unemployed now are spouses, single sons or daughters and other relatives living within family units having a breadwinner. Some economists have argued that because of this high number of nonbreadwinners comprising the unemployed, the unemployment rate should not be regarded as a measure of hardship. Rather, the component unemployment rate for married men (25-54 years) should be the measure used—not just for measuring hardship but also for determining the degree of slack (availability) and tightness (unavailability) of workers to fill jobs in the labour market. Others have argued that women and youths living at home should be counted fully with married male breadwinners because they have a right to, and a need for, job opportunities similar to anyone else. In other words, government policy should not discriminate against women and youths wanting jobs.[27]

Data on the CPI and unemployment rates are obviously not the only statistical information whose timing and content evoke political dispute. Data on energy and resource reserves, on crime rates, and on the various measures of the money supply, to name other examples, also influence the process and content of public policy.

Public Opinion Polls

All of Canada's political parties employ pollsters to help them gauge public opinion for immediate electoral purposes and between elections as well. The periodic publication of Gallup and other polls produces a similar tribal ritual to that described above for the announcement of CPI and unemployment data. Line departments and agencies have also used poll data in their own policy fields. Thus, there have been numerous polls: to gauge the "work ethic" and other values deemed to be important for programs such as unemployment insurance; to assess support for federalism versus separatism among citizens of Quebec; to gauge the popularity of wage and price controls; to assess attitudes about the bureaucracy; and to gauge support for nuclear power or for the National Energy Program.

Indeed, many departments subscribe to regular quarterly public opinion reports supplied by private firms. In addition to supplying views about particular policy fields, the polls survey the overall mood of the country, including the perceptions that Canadians have about their confidence in the future. Since the late 1970s the "communications plan" section of Cabinet documents have regularly included brief paragraphs setting out recent polling data on the subject at hand. The importance of such data is difficult to gauge precisely, partly because of the question of the degree to which ministers actually read Cabinet documents and partly because ministers are themselves often skeptical of polls and have greater confidence in their own political intelligence.

Interest groups, businesses and unions have also used polls not only to assess particular policies but to gauge how they are perceived by the public. Private polls by Gallup and others have shown important changes in the public perceptions of different institutions. For example, in the early 1970s businesses and then unions were more feared and distrusted than government. By the end of the 1970s and in the early 1980s government was the most distrusted.

Polls used for policy purposes, though not necessarily for electoral purposes, are almost always used with great caution and as a supplement to many other souces of information. Polls have inherent weaknesses in particular policy fields or as devices to help set priorities. This is because most polls do not allow persons to rank preferences, and where they do they are rarely tied to the *costs* of those preferences. They are therefore the political equivalent of "having your cake and eating it too." Despite this, they continue to be used. In addition, publicly financed polls raise important questions about who they belong to. Opposition parties argue that they should automatically be made public, a view difficult to dispute. The governing party meanwhile asserts that such polls are another form of advice to the government and that there is no obligation to make the polls public. In the context of elections, polls are undoubtedly of greater importance, particularly because they capture immediate moods of the electorate. Moreover, such polling data are given usually to only a small handful of persons and thus become an important instrument of power.

Political Intelligence

The sources of political intelligence about the views, concerns and preferences of Canadians are numerous and utterly essential to policy formulation. In the immediate political arena outside the Cabinet and the party the main sources are Parliament and the media. Parliament is composed of the opposition political parties and the government's own caucus. Both are a constant source of information and views about general priorities and about specific policy fields. The opposition's views are expressed in a decidedly public way, while those of the caucus usually arrive in the private confines of weekly caucus meetings and numerous telephone calls and private discussions. It is these forums that provide the regional views about the impact of current policies and programs. The individual member of Parliament has a communication network in his or her constituency which no bureaucrat or journalist can match. This is not to argue that these views are always listened to or that regional opinion is faithfully reflected in policy. The regional weakness of the Liberal party in Western Canada and of the Progressive Conservatives in Quebec has been a serious problem for decades. Ministers who do not cultivate their relations with their own party caucus or who are chained to their Ottawa desks can quickly lose touch with this kind of political intelligence.

Key party officials, such as Senator Keith Davey of the Liberals or Senator Lowell Murray of the Progressive Conservatives, are also an essential source of political intelligence. While these officials assume great strategic influence in election periods, their influence is by no means limited to these periods. For example, it is known that Senator Davey was instrumental in designing and helping coordinate the Liberal's "6 and 5" anti-inflation package revealed in the June 1982 Budget, a policy devised at a time of unprecedentedly low popularity for the Liberal government. Important party intelligence is also supplied to individual ministers by their executive and special political assistants.

We have already mentioned several facets of the media's role in the policy process. In terms of political intelligence the media provide an additional source of editorial opinion, especially that of the key political columnists. While "the media" hardly offers a consistent set of views or even necessarily accurate informative, it is nonetheless so critical in the development of political careers that its many views are listened to, if not necessarily agreed with. There is, of course, an intense mutual distrust between a "free press" and politicians. This has been in evidence in the early 1980s in the increasing use of advocacy advertising by governments to market their policies and, hence, themselves. The media is often critical of this practice but at the same time willingly pockets the profits from the advertisements.

Cabinet Documents and Papers
We have referred at length to the Cabinet's internal paper flow in Chapter 4 and in the brief analysis in this chapter of written versus verbal information and knowledge. We include these documents as an important source of information in this brief inventory of sources precisely because they are one form of documentation in which some (but not all) of the other sources are synthesized, summarized and interpreted for ministers by bureaucrats and political staffs.

Other Jurisdictions
The sheer volume of information and knowledge transmitted (and also withheld) by other jurisdictions is both awesome and unwieldy. Federal-provincial, international and public sector-private sector information is traded constantly in numerous forms and modes of communication. Of equal significance is the frequent withholding of information between and among sectors. This practice is caught up in the compulsory versus voluntary aspects of information discussed above, but is also influenced

by a number of principles such as commercial privilege, the sensitivity of international relations and national security, not to mention partisan distrust among ministers in different governments and among officials.

One example of the conflicting pattern of information exchange is found in environmental data. In a field such as the pre-testing of chemicals federal and provincial governments separately collect some of the same data from the same companies. The sharing of data is not permitted for fear of a breach of commercial privilege. In this instance "duplication" is hailed by companies as an administrative virtue. In other instances these same companies would complain bitterly of federal-provincial duplication and the growing paper burden of government. In the latter instance duplication is a bureaucratic sin. Similar problems exist, incidentally, in the exchange of data among countries in this field and in others.

Despite the extraordinary volume of information there are of course many policy fields and program areas where it is argued, often with great validity, that there is grossly insufficient information of the right kind either to make intelligent decisions in the first place or to evaluate them afterwards. This is an issue which we review in Chapter 18.

Specialized Policy Analysis Units

A further source of information, knowledge and advice is found in the burgeoning and relatively recent (post mid-1960s) emergence of a policy analysis industry. This industry is also discussed in Chapter 18. Within the government these specialized units include numerous policy and planning branches established in many departments.[28] In part these units were created out of genuine desire to improve analysis and to lengthen the time frame of decision making and planning. The units, however, were also established by departments as a protective device against the growing central agency "planners." Not surprisingly, the units have a very ambivalent role to play. Some do genuine research, while others are merely firefighters engaged in the short-term analytical trench warfare that often characterizes interdepartmental relations.

Other manifestations of this policy analysis industry are found in governmental advisory bodies such as the Economic Council of Canada and the Science Council of Canada, as well as the several private and university research bodies such as the Conference Board of Canada, the

C.D. Howe Research Institute, the Fraser Institute, the Institute for Research on Public Policy, the Ontario Economic Council, the Institute for Economic Policy and the Centre for Policy Alternatives. These bodies reflect ideas from almost the entire ideological spectrum and produce numerous reports and studies. Most studies are dutifully reported by the media, read by *some* bureaucrats in relevant departments, and discussed at conferences and seminars. It is doubtful that most are read by ministers and senior officials, who generally lack the time. These specialized units are nonetheless an important feature of the knowledge and information network, whose role as "evaluators" we explore in Chapter 18.

Conclusions

We began the chapter with the assertion that knowledge is not necessarily power. The analysis of some of the characteristic dichotomies of information and knowledge, written-verbal, facts-values, causal-uncertain, voluntary-compulsory and input-output, and our brief descriptive inventory of the major sources of information show the general need to be more careful about the usual "knowledge is power" thesis. It is essential to appreciate that knowledge and analysis embrace both intellectual thought and processes of social interaction. It is this fundamental reality which places limits on the utility of formal evaluation studies. And yet it makes public policy theory and practice not polar opposites but closely interconnected endeavours.

NOTES

1. See Herbert A. Simon, *Administrative Behavior,* Second Edition (New York: Free Press, 1957), Chapter 3.
2. See Yehezkel Dror, *Design for Policy Sciences* (New York: Elsevier, 1971).
3. Sir Geoffrey Vickers, *The Art of Judgement* (New York: Basic Books, 1965), Chapter 4.
4. See Aaron Wildavsky, *Speaking Truth to Power: The Art and Craft of Policy Analysis* (Boston: Little Brown, 1979).
5. Wildavsky, *op. cit.,* Chapter 5. See also Arnold J. Meltsner, *Policy Analysts in the Bureaucracy* (Berkeley: University of California Press, 1976).
6. Wildavsky, *op. cit.,* p. 120.
7. *Ibid.,* p. 139.
8. *Ibid.,* p. 123.
9. For one frank and succinct view by a provincial central agency policy analyst, see Philip G. Halkett, "Widening Gap: The Loss of Technical Inputs in Policy Advice; A Provincial Viewpoint." Paper presented to Conference on Mineral Policy Formulation, Centre for Resource Studies, Queen's University, Kingston, Ontario, June 22-24, 1982.
10. This is one of the weaknesses in such studies as Colin Campbell and George Szablowski, *The Superbureaucrats* (Toronto: Macmillan of Canada, 1979).
11. Sandford F. Borins, "Ottawa's Envelopes: Workable Rationality at Last," in G. Bruce Doern, ed., *How Ottawa Spends Your Tax Dollars 1982* (Toronto: James Lorimer Publishers, 1982), Chapter 3.
12. See David C. Smith, ed., *Economic Policy Advising in Canada* (Montreal: C.D. Howe Research Institute, 1981).
13. See Richard W. Phidd, "The Agricultural Policy Formulation Process in Canada." Paper presented to the Canadian Political Science Association Meetings, Montreal, June 2-4, 1980.
14. G. Bruce Doern, *Science and Politics in Canada* (Montreal: McGill-Queen's University Press, 1972); G. Bruce Doern, *The Peripheral Nature of Scientific and Technological Controversy in Federal Policy Formation* (Ottawa: Science Council of Canada, 1981). See also Dean Schooler Jr., *Science, Scientists and Public Policy* (New York: Free Press, 1971).
15. See Liora Salter and Debra Slaco, *Public Inquiries in Canada* (Ottawa: Science Council of Canada, 1981); and Doern, *The Peripheral Nature of Scientific and Technological Controversy in Federal Policy Formation, op. cit.*
16. Wildavsky, *op. cit.,* Chapter 15.
17. G.B. Reshenthaler, *Occupational Health and Safety in Canada: The Economics and Three Case Studies* (Montreal: Institute for Research on Public Policy, 1979).

18. Allan Maslove and Eugene Swimmer, *Wage Controls in Canada* (Montreal: Institute for Research on Public Policy, 1980); and Prices and Incomes Commission, *Inflation, Unemployment and Incomes Policy* (Ottawa: Information Canada, 1972).

19. See Sharon L. Sutherland, "The Ministry of the Solicitor General," in G. Bruce Doern, ed., *Spending Tax Dollars: Federal Expenditures 1980-81* (Ottawa: School of Public Administration, Carleton University, 1980), Chapter 7; and James Q. Wilson, " 'What Works' Revisited: New Findings on Criminal Rehabilitation," *The Public Interest*, No. 6 (Fall, 1980), pp. 3-17.

20. Mervin Daub, "Economic Forecasting in the Federal Government" (Ottawa: Ministry of State for Economic Development, 1982).

21. See G. Bruce Doern, Michael Prince and Garth McNaughton, *Living With Contradictions: Health and Safety Regulation and Implementation in Ontario* (Toronto: Royal Commission on Matters of Safety Arising from the Use of Asbestos in Ontario, 1982).

22. Douglas Hartle, *Public Policy, Decision Making and Regulation* (Montreal: Institute for Research on Public Policy, 1979).

23. John D. McCamus, *Freedom of Information: Canadian Perspectives* (Toronto: Butterworths, 1981).

24. See Wayne Cheveldayoff, *The Business Page* (Ottawa: Deneau and Greenberg, 1980), Chapter 9; and D.J. Desjardins, "Sharpening a Public Policy Tool: The CPI," *The Canadian Business Review* (Summer, 1982), pp. 36-38; and M.C. McCracken and E. Rudick, *Toward a Better Understanding of the Consumer Price Index* (Ottawa: Economic Council of Canada, 1980).

25. Cheveldayoff, *op. cit.,* pp. 108-110.

26. Employment and Immigration Canada, *Labour Market Development in the 1980s* (Ottawa: Minister of Supply and Services, 1981), Chapter 2.

27. Cheveldayoff, *op. cit.,* p. 129.

28. Michael Prince, "Policy Advisory Groups in Government Departments," in G. Bruce Doern and Peter Aucoin, eds., *Public Policy in Canada* (Toronto: Macmillan of Canada, 1979), Chapter 10.

PART III

POLICY FIELDS

- Ideas and Policy Fields: Economic, Social and Foreign
- Industrial Policy
- Energy Policy
- Labour Market Policies

CHAPTER 14

IDEAS AND POLICY FIELDS: ECONOMIC, SOCIAL AND FOREIGN

There are literally dozens of public policy fields, from agricultural to youth policy and from fisheries to fiscal policy. Everyone involved in the policy process, from the prime minister to the individual citizen, cannot avoid the inevitable mental and practical task of sorting public policy into manageable categories. At the same time, if one is studying public policy as a whole, a basic question arises, "How does one sort out the features that are common to all or most public policy fields?" Presumably, unless there is some common base to all policy fields, one faces the impossible task of somehow becoming an expert on, or at least passingly knowledgeable about, dozens of fields. Our approach in this and the next three chapters is to suggest that one overriding common ground is found in the dominant ideas stressed throughout the book and that this much smaller handful of ideas reveals the presence of social, economic and foreign policy content in all major policy fields.

This chapter describes and defines the evolving content of the broadest economic, social and foreign policy fields to show the reoccurrance of the dominant ideas and the slipperiness of the boundaries between our conventional major policy categories. The analysis therefore builds on and complements several dimensions of earlier chapters in which these boundary problems were implicitly present or explicitly discussed. These include the dominant ideas initially outlined in Chapter 2, economic versus social or collective rights associations and interests analyzed in Chapter 3, economic versus social regulation and taxation assessed in Chapters 5 and 12, the Cabinet structure and the envelope system with its social, economic, foreign and defence policy committees, and the historical review of priorities surveyed in Chapter 10. The assessment of the major policy fields is also linked to the formal models and approaches examined in Chapter 6.

In the next three chapters we then examine three policy fields: industrial, energy, and labour market policies. These are major and important policy fields in their own right. But we also examine them in an illustrative way to show how they might serve as a possible guide for viewing the evolution of other policy fields such as medicare, defence or environmental policy. The normal instinct of many persons may be to attempt to label industrial, energy, labour market or other policy fields as being a subcategory of "economic" or "social" policy, as the case may be. We suggest that, initially at least, this instinctive habit be avoided and that all public policy fields be examined to determine both their economic and social policy content as well as their foreign and domestic policy content. By doing so, one is forced to deal again with the underlying ideas of Canadian political life.

Eventually, of course, it is both necessary and desirable to categorize and subcategorize policy fields for many of the same practical reasons identified in Chapter 7. To be rendered manageable, policy fields must be delegated and broken into manageable chunks of reality. To be held accountable, ministers must be given some kind of definable task related to different political interests and structural definitions of power, even though it is recognized that the boundaries of the task are far from being well-defined.

Figure 14.1 presents a simple visual glimpse of the essential task at hand and of the basis of the policy reviews carried out in the next three chapters. It portrays a policy triad. Policy field X denotes the policy field being examined. While each side of the triad is shown to impart

FIGURE 14.1
THE PUBLIC POLICY TRIAD: POLICY FIELDS AND IDEAS

Economic
- Efficiency
- Stability
- Regional sensitivity
- National integration

Policy
Field
X

Social
- Individual liberty
- Stability
- Equity
- Equality and Redistribution
- Regional sensitivity
- National integration

Foreign/territorial
- nationalism
- internationalism
- continentalism

economic, social and foreign policy content, respectively, to the policy field, and an apparently distinct set of ideas, we already know from previous chapters that many of the dominant ideas show up under all three sides of the policy field triad. In short, one should approach the analysis of any policy field by expecting to find sometimes explicitly and sometimes implicitly beneath the first cloudy layers of the rhetoric of political debate the presence of dominant ideas such as efficiency, individual liberty, stability, equity, equality and redistribution, regional sensitivity and national integration. The territorial imperatives of foreign policy result in many of these ideas being expressed not only under the rubric of nationalism but under ideas such as internationalism and continentalism as well.

The organization of the chapter is straightforward. In each of the next three sections of this chapter we review the economic, social and foreign policy fields, respectively, in relation to dominant ideas, to the more specific objectives often enunciated in these fields, and in relation to major features of the public policy structures created to manage and exert power over these spheres. The chapter as a whole also provides other useful background information in preparation for the illustrative analysis of industrial, energy and labour market policies.

Economic Policy
Dominant Ideas
At its core economic policy has been historically associated in liberal democracy with the idea of efficiency and economic growth and productivity. The private market economy was the engine of growth and progress.[1] It would shape and mobilize the major factors of production— land, capital and labour—to yield the highest return. National wealth would be maximized in this way. The job of government was to allow this to happen. It was believed by some that there was a natural self-correcting equilibrium to the market which governments should not and ultimately could not interfere with. The idea of efficiency was also linked to the idea of private property and individual freedom. Thus, this view of economic policy was simultaneously a social view as well.

While efficiency remains an essential economic policy idea, it is evident from even a brief glimpse of Canada's political history that efficiency and individualism have only been embraced in a selective way by Canadians. As pointed out in Chapters 1, 2 and 10, Canada's creation as an east-west ribbon-like continental state was an act of political defiance against the efficiency of the north-south axis. The National Policy of Sir John A. Macdonald was an act of intervention mobilizing tariff, land, immigration and transportation policies to give sustenance both to eastern businesses and to the "national dream." As to individual liberty it must be stressed that the original, virtually anti-liberal democratic idea of Canada was precisely that it would avoid the excesses of American individualism. Loyalty would be to peace, order and *responsible* government and authority.

The second dominant idea in economic policy is that of stability of income over time. At its root is Keynesian economics, or what some called in the Canadian context, the second National Policy.[2] In the midst of the depression of the 1930s, Keynes articulated a powerful theoretical case against the claimed self-correcting capabilities of the market. Economic policy at the macro level would have as its overall purpose the stabilization of economic activity. By manipulating taxes and spending the government could "manage" the economy, stimulate demand and, therefore, investment and employment. Keynes supplied a paradigm that provided an acceptable justification for marginal intervention in a capitalist economy.

As many have pointed out, Keynesian stabilization was attempted but not wholly practised. It was a grand illusion, not just because both monetarists and those with a Galbraithian view later criticized it, but because macroeconomic policy was never the dominant concern of *only* the chief custodian of Keynesianism, the Department of Finance. Not only was Keynesian countercyclical activity not practised in most of the 1950s and 1960s, but other centres of economic power such as C.D. Howe's Department of Trade and Commerce were carrying out policies in the late 1940s and 1950s with even greater macro implications. These policies were centred on the encouragement of foreign ownership of the Canadian economy.[3]

It must be stressed as well, however, that the *idea* of stability of income over time has an importance that vastly exceeds the Keynesian notion of stabilization. In many respects stability is the opposite of efficiency. The latter implies unpredictability and change, especially for those elements of capital, labour and land that are being "mobilized" by someone else. Those who oppose such change are inherently expressing a higher preference for stability and predictability in their own lives.

Thus, economic policy is always a struggle between efficiency and change on the one hand, and stability and predictability on the other. Over the decades Canada has assembled policies that are intended to support both of these ideas simultaneously. This is because *both* are desirable and valued. In each of the next three chapters this fact will be evident. For example, in the field of labour markets, Canada has policies to ensure that labour is mobile and moves to where economic opportunities are. Canada also has policies whose intended effect is to keep labour where it is even when it is not "economic."

We can already see from the above discussion how difficult it is to visualize policies in watertight economic and social compartments. Efficiency, an economic idea, is linked to individualism, a broader social concept. Stability beyond the Keynesian sense also relates to a broader social view of the human value of predictability and orderliness.

Evolving Objectives

While influenced by these broad ideas, economic policy in the period since World War II has been more conventionally debated in relation to its success or failure in meeting the four primary objectives which have accompanied the Keynesian view.[4] The four objectives are:

- economic growth
- full employment
- reasonable price stability, and
- balance in international payments

Governments have nominally adopted these objectives, but their degree of commitment to any one has been in dispute since the dawn of the Keynesian era. Moreover, resolving the contradictions among them necessitates a constant ranking of these objectives, a task which governments for many good reasons often do not like to perform.

Each objective is a source of dispute because each economic purpose has a social dimension. Economic growth has been embroiled in a dual debate. First, there are those who are dissatisfied with the concept of national economic growth and who look for the regional distribution within it. The power of regional forces in Canada makes economic growth per se an insufficiently clear and acceptable objective.[5] A second attack on the concept of economic growth emerged in the late 1960s and early 1970s and was linked to a global view by environmentalists and others about the limits of growth, the need to conserve increasingly finite resources and the inadequacies of the GNP as a measure of growth or wealth. This was also a broader social movement. Indeed, many of the environmental policies this movement succeeded in having adopted were labelled, as we have seen in Chapters 5 and 12, as "social" regulation.

The commitment to, and meaning of, full employment has similarly been in dispute.[6] The political left has charged with some accuracy that there has never been a policy commitment to full employment. The left tends to argue that this is because government, supported by employers, needs a reasonable amount of unemployment to "discipline" labour and to make sure that the economy has flexibility, that is, "efficiency." Others argue that it is simply difficult to come up with a working definition of what a proper level of unemployment or employment is. We saw this in Chapter 13 when we noted the debate about data on unemployment. The definition of acceptable unemployment does seem to have changed but not the underlying intensity of the debate. For example, the growing employment participation rate of women in the 1970s was accompanied by dispute over whether this was a social frill occasioned by the emergence of the women's movement or an economic necessity.[7]

There were, of course, other challenges to the sanctity of the main objectives. In addition to regional disparities there were other distributional challenges. The inevitable concern about the redistribution of income to low income Canadians was reflected in several of the disputes over objectives, especially employment, growth and price stability. As the next section on social policy shows, studies began to appear in the late 1960s indicating that despite the arsenal of social programs, significant redistribution had not been achieved. The gap between the rich and the poor remained about the same or was in fact worsening.

While, as we can see, there was always criticism of Keynesian policy, the dominance of the Keynesian idea was not seriously challenged until the heady prosperity of the 1950s and early 1960s came to an end. In particular, it became especially difficult to explain the concurrent existence and increasing persistence of both high unemployment and high rates of inflation, which had heretofore been generally assumed by many to have an inverse relationship to each other. If unemployment rose, it was expected that the rate of price increases would decline. In addition, refinements of Keynesian strategy made it necessary to develop in the 1960s certain policies on the "supply" side of the economy (especially the supply of labour) to remove rigidities and bottlenecks in the flow of different factors of production. This was sometimes called the "new economics" and was reflected in the development of manpower policies and some related social policies which, almost by definition, could not operate on the same short-run time frame as had the early demand-management Keynesian strategies.[8] These so-called supply policies were also often directed towards secondary or redistributive goals which, in Canada in particular, meant both an attempt to secure a more equitable distribution of income in general, and the removal, or at least the lessening, of regional economic disparities.

As the economic malaise became more intractable in the 1970s, those seeking to produce both alternative (presumably non-Keynesian) explanations for the worsening economic condition, as well as grand prescriptions for its cure, tended to group themselves, sometimes quite misleadingly and artificially, under two other grand paradigms of economic policy, the Galbraithian and the monetarist paradigms. The former is led intellectually by John Kenneth Galbraith and the latter by Milton Friedman.[9]

Although each of these competing views defies easy or brief description and requires the reader to differentiate the "master" from his "disciples" and his "interpreters," they each clearly posit different causal and ideological links in the economic chain from which quite different policy prescriptions emerge. Briefly, Galbraith attributed the growing economic malaise to the pronounced existence of "market power," by which he meant the power of the largest corporations (and, by extension, the largest labour unions) to control the market rather than be subject to its competitive hidden hand. His prescriptions centre on the need for increased state intervention, including, in particular, permanent wage and price controls (or an incomes policy) over the "commanding heights" of the economy.

Aligned with Galbraith in a general way, but incorporating a more explicit acknowledgement of the growing international protectionism and of the need to maintain a high level of redistribution as a precondition of economic growth, is the work of liberal economists such as Robert Heilbroner and Lester Thurow. Both are institutional interventionists, the former advocating government-industry joint ventures and the latter favouring concerted international industrial policy collaboration.[10]

Monetarists, under Friedman's leadership, tend in general to attribute the economic decline to the failure of governments both to understand the central signals which money represents in economic transactions and in future price expectations, and to manage the supply of money in such a way as to allow "normal" market forces to operate. Monetarist prescriptions are centred on less government intervention, the control (if not reduction) of government spending and borrowing, and the proper management of the money supply.[11] Price and wage controls are the antithesis of the monetarist strategy.

In addition to the above ideas, there are other explanations and prescriptions, albeit somewhat more marginal in nature, at least in so far as they lack general political expression and tend to be confined more strictly to academic discussion. Clearly, the most important are the class analysis ideas which link the economic malaise to the role and "fiscal crisis" of the state, and to the claimed internal contradictions of capitalism. As outlined in Chapter 6, the central tenet is that the function of the state in a capitalist economy is three-fold: to facilitate the *accumulation* of capital; to *legitimate*, which involves the adoption of policies and practices (manpower, welfare, unemployment insurance); to buy off or at least ameliorate those victimized or displaced by capital accumulation, and where necessary, to *coerce*. The economic condition of the 1970s is portrayed in this view as being the result of the increasing conflict between the capacity to fulfill the first two functions, usually through state spending and taxation incentives, and the consequent need to coerce (for example, through the direct regulation of wages and prices, especially the former). The prescriptions that follow from this Marxist perspective are to change radically the nature of the state and to create ultimately a socialist state.[12] In the Canadian context of the late 1970s, this view in particular led to an assault against such concepts as "tripartism" which was seen as merely the first stage of greater state control of unions and the working class.

During the latter half of the 1970s and the early 1980s Canada's central economic policies and processes reflected an eclectic selection from the above ideas and objectives, both those from the Keynesian point of view and from the "new" contenders. Previous chapters have already conveyed some of these changes. The review of budget speeches in Chapter 10 showed the emergence in 1976 of a policy of monetary gradualism in response to the monetarist critique. For the more part, however, monetary policy was not supported by equivalent fiscal policy restraint, which monetarists would argue is a necessary policy companion. The wage and price controls program from 1975 to 1977 reflected a form of Galbraithian experiment, albeit not the permanent controls program advocated by the master. The federal policy paper, *The Way Ahead*, contained obligatory paragraphs which gave an intellectual nod to each of these schools of thought including, of course, the Keynesian view.[13]

In addition, one began to hear in the mid-1970s the return of the traditional efficiency idea. It occurred under the rhetorical guise of the call, during the 1975 to 1977 controls program, for a restructuring of the economy and in Ottawa's adoption in 1980 and 1981 of the disarmingly soothing notion of "adjustment" policies. It was present even earlier in the early 1970s search for an industrial strategy. We have already referred to this effort in Chapter 11 when we examined the economic development envelope. Chapter 15 examines it in greater detail. It is sufficient to note here that the notion of an industrial policy was intended to lead to a rediscovery of that element of the economy, the productive system, that had for too long been relegated to the realm of "micro" economic policy, the poor sister of the macro Keynesians. It also reflected the need to review these industries in the wake of two decades of increased regulation, especially social regulation. Moreover, there was the critical need to consider the underlying technological and geopolitical changes in the international economic order both in the realm of increasing oil prices and in the emergence of highly competitive, less developed countries in fields such as textiles and clothing, as well as resources.[14] To facilitate the future efficiency and adjustment of Canada's industrial policies, it would also be necessary to consider more seriously trade policy, competition policy and the effects of the foreign ownership of Canada's economy.[15]

Structure and Process

By the 1980s economic policy, despite the illusion of Keynesian economics, comprised an array of policies, including fiscal policy, debt policy, monetary policy, regional policy, industrial policy, trade policy, science and technology policy, competition policy, policies for small businesses, labour market policy and agricultural, energy and resource policies. Each of these corresponded to one or more departments and agencies of government (see Figure 14.2). In an earlier book we

FIGURE 14.2
ECONOMIC MANAGEMENT DEPARTMENTS, 1983

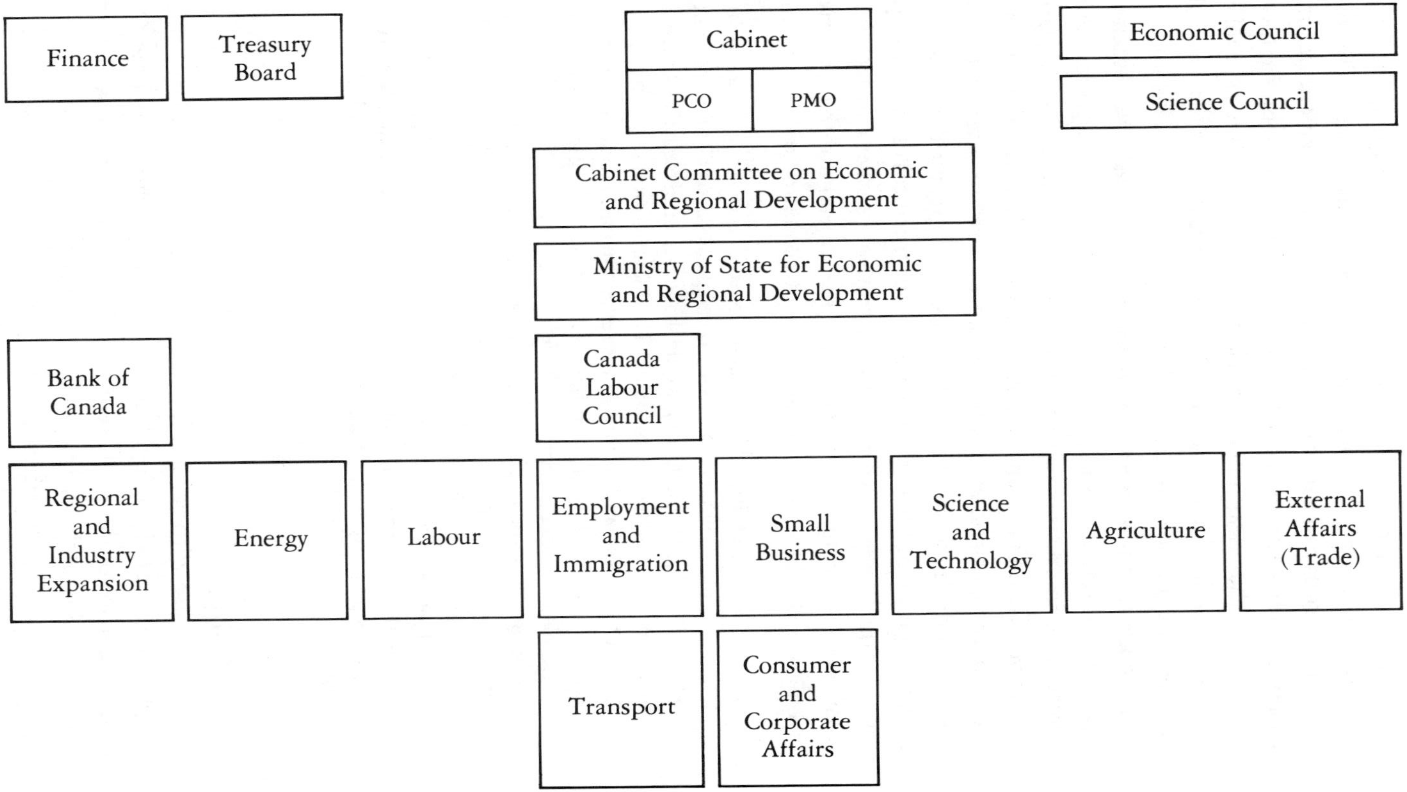

examined the emergence of these economic departments, showing how they interact in a larger process of economic management.[16] This process involves large organizations, each charged with an element of the total economic policy sphere. Economic management invariably involves not only all of the ideas uncomfortably contained within the rubric of economic policy, but also all the attributes inherent in Cabinet government and organization. Thus, it includes demand and supply management, short-term and long-term time frames, a variety of policy instruments, research and information, ministerial delegation, and the demands of interests, from provincial governments to interest groups.

Since Chapters 11 and 12 review some of these relations as they are revealed in the envelope process and since there are other sources which discuss these developments and processes in greater detail, we do not elaborate on them further. In terms of the structures of economic policy formulation, however, we can only reiterate our earlier conclusion about what these evolving ideas and changes have meant for the Department of Finance as Canada's nominal centre of economic policy making.

> In 1975 Michael Pitfield, Secretary to the Cabinet, described the Department of Finance as the "court of last resort" for economic policy. No such description would have accompanied the Finance department's role ten years earlier. The metaphorical reference to the court of last resort is an important reflection of how the processes of economic-policy formulation have evolved. It is simply no longer as plausible as it once might have been to speak of a single department "making" economic policy. The increasing complexity of goals, instruments, agencies, and research needs means that a broader managerial requirement has become necessary. The promotion and control of economic activity has become a highly important and pervasive governmental function. Economic policy making becomes, therefore, an important part of both politics and public administration.[17]

Social Policy

As was the case with economic policy the boundaries of social policy are slippery and ever-changing.[18] Its two contemporary component parts reveal the scope of ideas inherent in it. First, there is social welfare policy which contains both income security and social services and therefore includes ideas of redistribution, equity and stability. The second part of social policy has often been summarized under the phrase "quality of life." It includes cultural policy, broadcasting, language policy, multiculturalism, individual and human rights, justice, corrections and law enforcement, sports, recreation and a host of other policy fields.

An issue of particular importance in understanding the evolving content and dominant ideas of social policy is that of determining whether social policy is and should be a residual category of public policy or a primary category. As Wilensky and Lebeaux point out, "the first holds that social welfare institutions should come into play only when the normal structures of supply, the family and the market, break down. The second, in contrast, sees the welfare services as normal 'first line' functions of modern industrial society."[19]

As could be expected, the various policy analysis models examined in Chapter 6 (which are, in turn, based on broader ideologies) evaluate this residual versus nonresidual question differently. A class analysis approach views social policies as a residual series of "legitimating" adjustments needed to sustain the basic power of capitalism. This view asserts that social policy *ought* to be primary but could only be so if a capitalist state was replaced by a socialist one. In contrast, a public choice, self-interest or market model would at best support the residual notion. In extreme form it would argue that the market is itself a social forum because it is supposedly based on noncoercive or free exchange. An incremental liberal and/or pluralist view might regard the two fields as evenly balanced with existing social welfare programs being evidence of progressive change.

In addition to the residual versus nonresidual issue, social policy faces the problem of an ever expanding set of boundaries alluded to above. Rice and Prince's comprehensive analysis of Canadian social policy and administration shows the expansionary tendencies and supports the need to define social policy more broadly.[20] Social policy is usually most easily equated with social welfare policy and the welfare state, which in turn is usually broken down into income security and social services as portrayed below.

Income Security	*Social Services*
• old age security	• health
• pensions	• education
• unemployment insurance	• housing
• social assistance	• personal and community services (e.g., day care, family counselling, parks, playgrounds)

- disability allowance
- allowances for the blind
- mother's (family) allowances
- youth allowances
- income supplementation
  scheme

Income security programs usually provide cash benefits on the basis of the four techniques employed: demogrants, social insurance, social assistance and income supplements. In a very real political sense, therefore, they involve a direct relationship with citizens and intense federal-provincial cooperation and competition. Demogrants are universal flat-rate payments made on the basis of age or similar demographic characteristics (Old Age Security and Family Allowances) rather than on needs. They are the largest component of the Canadian income security package. Insurance programs are the next largest component and are based primarily on insurance principles. Unemployment insurance is thus financed out of employer and employee premiums but also partly out of federal tax revenues. Other insurance-based programs include pensions and workmen's compensation (the earliest program created).[21]

Social assistance, as Banting points out, "is the modern version of the ancient Poor Laws."[22] These programs define welfare in the stigmatized notion of the word. They are based on a needs or means test. Initially, these were the original and primary form of social welfare, but today they are "the residual element in the income security system, the last resort for needy Canadians who do not qualify for other income security programs or whose income from these other programs is still inadequate."[23] These programs are a provincial responsibility but are supported by federal contributions of 50 percent under the Canada Assistance Plan (CAP).

Income supplementation funds have grown in recent years partly in response to the need to target benefits to particular low income Canadians but without the full needs tests of social assistance programs. Examples of this type of program are the Guaranteed Income Supplement (GIS) for pensioners and the Child Tax Credit.

On the social services side social policy includes health, education and housing, and personal and community services. Generally, these services provide a benefit in kind rather than in cash. Health programs (including hospital and medicare assistance) and education are both in provincial jurisdiction but involve federal-provincial financing under the Established Programs Financing Arrangements (EPF).[24] Initially, these financial relationships were on a conditional grant basis. However, since program costs were tied to demand, and demand then grew, the federal government, anxious to avoid the escalating costs, changed the arrangement in 1977 and financed its share through block grants and tax points. By 1981, however, the perceived problem had changed again. The freedom of the 1977 arrangement had resulted in some provinces diverting the money to other needs, particularly away from education. New arrangements were worked out. Thus, the EPF arrangements involve both great cost and great federal-provincial controversy.

Housing services have typically involved programs and loan financing arrangements to supplement the private housing market. In the 1970s, however, it increasingly involved provincial rent controls, as well as special tax breaks to encourage home ownership and investment in housing. Mortgage rates and subsidies also became a major political issue not only for low income Canadians but for the middle class as well. Most of the other social services are provincial in jurisdiction and involve direct services such as day care, family counselling, probation and child welfare.

The boundaries of social policy, however, now go well beyond these traditional social welfare limits. To the extent that social policy seeks to foster an identity with the nation or community as a whole or seeks the full development of the individual, it then embraces law and justice, human rights, corrections, culture and broadcasting, sport, recreation and leisure, environmental and occupational health and safety, the conservation of resources (the so-called "conserver society"), and the nature and quality of employment and work.[25] It is this latter panoply of areas that constitutes another and even more ill-defined phase or sector of the social policy field.

Dominant Ideas
In the face of this array of activities it should be scarcely surprising that several dominant ideas compete for attention. As should also be expected, these ideas have an interdependence with economic policy. Indeed, they are usually the other half of the same policy coin. Most of these ideas were presented in Chapter 2 where we surveyed the

normative content of public policy and in Chapter 11 where we surveyed the social envelope.

The redistribution of income and power is certainly a major idea in social policy, but it has not been the central concept. In this sense social policy has been residual. Both the original "welfare" assistance programs of the prewelfare state era and the most recent income supplementation programs such as the GIS and the Child Tax Credit can be said to be redistributive. But the vast array of larger programs established between these periods have not been created for redistributive reasons. As we will see, other ideas have been present.

It must be stressed that the extent of redistribution is not easy to measure and agree upon. It involves assessments of the net effect of both taxing and spending decisions (and ideally of regulatory costs and benefits as well) and thus can change over time. Irwin Gillespie's research on redistribution indicates the broad trends. In an initial study using 1961 data, he concluded that together government taxes and expenditures are "clearly favourable to the lower income classes, and become less favourable as income increases."[26] Later, using 1969 data, he found that taxes were regressive on the poor. He noted that:

> In general ... at the all-Canada level of aggregation, tax incidence is regressive up to an income level of about $5,000, and beyond an income level of $15,000, with proportionality in between. The tax patterns of all three levels of government contribute to this regressive pattern, with the local level contributing relatively more to regression that the other two levels of government.[27]

In the 1970s this situation, he concluded, had become worse. As we have seen in Chapters 5 and 12, this was due in part to the growth of tax expenditures that favoured the rich.

For the tax regressiveness to be overcome and redistribution to occur, public expenditures would have to clearly redistribute income. On balance expenditures were redistributive. Gillespie's conclusions from 1969 data were that these redistributive impacts overcame the regressive impact of taxes. By the late 1970s, however, Gillespie concluded that

> The evidence does not support the belief that over time governments have been successful in increasing the degree of redistribution from the rich to the poor such that the "share" of command over resources of the poor have increased significantly. Quite the contrary: the small relative gain of the poor during the 1960s has been eroded during the

early 1970s leaving the poor with no improvement in their "share" over the longer period. On the other hand, the considerable gain of the rich during the 1960s has persisted during the early 1970s, thus giving the rich an improvement in their "share" over time.[28]

In 1981, Gillespie offered a further overall conclusion:

> Between 1951 and 1979, the last years for which data are available, there has been no substantial significant change in the distribution of money income in Canada: the poorest quintile of families and unattached individuals had 4.4 percent of total income in 1951 and 3.9 percent in 1979, while the richest quintile had 42.8 percent of total income in 1951 and 42.2 percent in 1979. This constancy in the distribution of money income is a well-documented fact. The income measure is a comprehensive one, including virtually all sources of money income.[29]

One of the ideas that served to counteract the redistributive idea was the notion of equity, often reflected in concepts such as equality and equalization. One notion of equity implies treating people in like circumstances equally. In public finance this is known as horizontal equity. The idea can, in principle, be applied to taxpayers and to governments. The strength of the idea of regionalism, reinforced and embodied by federalism, has elevated this kind of equity to a high plateau. It was initially reflected in the equalization arrangements of federal-provincial fiscal relations, whereby provincial revenues were equalized to some agreed-upon level to allow public services to be offered to Canadians without unduly burdensome tax levels. This notion of regional equity easily melded into the larger idea of national unity.

The use of the term "equalization" to describe what we would otherwise define as being closer to the idea of equity shows the importance of the rhetorical language of debate and the labelling of policies. Equalization payments to provinces and thus indirectly to taxpayers are not the same as paying redistributive benefits to low income Canadians, most of whom pay no taxes. They may be helped in a general way by the extra revenue given to their provincial government, but they are not necessarily the prime beneficiary of such "equalization" policies.

The latter appeal to remove other "regional disparities" is a further reflection of the equity idea. It is also a manifestation of a spatial-geographic definition of policy, one that only partially coincides with redistribution by income class. As noted in Chapter 8, the Diefenbaker government epitomized this sense of regional injustice and launched a series of programs that would later be consolidated under the Liberal's Department of Regional Economic Expansion (DREE). By the 1980s, however, it could be shown that "little if any improvement in the reduction of regional disparities"[30] had occurred. Moreover, any limited reduction in the income gaps could virtually all be attributable to transfer payments such as unemployment insurance payments. This evidence did not in itself destroy the *idea* or strength of regionalism or equity. It only questioned the results of policies intended to help solve these problems.

It can easily be seen how ideas such as regionalism and equity combine to form a stout defence of the idea of stability, the idea discussed earlier under the economic policy column. If incomes cannot be redistributed, regionally or otherwise, then they can at least be stabilized and made more predictable and therefore socially humane.

Also melding with the above ideas was the debate over universality versus the stigma of means tests. Universality implied that programs were a right and a condition of Canadian citizenship, not welfare handouts.[31] At a practical political level this could also be interpreted to mean that some social programs had to be offered to everyone so that the middle class would politically support welfare for the poor. At the same time, however, this greatly increased the costs of social expenditures, and by the late 1970s governments were looking for, and finding ways of, targeting programs to particular lower income groups without directly and openly attacking the universality idea. The universality idea had to be approached by stealth rather than by "rational" debate. This was evident in the emergence of programs such as the GIS and the Child Tax Credit noted above. We also saw it in our review of the social envelope in Chapter 11 where Liberal ministers had, in part, defined their social priorities in terms of the aged, single women with children, and the handicapped.

Even the above survey does not by any means exhaust the ideas inherent in social policy. For example, unemployment insurance has had to face a backlash linked to support for the idea of the work ethic.[32] As such it involves a political tussle between the idea of insurance against bad times and welfare. In the early and mid-1970s changes to this policy field brought it into significant partisan dispute among political parties as to its appropriate "welfare," "insurance" and "work ethic" components. Critics charged that it was harming the "efficiency" of Canada's labour markets as well.

Ideas collide in the effort to bundle several social policies under the catch-all concept of improving the "quality of life."[33] This was present not only in the social regulation fields identified in Chapters 5 and 12 but also in health care. For example, in the early 1970s the Department of National Health and Welfare launched an effort to gain support for a preventative lifestyle approach to health care as opposed to the curative doctor-dominated system now in place. It got nowhere but reflected an idea which had the support of a modest political constituency.[34]

A major social policy event of the early 1980s was, of course, the entrenchment of a Charter of Rights in the Canadian Constitution.[35] These rights included the rights of women, the handicapped, Canada's native peoples and the aged. While these represent an assertion of the idea of individual liberty and dignity, this idea was not entrenched in an absolute way. Room for manoeuvre was left in the "override" provisions whereby legislatures could temporarily infringe on some of these rights, a concession to Parliamentary sovereignty and to a collective view of the common will. Nonetheless, the Charter will undoubtedly affect social policy in many important ways as citizens, through the courts, seek redress of their rights.

One could go on and on in the realm of social ideas—consumer free choice in the realm of radio and television versus Canadian content; language policy, education and minority rights, multiculturalism versus a bicultural view of Canada, law and order policing versus citizen rights and the rights of criminals. The point to be stressed is that many ideas merge and separate and rise and fall as policies evolve and society changes.

Evolving Objectives: The Case of the
Social Security Review

There is no tidy list of objectives for social policy to match the four initially listed in our review of economic policy objectives. Nor are they as easily quantified or supported by theory (or paradigms) as compact as Keynesian economics or monetarism. This is a blessing or a curse, depending on one's point of view. Social policy could be said to include objectives such as a more equitable distribution of income, the reduction of regional disparities, the promotion of national unity, the stabilization of real income of those on fixed incomes, justice and fairness, and enhancing respect for law and order. But it is evident that the objectives are even more fluid and vague than those of economic policy. Moreover, there is an inevitable and necessary overlap between the two fields. These realities are evident not only from the discussion above, and from earlier analysis in this book, but from the abortive efforts in the 1970s to construct social indicators to parallel the commonly used economic indicators.

Perhaps the best way to see the changing pattern of objectives is to cite briefly the analysis of the Social Security Review begun in 1973 as chronicled in an article by Rick Van Loon.[36] In April 1973 the Minister of National Health and Welfare published a Working Paper on Social Security Review in Canada, known as the "Orange Paper." It led to an elaborate process referred to as the Social Security Review. Its scope was massive, embracing family allowances, social assistance, personal and social service programs for the elderly, unemployment insurance and job creation programs. As Lalonde's Orange Paper put it:

> We have sought, in developing our proposals, to comprehend the whole sweep of social security policy and to develop a comprehensive, logical, and hopefully imaginative approach to this field. We have sought, too, to exercise our ingenuity in finding new and, if necessary, radical, federal-provincial or constitutional arrangements, in order to achieve the kind of integrated social security system which will best serve the needs of the Canadian people.[37]

The impetus for the review in 1973 was not an overriding concern about the lack of progress in redistributing income nor was it due to escalating costs or a welfare backlash. Costs had not increased sharply nor was there anything like the backlash against welfare evident then in the United States. In Canada the only backlash was over the generosity of unemployment insurance. Rather, the impetus came from federal-provincial political problems, in particular the failed attempt from 1968 to 1971 to rewrite and patriate the Constitution. The effort failed at the last moment when Quebec Premier Robert Bourassa withdrew his support because the constitutional scheme failed to protect Quebec's claims and concerns regarding jurisdiction over social policy. Federal-provincial relations in social policy deteriorated further because of the major changes made by Ottawa in 1971 to the Unemployment Insurance program and in Ottawa's 1971-72 proposal to change family allowances from a demogrant to a means-tested program, both made without consultation with provincial governments. A further impetus was supplied by the 1970 Quebec report on health and social welfare, the Castonguay-Nepveu report, which was perceived by federal health and welfare officials as giving the innovative initiative to Quebec in social policy matters rather than to Ottawa. The Social Security Review addressed all these problems. As Van Loon concluded, the review "was initiated in an environment where welfare programs were in many respects a surrogate for broader political issues, a situation that left the reform process very much open to control by larger political and social forces."[38]

The overall objectives of an ideal social security system were set out in the Orange Paper:

> For people who are of working age, and are able to work, there would be employment at at least a living wage. To ensure that a living wage is paid, the state would legislate a minimum wage. If the minimum wage were sufficient to support small family units only, income supplements would be available to meet the costs of child raising in larger families whose incomes fell at or near the minimum wage.[39]

This ideal system flew in the face of several realities of the then existing system of social security. Van Loon's summary of these realities are paraphrased below.

- The system was founded on an assumption of full or nearly full employment and that when unemployment rose, macroeconomic policies would compensate.
- Income from employment was often inadequate, particularly in larger families. Thus, there was growing concern about the so-called "working poor."
- There was little incentive to get off social assistance once one was on it.
- Benefit levels varied widely in different jurisdictions and under different programs.
- Social insurance plans were inadequately funded, particularly the Canada and Quebec pension plans.
- There was a lack of coordination among the various elements of the system.
- There was a stigma to social assistance and some political concern about abuses of the system.[40]

The Orange Paper contained numerous proposals to address these problems. These included an employment strategy, increases in family allowance payments with benefits made taxable, a general income supplementation plan with built-in work incentives, and a guaranteed income to those people whose incomes are insufficient because they are unable or are not expected to work. There were other elements in the federal proposals including proposals to win provincial support, given the latter's jurisdiction in this field. The sweetener would be money, the provincial right under suitable national standards to use funds in federal program areas such as family allowances to supplement and adjust their own programs.

The process of negotiating these myriad proposals was centred in three federal-provincial working parties of officials: one on the employment strategy, one on personal social services, and the other on income maintenance and social insurance. The last of these clearly became the focal point. As could be expected, the policy process accompanying the review began to exert its inevitable influence. Not only did federal-provincial and interdepartmental conflict occur, but the policy environment changed since the review process took several years. For example, the employment strategy ran afoul of interagency dispute between the Department of Health and Welfare and the Department of Manpower and Immigration. For the initiators of the Social Security Review, Marc Lalonde and his deputy minister, A.W. Johnson, the employment strategy was not the centrepiece of their work. So they quickly decided not to spend scarce time and energy to overcome the bureaucratic wars in this aspect of the proposal.

The work of the social services group went on longer, extending until 1978. Its initial report led nowhere, but its work was later revived as a way to keep the review process going, particularly since the income maintenance group was stalled. The heart of the proposals in this sector was a federal proposal to change the funding from shared cost to block funding. The federal preference for block funding was similar here to their growing concern about cost escalation in other federal-provincial social policy fields such as health and education. Legislation incorporating block funding seemed certain to pass in 1978 except that it ran into the massive Trudeau budget cuts exercise of August 1978, referred to earlier in Chapters 10 and 11.

The working party on income maintenance was the most contentious arena in the review process. Work on family allowances and old age security and pensions moved fairly agreeably and led to significant increases in both (about $1 billion each annually). Since these areas arrived at the federal financial trough first, there was simply much less money available when the larger income supplementation proposals, costing about $2 billion annually, reached the treasury. The federal proposals in this field ultimately led to two options. One was based on refundable tax credits and therefore would be delivered federally, and the other was based on transfer payments and therefore would be delivered provincially. Because of opposition by the Department of Finance to using the tax system and because of the undertaking to cooperate with the provinces, Lalonde and Johnson somewhat reluctantly opted for the provincially delivered program funded on a shared costs basis.

The proposal went to Cabinet early in 1975 where the *idea* of income supplementation was supported, but the *funds* were not granted. It was a policy without resources. The opposition in Cabinet was led by Finance Minister John Turner, who opposed further social spending. He was joined by others who feared it would preclude expansion of their own policy areas. On this occasion Prime Minister Trudeau chose not to take sides between Lalonde and Turner.

Later in July 1975, when Bruce Rawson succeeded A.W. Johnson as deputy minister in the Department of Health and Welfare, a smaller $240 proposal was devised. Arriving at Cabinet after Turner had resigned and had left Finance, the proposal was approved early in 1976 with implementation targeted for 1978. In subsequent discussions with the provinces, however, Ontario rejected the program "in part because of opposition to any new shared-cost programs, in part because of a feeling that the program should be federally delivered via the tax system, in part because of a reluctance to take on any new expenditures, and in part because of inherent conservatism."[41] At this point income supplementation appeared to be a lost cause.

The idea of targeted income supplementation was revived, however, within two years. The catalyst was at first glance an unlikely one, the Trudeau $2.5 billion budget cutting exercise of 1978. Van Loon precisely sums up the sudden occasion that led to the tax-based Child Tax Credit.

> One of its major casualties had been the proposed Social Services block-funding arrangement. But no government likes to cancel

proposed programs while offering nothing in return—especially with an election in the offing. What better way of restraint than to replace part of a universal and poorly targeted program with a more sharply targeted income-tested program? If the times make it impossible to establish any new bureaucracy to implement the program, then why not utilize an already existing system to deliver it? And if you can experiment a bit with new forms of program delivery, in accord with the task-force report on tax and transfer program integration, then why not proceed that way?

Suddenly, in a period of expenditure restraint, the time for welfare reform was ripe! Within three weeks after it was proposed to Cabinet by a senior adviser to the prime minister and the Department of Health and Welfare, Cabinet approved an $800 million reduction in the Family Allowance program, elimination of some special child-related tax deductions, and the implementation of a refundable Child Tax Credit delivered via the federal income tax system. The credit is valued at $200 per child (indexed for inflation) and is fully payable to families with incomes up to $18,000. Above that level benefits are reduced at a 5 percent rate as income rises. A full supplementation program it is not, but it is an important beginning for it foreshadows sharper targeting of social programs and pioneers tax-credit delivery.

The legislation passed Parliament with little difficulty; scarcely a provincial voice was raised in dissent. The first benefits are payable in early 1979. Part of what planners had failed to gain through the lengthy Social Security Review they won, with apparent ease, through a conjunction of forces largely outside the welfare system after the Review was over.[42]

There are many other aspects of the Social Security Review process which need not concern us here but which reflect on issues raised continuously in the book, including comprehensive rationality versus piecemeal incrementalism, policies without resources, federal-provincial relations, and central agency-line department relations, all of which lend credence to the view that public policy is an interplay among ideas, structures and processes. Our concern here was primarily to use a specific but large case study to trace the elusive nature of changing social policy objectives. These included varying amounts of concern for increasing the redistributive thrust of social policy. It was not a major *cause* of the review, but it produced specific changes such as the Child Tax Credit. Thus, its *effect* was partly redistributive. Concerns for improving a form of horizontal equity were variously reflected in proposals to allow greater provincial flexibility. Concerns about the stigma of welfare were reflected in the decision to finally go with a tax-based scheme. As we have stressed in Chapters 6 and 12, instrument choice, and the use of the tax system, is a "valued" and not a neutral process.

The social security case study does not, of course, show all of the variations either in social policy ideas, objectives or processes. One must compare it with other analyses in other social policy areas. Space does not allow us to recount these, but there are excellent analyses available in fields such as health care policy, Indian policy, old age security policy and family allowances.[43] We return to major elements of social policy as they are reflected in the next chapters on industrial policy, energy policy and labour market policies.

Structure and Process

To parallel our brief review of economic policy structures, we also note some features of social policy structures at the federal level. As Figure 14.3 shows, social policy embraces several departments and agencies including National Health and Welfare, Employment and Immigration, Justice, Solicitor General, Correctional Services, Secretary of State, the Canadian Broadcasting Corporation, the RCMP, and Indian Affairs and Northern Development. It is instructive to compare and consider the departments and budgets that are part of the Cabinet Committee on Social Development which manages the social envelope and the justice envelope. Not surprisingly, it shows the slipperiness of the social-economic boundaries. First, the EPF fiscal arrangements (medicare and education) are controlled by the Cabinet Committee on Priorities and Planning. The Department of Labour is part of the economic development committee, though arguably could be viewed as a social department. The Department of Environment, despite its "social regulation" role, is part of the economic committee. Employment and Immigration is part of both the social and economic envelopes.

In the 1980s the organizational focal point for social policy has been the Cabinet Committee on Social Development and its agency, the Ministry of State for Social Development. We reviewed some of its resource allocation dilemmas in Chapter 11. The dynamics of this organization varies according to changes in both people and circumstances. The first Minister of Social Development, Jean Chretien, was concurrently Minister of Justice. During much of his tenure he was preoccupied with constitutional negotiations. These led to the en-

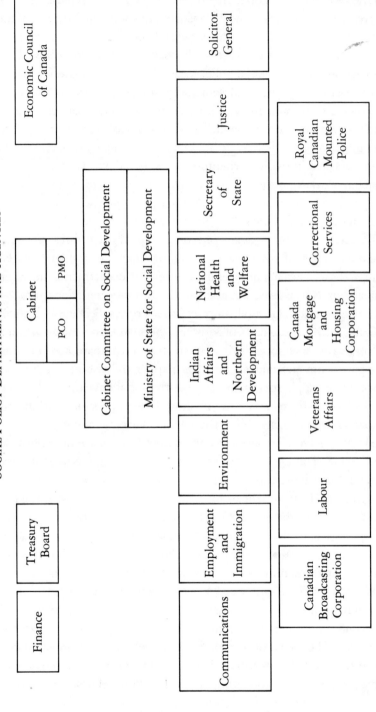

FIGURE 14.3
SOCIAL POLICY DEPARTMENTS AND AGENCIES

trenched Charter of Rights, arguably the most significant social policy initiative of the early 1980s, but forged with virtually no involvement by MSSD nor the Cabinet committee. The first deputy in MSSD was Bruce Rawson, a former Deputy Minister of Health and Welfare, whose interests were primarily in the income maintenance field. He knew little of other social policy domains now lumped in the envelope. Their successors were Senator Jack Austin as minister and Gordon Smith as deputy, the former an unelected politician with previous experience as the prime minister's Principal Secretary and the latter a long time central agency PCO official. These developments, as did the Social Security Review case study, show the increased influence of the central agencies in social policy formulation. This is undoubtedly a reflection of the evolving cost consciousness and fiscal restraint in the late 1970s and early 1980s, as social policy expenditures were projected to decline relative to other fields.

In earlier periods the focus of coordination for social programs did not reside in the central agencies to the same degree. The Department of National Health and Welfare was the focal point of social policy defined in social welfare and social service terms. The Department of Finance has always had a strong say in such matters, especially when the statutory fiscal arrangements were scheduled for renegotation. In the mid 1960s, in the Pearson era, a special planning secretariat in the PCO also sought, without much success, to impose some kind of order on Canada's then styled "war on poverty." Prior to the envelope system a Cabinet committee on social programs existed but suffered from the same problems as did all the committees then, namely the separation of policy approval from resource approval.

Each political regime makes its organizational mark on the broader structural reflection of its social policy preferences and styles. For the Diefenbaker regime social policy was equated, as much as anything else, with an eclectic collection of regional grievances, leading to a forestry and rural development department, the predecessor of DREE. The massive Pearsonian social welfare reforms saw the rapid expansion of the Department of National Health and Welfare, and to a lesser extent the Secretary of State with its new education policy role. With the important exception of the Charter of Rights and the Child Tax Credit, the Trudeau social reforms leaned to the vague "quality of life" view of social policy and witnessed the establishment of new ministers of multiculturalism, and also sports and recreation.

Foreign Policy

The evolving content of economic and social policy have thus far been examined in a domestic setting only. Both economic and social policies contribute to, or detract from, the achievement of national unity and integration and to an evolving state of national independence. But the other half of this domestic policy coin is found in foreign policy and Canada's international relations. Foreign policy is fundamentally a territorial definition of policy. Like other territorial or spatial definitions such as regional policy, it is therefore bound to cut across most or perhaps all of the domestic policy fields, albeit some fields more than others. Foreign policy is therefore a composite product of Canada's domestic policy ideas, structures and processes, and is influenced by those of other states in the world community.

Of critical importance in Canada's foreign policy is our economic dependence on foreign trade which accounts for about 25 to 30 percent of Canada's economic activity. Much of Canada's trade is in resource products, augmented by a very limited and truncated range of manufacturing products. The great majority of Canada's trade is with one country, the United States. Related to this economic reality is the extensive foreign ownership of Canada's economy, again primarily by American multinational enterprises. These economic realities, despite several efforts to construct counterweights to the north-south continental axis, have produced the inevitable problems of dependence. In the more extreme view this dependence is characterized as a virtual state of economic colonialism.

In Canada's early history the essence of foreign policy was to secure the real and symbolic levers of independence from the United Kingdom. These were largely achieved by the beginning of World War II. The not unimportant residue of the British connection in foreign policy is found in Canada's continuing support for the Commonwealth, an institution which, in its modern form, provides an important link as well to countries of the Third World. In the post-World War II era, however, Canada evolved more and more into the American axis. This was partly a product of war and post-war defence arrangements, and the official encouragement of foreign equity ownership and investments, but it was also a cultural phenomenon, propelled by the power and influence of Canadian exposure to the American media and by the geographic proximity of Canada's neighbour.

A further historical product of considerable importance to Canada's foreign policy was Canada's emergence out of the ravages of World War II as a significant middle power on the world stage, a power of even greater influence in the immediate post-war era because of the weakened state of Western Europe. It was in this era that Canada's foreign policy developed a highly articulate commitment to internationalism, the latter epitomized by the chief architect of this view, Lester B. Pearson.

Ideas

The central ideas of Canada's foreign policy are therefore a composite of the ideas embedded in domestic policy but often clothed in the language of international relations and the territorial definition of such policies. Certainly, nationalism, or national independence, is a central idea sometimes preached and sometimes practised. It is evident in such symbolic decisions as establishing the maple leaf as a national flag and in support for international sporting and cultural events and exchanges. More concretely, it is evident in policies such as rigid and even discriminatory immigration policies, the aggressive National Energy Program, the foreign ownership limits on broadcasting and banking, and the review and screening role of the Foreign Investment Review Agency.

The opposite of the nationalist idea is internationalism on the one hand and continentalism on the other.[44] The former usually evokes more positive connotations. It embraces policy support for the Western defence alliance centred in NATO, for the work of the United Nations, for the General Agreement on Tariffs and Trade (GATT), for humanitarian immigration policies, for the reduction of nuclear weapons and proliferation, for the international redistribution of wealth through development aid to Commonwealth and other Third World countries, and to international peace-keeping functions in at least some of the world's trouble spots. Internationalism can also embrace the Canadian role as diplomatic intermediary between the United States and Europe, and perhaps between the rich North and the poor South. Internationalism in these numerous contexts is thus an amalgam of ideas including equality, equity and the preservation of world peace.

Continentalism on the other hand evokes a less favourable view, an idea to avoid rather than support. It initially evokes a concern for Canada's stock of wealth in her natural resources and the American desire to utilize them, but it can also include American domination of the

Canadian economy and of Canadian cultural life. Nonetheless, continentalist policies have been explicitly or implicitly pursued, albeit usually clothed in the positive terms of economic development and efficiency. These policies include those on foreign investment, the auto pact, defence production sharing arrangements, energy policy in the 1960s and 1970s, and trade policy generally.

Somewhere between internationalism and continentalism Canadian foreign policy has also lent support to the idea of finding a counterweight to the dominance of the Canadian-American relationship.[45] This has been attempted and defined in various ways. For the Diefenbaker government it was a failed attempt to reassert a stronger trade relationship between Canada and the United Kingdom. For the Trudeau government it was an attempt in 1972 to devise a so-called "Third Option" between the status quo (Option One) and closer integration with the United States (Option Two). In part this implied seeking greater ties with Western Europe and Japan as a counterweight. The Minister of External Affairs, Mitchell Sharp, described it ultimately in nationalistic terms as follows:

> We will have a permanent test for each policy instrument we devise. What will it do to strengthen our economy and reduce its vulnerability? And we will be compelled to examine each policy instrument in relation to the others, because each will be introduced to support and reinforce the others. The proof of the pudding will be the kind of industrial strategy we pursue, the kind of energy policy we adopt, and so on.... The emphasis of the Third Option is on Canada—on decisions that have to be taken in this country by Canadians rather than matters to be negotiated with the United States.[46]

Evolving Objectives
The hydra-headed territorial imperatives of nationalism, internationalism and continentalism obviously produce a panoply of interdependent and sometimes contradictory objectives as diverse as those present in the economic and social policy fields discussed in the first two sections of this chapter. Numerous policy fields inject themselves into the foreign policy arena including defence policy, immigration policy, trade policy, foreign investment policy, foreign aid policy, agricultural policy, mineral policy and energy policy, to name only a few policy fields. The best way to see foreign policy objectives in practice is to briefly trace one or two foreign

policy cases or issues. In this respect the experience of the Trudeau era in foreign policy is instructive particularly because Prime Minister Trudeau placed such an initial emphasis on altering in a "rational" way the perceived thrust of the Pearson era, a foreign policy labelled by Trudeau as being both reactive (that is, unplanned) and internationalistic (that is, insufficiently attuned to national self-interest).

Trudeau's review of foreign policy led to a White Paper in 1970 which outlined six policy objectives.[47] These were: fostering economic growth; safeguarding sovereignty and independence; working for peace and security; promoting social justice abroad; enhancing the quality of life; and ensuring a harmonious natural environment. Though fostered by Trudeau's strong penchant for rationality, the presumed change in objectives were not without some foundation in the changing geopolitics of the world community in the early 1970s. There were clearly, for example, growing problems arising out of oil pollution from super-tankers and sea-based transport of resources through Canada's arctic waters, satellite communication, and a depleting fisheries stock off Canada's coasts. The social justice and quality of life objectives were partly a product of genuine concern expressed by other states and partly a reflection of Trudeau's domestic policy objectives especially in the early 1968 to 1971 period.

The need to elevate national self-interest and hence, almost by definition, to seek ways to reduce dependence on the United States was also congruent with Trudeau's professed view of developing counter-weights to prevailing tendencies, in short a desire to go against the grain of whatever tendency was prevalent. There is of course a special and specific foreign policy dimension to the counterweight thesis—the search for ways to reduce American influence. But Trudeau exercised a fascination with his concept in other fields as well. When federalism is too decentralized, then centralize. When market power is too great, then lean toward greater state power and control.

The formal reordering of priorities by Trudeau undoubtedly reflected some genuine concern about emerging world issues, but they were not as starkly in opposition to the Pearsonian concept as either Trudeau or his critics of the day believed. Michael Tucker captures the dilemma of internationalism and nationalism when portrayed as polar opposites.

Less well recognized, as it was obscured by the nationalist sovereignty-oriented rhetoric of the foreign policy review days, was the fact that Trudeau's nationalism was in its essence a form of internationalism. By this we mean that he conceived of Canada as a mentor state, taking initiatives on behalf of the world community. Canada, Mr. Trudeau mused in this vein, "is perhaps in the advantageous position of not making decisions which can imperil the future of the world. You know, it is easier for a small country like us to take a chance at having our trust betrayed, because if we are betrayed then we will suffer for it, but all humanity won't have to pay the price. . . ."

Trudeau's major foreign policy initiatives in the late 1960s were entirely congruous with this perspective. His "independent" overtures toward the People's Republic of China reflected in part his feeling that the continued alienation of the world's most populous community from the community of nations could only augur ill. The NATO review and Canada's subsequent troop reductions within the alliance reflected not only the prime minister's antimilitarism but also his view that military alliances were an anachronism, if not a danger, in a world of detente. This fundamental shift in Canadian foreign and defence policies away from the NATO cornerstone of the Pearsonian era was signalled to the Canadian public in Mr. Trudeau's Calgary speech of April 1969. The prime minister advised therein that the aims of Canadian foreign policy were "to serve our national interests." Yet he quickly entered the caveat that "when I say national interest I am not thinking in any egotistical sense of just what is happening to Canadians. It's in our national interest to reduce tensions in the world. . . ."

This might well have been a quote from the book of middle-power internationalism, if there were one. In terms of his belief in Canada's right and responsibility to help reduce global tensions Pierre Trudeau was a Pearsonian. The differences between the two men cannot be seen as quintessential but more a reflection upon their times. Trudeau felt, as did Pearson, that Canadian interests and values could often best be expressed through international relationships. For Pearson this was through activities in the military-security realms, in alliance membership and through peacekeeping. For Trudeau this was through environmental and arms control measures, and developmental assistance in the Third World. Down to the mid-1970s, Trudeau's thinking on this score remained in the mould of Canadian nationalist sentiment of the mid-late 1960s. While hardly hostile to the idea of international involvement as a vital aspect and expression of Canadian interests, this sentiment was strongly opposed to a particular practice of that involvement which at the time seemed out of step with a post-Cold War international environment.[48]

The above reference to the connection between foreign and defence policy also raises questions about the degree to which Trudeau succeeded in developing a more planned and less reactive foreign policy. The logic is that the clearer one is about one's objectives, the more assertive one can be—in short, the more one can do first things first. The evolution of defence policy within this set of reordered priorities in the 1970s is of considerable interest in this regard.

In Trudeau's view, the foreign policy review had revealed that

> NATO in reality determined all our defence policy. We had no defence policy, so to speak, except that of NATO. And our defence policy had determined all of our foreign policy. And we had no foreign policy of any importance except that which flowed from NATO. And this is a false perspective for any country. It is a false perspective to have a military alliance determine your foreign policy. It should be your foreign policy which determines your military policy.[49]

In light of this view Trudeau announced on April 3rd, 1969 that Canada's armed forces would have four priority roles:

(a) the surveillance of our own territory and coast-lines—for instance, the protection of our sovereignty;

(b) the defence of North America in cooperation with United States forces;

(c) The fulfilment of such NATO commitments as may be agreed upon; and

(d) the performance of such international peacekeeping roles as we may, from time to time, assume.[50]

Thus, defence policies would become more oriented to North America and away from a European focus through NATO. This view and the logical ambiguities behind it brought Prime Minister Trudeau and his chief foreign policy advisor of the day, Ivan Head, into a sharp conflict of views with senior officials in the Department of External Affairs. The differences were not merely a reflection of narrow bureaucratic infighting but also of differences in ideas and the logical relationships between objectives and ideas.

Thordarson's analysis shows how the Trudeau view misunderstood the connection between Canada's military commitment to NATO in Europe and Western Europe's view of Canada.[51] NATO was far more than a defence pact. It was rooted in broader foreign policy considerations, both economic and human in the broadest sense. Thus, DEA officials argued that it was not defence policy that produced foreign policy as Trudeau believed, but the reverse. When NATO defence commitments were reduced in real dollars in the early 1970s, Western Europe took this as a signal of Canada's reduced overall foreign policy interest in Europe, despite efforts to forge new links with Europe in matters of trade. NATO was an essential part, moreover, if one was to secure a counterweight to U.S. influence.

The relationships between ideas, structures and processes was evident in the foreign policy review process and its outcomes. Tucker describes the net effect of the early 1970s debate on the role of the Department of External Affairs (DEA).

> The move of the Trudeau government away from NATO Europe signalled and sustained a significant reduction in the policy-making influence of the Department of External Affairs. Policy advisers in the DEA realized, perhaps more clearly than others in Ottawa in the late 1960s, the subtle link between Canada's national economic interest in Europe and its internationalist commitment to NATO. It was for this reason that the DEA argued for the status quo. As a sensitive student of Canadian foreign policy observed at the time, the DEA "did not recommend that the same direction of policy the prime minister eventually chose should not be traced to some pavlovian instinct for the status quo.... Such an explanation would be both unfair and inaccurate." Yet in policy-making terms the net effect for the DEA was the same; because of its position on NATO the reservations harboured by the P.M. and his close advisers about the Department as a bastion of bureaucratic conservatism were heightened, and its authority was reduced accordingly. Also, for the DEA this deliberate move on the part of the prime minister paralleled a tendency in that direction which was perhaps inevitable. With the advent of new economic, environmental and social concerns which came to supplant the high politics of military-security matters in Canadian foreign policy, the DEA lost further ground to other departments whose expertise on the issues of low politics it could not match. Again the significance of this tendency as an underlying factor in Canadian foreign policy making in the 1970s should not be understated.[52]

The slipperiness of the objectives at stake and how they are ranked are revealed by the evolving defence-foreign policy connection later in the 1970s. In August 1971 the Nixon government imposed a 10 percent surcharge on manufactured goods entering the United States. Canada failed to obtain an exemption from this move, as had occurred in the past.

This "shock" led to an immediate search (again) for a counterweight to U.S. influence. In addition to initiatives such as the establishment of the Foreign Investment Review Agency (FIRA), the Nixon shocks led to the "Third Option" statement by Mitchell Sharp referred to earlier. This led, in turn, eventually to a search for a stronger contractual link with Western Europe and Japan. Western Europe's interests, however, were in part linked to a desire to see greater evidence of Canada's NATO defence commitment. Paradoxically, the United States was even more assertive about Canada's failing commitment to NATO. The American concern was itself caused by her own view that her commitments to Western Europe were too burdensome and that other allies should share the burden. Thus, in the mid-1970s the policy logic went this way. To counterbalance U.S. economic influence in general *foreign* policy, one needed Western Europe. To increase the prospects of securing this need, one had to support NATO more strenuously. To support NATO would be to support U.S. views of *defence* policy.

In addition to the interplay between these territorial and policy field definitions of policy, there were certain resource allocation realities which could no longer be postponed. These concerned the re-requipment of Canada's armed forces.[53] Canada's military hardware was deteriorating badly and its personnel reduced considerably. New aircraft, tanks, ships and other heavy capital equipment had to be acquired. Decisions on such equipment would be needed for domestic purposes as well as NATO purposes. The choice of such equipment, moreover, would have effects for the next decade on the military configuration of Canada's forces. The choices would also involve economic relations between potential American versus Western European arms suppliers. Foreign policy would therefore involve many departments in Ottawa and decisions would proceed over several years. For example, in 1971 the Defence Policy White Paper had spoken of the preference for "versatile forces" and "multipurpose equipment" to meet the broad sovereignty goods of foreign and defence policies. But later procurement decisions on the Aurora Long Range Patrol Aircraft and on fighter aircraft reflected the inevitable hodgepodge of defence, foreign, territorial, and national and regional procurement criteria, all forged in the midst of escalating defence equipment costs, technological advancement and a declining economy.

Tucker concluded that during this period there was no overall consensus about where the permanent direction of foreign and defence policies lay.

> There was, down to that time at least, no consensus about the paramount importance of Western Europe as a counterweight. Lacking this consensus, policy making in these areas could not but be consigned to the tortuous mill of the policy process. This was a mill of conflicting perspectives on Canada's military roles, whether these should be "sovereignty protection" or NATO-oriented, whether a Western European link was the best or the only feasible alternative to a continental embrace, whether attempts should be made to escape that embrace at all in an era of developing regionalism. These differing perspectives constituted part of the "domestic" sources of Canadian foreign policy on the related issues of a NATO commitment and a European economic link. As they all were at once influential and conflictual, it can be said that the architects of the "new" foreign policy for the 1970s had one of their wishes fulfilled, but with a vengeance: that Canada's foreign policy should reflect domestic interests and concerns.[54]

It can, of course, be argued that one cannot judge foreign policy only on the basis of one or two policy case studies within it. There were many other aspects of policy proceeding in parallel. Canada's initiatives on the Law of the Sea are acknowledged by many to be an example of an active and well-prepared area of policy development. On the nuclear front, Canada did devise perhaps the strongest rules of any nuclear exporter to help prevent nuclear proliferation—so much so that some argue it was at the cost of actual nuclear reactor export sales. Canada's foreign aid budgets increased in the early and mid-1970s, and thus reflected the goals set out in the foreign policy review. After declining in the latter part of the 1970s, such expenditures increased significantly in the early 1980s despite the serious economic downturn. The latter commitment is attributed directly to Prime Minister Trudeau's personal interest in the North-South dialogue.

All of these fields, however, reflected the almost inevitable ebb and flow of the dominant foreign policy ideas. The analysis of industrial, energy and labour market policies in the next three chapters will also show that our examples are not atypical.

Structure and Process
The brief account above of the defence-foreign policy changes and of the shocks to Canada-United States relations has already given us a glimpse

of changes in the organizations and processes of foreign policy making. It is evident, for example, that the Department of External Affairs (DEA) has gone through several phases in recent decades in its somewhat episodic role as the grand coordinator of Canada's foreign policy.[55]

In the first phase from World War II to the late 1960s DEA was clearly the leading agency, its role reinforced by its close connection to the prime minister, a fusion most epitomized by Lester Pearson's years as prime minister, but also in the earlier St. Laurent-Pearson era when Pearson was Secretary of State for External Affairs. The Diefenbaker era provided an aberration of this close relationship, but even in this period DEA's supremacy among Ottawa departments was not seriously challenged.

During the Trudeau era, DEA's role changed significantly. This was because initially its senior officials disputed the basis of Trudeau's rational foreign policy constructions, including, as we have seen, the downgrading of the economic and diplomatic implication of the NATO defence alliance. DEA's role also declined for reasons similar to the decline of the Department of Finance, namely the emergence in the Trudeau era of other central agencies, including the Prime Minister's Office where Ivan Head resided. Moreover, the more that the international economic order created stress, the more other line departments and agencies defended their turf and the policies within them. These fields involved expertise which DEA did not necessarily possess. Thus, issues such as the law of the sea and acid rain required the involvement of the Department of the Environment; immigration issues involved the Department of Employment and Immigration; nuclear exports brought in Atomic Energy of Canada and Industry, Trade and Commerce, foreign aid involved the Canadian International Development Agency (CIDA), energy policy involved EMR, Petro-Canada and the National Energy Board, and grain exports involved the Department of Agriculture and the National Wheat Board. This is not to suggest that other agencies were not part of foreign policy in earlier periods, but now there were more of them and they were struggling in an international and domestic economy that was less hospitable than the 1950s and 1960s.

Moreover, provincial governments and their agencies and Crown corporations were far more assertive in the foreign policy field. This was true not only in respect of Quebec in relations with France and the Francophone Commonwealth, but also of Western Canadian provinces in resource exports, tariffs and Crown corporation borrowings in foreign capital markets, and Atlantic Canada in the fisheries, law of the sea and off-shore resources. Even an issue such as regional development incentives were viewed increasingly as a nontariff barrier to international trade under GATT and consequently a concern to all provinces.

In the early 1980s the DEA role evolved in still a different direction. Foreign policy organization and process was affected by the envelope system and by the reorganization of DEA itself when its trade policy functions were increased in 1982 through the transfer to DEA of the Trade Commissioner Service previously located in the Department of Industry, Trade and Commerce. We did not examine the External Affairs or Defence expenditures envelopes in Chapter 11, but two aspects of the envelope system deserve mention. First, the Cabinet Committee on External Affairs and Defence Policy that manages the two envelopes is chaired by the Minister of External Affairs. The committee, however, in contrast to the economic and social committees, is not supported by a large ministry secretariat. Only a handful of officials support the committee. On balance this would appear to give the coordinative edge to DEA itself and so reinforces DEA's influence. DEA also chairs the two senior coordinating committees, the Interdepartmental Committee on External Relations and the Interdepartmental Committee on External Relations for Developing Countries.

This preeminence, however, is partly counterbalanced by the realities imposed by the content of the spending in the two envelopes and the sources of flexibility and discretion in each. DEA's own expenditures in the External Affairs' envelope are overwhelmingly personnel-oriented and thus there is little room for change. The greatest area of discretion is in CIDA's far larger budget, and it is here that discretion has been primarily exercised, both in increasing Canada's commitments to developmental aid, and, since these expenditures involve extensive domestic contracting, in promoting industrial development in Canada. The defence envelope is large but contains little room for manoeuvre. It is also highly personnel-oriented and, in addition, involves a heavy capital equipment and weapons component which cannot be changed easily in the short run. Moreover, when such major weapons procurement decisions do arise every few years, they immediately involve several departments because of their military and economic effects. As to other policy fields with foreign policy implications, it follows that DEA and its minister cannot actually allocate resources in these fields since they are lodged in the other envelopes examined in Chapter 11.

As to the trade promotion role of DEA envisioned by the 1982 reorganization, it is too early to judge the impact of this change. It clearly places the economic self-interest idea alongside the diplomacy role *within DEA*. This is bound to affect the internal career system of DEA, but it remains to be seen whether it affects the conduct or outcomes of foreign policy per se, since these ideas have always been, and still are, present *within the government* as a whole as well as the country in general.

One final attribute of foreign policy structure and process deserves comment. This is the link with the notion of diplomacy, namely the secretiveness of many aspects of international relations and the conduct of such relations at a very personal leader-to-leader or diplomat-to-diplomat level. While federal-provincial and intra-Cabinet relations also turn on heavy doses of secrecy and personal chemistry, it is fair to say that foreign policy trades on these characteristics to an even greater degree. It is not, however, a totally closed process. It must be emphasized that many of the interest groups examined in Chapter 3 as well as large individual enterprises, including Crown corporations, continuously attempt to influence foreign policy both in Canada and in countries whose decisions might affect them favourably or unfavourably.

Conclusions

This chapter reflects the problems policy makers face. We know that policy must be compartmentalized to be made more manageable, and yet we know simultaneously that policy fields are interrelated and must be given a semblace of coherence both in the current period in question and over longer periods of time. Some ranking of different ideas and objectives in the three overall economic, social and foreign policy fields undoubtedly occurs, but it is an elusive and never-ending task. Beneath the excesses of policy rhetoric and the genuineness of many new "initiatives" lie the bedrock realities of dominant ideas and changing views of political power reflected in policy structures and processes.

While we must eventually compartmentalize policy fields, the chapter has sought to guide the reader through the broader interdependence of the three fields. There is more to learn in breadth than in the precise details, although the latter is eventually necessary too. It is also necessary to analyze single policy fields by first being intellectually dispossessed of the notion that economic policy is only about markets and efficiency, and social policy only about redistribution. It is also necessary to know clearly that foreign policy imposes a territorial and therefore partly conflicting definition to all policy fields to a greater or lesser extent.

In the next three chapters we present an illustrative look at three major policy fields, industrial policy, energy policy and labour market policy. Our analysis is illustrative in the sense that by reviewing three policy fields we hope to show how a similar approach could be used to assist those studying other policy fields not examined in the book (see Appendix A for a guide to other policy field sources and literature). The next three chapters present a decade by decade review of the evolution of public policy in each field. They also show the economic, social and foreign policy content of each field by examining the persistence of dominant ideas and the interplay among ideas, structures and processes. Each chapter also reflects the idiocyncratic features of each policy field, including the policy paradigms and rhetorical language that influence and cloud the debate in each field. Together, the three fields cover a comprehensive domain and present a cumulative portrait of the drift and evolution of policy in Canada. In combination with our overall survey of the economic, social and foreign policy umbrella fields, they should allow the reader to venture into other policy fields with some greater sense of direction.

NOTES

1. Charles Lindblom, *Politics and Markets* (New York: Basic Books, 1977) and Joseph A. Schumpeter, *Capitalism, Socialism and Democracy,* Third Edition (New York: Harper Torch Books, 1962) and Lawrence C. Pierce, *The Politics of Fiscal Policy Formation* (Pacific Palisades, California: Good Year Publishing, 1971).
2. Robert Campbell, *Grand Illusions: The Keynesian Experience in Canada* (Manuscript: Publication in 1983).
3. Richard W. Phidd and G. Bruce Doern, *The Politics and Management of Canadian Economic Policy* (Toronto: Macmillan of Canada, 1978), Chapters 7 and 8.
4. Phidd and Doern, *op. cit.,* Chapter 2.
5. See Anthony Carless, *Initiative and Response* (Montreal: McGill-Queen's University Press, 1977); H. Lithwick, *Regional Economic Policy: The Canadian Experience* (Toronto: McGraw-Hill Ryerson, 1978); and Economic Council of Canada, *Living Together* (Ottawa: Minister of Supply and Services, 1980); and Special Symposium on "Regional Policy in North America," *Canadian Journal of Regional Science,* Vol. V, No. 2 (Autumn, 1982).
6. David Wolfe, "The State and Economic Policy in Canada, 1968-75" in L. Panitch, ed., *The Canadian State* (Toronto: University of Toronto Press, 1977), pp. 251-288; and Phidd and Doern, *op. cit.,* Chapter 2; and Employment and Immigration Canada, *Labour Market Development in the 1980s* (Ottawa: Minister of Supply and Services, 1981), Chapter 3.
7. Employment and Immigration Canada, *op. cit.,* Chapter 6.
8. Phidd and Doern, *op. cit.,* Chapter 10.
9. See Milton Friedman, *Inflation and Unemployment: the New Dimension of Politics,* 1976 Albert Nobel Lecture (London: 1977); John K. Galbraith, *The New Industrial Estate* (New York: Signet Books, 1967); and John K. Galbraith, *Economics and the Public Purse* (New York: Signet Books, 1973).
10. See Lester C. Thurow, *The Zero-Sum Society* (New York: Penguin Books, 1981); and Robert Heilbroner and Lester Thurow, *The Five Economic Challenges* (Englewood Cliffs: Prentice Hall, 1981).
11. James M. Buchanan and Richard E. Wagner, *Democracy in Deficit* (New York: Academic Press, 1977), Chapter 8; Fraser Institute, *The Illusion of Wage and Price Controls* (Vancouver: Fraser Institute, 1976); and Clarence L. Barber and John C.P. McCallum, *Unemployment and Inflation: The Canadian Experience* (Ottawa: Canadian Institute for Economic Policy, 1980).
12. See Ralph Miliband, *The State in Capitalist Society* (London: Quartet Books, 1973).
13. Canada, *The Way Ahead* (Ottawa: Minister of Supply and Services, 1976).
14. See M. Biggs, *The Challenge: Adjust or Protect* (Ottawa: The North-

South Institute, 1980); David H. Blake and Robert S. Walters, *The Politics of Global Economic Relations* (Englewood Cliffs: Prentice-Hall, 1976); David R. Protheroe, *Imports and Politics* (Montreal: Institute for Research on Public Policy, 1980); and Rianne Mahon, *The Politics of Industrial Strategy in Canada: Textiles* (Toronto: University of Toronto Press, 1983).

15. C. Green, *Canadian Industrial Organization and Policy* (Toronto: McGraw-Hill Ryerson, 1980).

16. Phidd and Doern, *op. cit.,* Chapters 3 and 4.

17. G. Bruce Doern and Peter Aucoin, eds., *Public Policy in Canada* (Ottawa: Macmillan of Canada, 1979), p. 67.

18. See James Rice and Michael Prince, *Social Policy and Administration* (Manuscript); Andrew Armitage, *Social Welfare in Canada* (Toronto: McClelland and Stewart, 1975); Dennis Guest, *The Emergence of Social Security in Canada* (Vancouver: University of British Columbia Press, 1980); Bruce D. McNaughton, *Public Finance for Political Profit: The Politics of Social Security in Canada 1941-1977,* Ph.D. Thesis, Department of Political Science, Carleton University, 1980; and Marsha A. Chandler and W.M. Chandler, *Public Policy and Provincial Politics* (Toronto: McGraw-Hill Ryerson, 1979), Chapter 6.

19. Harold Wilensky and Charles Lebeaux, *Industrial Society and Social Welfare* (New York: Free Press, 1968), p. 138. See also D. Guest, *op. cit.*

20. Rice and Prince, *op. cit.,* Chapter 1.

21. See K. Bryden, *Old Age Pensions and Policy Making in Canada* (Montreal: McGill-Queen's University Press), Chapters 3 and 4.

22. Keith Banting, *The Welfare State and Canadian Federalism* (Montreal: McGill-Queen's University Press, 1982), p. 11.

23. *Ibid.,* p. 11.

24. Economic Council of Canada, *Financing Confederation* (Ottawa: Minister of Supply and Services, 1982), Chapters 6 and 7.

25. See, for example, Canada, *Report of the Federal Cultural Policy Review Committee* (Ottawa: Minister of Supply and Services, 1982), Science Council of Canada, *Canada as a Conserver Society* (Ottawa: Science Council of Canada, 1977).

26. W.I. Gillespie, *The Incidence of Taxes and Public Expenditures in the Canadian Economy* (Ottawa: 1964), p. 181.

27. W.I. Gillespie, *The Redistribution of Income in Canada* (Draft paper, 1975, section II), p. 49.

28. W.I. Gillespie, "On the Redistribution of Income in Canada," *Canadian Tax Journal,* Vol. XXIV, No. 4, 1976, p. 435.

29. W.I. Gillespie, "The State and Income Redistribution," *Canadian Taxation,* Vol. 3, No. 3 (Fall, 1981), p. 153. See also Grant Reuber, "The Impact of Government Policies on the Distribution of Income in Canada: A Review," *Canadian Public Policy,* Vol. IV, No. 4, 1978, pp. 505-529; and

"The Measurement of Income Distribution" Panel Discussion in *Canadian Public Policy*, Vol. V, No. 4, 1979, pp. 493-517.

30. Harvey Lithwick, "Regional Policy: The Embodiment of Contradictions," in G. Bruce Doern, ed., *How Ottawa Spends Your Tax Dollars 1982* (Toronto: James Lorimer Publishers, 1982), p. 135.

31. See Bryden, *op. cit.*, Chapter 6 and Canadian Council on Social Development, *Social Policies for the 1980s* (Ottawa: Canadian Council on Social Development, 1981). See also Simon McInnes, *Federal-Provincial Negotiation: Family Allowances 1970-1976*, Ph.D. Thesis, Department of Political Science, Carleton University, Ottawa, 1978.

32. See Reuben Hasson, "The Cruel War: Social Security Abuse in Canada," *Canadian Taxation*, Vol. 3, No. 3 (Fall, 1981), pp. 114-147.

33. See G. Bruce Doern, ed., *How Ottawa Spends Your Tax Dollars 1982* (Toronto: James Lorimer Publishers, 1982), pp. 32-35.

34. Betty Muggah, "A New Perspective: The Making of a New Paradigm for Health Policy," *Macdonald Essays* (Ottawa: School of Public Administration, Carleton University, 1982).

35. See Robert Sheppard and Michael Valpy, *The National Deal* (Toronto: 1982).

36. Rick Van Loon, "Reforming Welfare in Canada," *Public Policy*, Vol. 27, No. 4 (Fall, 1979), pp. 469-504. See also Dennis Guest, *op. cit.*, Chapter 12.

37. Quoted in Van Loon, *op. cit.*, pp. 469-470.

38. Van Loon, *op. cit.*, p. 475.

39. Quoted in Van Loon, *op. cit.*, pp. 476-477.

40. Van Loon, *op. cit.*, pp. 477-479.

41. *Ibid.*, p. 497.

42. *Ibid.*, p. 499.

43. See Bryden, *op. cit.*; Malcolm Taylor, *Health Insurance and Canadian Public Policy* (Montreal: McGill-Queen's University Press, 1978); Sally M. Weaver, *Making Canadian Indian Policy* (Toronto: University of Toronto Press, 1981); and Simon McInnes, *op. cit.*

44. See Peyton V. Lyon and Brian W. Tomlin, *Canada as an International Actor* (Toronto: Macmillan of Canada, 1979), Chapter 3; and Brian Tomlin, ed., *Canada's Foreign Policy: Analysis and Trends* (Toronto: Methuen, 1978); and Stephen Clarkson, *Canada and the Reagan Challenge* (Ottawa: Canadian Institute for Economic Policy, 1982).

45. Andrew Axline, Maureen Molot, J. Hyndman and Peyton V. Lyon, eds., *Continental Community: Independence and Integration in North America* (Toronto: McClelland and Stewart, 1974).

46. Quoted in Michael Tucker, *Canadian Foreign Policy* (Toronto: McGraw-Hill Ryerson, 1980), p. 86.

47. See Bruce Thordarson, *Trudeau and Foreign Policy* (Toronto: Oxford University Press, 1972), Chapters 6 and 7; Lyon and Tomlin, *op. cit.*, Chapter 3; and Tucker, *op. cit.*, Chapters 1, 2 and 3.

48. Tucker, *op. cit.,* pp. 10-11.
49. Quoted in Tucker, *op. cit.,* pp. 228-229.
50. Prime Minister P.E. Trudeau, "A Defence Policy for Canada," *Statements and Speeches,* No. 69/7 (April 3, 1969).
51. Thordarson, *op. cit.,* Chapter 5.
52. Tucker, *op. cit.,* p. 229.
53. See Dan Middlemiss, "Department of National Defence," in G. Bruce Doern, ed., *Spending Tax Dollars 1980* (Ottawa: School of Public Administration, Carleton University, 1980), Chapter 3.
54. Tucker, *op. cit.,* p. 233.
55. See Tucker, *op. cit.,* Chapter 1; and Canada, *Royal Commission on Conditions of Foreign Service* (Ottawa: Minister of Supply and Services, 1981), pp. 60-86; and J.L. Granatstein, *A Man of Influence: Norman A. Robertson and Canadian Statecraft 1929-68* (Ottawa: Deneau Publishers, 1981), Chapter VII.

CHAPTER 15

INDUSTRIAL POLICY

Many see the primary concern of industrial policy to be that of ensuring that Canada's industrial and overall economic competitiveness is maintained and advanced domestically and in foreign markets. Accordingly, it focuses on the links between industrial structure and employment, international trade and Canada's balance of payments and investment. If Keynesian policy operated on the demand side of the economic equation and to facilitate stabilization, then industrial policy is concerned with the basic supply and productive capability of the economy set in an international competitive context. The focus on the need for new productive capability is seen in particular as a necessary antidote for an inflation-oriented economy.

Morici, Smith and Lea suggest that there are three major approaches to industrial policy:[1] one which favours a freer international trade and domestic nonintervention approach; one which favours interventionism in both territorial domains; and one which favours freer international trade and domestic intervention. While these classifications are useful at a very general level, especially since they specifically link the domestic and international dimensions, they are insufficient in dealing with the nature of interventionism. Our approach suggests the need to view industrial policy and the nature of the interventionism in a far more subtle way and in a larger historical context. In short, one must link industrial policy to key ideas, structures and processes, including the institutional imperatives present in Canadian political life.

Industrial policy in the post-World War II era has been a much more elusive beast than that implied by the above definition. Much of the elusiveness has been caused by the shifting conceptual categories into which it has been put. In the late 1940s and 1950s industrial policy was expressed in terms of overall economic and social reconstruction. In the 1960s there was an attempt to give a focus to the manufacturing sector while practising the ritual of Keynesian policy, but in a manner which we characterize in this chapter as ad hocism with a vengeance. In the 1970s there was an attempt to be comprehensive not only in the policy fields encompassed but in the effort to involve the major institutions of Canadian political life in different forms of consultations. In the early 1980s there was an apparently sudden public emphasis given to natural resources and to so-called mega projects, a focus which clouded the severe need to restructure the Canadian industrial system in the face of the new international economic order and the imperatives and contradictions between free trade and protectionism.

Particularly since the early 1970s, an industrial policy has often been referred to as an "industrial strategy." It seemed to denote the endorsement of a general framework by which the Government of Canada, provincial and other levels of government, exercised influence over the behaviour of public and private industrial firms. The degree to which these initiatives were coordinated could vary to a considerable degree. The nature of governmental policies pursued would be influenced by the degree of commitment held by political and business leaders to either a laissez faire or a highly interventionist ideology of industrial policy formulation.

Building on our earlier review of historical trends and priorities in Chapters 1, 10 and 14, the chapter shows in more particular ways how industrial policy deals with historically persistent ideas. These include:

- Sir John A. Macdonald's view of industrial policy as "nation building" in partial defiance of continental efficiencies;
- the free trade versus protectionism debate symbolized by the defeat of the free-trade oriented Laurier government in 1911;
- the on-going dilemmas of dependence and independence inherent in Canada-United States relations;
- the post-World War II notions of the positive state couched in reconstruction and Keynesianism and forged by the bitter memory of pre-war depression and war itself;
- the attempt to construct in the 1950s and 1960s a liberal international order for trade and investment under bodies such as GATT and the International Monetary Fund;
- the effort in the 1960s and 1970s to deal with the underlying technological changes in industrial production and hence to devise science and technology policies and changes to improve industrial productivity;
- and the need in the 1970s and 1980s to deal with internal barriers to trade induced both by demands for social and economic regulation, competitive federalism and aggressive "province build-

ing" as well as by international protectionism, oil cartels and
embargoes, nontariff barriers and by Third World demands for a
new international economic order.

In relation to policy structures, industrial policy formulation shows the
presence and influence of several changing loci of power and organization, including the Department of Trade and Commerce from the 1890s
to World War II, the Department of Reconstruction and Supply in the
1940s and early 1950s, Trade and Commerce in the 1950s, the separate
departments of Industry, and Trade and Commerce in the 1960s, and
then a panoply of structures in the 1970s, including an integrated
Department of Industry, Trade and Commerce, a Department of
Regional Economic Expansion, and other ministries for Science and
Technology, Small Business, and so on. By the late 1970s and early 1980s
other restructuring occurred, including the establishment of a Cabinet
Committee on Economic and Regional Development, the merging of
DREE and IT&C into one Department of Regional and Industrial
Expansion, and the transfer of IT&C's trade role to a Minister of Trade
serving under the Minister of External Affairs. All of these structural
changes showed the difficulties of locating appropriate centres of
political power to coordinate industrial policy. Throughout most of the
post-World War II period, industrial policy was also characterized by
many efforts to deal with the basic relationships of power among
institutions, public-private (business and labour), federal-provincial,
intragovernmental and international institutions. Thus, the idea of
consultation and even of vague notions of planning melded with all the
other ideas inherent in the field.

The brief capsule portrait of ideas and structures presented above is
obviously an imposing one. In this chapter we focus on major policy
events in the post-World War II period but present a somewhat more
detailed look as we move into the 1970s and 1980s. Before proceeding on
this roughly chronological journey, however, it is essential to appreciate
more of the historical legacy of industrial policy and to keep several
contending industrial policy paradigms and analytical categories in mind.

Industrial Policy: The Historical Legacy, Sectors and Policy Paradigms

The traditional view of Canada's industrial strategy, espoused by Sir John
A. Macdonald, was that in order to pursue a policy of building and
strengthening infant industries it was imperative to have a protective

tariff, behind which Canadian manufacturers could become entrenched in the domestic market. This protectionist approach was in contrast to the then prevailing economic ideas, which suggested that such action would be inefficient and would lead to the waste and misuse of resources, since enterprises that were encouraged to develop could not stand up against foreign competition. Macdonald's "National Policy" was an act of nation building in defiance of the efficiency of the north-south continental axis.

The main instrument for the National Policy was the tariff, raised substantially to provide protection primarily for Ontario and Quebec based manufacturers. The National Policy was subsequently strengthened by state support for a national transportation system and large-scale immigration, especially to develop the West's resources and to head off feared American expansionism. Consequently, Canada's early National Policy, or industrial strategy, consisted of three elements: the tariff, the railway and immigration. It produced an economic system which developed at a very rapid rate, especially later in the first decade of the twentieth century. It was national policy and regional policy rolled into one and constructed on significant amounts of state involvement.

As the National Policy evolved, Canada's industrial strategy was dominated by three main preoccupations: first, extending Canadian natural resource frontiers and getting natural resource products to markets via the building of transportation systems, subsidization of transportation rates, special tax concessions for individual producers, and importation of manpower (immigration); second, encouraging the production of manufactured goods via tariff protection through the National Policy of 1879 and later the British preferential system of 1932; and third, by attracting capital via minimum restraints on foreign capital. In the pre-World War II period foreign capital inflows were primarily in the form of debt rather than equity investment. A few industries such as railways were partially nationalized, but such action was forced largely by concerns about financial stability and regional pressure.

Industrial Sectors

In addition to this overall pre-World War II historical legacy, it is essential to keep in mind the underlying transformation of the Canadian economy as economic development occurred, sometimes in response to policy but just as often *despite* public policy. These major transformations help yield categories of analysis such as those referred to as the "primary," "secondary" and "tertiary" sectors of the economy. The first was the relative transformation of Canada from an agricultural economy to an industrial economy and the second is the current transformation from a primarily industrial economy to a service, knowledge-based or information economy. If the latter is often referred to as the "de-industrialization" of Canada, then the former must be belatedly and awkwardly labelled as the "de-agriculturalization" of Canada. Both transformations produced painful effects and responses, as well as opportunities. Nonetheless, the overall effect was to shift the pattern of employment from the primary agricultural and resource sector to the secondary manufacturing sector and from the latter to the tertiary service or information sectors in terms of relative growth and proportions of employment. Employment data on these changes is provided in Chapter 17 on labour market policy and discussed in greater detail.

The primary sector (agriculture, resources, fisheries), the secondary sector (manufacturing) and the tertiary sector (services) in turn introduce the concept of a sectoral approach to industrial policy. Sectors can be defined in many ways which may or may not correspond to business, producer and other interest groups. The sectoral approach usually refers to specific, even more precisely defined, elements of "industry" or "resources." Thus, one speaks of the automobile sector, the clothing and textile sector or the forestry sector and mining sector. But sectors can also refer to elements such as the small business sector, the export sector, the high technology sector, the foreign-owned sector, and the banking sector, to name only a few. Needless to say these sectoral slices can produce an extraordinary range of relations and cross pressures between governments and business interests, among the macro business associations examined in Chapter 3, and the more particular groups and "interests" referred to in Chapter 3 and in several other previous chapters as well. It is also little wonder why consultation with "business" and "labour" takes on such a will-of-the-wisp character as industries jockey for position to become more efficient, to become more stable, or to survive, and as governments strive to get the right national, regional and international political-economic mix and to coordinate the process without calling it planning and without losing office.

Industrial Policy Paradigms

The debate about industrial policy has been influenced by several policy paradigms, most of which we have referred to in previous chapters when we discussed broader aspects of policy formulation. One paradigm is the ultimate legacy of Macdonald's National Policy and has been characterized as a limited truncated industrialism designed to produce limited import substitution and a heavy dependence on a limited range of trade with one or two dominant markets, primarily in recent decades the American market. A second paradigm closely related to the first is the resources, or staples, paradigm, one which emphasizes Canada's resource wealth but which carries with it the usually unpalatable perception of Canada as an underdeveloped country composed of "hewers of wood and drawers of water," and, in foreign policy terms, with a continentalist and highly dependent posture vis-à-vis the United States. A third paradigm, which in many respects links these two but has its own mode of expression, is the "centre-periphery" or metropolis-hinterland paradigm which characterizes industrial policy in spatial terms, in short, in relation to the dominance of the Upper Canadian industrial heartland over the resource-based regions of the East and West. Located in some respects alongside these three paradigms, and in other respects "above" them, is the Keynesian paradigm to which we have referred repeatedly. Associated with macro economic policy fields such as fiscal, stabilization and indirectly even monetary policy, it clearly has had effects on industry and the economy but at the same time came to be viewed as something distinct from industrial policy.

Finally, it requires little imagination to see how this daunting array of paradigms, ideas, sectors, interest groups and interests presents problems that are reflected in the policy structures of government at the federal level and between the federal and provincial constitutional domains. Who or which agency should coordinate the industrial strategy? In short, who or which agency should have power over other agencies and ministers? To what extent will private interests and other governments behave in desired ways? Will provincial decisions counteract federal plans? Which ideas will prevail and for how long?

As industrial policy evolved, especially in the 1960s and 1970s, an attempt was made to make it even more comprehensive in scope. It moved beyond its trade-industry core concerns. Figure 15.1 attempts to convey its contemporary content and the many policy spillovers.

FIGURE 15.1
THE MAJOR COMPONENTS OF INDUSTRIAL POLICY

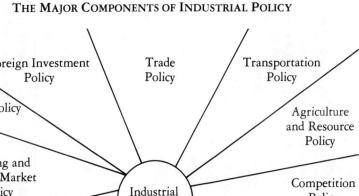

Effectively, industrial policy included tariff and trade policy, agriculture and resource policy, transportation policy, regional policy, immigration and manpower policy (later referred to globally as labour market policy), competition policy, energy policy, research and development (R&D) policy and technology and communications policy.

Table 15.1 presents a brief chronology of major industrial policy events since World War II. It is not meant to be exhaustive nor does it deal with all the policy fields noted above. Other aspects of the chronology are dealt with in Chapters 16 and 17 where energy and labour market developments are examined. The two figures should be viewed merely as a visual aid and as a device to convey as starkly as possible the expanding dimensions of the field. Our intention in the remaining sections of this chapter and in the next two chapters is to provide a broad appreciation of the dynamics involved in the policy field being examined as ideas, structures, and processes interact in each post-World War II decade.

TABLE 15.1

MAJOR INDUSTRIAL POLICY EVENTS*

	General Industry Development and Trade Policy	Consultative Efforts	Foreign Investment	Regional Policy	Competition Policy
Post World War II and 1950s	—White Paper on Employment and Income (1945) and Reconstruction Program —Bretton-Woods Monetary system (1944) —St. Lawrence Seaway —Trans Canada Pipeline —Cancellation of AVRO Arrow —Canada-U.S. Defence Production Pact (1959)	—Gordon Royal Commission on Canada's Economic Prospects (1957)	—Carte-blanche encouragement of branch plantism and Equity Foreign Ownership	—Diefenbaker "roads to resources" and Agricultural and Rural Development Program —McPherson Royal Commission on Transportation (1959)	—Restrictive Trade Practices Commission established (1952)
1960s	—Department of Industry established 1963 —Auto Pact (1965) —Department of Industry, Trade	—Economic Council of Canada (1963) —Science Council of Canada (1966) —Prices and	—Walter Gordon Budget of 1963 —Watkins Report 1968 —Canada Development Corporation proposed	—National Oil Policy (1961) —National Transportation Act of 1967 —Establishment of Department of Regional Economic	—Establishment of Department of Consumer and Corporate Affairs (1967) —Economic Council study of Competition Policy (1966 and

	Incomes Commission (1969)	Expansion (1969)		1969)
and Commerce established (1969) —Establishment of Telesat Canada and later the Department of Communications				
1970s —Nixon shocks of 1971-72 —OPEC shock of 1973 —"Third Option" Foreign-Policy Statement (1973) —Jean Luc Pepin's "Industrial Strategy" (1972) —Ministry of State for Science and Technology established (1972) —Tokyo Round Multi-National Trade Negotiations (1973-79) —Economic Council Study on Trade Policy (1975)	—Gillespie's "bottom-up" sector approach (1974) —John Turner's voluntary Price and Wage Guidelines Exercise of 1975 —23 Sector Task Forces and Tier II Exercise (1978) —Clark government's Consultative Effort with provinces (1979)	—Canada Development Corporation Established (1971) —Gray Report on Foreign Investment (1972) —Foreign Investment Review Agency Established (1973) —Petro-Canada Established (1975) —Science Council's Technological Sovereignty reports	—Regional Development Policy announced (1973) including General Development Agreements with the Provinces —Western Economic Opportunities Conference —On-going dispute over revenues and control of Natural Resource Development	—Competition Act passed (Phase I) —Skeoch-McDonald Report 1976 —Royal Commission on Corporate Concentration Report (1978) —Failure to pass Phase II proposals —Bank Act Review Process to allow controlled competition —Economic Council's Regulation Study (1979) urges deregulation to promote competition

(Table 15.1 continued)

General Industry Development and Trade Policy	Consultative Efforts	Foreign Investment	Regional Policy	Competition Policy
—Senate Foreign Affairs Committee Report on Free Trade with U.S. (1978) —Ministry of State for Small Business Established (1976) —Formation of Inter-Departmental Committee on Trade and Industrial Policy (ICTIP) (1976) —"DM 10" formed (1976-77) —Board of Economic Development Ministers formed (1978)				

	—Iranian Revolution and resulting oil price increases (1979) —Reisman Inquiry on Auto Pact (1978)		—National Energy Program (1980)	—National Energy Program —Western Development Fund (1980) —Ending of Crow's Nest arrangement (1982) —Abolition of DREE	—Draft federal proposals on Competition Policy (1980) —Transportation Ministry's partial disavowel of nation-building role for transportation (1981)
1980s	—Olsen Eight Point Agenda —Statement on Economic Development for the 1980s (1981) —Blair-Carr Task Force on Major Projects (1981) —Establishment of Department of Regional and Industrial Expansion and transfer of Trade to External Affairs Department (1981)	—"6 and 5" Consultative and Leverage Effort (1982)	—National Energy Program (1980) —Promise to strengthen FIRA (1980) —Office of Industrial and Regional Benefits established (1981) —Establishment of Canada Oil and Gas Lands Administration (1982)		

*See Chapters 16 and 17 for energy and labour market events and components.

Industrial Policy in the Aftermath of World War II: Reconstruction, Foreign Ownership and the Keynesian Illusion

In the immediate post-World War II era there was virtually no rhetorical reference to an industrial policy. Instead, national policy was couched in terms of reconstruction for a peace-time economy that would avoid the ravages of the pre-war depression.[2] The war effort had been the product of a virtually planned economy, including an arsenal of over 30 Crown corporations, most of which were privatized after the war.[3] The main vehicle for the expression of the reconstruction program was the White Paper on Employment and Income.[4] Although often associated only with the dawn of Keynesian policy, the White Paper embraced, in fact, an amalgam of social and economic programs, from family allowances to encourage family formation and consumer spending to a ready list of public works projects to implement if demand and employment slackened.

Reconstruction and the Second National Policy

The breadth of the policy initiatives, coupled with the then obvious dominance of Ottawa vis-à-vis the provinces, have led many to refer to the reconstruction program as Canada's second National Policy. In our brief historical review of priorities in Chapter 10 we also referred to it in these terms. Those who apply a class analysis perspective characterized the same reconstruction formula as part of a larger "post-war settlement" between capital and labour. This view linked the reconstruction program to the granting of basic collective bargaining rights to labour unions in 1944. These rights along with the social welfare programs were, according to this view, the price for future stability and a peaceful industrial society. Although the reconstruction program was in many respects a second National Policy associated in a general way with Keynesianism, it was really only the tip of the iceberg.[5] Two other overriding realities also characterized Canada's industrial policies of the day, the favourable state of post-war trade markets for Canada and the policy of encouraging foreign equity ownership.

It must be remembered that the Western European post-war economy was in a state of disrepair, ravaged by war and its capital stock depleted and destroyed. It would take time to grow. From 1945 to the mid-1950s Canada enjoyed not only a healthy access to world markets but also a foreign policy influence well beyond its relative size in the world of nations. This was aided by the post-war international monetary system constructed at Bretton Woods.[6]

Foreign Ownership and Truncated Branch Plantism

By far the most important element of Canada's industrial policy was the official encouragement of foreign equity ownership. Though, as we have stressed, Keynesianism received the rhetorical attention and was the dominant paradigm, it was Canada's foreign investment policy that was ultimately the real "macro" economic policy in the post-war era until the late 1960s.

The formulation of an industrial strategy obviously requires close coordination between trade, investment and industrial policies. This relationship had been evident earlier during the 1930s when Canada considered a negotiated free trade arrangement with the United States. Thereafter, her post-war economic policy was based on the American connection. The post-war industrial strategy included the strong encouragement of American equity investments in resource industries and in manufacturing. Within a few years American investors directly owned more than half of the resource and manufacturing sectors of the Canadian economy. Canada thus had branch plantism, an economic system that was a halfway house union between full continentalism and the National Policy. The execution of this policy was under C.D. Howe's Department of Trade and Commerce (T&C).[7]

In his detailed historical analysis of industrial policy and T&C, Glen Williams summed up the industrial policy as "import substitution industrialization" (ISI).

> ISI is the industrial strategy most typical of the Third World. It is basically simple, rapid and painless in execution. This has accounted for its widespread popularity. Tariffs are erected on selected commodities with established markets formerly serviced by imports at levels at which domestic production becomes feasible. Foreign technology (usually both machinery and processes) is freely employed by a domestic licencee or foreign-owned subsidiary to create an instant industry. The new factory cannot compete on world markets as it has nothing distinctive to offer them. In addition, a condition of use of the foreign technology is usually that production be restricted to the domestic market. Further, the ISI factory provides few backward linkages in the rest of its economy as it needs no domestic capital

goods industry to keep it supplied with new processes and machines. Thus, the ISI manufacturing sector tends to stagnate as a mere supplement to other production activities (usually resource extraction).[8]

It is essential to see this policy paradigm in relation to economic and industrial policy structures. In the 1950s the Trade and Commerce department was the central structure. Williams's capsule summary of the department's growing recognition of the problem of this approach and of the shifting balance between manufacturing and resource exporters is worth quoting in full.

> Although some transportation and merchant interests were alive to an expanded role for Trade and Commerce in overseas markets, the department was drawn mainly into the orbit of industrial concerns. A close relationship with Trade and Commerce in its formative years before the Great Depression of the 1930s was earnestly cultivated by the small minority of Canadian industrialists who seriously pursued export trade. This level of involvement was not matched by the exporters of Canada's staple resources. Those trading in commodities such as wheat, flour, cheese and timber had developed their own export channels and found little use for Trade and Commerce services in ordinary circumstances. As late as 1929, a Minister of Trade and Commerce spoke of the essentially private organization of the staples trade and how the department could not be "of very much assistance" to it.
>
> Yet the affinity between Canada's manufacturers and the department was not as close as it seemed. In practice, the relationship was frequently an uncomfortable one for both parties. The trade commissioners found that most of their clientele were unwilling or unable to develop the specialized world competitive products necessary to enter export markets. This was because of the dual ISI dependencies referred to earlier—foreign technology and the small domestic market. If export was attempted, it was often half-hearted, amateurish, and related to a temporary glut on the domestic market. In this context the trade commissioners were frequently discouraged or disgusted—sentiments often reflected in their published reports. The manufacturers found it necessary to plead for more discretion and, as a result, in the mid-1920s the Director of the Trade Commissioner Service ordered his officers to stop "unfavourable appraisals" in their reports and to emphasize the "good features" of Canadian export practice.
>
> As the twentieth century progressed, Trade and Commerce shared in the spoils of the general growth of government activities

and began to take on the characteristics of an omnibus department with many diverse responsibilities, some of which, like the Dominion Bureau of Statistics (1918), bore little or no relation to the promotion of export trade. Nevertheless, the central "raison d'etre" of the department remained its overseas activities. The Trade Commissioner Service grew from 20 offices in 15 countries in 1911, to 34 offices in 27 countries in 1939, to 53 offices in 43 countries in 1955.

Although this expansion, as we have already noted, was initially propelled by the export needs of a select minority of Canadian manufacturers, the special circumstances of the 1930s, 1940s and 1950s permanently widened the mandate of Trade and Commerce to include some resource exporters. In this era, the growing complexity of the post-Depression economy with its increasing need for state intervention drew Trade and Commerce and other related departments into new involvements in resource production and trade. These activities included the encouragement of orderly marketing and price stabilization through cartelization and supply management to reduce surplus capacity. The strategic demands of World War II production and Cold War stockpiling reinforced these trends.

The emergence of resource exporters as major consumers of Trade and Commerce services led to a personality crisis within the department which brought it to a state of near-schizophrenia. On the one hand, its traditional experience taught it that there was something radically wrong with the import substitution pattern of Canadian industrialization which had prevented it from reaching maturity as an actor in world markets by transforming more of our raw materials into fully manufactured exports. It was also becoming apparent that the advancing importance of foreign branch plant industries had only supplemented and consolidated the earlier problems of the inward-looking technologically dependent pattern. Here, within this perspective, a potential challenge to foreign investment and resource exports was gathering force. On the other hand, Trade and Commerce had now developed new allegiances. By submitting itself to the power of continental market forces, especially under C.D. Howe, and by facilitating Canada's role as a resource hinterland of U.S. capital, it was accepting a significantly more limited future for Canadian industry.[9]

Canada enjoyed considerable economic prosperity during the 1950s, and thus the reconstruction-cum-foreign investment policy bundle described above was not challenged in any significant way until perhaps the late 1950s. The giant St. Lawrence Seaway project and the Trans Canada Pipeline project (see Chapter 16) helped add a sufficient economic impetus to sustain relative prosperity, though the controversy over the latter helped bring down the Liberal government after 22 years in power. The Diefenbaker government represented, in part, a regional reaction to the unevenness of Liberal prosperity, but the Diefenbaker Tories did not really have a cohesive alternative industrial view. Diefenbaker spoke hopefully of increasing trade with Britain and the Commonwealth and advanced his concept of a northern vision and "roads to resources." But the underlying vulnerability of Canada's post-war industrial policy was not addressed.

The AVRO Arrow, the Defence Production Pact and the Gordon Commission

As the decade of the 1950s ended, the frayed edges of the policy were in some respects symbolized by three events, the cancellation of the AVRO Arrow aircraft, the Defence Production Pact with the United States which followed in the wake of the Arrow, and the report of the Gordon Royal Commission on Canada's Economic Prospects. The Diefenbaker government found continued work on the all-Canadian Arrow jet fighter aircraft to be too expensive in the face of no assured markets. By cancelling the Arrow, it aborted the prospects of a longer-term high technology strategy in the defence industry sector. To fill the gap, the Tories reached an agreement in 1959 with the Americans on the Defence Production Sharing Arrangements. This enabled Canada, as a quid pro quo for a North American defence pact, to obtain a guaranteed industrial access to the United States defence market. Thus, the Diefenbaker Tories, despite the professed desire to diversify trade, found itself adopting an arrangement which produced greater continental industrial dependence on the United States.[10]

The Gordon Royal Commission reported in 1957 and its work also symbolized a partial recognition of the underlying problems. It drew attention to the severe problems of foreign investment, to the historical weakness of the industrial sector and to issues such as the weak domestic sourcing and contracting in the energy and resource sector (an item that surfaced more visibly in the late 1970s and early 1980s). In addition, the inquiry elevated Walter Gordon himself to a position as chief idea man for the Liberal party, a position he did not relinquish until the debacle of his nationalist Budget of 1963 as the Pearson government's first Minister of Finance.[11]

Industrial Policy in the 1960s:
Ad Hocism With a Vengeance

While the 1960s testified to some continuing concern about Canada's industrial and trade vulnerability, the prosperity from 1963 to the end of the decade and the social policy reforms it spawned made it difficult to obtain any sustained political attention to the underlying industrial dilemma. The decade was characterized by small sporadic bursts of concern about individual dimensions of industrial policy. Industrial policy was "ad hoc-ism" practised with a vengeance.

The Search for an Industrial Manufacturing Focus:
The Auto Pact and Technological Weaknesses

One delayed spin-off from the Gordon Commission was the establishment in 1963 of a separate Department of Industry to improve the position of Canada's manufacturing industries.[12] It also led to a relative downgrading of the support for resource development. A number of measures were adopted to give the manufacturing sector a new impetus:

- There was a reduction of reliance on tariff protection through the Kennedy round of GATT negotiations in return for improved access to foreign markets. This was reinforced by greater assistance for exports and product innovation;
- Research & Development (R&D) in government and support for R&D in industry were expanded to a limited extent;
- T&C programs for productivity, efficiency and design were expanded;
- Financing was provided for industrial restructuring;
- Regional industrial development incentives were increased;
- A somewhat more discriminatory approach to foreign investment was adopted through the tax system, through regulations in key sectors where foreign ownership or control was limited, through negotiations for offsets, and through somewhat greater efforts to ensure that R&D facilities and export rights accompanied the new investment;
- Full or partial direct government ownership of Crown corporations such as Telesat Canada and the Canada Development Corporation were instituted.

By the end of the decade in 1969 the two main industrial policy departments were merged into one, the Department of Industry, Trade and Commerce (ITC). Williams's analysis of the reversal which produced the merger shows the familiar themes.

Strikingly, the government justified this reversal by explicitly recognizing that Trade and Commerce had been, to some extent, riding the
wrong horse, that the historic trend in world trade was more
favourable to industrial, not resource, exporters. The new minister,
Jean-Luc Pepin, also made the key connection between industrial
development and trade expansion which fundamentally contradicted
the earlier inward-oriented ISI model when he suggested that Industry,
Trade and Commerce would promote the establishment of world
competitive manufacturing sectors. "To produce ... goods competi-
tively, we must win as many domestic and foreign markets as possible,
so as to make economies of scale and specialization. In other words, to
sell mining, logging, school and medical equipment on the Canadian
market, we must also be able to sell it on the foreign market, so as to
achieve competitive prices.

It would seem that the merger at least initially reduced tensions
between the two departments over economic development strategy.
As one senior civil servant noted, "in the early 1960s ... they each
came up with opposite solutions to problems. Bringing those two
together produced a unit that came up with a reasonably balanced
policy".[13]

Perhaps the most significant single policy initiative to emerge out
of the initial Department of Industry was the Canada-United States Auto
Pact of 1965. The Auto Pact provided for a form of sectoral free trade and
was viewed by some as a model in addressing the classic Canadian
problem: too many firms producing inefficient short production runs for
a small Canadian market.[14] The Auto Pact gave Canadian producers
access to the larger American market. At the end of the decade this
initiative looked promising indeed, since investment, employment and
productivity increased greatly, albeit concentrated primarily in Ontario.

Other industrial development initiatives in the 1960s were the
establishment of the Economic Council of Canada in 1963 and the
Science Council of Canada in 1966. These bodies are examined in
Chapter 18 but are noteworthy in an industrial policy context because
they signalled a concern for two recurring and persistent dimensions of
such policy, namely the search for consultative or even "planning"
forums between government, business and labour, and the recognition of
Canada's weaknesses in industrial research, technology and development.[15] The Economic Council was also influential in the 1960s in the
field of labour market policies. These are examined in Chapter 17 but
should also be noted here since in 1966 major manpower policy
initiatives were launched ostensibly to promote greater industrial

efficiency and to respond to structural problems in the economy.

The foreign investment aspects of industrial policy were also addressed in other episodic ways. Three events signalled both the importance of the issue and yet the political unwillingness to address it squarely in the midst of prosperity. The first event was the Walter Gordon Budget of 1963. Gordon's proposed taxes on foreign investment had to be withdrawn in a flurry of opposition by partisan and business critics. The issue reappeared in 1967, however, in the form of federal "guidelines" for foreign corporate citizenship, and in the publication in 1968 of the Watkins' report on foreign ownership. The latter showed the increased pace of foreign ownership, but in most other respects repeated the familiar diagnosis of Canada's industrial ills—branch plantism, technological underdevelopment, weak market penetration abroad, and the extraterritorial application of U.S. laws in Canada regarding the behaviour of branch plants. A further event was the proposed establishment of the Canada Development Corporation (CDC), an entity not established until 1971. While economic "nationalists" wanted it to be an aggressive vehicle to "buy-back" Canada and to restructure industry, the CDC was a much more modest entity. It was not a Crown corporation, but rather a joint holding company half owned by the Government of Canada and half by private investors. It was to operate according to commercial investment principles.

Regionalism and Industrial Policy:
Regional Policy Before DREE

The regional dimensions of industrial policy in the 1960s were reflected in numerous ways and again raised the intractable problems of the resource versus manufacturing components of industrial policy and their underlying paradigms. As we saw in Chapters 8 and 10, the Diefenbaker government expressed its regional "industrial" concerns through reforms to programs in rural agricultural development and forestry. Regional concerns were at the heart of the National Oil Policy of 1961, which divided the national oil market at the Ottawa river and hence provided an assured Ontario market for Alberta oil, with Ontario consumers paying higher than world prices, the reverse of the situation in the late 1970s. It was also central to the increased oil and gas exports allowed in the 1960s. In 1967 the National Transportation Act was passed. It reflected the extraordinary regional dependence on transportation policies and subsidies stressed in the 1959 report of the McPherson Royal Commission. The legislation rejected the classic definition of competition among firms and opted instead for closely controlled competition among "modes" of transport, since transportation was itself an instrument of national and regional policy.[17] How to arrest regional decline was also a central concern in Ottawa's establishment of the Cape Breton Development Corporation (DEVCO) in 1967. DEVCO was to help phase out the coal industry and find alternative employment opportunities for local workers in Cape Breton. As we show in Chapter 16, in the late 1970s and early 1980s changing energy prices made expansion of the coal industry possible again.

Regional policy was also being influenced by the policies and actions of provincial governments as well. The 1960s represented the real birth of "province building" as key provinces sought to build and protect their regional economic and political bases. In the late 1960s and early 1970s provincial development agencies and corporations emerged. There were also conspicuous industrial development failures and boondoggles. As Mathias's account shows, the politics of "forced growth" in some of these provincial initiatives proved to be salutory in showing the limits of trying to locate plants at the margin of market forces and yet the understandable political compulsion in needing to continue to try.[18]

Finally in 1969 the name "regional policy" showed up with its own federal departmental home. It is essential to note, however, that *none* of the above examples of regional policy in the energy or transportation fields were part of the mandate of the then new Department of Regional Economic Expansion (DREE). DREE was an ad hoc merger of the previous Department of Industry "area incentives" and of some agricultural and rural infrastructure grants.[19]

Competition Policy: Domestic Versus International Efficiency

The brief reference above to the transportation concept of "intermodal" competition and to the theme of Canada's industrial policy need for larger, efficient industrial entities also points out the Canadian difficulties in devising "competition" policies as part of industrial policy.[20] They also inherently raise the different views of market efficiency. In 1967 a Department of Consumer and Corporate Affairs was established. It was visualized as a kind of "attorney general" of the market place. The market must be regulated to keep it competitive and efficient, to avoid "excessive" corporate concentration and to prevent restrictive trade practices.

What then is competition policy? To some its quintessential form is the existence of many firms competing in the same industry so as to reduce prices and meet consumer needs. For others it implies the need for fewer and larger firms in strategic industries so as to enhance Canada's *international* competitiveness. In particular contexts such as transportation policy, it is competition among modes rather than firms in a stable, controlled way so as to maintain national unity. In the banking sector competition was also to be muted and stable so as to promote respect for the "integrity of the financial system." Each of these versions has its own claim to legitimacy. In the 1960s their persistent and conflicting existence easily showed why later in the 1970s several competition policy bills floundered and sunk in the larger sea of industrial policy.

Industrial Policy in the 1970s:
The Attempts To Be Comprehensive

Industrial policy in the 1970s was characterized by an attempt, indeed several attempts, to be comprehensive. Ottawa increasingly recognized the need to reinvigorate the industrial sector in all its dimensions. In our analysis in Chapter 11 of the resource allocation dynamics of the economic development envelope, we provided a capsule summary of these several abortive efforts in the 1970s to bring together the tangled threads of industrial policy. We now need to take a somewhat closer look at these events, because our concern is no longer only about the intra-Cabinet resource allocation process but also about how ideas, structures and processes interact in the larger institutional setting as an attempt is made to secure some kind of democratic consensus as to what industrial policy should be. To do this we first summarize some of the data which was known at the *end* of the 1970s about Canada's industrial condition. Some aspects of this condition were known at the start of the decade as well, but it is useful to remind ourselves of the advantages of our analytical hindsight. Ottawa's decision makers, however, were operating in the midst of uncertainty, not to mention the welter of theories and ideas about which road led to industrial salvation.

Trade Policy and Industrial Vulnerability

Tables 15.1 and 15.2 portray major features of Canada's trade vulnerability. Table 15.2 shows the rapidly deteriorating commodity trade balance in end products, a major indicator of industrial maturity and prosperous employment. Table 15.3 shows the growing vulnerability to outflows of interest, dividends, and income from services. Many experts of varying ideological persuasions would have little difficulty in agreeing with the summary diagnosis of the Senate Committee on Foreign Affairs report.

> In the ten-year period to 1979, Canada's share of world trade in manufacturer goods declined from 4.8 percent to 3.1 percent. Canada's trading performance worldwide and with the United States, has, at best, marked time since 1978. In spite of strenuous efforts by the government, the deficit in end product trade continues to grow. Canada appears to be in danger of being pushed out of world markets in manufactured goods.
>
> The problem remains that too many fragmented and inefficient firms are producing mainly for the small Canadian market. It is important to observe that Canada is the only major industrialized country without free access to a market of from 100 to 300 million

TABLE 15.2

TRADE BALANCE BY COMMODITY CATEGORY

($ billions)

Year	Edible[a] Products	Crude[b] Materials	Fabricated[c] Materials	End[d] Products	Other	Total
1970	+0.8	+1.8	+ 3.0	− 3.1	—	+2.5
1971	+1.0	+1.9	+ 2.7	− 3.6	−0.2	+1.8
1972	+1.0	+2.0	+ 3.0	− 4.8	−0.2	+1.0
1973	+1.3	+2.9	+ 3.9	− 6.4	−0.2	+1.5
1974	+1.4	+3.7	+ 4.2	− 9.0	−0.2	−0.5
1975	+1.4	+2.8	+ 3.8	−10.3	—	−2.3
1976	+1.4	+3.2	+ 6.0	−10.0	−0.5	+0.1
1977	+1.3	+3.5	+ 7.9	−10.9	−0.4	+1.4
1978	+1.4	+2.9	+10.4	−12.4	−0.1	+2.2
1979	+2.1	+4.6	+12.4	−17.2	−0.5	+1.4
1980	+2.6	+3.4	+16.6	−17.8	+0.4	+5.2

Notes: [a]Live animals, food, feed, beverages, tobacco, etc.

[b]Fibres, industrial vegetable products, pulpwood, ores, petroleum, natural gas, etc.

[c]Leather, chemicals, metals, electricity, paper, etc.

[d]Machinery, equipment, consumer goods.

Source: Statistics Canada, Cat. Nos. 65-202 and 65-203. Reproduced by permission of the Minister of Supply and Services Canada.

TABLE 15.3

BALANCE OF CANADA'S INTERNATIONAL PAYMENTS
($ billions)

Year	I Commodity Trade Balance	II Interest and Dividends	III Other Services and Transfers	IV Net Foreign[1] Direct Investment	V Other Long-Term Capital Movement	VI Short-Term Capital Movement	VII Errors and Omissions	VIII Net Official Monetary Movements and SDR Allocation
1970	+3.1	-1.0	-0.9	+0.5	+0.5	-0.2	-0.4	+1.7
1971	+2.6	-1.1	-1.0	+0.7	-0.1	+1.0	-1.3	+0.9
1972	+1.9	-1.0	-1.2	+0.2	+1.4	+0.5	-1.5	+0.3
1973	+2.7	-1.2	-1.4	+0.1	+0.5	-0.6	-0.6	-0.5
1974	+1.7	-1.6	-1.6	—	+1.0	+1.3	-0.9	—
1975	-0.5	-2.0	-2.4	-0.2	+4.1	+1.6	-1.2	-0.4
1976	+1.4	-2.5	-2.7	-0.9	+8.8	+0.1	-3.7	+0.5
1977	+2.7	-3.7	-3.4	-0.3	+4.6	+0.6	-2.0	-1.4
1978	+3.6	-4.5	-4.1	-1.9	+5.3	+1.2	-2.8	-3.3
1979	+4.0	-5.3	-3.8	-1.3	+4.1	+7.8	-3.9	+1.9
1980	+8.0	-5.6	-3.9	-2.1	+3.5	+1.2	-2.5	-1.3

Note: [1]Excludes retained earnings and repatriated dividends and includes Canadian direct investment abroad and repatriated capital by foreign investors. The inflow of capital (columns IV, V and VI) provided a short-term support to the Canadian dollar during the early seventies. By the end of the decade the dollar was being weakened by direct disinvestment (column IV) and by the interest and dividend outflows (column II) needed to service the earlier borrowing.

Source: Statistics Canada, Cat. No. 67-001. Reproduced by permission of the Minister of Supply and Services Canada.

people. The manufacturing sector is, with a number of notable exceptions, producing standard technology products, using technology which has been largely imported. R&D in Canada has been at seriously low levels. Productivity is rising relatively more slowly in Canada than in competing countries and remains markedly lower than in the United States.

The remedies are generally accepted and not particularly controversial: economies of scale are essential; the Canadian manufacturing sector must rationalize; it must specialize in particular product lines instead of a broad diversity of products; it must modernize its production processes and achieve economies of scale and higher productivity rates through long, efficient production runs; it must seek out the areas where Canada has natural advantages.

Where opinions differ is on how to accomplish these changes.[21]

As the decade evolved, however, the "how" question begged others; what does one actually do about it? How is the political and economic power mobilized and *sustained*? Towards the realization of what objectives or in pursuit of whose ideas? In what order? Who will take the risks? Who will we blame if things go wrong?

In the industrial policy field per se the links between industry and trade were even more in evidence. A specific catalyst early in the decade was the so-called "Nixon shocks" referred to in the previous chapter. They jolted Canada's foreign policy makers out of the assumption that Canada had an inviolable special relationship with the Americans. The Nixon shocks were followed by the OPEC shock of 1973 and the consequent shortage of oil and a four-fold increase in oil prices. Other external events were less shocking and more subtle, but were increasingly understood. One was the emergence of the industrial prowess of some less-developed states, whose low labour costs allowed them to produce goods such as footwear and textiles at much lower prices than Canadian firms.[22] This was simultaneously good for the consumer but bad for employment, especially in Quebec. The other was the technological prowess of the Japanese in the burgeoning computer and micro-chip industries, which not only brought in a flood of imports but also revolutionized the production process in sectors such as automobiles through the use of industrial robots. By the end of the 1970s these developments were contributing to increasingly unfavourable trade balances in the Canada-U.S. Auto Pact and in other "end product" data shown in Table 15.2.

The Pepin Industrial Strategy

One explicit policy response to these unfolding events early in the decade was the Third Option foreign policy statement discussed in Chapter 14. Of related importance was Jean-Luc Pepin's unveiling of an "industrial strategy statement" in 1972. He suggested that "a strategy is an ensemble of coordinated objectives and instruments, that is, policies, programs and institutions. Applied to industry, the term means the proper planning by government (federal) for optimum coordination of policies and decisions, on the use of all productive resources, in order to achieve defined (and accepted) social and economic goals." To that end "the strategy must embrace all sectors of economic activity from resources to services but must emphasize manufacturing and processing." The Pepin statement concluded that because of a variety of difficulties "an industrial strategy will have to be fairly general, the broad design by which the government strives to influence the use of resources to the best advantage of Canada as a whole and flexible in its implementation." He also conceded that "the more general the objective the easier the consensus ... but the less useful the objective. So it should not be too general either."[23]

The Pepin strategy involved "the soliciting of input from those who actually make the system work"; that is, the private sector. Thus, plans were put in place to achieve at least two things: first, to form small consultative bodies of senior statesmen from business, labour and government to assess findings and recommendations; and second, to encourage consultations on various aspects of the developing policy with the provinces and industrial associations. Pepin's approach, however, was not totally carried out in isolation from broader fiscal policy. As we saw in Chapter 10, the Turner Budgets of 1972 and 1973, in the midst of a minority Parliament, were fairly expansionary in nature and included new capital cost allowances for the manufacturing sector. The events of the early 1970s demonstrated, however, that if a comprehensive industrial strategy was to be formulated, conflicts would have to be resolved in at least three spheres: within the federal government, among and between different levels of government, and between government, business and labour. The required cooperation was never achieved, given the fact that the participants were not able to agree on the need for, or the components of, an industrial strategy.

The failure of the initiatives by Jean-Luc Pepin led to the adoption of another approach to the formulation of an industrial strategy. Pepin's successor, A.W. Gillespie, placed strong emphasis on a "bottom up" approach and, accordingly, on improving the machinery for consultation with the various industrial sectors.[24] The nine industrial sectors already identified in the organizational structure of IT&C were subsequently broadened and provided the base for the later 23 sector task forces which reported to the minister in 1978. Gillespie attempted to improve consultation with the shipbuilding, textile, clothing, electrical and footwear industries, among others. By the mid-1970s Gillespie had identified his own list of the critical problem areas faced by the government with respect to the formulation of an industrial strategy; first, the necessity to develop measures to avoid the pervasive effects of inflation; second, the need to increase industrial productivity and to insure its fast distribution; and third, the need to avoid the pitfalls of protectionism.

Technological Sovereignty and Foreign Ownership

Of increasing concern was Canada's science and technology policies as an underlying weakness in industrial productivity and competitiveness. The Science Council of Canada had begun to assess these issues, but there was no Cabinet-based mechanism to mobilize the power or ideas needed. Accordingly, a Ministry of State for Science and Technology (MOSST) was established in 1971, but was given policy advisory powers only and, hence, could scarcely even contemplate dealing with the tasks at hand.[25] In the meantime the technological dilemmas were real and sharp controversy arose over how to deal with them. Two aggregate policy indicators were judged to be distinctly unfavourable. One was the low percentage of GNP spent on R&D in Canada in comparison with our trading partners. Despite a decade of science policy debate the volume of real dollars spent actually declined in the 1970s. The second unfavourable indicator was the degree to which Canada's R&D activity, in stark comparison with other industrialized states, was concentrated in government laboratories. Though efforts were made to contract out more R&D work to industry, the expenditure restraints as well as the absence of any internal centre of coordinative power made any progress in this direction slow and gradual.[26]

By the mid and late 1970s the technological debate was linked even more explicitly with foreign ownership. The Science Council viewed branch plantism as the primary cause of technological weakness. The federal government, meanwhile, through the aegis of MOSST and IT&C and later the Ministry of State for Economic Development, promised increased resources for technology and attempted to target funds towards areas such as the "high technology-communication" field. Old dilemmas arose here as well, however, especially over whether to use the tax system or grants to target the support. The former was favoured by industry spokesmen, but the latter was more suitable for targeting on smaller Canadian firms and for obtaining visible political credit.[27]

The Multinational Trade Negotiations and the Search for Industrial and Trade Policy Structures of Power

A larger but clearly related problem throughout the decade was the sluggishness and uncertainty of the world economy in the wake of OPEC and in the context of the Multinational Trade Negotiations (MTN), under the General Agreement on Tariffs and Trade (GATT). The GATT Tokyo Round, as these negotiations were referred to, involved six years of bargaining which ended in 1979.[28] One major projected effect of the Tokyo Round is that by 1987 80 percent of current Canadian industrial exports to the United States will enter duty free and up to 95 percent will be subject to tariffs of 5 percent or less. For the United States the comparable figures will be 65 percent and 26 percent for the two categories. The Tokyo Round also dealt with nontariff barriers. While definitions of a nontariff barrier vary, they could include many items that are part of the arsenal of industrial policy measures and which in every industrialized state had grown in use in the 1960s and 1970s. These included countervailing duties, procurement policies, tax measures, regional incentives, special export financing measures, and "emergency" actions.

Once again, the Canadian-American dimensions of these nontariff trade issues were especially important and were to build to somewhat of a crescendo in 1981 and 1982 when, as we see below, the National Energy Program and FIRA were targets of severe American criticism. In the meantime, much more quietly and less visibly, the Americans at the federal and state government levels were marshalling an imposing array of sector by sector protective devices.[29]

By mid-decade the Economic Council of Canada had concluded, in the light of some of these general developments, that time was not on the side of Canada's manufacturing industry.[20] Later, the Senate Foreign Affairs Committee in both its 1978 and 1982 reports concluded in an even more gloomy vein:

> In sectors where the traditional tariff protection is diminishing, increased import competition from efficient foreign producers will challenge the less-protected Canadian manufacturers who are not structured to resist such competition and whose position will be gradually eroded. At the same time, many Canadian manufacturers will not be in a position to take advantage of the increased export opportunities in the U.S. market, also less protected by tariffs. In that market they will face stepped-up competition as stronger, more efficiently structured Japanese or European competitors move in. At the same time, relatively high U.S. duties will remain on a number of items of importance to Canadian industry, most notably on petro-chemicals where Canadian producers stand ready to compete inter-nationally.
>
> In the trading world of the 1980s, tariffs are no longer the most important influence on trade flows for most products. Much more worrying in the Canada-U.S. context are the uresolved problems related to nontariff restrictions and particularly the U.S. nontariff barriers.... The economic distortions to trade arising from such nontariff restrictions may prove to be more costly than any remaining tariffs....
>
> The Tokyo Round has, in effect, left Canadian industry in the worst of both possible worlds—with tariffs too low to be an effective protection and, at the same time, still without free access to a high assured market as enjoyed by its competitors, the European Com-munity, Japan and the United States.[31]

The Senate Committee went on to recommend that Canada should negotiate a bilateral free trade arrangement with the United States. It attempted a defence of why this would be economically desirable for Canada without any loss of political independence. Both the Economic Council and Senate reports received only limited discussion, and their arguments were labelled as "continentalism." Their reception is a major manifestation of the difficulty of holding a serious and concerted debate on industrial policy options. Important ideas are often sacrificed at the altar of short-term rhetorical overkill. The same occurred, as we show below, over other threads of industrial policy such as foreign ownership and the energy mega-projects.

The trade negotiations of the 1970s are also an item on which it is useful to pause and appreciate the structures and processes of industrial policy formulation as all these events unfold. They raise the familiar issues of consultation, coordination and "planning" in an intragovernmental, public-private sector and federal-provincial context. The federal-provincial dimensions are discussed later.

Within the federal government the MTN process required a special mechanism to coordinate Canada's negotiating effort. In short, it required a miniature replica central agency. This came in the form of the Office of the Canadian Coordinator for the Multilateral Trade Negotiations headed by J.H. "Jake" Warren, a former Ambassador to the United States. Early in the negotiations an interdepartmental Canadian Trade and Tariffs Committee was established as a channel for input from interest groups. Over four hundred briefs were submitted and dozens of meetings held.[32] Later, the coordinating problems among departments in Ottawa necessitated another parallel higher-level committee whose name conveyed even broader realities. It was the Interdepartmental Committee on Trade and Industrial Policy (ICTIP). ICTIP supported a special Cabinet committee, chaired by the Minister of External Affairs, Allan MacEachen, to forge the MTN negotiations, but also to link them to industrial policy per se.

Alas, the world was not conveniently standing still while the new trade policy structures were created. Other consultative forums, structures and events were underway. First, as we have seen, Pepin's initial efforts bore little fruit since they were unable to bring much rhyme or reason out of the patchwork of industry-by-industry and selected across-the-board industrial tax and expenditure incentives, then in existence in the industrial policy arsenal. This was also the time when regional economic development, reflected in the establishment of the Department of Regional Economic Expansion (DREE), was as much in the political forefront as a national industrial strategy.

The mid-1970s was also a period in which debate over fundamental economic ideas was beginning to be openly readdressed, albeit in somewhat confined quarters. For example, the reports of the Science Council of Canada advanced a nationalist "technological sovereignty" line of argument focusing, as we saw above, on technology and on the obstacles that foreign ownership placed on the development of the Canadian economy. On the other hand, the Economic Council of Canada, as we noted above, expressed the more classic "freer" trade preferences of classic liberal economics. In comparison with the later developments after 1980, however, this period of debate was noticeably silent on the issue of the role of resources in Canada's future economic development.

By the mid-1970s a new series of approaches was attempted. Again, the focus was on the manufacturing sector, but this time there was a greater breadth of view and a somewhat more concerted attempt by the federal government to consult business and labour organizations. The previously mentioned ICTIP was itself an outgrowth of two IT&C task force studies carried out in 1974 and which led in 1975 to the formation of an Interdepartmental Committee on Industry Sectors and to a program called the Enterprise Development Program. ICTIP began as a two-tiered committee of deputy ministers and assistant deputy ministers. It reviewed the medium-term forecast of the economy prepared by the Department of Finance. With the changes anticipated from the Multinational Trade Negotiations, the committee performed a role in reviewing the necessary adjustment policies and programs which should be developed. The committee, chaired by Industry, Trade and Commerce, provided an additional mechanism by which the department's work could be coordinated with the Department of Finance. It was at this stage that an attempt was made initially to distinguish and ultimately relate the micro and macro aspects of industrial change processes. ICTIP consisted of the following departments: Industry, Trade and Commerce; Finance; Regional Economic Expansion; Privy Council Office; Treasury Board; Energy Mines and Resources; and Employment and Immigration. In this respect IT&C had begun to function as a type of central agency and, accordingly, its operation between 1977 and 1978 provides an illustration of the problems encountered by lead agencies in the coordination of industrial policies. As indicated above, the creation of the committee was a natural response to the economic problems faced in the 1970s.

The 23 Sector Task Forces and Public-Private Sector Consultation

In 1977 the Department of Industry, Trade and Commerce (IT&C), on the initiative of its then deputy minister, Gordon Osbaldeston, launched its Enterprise 77 program. This was the centrepiece of an extensive review of government policies affecting economic performance. It included interviews with five thousand individual firms across Canada. This led directly, following the concern expressed at the February 1978 First Ministers' Conference on "Medium Term" economic development, to the establishment by IT&C of 23 sector task forces (called Tier 1 committees). The task forces comprising industry and labour representatives recommended detailed proposals for these sectors in virtually all areas affecting economic performance, including tax policy incentives, trade policy, labour supply, and the like.

Later in July 1978, a so-called "Second Tier Committee" was created, whose task was to work directly from the task force reports to identify and make recommendations about factors and policies that cut across sector lines. This committee was composed of five representatives from industry, five members of the executive of the Canadian Labour Congress, an academic, and a chairman from the private sector who had not been involved in the task force studies.

By the time the Second Tier Committee had been created, there was already a strong feeling among senior officials that the machinery for economic coordination would have to be strengthened. The 23 sector task forces were already demonstrating how little industry knew about the availability of existing governmental industrial development incentives, and about confusion as to where to get information. It was also being recognized that government officials were surprisingly unaware of many programs as well.

The period of wage and price controls from 1975 to 1977 was also an important catalyst in pressuring the government to consult these major interests or, at the very least, to be *seen* consulting them, especially to help achieve a restructuring of the economy during the supposed hiatus provided by the controls program.[33] Even though it was thought to be necessary, the consultations with major business and labour interest groups were not particularly successful, partly because, almost inevitably, it was difficult to know what success meant—especially short-term success. For example, though the 23 task forces produced specific suggestions for each sector, many were in the form of a veritable flood of requests for tax benefits. Had they been granted they would have cut federal revenues virtually in half. The "tier-two" group did, however, produce general recommendations concerning such questions as manpower skill shortages, research and development and the need to encourage capital investment to avoid the further "de-industrialization" of Canada.[34] Accordingly, it contributed to a greater awareness of the problems of industrial efficiency.

This period was also characterized by another attempt to coordinate the federal government's own initiatives. One attempt was reflected in the formation of "DM 10," a group of economic deputy ministers created in the midst of the wage and price controls program. In many respects "DM 10" was merely the previously mentioned ICTIP committee, except that its scope was broader. For example, it was one of the catalysts that addressed the issue of regulatory reform, examined in Chapter 12. "DM 10" also led, in part, to the creation in the fall of 1978 of the Cabinet's Board of Economic Development Ministers (BEDM). The specific impetus for the creation of BEDM was the sudden $2 billion budget cut launched in August 1978 by Prime Minister Trudeau. It included an effort to shift spending to the economic and industrial policy field, but the central planners became finally convinced that there was no mechanism to decide where the money should go. BEDM later became the Cabinet Committee on Economic Development and was renamed in 1982 the Cabinet Committee on Economic and Regional Development.

It is important to mention at this point that the Blair-Carr Task Force on Major Projects to be discussed below was a later by-product of the initial 23 task forces. It was seen by Ottawa officials as a way of keeping up some momentum in the bilateral business-labour cooperation reflected in the original task forces. The Blair-Carr subject matter, major projects (later dubbed "mega-projects"), was certainly not at this stage envisioned as the centrepiece of industrial policy. They were merely one component of a complex industrial puzzle.

The discussion above of public-private sector and intra-Cabinet structural relations cannot be viewed glibly as bureaucratic musical chairs. Fundamental ideas were at stake and so were questions of political power. In this regard it is useful to return to our brief comments made in Chapters 7 and 9 about Richard French's analysis of industrial policy. We stressed then that French's interpretation of the failure of Ottawa's industrial policy in the 1970s was too narrowly constructed. Though his analysis deals with many of the events described above, he attributes, in our view, far too much to the conflict among what he calls Ottawa's "three planning systems," that of the PCO, the Department of Finance and the Treasury Board's planning branch. While we agree that there was conflict among central agencies, it is not at all sufficient to interpret these as "planning" since they were not well-defined or viewed in that way. But, more important, the industrial policy dilemmas dealt with a far broader terrain of ideas and interests. French recognizes some of these ideas but fails to give them sufficient weight by subsuming them under the central agency "planning" debate.

Our examination of interest groups in Chapter 3 also needs to be seen in the context of industrial policy structures and ideas during the 1970s. For example, while the Canadian Manufacturer's Association and the Canadian Chamber of Commerce continued to lobby strongly for pro-market approaches, they were joined by two other associations whose interests, while similar, were by no means identical. The Canadian Federation of Independent Business lobbied for particular issues affecting small business and succeeded in gaining political and structural recognition not only for the small business sector but also, to a certain extent, for the tertiary service sector. The establishment of the Ministry of State for Small Business symbolized this recognition. Meanwhile, the Business Council on National Issues was also established partly because of a perceived failure of other business lobbies to anticipate and deal with wage and price controls in 1975 and to build a new higher-level "corporate executive to political executive" link conducted in a regular behind-the-scenes statesmanlike way. All of these groups struggled for a piece of the consultative action. However, apart from their overall support for pro-market ideas, they did not necessarily agree on the important component issues of industrial policy.

Similar problems occurred within the Canadian Labour Congress. The CLC craved recognition and took an interventionist stance, but at the same time did not want to be co-opted by the state nor violate fundamentally its formal alliance with the New Democratic party. And yet business and labour both knew that at a practical level new relationships between themselves and with government had to be forged.

The Olson Eight Point Agenda: Breaking The "Industry" Focus
Difficult though it may be, and no matter how tortuous the journey, all of these ideas, structures and processes must be examined together. The new Cabinet Committee on Economic Development in place as the 1980s began can only be understood in this context. The Cabinet Committee on Economic Development was advised by the new team of

central agency advisors in the Ministry of State for Economic Development (MSED). As we saw in Chapter 11, the Committee took charge of the economic development "envelope" of funds in the new federal system of expenditure management. Once again, it is both intellectually and practically necessary to appreciate the interplay between ideas, structure and process and between ministers and bureaucrats. Not surprisingly, the instinct of practical politicians is to think of the industrial and economic decisions they make in terms of benefits and support for particular industries or sectors in their regions and constituencies. It is not easy or even comfortable for them to think in terms of longer-term economic *development* needs, nor is it easy for politicians, or anyone else, to understand the "economic development process" since such "understanding" is not only difficult but is invariably tied to ideologies.

Officials in MSED, however, began to try to persuade ministers on the committee to think (and hopefully act) differently on the subject. This effort, plus the obvious evidence of economic malaise in the late 1970s, resulted in the announcement in 1980 by Senator Bud Olson, the Minister of State for Economic Development, of an eight-point agenda for economic development. The agenda was expressed essentially in terms of the factors of production, in short of the elements that contribute to economic development rather than in terms of particular industries. The "industry" focus of the earlier phase was broken, at least symbolically. The Olson agenda stressed eight factors: human resource development, capital investment, energy development, natural resources, technology, infrastructure, institutions and market development. The general thrust was to guide more decisions in the direction of support for capital development and to de-emphasize current consumption and "uneconomic" subsidies. The latter were to be viewed as welfare. The influence of this economic efficiency view was evident in such decisions as the reduction of VIA Rail subsidies and the Crow's Nest freight subsidies.

FIRA and the Changing Pattern of Foreign Investment

The foreign investment and foreign ownership aspects of industrial policy continued their episodic journey through the political and industrial policy agenda of the 1970s. The Gray report echoed much of what the Watkin's report had said and led to the establishment of the

Foreign Investment Review Agency (FIRA) in 1973, in the midst of a minority Parliament and as a response to the Nixon shocks referred to earlier. FIRA screened foreign investment. It functioned as a kind of negotiating and jawboning chamber in which foreign firms applying to acquire Canadian firms were persuaded to do more things "for the benefit of Canada" or, if they did not, would have their plans disallowed by the Cabinet. As the decade ended, FIRA satisfied no one, since it was viewed as weak by its economic nationalist critics and as a bureaucratic irritant and nuisance by those who favoured a laissez-faire approach. Provincial governments were also divided in their views of FIRA. The "have not" provinces increasingly regarded it as a discouragement to badly needed foreign investments in their regions.

While foreign investment policy as a whole continued in a haphazard way, the underlying patterns of foreign investment were changing. The degree of foreign control of Canadian corporations peaked in the early 1970s and declined in the rest of the decade. As measured by profits, foreign-controlled firms had accounted for 60 percent of taxable income in the late 1960s and 43 percent in 1979.[36] In terms of assets the large number of corporate takeovers referred to later in the chapter increased the percentage of assets held by Canadian controlled companies in the top one hundred companies. The decade was also characterized by a sharp increase in Canadian direct investment abroad, which for the first time exceeded foreign direct investment in Canada. This occurred *before* the large capital outflows of 1981-82 that followed in the wake of the National Energy Program.

As to specific sectoral approaches to foreign investment in the 1970s, it is essential to stress the establishment of Petro-Canada, whose role we explore in Chapter 16. It was established in part in response to the high level and consequences of foreign control of Canada's oil industry. Foreign investment was also increasingly linked in an explicit way with research and development policy and with demands for product mandating to enable Canadian subsidiaries to compete more aggressively in world markets.

Regional Policy, Province Building and the Limits of an Industry Focus

As was the case in the 1960s, the regional dimensions of industrial policy again took many forms. In 1973, following criticisms that DREE's incentive grants were a form of patronage and following a review of the prior ad hoc programs that DREE had bought under one roof in 1969, a new regional policy was announced. Basically, it asserted the notion that regional policy was not a form of welfare, but that DREE's goals were those of "development." Accordingly, DREE switched its emphasis to a series of bilateral general development agreements (GDA's) with the provinces and de-emphasized the earlier incentive payments to companies that located in designated areas. By the end of the decade, however, as the analysis cited in Chapter 14 showed, the disparity among regions had not been narrowed. They had at best been stabilized.[35]

Regional industrial policies also brought into play the importance of federal-provincial relations and the need to somehow accommodate and meld numerous provincial incentives and industrial policies forged by aggressive and assertive provincial governments which, by the late 1970s, were run primarily by Progressive Conservative premiers. There were no Liberal governments at the end of the decade, whereas there had been four at the start of it. Provincial industrial policies reflected the variety and nature of the regional economies in question, including their relative dependence on United States and foreign markets. Most of the issues involved in dealing with the Western provinces, for example, were on the agenda of the 1973 Western Economic Opportunities Conference (WEOC). WEOC was held to counterbalance the perception in the West that DREE was essentially a department for Quebec and Atlantic Canada and as an effort by the Trudeau Liberals to gain some ground in the barren electoral territory Western Canada had become for them. The Western issues were familiar: railway infrastructure and freight rates for Alberta and Saskatchewan, petrochemical and energy-based diversification for Alberta, forestry and mineral development, as well as ocean-based tanker traffic and environmental concerns for British Columbia. Eventually, after OPEC, Western Canadian concerns came to be symbolized by the issues of the control and management of natural resources, including not only oil and gas but coal, sulphur and potash, as well. The post-OPEC growth in resource revenues gave new wealth and hence the prospect for new leverage over Eastern Canada to address deep-seated historical concerns. These are discussed in greater detail in relation to the energy policy in Chapter 16. But, while energy issues hogged the political spotlight, the underlying dynamics of regional policy involved virtually every industrial sector, depending upon the characteristics of the provincial economies involved. The 1970s were also characterized by the aggressive initiation and expansion of public enterprises by provincial governments. Data on this growth was presented in Chapter 5. Of particular importance were provincial investments in the energy, resource and transportation sector, particularly by Saskatchewan, Alberta and Quebec. Tupper's analysis of the provincial view of the overall regional impact of federal industrial policies and of provincial actions concluded as follows:

> Over the past twenty years, every province, with the exception of Ontario, has denounced federal industrial policies for exerting perverse influence on the course of provincial economic development. In particular, our analysis reveals how governments of the hinterland provinces, and now the government of Quebec, have argued that on balance federal policy has maintained Ontario's economic hegemony. Two points must be made about such long-standing provincial grievances. First, there is some evidence which suggests that provinces may have overestimated the significance of "discriminatory" federal policy as an obstacle to industrial development. Such evidence has not, however, exerted much influence on intergovernmental conflict, particularly when controversies centre around questions of industrial location. Second, the provincial governments wield important economic powers which may be employed to offset the "centralizing" or "discriminatory" impact of federal policies. What emerges under federalism, therefore, is not merely a war of words, but often a clash of governments, each armed with potent instruments of intervention. And in the modern era, the activities of the Alberta state remind us that the provinces differ in their capacity to limit federal influence over provincial priorities . . . the provinces also employ their policy-making powers against one another. . . .[37]

Competition Policy Malaise Amidst Growing Corporate Concentration

In the field of competition policy three events or items were especially noteworthy in the 1970s[38]: the elusive attempt to pass new legislation on competition policy, the Skeoch-McDonald Report of 1976 and the Royal Commission on Corporate Concentration which reported in 1978. The First Competition Bill was introduced in 1971, several years after a major study on the subject by the Economic Council of Canada. Intended to provide teeth for Ottawa's merger policy, the legislation was severely criticized by the business community not only for its content but because the business interest groups felt themselves to be already besieged at the time by the post-Carter tax reforms, examined in Chapter 12, and by the liberalization of unemployment insurance legislation, analyzed in Chapter 17. As a result, the competition legislation was split into two phases, with the more difficult merger issues postponed until the second phase. The Skeoch-McDonald Report was a major study prepared for the second-phase activity and was followed by another bill which was also attacked by business interests.

While competition policy has many features, the key disputes centred on the problem of how one decides when a merger is anti-competitive, who shall determine such questions, and what penalties and remedies apply. Previous "anti-combines" policy had been based on the federal criminal law constitutional powers. It had proven to be extremely difficult to secure successful prosecutions. The proposed new law would be civil in nature to enable economic criteria to be applied. A new tribunal would be established with powers that the business community found draconian. The legislation, in several forms, was never passed because the business lobby was mobilized again in the late 1970s and early 1980s, when another round of competition policy consultations began.

In the meantime, a Royal Commission on Corporate Concentration had reported in 1978 after three years of study. It also adopted a hands-off approach. This occurred despite evidence of growing corporate concentration. As Stanbury and Burns concluded:

> Yet all the while between November 1977, when Bill C-13 was introduced, and the end of 1981, Canada experienced the greatest merger boom in its history. Between 1977 and 1981 the average number of mergers was over 430 per year. This compares with an annual average of 378 in the period 1970-74 and 192 in the period 1960-64. But of particular concern is the number of large mergers/takeovers that occurred. For example, between 1978 and 1981 there were 55 takeovers of companies in Canada in which the transaction price exceeded $100 million. In 20 of these takeovers the value of the transaction exceeded $400 million.
>
> The National Energy Program was a powerful stimulus to the takeover of foreign-owned petroleum enterprises by Canadians. For example, 23 of the 55 takeovers referred to above were in the petroleum industry. At the same time, however, a major part of the takeover activity was generated by eight large conglomerates, seven of

which are effectively controlled by a single family. The eight are: the Thomson family interests; Olympia and York (the Reichmans); the Ravelston group (Conrad and Montegu Black); Power Corporation (Paul Demerais); George Weston Ltd., Cempt Investments (Bronfman family); Edper Equities (Edward and Peter Bronfman); and Canadian Pacific Ltd. While definitive figures are not available, between 1975 and 1981 these eight conglomerates probably tripled their assets, in large part due to takeovers. Overall, between 1975 and 1980, one-third of all mergers in Canada were of the conglomerate type. Horizontal mergers, those most threatening to the extent of competition in individual markets, accounted for about 56 percent of the total during the same period.

Despite this record, not one merger was challenged in court.[39]

While competition policy of a general kind was being stalemated, in specific sectors, other forces were at play to show the inherent difficulty of obtaining a consistent approach. In the energy sector the National Energy Policy was intended to help Canadian firms to compete, but also sought to help establish one or two Canadian "major" firms such as Petro-Canada and perhaps NOVA and Dome Petroleum among the energy giants. In the banking sector some greater competition was allowed in the new Bank Act, mainly by allowing judicious amounts of foreign competition.[40] In the transportation field Ottawa's planners began to see overall transportation policy less and less in terms of grand nation-building purposes and seemed to be becoming cautiously more pro-competition or at least efficiency-oriented, a posture partly forced by expenditure restraint.[41] Almost inevitably in these several policy fields, the macro and the micro notions of "competition" could not quite fit, in part because the politics of each sector is somewhat different, as are the underlying ideas about what competition means in the context of Canada's truncated branch plant system.

Industrial Policy in the 1980s: Energy, Resources, Mega-Projects and the Meaning of Economic "Development"

It is little wonder, then, that there was both growing concern and at the same time confusion about Canada's industrial policy at the beginning of the 1980s. The concern and the ideas about what to do about it occurred at several levels. For example, during the intensive constitutional debate of 1980 following the Quebec referendum, the federal government attempted to seize the constitutional initiative by publishing its "powers over the economy" paper, in which it decried the balkanization of the Canadian economy and compared the barriers to trade within the Canadian common market *unfavourably* with those of the European Economic Community. It sought to suggest ways in which the "Canadian economic union could be better secured in the Constitution. . . ."[42]

The Liberal Pursuit of Federal Visibility and the New Nationalism

In 1980 and 1981, industrial policy, constitutional reform and the National Energy Policy converged at approximately the same point in the political agenda, as part of the aggressive Trudeau Liberal priorities. Industrial policy was announced in the "resources first-economic development" statement appended to the second MacEachen Budget of November 1981, where it was linked to the issue of energy mega-projects.[43] The mega-projects themselves, a list of large (over $100 million) projects planned or envisioned over the next 20 years, were the focal point of the Blair-Carr business-labour task force on major projects which reported in the summer of 1981.[44] All three of the above policy events were, in turn, part of a larger set of priorities launched by a refurbished and aggressive Trudeau government re-elected in February 1980. As we stressed in Chapter 10, the Trudeau Liberals emerged reinvigorated from their 1980 election victory. They launched a series of extremely aggressive initiatives designed above all to re-establish the identity of Canadians with national institutions by facilitating more direct contact of individuals with Ottawa rather than through provincial governments. The central elements of the Liberal approach were the Constitution with its Charter of Rights and the National Energy Program (NEP). On both issues the Liberals could work a generally supportive public opinion to their political advantage.

The three other initiatives which the Liberals launched in 1981, but which, by their own choice, played second fiddle to the Constitution and the NEP, were the new approach to economic development (then simply referred to as an industrial strategy), the related question of the Western Development Fund and a strategy to improve relations with Western Canada, and the renegotiation of social program funding and equalization payments with the provinces. By the fall of 1981 the full weight of this agenda had begun to create unmanageable problems. These problems emerged from the fact that it was virtually impossible for any federal government—let alone one without a strong base in all regions—to politically manage what was effectively the nonmilitary equivalent of a five-front war. Motivated to an excessive degree by the consuming desire for federal visibility and identity, the Liberal initiatives on the Constitution, the NEP, economic development, Western Canada, and social programs were constructed on too fragile a political and philosophical base. The depressed economy of 1981-82 imposed an even more crushing burden to an already unmanageable political agenda. The overall Liberal strategy was founded on the fundamental belief among senior Liberals that the national government could not restrict itself to acting merely as a referee between competing interests of the Canadian "communities." They profoundly rejected the short-lived Clark government's "community of communities" concept of Canada.

The National Energy Program and Industrial Policy

It is no small point to observe that in federal policy priorities during this period, if one excludes the constitution, energy policy came first and economic development came second. The fact that the National Energy Program (NEP) came first in the priorities of the re-elected Trudeau government can undoubtedly be attributed to the central place energy issues had in the 1980 election campaign and to the power and influence of Energy Minister Marc Lalonde. Needless to say, the NEP is itself a massive policy undertaking, which is not examined in depth in this chapter. Our interest in it here is a limited, but not an unimportant one.[45] We are concerned with the fact that it came first on the policy agenda and with how it fits in with the federal view in the early 1980s of economic development (the new name for industrial policy) and the mega-project issue.

The official objectives of the NEP were to promote security of oil supply, opportunity for Canadians to participate in their oil and gas industry, and fairness in the distribution of energy benefits and burdens. Though it had enormous effects on economic development, the NEP was *not* explicitly devised as a part of a larger economic development concept per se. Energy came first and economic development came second. Within the Ottawa labrynth the NEP was not forged through the normal Cabinet structures for economic policy, but rather emerged from a small cabal of ministers and officials. It was shaped by the Liberal election platform group that devised its broad contours before and during the 1980 election campaign and by an Energy, Mines and Resources (EMR) senior bureaucracy frustrated by its inability, even under the Clark government, to get anywhere in energy revenue negotiations with Alberta.[46]

The key element in the genesis of the NEP was the struggle over the share of resource revenues. In this context the Ottawa-Alberta battle was central. All other factors—security of supply, fairness and Canadianization—were of secondary importance. This is not to suggest that the revenue issues was only a partisan self-interested struggle for power between Ottawa and Alberta. Revenue was a genuine issue and a surrogate for many of the normative concerns that are inherent not only in energy policy but in Canadian politics in general—different views of federalism, the role of Western Canada, the control of resources, regional disparities, growing budgetary deficits and Canadian ownership of the economy.

The fact remains, however, that the NEP was not devised in an explicit economic development context—that is, in a coherent larger view of Canada's economic future. It is also essential to note that the NEP itself did *not* draw particular attention to mega-projects even though the list of projects produced by the Blair-Carr task force was dominated by energy and resource projects. The importance of Alsands, Hibernia, the Beaufort Sea and the High Arctic were stressed in the NEP's geological and political view of future sources of supply, but mega-projects and their subcontracting practices were not given any particular emphasis. Nor can it be said that the NEP gave particular emphasis to the notion of an overall "resources first" strategy of economic development. It implied, of course, that energy development would be an essential engine of economic growth, but there was little in the NEP to indicate a more catholic economic view.

Forging a New "Economic Development" Approach: The Gray Initiatives and the MSED "Resources" Paper

This is why the federal Liberal government's *Statement on Economic Development for Canada in the 1980s*, tabled with the ill-fated MacEachen Budget on November 12, 1981, was so surprising a document. Given the history of industrial policy which we have already traced, it is useful to see in greater detail how the statement was constructed. It shows even more concretely the interplay between ideas, structure and process.

In the eighteen months prior to the release of the 1981 Economic Development Statement, the forging of the "national development policy" promised in the April 14, 1980 Liberal Throne Speech was crystalized around two competing policy documents and sets of policy ideas.[47] The first emerged from the Honourable Herb Gray, Minister of Industry, Trade and Commerce. It articulated the nationalistic, more industry-based focus.[48] The Gray proposals took several forms as a Cabinet Discussion Paper in 1980. The second set of ideas was contained in work prepared in the Ministry of State for Economic Development (MSED). It presented a view which supported the need to take advantage of the increased value of the resource sector in the economy. The line of argument was set out in the MSED's Medium Term Track document (MTT) of November 1981 (hereafter referred to as the MTT document).[49] We examine both documents briefly below. It is essential to stress, however, that neither set of proposals gave a particular focus to mega-projects.

The Gray proposals were first presented in a Cabinet paper in the summer of 1980. It was extremely critical of the overall performance of multinational subsidiaries, and thus reinforced previous electoral pledges to broaden and strengthen the mandate of the Foreign Investment Review Agency, to broaden the review of foreign-owned and Canadian-owned companies in general, and to require product mandating and similar measures. It urged an end to measures designed to prop up industries such as textiles and clothing, preferring instead targeted measures to support high technology companies and other growth sectors. In a later Cabinet paper this included proposals for an expanded role for the Canadian Development Corporation in the manufacturing sector. There was a strong export focus in the first paper, including strong support for aggressive low-cost loans and financing for exports to match the support supplied by other countries. Finally, the document criticized the tax incentive structure for corporations, particularly regarding research and development incentives. It advocated more targeted incentives, especially to encourage venture capital for small businesses.

The initial Gray proposals also advocated the introduction of industrial benefits legislation to ensure that Canadian companies have access as suppliers and subcontractors for major energy and other projects worth more than 100 million dollars. The mega-projects were thus discussed in the document and reflected genuine concern about energy procurement, but mega-projects per se were not given a very strong focus. It must be stressed that in governmental projections of capital investment needs over the 1980s, mega-projects were expected to account for only about 7 to 10 percent of total investment.

It is worth noting that in terms of *formal* timing, the Gray initiatives reached the Cabinet Committee table in August 1980 *before* the NEP. In real terms, however, the NEP was at the apex of power. It was already being visualized as a Budget measure and thus devised in a secretive way by a handful of Energy and Finance ministers and officials. In any case, the interventionist Gray initiatives were not well received even in the post-NEP months by a majority of economic development ministers.

It was these concerns which led to the production and development of an MSED paper on "Economic Development in Canada." As noted earlier in this chapter, Olson and the MSED were already well into trying to view the world through the prism of their Eight Point Agenda, an approach which was not particularly interventionist. The analysis was done in conjunction with the MSED effort to prepare annually a medium-term view of the economy. The MSED paper was being circulated in May and June 1981, and its basic analysis emerged in the November 1981 Medium Term Track document (MTT). The intricate and careful nature of the arguments assembled in the MTT document were not all reflected in the federal Statement on Economic Development tabled with the MacEachen Budget in the fall of 1981. Whereas the final public Statement on Economic Development gave the easy impression of an almost unthinking "resources first," "let's cash in on the mega-projects" approach (see below), the MSED work, though focusing on the increased economic importance of resources, was a far more subtle and careful (albeit still extremely controversial and debatable) line of argument. Four major features of the thesis in the MSED document should be highlighted: the overall thesis regarding the changing terms of trade and future resource prices, the assumptions about future labour markets, the implications of both for regional economic adjustment and the absence of any reference to mega-projects.

It is essential to quote the MTT document at some length. It initially and necessarily emphasizes that "economic development is a complex process to understand in the simplest of times," especially given Canada's open and diverse economy. It proceeds quickly, however, to its central thesis.

> It is certainly tempting in circumstances such as these to try to set out an exhaustive review of all the factors and relationships that are relevant to economic development. But the complexities multiply very quickly, and comprehension and a sense of direction soon become impossible. Therefore, the MTT takes the opposite approach. It develops a simple but basic theme about economic change in Canada, namely that a fundamental and essentially permanent shift has taken place during the 1970s, one that strengthens Canada's traditional comparative advantage in the production of basic commodities, related manufacturing products, and high productivity, high technology manufactured goods on the one hand, and increases the comparative disadvantage of many standard manufactured end products on the other.[50]

The document then set out the current regional and sectoral distribution of economic activity and related it to the changing terms of trade of resource products to manufacturing goods, stressing that Canada "is not a dominant world supplier in most products (either basic or manufactured) [and] that it is a price-taker and not a price-setter (for goods which tend, in addition, to be price elastic)." The report next posed the question, "what evidence is there that these changes over the past decade in the terms of trade between resource and manufactured goods are fundamental and essentially permanent (thereby requiring 'fundamental and essentially permanent' changes of a similar type in policy?"[51] The document included Figure 15.2 which shows the terms of trade of Canadian resource products to manufactured goods. The resource products included are imported oil and exported grains, forest products, metals and minerals, natural gas and oil. Automobiles and parts, which Canada both imports and exports, account for a large part of the manufacturing group. The interpretation of Figure 15.2 in the MTT document also deserves to be quoted at length.

> The chart shows how the relative prices of resource products increased dramatically from 1972 to 1975, were only slightly eroded in the period to 1978 and then experienced a second major price increase (concentrated primarily in oil and forest products). Such a shift in the terms of trade of resource products during the 1970s marks a reversal of the trend of the previous two decades. It should be remembered

FIGURE 15.2
TERMS OF TRADE OF RESOURCE PRODUCTS
TO MANUFACTURED GOODS

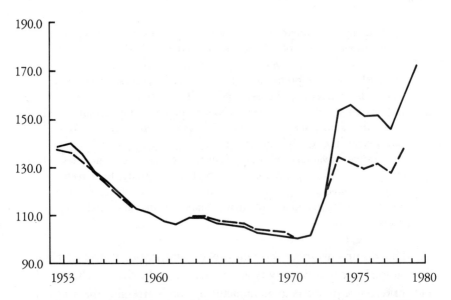

Note: Index, 1971 = 100. Calculated on the basis of import and export prices of commodities (Bank of Canada classification). The dashed line indicates the terms of trade of resources *excluding oil and gas* to manufactured goods.
Source: MTT Document. See note 18.

that during the fifties, the terms of trade for agriculture and forest products in particular declined quite sharply. It was also the period of ample world supplies of oil. That basic commodities could be in scarce supply had almost been forgotten until the early seventies. So far in 1981, prices of resource commodities appear to have lost some ground to prices of manufactured products, most likely as a result of weakness in world markets. By no means, however, does this loss threaten to undo the enormous changes of the past decade.

Will this situation which developed in the seventies last? The evidence here is necessarily more speculative but nevertheless arresting. In general, basic commodity trade is comprised of four major groups. These are energy commodities, food stuffs, forest products, and a wide range of mineral ores and concentrates. A reversal in the terms of trade to the 1971 level would require fairly sharp declines in the real price of one or more of these groups of commodities. Which ones?

The room for differences of view in the trend of real energy prices is wide but at currently and reasonably anticipated price levels, the scope for bringing on additional supplies as well as the ability to substitute other forms of energy and the incentives for conservation are all significant. Thus, while significant increases in real prices are not impossible, it is more likely that if there is to be an increase at all, it will be small. However, the question which is relevant here is rather whether there will be a persistent significant decline. The answer would seem to be that for a host of reasons, there is some possibility of a decrease but not of a significant nature in particular because the OPEC countries would not find it in their economic interests to allow this to happen indefinitely. Thus, while there may be some scope for modest fluctuations in the real price of energy, a reasonable assumption seems to be that it will remain constant or slightly increase.

The projection of real price trends for food stuffs is more certain. Consider that one of the more recent studies for the U.S. postulates that the real price of food will double by the year 2000. Although this may be somewhat excessive, even a more modest expectation would imply a significant further increase in the terms of trade in favour of staple food products. Growing demand from Communist and developing countries is anticipated even though the level of wealth is modest. The most likely assumption, therefore, is that the terms of trade for food will improve.

Forest products have recently been strong and the Canadian competitive position has been assisted by the devaluation of the dollar. But additional supplies from tropical and subtropical areas are a major possibility. Therefore the scope for further real price increases would be dependent upon rapid growth in demand. This does not seem as certain as the increase in the demand for food stuffs.

The fourth group of basic products, "minerals," is more difficult to predict. The real prices of many of these minerals are still relatively low. Some deterioration is possible, but basic demand is likely to prevent much decline. On the other hand, there are substantial reserves of many of these basic minerals elsewhere in the world. Thus, a significant persistent increase cannot necessarily be anticipated either. The most likely assumption is that real mineral prices will remain relatively steady or increase slightly.

In summary, the shifts in the terms of trade toward basic materials can be expected at least to be maintained in the medium term, and perhaps even to strengthen. There is more.

Because the real prices of most resource products are not expected to change markedly over the next decade or more (with the possible exception of food stuffs), Canada's international terms of trade may improve somewhat because of this. International terms of trade relate to the price of exports and imports. Changes in the international terms of trade give rise, therefore, to effects analogous to changes in the commodity terms of trade. In particular, since Canada is a net exporter of resource products and a net importer of manufactured ones, its international terms of trade tend to move in the same direction as the terms of trade of resources to manufactured goods.

Figure 15.3A (not reproduced here) shows the large swings in Canada's international terms of trade during the seventies compared to earlier years. It has been estimated that for every 10 percent rise in the terms of trade of resources to manufactured products, Canada's international terms of trade improve by roughly 2 percent (other factors also play a role, in particular exchange rate changes). An increase in the international terms of trade has an immediate effect on the real income of the country. This arises from the fact that with each dollar earned on export sales, more imports can be bought. This real gain is proportional to the value of international trade. Since Canada's international trade is 20-30 percent of GNP, and the terms of trade improved by 8 percent during the seventies, it means that Canadians became better off by about 2-2.5 percent of GNP.

The quantum jumps of the past decade are not projected to recur. Rather, a gradual improvement in the terms of trade is expected as Canada adjusts the content of its trade to the new prices. Among these adjustments, the potential for drastically cutting back imports of oil and oil products is important. By eliminating this high-priced import item, the overall price of imports will be substantially lowered. Thus, projected changes in trade and trade prices may bring as much as 10 percent further gain in terms of trade and thus a 3 percent further real income gain, by the year 1992.[52]

The report went on to assess the likely impact of these changes on specific industrial sectors and on Canada's regions. It showed naturally enough that sectoral and therefore regional impacts vary greatly, and thus presented different policy problems not easily solved by insensitive and blunt macro policy levers. It also related the employment creation potential of these shifts to the fact that Canada's future job creation needs in the 1980s would not *in the aggregate* be as gigantic as they were in the previous two decades when the post-war baby boom and a large intake of immigrants had to be employed, not to mention increased participation by women. Echoing the work of the Dodge Task Force (examined in Chapter 17), the MSED document saw the labour market problem as being more qualitative, not quantitative.[53] Although still debatable, this assertion at least countered somewhat the problem usually identified with a resource emphasis, namely the lack of significant job content in a resources first-mega-projects strategy.[54] The MSED argument was once again much more carefully argued than the public pronouncements contained in the 1981 Statement on Economic Development.

Mega-Projects, Resources, Regionalism and Industrial Benefits
It must be stressed that there is scarcely any mention of mega-projects in these documents. The mega-projects issue followed its own route to the Cabinet table, eventually being given a prominence that the MSED document did not intend. By examining these two sets of documents we do not wish to argue that written documents *are* policy. Indeed, it is questionable just how closely these documents were read by ministers. After all, the flood of paper in the Ottawa policy process puts an even greater premium on verbal policy advice. Thus, the "industrial" interventionism of the Gray initiatives and the resource-based "terms of trade"-driven economic development notions of the MSED papers can never be said to penetrate the collective Cabinet and bureaucratic psyche in a pure form. Nonetheless, the thrust of verbal advice was very similar to the documents cited above. Moreover, the ideas expressed in both documents raise genuinely historic controversies about Canadian politics and economics. Both approaches *are* highly debatable. This debate was unnecessarily deflected into the relative "side show" of the mega-projects issue.

It was the Blair-Carr "Major Projects Task Force on Major Capital Projects in Canada to the Year 2000"[55] which first focused attention on the mega-projects issue in a more generic way. As noted earlier, the Task Force was put to work in November 1978 by the Federal-Provincial Ministers of Industry Conference. The chief impetus was one of keeping business and labour in a process of consultation to maintain the momentum of the initial 23-sector task force exercise. Co-chaired by Robert Blair, President of Nova, and Shirley Carr, Executive Vice President of the Canadian Labour Congress, the task force involved an autonomous bipartite group of about 80 senior Canadian business and labour representatives.

The Blair-Carr Task Force report was released on June 23, 1981. Thus, some of its work was reflected in the Herb Gray initiatives described above. The report presented an inventory of projects to be implemented by the year 2000, showing a list of actual projects totalling

$440 billion spread across the country in all regions.[56] The projects were overwhelmingly in the energy and resource field. The report made several recommendations to help maximize the flow of benefits from these projects to Canadians. These included:

- formation of a "Major Projects Assessment Agency" comprised of business and labour representatives with governments participating as observers.
- provision of continuously updated information regarding major projects, since this is seen to be critical to the objective of maximizing industrial and regional benefits.
- a clear statement by governments and project participants of policies and procedures to be followed to expand Canadian ownership and participation, encourage regional equity and streamline regulatory and administrative practice.
- specific actions to improve training and utilization of manpower.
- support of good labour practices through recognition of the right of employees to organize and bargain collectively.
- high priority efforts to develop technology while limiting any disruptive effects, particularly on workers and communities.
- assistance to facilitate development of Canadian manufacturing and service capability.[57]

There were dissenting opinions contained in the report from five corporate executives. Their objections generally centred on the recommendation for a procurement premium of 3 percent for Canadian-based companies contained in the report and on the powers and role of the proposed Major Projects Assessment Agency.

The federal government did not support the concept that a review agency with regulatory powers could be a bilateral business-labour body. Nor did it adopt the general proposal in the Gray initiatives to establish a general body with statutory powers over Canadian benefits. It also rejected the procurement premium policy, at least as an overt policy.[58] The government's main initial response to the report was its announcement on August 27, 1981 that it was creating an Office of Industrial and Regional Benefits (OIRB) *within* the Department of Industry, Trade and Commerce. It would be supported by an Interdepartmental Committee on Industrial Benefits and by a bilateral business-labour board with information and research powers only.[59] A list of industrial benefits objectives and guidelines for owners/sponsors of projects were also released.

The 1981 Statement on Economic Development

The two contending sets of documents reflecting two quite different orientations and sets of ideas somehow had to be resolved in the Trudeau Cabinet. The 1981 Statement became a product of drafting and creative writing by an ad hoc Cabinet Committee chaired by Finance Minister Allan MacEachen. To the economic development stew was added the mega-projects broth. The publication of the Statement on Economic Development was followed by a restructuring of federal economic ministries.[60] This included a merger of parts of the Department of Industry Trade and Commerce (ITC) and the Department of Regional Economic Expansion (DREE) into a new Department of Regional and Industrial Expansion (DRIE) and an attempt to strengthen the economic and trade role of the Department of External Affairs by transferring the Trade Commissioner Service from ITC to External Affairs.

In addition to stressing the mega-projects the statement on economic development focused on three priority concepts. These were that:

- The leading opportunity for the Canadian economy "lies in the development of Canada's rich bounty of natural resources." Natural resources include not only energy, but also mining, forestry, agri-food and fisheries, four sectors singled out specifically. Linked to this resource-driven approach, but taking second place to it, is manufacturing activity "to supply machinery, equipment and materials needed for resource development and to extend the future processing of resource products beyond the primary stage." The resource approach will also be tied to strategic international trade opportunities in selected industries. The manufacturing sector is by no means ignored in the statement. Support for high technology industry is indicated, but the impression is clear that resources will be the engine of growth.
- Economic development based on resources carries with it the prospect that such development for the first time can benefit all of Canada's regions concurrently. The statement notes that "seldom in this century has it been possible to identify genuine prospects for growth in every region."
- The process and pace of resource development and the industrial restructuring that will accompany it must be "managed." This is because "only a reasoned pace will permit us to marshal the enormous financial resources needed to fund this development. Only a reasoned pace will permit local indigenous manufacturing and service industries to flourish and thus build an enduring and diversified economic base."[61]

The first sections of the Liberal government's statement on economic development implied a strong interventionist approach. Later sections set out assurances to business and American audiences about nonintervention. These assurances include a commitment to preserve and enhance the Canadian "common market," to reduce regulatory obstacles for businesses, to support research and development and to resolve uncertainties over federal competition policy. Above all, the Liberals offered assurances that the special NEP measures then "being employed to achieve Canadian ownership and control of the oil and gas industry are *not*, in the Government of Canada's view, appropriate for other sectors." The paper also said that the changes to the mandate of the Foreign Investment Review Agency (FIRA), promised in the previous Liberal Throne Speech, would not be carried out "for the time being."

Such assurances to the business community and to placate growing American criticism of FIRA and the NEP were thought by some members of the Liberal Cabinet and senior bureaucracy to be essential to produce a proper climate for economic development. For other ministers and officials the need to give assurances was more akin to a tactical retreat. For them the early part of the statement contained the heart and soul of Canadian economic development in the 1980s.

The above chronological account does not capture all the policy circumstances. A further reality was that the Statement on Economic Development was part of the disasterous MacEachen Budget of November 12, 1981. Moreover, it was followed several months later by the third MacEachen Budget, which imposed the "6 and 5" public sector wage control program, and by the Lalonde unofficial Budget of October 1982, which focused on a modest job creation package in the midst of the worst recession since the 1930s. These coincidental policy events show in obvious ways that the approach to economic development cannot be divorced from the exigencies of short-term macro fiscal and monetary policy. To reach the promised land of the medium term one must first wend one's way through, or for many Canadians often struggle merely to survive, the swamps of the short term. The three Budgets of 1981-82 placed more than normal obstacles along the course of this difficult journey.

Meanwhile, in October 1981 the Office of Industrial and Regional Benefits had released a more up-to-date and somewhat more economically realistic inventory of major capital projects.[62] The Statement on

Economic Development followed in November, however, and triggered an even larger political focus on the mega-project strategy. Within months, the MacEachen Budget debate, the seriously depressed economy, high interest rates, plummeting oil prices, declining federal revenues and a doubling of the federal deficit had conspired to bring the federal approach to the economy, both short term and medium term, into severe political disrepute. The most visible symbolic victims of this malaise were the Alsands and Cold Lake energy mega-projects, especially the former.

On the larger intervention questions inherent in industrial policy and economic development, it is evident that the normative basis of the aggressive post-1980 election interventionism of the Liberals was extremely narrowly based. The only seemingly coherent view was the new nationalism of enhancing federal visibility. This is not an unimportant issue, but it is not a normative base on which one can construct policies that address the main policy ideas inherent in governing Canada—facilitating the creation of wealth and efficient economic growth, redistributing it fairly among Canadians both regionally and in relation to income groups, and enhancing national unity and independence.

All public policy involves some kind of intervention, but the capacity to intervene in an overall sense and to have such intervention accepted and understood in a democratic way requires a greater clarity and breadth of thought than was evident in 1981 and 1982. Future directions for economic development were not debated in such a way as to bring out the issues that were being addressed, in part at least, in the more private confines of the executive and bureaucracy.

At the same time, however, it is evident that the two broad alternatives, the Gray package and the MSED package, were inherently filled with uncertainties and risks. The former created uncertainty because it expressed a faith in the wisdom and foresight of state managers and regulations. Moreover, it issued a challenge to United States corporate and political power, precisely at a time when the United States was headed by a president who was avowedly and energetically pro-private enterprise.[63] The MSED package rested seemingly on a faith that future resource prices in the late 1980s would confirm trends in the last half of the 1970s. It presented a plausible, even careful scenario, but the question was, should it be believed? Was it a good bet? Could the ideas inherent in it be "sold" and communicated to the Liberal party or to the Canadian people?

The sharpening of the intervention scenarios and alternatives and of the industry versus resource dimensions in the early 1980s (as reflected in the documents but not necessarily in the public debate) should perhaps be expected. There is, after all, a relationship between uncertainty and ideology. The more that it was felt in the early 1980s that "nothing works" or the greater the uncertainty about the future, the more important ideologies may become.

The Liberals had occupied the supposedly nonideological middle of the political spectrum with considerable electoral political success but increasingly dubious "industrial policy" success. The Liberal party was not idea-less, but it had become perversely narrow and unable to deal with its own contraditions. The slippery emergence of the mega-projects to a place in the rhetorical political sun illustrated this reality well.

Concluding Observations

The prime concern of industrial policy is undoubtedly one of ensuring that Canada's industrial and overall economic competitiveness is maintained and advanced in the context of both domestic and international trade markets. But industrial policy must be placed in the broader context of the Canadian political economy. From Sir John A. Macdonald's National Policy to the post-World War II reconstruction policy and from the ad hocery of the 1960s to the search for a comprehensive industrial strategy in the 1970s, industrial policy has attempted to embrace a wide range of ideas and structures. In the 1980s industrial policy involves: manufacturing, resources and the burgeoning service sectors of the economy as well as other sectoral definitions; interdepartmental, intergovernmental, international and public-private sector consultation; conflict and consensus; short-term flexibility and long-term planning; numerous policy fields including trade, regional, competition, energy, resources, labour market, defence, transportation, foreign investment, banking and research and development policy. All of these involve an interplay of ideas, structures and processes and of economic, social and foreign policy content which are not necessarily compatible. This has led to a search for a locus of coordinating power.

The ideas of industrial policy are not always reflected in the pristine form of the formal list of ideas presented in Chapters 2 and 14. There is a considerable rhetorical variety for the ideas including expressions such as, "improving labour productivity," "promoting a climate for investment," avoiding "continentalism," or a "resource sell-out, "preserving the 'integrity' of the banking system," "equalization payments," "Canadianization," "better business-government relations," "avoiding the balkanization of the Canadian common market," "demand management," "supply management," "labour mobility," "industrial democracy," "free trade," "adjustment policies," "nontariff barriers," avoiding "protectionism," "third options," "tripartism", the "national policy" and "Western economic opportunities." The rhetoric varies but the dominant ideas persist.

NOTES

1. Peter Morici, Arthur Smith, Sperry Lea, *Canadian Industrial Policy* (Washington: National Planning Association, 1982), p. 4. On the general issues of industrial policy, see Richard W. Phidd and G. Bruce Doern, *The Politics and Management of Canadian Economic Policy* (Toronto: Macmillan of Canada, 1978), Chapters 8 to 12; Richard French, *How Ottawa Decides* (Ottawa: Canadian Institute of Economic Policy, 1980); Allan Tupper and G. Bruce Doern, eds., *Public Corporations and Public Policy in Canada* (Montreal: Institute for Research on Public Policy, 1981); W. Diebold, *Industrial Policy as an International Issue* (New York: Council on Foreign Relations, 1980); David H. Blake and Robert S. Walters, *The Politics of Global Economic Relations* (Englewood Cliffs: Prentice-Hall, 1976); and C. Green, *Canadian Industrial Organization and Policy* (Toronto: McGraw-Hill Ryerson, 1980).
2. Robert Bothwell, Ian Drummond, John English, *Canada Since 1945: Power Politics and Provincialism* (Toronto: University of Toronto Press, 1981), Chapter 9.
3. Sandford F. Borins, "World War Two Crown Corporations: Their Wartime Role and Peacetime Privatization," *Canadian Public Administration*, Vol. 25, No. 3 (Fall 1982), pp. 380-404.
4. Department of Reconstruction, *White Paper on Employment and Income* (Ottawa: King's Printer 1945).
5. See Robert Campbell, "The Keynesian Politics—Economic Synthesis: Canadian Economic Policy 1945-1968", paper presented to the Canadian

Political Science Association Meeting, Halifax, 1981.

6. See A.F.W. Plumptre, *Three Decades of Decisions: Canada and the World Monetary System 1944-75* (Toronto: McClelland and Stewart, 1977), Chapters 1 to 4.

7. See Robert Bothwell and William Kilbourn, *C.D. Howe: A Biography* (Toronto: McClelland and Stewart, 1979), Chapters 12, 13 and 14.

8. Glen Williams, "Trade Promotion and Canada's Industrial Dilemma: The Demise of the Department of Industry, Trade and Commerce" in G. Bruce Doern, ed., *How Ottawa Spends Your Tax Dollars 1982* (Toronto: James Lorimer Publishers, 1982), p. 129. For a more detailed account, see Glen Williams *Not For Export: A Political Economy of Canada's Arrested Industrialization* (Toronto: McClelland and Stewart, 1983).

9. Glen Williams, "Trade Promotion and Canada's Industrial Dilemma: The Demise of the Department of Industry, Trade and Commerce," *op. cit.,* pp. 117-118. See also M.H. Clark, "The Canadian State and Staples: An Ear to Washington," Ph.D. Dissertation, McMaster University, 1979.

10. On the Arrow and Defence Production, see James Dow, *The Arrow* (Toronto: James Lorimer Publishers, 1979); and Stephen Clarkson, *Canada and the Reagan Challenge* (Ottawa: Canadian Institute for Economic Policy, 1982), Chapter 11.

11. See Denis Smith, *Gentle Patriot: A Political Biography of Walter Gordon* (Edmonton: Hurtig, 1973), pp. 31-50.

12. See Phidd and Doern, *op. cit.,* Chapter 2.

13. Glen Williams, "Trade Promotion and Canada's Industrial Dilemma," *op. cit.,* pp. 118-119.

14. See Ross Perry, *The Future of Canada's Auto Industry* (Ottawa: Canadian Institute for Economic Policy, 1982) and Inquiry into the Automotive Industry (the Reisman Commission), *The Canadian Automotive Industry: Performance and Proposals for Progress* (Ottawa: Minister of Supply and Services, 1978).

15. See Richard W. Phidd, "The Economic Council of Canada 1963-1974," *Canadian Public Administration,* Vol. 18, No. 3 (1975); and G. Bruce Doern, *Science and Politics in Canada* (Montreal: McGill-Queen's University Press, 1972).

16. See J. Fayerweather, *Foreign Investment in Canada* (Toronto: Oxford University Press, 1973); and Richard Schultz, "The Cabinet as a Regulatory Body: The Case of the Foreign Investment Review Act" (Ottawa: Economic Council of Canada, Working Paper No. 6, 1980).

17. See John Langford, *Transport in Transition* (Montreal: McGill-Queen's University Press, 1976); A.W. Currie, *Canadian Transportation Economics* (Toronto: University of Toronto Press, 1967), Chapter 1; and R. Schultz, *Federalism, Bureaucracy and Public Policy: The Politics of Highway Transportation Regulation* (Montreal: McGill-Queen's University Press, 1980).

18. Philip Mathias, *Forced Growth* (Toronto: James Lewis and Samuel, 1971),

Chapter 1. See also Harvey Lithwick, *Regional Economic Policy: The Canadian Experience* (Toronto: McGraw-Hill Ryerson, 1978).

19. Phidd and Doern, *op. cit.,* Chapter 9.

20. *Ibid.,* Chapter 10. See also W.T. Stanbury, *Business Interests and the Reform of Canadian Competition Policy* (Toronto: Carswell Methuen, 1977).

21. The Standing Senate Committee on Foreign Affairs, *Canada-United States Relations,* Vol. III, Canada's Trade Relations with the United States (Ottawa: Minister of Supply and Services, 1982), p. 18. See also "Canada-United States Trade and Policy Issues," Special Supplement, *Canadian Public Policy,* Vol. VIII (October, 1982).

22. See Rianne Mahon, *The Politics of Industrial Strategy in Canada: Textiles* (Toronto: University of Toronto Press, 1983). See also G.K. Helleiner, "Canada and the New International Economic Order," *Canadian Public Policy,* Vol. II, No. 3 (Summer, 1976), pp. 451-465.

23. Honourable Jean-Luc Pepin, "Industrial Strategy—Notes for a Speech to the Annual General Meeting of the Canadian Manufacturer's Association," Edmonton (June 5, 1972).

24. See Richard French, *How Ottawa Decides* (Ottawa: Canadian Institute for Economic Policy, 1979), Chapter 6.

25. See Peter Aucoin and Richard French, *Knowledge and Power* (Ottawa: Science Council of Canada, 1974); and G. Bruce Doern, *Science and Politics in Canada, op. cit.,* Chapter 8.

26. See Mel Skinner, "The Federal 'Make or Buy' R and D Policy: A Preliminary Assessment of Policy Development and Implementation," (Ottawa: Masters Thesis, School of Public Administration, Carleton University, 1979). See also Donald G. McFetridge, "Research and Development Expenditures" in G. Bruce Doern, ed., *How Ottawa Spends Your Tax Dollars 1981* (Toronto: James Lorimer Publishers, 1981), Chapter 8; and H.H. Harvey, "Inflation: A Powerful Tool in Government Science Policy," *Canadian Public Policy,* Vol. II, No. 3 (Summer, 1976), pp. 439-450.

27. On the Science Council's technological sovereignty approach, see John N.H. Britton and James Gilmour, *The Weakest Link: A Technological Perspective on Canadian Industrial Underdevelopment* (Ottawa: Science Council of Canada, 1978); Science Council of Canada, *Forging the Links: A Technology Policy for Canada* (Ottawa: Science Council of Canada, 1979); Kristian S. Palda, *The Science Council's Weakest Link* (Vancouver: Fraser Institute, 1979); and Steven Globerman, "Canadian Science Policy and Technological Sovereignty," *Canadian Public Policy,* Vol. IV, No. 1 (Winter, 1978), pp. 34-45.

28. On the making of trade policy, see David R. Protheroe, *Import and Politics* (Montreal: Institute for Research on Public Policy, 1980), Chapter 7; and M. Biggs, *The Challenge: Adjust or Protect* (Ottawa: The North-South Institute, 1981).

29. See Standing Senate Committee on Foreign Affairs, *op. cit.,* pp. 9-11 and S. Clarkson, *op. cit.,* Chapter 5.

30. Economic Council of Canada, *Looking Outward: A New Trade Strategy for Canada* (Ottawa: Information Canada, 1975).

31. Standing Senate Committee on Foreign Affairs, *op. cit.,* pp. 17-18.

32. See Protheroe, *op. cit.,* pp. 156-163.

33. See Phidd and Doern, *op. cit.,* Chapter 14; French, *op. cit.,* Chapters 5 and 6; Douglas Brown and Julia Eastman, *The Limits of Consultation* (Ottawa: Science Council of Canada, 1981), *Consultation and Consensus: A New Era in Policy Formulation?* (Ottawa: Conference Board in Canada, 1978); A. Maslove and E. Swimmer, *Wage Controls in Canada 1975-78* (Montreal: Institute for Research on Public Policy, 1980), Chapter 2; and Leo Panitch, "Corporatism in Canada," *Studies in Political Economy,* Vol. 1, No. 1 (Spring, 1979), pp. 43-92.

34. See Brown and Eastman, *op. cit.,* Part C, pp. 117-134.

35. See Economic Council of Canada, *Living Together: A Study of Regional Disparities* (Ottawa: Minister of Supply and Services, 1977); and Donald J. Savoie, *Federal-Provincial Collaboration: The Canada-New Brunswick General Development Agreement* (Montreal: McGill-Queen's University Press, 1981).

36. See *Companies and Labour Unions Returns Act, Report for 1979* (Ottawa: Statistics Canada, 1981), pp. 20 and 39-41; and Organization for Economic Cooperation and Development (OECD), *Economic Surveys, Canada* (Paris: OECD, 1981), pp. 64-66.

37. See Allan Tupper, *Public Money in the Private Sector* (Kingston: Institute for Intergovernmental Relations, Queen's University, 1982), p. 53. See also Brown and Eastman, *op. cit.*

38. See Stanbury, *op. cit.;* and Irving Brecher, *Canada's Competition Policy Revisited: Some New Thoughts on an Old Story* (Montreal: Institute for Research on Public Policy, 1981).

39. W.T. Stanbury and Susan Burns, "Consumer and Corporate Affairs: Portrait of a Regulatory Department," in G. Bruce Doern, ed., *How Ottawa Spends Your Tax Dollars 1982* (Toronto: James Lorimer Publishers, 1982), pp. 190-191.

40. R.M. Rickover, "The 1977 Bank Act: Emerging Issues and Policy Choices," *Canadian Public Policy,* Vol. 11, No. 3 (Summer, 1976), pp. 372-379.

41. John Langford, "Transport Canada and the Transport Ministry: The Attempt to Retreat to Basics" in G. Bruce Doern, ed., *How Ottawa Spends Your Tax Dollars 1982* (Toronto: James Lorimer Publishers, 1982), Chapter 7.

42. Government of Canada, *Powers Over the Economy: Securing the Canadian Economic Union in the Constitution* (Ottawa: Government of Canada, July 1980). See also Robert Sheppard and Michael Valpy, *The*

National Deal: The Fight for a Canadian Constitution (Toronto: Fleet Books, 1982), pp. 48-50.

43. See Government of Canada, *Statement on Economic Development for Canada in the 1980s* (Ottawa: November 1981). Hereafter referred to as Statement on Economic Development.

44. *Major Canadian Projects: Major Canadian Opportunities.* A Report to the Major Projects Task Force on Major Capital Projects in Canada to the Year 2000. (Ottawa: Supply and Services Canada, 1981). Hereafter referred to as the Blair-Carr Task Force.

45. See Chapter 16. See also Larry Pratt, "Energy: The Roots of National Policy," *Studies in Political Economy*, No. 7 (Winter, 1982), pp. 27-59; David Crane, *Controlling Interests* (Toronto: McClelland and Stewart, 1982); and G. Bruce Doern and Glen Toner, *The NEP and the Politics of Energy* (Toronto: Methuen, 1984).

46. Doern and Toner, *op. cit.*, Chapter 3.

47. See G. Bruce Doern, "Energy Policy and Mega Projects as an Instrument of Economic Development," paper presented to Conference on "The Limits of Government Intervention," School of Public Administration, Carleton University (Ottawa: October 6, 1982).

48. See *Financial Times*, Vol. 69, No. 16, September 15, 1980, pp. 1-2.

49. Minister of State for Economic Development, "Sectoral and Regional Economic Development in the Medium Term Perspective and Outlook." Unpublished paper dated November 1981. Hereafter cited as the MTT Document.

50. MTT Document, pp. 27-28.

51. *Ibid.*, p. 29.

52. *Ibid.*, pp. 32, 34, 35, 36 and 38.

53. See Employment and Immigration Canada, *Labour Market Development in the 1980s* (Ottawa: Minister of Supply and Services, 1981), Chapter 4.

54. This was the main line of criticism of the NDP. See Ed Broadbent, "A New Employment Option for Canada," A Policy Statement. (Ottawa: February 18, 1982).

55. Blair-Carr Task Force Report. See note 44 above.

56. *Ibid.*, p. 27.

57. *Ibid.*, pp. 10-11.

58. Some incidental premiums may be creeping into federal policy in the general procurement of supplies. See Douglas McCready, "The Department of Supply and Services: Efficiency Canada?," in G. Bruce Doern, ed., *How Ottawa Spends Your Tax Dollars,* National Policy and Economic Development 1982 (Toronto: James Lorimer Publishers, 1982), pp. 235-236.

59. Department of Industry, Trade and Commerce, News Release, "Major Projects Benefits Board to be Formed" (Ottawa: May 20, 1982).

60. Office of the Prime Minister, "Reorganization for Economic Develop-

ment" (Ottawa: January 12, 1982).

61. Economic Development Statement, p. 2.

62. Office of Industrial and Regional Benefits, *Major Capital Projects Inventory* (Ottawa: Industry, Trade and Commerce, October 1981).

63. See Stephen Clarkson, *op. cit.,* Chapter 1; and Mildred Schwartz, *The Environment for Policy Making in Canada and the United States* (Washington: National Planning Association and C.D. Howe Research Institute, 1981).

CHAPTER 16

ENERGY POLICY

Energy policy is often viewed to be merely another subsector of industrial policy, much like the auto industry is. Canada's history, however, testifies that it is far more than a subsidiary component. Energy is essential for all socioeconomic activity. As David Brooks reminds us, energy use also serves to "measure the efficiency and effectiveness of that activity." It is not, as many too often believe, a commodity "determined by the level of other variables such as population and income," but has an independent role of its own.[1] Thus, it is an important, indeed crucial, determinant in a host of policy fields including food and agricultural policy, industrial policy, transportation policy, resource policy, foreign policy and social policy, to name only a few policy areas.

The focus of this chapter is on the oil and gas aspects of energy policy. They have been the dominant fuels in the past three decades, but they were not before the 1950s and they may not be again in the next century. Coal, hydroelectric and nuclear energy sources are also an essential part of energy policy, especially in some regions of Canada. Though space does not allow a full treatment of them here, they do enter the overall mosaic of energy policy.[2] For example, hydroelectric power is a major source in Quebec, including post-James Bay project develop-ment. Nuclear power is a major part of Ontario's and New Brunswick's energy equation. Coal in Nova Scotia was a major industry in the 1940s and 1950s, was to be phased out or scaled down through the aegeis of the Cape Breton Development Corporation in the 1960s and 1970s, but in the 1980s is expanding again.

Because of varying national and regional fuel and resource endowments, energy policy has been conceptualized in different ways and has involved structural change within and between governments. While energy policy has always been linked with industrial policy, until the early 1960s the phrase "energy policy" was scarcely used. If any catholic phrase was used it was more likely to be "natural resource" policy or simply the particular fuel such as "oil policy." In the 1960s and early

1970s the links between industrial and energy policies became a source of more explicit concern. After the shock of the Arab-based OPEC oil embargo, which resulted in a fourfold increase in prices and concerns about security of supply, energy policy was elevated to an even more central place in the policy sun. By the end of the 1970s and in the 1980s energy policy was being linked to an even more fundamental transformation of the industrial system where energy and micro-chip communications and the movement of information became intricately linked in the revolution in industrial productivity. It was also a central feature of the fiscal debate about the proper share of resource rents between the two levels of government and industry. In short, energy came to be explicitly recognized as an underlying structural feature of the economy rather than as a mere industrial sector.

In energy policy structures a similar pattern of development and increasing comprehensiveness occurred. At the provincial level in earlier decades the structure of energy policy focused first on debates about nationalizing hydroelectric utilities. In Ontario, Canada's industrial heartland, Ontario Hydro was made a Crown corporation, primarily because of the pressure of the small business community which feared a private sector monopoly. In Quebec, Hydro Quebec was nationalized in the 1960s to become a symbol of French-Canadian industrial nationalism. Both these structures became dominant in their provinces and, in the absence of strong energy departments until the 1970s, "made" energy policy in their respective domains. Eventually, in the 1970s, provincial energy departments emerged to coordinate policy. At the federal level energy policy structures also became increasingly more complex. In the early 1960s the National Energy Board held sway. Gradually, it was joined by the Department of Energy, Mines and Resources in 1966, Pan Arctic Ltd. in 1966 and Petro-Canada in 1975. Coupled with the energy envelope in 1980, EMR became virtually a central agency. By the late 1970s, if not sooner, the large energy bureaucracy exerted its own influence, in some peoples' view constructively and in others destructively. The National Energy Program (NEP) of 1980 was undoubtedly the most obvious and important product of the widening debate and of the growing energy structure.

Nothing evokes the conceptual breadth of energy policy more than the stated goals of the 1980 NEP. As we outlined in Chapter 12, these goals are security of supply, opportunity for Canadians to participate in their oil and gas industry, and fairness in the distribution of energy benefits and burdens.[3] When one scratches beneath the surface of these goals, familiar ideas emerge. Security of supply, particularly in oil, combines a concern for both stability and national independence. The Canadianization aspects of the NEP also demonstrate a concern for national independence and are viewed, in some quarters at least, as a commitment to harness and promote the efficiency and drive of smaller Canadian firms. Fairness as a goal incorporates a decidedly mixed bag of ideas including equity, regional sensitivity and redistribution.

While previous periods in Canadian history have not seen the rhetorical zest of the NEP's expression of goals, they have borne out the presence of these ideas in successive energy policies. Following the pattern of the previous chapter, we trace below Canada's evolving energy policies in each of the post-World War II decades by reviewing major policies and events. For each decade of the 1950s, 1960s, 1970s and 1980s we focus on the major ideas, but we also relate these to structures and to the dynamics of energy policy. Figure 16.1 portrays the key ideas and related policy components at a glance. Table 16.2 at the end of the chapter provides a list of the key policy events. Before proceeding, however, it is essential to set out certain other distinguishing features of energy policy.

The first point to stress about energy policy is the importance of physical/geographical realities. While this seems to be an elementary point, it is remarkable the extent to which past policies have often been criticized or evaluated without reference to these realities. Energy sources are first a function of geological and geographical determinants.[4] Oil and gas, hydroelectric, nuclear, coal and other sources are not distributed evenly or conveniently across Canada. From these realities flow many of the main economic and political configurations. The economic configurations arise when energy sources are linked to transportation and then to markets and hence population centres. Political realities emerge when producer provinces and regions must interact with consumer provinces and when the national government must devise policies that balance these sources and concerns within the physical limits set by nature.

A second reality is the extent and nature of foreign ownership and control of Canada's energy industry.[5] While hydroelectric, nuclear and, to a lesser extent, coal have Canadian ownership (including public

FIGURE 16.1
ENERGY POLICY: IDEAS AND POLICY COMPONENTS

Stability and Security
- frontier exploration incentives
- stable fiscal regimes
- export controls

Efficiency
- let U.S. markets subsidize construction costs
- exports
- conservation

| ENERGY POLICY |
| NATIONAL ENERGY PROGRAM |

Equity
- blended national price
- national oil policy
- treating foreign and Canadian investment equally
- NEB procedural fairness

Redistribution
- energy pricing and regressive effects
- energy tax credits for low-income Canadians

Regional Sensitivity
- producer provinces versus consumer provinces
- different energy sources of provinces
- offshore resources management
- resource control
- provincial benefits

National Unity and Integration
- pipeline construction and extension
- Canadian ownership and PIP grants
- equalization payments and resource rents
- Petro-Canada
- Canadian Benefits

ownership), the dominant energy sources, oil and gas, have been controlled by foreign (primarily American) multinational corporations. Linked to the dominant foreign firms and dependent upon them are numerous smaller Canadian-owned firms, especially in the exploration and development (upstream) sectors of the industry, and in the subcontracting elements of parts of the downstream sector, that is, refining, transportation and marketing. Only with the establishment of Petro-Canada in the mid-1970s and with the growth of Dome Petroleum and AGTL (later called NOVA) in the late 1970s can it be said that any Canadian firms were positioned to challenge firms such as Imperial Oil, Gulf Canada, Texaco and Shell. These ownership realities are also more or less reflected in the two major oil and gas industry interest groups. The Canadian Petroleum Association (CPA) tends to be dominated by the larger American firms, while the Independent Petroleum Association of Canada (IPAC) contains more of the smaller Canadian firms. Many firms are members of both associations.

A third feature is a constitutional one. The ownership of resources, at least in land-locked provinces, is under provincial jurisdiction. Sections 109, 92(2), 92(5) and 92(13) of the British North America Act provide the basis of the provincial ownership claim. The ownership of off-shore resources is constitutionally less clear and a point of major dispute, especially in the early 1980s, between Ottawa and Newfoundland. Moreover, much of the land under which oil and gas exploration is conducted is Crown-owned land, especially in Alberta and British Columbia. Producer provinces have, however, fought hard for greater constitutional protection of resource rights because the federal government, through its many indirect ways of controlling resources such as through its taxation, interprovincial trade and foreign policy powers, has increasingly exercised such powers for fiscal or other reasons.[7]

The constitutional and fiscal features of energy policy merged in the late 1970s and early 1980s in a highly emotive way. Producer provinces obtained increased clarification and protection of their resource powers in the Constitution Act of 1982, including the power to levy indirect taxes in respect of nonrenewable resources and electrical energy. The constitutional negotiations occurred in the midst of the divisive national energy policy debate of 1979 and 1980 that led to the NEP. The central conflict over the NEP concerned the distribution of resource rents. Price increases had resulted in a massive transfer of wealth, to the Alberta treasury, in particular, and thus had enormous fiscal consequences affecting the national debt. It also affected the intricate formula regarding equalization payments to the provinces, depending upon whether the formula led to a province being defined as a "have" or "have not" province.[8]

A further feature to note is the importance in the politics and economics of Canadian energy policy of large projects.[9] As pointed out in Chapter 4, a *project* assumes a high level of political visibility and can become a surrogate for many policy issues. In each decade energy projects have been important political events. These include the Pipeline debate of 1956, nuclear and giant hydroelectric projects in the 1960s and 1970s and the Alaska Pipeline in the 1970s. In the 1980s energy policy was tied to the federal mega-project strategy, and thus involved projects such as the Beaufort Sea, Hibernia, Sable Island and Arctic Pilot. In most of these cases energy policy is almost inevitably linked to issues involving transportation infrastructure and industrial spin-off and procurement benefits as well.

Finally, there is the partisan dimension of energy policy. The comprehensive energy policy debate of the late 1970s occurred at a time when the federal Liberals faced a sea of partisan opposition at the provincial level in the key producer provinces of Alberta, Saskatchewan, British Columbia and also Newfoundland and Nova Scotia. In addition, the federal Conservative party, led by a Western Canadian, increasingly aligned itself with the provincial producers, even at the cost of some of its Ontario Conservative party support. The partisanship was intense, often highly personal, among the leaders involved, but underlying these disputes were genuine historic principles and grievances, as well as visions of Canada.

Energy Policy in the Post-War Period and the 1950s

From the period following the Leduc oil discovery in 1947 to the promulgation of the National Oil Policy in 1961, Canadian energy policy can be characterized primarily as a policy intended to promote the rapid growth of a domestically sourced oil industry, and to facilitate the transformation from a coal-based to an oil-based economy.[10] In general, this was to be done with a minimum of governmental intervention, save for suitable tax incentives and encouragement for the building of the proper transportation infrastructure to bring Alberta oil and gas to an expanded Canadian market on the West coast and in Eastern Canada. Therefore, the overt concern was one of efficiency coupled with a need to expand secure domestic supplies. Four major policy events in the 1950s need to be understood, however, to appreciate the presence of other underlying ideas and issues. These are: the Alberta government's decision in 1954 to create a mixed public and private company, the Alberta Gas Trunk Line (AGTL), which late in 1979 became NOVA Corporation; the 1956 "Pipeline Debate" on the building of the Trans-Canada Pipeline; the Royal Commission on Energy (the Borden Commission); and the establishment of the National Energy Board in 1959.

AGTL and Regional Sensitivity

In 1954 the Social Credit government of Alberta of Premier Ernest Manning established AGTL to act as a single monopoly gas gathering system.[11] AGTL would act as a common carrier inside Alberta and distribute pooled gas to export companies (such as the then contemplated Trans-Canada pipeline company) at the provincial border. AGTL's ownership structure was a mixed public and private one and was intended to ensure that control would not fall into the hands of Eastern Canadian interests. In picking this corporate vehicle Premier Manning rejected two alternatives, a wholly privately owned firm and a full Crown corporation. The former might lead to external control and the latter was rejected by Manning on ideological grounds, despite the strong advice of government lawyers who felt that public ownership would solidify Alberta's constitutional position. The AGTL decision reflected a deep concern for regional sensistivity or what Richards and Pratt refer to, in Aitken's words, as "defensive expansion" by Alberta. They conclude succinctly:

> On constitutional grounds the Manning government had long worried that federally incorporated pipelines could, by extending their gathering lines across Alberta's borders into its major gas fields, thereby also extend Ottawa's jurisdiction into the province and give the federal authorities wellhead control over Alberta's gas; this in turn could be used by the Dominion to undermine Alberta's emphasis on local priority in regard to supply and price, and to provide consumers in Eastern Canada or the United States with cheap Western Canadian gas.
>
> In light of Howe's constant intercessions on behalf of American corporate and security interests and his single-minded pursuit of the Trans-Canada project, there was more than a little truth in this skeptical appraisal of federal policy. Fear of outside monopoly under federal jurisdiction was behind the enactment of the Gas Resources Preservation Act in 1949, and it was also the dominant consideration underlying the idea for a provincial monopoly over gas-gathering within the province.[12]

This view, in turn, was fostered by the deeper fears and concerns rooted in the prairie populism and depression of the 1920s and 1930s, which we stressed in Chapters 1 and 2. Richards and Pratt again capture this larger Alberta view in the context of both oil and gas.

> Social Credit, like the CCF in Saskatchewan, was eager to diversify Alberta's economic base out of its heavy dependence on agricultural commodities. Memories of the recent depression were still intense, and before Imperial's discovery of oil at Leduc in February 1947, the province's economic prospects were not particularly bright. Alberta's coal industry had been plagued for years with marketing problems; Turner Valley oil production was declining, and the outlook for

agriculture was at best uncertain. Alberta's future, it seemed in 1946, would largely revolve around the wheat farm, the ranching and livestock industry and mixed farming; much would depend on the export demand for wheat and other farm products and on cost reductions in agricultural production. The mechanization of agriculture promised to reduce the number of farms: many anticipated a gradual long-run decline in both the rural and the total provincial population. Oil promised growth and the prospect of diversification; it also held out hope that Alberta's public debt burdens could be eliminated without increasing personal taxation.[13]

The 1956 Pipeline Debate: Efficiency, Stability and National Unity

The impending event to which Alberta was reacting was the long-mooted Trans-Canada pipeline project being actively encouraged by C.D. Howe and the federal Liberals, the latter then in its twentieth consecutive year in power.[14] Initially, two groups wanted to build a pipeline to bring Alberta gas to Eastern Canada and to the United States. An American group wanted to build on an all-Canadian pipeline route. A Canadian group wanted a line east to Winnipeg and then south through the United States to Eastern Canada. Ontario business interests were promoting the idea of serving the Toronto market with Texas gas, and there was pressure from Alberta on the federal government to allow exports to the United States. Ontario's Premier Frost wanted first and foremost a stable, secure supply to fuel Ontario's industries and homes. Alberta Premier Manning supported the idea of one Canadian company but also wanted the Winnipeg line, since exports would assist in financing and keep Alberta's options more flexible. C.D. Howe succeeded in having one combined consortia to build the pipeline, Trans-Canada Pipelines (TCPL). In 1954, however, TCPL was in financial difficulties and had few secured supply or market contracts for gas. Early in 1955 TCPL asked Ottawa for government bond guarantees. Howe supported the proposal, but the Minister of Finance did not and carried the day. Later in 1955 it was proposed by senior bureaucrats in Ottawa that a Crown corporation be created to finance and operate the northern Ontario part of the all-Canadian route. It would eventually pay for itself but in the meantime would avoid further delays in the project.

C.D. Howe became increasingly concerned about the need to complete the project before the expected 1957 general election and the deadline of the winter nonconstruction season. Moreover, TCPL had already acquired an option on steel pipe and needed a decision. To ease TCPL's difficult financial circumstances and to meet other deadlines, Howe and the St. Laurent Cabinet acceded to a temporary arrangement, allowing 51 percent ownership control to reside with American interests. Later, further loan assistance for TCPL was needed. Howe forced the TCPL legislation through an embattled House of Commons by applying closure. Howe portrayed the TCPL as a necessary centrepiece for a new phase of national economic development and thus an essential national undertaking. The Conservative Opposition with soon-to-be-leader John Diefenbaker leading the fight portrayed the issue as one of Liberal arrogance and, in somewhat more muted tones, as a sell-out to American interests.

There is little doubt that the Pipeline debate and the TCPL decision led to the defeat of the Liberals after 22 years in power, but it also lay bare the inevitable compromises between efficiency, which in this case also meant some form of continentalism, and broader national and regional aspirations. Moreover, TCPL was to go on to be another symbol of Eastern control of Western resources. Eventually, a controlling interest in TCPL passed to the Canadian Pacific Railway through C.P. Investments. The CPR had long been a historic and despised corporate symbol of Eastern financial control in the eyes of many Westerners. We return to this point later.

The Borden Commission and the National Energy Board: Structures To Ensure Equity to All the Players

To help depoliticize the volatile energy issue, the newly elected Diefenbaker government established the Borden Royal Commission on Energy in 1957. The key recommendations it made were the adoption of a National Oil Policy (discussed in the next section) and the establishment of a National Energy Board (NEB), the latter promulgated by law in 1959.[15] As the 1950s ended the new focus was to create a structure which would ensure some predictable fairness and equity to all the key energy players. The NEB was to be the central and hopefully more dispassionate regulator of the certification of pipelines, interprovincial tariffs and marketing, and aspects of export marketing and energy trade. In addition, it would become the key advisor to the Cabinet on energy policy matters.

It must be remembered that at this point there was no Department of Energy, Mines and Resources. Energy policy had been forged in C.D. Howe's Department of Trade and Commerce. The then existing Department of Mines and Technical Surveys possessed considerable geological and technical expertise, but it was clearly not an energy department. The Borden Commission, however, was not exercised by the overall energy policy analytical weakness of the Ottawa bureaucracy. These concerns were actually much more in evidence in the Gordon Royal Commission on Canada's Economic Prospects which had reported in 1957.[16] Borden saw the energy policy mood much more in relation to the desire for equity and stability, in the wake of the intense energy politics of the 1956-57 period. Energy policy structures per se were thus not greatly in evidence. The NEB emerged as the new focal point, and its mandate and technical habits and behaviour were to later influence energy policy, particularly in the realm of export policy and the assessment of energy reserves.

The 1960s and the National Oil Policy: Stability and Continental Integration

A major factor in Canadian energy policy in the 1960s was the growing availability of cheap foreign oil which caused world oil prices to fall. This was evident to the Borden Commission even earlier and their recommendations led to the adoption in 1961 of the National Oil Policy (NOP) by the Diefenbaker government. The NOP encapsulated a delicate and surprisingly noncontroversial balance between stabilizing markets for Alberta producers and thus demonstrating regional sensitivity, some increase in national integration, and the efficient supply of oil to Quebec and Atlantic Canada through lower-priced foreign sources. The NOP divided the domestic oil market in half with those in Ontario (west of the Ottawa River) and the West supplied by higher-priced Alberta oil.[17] Thus, for the 1960s and early 1970s Ontario consumers in particular subsidized and helped sustain Alberta producers, the reverse of the situation from 1973 on when Canadian oil prices were below the world price. The NOP also allowed a much greater penetration of the Ontario market by Alberta oil than might have occurred if lower-priced offshore supplies were not restricted.

Given the pace of oil discovery, however, the second major effect of the NOP was the creation of a surplus of oil for export purposes. A gas surplus was unintentionally created because Canadian gas was not allowed to compete with imported oil in Canadian markets. Much of the rest of the decade was spent debating the degree to which oil and gas exports to the United States should be encouraged and also the exact size of Canada's proven reserves. By definition this raised the territorial imperatives of energy policy and its related effect on those who urged continentally "efficient" decisions. Ottawa's energy policy makers successfully increased gas exports to the United States. Oil exports were harder to achieve because of U.S. quotas, but these exports increased as well, at least for a brief period in the pre-OPEC 1970s.[18]

The choice involving greater north-south continental integration, as opposed to more extensive domestic east-west expansion beyond Ontario, was one which the multinational oil companies favoured, but the causes of the NOP and the export push it generated also reflect transportation and financial economics that made increased exports attractive. Thus some concern for efficiency was present and reflected in the policy.

The growing difficulty in determining the size of Canada's energy reserves was a more gradual and intractable dilemma and shows some of the issues raised in Chapter 13 regarding knowledge and information, as well as the role of structure. The National Energy Board had to determine the extent and adequacy of reserves. The dilemmas were two-fold.[19] The first concerned the very real problems of forecasting and estimating reserves. There were controversies not only among geologists and among economists but between the geological and economic definitions of reserves. The second concerned the issue of trust and dependence as to which institutional sector was supplying the estimates and interpreting them. The government was for the most part dependent upon the oil and gas industry's expertise. The NEB had some expertise. Moreover, in 1966 Ottawa established the Department of Energy, Mines and Resources partly to increase its expertise and reduce its dependence, but little was achieved in the 1970s to overcome the dependence on the industry.

These structural and informational issues were of no small importance. A large estimate of reserves would lead to a larger exportable surplus. The politics of information, aided by the buoyancy and optimism that characterized the 1960s in general, helped contribute to extravagant interpretations of estimates. The extent of the extravagance was reflected in the now famous claim by Energy Minister Joe Greene in 1971 that Canada's oil and gas reserves were adequate for 923 and 392 years, respectively.[20]

In general, then, the 1960s were characterized by further growth in oil and gas consumption in a buoyant economy and a general effort to stabilize and increase markets through the aegeis of the NOP and the NEB. The only other public policy item of importance was the establishment in 1966 of Panarctic Oils Ltd. Ottawa purchased a 45 percent equity share and controlling interest in the company. Its task was to undertake risky oil and gas exploration in the high Arctic. For Ottawa it was a modest act of intervention which presaged many of the issues of the 1970s and 1980s, including not only public ownership but the emerging concern for security of supply, and the related problems of regional development in the north including environmental issues and territorial sovereignty regarding northern waterways. In December 1968 EMR and the Department of Indian Affairs and Northern Development established a task force on northern oil development.

The 1970s and the Post-OPEC Era

Energy policy in the 1970s took on a vastly increased amount of related public policy baggage. The issue of the economics and fiscal consequences of resource rents and equalization payments became explicit and took a quantum leap in dollar amounts. Trade and industrial policy issues, including procurement, emerged as part of the larger debate on restructuring the economy. Security and foreign policy concerns about energy supply increased markedly and the issues of environmental policy, native peoples' rights and land claims and pollution were raised far more explicitly. This broader range of concerns affected not only oil and gas but also other energy sources such as uranium, nuclear power exports, nuclear proliferation, nuclear waste management and hydro-electric exports and projects.

In the early 1970s the energy stability of the 1960s came unstuck—with a vengeance. In the wake of the October 1973 Yom Kippur Middle East War, the Arab members of the Organization of Petroleum Exporting Countries (OPEC) imposed a partial oil embargo and oil prices increased four-fold. Canada, as well as other Western states, was unprepared for the OPEC shock. Toner and Bregha succinctly explain why the shock was so traumatic:

The reasons for Canada's unreadiness were simple. First, the government had no direct access to information on which it could base policy. In 1974 Donald Macdonald, the Minister of Energy, Mines and Resources, was forced to admit that "one of the difficulties facing the Canadian government is that it is virtually dependent on major international companies for its sources of information." Second, the government only had an embryonic policy-making ability. According to Bill Hopper, Petro-Canada's president, "You could [have] put the people in Energy, Mines and Resources who knew anything about oil and gas in one corner of Imperial's corporate economic department."

With no means to gather information independently and, in any event, no means to digest it, the government predictably reeled from crisis to crisis in 1973 to 1974. Thus, in quick succession, the government imposed oil export controls, similar controls over the export of refined products, announced the extension of the Inter-provincial oil pipeline to Montreal (only two months after having reaffirmed the National Oil Policy), froze domestic oil prices, levied an export tax on crude oil, developed an oil import compensation scheme to protect consumers dependent on imported oil, considered and rejected acquiring a subsidiary of one of the major multinational oil companies, and contemplated the imposition of oil rationing.[21]

The 1970s are much less easy to summarize than the preceding two decades, but several main policy events and decisions reflect the ever more delicate balance of ideas inherent in Canadian energy policy, as well as its increasing scope. These are the establishment of Petro-Canada as Canada's national oil company, the establishment and operation of the oil import compensation fund, the Ottawa dispute with the producing provinces over revenues, prices and the control of natural resources, the Alaska Pipeline debate, the issue of energy conservation, and the Clark government's energy policies reflected in the Crosbie Budget of December 1979. As these events and issues are summarily discussed, it is essential to keep firmly in mind the other items concurrently on the public policy agenda, not only in the industrial policy field set out in Chapter 15 but also the larger macro priorities examined in Chapter 10.

It is also essential to appreciate the kinds of decisions and uncertainty faced by the major oil companies during this period, since they were also making exploration and investment decisions with large public policy impacts. The case of Imperial Oil of Canada, the largest of the multinationals in Canada, is instructive in this regard.[22] In the late 1960s Imperial shifted its focus from the conventional fields in Western

Canada to frontier exploration at a time when frontier prices were low and the uncertainties great. It found promising reserves of gas in the Mackenzie Delta, but when the pipeline consortia it backed, the Arctic Gas Consortium, lost out in 1978 to the Canadian consortium headed by AGTL President Bob Blair, it experienced severe market problems. Meanwhile, as it was focusing on the frontiers, Imperial also lost out in the renewed Alberta "Pembina" oil boom of the mid-1970s and had to scramble to get back into land holdings it had given up. These difficulties also helped influence Imperial to become more involved in heavy oil developments such as the huge Cold Lake project which was also aborted in 1982. This brief aside regarding Imperial's experience is not intended to suggest that Imperial was a candidate for governmental welfare but rather to show that underlying the "high policy" machinations were indeed some giant risk-taking problems of both a geological and economic kind. Each of the multinationals and the emerging Canadian firms such as Dome Petroleum faced their own configuration of risks, *some* of which they strenuously sought to have absorbed by the state.[23] Indeed, in the case of Dome a private company became, in a sense, a partial tool of public policy, strategically supported by Ottawa through special depletion allowances and viewed by Ottawa as a suitable counterweight both to Alberta's AGTL and its own Petro-Canada.

Petro-Canada, Security and Energy Nationalism

In the wake of the OPEC crisis and in the midst of a minority Parliament, Prime Minister Trudeau presented in December 1973 an eleven point oil policy statement. The major element was the decision to establish Petro-Canada. The initial emphasis in the rationale for creating Petro-Canada was that of energy security. The overt Canadianization aspects of Petro-Canada were to be emphasized later in the NEP of 1980. Petro-Canada was to engage in accelerated frontier exploration both on its own and in joint ventures, especially with smaller Canadian firms.[24] Its mandate was also initially expressed in terms of a "window on the industry" role and hence was in part a structural response to the government's weaknesses in energy knowledge and information. It was also, however, a response to the oil industry's own policy reversals in the post-OPEC period. Instead of reassurances about the existence of long-term supply, the industry now campaigned about the need for security and for increased prices to find new supplies. This reversal greatly increased public suspicion and mistrust of the oil giants, a mood on which the Trudeau Liberals later capitalized.

Petro-Canada was established by the passage of the Petro-Canada Act in 1975. It experienced extraordinarily rapid growth both prior to and especially after the NEP when it acquired Petrofina and the refining and marketing assets of British Petroleum. In the period from 1978 to 1980, in particular, it became the object of partisan political controversy at both a symbolic and substantive level. The Clark Tories promised to privatize it and used the Petro-Canada issue in a broader nonenergy context to signal their determination to reduce state involvement in the economy and to appeal to Western Canadian regional views. This promise was not carried out in the brief nine-month tenure of the Clark government in 1979. Popular political support was decidedly on the pro-Petro-Canada side and against the multinational oil companies. In 1980 the Liberals rode this issue, along with other doubts about the Clark government by Ontario voters (such as energy prices and mortgage deductability) to electoral victory.[25]

By the early 1980s Petro-Canada came to encapsulate in an undiluted form the national identity aspects of energy policy. Even in Western Canada, Petro-Canada had majority support in public opinion polls. Its nationalism, however, was no longer tied vaguely to energy security and frontier exploration. It now included a view that Petro-Canada would be a tool of economic development through its procurement and other investment policies, and that it would operate visibly in upstream and downstream activities, from the high Arctic to the corner filling station.

In terms of energy policy structure, Petro-Canada significantly changed the Ottawa scene. It joined the NEB and EMR as the main energy agencies, but it also raised new concerns about how to control the new energy leviathan. Petro-Canada's capital budgets required the approval of both the Energy and Finance ministers. There was an overall sense of direction and confidence in Petro-Canada's early years primarily because of the close connection between senior Petro-Canada officials such as Bill Hopper and Joel Bell and the prime minister and his senior energy colleagues. But uncertainty remains about whether the Crown corporation tail will wag the Cabinet dog as the company becomes larger and as personalities change.

The Oil Import Compensation Program and Regional and Consumer Equity

If Petro-Canada symbolized the national identity idea in energy policy, then the Oil Import Compensation Program (OICP) expressed the need to cater to the idea of equity and fairness for regionally based and disadvantaged consumers. It was also a commitment in the December 1973 Trudeau statement and was put into place in 1974.

Under OICP, refiners processing imported oil were paid federal subsidies to reduce their costs to the same level as refiners using Canadian oil. In July 1978 the per barrel difference between world prices and domestic prices was less than $3. By late 1980, however, following the Iranian revolution, the differential was about $20 a barrel. This extraordinary and uncontrolled increase resulted in a 300 percent increase in EMR's expenditures between 1979-80 and 1980-81. In 1981-82, following the October 28 Budget and the announcement of the NEP, this subsidy was transformed from an EMR recorded expenditure to a separate account reflecting its revised status as a price (part of Ottawa's "blended" price) charged to the oil consumer rather than the taxpayer. Under this system all domestic refiners pay a new Petroleum Compensation Charge to cover the cost of oil import compensation. Revenues from this charge are used to pay importing refiners an amount sufficient to reduce the "average" cost of imported oil to the average cost of oil to Canadian refiners.

Extraordinary fiscal pressure resulted from the rapid growth of OICP. In 1980-81 the estimated expenditures of over 3.5 billion dollars on OICP made it larger than all but three of the federal departments. The OICP accounted for a significant part of the rapid growth in the federal deficit.[26]

As we outlined in Chapters 10 and 11, it was the growing view by senior Liberals that Ottawa was perceived as a deficit-ridden, mismanaged government that helped persuade them to take on the provinces and their balanced budgets in 1980 and to promote a "new nationalism" based on federal visibility. The billions involved in OICP were also part of the federal-provincial revenue imbalance discussed below. At its core, however, the OICP was a necessary follow-up to the consequences of the 1961 NOP. Energy policy had to embody regional equity both for its own sake and to promote national unity and stability.

Federal-Provincial Dispute Over Revenue Shares, Prices and Resource Management: Nationalism, Regionalism and Efficiency

Petro-Canada and OICP were part of a larger and inevitable federal-provincial and interregional conflict between energy producers and consumers. It embodied virtually all the dominant ideas played out in the context of intense partisan politics, and it involved energy revenue shares between governments, prices, and the control and management of resources. OPEC triggered all these concerns simultaneously both in the first OPEC shock of 1973 and in the second shock in 1979 following the Iranian revolution. The increased world prices for oil sharply increased provincial royalties and resulted in a massive transfer of fiscal wealth, especially to Alberta. This, in turn, upset delicate federal-provincial fiscal and equalization payments. Although royalties were not fully a part of the equalization formula, the dollar volumes were such as to seriously distort the fiscal system.[26] OPEC led to the obvious realization by Western Canadian provincial governments that this wealth would finally give them increased political and economic leverage relative to Eastern Canada and an opportunity to realize the long sought-after diversification of the Western economy, especially as a source of stability against a depleting resource. It therefore involved the deepest issues of past Western resentment as well as future optimism and buoyancy. Resources were the key and, hence, control of those resources, reflected in the earlier AGTL decision, was a central concern. As we saw in the previous chapter, resource issues and diversification were the central items at the 1973 Western Economic Opportunities Conference and in the subsequent debate about the regional dimensions of an industrial strategy. For economically depressed provinces with newly found energy resources such as Newfoundland, the issue was, if anything, even more deeply felt.

In terms of prices, an array of ideas were melded in the energy policy dispute. By moving rapidly to world prices, many argued that this would enable the Canadian economy as a whole to adjust more quickly, become more efficient, and thus be better able to compete with their trading partners,[28] which had already made many of these adjustments. Energy policy was therefore an issue concerning the underlying structure of the economy and the need for major adjustments. Less than world prices implied to Westerners a subsidization by the West of Eastern consumers. The federal Liberals, with their electoral power base in Ontario and

Quebec, asserted the need for "made in Canada" prices and a slower upward movement in prices in the interests of stability and overall equity.

All of these ideas were present in the various federal-provincial disputes of the 1970s. Ottawa's 1973 tax on oil exports and other features of the Turner Budgets of 1973 and 1974 were viewed by Alberta and Saskatchewan as an attack on provincial resource control. Alberta then increased its royalty charges. This reduced federal revenues because royalties were deductible under federal tax provisions. Ottawa, in turn, eliminated their status as a deductible item. Later Supreme Court cases involving Saskatchewan measures upheld Ottawa's trade and commerce and taxation powers and then escalated the Western concern about the need for further constitutional protections.[29] As we have seen, these concerns entered the larger and heated nonenergy arena of constitutional reform which also peaked in 1980-81.[30]

We have by no means dealt with all the other specific issues of federal-provincial energy disputes. The issues must be seen in a cumulative multidimensional way. Both Petro-Canada and OICP were part of the federal-provincial context even though we have treated them separately. The same applies to the next issue, the Alaska Pipeline Debate.

The Alaska Pipeline Debate: Security, Ecology, Continentalism and Efficiency

Just as the Pipeline debate of 1956 became a surrogate for many energy and nonenergy controversies and ideas in the 1950s, so also did the Alaska Pipeline debate in the 1970s.[31] We cannot do justice to the full panoply of decisions and events, but a brief account will illustrate again the ideas inherent in energy policy, including the economic and political uncertainty of large energy projects.

The debate began over the route that would be taken to transport the massive gas supplies found in Prudoe Bay, Alaska to American markets. Initially, the United States government preferred a tanker route down the West coast. Environmental and other security concerns eventually conspired to force a preference for an overland route through Canada. Eventually, two major energy groups bid for the right to construct the pipeline. One group, the Arctic Gas Consortium composed of an Eastern consortium and several of the multinationals, as well as

Trans-Canada Pipelines and Ontario-based gas companies, favoured a route along the Mackenzie Valley corridor. The second group was the Foothills group headed by Robert Blair, the head of AGTL, the second largest gas transmission company after TCPL. The Foothills group favoured a route adjacent to the Alaska Highway. Blair had briefly been a part of the larger eastern consortium but left it over a dispute regarding Canadian control over the Canadian parts of the line. Since the Arctic Gas group believed that financial clout and backing would be the key, it was headed by William Wilder of Wood Gundy, an investment firm. In contrast, Blair calculated that environmental and other political issues would be the key. The latter included his own judgement that he might be looked on favourably by Ottawa as an acceptable intermediary with Alberta in the otherwise intense partisan debate then underway in the early and mid-1970s.

In 1977 the NEB and the Ottawa Liberals sided with Blair's group and the Alaska Highway route, but the decision process was a tortuous one that few could have predicted early in the 1970s. The Trudeau government in 1972 initially expressed a preference for the Mackenzie Delta route. The NDP, with its additional leverage in a minority government situation, and the environmental lobby forced the Liberals to establish the Berger Inquiry in 1974. Berger's final report, following an elaborate hearing process in the far north as well as in southern Canada, recommended in 1977 a ten-year delay and opposed the Mackenzie Delta route.[32]

Another key factor in the process were the deliberations in the United States by the Federal Power Commission which split between the two proposals, thus leaving the choice of route more exclusively in Canadian hands than it might otherwise have been. The continental implications of the line were obviously essential from the very beginning and contained all the issues explored earlier in the 1956 pipeline debate. United States' markets and financing would make the future transport of Canadian gas more efficient. At the same time it would produce an inexorable pressure to export future gas reserves whose dimensions, not to mention prices, were unknown. These issues were debated again in miniature form in 1980 when the special "pre-build" line, part of the larger Alaska project, was approved at a time of even greater financial uncertainty than had been the case in 1972. The "pre-build" would allow the immediate export of cheaper domestic gas to the United States, leaving Canadians with the later, more expensive frontier sources of supply.

Conservation and CHIP: The Emergence of A New Energy Policy Paradigm and How To Implement It

Throughout the 1970s the energy policy debate also began to be influenced, albeit very slowly, by the emergence of a conservation ethic and policy paradigm.[33] This contending view was originally articulated in a very broad environmental context and stressed the finite limits of resources, the delicate ecological balance, and the need to pursue "no growth" policies. In more specific energy policy terms it opposed the prevailing growth and supply-oriented view which consistently favoured the expensive search for new sources. The notion of a "conserver society" applied to energy policy meant that the focus should be on securing future supplies by conserving and eliminating waste through the reduction of demand. Conservation also meant a better matching of energy sources to different types of energy use. To some this meant, in addition, the need for a larger focus on renewable energy. The net effect of the debate was that by the end of the decade, energy policy was perceived to be one which could operate on both the supply and demand side of overall economic policy.

The conservation issue, however, can hardly be said to have dominated energy policy in the 1970s. A renewable energy branch was installed in EMR in 1977-78 but given limited resources. A somewhat more specific manifestation of the gradual influence of the conservation paradigm emerged in the establishment in 1977 of the Canadian Home Insulation Program (CHIP). CHIP paid taxable grants to Canadian homeowners to reimburse them for part of the costs of buying and installing insulation. While in Chapter 18 we use the CHIP program to illustrate the problems of evaluation, here we are concerned with the ideas inherent in it and their links to the previous energy policy items. Chief among these is the connection between prices, CHIP grants and the consumer role in "implementing" energy policy.

It was certainly argued by some energy advisors in Ottawa that the most *efficient* way to encourage insulation and conservation was to allow oil prices to rise to world levels. This would both signal and eventually result in approriate consumer action if coupled with suitable information for consumers. By relying on grants, one would never know how much of an expediture incentive would be needed to induce the right behaviour. Money would inevitably be wasted. On the other hand the price mechanism would also have undesirable side effects, both punitive redistributive effects on the poor and in relation to equity and regional concerns (arising from different kinds of housing stock, and regional energy sources and costs).

We have already seen how energy prices were the object of a higher level of political and economic dispute and, thus, in a sense, unavailable as an "ideal" conservation instrument. CHIP was launched and involved the spending of billions of federal dollars. As we see in Chapter 18, it was later evaluated after it had accumulated other policy and political baggage, including the need to reduce expenditures to fight growing government deficits, fraudulent practices by some insulation companies, regionally varied "take-up" rates, and even health and safety concerns about urea-formaldehyde insulation.[34] It also had to be somehow integrated with broader conservation concepts in the NEP, particularly the desire to persuade consumers to switch off oil.

The Clark Conservative Government and the Crosbie Budget: Regionalism and Redistribution

As the 1970s ended, the contending ideas of energy policy were at the centre of partisan and regionally based electoral politics. In 1979 the Clark Conservatives came to power, only to be defeated following the demise of the Crosbie Budget of December 13, 1979. The Tory energy policy package, while not complete in all its details at the time the budget was brought down, was sufficiently detailed to describe the direction of the government's policy. It aimed at reducing the domestic demand for energy while ensuring future energy supplies. The package included larger increases in the well-head price of oil such that prices would rise to 85 percent of the world level, a new energy tax that would extract half the future price increases in excess of $2 per barrel (to reduce windfall profits), and an increase in the federal excise tax on gasoline of $.18 per gallon.[35] The latter tax was first introduced by the Liberal government at $.10 per gallon and reduced to $.07 in the 1978 budget.

Significantly, the Crosbie Budget also included a refundable energy tax credit. The Conservatives recommended a refundable energy tax credit, modelled upon the refundable Child Tax Credit of 1978. The credit would have amounted to $80 per adult and $30 per child, with benefits reduced by 5 percent over a family income of $21,380—and it would have been phased in over two years. No similar redistributive idea was contained in the later Liberal Budget of October 1980, when the NEP was launched.

Another substantive difference between the two budgets concerned the implied sharing of resource rents among the Western provinces, the oil and gas industry, and the federal government. The exact shares implied by each budget are open to dispute, but it is safe to say the Liberal Budget proposed to significantly increase the federal share at the expense of industry and the provincial sectors, relative to the sharing of rents implied by the Conservative Budget. The Liberal Budget claimed that a 24-43-33 federal-provincial-industry split would result from its tax measures. Alberta, however, claimed its share would be less than 43 percent, while figures given in the Crosbie Budget of December 1979 suggest that the split generated by its tax proposals would be 19-44-37.[36] To a greater extent than the Conservatives, the Liberals were clearly prepared to take on oil and gas producers, and to some extent the Western Canadian producing provinces as well, not just in favour of voters in central Canada but in the interests of Ottawa's own revenue needs.

Other contrasts between the Tory energy package and the NEP are identified below. In general, though, the 1970s witnessed the presence of the same underlying ideas as in previous decades. Energy policy itself, however, had clearly moved to centre stage much more than it had been in the 1950s and 1960s. It was also conducted in a more volatile and uncertain environment, especially compared to the relative stability of the 1960s.

By the early 1980s energy policy structures reflected and influenced the new comprehensiveness and illusiveness of energy policy. The additional power of these structures was symbolized by the virtual central agency status which EMR had achieved in 1980 and its subsequent de facto control of the energy envelope examined in Chapter 11. Aspects of the NEP, as we saw in the previous chapter, were also premised on EMR's own economic forecasts of future world oil prices, forecasts that proved to be wrong in 1981 and 1982, though not necessarily for the late 1980s. Petro-Canada also continued to expand its tentacles and was joined by other bodies such as the Petroleum Monitoring Agency, established to increase Ottawa's knowledge of the financial operations of the oil and gas industry. Meanwhile, the NEB's role had become politically different. While it had been viewed by the energy industry in the 1960s and early 1970s as at best a benign institutional presence, the NEB was increasingly viewed in the 1980s as perhaps the only structural friend the oil and gas industry had in Ottawa. In general, the perceived power of the energy "super bureaucrats" was great. Indeed, in some quarters the blame for the NEP and its consequences was laid much more specifically on the bureaucrats in the energy policy structures and not on the ministers.[37] While there can be little doubt that the NEP was interventionist and that Ottawa's bureaucratic power was a factor, such judgements seriously underplay the structural and partisan competition between Ottawa and the provinces, as well as the full range of ideas inherent in Canadian energy policy. For example, Peter Foster's verdict on the NEP, while representative of a genuine political view, links energy policy structures, the NEP and the entire Trudeau regime to a seemingly simple trade-off between equality and efficiency, with nationalism as a smokescreen:

> Ottawa's enlightened interventionists continue to believe in their ability to perpetrate a more efficient society. Blinded by their own fervent desire to rectify inequality and "do good," they do not consider for a second that gross inefficiency might result, and that the very health of society could be in danger from their very prescriptions. They are experts at the game of false logic: that supporting the health of corporations is in some way depriving the much-invoked "little-man"; that because their intentions are good, the results cannot be bad. Danger from their recommendations? Do we really think the men in the brown uniforms will come next? they scoff. And as for opposing the NEP, well that just means, they say, that you don't support Canada!
>
> Appeals to our concern about the "little man" and the "national interest" are at the very root of the interventionists' conscious or unconscious false logic. By asserting that the National Energy Program is synonymous with both concepts, while the interests of foreign-owned oil companies are diametrically opposed to them, they seek to win their case by default. Unfortunately, in many cases they are successful. When they are forced to make their case explicitly, however, the cracks begin to appear.
>
> Higher prices and tax incentives have been given in pursuit of the national objective of finding additional petroleum supplies. Their inevitable concomitant has been that the companies who have produced the largest supplies of oil and gas, do the bulk of exploration,

and find the new reserves, get richer. One cannot stimulate the nation's resource wealth in a free-market economy such as Canada's without enriching the private sector in the process. That is the very basis of economic growth but, due to the dominant position of foreign companies in the industry, it is a fact that militant economic nationalists abhor. They struggle, therefore, to prove that the wealth of corporations and the wealth of society are not synonymous but contradictory. They yearn for the benefits of free enterprise without the corporate intermediaries that provide them. They display an inability to see the great Canadian economic wood for the foreign trees within it. More than that, they seem to seek—and indeed, to believe that it is possible to find—a system whereby we can have woods *without* trees.

Such a view means that features of capitalism previously considered praiseworthy, such as reinvestment, have to be condemned because they are the means whereby foreign-owned or controlled oil companies have grown. This argument is perverse because it takes the view that only the original cross-border flow of investment from a foreign country should be counted as investment at all. Reinvestment of domestically generated profits, instead of being viewed as the admirable engine of job creation and economic growth, has, instead, to be treated as a sneaky and reprehensible method of gaining a stranglehold on the economy. Meanwhile, the fact that governments have allowed companies to write off reinvestment against corporate taxes on their own profits is treated as tantamount to Canadian taxpayers financing the buy-out of their country.[38]

Foster is of course not alone either in espousing a pro-market view, or in force-feeding policy into the simplistic equality-efficiency dichotomy and in laying blame on bureaucrats. It is a polemical view which easily comes to those who choose to study public policy in an a-historical way and without reference to the broader realities of Canadian political life. As we show below and as the foregoing events in this chapter and in Chapter 15 indicate, the NEP was much more a marriage of interests between ministers and bureaucrats spawned by intense partisan conflict, rather than the bureaucratic imposition implied by Foster's polemics.

The 1980s and the NEP: Security of Supply, Canadianization and Fairness

Energy policy in the 1980s obviously revolves around the aggressive interventionist National Energy Policy announced in October 1980. The goals of the NEP are:

- to establish the basis for Canadians to seize control of the energy future through security of supply and ultimate independence from the world oil market.
- to offer to Canadians, all Canadians, the real opportunity to participate in the energy industry in general and the petroleum industry in particular, and to share in the benefits of industry expansion.
- to establish a petroleum pricing and revenue-sharing regime that recognizes the requirement of fairness to all Canadians no matter where they live.[39]

As we pointed out at the beginning of the chapter, these goals expressed a concern for the ideas of stability, national identity and equity, including regional equity.

The NEP-related Budget measures included a radical new fiscal regime in which the basic incentives to the oil and gas industry would be shifted from tax-based incentives to expenditure grants. This would allow Ottawa to target its support to Canadian-controlled firms and to shift exploration and development activity to the federally controlled Canada Lands in the north and offshore. The NEP Budget also contained several tax measures including:

- an 8 percent surtax on net corporate revenue from oil and gas production.
- a natural gas and gas liquids tax (whether exported to the U.S. or not).
- the petroleum compensation charge to be levied on all refiners, designed to produce a blended price of oil in Canada that reflects both the cost of domestic oil as well as the higher cost of foreign imports, but a price which is still no higher than 85 percent of the price of imported oil.
- the elimination of depletion allowances for oil and gas exploration, except with respect to tar sands projects and frontier exploration.
- the extension of the oil export charge to marine and aviation fuel.[40]

In light of the heated short-term partisan politics of the 1979 and 1980 elections and the defeat of the Tory Budget, the Liberal NEP Budget emphases and strategies clearly did not go unnoticed. General personal income tax increases would have met strenuous opposition in Ontario and Quebec, given the low rate of growth in real incomes there. The booming energy sector was the obvious alternative source of additional revenues. The energy-related tax increases promised to capture for the federal government a significant part of the increase in natural resource rents generated by the oil and gas price increases the government was prepared to allow. At the same time, the blended price increase would reduce the oil import compensation payments required to keep the price to consumers of imported oil at lower than world price levels. The rise in the blended price would be expected to eliminate petroleum compensation payments and hence help give the appearance of reducing the deficit.

This program of direct taxes levied on corporate incomes, indirect taxes levied at the well-head, and an Ownership Charge levied on consumers, but earmarked for the Canadianization program, was a marked contrast to the Tory energy tax package.

The NEP was therefore a comprehensive but highly debatable response to the several separate strands of energy policy that had evolved in the 1970s and before. Table 16.1 lists the major component features of the NEP and shows how it had a "little bit for everyone," clearly a necessity if one was to garner broadly based political support. In regional terms, while the West received its Western Development Fund (discussed in Chapter 11), the Maritime provinces were shown a Special Atlantic Canada program. This was not just political marketing. Atlantic Canada's energy sources and problems *are* different and needed to be treated differently. Conservation and renewables is the longest list in Table 16.1 but, save for the CHIP program, is the least well-funded. The great bulk of the then proposed funds were to go to industry incentives and the off-oil conversion activities. These included an extension of the pipeline beyond Montreal to the rest of Quebec and the Maritime provinces, a critical commitment both for national integration and efficiency.

One must also place the NEP in the context of the broader policy agenda, which we have already examined in previous chapters in detail and thus will not repeat here. This broader agenda included the Liberals' view of asserting federal visibility to counter the Clark government's decentralized "community of communities" view of federalism, the Western Canadian strategy devised by the Trudeau PMO, and the resources, mega-project and industrial benefits-based economic development strategy examined in the previous chapter. In short, the NEP was more than just energy policy. Like any broad policy field it both encompassed and could not avoid dealing with the underlying ideas of political life.

TABLE 16.1
ENERGY EXPENDITURES FOR 1980-1983 AS PROPOSED IN THE NEP
($ millions)

Industry Incentives	2,550	• Municipal Energy Management Program	
• Exploration		• New Housing Guidelines	
• Development		• Remote Communities Initiative	
• Nonconventional Oil		• Agricultural Sector Initiatives	
• Heavy Crude Oil Upgrading		• Super-Efficient Housing Demonstration	
Gasbank	440	• Small Projects Fund	
Oil Substitution	1,620	• Super-Retrofit (Newfoundland, P.E.I., Yukon, N.W.T.)	
• Conversion Grants			
• Conversion of Federal Buildings			
• Distribution Systems Incentives		*Special Atlantic Canada*	
• Transmission System Support		*Program*	460
• Propane Vehicle Initiative		• Utility Off-Oil Fund	
• Propane Demonstration (Government fleets)		• Lower Churchill Development Corporation	
		• Coal Utilization Package	
Conservation and Renewables	1,150	• Coal R&D	
• Expanded CHIP		• P.E.I. Conservation and Renewable Energy Agreement Extension	
• Industrial Audits			
• Seminars and Workshops			
• Mileage Standards		• Industrial Conservation	
• Retrofit Federal Buildings		Upgraders	310
• Arctic Community Demonstration		Research and Development	260
• Arctic Housing Demonstration		Petro-Canada International	200
• Solar Demonstration (Residential Hot Water)		Future Initiatives	1,200
• FIRA Extension			

Source: *National Energy Program*, p. 90.

The NEP must also be seen in relation to several other structural aspects of public policy formulation. The NEP was preceded by a decade of consultation and discussion mixed with ploy and counterploy and deep-seated partisan distrust. The NEP itself, however, was a rare example of a policy based on an "act first, talk later" strategy carried out in the face of the Ottawa-Alberta revenue deadlock.[41] It was an outburst of policy aggressiveness and risk taking. Key features of the NEP were forged while the Liberals were in opposition and by a small Liberal party committee in the context of the 1980 election and announced in Prime Minister Trudeau's mid-election campaign speech in Halifax.[42] When they returned to power, the key Liberal ministers, Marc Lalonde and Prime Minister Trudeau, found senior EMR bureaucrats who were also anxious for radical change because of their frustration, even under the auspices of a Conservative government, at being unable to get an energy agreement with the Alberta Tories. Thus, as we noted above, the NEP was far from being a bureaucratically imposed policy by wild-eyed socialist bureaucrats "with Ph.D.'s," as Foster has implied in his policy polemic.[43] It reflected a much more even-handed marriage of the ideas of key ministers and the bureaucracy, but only forged after a decade of debate and intensely partisan and regional politics.

Within the Ottawa executive it is also essential to appreciate that the NEP, linked as it was to a Budget, was forged in great secrecy. A bare handful of ministers and senior bureaucrats were involved, a fact about which many of the "left out" ministers bitterly complained, especially as the economy unravelled in 1981 and 1982. The NEP shows that decisive action can be taken, but that it requires a concentration of power and an "act first, talk later" approach. The NEP, however, does not reflect a policy devised through a typical policy process. It was achieved by breaking all or most of the policy formulation rules. It was not merely a case of the proverbial "end-run" but rather a case where the team owners took the ball and moved to another stadium. No government could survive the stress if the NEP process was the typical policy process.

The NEP was also premised on assumptions about how others would act, as well as on other uncertain propositions. The reaction of the Americans was expected to be unfavourable, but the intensity of it was not foreseen, partly because it was not expected to be linked to parallel developments such as the FIRA and trade issues examined in the previous chapters.[44] Particular features of the NEP were especially susceptible to foreign criticism, especially by a decidedly pro-business Reagan government and by its domestic equivalent in the Conservative party in Canada. Chief among these was the 25 percent "back in" Crown interest (especially its initial retroactive application) which Ottawa would take in developments on the Canada Lands. This triggered a defence by Conservatives of the idea of property rights and unfair expropriation.

Another area of uncertainty was the question of future energy prices. As we saw in Chapter 13, forecasting is a risky art. The NEP was constructed on a hypothesis and expectation that world prices *over the full decade of the 1980s* would rise significantly and steadily. EMR forecasters held this view, but so in most respect did the Alberta government and energy industry forecasters. The fall in prices in the midst of an oil glut and a deep recession in 1981 and 1982 was not foreseen.[45]

Finally, as we saw in the analysis of the energy envelope in Chapter 11, there was great uncertainty as to how quickly individual Canadians would take up or respond to the new incentives to conserve and to shift off oil. This was simply a larger manifestation of the problem discussed in the previous section regarding the CHIP program. In the case of the total NEP, however, the cost implications were enormous. There was little that could be done to estimate the full costs, let alone effects, of the NEP when so many features of it depended upon private behaviour, including behaviour by an industry that would oppose the program. In this sense the NEP was an act of faith that some of these problems could be sorted out later.

The NEP, in contrast to earlier energy policy in the 1970s and certainly in comparison with industrial policy, shows the analytical importance of a point stressed in Chapters 6 and 8. In Chapter 6 we pointed out, in reference to Allison's first model, the importance of asking whether in any policy field at any period of time the government is acting as a single, cohesive purposeful actor. In Chapter 8 we stressed the need to ask whether the prime minister was prepared to invest his power in a given issue. In other words, is the Cabinet or its key leaders solidly coalescing around a position or is the consensus a flabby one? In the case of the NEP, the cohesiveness was hard and aggressive, albeit virtually an imposed one by Trudeau, Lalonde and, to a lesser extent, MacEachen. In contrast, the industrial policy initiatives of the 1970s and the early 1980s had no such commitment. Neither did energy policy in the early and mid-1970s.

Space does not allow us to go beyond the broad contours of the NEP. Table 16.2 lists some important post-NEP events, including the passage of the major energy bills amidst Parliamentary furor, the Petro-Canada acquisitions of Petrofina Canada and B.P. Canada, and other acquisitions by Dome Petroleum and the Canada Development Corporation, the release of the Bertrand Report which alleged that the oil companies had engaged in anti-competitive restrictive trade practices, the Ottawa-

TABLE 16.2
MAJOR ENERGY POLICIES AND EVENTS

1950s

- Formation of Alberta Gas Trunk Line Co. (AGTL) by Alberta Government (1954)
- Trans-Canada Pipeline Debate (1956)
- Borden Royal Commission on Energy established (1957)
- National Energy Board (NEB) established

1960s

- The National Oil Policy (NOP) is announced by the Diefenbaker government (1961)
- Creation of the Department of Energy, Mines and Resources (1966)
- Federal government acquires a 45 percent equity share and controlling interest in Panarctic Oils Ltd. (1966)
- Task Force on Northern Oil Development is formed

1970s

- Ottawa restricts exports of crude oil and imposes export tax (1973)
- Ottawa releases *Energy Policy for Canada—Phase I* (1973)
- Yom Kippur War and OPEC oil embargo and quadrupling of oil prices (1973)
- Prime Minister Trudeau announces 11-point Energy Policy including the establishment of Petro-Canada (December 1973)
- Alberta and Saskatchewan introduce new increased royalty schemes which reduce federal revenue shares (1973-74)
- Federal Budget disallows the deductability of provincial royalties in corporate income tax calculations (1974)
- Oil Import Compensation Program (OICP) for subsidizing eastern refiners (1974)
- Berger Commission is established to inquire into Mackenzie Delta pipeline (1974)
- Syncrude Project saved by Federal-Alberta-Ontario equity package (1975)
- Petro-Canada established (1975)
- Ottawa publishes energy policy document, *An Energy Strategy for Canada* (1976)
- CHIP program of home insulation grants begun (1977)
- Renewable Energy Branch established in EMR
- Petroleum Corporations Monitoring Act is passed (1978)
- The Clark Conservative government's Budget, including the .18¢ transportation tax, and the refundable energy tax credit, is defeated
- Iranian Revolution results in doubling of world price of oil

1980s

- Trudeau government returned to power on policy of defence of Petro-Canada, a promise to keep energy taxes below the Tory increase, and a promise to adopt a blended made-in-Canada price below the world price (1980)
- Announcement of the National Energy Program (NEP) (1980)
- Petro-Canada acquires Petrofina Canada Inc. (1981)
- Dome acquisition of Hudson Bay Oil and Gas and Canada Development Corporation's acquisition of Aquitaine (1981)
- Bertrand Report on Competition in the Petroleum Industry released (1981)
- Ottawa-Alberta energy agreement signed. Agreements with Saskatchewan and B.C. (1981) and Nova Scotia (1982) are reached
- NEB concludes there are insufficient gas reserves for export (1981)
- NEP Energy Legislation passed but only after intense Parliamentary conflict including Clark Tories' tactic of closing down the Commons through a refusal to answer the division bells (1982)
- Alberta offers fiscal relief to the oil and gas industry totalling over $5 billion
- NEP Update published. Includes federal tax concessions (1982)
- Alsands and Cold Lake Mega-Projects cancelled or postponed (1982)
- Petro-Canada acquires refining and marketing assets of B.P. Canada (1982)
- Announcement of "bail out" package to prevent receivership of Dome Petroleum
- Break-up of effective OPEC Cartel and drop in world oil prices (1983)

---

provincial energy agreements, the fiscal relief provided by Alberta, the NEP Update of 1982 in which Ottawa sweetened the fiscal incentives to the oil industry in response to slumping prices, and the problems encountered by the Alsands and Cold Lake projects, and by Dome Petroleum.

Concluding Observations

The implementation and effects of the NEP is another story that cannot be adequately examined here. Our purpose in this chapter has been a limited but important one, namely, to survey the broad evolution of energy policy over several decades by focusing on the underlying ideas inherent in it and by showing their links to structure and process and to other policy fields—economic, social and foreign. There are many other detailed aspects of energy policy, not only in oil and gas, but in other fuels such as coal, nuclear and electricity which we have not dealt with here. By focusing on the ideas one invariably must also deal with major institutional features, including partisan, federal-provincial, government-business and interest-group elements, as well as problems of information, knowledge and uncertainty.

Energy policy has been influenced by the changing position of primary resource fuels, not only in a national context but regionally as well. It has acquired an ever-broadening range of policy concerns, especially since OPEC, and is now central to industrial restructuring procurement and transportation policy, resource rents, fiscal policy and equalization, trade and security matters, native peoples' rights and environmental safety. The increased comprehensiveness has led to, and been influenced by, expanded energy policy structures, including a growing number of public enterprises, mixed enterprises, as well as quasi-central agency envelope machinery and regulatory boards. The NEP also shows in very explicit ways the degree to which instrument choice is linked to structural control, to essential ideas of power purpose and control and to ideas about intervention and the proper and the de facto role of bureaucrats and politicians.

NOTES

1. David Brooks, *Zero Energy Growth for Canada* (Toronto: McClelland and Stewart, 1981), p. 39.
2. On the nuclear, coal and hydroelectric aspects of energy policy, see G. Bruce Doern, *Government Intervention in the Nuclear Industry* (Montreal: Institute for Research on Public Policy, 1980); G. Bruce Doern and R.W. Morrison, eds., *Canadian Nuclear Policies* (Montreal: Institute for Research on Public Policy, 1980); J. Gander and F. Belaire, *Energy Futures for Canadians* (Ottawa: Minister of Supply and Services, 1978), Chapters 2 and 5; John McDougall, *Fuels and the National Policy* (Toronto: Butterworths, 1982), Chapters 2 and 3; Neil A. Swainson, *Conflict Over*

the Columbia (Montreal: McGill-Queen's University Press, 1979); and Allan Tupper, "Public Enterprise as Social Welfare: The Case of the Cape Breton Development Corporation," *Canadian Public Policy,* Vol. IV, No. 4 (Autumn, 1978), pp. 530-546.

3. Canada, *National Energy Program* (Ottawa: Minister of Supply and Services, 1980), p. 2. See also Canada, NEP *Update* (Ottawa: Minister of Supply and Services, 1982).

4. See John N. McDougall, *op. cit.,* Chapter 1; and James E. Gander and Fred W. Belaire, *op. cit.*

5. See Canada, *National Energy Program, op. cit.,* pp. 16-21; and David Crane, *Controlling Interest* (Toronto: McClelland and Stewart, 1982), Chapters 2 and 8.

6. See G. Bruce Doern and Glen Toner, *The NEP and the Politics of Energy* (Toronto: Methuen, 1984), Chapter 5.

7. See Barbara Hodgins, *Where the Economy and the Constitution Meet in Canada* (Montreal: C.D. Howe Institute, 1981), pp. 14-30; Marsha A. Chandler and William M. Chandler, *Public Policy and Provincial Politics* (Toronto: McGraw-Hill Ryerson, 1979), Chapter 7; L. Copithorne, "Natural Resources and Regional Disparities: A Skeptical View," *Canadian Public Policy,* Vol. V. No. 2 (Spring 1979), pp. 181-194; and L. Copithorne, "A Search for Common Ground: Canada's Regional and National Energy Policy Conflicts Defined," Discussion Paper, Economic Council of Canada (May 1982).

8. See Economic Council of Canada, *Financing Confederation* (Ottawa: Minister of Supply and Services, 1982), Chapter 4.

9. See Chapter 15. See also G. Bruce Doern, "Mega Projects and the Policy Process" (Ottawa: School of Public Administration, Carleton University, 1982).

10. McDougall, *op. cit.,* Chapters 3 and 4.

11. See John Richards and Larry Pratt, *Prairie Capitalism* (Toronto: McClelland and Stewart, 1979), Chapter 3. See also Larry Pratt, *The Tar Sands: Syncrude and the Politics of Oil* (Edmonton: Hurtig, 1976), Chapters 9, 10, 11 and 12.

12. Richards and Pratt, *op. cit.,* p. 66.

13. *Ibid.,* p. 83.

14. See William Kilbourn, *Pipeline* (Toronto: Clarke Irwin, 1970); and Robert Bothwell and William Kilbourn, *C.D. Howe: A Bibliography* (Toronto: McClelland and Stewart, 1979), Chapters 17 and 18.

15. For analyses of the NEB, see Alistair R. Lucas and Trevor Bell, *The National Energy Board: Policy Procedure and Practice* (Ottawa: Minister of Supply and Services, 1977); and McDougall, *op. cit.,* Chapter 5 and 6.

16. See Crane, *op. cit.,* Chapters 2 and 8.

17. See McDougall, *op. cit.,* Chapter 6; and Robert Bertrand, *Canada's Oil Monopoly* (Toronto: James Lorimer Publishers, 1981), pp. 155-199.

18. McDougall, op. cit., Chapter 7; and Glen Toner, "Oil, Gas and Integration," in Jon Pammett and Brian Tomlin, eds., The Integration Question: Political Economy and Public Policy in Canada and North America (Manuscript, 1983).

19. See David Brooks, op. cit., Chapters 5 and 6.

20. Honourable Joe Greene, Speech to Petroleum Society of the Canadian Institute of Mining and Metallurgy, Banff, Alberta, June 1, 1971.

21. Glen Toner and Francois Bregha, "The Political Economy of Energy" in Michael S. Whittington and Glen WIlliams, eds., Canadian Politics in the 1980s (Toronto: Methuen, 1981), pp. 12-13. On the broader international post-OPEC dimensions, see Peter Odell, Oil and World Power, 6th Edition (London: Penguin, 1981), pp. 71-116 and 194-278.

22. See Peter Foster, The Blue Eyed Sheiks: The Canadian Oil Establishment (Toronto: Collins, 1979), Chapter 5.

23. See Crane, op. cit., Chapter 6 and Foster, op. cit., Chapter 12 and Leonard Waverman, "The Distribution of Resource Rents: For Whom the Firm Tolls," in P.N. Nemetz, ed., Energy Crisis: Policy Response (Montreal: Institute for Research on Public Policy, 1981), Chapter 13.

24. Larry Pratt, "Petro-Canada: Tool for Energy Security or Instrument of Economic Development?" in G. Bruce Doern, ed., How Ottawa Spends Your Tax Dollars 1982 (Toronto: James Lorimer Publishers, 1982), pp. 87-114.

25. Jeffrey Simpson, Discipline of Power (Toronto: Personal Library, 1980), Chapters 12 and 13.

26. See Irwin Gillespie and Allan Maslove, "The 1980-81 Estimates: Trends, Issues, Choice" in G. Bruce Doern, ed., Spending Tax Dollars (Ottawa: School of Public Administration, 1980), Chapter 1.

27. Economic Council of Canada, Financing Confederation, op. cit., Chapters 2, 3, 4 and 5.

28. See, for example, Judith Maxwell, A Time for Realism, C.D. Howe Institute, Policy Review and Outlook, (Montreal: C.D. Howe Research Institute, 1978), Chapters 2, 3 and 6.

29. See Richards and Pratt, op. cit., Chapters 10 and 11.

30. Robert Sheppard and Michael Valpy, The National Deal (Toronto: Fleet Books, 1982); and Hodgins, op. cit., pp. 14-30.

31. See Francois Bregha, Bob Blair's Pipeline, Second Edition (Toronto: James Lorimer Publishers, 1981). See also Edgar Dosman, The National Interest (Toronto: McClelland and Stewart, 1975) and Gurston Dacks, A Choice of Futures: Politics in the Canadian North (Toronto: Methuen, 1981).

32. Canada, Report of the Mackenzie Valley Pipeline Inquiry (Ottawa: Minister of Supply and Services, 1977).

33. See Brooks, op. cit., Chapters 8 to 12; and C.A. Hooker and R. MacDonald, et al., Energy and the Quality of Life: Understanding Energy Policy (Toronto: University of Toronto Press, 1980), pp. 1-96.

34. See Doern and Toner, *op. cit.,* Chapter 11.

35. See G. Bruce Doern, ed., *How Ottawa Spends Your Tax Dollars 1981* (Toronto: James Lorimer Publishers, 1981), Chapter 1; and Simpson, *op. cit.,* Chapter 8.

36. *The Budget,* October 28, 1980 (Ottawa: Minister of Supply and Services, 1980), p. 11. For critical assessment, see B.L. Scarf, J.F. Helliwell and R.N. McRae, "Energy Policy and the Budget," *Canadian Public Policy,* Vol. VII, No. 4 (Winter 1981), pp. 1-27; Wendy Dobson, *Canada's Energy Policy Debate* (Montreal: C.D. Howe Research Institute, 1981); and G.C. Watkins and M.A. Walker, eds., *Reaction: The National Energy Program* (Vancouver: The Fraser Institute, 1981).

37. See Peter Foster, *The Sorcerer's Apprentices: Canada's Super Bureaucrats and the Energy Mess* (Toronto: Collins, 1982).

38. *Ibid.,* pp. 372-373.

39. Canada, *National Energy Program, op. cit.,* p. 2.

40. List adapted from *The Budget,* October 28, 1980, Table 3.

41. See Doern and Toner, *op. cit.,* Chapter 3. See also Larry Pratt, "Energy: Roots of National Policy," *Studies in Political Economy,* No. 7 (Winter 1982), pp. 27-59.

42. Notes for Remarks by the Right Honourable P.E. Trudeau, Halifax Board of Trade, Halifax, Nova Scotia (January 25, 1980).

43. Peter Foster, *The Sorcerer's Apprentices: Canada's Super-Bureaucrats and the Energy Mess, op. cit.,* Chapter 6.

44. Stephen Clarkson, *Canada and the Reagan Challenge* (Ottawa: Canadian Institute for Economic Policy, 1982), Chapters 1, 2, 4 and 6.

45. R.G. Wirick, "The World Petroleum Market and Canadian Policy," *Canadian Public Policy,* Vol. VIII, No. 4 (Autumn 1982), pp. 534-553.

CHAPTER 17

LABOUR MARKET POLICIES

Labour market policy generally has been defined as a set of ideas and actions designed to enable the supply of labour to adjust more rapidly to changing demands, including geographical, industrial and occupational demands. Somewhat like industrial policy, labour market policy is typically viewed as a supplement to the macroeconomic policy levers. It deals with the medium-term structural adjustment of the economy rather than with short-term demand management. Figure 17.1 presents a visual portrait of the medium-term supply and demand side activities in labour market policy and the kinds of decisions employers and workers make. The linchpin is found in labour market intelligence, a system of information, services and incentives designed to bring demand and supply together.

As the three previous chapters have shown, however, all policy fields have imperialistic tendencies. Depending upon how one looks at the policy kaleidescope, the boundaries of the policy fields expand and extend to the interconnected parts of society, economy and government. So it is with labour market policies. The very name "labour market" evokes different perceptions.[1] On the one hand, as the classic definition above suggests, it rings with the ethos of efficiency. Labour, according to this view, is a factor of production, along with other factors such as capital, land and knowledge. Labour should be mobile so as to be used in an "optimal" way. This perception immediately evokes its polar opposite. Labour market policy should deal with the human dimensions of the industrial system and hence should be governed by other ideas as well. Labour market policy should involve the entire panoply of social policy: from daycare to pensions and from occupational health and safety to affirmative action policies for disadvantaged groups, including the handicapped. In the 1970s and 1980s the role of women in the family and in the economy and politics both affected labour market policy and, in turn, were influenced by such policies. Women's vastly increased participation in the labour market led to divergent views about the extent to which this was a social frill to be tolerated by a male-dominated

FIGURE 17.1

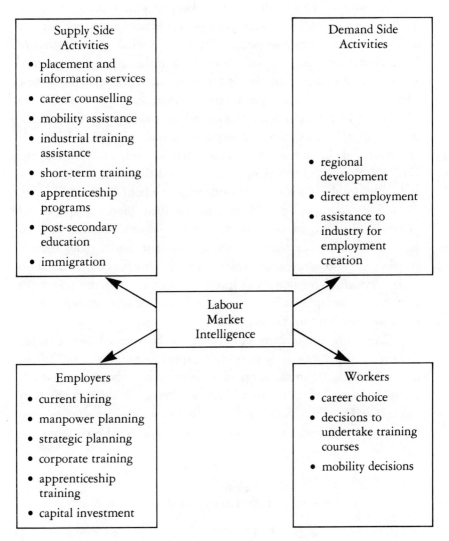

Source: Employment and Immigration Canada, *Labour Market Development in the 1980s*, p. 83.

economy or an economic necessity both for women themselves and for the future productivity of the economy. In all the above dimensions labour market policy has been influenced by the same arguments about whether such policies are "primary" or "residual," as we outlined in our broader treatment of social and economic policy in Chapter 14.

We have already noted in Chapters 1 and 2 how both these economic and social views of labour market policy exist and are reflected in Canada's policies. Canada has policies to enhance labour mobility and to make labour immobile because both are desirable, are rooted in fundamental ideas and are supported by significant political constituencies. To appreciate why this is the case, one ultimately has to view labour market policies in a broader context than that suggested in Figure 17.1 Figure 17.2 therefore portrays the related public policy fields which in fact comprise this sphere of policy activity and which affect the supply of labour and the demand for labour, quantitatively and qualitatively. Labour can refer to all working Canadians and those who wish to work and therefore deals with all the categories of labour: male and female, youth and older persons, skilled and unskilled, highly qualified and professional versus manual and apprenticed labour, handicapped and able-bodied, and Canadian and immigrant. The policy fields include employment and job creation, training and mobility programs, education policy, industrial relations and incomes policies (including minimum wage laws), unemployment insurance and other income security policies, regional policy and immigration policy.

One major preliminary point needs to be stressed. While in the context of the 1980s it is possible to speak conceptually of "labour market" policies with the array of elements noted above, this has not always been the case in the past. There were certainly theories of labour markets and how they functioned, but the policy elements often evolved separately, even when it was known that they affected each other.

FIGURE 17.2
THE COMPONENTS OF LABOUR MARKET POLICY

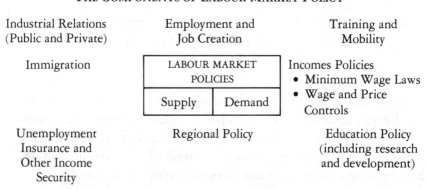

The importance of overriding ideas in the evolution of labour market policies is best reflected in the Dupre, Cameron, et al. analysis of training programs during the first post-war decade.

The view of the labour market has been at two extremes a view of pure competition as opposed to one of a market shaped only by institutional forces. The classical and neoclassical theorists produced models of competitive market behaviour relying on the role of wages as the allocator of labour. In these models, which assumed standardized labour and complete knowledge, both employers and employees responded to wage changes in an uncomplicated way, that is, workers moved to positions of higher wages, vacating positions providing lower wages, while employers continued to hire workers "to the point where the decreasing value of hiring more labour matches the cost of hiring extra labour." In these models, unemployment was not considered, since analysis was concerned with the equilibrium price that would "clear the market." Since workers and employers were assumed to respond immediately to price changes in a fully competitive setting, the market was labelled "perfect."

The so-called Keynesian revolution did not challenge the classical and neoclassical view of the labour market. Focusing as it did on the concept of aggregate demand, Keynesian economics assumed that, given the application of the macroeconomic tools of monetary and fiscal policy to produce the desired level of aggregate demand, the labour market would continue to do its job. But this comfortable assumption was challenged as postwar experience indicated *with increasing clarity that the labour market was anything* but perfect. It was found that increasing aggregate demand beyond a certain level in an effort to solve unemployment often resulted in unacceptable price increases. Also, the Keynesian macroeconomic tools were too blunt an instrument *to affect all regions of the economy in the same way*. The fact was that the "perfect" labour market could neither solve problems of matching skills and jobs nor overcome obstacles of geographic and other types of immobility. Thus, it came to be recognized that many imperfections existed in the labour market, and while workers might behave in the manner indicated by the classical and neoclassical school—move to jobs with greater "net advantages"—the "net advantages" were as yet unexplored by economists, but were highly significant. The employers and employees had ties to particular markets for goods and services that constrained their behaviour. The imperfections in the supply of labour, barring a "perfect allocation," included its occupational heterogeneity, its lack of knowledge, and the ties that employees might have with a particular firm or community. The outcome was to make labour supply more inelastic since there was limits to the response of the worker to changes in the market. Complicating the matter further in Canada was the question of labour market boundaries. Few workers are able or willing to move anywhere in Canada for employment. Few employers extend their search for employees in most occupations across the breadth of the economy.[2]

As was the case with both industrial and energy policies, labour market policy was scarcely even a recognizable phrase or concept in the policy lexicon in the pre- and immediate post-World War II period. In the 1940s and 1950s, if labour market policies could be said to exist, then they included primarily industrial or labour-management relations policy and unemployment insurance policy and a mixture of modest vocational training activity and immigration policy. In the 1960s the economic notions of labour market policy flowered as part of the new supply economics. Accordingly, it embraced training, education and mobility incentives under the policy name of manpower policy. In the 1970s and 1980s policy imperialism reached new levels as regional policy, employment and job creation, social security, policies for women, and incomes policies were increasingly viewed to be part of the field.

These developments were accompanied and influenced by parallel changes in public policy structures. The Department of Labour and the Unemployment Insurance Commission were joined by the Department of Manpower and Immigration, later renamed the Department and Commission on Employment and Immigration, as well as by large education bureaucracies at the provincial level and in the universities and community colleges, and incomes policy tribunals and consultative exercises.

Labour market policies were influenced by, and in turn affected, the macroeconomic state of the economy, particularly the evolving changes in and debate about unemployment and inflation. While we have examined these macro dimensions in Chapter 14, as well as in Chapters 10 and 11, we need to see the trends somewhat more specifically. Figure 17.3 shows the consumer price index and unemployment rates from 1953 to 1980.[3] It shows that the unemployment rate has drifted upward over time and indicates the persistently higher rates of inflation in the 1980s which occurred despite the higher unemployment rates.

At a somewhat more technical and analytical level, however, there were different views, especially among economists, about the nature of unemployment.[4] Of particular concern was how how much unemploy-

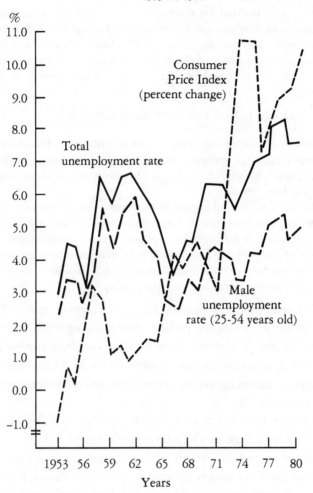

FIGURE 17.3
CONSUMER PRICE INDEX AND UNEMPLOYMENT RATES,
1953 TO 1980

Source: Employment and Immigration Canada, *Labour Market Development in the 1980s* (July 1981), p. 8.

ment stemmed from a deficiency of aggregate demand and how much was noncyclical. Noncyclical factors consisted of:

- frictional unemployment, a normal characteristic of a dynamic labour market in which job turnover is continually occurring as people search for better jobs;

- seasonal unemployment, attributable to the seasonal nature of economic activity in some industries such as construction, fishing and agriculture; and
- unemployment resulting from structural factors such as technological change or changes in the industrial structure which cause mismatches between requirements of available jobs and the skills, experience, or location of unemployed workers, as well as barriers in hiring practices and procedures which deny access to some groups.[5]

As the 1981 Dodge federal task force study concluded:

> With the exception of the seasonal component, noncyclical unemployment has never been defined in a way which permits direct measurement with available data.... The major debate in the early 1960s was between:
> - those economists who argued that the high unemployment of the time was a consequence of longer-run structural factors and was not amenable to influence by aggregate demand policies; and
> - those who argued that a significant portion of unemployment was of a demand-deficient or cyclical nature which could be eliminated by expansionary fiscal and monetary policy.[6]

Though the details of this debate change throughout the 1960s and 1970s, the broad nature of the politics accompanying it did not change appreciably. By the late 1970s there was growing recognition of the structural causes of unemployment, much as we saw in Chapters 15 and 16 on industrial and energy policy, respectively, but no evident consensus on what to do about it.

Inevitably, there are also constitutional and jurisdictional issues to respect and to overcome in the labour market field. Education was a jealously guarded area of provincial jurisdiction. To the extent that manpower and skill training could be shown to be economic, the federal government claimed primary jurisdiction. Labour relations, the professions, minimum wage laws and apprenticeship rules were primarily in provincial hands.[7] Immigration was a concurrent power, but Ottawa held most of the controls. Job creation is also a dual realm, as is incomes policy, unless the federal government could justify action, as it did in 1975 on the ground of a national emergency. Unemployment Insurance was a federal responsibility but only after a 1940 constitutional amendment made it so. Many of these de facto powers were also influenced by the fiscal capacity of the governments involved. Even when aided by federal equalization payments, the "have not" provinces almost invariably could not keep up.

The result was to produce inequity and the inevitable demand to be treated fairly.

Changing Demographic and Labour Force Characteristics

As we take a retrospective look at policy, it must be remembered that we again have the immense advantage of hindsight. It allows us to set out certain essential information about the labour force which is necessary to understand the changes that occurred in each decade discussed below. Policy makers in these earlier periods, however, had less certain information and inevitably were setting their known "facts" against a hypothesized but uncertain future. The first data to stress show the changing composition of the labour force and the changed participation rates it reflected among men, women and young people. Table 17.1 displays the composition at five-year intervals since 1955. Figure 17.4 reflects the participation rates and includes federal projections into the 1990s. We refer to these projections later. The trends are fairly clear. For men over 25 it has been fairly high and stable. For youths aged 15 to 24 there was a significant increase from the mid-1960s to the mid-1970s as the post-war and early 1950s baby boom moved through the economy. By the 1980s the youth proportion levels off. The most persistent change has been for women 25 and over. These data are important in seeing the changing content and target groups for job creation programs and other aspects of training and education in the 1960s and 1970s.

TABLE 17.1
COMPOSITION OF LABOUR FORCE FOR SELECTED AGE/SEX GROUPS

	Youth	Adult Women	Adult Men	Total
		(percent)		
1955	22.8	14.1	63.1	100.0
1960	21.9	17.3	60.8	100.0
1965	23.4	19.6	57.0	100.0
1970	25.4	22.4	52.2	100.0
1975	27.2	24.6	48.2	100.0
1980	26.4	27.7	45.9	100.0

Source: Employment and Immigration Canada, *Labour Market Development in the 1980's* (July 1981), p. 10.

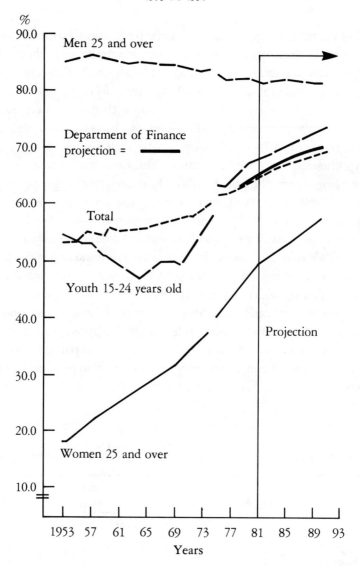

FIGURE 17.4
PARTICIPATION RATES AMONG CERTAIN DEMOGRAPHIC GROUPS,
1953 TO 1990

Note: The historical series break in 1975, the year in which major revisions were made to the labour force survey. The most abrupt break occurs in the case of the less-than-25 group. Prior to the revisions, this group consisted of 14-25 years olds. With the revisions, it was redefined to comprise 15-24 years olds.

Sources: Historical data based on Statistics Canada. *Labour Force Survey*. Projection developed by Labour Market Development Task Force. Department of Finance projection from *Participation Rate and Labour Force growth in Canada*. April 1980.

Another underlying trend is found in the occupational composition of the labour force. Data shows on an overall basis a very high growth in the service sectors, moderate growth in manufacturing and construction and a considerable decline in primary industries due primarily to productivity increases in agriculture. Since the early 1970s, however, service sector growth rates have declined somewhat, manufacturing has maintained stable growth rates, and primary industries have experienced greater growth than before. The service sector has been able to employ women and youth at entry level positions more readily than other sectors, and hence the occupational trends discussed here separately must be linked to the data on the composition regarding men, women and young people.

A further set of data concerns the mobility of labour within Canada. Table 17.2 indicates some of the flows in interprovincial migration since 1961. It shows Alberta and British Columbia with strong net gains and Quebec, Manitoba and Saskatchewan with significant net outflows. Ontario had major gains in the 1960s but losses in the 1970s. The Dodge Report's interpretation of these and other migration data drew particular attention to the situation in Atlantic Canada in the 1970s, a point to which we return later in the chapter.

TABLE 17.2
INTERPROVINCIAL MIGRATION FLOWS*
(annual average '000)

	In-migration		Out-migration		Net migration	
	1961-71	1971-80	1961-71	1971-80	1961-71	1971-80
Newfoundland	7.7	11.4	11.1	12.5	− 3.5	−1.1
Prince Edward Island	3.7	4.6	4.3	3.9	− 0.6	0.7
Nova Scotia	22.1	24.0	26.5	22.7	− 4.4	1.3
New Brunswick	18.5	20.9	23.0	18.4	− 4.5	2.5
Quebec	41.4	32.2	55.7	56.6	−14.3	−24.4
Ontario	104.2	95.7	80.7	102.7	23.6	− 7.0
Manitoba	27.4	27.0	33.8	34.5	− 6.4	− 7.5
Saskatchewan	22.8	26.6	35.2	29.4	−12.4	− 2.8
Alberta	52.0	81.5	49.0	61.7	3.0	19.8
British Columbia	62.0	73.7	42.7	54.8	19.3	18.9

*For all adults and children.

Source: Employment and Immigration Canada, *Labour Market Development in the 1980's* (July 1981), p. 29.

One might expect that net internal migration flows would be related to movements in provincial unemployment rates, with a pattern of rising provincial unemployment rates associated with an increased tendency toward out-migration and falling unemployment rates associated with a corresponding tendency toward in-migration. As can be seen, net migration did play an adjustment role of this kind with respect to the Western provincial economies, but in three of the four Atlantic provinces internal migration operated in the opposite direction to that which might have been expected.

In fact, the net in-migration to the Atlantic region as a whole which occurred in the 1970s was a reversal of the long-standing tendency for out-migration from the region. Strong employment growth undoubtedly reduced the incentive for people to move out of the region and increased its attractiveness to in-migrants. Further analysis of this question suggests that the 1971 changes in the unemployment insurance legislation may also have been an important contributing factor.[8]

Finally, it is important to stress the territorial and foreign policy aspects of labour market policies. One obvious aspect is found in the evolving markets for Canada's resources, goods and services, which in turn helps determine the structural and technological determinants of employment and unemployment, as well as needed job skills. These were examined in Chapter 15. The second aspect is immigration.[9] As we stressed in Chapters 1 and 10, immigration has played a critical role in Canada's development. It was one of the three pillars of Macdonald's National Policy and has always had great economic, social and cultural importance. Immigration, to meet skill shortages, was particularly pronounced in the 1950s and early 1960s. Even in the late 1960s official policy took an expansionary view of immigration, a view that abated only in the 1970s when unemployment rates rose. Table 17.3 shows the economic and social patterns of the immigrant population. While all the categories—family class, independent, assisted relative and refugees—contain persons who may bring economically needed skills, it is the independent immigrant which most brings the economic skills. This group's percentage has declined significantly since 1965 in part, as Green's analysis stresses, because skilled labour was also in great demand in Western Europe's buoyant economy and Canada was no longer quite as attractive as it once was.[10]

Domestic settlement patterns are also important. Most immigrants settle in Ontario, Alberta, British Columbia and Manitoba. These

TABLE 17.3
IMMIGRATION BY CLASS, 1965-1980

Year	Total	Family class		Assisted relative		Independent		Refugees	
		Number	Percent	Number	Percent	Number	Percent	Number	Percent
1965	146,758	57,073	38.9			89,685	61.1		
1966	194,743	66,562	34.2			128,181	65.8		
1967	222,876	74,427	33.4			148,449	66.6		
1968	183,974	38,307	20.8	35,040	19.1	110,627	60.1		
1969	161,531	33,548	20.8	39,084	24.2	88,899	55.0		
1970	147,713	32,263	21.8	35,151	23.8	80,299	54.4		
1971	121,900	33,450	27.4	29,328	24.1	59,122	48.5		
1972	122,006	33,019	27.1	30,692	25.2	53,115	43.5	5,180	4.2
1973	184,200	41,677	22.6	44,278	24.0	95,886	52.1	2,359	1.3
1974	218,465	54,232	24.8	53,161	24.3	109,406	50.1	1,666	0.8
1975	187,881	64,124	34.1	45,727	24.3	72,464	38.6	5,566	3.0
1976	149,429	60,830	40.7	32,528	21.8	44,320	29.6	11,751	7.9
1977	114,914	51,355	44.7	26,114	22.7	30,145	26.2	7,300	6.4
1978	86,313	45,540	52.8	17,199	19.9	19,319	22.4	4,255	4.9
1979	112,096	46,763	41.7	11,474	10.2	25,980	23.2	27,879	24.9
1980[1]	142,634	50,936	35.7	13,406	9.4	38,172	26.8	40,120	28.1
1965-80	2,497,433	784,106	31.4	413,182	16.5	1,194,069	47.8	106,076	2.2

[1] 1980 data are preliminary.
Source: Employment and Immigration Canada, Labour Market Development in the 1980's (July 1981), p. 180.

TABLE 17.4
MAJOR FEDERAL LABOUR MARKET POLICY EVENTS

Period	Education, Training, Immigration	Industrial Relations and Incomes Policy	Unemployment Insurance, Income Security and Regional	Employment and Direct Job Creation
World War II, Post-War to Mid-1960s	• Vocational Training Coordination Act (1942) • Massey Commission (1951) on the Arts, Letters and Sciences • Federal University Grants of fifty cents per capita for each province (1951-52) • Technical Vocational Training Assistance Act (1960) • Economic Council of Canada's First and Second Annual Reviews (1963, 1964)	• Basic collective bargaining rights won by labour (1944) through wartime Labour Relations Regulations later legislated in the 1948 Industrial Relations and Disputes Investigation Act • War Time Price and Wage Controls	• Unemployment Insurance Act (1940) • White Paper on Employment and Income (1945) • Gill Committee (1962) on the Unemployment Insurance Act • Canada Pension Plan (1965)	• Winter Works Programs (1958)

Mid-1960s to 1980			
• Adult Occupational Training Act (1967) • Bladen Report on Financing Higher Education (1965) • Federal support for higher education through tax points and grants equal to 50 percent of operating cost. Coupled with improvements in equalization formula (1966-67) • White Paper on Immigration (1966) • Department of Manpower and Immigration established (1966) • Green Paper on Immigration (1974) • Department of Employment and Immigration established (1976)	• Public Service Staff Relations Act permits collective bargaining for federal public servants (1967) • Prices and Incomes Commission (1969) • John Turner voluntary restraint exercise with business and labour (1974-75) • Wage and price controls and Anti-Inflation Board (1975-78) • Frequent use of Back to Work Legislation in 1970s	• Mackasey Reforms to Unemployment Insurance Act (1971) • Social Security Review (1973 to 1976) • Establishment of Department of Regional Economic Expansion (1969) • Tightening of Unemployment Insurance Act (1974)	• Company of Young Canadians (1966) • Opportunities for Youth (OFY) 1970 • Local Initiatives Program (LIP) 1971 • Local Employment Assistance Program (LEAP) 1971 • Canada Works • Young Canada Works

(Table 17.4 continued)

| 1980s | • Dodge Report on Labour Market Policies in the 1980s (1981)
 • New Federal Education Financing to obtain better visibility and targeting for economic skills
 • National Training Program announced (1982)
 • Special measures for handicapped workers and affirmative action | • "6 and 5" Wage Control Program and virtual elimination of collective bargaining for public servants | • Task force on Unemployment Insurance Benefits in the 1980s | • Job sharing
 • Jobs directed at "exhaustees" of UIC Benefits |

patterns affect other social issues such as language policy, education, social services and Canada's views of relations with Third World and with particular ethnic and racial groups in and outside of Canada.[11] In the realm of language policy, for example, it was the strong preference of immigrants settling in Quebec to obtain their children's education in English which helped propel the Quebec government under both Robert Bourassa, and later Rene Levesque, to adopt unilingual language legislation under Bill 101. The continued concentration of diverse immigrant groups in Western Canada and in Toronto led to the adoption of policies on multiculturalism in the mid-1970s as a symbolic counterweight to the bilingualism and biculturalism focus of the late Pearson and early Trudeau years.

All of the above demographic and labour force characteristics are part of the dynamics of change, some of which policy makers knew were emerging but whose magnitude and interactions one could not anticipate in forcasts in any precise way. And even if one could, there were significant interests to both force or resist change and there were ideas in conflict.

An examination of all these policy fields in detail is impossible. It is also unnecessary, given our intention to survey the overall field in the period since post-World War II and to highlight the relations between ideas and policies. Accordingly, we review for each decade major groups of policy components in the labour market field, showing how they have evolved. Thus, we look at education, manpower training and immigration together, as well as industrial relations and income policies. We also group unemployment insurance, income security and regional policies. Employment or job creation activity is treated separately. In short, we need to see some of the policy trees, but we are interested primarily in the forest and in broad trends. Table 17.4 provides a compilation of policy events.

The Post-War Era to the Early 1960s: Efficiency and Stability

Compared to later decades, the scope of labour market policy was quite limited. In the field of occupational training, until 1960 there was only a modest succession of federal conditional grant programs in which the federal government provided matching funds to the provinces to supply technical and occupational education. The Vocational Training Coordination Act of 1942 provided a wartime impetus to this activity. The prosperity of the 1950s, however, and the heavy resort to "buying" skills through immigration, rather than "making" them through training, meant that the intervention was a minimum one. This unwillingness to intervene for most of the 1950s was also aided by the sensitive issue of jurisdiction over education. The federal government was extremely cautious about education. Even the recommendation of the Massey Royal Commission on the Arts, that Ottawa support higher education, elicited only a modest per capita grant program paid directly to the universities.[12]

By the early 1960s, however, the impetus for intervention increased. The recession of 1959-60 prompted the Diefenbaker government to pass the Technical and Vocational Training Assistance Act of 1960 (TVTA).[13] Grants to the provinces to train unemployed workers were increased to 75 percent from the previous 50 percent. The new program also included assistance for capital development. To be efficient, training had to be done with the best capital equipment, but the latter investments had not been forthcoming from the provinces under the previous arrangements. The TVTA produced a quantum jump in federal spending, an eight-fold increase between 1960 and 1967 over what had previously occurred between 1913 and 1960.

An impetus for efficiency produced its inevitable inequities. These were most in evidence among provinces. The "have not" provinces, even with the sweetened federal grants, could still not afford a high take-up rate. Quebec also presented problems. In the midst of its "quiet revolution," Quebec did not yet have an education department to give impetus to its use of federal dollars. The province was in the midst of revising its previously church-dominated educational system and, moreover, objected strongly to federal invasions of its cultural domain.[14]

In other labour market domains in this period there were similar instances of only hesitant and uncertain intervention. In the field of industrial relations, it must be recalled that basic collective bargaining rights for Canada's unionized workers were only won in 1944.[15] Prior to this time labour unions had limited rights compared to the rights of property holders and the owners of capital. There was, moreover, little or no collective bargaining in Canada's public service institutions. While wage and price controls had been in place during the war and later, in a more limited way, during the Korean War, collective bargaining was in general allowed to operate in a normal way from the mid-1950s to the late 1960s.

In the realm of unemployment insurance, the first post-war decade and a half was a period of consolidation. The Unemployment Insurance Act of 1940 had been preceded by a constitutional amendment making this field a federal jurisdictional item.[16] The very notion of "insurance" was one of providing some stability for workers to help overcome the worst ravages of unemployment. At the same time, the insurance benefits were constructed so as to not unduly harm the dictates of an efficient and mobile labour market. To aid efficiency, by matching jobs to workers, the Unemployment Insurance Commission also took charge of the employment placement services previously run by the provinces. The National Employment Service was later in 1962 severely criticized by the Gill Committee, whose broader views of labour market policy we examine in the next section.

On the employment and job creation aspects of labour market policies, this period was typified by the experience with Ottawa's Winter Works program established in 1958 and cancelled in 1968.[17] At one level it shows the evolving debate among economists about the ideas inherent in defining unemployment, and at another it shows the exigencies of federal-provincial expenditure relations and equity. The Winter Works program was ostensibly a response to the not inconsiderable Canadian problem of winter seasonal unemployment, especially in the construction industry, where winter construction technologies and protections were still quite primitive. The Labour Department urged that a grant program for municipal-based projects be established. The Finance Department opposed it because it believed that "normal" macro fiscal policies would resolve most of the problem in a sensible Keynesian way. The program was launched in the midst of the 1957 and 1958 elections by the Diefenbaker Tories. The program did help the seasonal problem, but over time it evolved in a program that came to mean different things to different federal, provincial and municipal interests, and its seasonal aspects became distinctly secondary. It was the victim of the Trudeau government's expenditure cuts exercise of 1968.[18] While considerable amounts of money were spent, direct job creation programs of this kind were, relatively speaking, a sidelight in this period. Federal policy relied primarily on other devices, including, as we saw in Chapter 15, tax policies, tariff and foreign investment policies.

Public policy structures in the labour market field during this period were correspondingly quite simple, reflecting and influencing the modest interventions examined above. The focal point was the Department of Labour. The department did not regard itself as a department *for* labour but rather as a department *of* labour management relations. This was its dominant role. Although the first stirrings of labour market policy of a broader kind emerged from the handful of labour economists in the department, they were operating in the shadow of the larger collective bargaining "referee" role that the Department of Labour played. The second structure of importance was the Unemployment Insurance Commission (UIC). A quasi-independent body, it reported through the Minister of Labour but also operated in a separate realm. It focused on the task of administering the unemployment insurance provisions, leaving the National Employment Service, as we stressed above, to a decidedly second-class status. Finally, there was the Department of Citizenship and Immigration, which at that time dealt with immigration issues.

The Mid-1960s to 1980: The Dynamics of Contending Paradigms and Ideas

If the notion of labour market policy in the 1950s and early 1960s was narrow, it was also fairly clear-cut, at least in relation to the contending views which had emerged by the mid-1960s. All of the policy components, education and training, industrial relations, income security, and employment programs came to be challenged by contending and generally broader and less clear-cut paradigms, ideas and approaches, making the need for policy coordination more imperative but at the same time much more difficult.

The underlying dynamics were led by the inexorable aging of the Canadian post-war baby boom population (proportionately the largest among Western states) from childhood to youth and hence the need to educate and train them at the post-secondary level. The demographic reality had to be dealt with in a federal-provincial context and thus involved the complex fiscal system and jurisdictional disputes then in place.[19] A further cause of the changes in policy was the crystalizing of views among economists about the need for the "new economics," referred to briefly in Chapter 14. Reflected in the United States and in the first two reviews of the then new Economic Council of Canada, the new view endorsed the need for a middle-level and medium-term supply side tool to augment the macro Keynesian "demand management" approaches, which invariably operated only in a short-term context. The key phrase was "manpower policy."

There was a receptive community for this paradigm in the mid-1960s in two different contexts. First, it was an area on which labour and management could express agreement, at least in principle if not on all details. The labour and management representatives on the Economic Council found such agreement quite readily, much more so, in fact, than on most other policy subjects dealt with in later years by the council.[20] Of greater importance was the way in which the supply side manpower paradigm allowed Ottawa to alter the entire pattern of federal-provincial financing and the operation of training activity.

Ottawa's new policy enshrined in the Adult Occupational Training Act of 1967 changed the federal-provincial relationship from a conditional grant-based one to a "buy-sell" one. Henceforth, Ottawa would act as a buyer of training, primarily from provincial education institutions, especially the community colleges, and the provinces would be the seller. Ottawa, advised by local committees and other sources of advice, would determine the quantitative and the qualitative dimensions of supply in each province.[21] Gone would be the across-the-board "equal" conditional grant which produced unequal results, and replacing it would be regionally unequal patterns of "buy-sell" spending which would hopefully treat regions "equitably" and bilaterally, that is, "fairly," in recognition of their different needs. Moreover, by defining the training as being for "adults" and as a device to promote better labour market mobility—in short, as manpower policy—Ottawa claimed in good conscience that this was in federal jurisdiction and was not "education." Thus, Ottawa appealed to the idea of efficiency and equity simultaneously.

Twinned with the manpower package were major changes in Ottawa's heretofore modest involvement in education. The Pearson government's dilemmas here were somewhat more complex. In the buoyancy and optimism of the 1960s there were strong demands on the Liberals for greater federal involvement in education. Redistribution was the key idea, albeit clothed in the then often heard phrase "reducing the economic barriers to higher eduction." There was a social need to make universities less elitist and more a reflection of society. Given the voter-aged baby boom segment of the population, this was not only a good idea but could attract votes as well. One good idea, however, immediately clashed with another: the need to preserve education as a provincial responsibility. The answer was found by financing greater federal involvement, primarily by Ottawa ceding tax points to the provinces. These would be supplemented by limited grants so as to contribute 50 percent of the cost of post-secondary education in each province. In addition, a floor provision would be established and there would be broader changes in equalization to ensure equity among provinces.[22] Dupre, et al. sum up the federal government's educational grand design as follows:

> With a single stroke, the federal government had coupled tax sharing with support for post-secondary education. For all practical purposes it had obliterated distinct assistance for operating and capital programs. Of key importance as well, it had neatly sidestepped the institutional trap set by the proliferation of post-secondary systems whether of the university, technical or composite stripe. In Mr. Pearson's words, "the action of the federal government can be essentially neutral in its effect on the institutional structure of post-secondary education within any province.... The federal government's proposals ... eliminate any bias, arising from federal fiscal contributions, in favour of any particular pattern of institutional development in any province."[23]

The immigration aspects of labour market policy did not change appreciably in the late 1960s and early 1970s. The immigration link was symbolized by the establishment in 1966 of the Department of Manpower and Immigration. A 1966 White Paper on Immigration took an expansionist view, emphasizing the continuing need for skilled immigrants and giving only slight recognition to the broader social and humanitarian aspects of immigration, then being urged by Third World countries and, in some respects, by domestic immigrant and multicultural groups.[24]

In industrial relations there were also major changes. Public servants won the right to strike and bargain collectively.[25] As pointed out in Chapters 3 and 9, this eventually affected other ideas and institutions beyond the confines of labour market policy per se. It helped alter public views of the bureaucracy and of public servants, especially in the wake of highly visible strikes by postal workers and air traffic controllers. It likewise affected the labour movement, since public service unions expanded rapidly and gained influence within the Canadian Labour Congress, and made the latter somewhat more radical than it had been.

In addition, industrial relations were affected by two kinds of de facto "incomes" policies. The first kind was overt and was reflected in the work of the Prices and Incomes Commission, which pursued the voluntary route, the 1975 voluntary exercise led by Finance Minister John Turner, and the compulsory Anti-Inflation Board program of 1975 to 1978. The second kind of incomes policy was an ad hoc but equally persistent one, namely, the greatly increased tendency in the 1970s for Ottawa and the provinces to pass "back to work" legislation, in specific strikes, even while arguing that it supported free collective bargaining. Between 1950 and 1970, over a period of twenty years, such legislation was used thirteen times by both levels of government. In the 1971 to 1978 period it was used 34 times.[26] The varieties of incomes policies were invariably accompanied by appeals to national unity and to keep Canada competitive with its trading partners. The underlying inequality of incomes policies, arising from the simple fact that it is easier to control wages than prices, was not acknowledged by Ottawa.[27]

While these were the dominant aspects of industrial relations, there were other elements as well. The issues of occupational health and quality of work life increasingly entered public debate, albeit usually on the fringes. Nonetheless, new ideas were advanced and some modest policy and structural reforms occurred.[28] Even the heretofore relatively sacred issue of minimum wage laws came to be challenged to some degree by the political right and by "public choice" analysts.[29] The issue was a classic one. The modest redistributive effects of such laws were held to be inefficient and even unfair because by definition such laws cost jobs. It was argued that, in particular, they resulted in lost jobs and work experience for young people.

In the realm of income security there was an equally complex array of changes, some devised in the explicit context of labour market policies but many approached in a broader and more traditional social policy context. These items were the Gill Report and subsequent changes in unemployment insurance policy, the Canada Pension Plan, regional policy, and the social security review already examined in Chapter 14.

The Gill Report of 1962[30] is best seen as merely one analytical catalyst for a series of later events and debates about unemployment insurance in which the "economic" efficiency ideas clashed with the "social" ideas of stability, redistribution and equity (later including the issues of the rights of women). Gill criticized the absence of a broader view, helped legitimize the "manpower policy" paradigm referred to above and urged the need for more integrated placement services.

Most of these issues formed the agenda of the reforms pushed through Cabinet by Bryce Mackasey in 1970.[31] We referred briefly to the dynamics of this reform package in Chapter 9 in our analysis of ministers and bureaucrats, since it is an example of a minister who was embued by social reform instincts, pushing a package of reforms through at a particularly propitious time. As Johnson's analysis shows, Mackasey's reforms built on the Gill agenda and on the increasing vacuum that existed within the Trudeau Cabinet's social policy agenda of the early 1970s in the wake of the withering of Trudeau's "just society" promises.[32] As the more generous benefits created by the Mackasey reforms, aided and abetted by growing unemployment, pushed up UIC costs, a conservative reaction set in. Subsequent ministers were brought in to make the program more efficient and to cut costs, a goal partly achieved by partially rolling back some of the Mackasey provisions.

If unemployment insurance became less of an insurance program and somewhat more of a social security program, it was inevitable that it would have to be viewed in the broader context of social security programs. This is precisely what happened. Ottawa's social security review exercise of the mid-1970s was a response to a federal-provincial social policy impasse, one element of which was the aforementioned unilateral changes in the unemployment insurance package.[33] The attempt to be comprehensive in the review was doomed to failure. There were too many policy balls bouncing in the air at the same time. The labour market part of the social security review became the first casualty. The key actors, Health Minister Marc Lalonde and his deputy, A.W. Johnson, focused on items such as the guaranteed income concept. The most significant and unexpected net result of the review was the eventual adoption of the Child Tax Credit.

While the review failed to link labour market policies with overall social security policy in any legislative or recognizable policy sense, the fact remained that such policies do effect the mobility of labour, albeit in imprecise ways. The Canada Pension Plan and even Medicare, the leading social policy initiatives of the 1960s Pearson era, were presented not just as social redistributive policies and as rights of citizenship, but as part of a social infrastructure that would assist efficiency, stability and the mobility of labour by increasing the portability of such benefits.

But the by now familiar array of labour market ideas is not yet complete. Regional policy more explicitly enters the normative kaleido-scope in the mid-1960s.[34] The essence of regional policies was to reduce the need for massive labour mobility between regions by bringing jobs and capital to where they did not exist, that is, in Canada's depressed regions. An array of infrastructure and industrial incentive programs were constructed by the then new Department of Regional Economic Expansion established in 1969 and even earlier by the Department of Industry. By the end of the 1970s, however, it was evident that the regional income disparities had not been reduced.[35] Even if they had prevented things from getting worse—in short, stabilized relations—much of this, as measured by incomes, was accounted for by the enormous flow of unemployment insurance payments into these regions, rather than by the efforts of DREE.[36] Such programs did not prevent labour mobility, as the data in Table 17.2 show, since Canadians decided to move in response to many cues despite risks and uncertainties. As we noted above, the 1981 Dodge Report attributed the theoretical unexpected net in-migration to Atlantic Canada partially to the generosity of unemployment insurance benefits.[37] Not surprisingly, it concluded that this result may have been equitable, but it was not efficient.

The on-going experimentation with employment and job creation programs in the late 1960s and 1970s also revealed the larger social dimensions that lay within the changing labour market. Even before the Winter Works program met its demise in 1968, there were important experiments underway. One of these was the Company of Young Canadians, a precursor to the larger Opportunity for Youth Program (OFY) established in 1970.[38] The CYC was launched in the mid-1960s as a vehicle of social and community development. It was a controversial agency, but its work provided the model for the later OFY job creation program. The differences between OFY and the earlier Winter Works scheme are significant. The OFY involved Ottawa's direct action rather than through the provinces and municipalities. This was to allow young people to have a say in the quality and nature of the work they wanted to do. The Winter Words scheme, as we saw, had seasonal objectives and affected adult male workers in the construction industry. The OFY program continued until 1976 and was replaced in 1977-78 by the Young Canada Works Program.

Running parallel with the youth programs were a succession of more general direct job creation programs, including the Local Initiatives Program (LIP) and the Local Employment Assistance Program (LEAP). In the 1970s about $2 billion was spent by Ottawa on direct job creation (as opposed to tax expenditure incentives). These funds yielded about 260,500 person-years of employment at an average cost of $7,500 per person-year.[39] Both general and particular evaluations of these programs were conducted.[40] Some internal evaluations of the youth programs suggested that the prime beneficiaries were young people from middle class socioeconomic backgrounds rather than poorer disadvantaged young people. As the decade ended, conservative critics were increasingly arguing that "real jobs" and "productive" jobs could only be established by the private sector with suitable tax incentives.[41]

This idea began to meld with an overall view that excessive Keynesian and "stop-start" expenditure "fine tuning" had to end. Keynesianism was part of the problem, not part of the solution.[42] This larger view was reflected in the Budget Speeches of 1976 and 1977 and even in the re-naming of the Department of Manpower and Immigration as the Department of *Employment* and Immigration. It was also linked to the call to control government spending and hence to the need to target policy and expenditure activity where it was most needed and most efficient.

In 1981 the Dodge Report summarized the decade's experience with direct job creation programs as follows:

> ... the job creation programs begun in the 1970s started with a concern for seasonally unemployed youth and evolved into a counter-cyclical effort to assist areas of chronically high unemployment. For the most part, these programs were designed and considered as short-term measures to reduce unemployment in periods of temporary downturn in the economy. A realization of the need to deal more effectively with structural problems of the disadvantaged or chronically unemployed led to later inclusion of more elements of training and a longer time frame, and programs gradually became quasi-permanent features of labour market policy. Aspects of most job creation programs have touched segments of seasonal, cyclical and structural unemployment, with poorly defined targets. This has seriously limited the impact and effectiveness of the programs.
>
> The political rationale for direct job creation rests on two further factors which have also limited the effectiveness of job creation

program design. The first is that some of the appeal of job creation stems from frustration over the apparent failures of early labour market programs in the late 1960s, such as training and education for the unskilled, to correct supply-side deficiencies. The second factor is that increasing public dissatisfaction with growth of the income support system and the hint of linking welfare with some work requirement led policy makers to place more emphasis on fitting individuals into a job slot and less on the value of their output. . . .

Any assessment of the effectivness of direct job creation measures in the last decade is hampered by a score of unresolved issues, such as agreement on global objectives, macro or micro level goals, targeting and evaluation methodologies.[43]

What the Dodge Report and other critics did not stress was the extent to which these program are also a function of the government's need to respond "now" to unemployment in the face of the ritual of Parliamentary debate. Even when urging the need for less fine tuning, for example, the Tory and even the NDP parties were still wanting action "now" and results "immediately."

Needless to say, by the end of the 1970s the structures of labour market policy were decidedly more complex and unwieldy. The attempt to devise a more integrative approach and the evolving paradigms of "manpower" and then "employment" concepts were reflected in the establishment of the Department of Manpower and Immigration in 1966 and its restructuring as the Department of Employment and Immigration in 1976.[44] The latter also involved a more catholic name for the old Unemployment Insurance Commission, which became the Canada Employment and Immigration Commission and retained its tripartite business, labour, and government representation on the commission. The Department of Labour continued to operate, but it was joined in the overall labour market policy structures by the Treasury Board with its major collective bargaining role, and by temporary bodies such as the Prices and Incomes Commission, and later the Anti-Inflation Board. In the regional policy field, DREE was in place and the Economic Council of Canada continued to tender advice on these related fields throughout the decade.

It is essential to stress that the Department of Labour could have been strengthened in influence and power had it been given the original manpower mandate forged in 1966. But structurally the Labour department was left to preside over its traditional referee-like role in the labour-management relations process. In part, this was done to weaken the focal point for labour representation, but it also reflected a divergence of professional views between traditional labour relations specialists, who were often lawyers, and the then newer breed of manpower economists. To a considerabl extent this difference of view exists to this day, not only in government but in university education as well. The Dodge Report, for example, left out industrial relations and thus excluded a large chunk of the reality of labour market policy.

Somewhat less conspicuous in an Ottawa setting but of major structural import in the broad scheme of things were two elements, the burgeoning white collar education bureaucracies at both the university and community college levels and the often beleaguered Canada Manpower offices located in the regions. By the end of the 1970s the former had acquired an enormous vested interest in "labour market" funds and had enjoyed years of generally heady expansion.[45] The two sectors respectively continued to personify the two "education" versus "training" paradigms stressed above. For Canada Manpower offices the problems were distinctly different but clearly traceable to the earliest days of the Gill Report's debate about the efficacy of the then existing placement offices. In theory these officies were to be, as Figure 17.1 showed, the linch-pin between the demand and supply sides of the labour market. In practice, however, they show how "implementation," as a marriage of private and public behaviour, affects policy development. The net effect of the virtual parade of new labour market initiatives in the 1960s and 1970s was to convert regional and local manpower offices into veritable supermarkets of labour market services. They became loaded with such a panopoly of tasks, from information services to placement counselling to direct job creation grants, that they could scarcely cope in the face of "yet another" initiative from Ottawa.[46]

The above array of concerns about public policy and decision-making structures, and thus about the organization of power, resulted in a larger debate about structural reform, especially in the 1976 to 1980 period. In the midst of the wage and price controls debate about tripartism and corporatism, the Canadian Labour Congress advocated the establishment of a powerful tripartite "labour market board" that would have a full range of decision making, investment and regulatory powers over the policy levers that impact on labour markets. The government rejected this idea of shared power by arguing it would violate the idea of responsible Cabinet-Parliamentary government and ministerial accountability. When the Liberals returned to office in 1980, the Minister of Employment and Immigration, Lloyd Axworthy, considered briefly the idea of broadening the representative basis of the Employment and Immigration Commission, possibly to incorporate representation from women's groups and small business. In the final analysis no restructuring occurred. This was partly due to the fact that Axworthy was being asked to consider another structural reform package as well. This one emerged as a rare joint proposal from the Canadian Labour Congress and the Business Council on National Issues (BCNI). As we saw in Chapters 3 and 15, the BCNI, as a relatively new elite business lobby of corporate chief executive officers, was attempting to cultivate better bilateral relations between itself and the CLC. The BCNI-CLC proposal was for a new labour market institute.[47] It would be incorporated and given a bipartite business-labour board but would be funded primarily by federal and provincial governments. Its purpose would be a limited one focused on improving labour market supply-demand information. The BCNI-CLC proposal was thus premised on two issues of policy and decision-making structure: the need to foster and actually experience greater business-labour trust and cooperation through a practical joint endeavour, and the need to overcome the perceived weakness of bureaucratic approaches to providing labour market information. On the latter point the two organizations believed that they, through the first-hand knowledge of member companies and union locals, and with an appropriate committee structure, could do a better job than the governmental bureaucracies in providing the critical advance knowledge and intelligence about demand and supply.

At the time of writing, the BCNI-CLC proposal was still being negotiated with Ottawa and with several provinces. All of the above structural reform proposals represent an effort to deal with, maintain, or radically alter the realities of labour market power, policy, decision making, and implementation in recognition of the realms of public and private behaviour involved and of the varying kinds of knowledge required, including the timeliness of such knowledge. The battle over structural power was engaged at several levels. For example, at the same time as the above initiatives were being debated, business, labour and government were advocating their own versions of "industrial democracy." For organized labour this came in the form of Western European-inspired industrial democracy.[48] For business organizations the topic was cautiously raised under the heading of the "social responsibility of corporations" or "corporate governance." For Ottawa, it came in the diffuse form of a fourteen-point labour reform package, which included reform gestures towards better "quality of work life" practices, new occupational health machinery, and increased protection for nonunionized workers.[49]

For much of this period, however, labour and government skirted around the issue of major tripartite structural reform. They engaged in a series of monologues rather than dialogues, each suspicious of the other's motives. But major structural reform cannot long be postponed. Consider, for example, three aspects of the Dodge Report's forecasts for the 1980s, outlined earlier in the chapter, especially in the context of the industrial policy debate set out in Chapter 15. Even if one issues the normal caveats about the reliability of forecasts, three of the Dodge forecasts seem eminently plausible, namely, the need for a large westward flow of labour to Western Canada, the need for significant increases in the participation of women in the labour market in nontraditional occupations (presumably also in an east to west regional context), and the need for massive "adjustments" in industries such as automobiles and in other manufacturing industries that may also have to shift to the West while simultaneously undergoing technological modernization to promote greater productivity. All of these tasks require new joint decision-making centres of power and therefore structural forums that involve labour, business and government in more concerted actions and in which women must have significantly increased representation. Moreover, the structures must somehow deal with both manpower issues and industrial relations. To a significant extent labour will move despite what policy incentives they are given, but the labour market policies of the 1980s cannot be addressed by dangling the right mix of carrots and incentives. It must embrace structural and institutional reform that cannot help but challenge other major institutional bases of power and the ideas they represent, including federalism and Parliamentary government.

The 1980s: The Rediscovery of Efficiency?

By the 1980s there were a confluence of ideas, events and pressures which suggested strongly that labour market policies were leaning toward a rediscovery of efficiency. The labour market policy events joined the larger general industrial and energy policy events we have examined in previous chapters, including expenditure restraint, declining comparative industrial productivity, the multinational trade negotiations, the need for industrial adjustment, the claimed need for regulatory reform including deregulation to promote competition, and the constitutional debate about power over the economy and the promotion of the Canadian common market by reducing the domestic barriers to trade.

The concentrated 1980-81 review of labour market policies by the Dodge task force also took place in the midst of an economic depression, 12 percent unemployment and soaring deficits, of three Budgets in less than one year, of the Liberal's new visibility strategy and of the National Energy Program and the Charter of Rights. The review was also a reflection of earlier criticism of labour market "bottlenecks" by the 23 sector task forces, and it revealed thinking in line with the Ministry of State for Economic Development's "economic development eight point factors of production" approach, an approach that leaned, as heavily as politics would let it, toward efficiency and away from welfare.

In the field of training and education, in addition to the report of the Task Force on Labour Market Development headed by David Dodge, there was the need to contend with the renegotiation of university finances as part of the Established Programs Financing (EPF) arrangements with the provinces.[50] The Dodge Report reviewed major aspects of labour market policy except for industrial relations, incomes policy and university education. Its basic approach was to call for the need to target federal funds in the training field to meet critical skill shortages needed by the economy. It downplayed other aspects of earlier programs such as literacy and language upgrading. It assumed that immigration would not be as ready a source of supply of needed skills as had been the case in previous decades. It also projected, as Figure 17.4 indicated, a sharply increased participation rate by women in the economy. This participation by women would no longer be a "social" phenomenon as it was often portrayed to be in the 1970s but would be an economic necessity, since there could conceivably be male full employment and thus "nontraditional" jobs would have to be assumed by women. The report also projected lost jobs not only in industries such as textiles but also in key industries such as the automobile industry. Hence, there would be a great need for "adjustment" policies. Last, but certainly not least, it projected the continued westward migration of Canadians, especially to Alberta and British Columbia.

Major features of the Dodge Report found their way into the National Training Program announced early in 1982 by Employment and Immigration Minister Lloyd Axworthy. It replaced the fifteen-year-old Adult Occupational Training Act. The focus was to give Ottawa a larger role in determining and dealing with skill shortages in "national" occupations. The program also included an occupational growth and adjustment fund to provide capital and operating expenses for training facilities and promised an emphasis on equal opportunities for women in the labour market.[51]

On the issue of financing higher education, the broader EPF negotiations revealed the rediscovery of efficiency. The Secretary of State disclosed one strand of the federal position. Federal policy, he said, is based on achieving several objectives:

> General support of the post-secondary system objective: to assist in maintaining and strengthening a general knowledge, learning and critical capacity in the post-secondary system ... which provides the infra-structure ... to meet more specific objectives ... with particular emphasis on pan-Canadian concerns.
>
> Manpower objectives: to promote adequate levels of training ... particularly for occupations requiring highly skilled nationally and internationally mobile manpower.
>
> Mobility objective: to minimize barriers to interprovincial mobility of students and teachers ... and of graduates wishing to work in other provinces.
>
> Research and economic growth objectives: to support research and development ... in order to promote economic growth and to support graduate training for the nation's overall research and development needs.
>
> Citizenship, language and cultural identity objective: to promote ... a sense of Canadian citizenship and identity, with particular emphasis on the nation's bilingual nature and to increase access by members of official language minorities to a full range of educational opportunities in their own language.
>
> Accessibility objective: to support equality of opportunity in (student) access to the ... system, by reducing geographic, socio-economic and other constraints on participation.
>
> International relations objective: to promote Canada's international interests in mattters relating to education ...[52]

These objectives reflect both the broader social and economic roles of universities. They were, however, hardly a ringing endorsation of the need to ensure that universities remain as reasonably independent centres of research and critical analysis in the main domains of human knowledge—the arts and humanities, the social sciences and the natural sciences and engineering.

The role of universities as an economic tool was the focal point of statements by the Minister of Finance who was the key figure in the FEP negotiations. Indeed, it was virtually the only point he made on the subject in several of his statements.

> The post-secondary ... transfer ... to the extent it serves federal policy ... is mainly related to long-term economic development. The existence of a large number of highly qualified managers, professionals and technicians is essential for future development. It is also in the university atmosphere that a good deal of the research which generates scientific advance, invention and industrial innovation takes place. However, the program as it now exists provides no link between these obvious federal policy interests and provincial outlays financed by these transfers.[53]

In a later statement the economic focus was again clearly present.

> The government is of the view that existing federal-provincial arrangements for the financing of post-secondary education are not consistent with the country's present or future needs. Because of provincial jurisdiction over education, these transfers have in effect been unconditional. This was not an important issue when the main priority of both orders of government was the expansion and improvement of a national system of post-secondary educational institutions to which all Canadians would have access. However, social and economic circumstances have changed in recent years. The institutional infrastructure is now in place, and the growth in student population has abated.
>
> Canada's economic development depends increasingly on our ability to make the most effective use of our human resoures. This will require better coordination of higher education and related activities. Federal support for human resources development should accordingly be reassessed. The issue is no longer simply growth and program expansion, but the focus and direction required to restore and maintain the vitality of Canada's economy. Concerted and sustained efforts are required to avoid university and college graduates finding themselves unemployed because of an over-supply of their particular skills, while industrial expansion is hampered by shortages of other skills. Although regional concerns remain important, long-term

planning for the country as a whole has become vital, and the federal government has national responsibilities in this regard which cannot be ignored. Otherwise, potential waste through duplication and wasteful competition could impede efforts to accelerate growth of the Canadian economy.[54]

As we saw earlier in this chapter, an original impetus for federal involvement in education in the 1960s was to promote accessibility to education and equality of opportunity. The 1981 Parliamentary Task Force on Federal-Provincial Fiscal Arrangements pronounced itself to be "impressed by the extent to which the objectives of mobility and equality of access are being met in Canadian post-secondary education."[55] It went on to express its concern about "the negative consequences that *could* flow from continuing financial constraint in the years ahead."[56] There was other evidence that showed, however, that the accessibility objective was not just threatened by *future* restraint but had, since the early 1970s, already been threatened. A study showed that university financing had been increasingly "pro-rich."[57] These tendencies would be exacerbated the more that federal (and provincial) funding encouraged the need for higher student fees and the more that student support was in the form of loans as opposed to grants.

Briefs from student unions stressed these current and future funding effects.[58] It is, of course, perfectly reasonably to argue in rebuttal that university education is an investment that pays handsome returns to those who benefit from it and that they should therefore pay a fair share. But the real accessibility impact was on those who, despite having the ability, could not afford to attend university and whose voice was not heard through *current* student unions. The point to stress is that, although there are always disputes as to "how much" is enough, there was no question that accessibility was declining already, had been for several years, and was not merely a future prospect.

The only aspect of federal policy in the early 1980s that might help (but only to a very limited degree) work against this pro-rich tendency of university financing was the stated preference in federal policy of increased support for engineering and related high technology areas. Studies show that these programs tend to have a higher intake of persons from lower income families.[59] In virtually all other respects, however, federal policy could not be said to be supportive of increased accessibility to university education. Indeed, it was increasingly reducing accessibility.

If efficiency was the dominant idea, it was not alone in the education-training realms. It is worth noting how the ideas of accountability and visibility (a narrow view of nationalism) entered the debate and influenced and was affected by structures and instruments.

A major federal concern was to secure greater identity and accountability for federal funds and to influence university priorities in a general way, particularly towards economic goals. Several ways of achieving these objectives had been suggested either separately or in combination, including giving funds directly to the universities and vouchers to students. A voucher system could be a real one in which students would have some discretion to "shop" for the educational program they wanted. Or it could be a symbolic voucher in which students receive visible notification of how much federal money is supporting their education. This latter version of a voucher could easily be implemented by sending letters to universities and other students suitably emblazened with the maple leaf and looking similar to the logo of the Liberal party. The question of a real voucher system and/or increased direct federal funding of universities was a larger one and embraced several ideas other than just visibility.

At one level it could be argued that universities would be more independent if they were less nominally beholden to only one level of government. This would require, however, a more direct frontal invasion of provincial jurisdiction by the federal government with all its adverse side effects both in this and, inevitably, in other areas of federal provincial relations. A direct federal funding concept may also make it more difficult for universities to plan their finances, thus reducing their independence in other ways.

A full-fledged voucher system could create maximum federal visibility but also potential maximum instability for the universities. Admittedly, no voucher system would allow students a totally unrestrained right "to shop" since this would defeat the goal of targeted priorities for education. A voucher system would, however, create greater uncertainty for the universities than the current system since they would have to compete somewhat more for students. Moreover, several local smaller universities might be in jeopardy, thus raising regional and local identity concerns, especially for the several Cabinet ministers who had such institutions in their riding.

While the Dodge Report and the EPF negotiations on university financing were the focal point of labour market policy in the early 1980s, there were other key developments. The federal government's "6 and 5" anti-inflation Budget in June 1982 effectively removed collective bargaining in the federal public sector. Presented as a temporary measure, it continued, this time in a stark way, the tendency to control industrial relations and hence worker incomes with a "continuous" array of ad hoc temporary measures, again in pursuit of the efficiency idea. On the job creation front the severe depression of 1981-82 produced its inevitable contradictions in ideas—namely, that the underlying problems were structural and little could be done in the way of "quick fixes," but that, nonetheless, short-term help was critically needed. This came in the form of a new package of work-sharing arrangements (linked to unemployment insurance funds), to special jobs for so-called "exhaustees" (unemployed persons whose unemployment insurance benefits had run out) and, in 1982-83, an old-fashioned "public works" project list. In the unemployment insurance field, a second task force had reported in parallel with the Dodge Task Force. Though it concerned itself more with issues of income security and regional equity, it nonetheless also stressed the efficiency and adjustment aspects and kept a sharp eye out for the ballooning costs of the program.[60]

Concluding Observations

Labour market policy is the third of the policy fields we have surveyed in an illustrative way. While there is a core definition for labour market policies, we have shown how initially in the post-war period there was scarcely any reference to such overall policies and how subsequently in the 1960s and 1970s different paradigms were articulated and partly acted upon as the policy field spilled over its arbitrary boundaries. We have also demonstrated the underlying dynamics and processes triggered by the changing nature of industry and the changing composition of the labour force and showed their two-way interactive connection to the evolving policy structures and to evolving institutions and interests.

Like the two previous fields we have examined, labour market policies evolve in a double-edged manner. Each field is lodged within the broader umbrella policy fields—economic, social and foreign—examined in Chapter 14, but at the same time they are filled with the dominant ideas of political life. Each policy field has, of course, its own idocyncratic language of debate, policy paradigms, structural arrangements and dynamics. In discussing three umbrella policy fields, and then three major policy categories such as industrial, energy and labour markets, we have threaded our way through numerous other policy fields as well, including education, industrial relations, social security, trade, foreign investment, transportation and resources.

We have not done full justice, of course, to all these fields. We have discussed them illustratively and have erred on the side of historical breadth rather than tantalyzing details. For persons interested in other policy fields such as health care or defence, and broadcasting or forestry, our analytical advice is the same. We suggest you "think big" rather than start out "thinking small." The main common ground among diverse policy fields are the dominant ideas. If one appreciates this overriding fact, the details then become more interesting, even while they become more complex. One should also look for the existence of ideologies and of more or less well-defined paradigms. One should treat structures not as sterile names in the government organization chart but as repositories of ideas and forums for the organization of power. And one should understand the presence of uncertainty and the risks it presents both for those who have power and for those who do not.

NOTES

1. See Employment and Immigration Canada, *Labour Market Development in the 1980s* (Ottawa: Minister of Supply and Services, 1981), hereafter cited as the "Dodge Report"), Chapters 1 and 2; David Gordon, *Theories of Power and Underemployment* (New York: Heath, 1972), Chapters 1 to 5; S. Dupre, D. Cameron, G.H. McKechnie and T.B. Rotenberg, *Federalism and Policy Development: The Case of Adult Occupational Training in Ontario* (Toronto: University of Toronto Press, 1973), Chapter 2; Economic Council of Canada, *In Short Supply: Jobs and Skills in the 1980s* (Ottawa: Minister of Supply and Services, 1982) and Parliamentary Task Forces on Employment Opportunities for the '80s, *Work For Tomorrow* (Ottawa: House of Commons, 1981).
2. Dupre et al., *op. cit.,* pp. 31-32. Reproduced by permission. For related early views of labour market policy, see the Economic Council of Canada's first two annual reviews in 1964 and 1965 (Ottawa: Queen's Printer, 1964, 1965).

3. Dodge Report, *op. cit.*, p. 8.
4. See Economic Council of Canada, *People and Jobs* (Ottawa: Information Canada, 1976).
5. Dodge Report, *op. cit.*, p. 9.
6. *Ibid.*, p. 9.
7. Dupre et al., *op. cit.*, Chapters 1 and 2.
8. Dodge Report, *op. cit.*, p. 29.
9. See Freda Hawkins, *Canada and Immigration* (Montreal: McGill-Queen's University Press, 1982); Dodge Report, *op. cit.*, Chapter 10; Alan G. Green, *Immigration and the Postwar Canadian Economy* (Toronto: Macmillan of Canada, 1976); and Gordon W. Davies and S. Sharir, "Towards 'A Rational Immigration Policy': Comments and a Proposal," *Canadian Public Policy*, Vol. II, No. 3 (Summer 1976), pp. 492-496.
10. Green, *op. cit.*, *passim*.
11. See, for example, the shocking and unconscionable immigration policy towards Jews in the pre- and post-war periods in Irving Abella and H. Troper, *None Too Many* (Toronto: Lester and Orpen Dennys Ltd., 1982).
12. *Ibid.*, pp. 20-23.
13. *Ibid.*, pp. 13-20.
14. *Ibid.*, pp. 22-23.
15. See Leo Panitch and Donald Swartz, "From Free Collective Bargaining to Permanent Exceptionalism: The Economic Crisis and the Transformation of Industrial Relations in Canada," in G. Swimmer and M. Thompson, eds., *Public Sector Industrial Relations in Canada* (Montreal: Institute for Research on Public Policy, 1983), Chapter 3.
16. Pierre Issalys and G. Watkins, *Unemployment Insurance Benefits*. Study prepared for the Law Reform Commission of Canada (Ottawa: Minister of Supply and Services, 1977), Introduction; and *Report of the Committee of Inquiry into the Unemployment Insurance Act*—hereafter cited as the Gill Report (Ottawa: Queen's Printer, 1962).
17. See R.M. Burns and L. Close, *The Municipal Winter Works Incentives Program* (Toronto: Canadian Tax Foundation, 1971).
18. *Ibid.*, Conclusion.
19. Dupre et al., *op. cit.*, Chapters 1 and 2; and Vincent W. Bladen et al., *Financing Higher Education in Canada* (Toronto: University of Toronto Press, 1965).
20. See Richard W. Phidd and G. Bruce Doern, *The Politics and Management of Canadian Economic Policy* (Toronto: Macmillan of Canada, 1978), Chapter 10.
21. Dupre et al., *op. cit.*, Chapters 2, 5 and 6.
22. Economic Council of Canada, *Financing Confederation* (Ottawa: Minister of Supply and Services, 1982), Chapters 3 and 6.
23. Dupre et al., p. 25. Reproduced by permission.
24. See Hawkins, *op. cit.*, Chapter 6.

25. See Swimmer and Thompson, *op. cit.*

26. See Panitch and Swartz, *op. cit.*, p. 24.

27. Allan M. Maslove and Eugene Swimmer, *Wage Controls in Canada 1975-1978* (Montreal: Institute for Research on Public Policy, 1980).

28. G. Bruce Doern, Michael Prince and Garth McNaughton, *Living with Contradictions: Health and Safety Regulation and Implementation in Ontario* (Toronto: Royal Commission on Matters of Health and Safety Arising Out of the Use of Asbestos in Ontario, 1982).

29. E.C. West and M. McKee, *Minimum Wages: The New Issues on Theory, Evidence, Policy and Politics* (Ottawa: Minister of Supply and Services, 1980).

30. Gill Report, *op. cit.*

31. See *Report of the Study for Updating the Unemployment Insurance Programme* (Ottawa: Unemployment Insurance Commission, 1969) and Hon. Bryce Mackasey, *Unemployment Insurance in the 70's* (Ottawa: Queen's Printer, 1970).

32. Andrew F. Johnson, "The Minister as an Agent of Policy Change: The Case of Unemployment Insurance in the Seventies," *Canadian Public Administration*, Vol. 24, No. 4 (Winter 1981), pp. 612-633.

33. Rick Van Loon, "Reforming Welfare in Canada," *Public Policy*, Vol. 27, No. 4 (Fall 1979), pp. 469-504.

34. Economic Council of Canada, *Living Together* (Ottawa: Minister of Supply and Services, 1977).

35. See Harvey N. Lithwick, "Regional Policy: The Embodiment of Contradictions," in G. Bruce Doern, ed., *How Ottawa Spends Your Tax Dollars 1982* (Toronto: James Lorimer Publishers, 1982), pp. 131-146; and Senate Committee on National Finance, *Government Policy and Regional Development* (Ottawa: Minister of Supply and Services, 1982).

36. Lithwick, *op. cit.*, pp. 135-142.

37. Dodge Report, *op. cit.*, p. 29.

38. See Robert Best, "Youth Policy" in G. Bruce Doern and V.S. Wilson, eds., *Issues in Canadian Public Policy* (Toronto: Macmillan of Canada, 1974), pp. 137-165.

39. Dodge Report, *op. cit.*, p. 135.

40. See Economic Council of Canada, *People and Jobs, op. cit.;* and S.F. Kaliski, "People, Jobs and the 'New Unemployment'," *Canadian Public Policy*, Vol. II, No. 3 (Summer 1976), pp. 497-503. See also Employment and Immigration Canada, "Evaluation of the 1977 Young Canada Work Program" (Ottawa, 1977) and Best, *op. cit.*

41. See, for example, Canadian Manufacturer's Association, *Agenda for Action* (Toronto: 1977), pp. 14-16.

42. See James M. Buchanan and Richard E. Wagner, *Democracy in Deficit: The Political Legacy of Lord Keynes* (New York: Academic Press, 1977).

43. Dodge Report, *op. cit.*, p. 135.

44. Phidd and Doern, *op. cit.*, Chapter 10.
45. Peter M. Leslie, *Canadian Universities 1980 and Beyond: Enrollment Structural Change and Finance* (Ottawa: Association of Universities and Colleges of Canada, 1980).
46. Dodge Report, *op. cit.*, Chapter 5.
47. See "A Proposal by the Business Council on National Issues and the Canadian Labour Congress for the Establishment of a National Manpower Board" (Ottawa: January 17, 1980).
48. See Anthony Giles, "The Politics of Wage Controls: The Canadian State, Organized Labour and Corporatism." Masters Thesis, School of Public Administration, Carleton University (Ottawa, 1980).
49. C.J. Connaghan, *Partnership or Marriage of Convenience: A Critical Examination of Contemporary Labour Relations in West Germany* (Ottawa: Labour Canada, 1976). See also *How to Improve Business Government Relations in Canada,* a Report to the Minister of Industry, Trade and Commerce (Ottawa: "Task Force in Business-Government Interface," 1976).
50. See House of Commons, *Fiscal Federalism in Canada.* Report of the Parliamentary Task Force on Federal-Provincial Fiscal Arrangements (Ottawa: Minister of Supply and Services, 1981).
51. Minister of Employment and Immigration, Press Release on National Training Program (Ottawa: January 6, 1982).
52. Quoted in House of Commons, *op. cit.*, p. 127.
53. *Ibid.*, p. 126.
54. Hon. Allan J. MacEachen, *Fiscal Arrangements in the Eighties* (Ottawa: Department of Finance, 1981), pp. 38-39.
55. House of Commons, *op. cit.*, p. 130.
56. *Ibid.*, p. 130.
57. Ronald Meng, Charles Seeto and Jim Sentang, *A Reconsideration of Canadian Universities and the Redistribution of Income* (Ottawa: Centre for Policy and Program Assessment, School of Public Administration, Carleton University, 1982).
58. Council of Ministers of Education, *Report of the Federal-Provincial Task Force on Student Assistance* (Ottawa: Minister of Supply and Services, 1981); National Union of Students, "Student Loans: Making a Mockery of Equal Opportunity," submission to the Federal-Provincial Task Force on Student Assistance (Ottawa, July 1980).
59. See R. Meng, et. al., *op. cit.*, p. 20.
60. Employment and Immigration Canada, *Unemployment Insurance in the 1980's* (Ottawa: Minister of Supply and Services, 1981). See also Lars Osberg, "Unemployment Insurance in Canada: A Review of the Recent Amendments," *Canadian Public Policy,* Vol. V, No. 2 (Spring 1979), pp. 223-235; and H.G. Grubel and M.A. Walker, eds., *Unemployment Insurance: Global Evidence of its Effects on Unemployment* (Vancouver: Fraser Institute, 1978).

PART IV

CONCLUDING OBSERVATIONS

- Policy Evaluation and Analysis
- The Study and Practice of Canadian
  Public Policy

CHAPTER 18

POLICY EVALUATION AND ANALYSIS

We have come full circle. The book began with a focus on the dominant and other institutional ideas, and we conclude with the role of these ideas by focusing on how policies and decisions are evaluated and analyzed.[1] Ideas are at the heart of analysis and are mobilized both to promote and to prevent the implementation of the results of evaluation studies and of other forms of policy advocacy. In this chapter we examine the main institutional sources and locales for policy evaluation and analysis and the relationships among them. These sources include line departments and agencies, central agencies, and the Cabinet ministers who head them. They include Parliament, royal commissions, advisory councils, private policy institutes and universities, as well as the media, interest groups and other governments. We also refer briefly to evaluations of the policy fields examined in the three previous chapters. In general, however, we are interested in the broader issues of policy evaluation and analysis.

Many attempt to reserve the word "evaluation" only for formal ex-post program evaluations, that is, studies which attempt to measure and assess the *causal* effects or impacts of designated and identifiable packages of governmental activity on external (nongovernmental) behaviour.[2] Evaluations of this kind purport to show how well a program is progressing either in meeting its objectives measured against specified criteria, or at least in showing the concrete effects that can be attributed to the program in question. Thus, ex-post "evaluations," it is argued by some, can be distinguished from a priori "analysis." Analysis, according to this view, would consist of modelling, analyzing or thinking about a proposed new policy prior to its adoption. Different formal techniques could be applied at this stage, including formal cost-benefit analysis, various kinds of econometric modelling, statistical analysis and even public opinion polling.

Ideas and the Scope of Evaluation and Analysis

To appreciate the fact that ex-post evaluation and a priori analysis are not nearly as distinct categories as many seem to believe, we must first reassemble several concepts and threads of analysis from earlier chapters. They again show the interplay of ideas, structures and processes in the evaluation and analytical aspects of policy making.

First, our approach suggests that there is no single, easily identifiable "phase" in the policy cycle at which it can be said that evaluation and analysis occurs. Evaluation and analysis, in one sense, occur in an episodic way through the development of an individual policy as ideas meld or conflict, resources are allocated, structures of power and the dynamics of uncertainty evolve and the degrees of causality and evidence are discovered, synthesized and wholly or partially rejected. There may, of course, be periods in the evolving life of a policy field or program area where bursts of change occur, followed by implementation and varying kinds of criticism, comment and study. In previous chapters we have seen this in areas such as energy policy, foreign policy, the social security review, reassessments of manpower training, foreign owner- ship, and in numerous other fields.

A second reality is that the definitions and scope of evaluation vary greatly in keeping with the many institutions, professional knowledge groups, interests and advocacy perspectives involved. Definitions and scope vary according to whether the analysis is applied to outputs versus outcomes or impacts or to structures and processes; deal with a priori versus ex-post decisions; and short-run versus longer-run time periods. They also vary according to whether one is dealing with notions of systematic planning intended to meet the "top-down" needs of central agency officials or the "bottom-up" needs of line department managers. The scope and purpose of evaluation and analysis also varies in relation to the institutionalized ideas and expansionary habits of knowledgeable professionals such as accountants, economists, and scientists. Thus, analytical activity involves some degree of advocacy rather than just dispassionate objectivity. For example, accountants, led by the Auditor General of Canada, have devised an expanded concept of auditing called "comprehensive auditing" and "value for money" auditing. Economists have both practised and propagated the utility of cost-benefit analysis and other analytical concepts. Scientists and engineers have promoted a belief in rationality and, to a certain extent, in "planning." When examining a particular study or report, or a new demand for evaluation and analysis, these several potential dimensions must be kept in mind.

Different views of evaluation can be shown more specifically in the position taken by the Auditor General as opposed to that of the Comptroller General. In the early 1980s they effectively symbolized at least two official Ottawa views of "program evaluation."[3] In one important usage, program evaluation is scientifically defensible research whose purpose is to make absolute and quantified determinations as to the nature and extent of the effects of specific government activities. In this conception the program is conceived of as a direct intervention by some government instrument or instruments (generally spending, regulation or persuasion rather than the so-called tax expenditures) into a public or social problem. The purpose of the intervention is, of course, to alleviate the undesired state of affairs, or to bring about a qualitatively different situation. The program evaluation itself would be replicable in all its details. It is in this sense that the term "program evaluation" is used by the Office of the Auditor General: program evaluation is to definitively establish the quantified accomplishments of government programs so that the information can be used for accountability purposes. In the alternative conception of program evaluation it is thought of as providing softer, more judgemental "findings," which nonetheless have some basis in evidence and which are documented to the extent possible and practical. This less rigourous conception of program evaluation is the one promulgated by the Office of the Comptroller General: program evaluation is to provide indications which will be used in conjunction with other sources of information to suggest possible program improvements to senior management.

A third reality in policy analysis is the importance and persistence of the dominant ideas as the explicit and/or implicit criteria for evaluative judgement. This reality is especially evident when it is recognized that the government or even Parliament's statutes and laws cannot control the *political scope of the analytical debate*. Efficiency versus stability; redistribution versus equity; individual rights versus collective goals; national unity and identity versus regional sensitivity. These are the ideas that matter. They are institutionalized as part of the agency philosophy of different structures in executive government tugging the Cabinet in different directions at the same time and ensuring some degree of persistent adherence to these ideas. The evaluation process is also affected by other ideas that matter, namely those rooted in the core institutions examined in Chapter 1, 2, 3 and 7. These ideas also affect and help govern judgements about how the processes of policy development, implementation and even evaluative activity itself occurs. Thus, elections produce a rough-and-ready form of evaluation of a critically important kind. Parliament, federalism and interest groups generate ideas not only about the substance of public policy fields, but also about the adequacy of consultation and about who or what structures of power *ought* to make decisions of different kinds.

Evaluation and analysis for all these reasons is both a process of social interaction and of cerebral thought. It is conducted by many structures and institutions in the face of contending ideas and uncertainty about the future. In short, evaluation must embrace a form of learning where power and knowledge are each understood to have limits. These limits arise partly because public policy involves changing or sustaining the behaviour of *both* public officials and private citizens and corporations not only within Canada but to a greater or lesser extent in other countries as well.

Institutions and Structures for Policy Evaluation and Analysis

It is in this total context that we review the roles of major institutions and structures in the analysis of public policies. We have already dealt with the broader roles of these institutions. Their analytical roles must be examined in more detail and in relation to each other.

Table 18.1 portrays the array of evaluation modes and mechanisms contained within each of the major structures and institutions. While purists in the cause of formal evaluation studies assert that most of these structures do not actually do *real* evaluations, it is our view that this is an unduly narrow, indeed naive, view of what evaluation is in a democratic and political setting and presents a needlessly artificial separation between a priori and ex-post activity and between evaluation as cerebral thought, that is, studies which result in formal reports claiming authoritative knowledge, and as social interaction. A further point about Table 18.1 deserves mention. It is not constructed to show any *hierarchical* paths for analysis or views of the legitimacy of evaluations and of the evaluators. For example, one could envision a table which showed Parliament at the apex to reflect its primacy as an *elected* evaluative body. Table 18.1 merely reflects the order in which we discuss

TABLE 18.1

INSTITUTIONAL FORUMS OF EVALUATION: MODES AND MECHANISMS

Cabinet and Central Agencies	Line Departments and Agencies	Central Agencies	Advisory Councils	Parliament and Political Parties
• Collective Cabinet and	• Senior officials	• PMO, PCO, Finance, Treasury Board	• Economic Council	• Evaluation by partisan anticipation
• Individual ministers as evaluators through social interaction and analysis	• Evaluation and Planning Branches	• Ministry of State for Economic and Regional Development	• Science Council	• Question Period
	• Special Study Teams		• Other departmental advisory councils	• Committees
• Cabinet committees	• Cost-Benefit and Socioeconomic Impact Analysis (e.g., for social regulation)	• Ministry of State for Social Development		• Auditor General
		• Office of Comptroller General		• Commissioner of Official Languages
	• Environmental Assessment Panels			• Human Rights Commission
				• Senate committees
				• Political party research
				• Party Caucus

Policy Institutes	Royal Commissions and Task Forces	Academics and Universities	Media	Interests and Other Governments

• C.D. Howe Research Institute
• Conference Board of Canada
• Institute for Research on Public Policy
• Canadian Institute for Economic Policy
• Fraser Institute
• Centre for Policy Alternatives
• National Foundation for Public Policy Development
• Canadian Council on Social Development
• Canadian Tax Foundation
• Canada West Foundation
	• e.g.—Gordon Commission
	  —Massey Commission
	  —Porter
	  —Hall
	  —Carter
	  —Berger
	• As well as White Paper and Green Paper Consultative Processes
	• 23 Sector Task Forces of 1977-78
		• Royal commission and policy institute research contracts
		• research grants
		• special policy field institutes
			• General coverage
			• In-depth series on policy fields
			• Coverage of Policy Institute and royal commission studies
				• Interest Group briefs
				• Provincial studies
				• International agencies
				  —OECD
				  —GATT
				  —World Bank
				  —United Nations

the analytical forums. It should be read by keeping in mind the varying levels, scope and views of evaluation outlined above.

The Cabinet, Central Agencies and Departments

The Cabinet itself is a political crucible for evaluation in the broadest political sense in that it is the main point at which priorities and actual resource allocation occur. As we have stressed, it pulls ministers in sometimes contradictory directions, reflecting the collective and individual as well as regional and representative norms of Cabinet government. Ministers and bureaucrats in part analyze and checkmate each other, as does the structure of vertical and horizontal portfolios set out in Chapters 7 and 9. The Cabinet's decisions and its behaviour, moreover, represent the most concrete composite summary of what the governing political party stands for relative to other parties. Throne Speeches, Budget Speeches and major addresses by the prime minister are themselves not only statements outlining Cabinet priorities but also macro evaluations of the state of the country and of the economy. The Cabinet is also the ultimate receptacle for both formal analysis and social interaction.

The central agencies are obviously involved in evaluation and analysis in several ways. They exist to ensure that an elaborate form of interdepartmental consultation and evaluation occurs, its contents being partly symbolized by the headings in the Cabinet papers outlined in Chapter 4. The central agencies frequently initiate evaluation studies and reviews or utilize those initiated elsewhere. Reviews examined in previous chapters such as the foreign policy review of 1969, the society security review of the mid-1970s and the labour market task force of 1980-81 were initiated at the centre.

Line departments and agencies engage in a wide variety of evaluative activity, but their focus must usually be somewhat more specific than that of central agencies and may be linked more explicitly to their several statutory mandates. Beginning in 1979-80 they were required to submit annual five-year strategic overviews and operational plans, as well as indicate the schedule of evaluation studies they had planned and how past studies had been utilized. Evaluation branches have been created in many departments, but their relationship to line program managers and with central agency evaluators is almost always a stressful one.[4] In suggesting that departments and central agencies engage in continuous assessment and analysis we do not wish to imply that the analytical process is always rigourous or produces good policy or even acceptable decisions. The analysis in Part II of resource allocation shows the mixed and sometimes curious results. Later in this chapter we again refer in a summary way to analytical efforts in the industrial, energy and labour market fields.

The Economic Council and the Science Council

The two major federal advisory councils, the Economic Council of Canada and the Science Council of Canada, have been involved in various kinds of public policy analysis and evaluation since their establishment.[5] Both were created in the Pearson era to improve on-going advice about economic policy and science and technology policies, respectively. Their principal vehicle for transmitting advice was their right to publish reports. In addition, their chief ministerial sponsor in the Pearson Cabinet, Maurice Lamontagne, saw them as a possible vehicle for French-style "indicative planning," particularly because they were to take a medium-term view of economic and technological issues somewhat as if they were permanent royal commissions. Neither body was capable of playing this role, not only because of the general antipathy to planning in a liberal federal state but because the internal structure of both councils created the seeds of their own ambivalence.

The councils had to combine a research role, a quasi-representative role and an arm's-length advisory and advocacy role in relation to their respective ministers, the prime minister and the Minister of State for Science and Technology. These roles invariably tugged the councils in different directions. The research role was important and the councils have published numerous reports and studies. But the research frequently ran into problems of communication and timing since invariably medium-term advice must arrive in the midst of a crowded short-term agenda. This was particularly the case for the Economic Council's annual reviews which were not published (until the 1980s) so as to be a timely input into Budget Speeches. The councils were also structured as quasi-representative institutions to serve as an intermediary between interests and the government, a role which therefore mixed analysis with advocacy. The business, labour and agricultural members of the Economic Council did not actually represent *interest groups*, but rather were there to ensure that the council's research and advice was screened through the views of persons from these "interests" and sectors. The Science Council was less broadly based but nonetheless brought together persons from all major sectors of science and technology, academe, government and business, as well as from major scientific disciplines. The quasi-representative roles of the councils often led, as one might expect, to advice that was watered down to reflect both councils' compromise of interests. Thus, their advice did not flow directly and self-evidently from research, but rather through dialogue and compromise. The research enterprise itself on any given subject was also often preceded by fairly elaborate kinds of consultation, including conferences and meetings.

The arm's-length nature of the councils' advisory role also presented dilemmas. The councils were not a small compact "eminence gris" whispering timely and strategic advice into their minister's ears. They were to be independent in nature and were also to look at the medium-term future rather than the short-term. But the natural instinct of many council members and of many of the councils' critics was to judge the councils' influence by a kind of advisory scorecard—a ratio of advice given to advice accepted by the Cabinet. Such scorecard approaches doom most individual advisory bodies to a life of failure simply because the Cabinet is the receptacle for numerous kinds and forms of advice, and thus almost by definition high batting averages are not likely to occur, especially if one's access is indirect and limited. The arm's-length role also presented problems with regard to access to information from the bureaucracy. The councils were in many ways dependent on the bureaucracy for cooperation but were invariably, in some degree at least, its critic as well.

The personal influence of the council chairmen also affected their role. John Deutsch, the Economic Council's first chairman, knew the Ottawa bureaucracy well and this, coupled with his personal knowledge of, and identification with, the then emerging problems such as manpower training, enabled the Economic Council to have some early influence in this policy field. It had less influence in macro-fiscal policy, however. Later chairmen such as Arthur Smith, Andre Raynauld, Sylvia Ostry and David Slater had fewer points of leverage and personal influence.[6] Science Council chairmen have generally had much less political clout. However, one of its executive directors, John Sheppard, did exert considerable influence, at least at the level of ideas. Sheppard led a concerted effort by the Science Council in the mid-1970s to articulate, as we have seen in Chapter 15, an interventionist and nationalist technological sovereignty approach to Canada's industrial policy.

For a time the Science Council abandoned its broader and very vague notion of a national science policy and became an aggressive policy advocate, in effect Canada's second "economic council." The Council focused its attack on the dependence created by foreign ownership of the economy and advocated a nationalist interventionist position. This position increasingly contrasted with the general and more traditional views taken by the Economic Council of Canada, whose permanent research staff of economists was generally more inclined to favour a hands-off approach. The Economic Council, it must be remembered, was concerned with more than just industrial policy and, hence, it is partly unfair to compare their positions on a strictly one-to-one basis. Nonetheless, perhaps the most important contribution of the two councils in the 1970s was the debate they helped engender on these questions.

At the same time their contributions must be kept in perspective. Theirs was a quiet, restrained debate conducted largely among economic experts and policy analysts and not necessarily or persistently in the larger political setting. Moreover, both councils studied and examined numerous other policy fields and issues. Some of their studies were read with interest, much of their content was rejected, and some were left to percolate amidst the welter of ideas that constituted the real world of policy analysis and evaluation. Thus, the Science Council contributed views and research on such areas as the "conserver society," occupational and environmental health and safety, energy research, technology transfer from governmental to private laboratories, and overall research and development policies. The Economic Council, as we have seen in earlier chapters, has conducted the most thorough review of government regulation in Canada's history, examined banking policy, labour market and employment policies, regional policy, federal-provincial fiscal arrangements and Canada-U.S. trade relations, to mention only a few of the studies it has published in its first twenty years of existence.

There is also a connection between the two major councils and other policy research bodies which now compete with them. John Sheppard, the Science Council's architect of technological sovereignty and of the need to deal firmly with the foreign ownership issue, left the council and was instrumental in establishing the Canadian Institute for Economic Policy in concert with former Liberal Finance Minister, Walter Gordon. Arthur Smith became Chairman of the Economic Council after a lengthy association with the Private Planning Association of Canada, which later evolved into the C.D. Howe Research Institute. Early work on economic modelling done by individual Economic Council of Canada economists such as Mike McCracken became the basis for some private economic forecasting firms such as McCracken's Ottawa-based Informetrica.

Private and Nongovernmental Public Policy Institutes

While the two councils referred to above were the creatures of government, they were joined in the 1970s by several other private and nongovernmental bodies that were only partly financed by government.[7] These included the C.D. Howe Research Institute, the Conference Board of Canada, the Institute for Research on Public Policy, the Fraser Institute, the Canadian Institute for Economic Policy, the Centre for Policy Alternatives, and the National Foundation for Public Policy Development. A complete list of policy research and advisory bodies would also have to include the Canadian Council on Social Development and bodies like the Canadian Tax Foundation and the Canada West Foundation.

While our brief review here cannot do justice to the work of each of these bodies, a summary profile of them is essential because their work in total reflects a wide range of ideas and because, in a fairly brief period of time, the public policy scene in Canada has changed from a situation in the early 1960s, where there were virtually no such external bodies, to one where there is a surfeit of such bodies, each jockeying for the attention of decision makers and the media and producing reports increasingly found on university and other educational course reading lists.

The C.D. Howe Research Institute (HRI) was founded in 1973 through a merger of the C.D. Howe Memorial Foundation and the Private Planning Association of Canada. The HRI exists to undertake research into Canadian economic policy issues, especially in the era of international finance and major government programs. HRI in particular builds on the earlier work of the Private Planning Association (PPA) an offshoot of the National Planning Association of the United States. The

PPA's Canadian-American Committee had sponsored work on Canada-U.S. relations since the mid-1950s. This legacy has led to a labelling of the C.D. Howe Research Institute as having strong continentalist leanings. Like most labels, this one is partly true and partly erroneous. It has certainly looked sympathetically at Canada-U.S. relations, but on an overall basis its reports can hardly be said to be dominated by continentalism. It has undertaken useful work on the question of the vulnerability of the Quebec economy and its annual policy reviews, while usually very critical of federal fiscal and energy policies in the late 1970s and early 1980s, have been quite measured in tone and substance. Its director, economist Carl Beigie, commanded considerable respect as an informed and responsible critic. In the midst of the 1979 election campaign, for example, a C.D. Howe report on the Clark Conservative party's proposal for the deductability of mortgage interest rates, then a major election issue, criticized the proposal as being both unfair, regressive and inefficient. If one had to locate the HRI on the ideological spectrum (admittedly a slippery business), it would have to be in a centrist or moderately right of centre position.

The Conference Board of Canada was initially just a modest branch plant of its American parent but in the 1970s greatly strengthened the independence of its operations in Canada. It does not view itself as a policy advisory or advocacy body but as a research body. It publishes research but does not take positions on its findings. Its quarterly economic forecasts and its reports on labour market data are probably the most respected private forecasting documents. The board's numerous large conferences and meetings are a forum for the exchange of views, particularly between business and government. Though several government departments are subscription members of the Conference Board, the board is still predominantly a conservative business organization. One of its former chairmen, Robert de Cotret, became the Minister of Economic Development in the short-lived Clark government of 1979.

The Institute for Research on Public Policy (IRPP) was founded in 1972 and given endowment funds initially provided by Ottawa but with Ottawa providing matching dollars for those raised by the Institute from the provincial and private sectors. Its first three presidents reflect the changing approach of the IRPP. Initially, it was viewed as a vehicle for long-term policy analysis. Its first director, Dr. J. Carrothers, took this temporal mandate somewhat too literally. Early work centred on such matters as the underlying demographic changes (clearly not an unimportant public policy determinant), but there were so few reports published that many wondered what had happened to the IRPP. This is merely another instance where the long run and short run frustrate each other. Carrothers' successor, however, was Michael Kirby who came from a position as senior policy advisor in the Prime Minister's Office. Kirby energetically mobilized the IRPP, improved its contacts with academics and with government and business, and quickly had the IRPP studying virtually everything. In short order the IRPP went from the excesses of the long run to the frenetic exigencies of the short run. When Kirby rejoined the federal Liberals as a key constitutional advisor in 1980, his place at the IRPP was taken by Gordon Robertson, former Clerk of the Privy Council. A more cautious individual, Robertson has reduced the pace of the IRPP research to a more manageable one.

The IRPP's connection to the government in the Kirby-Robertson interchange has undoubtedly given it a perceived Ottawa-Liberal tinge and a middle of the road position. This has happened despite its elaborate governing board of trustees which is drawn from a broad partisan and regional base and despite its numerous reports. Indeed, its reports have been so numerous since 1977 and have dealt with so many policy fields that it is impossible to detect a firm ideological position, other than the flexible fuzzy middle. As with some of the other councils and institutes, the IRPP's work is primarily the work of many individual authors rather than a considered institutional position.

Some of the earlier designers of the IRPP also envisioned it as serving, much as the Washington-based Brookings Institution had done, as a form of "bureaucracy in exile"; that is, as place where advisors who were out of power would have a place to conduct research, increase their knowledge and renew themselves for a return to power. The IRPP has brought in individuals such as David McDonald, a former Clark government minister, as resident fellows, but the bureaucracy in exile notion in which experts did their own research has never really caught hold. This was due not only because of the Ottawa-Liberal stripe created by the Kirby-Robertson team but also because of the obvious fact that the Liberals are virtually always in power. As we see below, this institutional absence prompted some Conservative party members to establish their own policy institute in 1982, despite the existence of the neoconservative Fraser Institute.

Located in Vancouver, the Fraser Institute was formed in the early 1970s with a more explicit conservative or market-based ideological rationale. Its objective is

> the redirection of public attention to the role of competitive markets in providing for the well-being of Canada. Where markets work, the Institute's interest lies in trying to discover prospects for improvement. Where markets do not work, its interest lies in finding the reasons. Where competitive markets have been replaced by government control, the interest of the Institute lies in documenting objectively the nature of the improvement or deterioration resulting from government intervention.[8]

Intellectually led by its director, Michael Walker, the Fraser Institute has published numerous studies which in fact usually do favour market solutions. These include studies of wage and price controls, industrial policy, rent controls, privatizing public enterprises, affirmative action programs and public sector labour relations. It has also published work in direct rebuttal to the views of the interventionist Science Council of Canada.

In 1982 the Canadian policy institutes on the political right were joined by the National Foundation for Public Policy Development. Forged partly in the context of a national Progressive Conservative policy conference, the foundation will not only conduct research from a conservative perspective but will attempt to be a forum for the nourishment of the "bureaucracy in exile" referred to above. While it is premature to judge this foundation, it is perhaps the first to link its role to what is undoubtedly a weakness of the Conservative party as a "government in waiting." The Tories have demonstrated their lack of disciplined preparation and research on the policies they will adopt on the assumption of power.

On the left of centre position on the ideological spectrum there are two policy institutes, the Canadian Institute for Economic Policy (CIEP) and the Centre for Policy Alternatives. The former is the body we portrayed above as a spin-off from the Science Council. The CIEP was established in 1976 and its nationalist and interventionist inclinations are reflected in its overall goal to "engage in public discussion of fiscal, industrial and other related public policies designed to strengthen Canada in a rapidly changing international environment."[9] It has published studies critical of monetarism, in defence of the National

Energy Program, and critical of previous industrial policies. It has also looked at specific industrial sectors such as energy and fisheries and the drug and automobile industries with a view to enhancing Canadian industrial benefits. The Centre for Policy Alternatives has to date produced little analysis. One of its initial reports was severely critical of the federal "6 and 5" program against public service unions. Thus, its overall concerns appear to encompass a broader social democratic perspective that spans industrial policy and includes social programs as well.

In addition to the above bodies there are other public policy institutes that have found a particular niche among this already imposing array of institutions. The Canadian Council on Social Development monitors social policy. The Canada West Foundation, formed in the mid-1970s, monitors and advocates policies favourable to an increased role for Western Canada in Confederation, including major studies of issues such as an elected Senate to strengthen regional representation in national institutions. The Canadian Tax Foundation and its journal, *The Canadian Tax Journal*, monitors taxing and overall spending in a general, technical and professional way. This traditional tax and expenditure watcher has been joined by others. The School of Public Administration at Carleton University in Ottawa publishes an annual review of federal expenditure priorities called *How Ottawa Spends Your Tax Dollars*.[10] A new journal, *Canadian Taxation*, based in the Osgoode Hall Law School, encourages articles that are more reformist and left of centre in perspective than those usually found in its much older competitor, the *Canadian Tax Journal*. The Institute of Intergovernmental Relations at Queen's University publishes work on several policy fields from a federal-provincial relations perspective, including an annual review of federal-provincial relations.

What does one make of the emergence of these numerous bodies? Canada has never had more policy analysis than it has now. While the cynic may be tempted to add that we have never had such unsuccessful public policy either, it would be unfair to link one to the other in a direct causal way. The institutes reflect both a healthy and worrisome trend. It is generally healthy to have a diverse market of ideas, advocates and studies. These are feeding into the general education process and provide some challenge to the earlier, virtual bureaucratic, monopoly of research and information. At the same time there are limits to how much analysis can be absorbed by decision makers, a point we have emphasized in Chapters 4 and 13. There are also problems in the links between these bodies and other political institutions, a point we review in more detail below in our discussion of Parliament and the media.

Royal Commissions and Task Forces

Royal commissions and task forces have been a favoured device used by numerous governments to analyze, evaluate and advocate public policy.[11] They are also the object of some ridicule because the inevitable short-term view of them is also governed by a scoreboard mentality. How much did the commission cost? How many recommendations did it make and how many were adopted by the government? Until the establishment of the Economic Council in 1963, royal commissions were arguably the only major external arms-length device for independent analysis. As pointed out in Chapter 12 and 13, royal commissions, task forces and other major study committees are not only an input to policy development but also an output, created in some instances to express symbolic concern, to "buy time" politically and/or to educate the public and involve groups in the policy process. Occasionally governments have followed up on commission reports by issuing White Papers or Green Papers, the former staking out a somewhat firmer position on the subject than the latter, but both being used to involve public interest groups and individual Canadians in some kind of further consultative exercise.[12]

To the extent that royal commissions engage in consultation, they are embroiled in all the dilemmas of consultation set out in Chapter 3. There can be little doubt that many major inquiries have served as a public catalyst for debate, and have produced or educated commission leaders and staff who have subsequently gone on to exercise influence in their own right in these fields by assuming positions of authority. In particular cases their main recommendations have been adopted, though usually only part of the cause can be attributed to the commission itself. Thus, the 1950s Gordon Commission on Canada's Economic Prospects helped set the agenda for later economic policy, the Massey Commission in culture and the arts, the Aird and the Fowler commissions on broadcasting and the Rowell-Sirois Commission in matters of federal-provincial fiscal relations. The Porter Commission influenced aspects of banking policy and the Hall Commission on Health Services added considerable impetus on the road to medicare. In the early 1980s a second

Hall Commission was used to build a renewed defence of medicare in the face of threats to its basic principles. In the 1960s there was also a Royal Commission on Bilingualism and Biculturalism which served as a major forum for the emotive debate about bilingualism. In addition, there was the Carter Commission on Taxation, some of whose effects were surveyed in Chapter 12. The McPherson Royal Commission on Transportation which reported in 1959 articulated and reinforced the broad nation-building role of transportation policy stressed in Chapters 1 and 15, as well as the controlled competition among "modes of transport" rather than among firms. In the early and mid-1970s the Berger Inquiry served as a forum which increased the consciousness of many Canadians about the interrelated issues of energy development, the north, the environment and Canada's native peoples.

By the 1970s the effect of any particular royal commission was all the more difficult to discern precisely because of the work of the new array of permanent policy institutes, as well as Senate committees and House of Commons committees and task forces. Moreover, several provincial inquiries earned national attention in fields such as nuclear and uranium policy, occupational health, and health care and social services.

Academics and Universities

There has always been a connection between academics as evaluators of various public policy fields and the world of royal commissions and policy institutes examined above, but the academic role is a broader one and filled with its own ambivalence and contradictions. The connection with royal commissions and policy institutes arises from the fact that individual academics are usually hired on contract to carry out many of the studies. Many are later recruited permanently into government work through this network.

Individual academics and universities as institutions face a double-edged sword regarding their role and independence in policy analysis. Universities must have a primary concern for the promotion of high-quality research and free, independent inquiry. At the same time, they are very dependent upon government grants and are under constant pressure to produce or do so-called "relevant" applied research. Many universities have set up special policy institutes in different policy fields funded in whole or in part by line departments of government. These exist in the energy, resource, agriculture, mining, transportation and social policy fields.

New pressures have also been created for academics by the existence of the other policy institutes described above. One problem concerns the mode of academic publishing and communication. The classic forum for academic communication is publication in scholarly journals which accept articles after they have been reviewed ("refereed") by other academic experts. But the new institutes, aided by word processing technology, have become adept at churning out studies at a pace that forces academics to face the realities of modern communication. New pressures exist as to how much effort researchers should devote to communicating their research to their peers and to students through teaching, and how much to the country's decision makers who have no time to read academic articles given existing pressures on their time, given the new volume of studies being spewed out by the policy institutes and other bodies, and taking into account their sensitivity to, and dependence on, day-to-day media coverage and the perceptions of policy that media relations help induce. The need and the pressure to communicate research through the mass media also creates new tensions between journalists and academics and among researchers, some of who become good "journalistic" communicators, but often only at the cost of the disapproval of their more traditional colleagues. Academics are also extremely and justifiably skeptical of the need imposed by the media to say something brief in a "three-minute interview" when the subject is complex, as it almost always is.

There is also a regional and international connection to the role of Canadian academics and universities which parallels the broader features of Canadian political life. Thus, there is often a deserved suspicion of academics and universities in the Toronto-Ottawa-Montreal axis by academics elsewhere in Canada. There is also a strong connection between Canadian academic voices and internationally prestigious academics, universities and institutes. Certain basic policy paradigms such as monetarism or Keynesianism are international commodities, as, of course, are most of the key ideas of political life.

The connection between academics and political parties is of a distinctly mixed kind. Socialist and social democratic thinkers have had a fairly close link to the NDP, but it is not without its stresses, including those between intellectuals and union leaders. The Liberals as the perpetual governing party have garnered intellectual support sometimes out of genuine belief but often because of their control of the spoils of office and contract funding. The Progressive Conservatives have had too few academics who were prepared to associate themselves with the Tory party, although this sad state may be improving in the 1980s in the wake of neoconservative (it is really neoliberal), intellectual revival identified in Chapters 2 and 6.

Parliament, Political Parties, the Auditor General and the Media

At first glance this quartet of institutions might seem to be an unholy alliance in the business of public policy evaluation. In keeping with our view that key institutions must be understood in relation to each other rather than in isolation, we believe that the realities of analysis and the prospects for reform are best understood by looking at them together. In previous chapters we have stressed four major aspects of the role of Parliament in the policy process. Its major role arises out of the fact that the government must constantly anticipate its partisan Parliamentary critics. This is a form of evaluation of no small importance. Second, Parliament is above all a place of partisanship, adversary politics, and political party discipline, where the rules of want of confidence in the government severely restrain the ability of individual members of Parliament to take initiatives and where admitting errors is extremely difficult.[13] Third, the power to initiate most legislation and to initiate all money bills resides with the government. Finally, the second and third points conspire to create weak committees, since the selection of topics and issues and the funding of adequate staff is also a governmental prerogative. While the package reforms adopted by Parliament in 1982 strengthened the committee process, it still did not fundamentally challenge the essential discipline of Cabinet-Parliamentary government conducted through political parties.

When one adds the mass media to this setting, certain features of public policy analysis are accentuated and others are stifled. The media, interested first in "news," feed on the partisanship of the House of Commons and the personalities within it. Issues and ideas are not totally ignored, but the attention span of the media, aided by ritualistic monthly events such as the updated unemployment and inflation statistics and public opinion polls, produces an often ludicrous short-run time frame. It contributes to the importance of perception and to instant evaluation that usually underplays ideas and their persistence over time. There are, of course, many good (and bad) "in-depth" (that is, full page or one half-hour) analyses of particular policy fields and issues. The media also dutifully reports on the content of major studies by the several policy bodies examined above. But the limits to evaluation of this kind are acknowledged to be severe by both journalists and their critics. The media coverage of the House of Commons includes television coverage of Question Period and the House as a whole but not its committees. Only in the case of the 1981 special committee on the constitution has a committee's work been televised. For the first time it allowed Canadians to see M.P.'s in something other than the bearpit partisanship of question period. Moreover, it allowed Canadians to see the testimony of interest groups in a direct way rather than through the screening role of the media itself. The failure to extend television coverage to committees is perhaps the greatest single weakness in the modern role of Parliament in a strict accountability sense.

All of the above must be kept in clear perspective, however. Television coverage of Parliament, in an age of massive public choice in home entertainment, will not top the ratings. Partisanship and party discipline serve useful democratic purposes despite their weakness in other aspects of more narrowly defined policy evaluation. Parliamentary committees from time to time show a modest streak of independence. For example, as we saw in Chapter 17, in the field of labour market policy a 1981 Parliamentary task force reached quite different social conclusions and emphasized different ideas than the efficiency-oriented Dodge Report prepared for the Liberal government.

There are also inherent limits, just as there are with ministers, in the capacity and inclination of M.P.s, even when aided by increased personnel and committee staff, to absorb all or even most of the incoming reports and information. While the reports and studies of the various policy institutes are sometimes read by M.P.s, there is not institutional focus within Parliament to focus on or use such studies. For example, the annual reviews of the Economic Council of Canada have never been the basis of focused committee work or other debates in the House. It must also be remembered that M.P.s have roles other than that of policy critics. They are also engaged in constituency matters, including weekly travel to their home political base, as well as committee work.

The Auditor General of Canada (A.G.) is an officer of Parliament whose role in, and views of, evaluation reflect the contradictions inherent in the Parliamentary-political party-media nexus.[14] As an expenditure watchdog the A.G. has played an important role, particularly in alliance with the media, for whom he is both good copy as well as a heroic gladiator against the bureaucratic dragons. For most of its history, the A.G. "evaluated" spending in relation to the idea of honesty and probity. He was, in short, a traditional "auditor." In Chapter 12 we saw how in the early 1970s auditing became something different. Articulating—indeed, preaching—the need for "value for money" auditing, the A.G. tried and in part succeeded in selling the view that if only managers would seriously try to set objectives and evaluate results, one could discover government's "bottom line" and keep government accountable. The refurbished A.G.'s office would not itself evaluate programs but would now ensure that the right systems were in place. To this extent it would also conduct comprehensive audits.[15] Thus, the views and advocacy of a knowledge profession—accountants—were brought to bear and indeed were expanded to provide an even more comprehensive scope to their self-styled role.

The A.G.'s view was alas premised on a truly heroic assumption that "systems" and processes were somehow distinctly separate from policy and program substance and that by identifying objectives and measuring results "caused" by different program elements one could not only achieve economy and efficiency and get things right, but also keep ministers accountable. The A.G. also believed that providing more objective and better information to M.P.'s would close the accountability gap. Evaluation, moreover, was viewed to be clearly distinct from "policy analysis." Thus, the work of the other policy institutes examined above was not viewed as evaluation.

The new auditing teams would be anchored by accountants but would include other discipline experts as well. Though he called the new process "comprehensive auditing," a natural outgrowth of his own accounting profession, the A.G. in fact had an unbridled faith in social science methods that virtually no social scientist would dare to have. Evaluation was viewed almost exclusively as cerebral cogitation and not social interaction. It deals with objectives and not with the scope of ideas that exist. Parliamentary government would be the chief beneficiary of the auditing "revolution," when in fact there was little thought given to the real dynamics of Parliament and its capability to absorb new information, even if one could assume that the studies would be well done, that is, both the comprehensive audit studies and the "actual" evaluations carried out by central agencies or departments.

The A.G.'s role is not to be dismissed glibly. There is a role for auditing. Honesty and probity are important ideas and watchdogs are needed. The later pitch by the A.G. for "value for money" is an appeal for efficiency in a broad sense—again, an important idea whose power is not to be underestimated and for which there is a deservedly significant political constituency. There are, moreover, problems of expenditure control, as we saw in Chapter 11. But the broader effort by the A.G. to peddle these concepts as a virtual theory of governing is filled with contradictions and represents a failure to understand the broader nature of politics and public policy, and of the ultimate balance that is needed in the evaluation process between formal analysis and social interaction. It fails, moreover, to understand the relationships among major political institutions and policy and program areas.

We have focused in this section on the relations among the media, Parliament, political parties and the Auditor General precisely to highlight the key questions involved in the evaluation process. We have by no means fully covered the subject, however. Parliament, for example, also has an evaluation role through the work of the Public Service Commission, the Commissioner of Official Languages and the Human Rights Commission. These institutions reflect other ideas including the "merit principle," which is rooted in the right of individual Canadians who are qualified to compete for available government jobs; language rights which embrace both a collective idea of Canada's linguistic duality as well as the language rights of individual Canadians; and individual rights including prohibitions against discrimination.

Parliament also includes the Senate where a less partisan atmosphere prevails. Senate committees have held hearings and published good reports on numerous policy fields and issues, including poverty, agricultural stabilization, science policy, the mass media, Canada-United States trade relations, and regional policy, to name only a few. The role of the Senate as a regional forum has never been strong due to its lack of electoral legitimacy and the peculiar construction of the regional divisions on which Senate seats are based. If, as is possible, an elected regionally based Senate was established, then a new layer of regional evaluation could be added to blunt the apparent monopoly voice of provincial premiers as the allegedly only legitimate regional representatives.

Interest Groups and Other Governments

Last, but certainly far from least in the already imposing analytical arsenal of Canadian public policy, are interest groups and other governments, provincial, local and foreign. In Chapter 3 we focused on the evolving structure and influence of the major business-producer and collective rights or public interest groups. We stressed their role not only in initiating change but also in stabilizing relations and preserving the status quo. Such groups are an essential aspect of the evaluation process. They maintain constant contact with officials and monitor and study public policies not only in the different policy fields which most concern them (be it in banking, competition policy or social services and education) but also in an aggregate sense.

For example, in 1977 macro business associations such as the Canadian Manufacturer's Association (CMA) responded to the federal government's discussion papers, *The Way Ahead* and *Agenda for Cooperation*. The CMA policy document "Agenda for Action" focused on policies to strengthen the market system.[16] In 1981 and 1982 the Business Council on National Issues conducted an extensive, indeed, in business quarters, unprecedented detailed and intense debate on incomes policy. Five years earlier in-depth discussions of such a heretical topic would have been anathema to most of the corporate heads with membership in the BCNI. Three of the major associations also collaborated to coordinate their views about regulatory reform both during and after the Economic Council's study referred to in Chapters 5 and 12. These macro evaluative exercises are in addition to their normal activity in the pre-Budget Speech period when the associations lobby the Minister of Finance and present their own evaluation of the state of the economy.

Similarly, on the other side of the interest group coin labour federations such as the Canadian Labour Congress have submitted a stream of briefs on both macro issues and a host of policy fields from industrial relations to pensions and occupational health and safety policies. Public interest groups, though always leery of their fragile finances, have been active not only in presenting briefs but also in appearing before hearings and in appealing for support through the media.

We will not repeat here all the problems and internal tensions among interest groups, which we reviewed in Chapter 3 and elsewhere. These affect their capacity to evaluate, the quality of their formal studies, the level and range of expertise they can afford to hire, and how their evaluations are perceived and dealt with by decision makers. What cannot be disputed is that they are heavily involved in the full range of analytical activities. Moreover, they interact with other forums of evaluation such as royal commissions, policy institutes and Parliament. In addition, interest groups or segments of these groups, including large individual firms or unions, are fully capable of aligning themselves with and securing the support of provincial governments, depending upon the particular configuration of a province's economy.

Provincial and foreign governments are also particularly well equipped to take on Ottawa's expertise. Provinces, particularly the larger ones, can call on their own battery of analysts in most of the major policy fields. They possess some degree of power to back up their evaluative preferences at least on a selective basis, depending upon when, where and how they may wish to challenge Ottawa. The analytical tentacles and power of foreign governments and international agencies are also of increasing importance. The release of studies by American agencies may trigger the need for a Canadian response, particularly in fields such as health and safety where the media often pick up American sources more readily than Canadian sources.[17] The General Agreement on Tariffs and Trade (GATT) arrangements add an expanding evaluative forum for foreign governments as the definition of nontariff trade barriers widens to include many policy fields previously viewed to be domestic issues. The studies, comparative data and forums of discussion supplied by the Organization for Economic Cooperation and Development (OECD), NATO, the World Bank, and the United Nations also exert pressure on Ottawa in particular policy fields and in relation to overall economic performance.

Policy Fields and the Dynamics of Analysis and Evaluation

It is only in the light of this broader array of institutions, structures and perceptions by knowledge groups and professions that the realities of policy analysis and evaluation in general and in particular policy fields can be fully appreciated. The experience of the Department of Energy, Mines and Resources with energy policy, the Department of Industry,

Trade and Commerce in industrial policy, and of the Department of Manpower and Immigration and its renamed successor, Employment and Immigration Canada, with the labour market, manpower training and job creation fields illustrates the analytical dynamics and dilemmas. Experience shows the importance of a climate of political receptivity for the findings of evaluation studies and illustrates the way analysis through social interaction operates sometimes parallel to, but separate from, formal evaluation studies. An appreciation is also required of the potential cumulative influence of several studies and reports over time.

In the case of energy policy and the relations between EMR and the central agencies, two illustrative examples can be cited, one concerning the NEP itself and the other concerning the Canadian Home Insulation Program (CHIP), which pre-dates the NEP but which was affected by it.[18] In the case of the NEP it is possible to argue that at a broad political level, including the forum of electoral politics, evaluation was occuring all the time. In the pre-NEP and post-1973 OPEC period several kinds of evaluation were conducted. These included internal central agency and EMR reviews which led to the prime minster's energy pronouncements of December 1973 (including the decision to create Petro-Canada), as well as the EMR exercise which led to the 1976 report, *An Energy Strategy for Canadians*. The Berger inquiry was also a form of evaluation of aspects of energy policy. In the year prior to the NEP's announcement the Clark government assessed and tried to devise its own overall energy policy. Meanwhile, the Liberals in opposition, both prior to and during the 1980 election, had assessed and forged major elements of what became the NEP. The EMR bureaucracy was also preparing its case in the wake of the failed negotiations with Alberta.

None of the above assessments can be said to have been constructed on the analytical base of elegant formal program evaluations of the then existing *program* elements of energy policy. As an aside, it is useful to note that there is no uniform way of defining what a program is. For example, the NEP is a National Energy *Program*. EMR's activity for the purposes of presenting the Estimates to Parliament is composed of two programs. But many other elements of EMR's activity are also called programs (for example, the off-oil program, the Special Atlantic Canada program). The Comptroller General of Canada refers to the existence of both "big-P" and "little-p" programs. In EMR some studies of big and little programs were carried out, but the overall process was a much broader one. It is difficult to see in practical terms how evaluation could be carried out in any other way given the intricate political, economic, regional and social issues involved. There were undoubtedly major examples where more formal evaluation and prior analysis may have or could have helped. For example, the Petroleum Incentives Program (PIPs) was not preceded by extensive formal analysis. Rather, it became a program element of the NEP almost automatically once it was decided that the NEP would encourage *Canadian* firms operating in the Canada Lands, and that the tax system incentives had therefore to be replaced in part by a system of grants. It was, moreover, difficult to estimate future costs, a point we stressed in Chapter 12 in our review of the energy envelope. More analysis may have helped, but in the final analysis the PIPs element was an act of political judgement.

A second energy example is the CHIP program. Established in the mid-1970s to encourage the installation of energy saving insulation in Canadian homes through limited grants to householders, CHIP was initially a program operated by Canada Mortgage and Housing Corporation. When the NEP was passed, it included a further program of grants to encourage Canadians to switch from oil to other fuel sources. In one sense this new post-NEP program necessitated an evaluation of CHIP, but the situation was in fact far more complicated. A formal CHIP evaluation was undertaken by EMR in 1982, but it was preceded by other less elegant but equally real evaluations operating at a distinctly political level through social interactions. CHIP had led to many "fly by night" operators in the insulation industry and virtually every Member of Parliament had dozens of "horror" stories to tell. Moreover, CHIP grants were also embroiled in a health and safety controversy concerning urea-formalde-hyde insulation. Thus, more than energy issues were involved in the CHIP evaluation. Later, as the formal CHIP evaluation proceeded, the size of the federal deficit and the need to save money entered the CHIP evaluation agenda. The net effect was that the CHIP program was changed in 1982, but the changes could only be partially, indeed tenuously, attributed to the formal evaluation study, part of which had not yet even been concluded. The CHIP example is not cited as an argument against doing or attempting to build into large programs a formal evaluation component. Rather, it is cited to show the interaction between different forums, levels and modes of evaluation.

In the field of industrial policy, our analysis in Chapter 15 showed the litany of studies, consultative processes and other modes of assessment carried out from a variety of ideological perspectives and dealing with different components of industrial policy. These included ITC's numerous reports by its trade commissioner service, its own initiation of the 23 sector task forces, studies by the Senate Foreign Affairs Committee and the Economic Council of Canada on trade relations with the United States, several reports on competition policy, the Watkins and the Gray reports, and the Science Council's advocacy documents on controlling foreign investment, and several evaluation exercises on regional policy and research and development policies.

In the field of manpower training and labour market policy, similar aspects of evaluation can be cited over the entire period from the late 1960s to the early 1980s as studies were carried out and the climate of receptivity for change was altered. A 1968 study by the Economic Council of Canada showed major problems with the then new training programs and also revealed problems of how one evaluated them.[19] In the mid-1970s the main department involved, Employment and Immigration Canada, had produced internal studies that showed the economic weakness of the training and job creation programs. So did a 1976 Economic Council of Canada study, *People and Jobs*.[20] But the early 1970s were a time of relative prosperity and even the private sector was not complaining too vociferously about the programs. Moreover, the training programs were the subject of a federal-provincial agreement and so could not be easily changed, especially given other elements of a crowded federal-provincial agenda. By the late 1970s, however, as we have seen in Chapters 11, 15, 16 and 17, the economic climate changed and similar things said about manpower training in the earlier 1970s now gained a more receptive hearing. In part this evaluation was transmitted through the 23 sector task forces exercise in 1978, through the effort by the then new central agency, MSED, to foster a concern for economic development and, finally, by the Dodge Task Force itself which articulated a primary concern for efficiency.[21]

A brief glimpse at these energy, industrial and manpower training examples indicates some of the inevitable difficulties faced by the Office of the Comptroller General (OCG). Established in 1977 to oversee and encourage the development of evaluation systems in all departments and agencies, the OCG confronts all the dilemmas inherent in the evaluation game.[22] Its mandate deals with formal evaluation studies and systems. It must attempt to schedule regular evaluations over about a five-year cycle of virtually the entire expenditure base of government, but which is comprised, as we noted above, of entities "programs" whose boundaries are not clearly fixed. It is also caught in the middle of different views regarding the purposes and levels of evaluation. As we stressed early in the chapter, the OCG cannot fully adhere to the needs of the Auditor General because the latter is most interested in accountability and "value for money." The OCG must also adapt to the needs of departmental managers who may want evaluations to help improve certain operations and to central agency analysts who impatiently want assessments "not next month but *now!*"

The analytical dilemmas are evident, but decisions about what is an ex-post evaluation obviously involve judgements about the temporal dimension of all policies. Is a problem, policy or program to be judged to be mature in terms of its perceived or real effects over one year? Five years? Ten years? Other pressures are also obvious. Is the evaluation part of a larger planning exercise requested by the central agencies or one emanating from the "bottom-up" by line managers? If so, then how much time, energy and resources are to be spent on formal evaluations and studies? Judgemental issues arise about whether the reality of the political agenda allows time for analysis of this kind. Will it produce better decisions? Does it yield more acceptable decisions? Does too much analysis produce paralysis and an incapacity to make decisions, or will routine incessant evaluation produce complacency and a lack of attention to emerging problems?

The answers to such questions obviously vary according to the different levels and purposes of evaluation as well. Are we evaluating the government as a whole or individual ministers to keep them accountable? Is our concern one of economic and social policy in general, or specific elements within these fields (for example, trade policy or family allowances)? Are we judging specific projects such as the Alaska Pipeline or Mirabel airport which invariably involve several policy and program fields *concurrently?* Do we evaluate programs and projects on the basis of our relations with different foreign countries or in relation to different regions within Canada?

Concluding Observations

It is rational for people to want to set objectives for public policy and to analyze and evaluate performance. It is irrational to expect that formal evaluation studies can or should lead to changed public policy behaviour in any direct causal or automatic way. This is because evaluation and analysis are both a cerebral and a social activity in which it is never easy to separate the past (ex post "evaluation") from the present and the future (analysis) and in which causality in the social science sense of objective knowledge is the exception and not the rule. Analysis involves social interaction because interests are often able to act purposefully to counter the findings of a study or to limit action taken in response to such a study. It is also the ideas of political life that happily and persistently get in the way of pristine formal studies. This is merely another way of saying, as we said in Chapter 13, that knowledge is usually not power, and of reasserting that the ideas and the dynamic relations *among* structures and institutions must be understood even when it is maddeningly difficult to do. Analysis is in part dependent upon the timeliness of studies and the existence of a climate of receptivity. At the same time within the rubric of formal evaluation studies there are important issues about the methodologies used, the temporal and other "program" boundaries arbitrarily set, the quality and reliability of the data, and the explicit or implicit assumptions and advocacy stances of the persons, institutions, and professional experts conducting and interpreting the analysis.

NOTES

1. See Harry Rogers, "Program Evaluation in the Federal Government," in G. Bruce Doern and Allan Maslove, eds., *The Public Evaluation of Government Spending* (Montreal: Institute for Research on Public Policy, 1979), pp. 79-90; W. Irwin Gillespie, "Fools' Gold: The Quest for a Method of Evaluating Government Spending," in Doern and Maslove, *op. cit.*, pp. 39-60; D. Nachmias, *Public Policy Evaluation Approaches and*

Methods (New York: St. Martin's Press, 1978); Aaron Wildavsky, *Speaking Truth to Power: The Art and Craft of Policy Analysis* (Boston: Little Brown, 1979); and Arnold J. Meltsner, *Policy Analysts in the Bureaucracy* (Berkeley: University of California Press, 1976). See also Guy Benveniste, *The Politics of Expertise* (Berkeley: University of California Press, 1973). For a review of institutions similar to those reviewed in this chapter but cast in the context of "participation," see L. G. Smith, "Canadian Participation Mechanisms," *Canadian Public Policy,* Vol. VIII, No. 4 (Autumn 1982), pp. 561-572.

2. See Leonard Rutman, *Planning Useful Evaluations* (Beverly Hills: Sage Publications, 1980). Rutman's views are of more than just passing interest because he was one of the main advisors to the Auditor General of Canada in the late 1970s and early 1980s.

3. See Harry Rogers, *op. cit.;* S.L. Sutherland, "On the Audit Trail of the Auditor General: Parliament's Servant 1973-1980," *Canadian Public Administration,* Vol. 23, No. 4 (Winter, 1980), pp. 616-645; H.G. Rogers, M.A. Ulrich and K.L. Traversy, "Evaluation in Practice: the State of the Art in Canadian Governments," *Canadian Public Administration,* Vol. 24, No. 3 (Fall, 1981), pp. 371-386; and R. Dobell and David Zussman, "An Evaluation System for Government: If Politics is Theatre Then Evaluation is (Mostly) Art," *Canadian Public Administration,* Vol. 24, No. 3 (Fall, 1981), pp. 404-427.

4. Michael Prince, "Policy Advisory Groups in Government Departments," in G. Bruce Doern and Peter Aucoin, eds., *Public Policy in Canada* (Toronto: Macmillan of Canada, 1979), Chapter 10.

5. See articles on the two councils by Phidd and Doern, respectively, in G. Bruce Doern and Peter Aucoin, eds., *The Structures of Policy Making in Canada* (Toronto: Macmillan of Canada, 1971), Chapters 8 and 9.

6. On the Council's first decade see, Richard W. Phidd, "The Economic Council of Canada 1963-1974," *Canadian Public Administration,* Vol. 18, No. 3, 1975. On the Science Council's work and criticisms of it see John N.H. Britton and James Gilmour, *The Weakest Link: A Technological Perspective on Canadian Industrial Underdevelopment* (Ottawa: Science Council of Canada, 1978); Donald J. Daly, "Weak Links in 'The Weakest Link'," *Canadian Public Policy,* Volume V, No. 3 (Summer 1979), pp. 307-317; and A.E. Safarian, "Foreign Ownership and Industrial Behaviour," *Canadian Public Policy,* Volume V, No. 3 (Summer 1979), pp. 318-336.

7. On the larger international world of policy institutes, see Paul Dickson, *Think Tanks* (New York: Ballantine Books, 1971). See also Ronald Ritchie, *An Institute for Research on Public Policy* (Ottawa: Information Canada, 1971).

8. This statement of purpose can be found on the inside cover of any of the Fraser Institute's reports.

9. See any of the CIEP's reports for this stated purpose.

10. See Chapters 11 and 12 where some of this work is incorporated into this book as well.

11. See V. Seymour Wilson, "The Role of Royal Commissions and Task Forces," in G. Bruce Doern and Peter Aucoin, eds., *The Structures of Policy Making in Canada* (Toronto: Macmillan of Canada, 1971), Chapter 4; M.J. Trebilcock, R.S. Prichard, D.G. Hartle and D.N. Dewees, *The Choice of Governing Instruments* (Ottawa: Minister of Supply and Services, 1982), Chapter 4; and Liora Salter and Debra Slaco, *Public Inquiries in Canada* (Ottawa: Science Council of Canada, 1981).

12. See Audrey Doerr, "The Role of Coloured Papers," *Canadian Public Administration,* Vol. 25, No. 3 (Fall, 1982), pp. 366-379. See also L.G. Smith, *op. cit.*

13. See Robert J. Jackson and Michael M. Atkinson, *The Canadian Legislative System,* Second Edition (Toronto: Macmillan of Canada, 1980); and T. d'Aquino, G. Bruce Doern and C. Blair, *Parliamentary Government in Canada; A Critical Assessment and Suggestions for Change* (Ottawa: Intercounsel Ltd., 1979).

14. See Auditor General of Canada, *Annual Report 1980* (Ottawa: Minister of Supply and Services, 1980) and S.L. Sutherland, *op. cit.*

15. James J. Macdonell, "Comprehensive Auditing—A New Approach to Public Sector Accountability in Canada." Paper presented to the Second Seminar of Senior Government Audit Institutions, Mexico City (May 14, 1980). For a private accounting firm's approach to comprehensive auditing, see Coopers and Lybrand, *Clear: An Approach to Comprehensive Auditing* (Ottawa: Coopers and Lybrand, 1982).

16. See Canadian Manufacturer's Association, *Agenda for Action* (Toronto: September, 1977).

17. See G. Bruce Doern, *The Politics of Risk in Canada* (Toronto: Royal Commission on Issues of Health and Safety Arising Out of the Use of Asbestos in Ontario, 1982).

18. G. Bruce Doern and Glen Toner, *The NEP and the Politics of Energy* (Toronto: Methuen, 1984). Chapter 11.

19. Economic Council of Canada, *Eighth Annual Review* (Ottawa: Queen's Printer, 1968).

20. Economic Council of Canada, *People and Jobs* (Ottawa: Information Canada, 1976).

21. Employment and Immigration Canada, *Labour Market Development in the 1980s* (Ottawa: Minister of Supply and Services, 1981).

22. See Harry Rogers, *op. cit.*

CHAPTER 19

THE STUDY AND PRACTICE OF
CANADIAN PUBLIC POLICY

The study and the practice of Canadian public policy are not the separate
worlds they are often alleged to be. Both must deal with the slippery task
of discovering causal relations among complex social structures and
institutions. Both must interpret and understand the ideas that lie
beneath the rhetoric of political debate. Both must understand that while
personalities and individual decision makers matter, ideas and structures
persist well beyond their current encumbents. Both must deal with the
problems posed by uncertainty.

In this book we have viewed public policy as an interplay between
ideas, structures and processes. Our final task is to provide our concluding
views about this approach and to offer some observations which emerge
from its use about the practice of public policy in Canada, especially in the
past two decades, a period bounded primarily by the Trudeau era.

We have stressed throughout the book that understanding Ottawa's
decisions and the theory and practice of Canadian public policy are not
easy tasks. One must look at policy fields historically, as well as in the
context of short-term constraints. Part I provided the basic concepts
necessary to deal with the subject—an appreciation of the environment
of Canadian political life; an understanding of the importance of the key
political institutions, including the relations *among* them, and the ideas
embedded in them; the role of different levels of normative content,
including ideologies and dominant ideas; the role of interests and interest
groups and the dilemmas of consultation; the main features of the public
policy routine and the dilemmas of doing first things first; the
importance of major governing instruments such as taxation, expenditure, regulation, public enterprise and exhortation; and, finally, the other
contending approaches for studying public policy and the ideologies and
ideas embedded in them. In Parts II and III we have related these
concepts in two different but necessary and complementary ways. Part II
examined the detailed structures and processes of the public policy

system with the focus on the Ottawa executive arena and the ways in which ideas, structures and processes relate to actual resource allocation and priority setting and to knowledge and information. Part III examined the broadest economic, social and foreign policy fields and then looked at the historical evolution of three policy fields, industrial policy, energy policy and labour market policy. Our concern here was not only to examine three critically important fields, but also to show how a focus on ideas in particular could help provide a way of examining any policy field, including fields not examined in detail in this book. This helps bring some order to the otherwise daunting task of finding some common ground among policy fields as diverse as cultural policy, policies for the aged and fisheries policy.

Ideas, Structures and Processes

Canadian public policy is best viewed as an interplay among ideas, structures and processes in which the direction of causality operates both ways, from society and economy to politics and government and vice versa. The validity of our approach rests upon both logic and evidence but must be seen as well in relation to the weakness of other approaches in meeting both of these tests. Our defence on logical grounds can be summarily presented. Ideas are a central element, not in some abstract philosophical sense but because ideas are inherent in behaviour and are present in structure and process. Ideas are not separate from "data," they *are* in many ways data. Ideas operate on both the input and output sides of the political system. The ideas we focus on are of two kinds and they are interrelated. The first kind include the general ideologies as well as the dominant ideas of efficiency, individual liberty, stability, redistribution and equality, equity, national identity and integration, and regional sensitivity. The second kind are the ideas embedded in key political institutions and in the relations among them, including the idea of responsible Cabinet-Parliamentary government, individual and collective ministerial responsibility, the idea of the policy-administration dichotomy between ministers and bureaucrats, the idea of freedom of association and the right to be consulted, freedom of the press, and the centralization and decentralization ideas inherent in federalism itself. These ideas do not exist in some abstract environment only but are present in the structure of public policy as power is organized and resources are allocated. Structures in the executive of Cabinet-Parliamentary government are not merely passive receptacles "pragmatically" responding to the forces outside it nor are they dominated only by powerful personalities. Pragmatism too often implies the existence of idea-less politics and policy. It is a term which provides a smokescreen behind which one can avoid the asking of important questions and where ideas are expunged in a way that defies reality. Ideas are also inherent in process, that is, in the need to deal with uncertainty and with the dynamics which occur when several (usually *good*) ideas clash over what to do in the future and when ideologies help guide conduct and/or foreclose certain options both among Canada's political parties and within them.

In asserting the presence and persistence of ideas we are not arguing that the ideas are always presented in a pristine form. We have seen how they are often reflected in the changing rhetorical language of general political debate or in the idiocyncratic terminology of particular policy fields. Thus, ideas are reflected in concepts such as "the just society," the "community of communities" concept, a "climate for investment," "productive jobs," "Canadianization," "industrial democracy," "universal social programs," the "targeting" of social spending and others explored in previous chapters. But ideas are nonetheless present, and the first pre-eminent task of policy analysis is to penetrate the rhetoric and examine the underlying ideas.

The identification of a few core ideas also helps us deal with the legitimate question often raised about public policy studies, namely, what is the common core among such diverse policy fields as agriculture, medicare, transportation and youth policies. The answer lies, partially at least, in looking first for the core ideas, a much more manageable task and one that makes each field intrinsically more interesting. Each policy field does, of course, have other ideas or concepts within it that may or may not be linked to, or be a subset of, the larger ideas. Thus, other ideas are also present such as "the right to life," the work ethic, the right to privacy, the right to a safe working environment, the right to self-determination, the right of commercial privilege, the confidentiality of the doctor-patient relationship, and so on.

In asserting the advantages of an approach that stresses the interplay between ideas, structures and processes, we are invariably expressing our dissatisfaction with the other major approaches examined in some detail in Chapter 6 and referred to throughout the book. None of them on their own offer a very satisfying description or explanation of reality or encompass the full range of ideas that exist. While each offers insights of great value, particularly about the existence of particular ideas and ideologies, each is separately flawed in a major way.

The rational model undoubtedly retains some normative appeal as to how decisions ought to be made, especially among some professional knowledge groups. But it is flawed in that it assumes that there is virtually no difference between the public and private sectors and fails to deal with the importance of coercion and power. It too easily assumes that knowledge is power and "the facts" will carry the day in an orderly, planned way. Incrementalism implants an appreciation of the importance of marginal choice and the need to take small steps so as to avoid large errors and to deal with limited information. It fails, however, to deal with the full range of ideas by focusing seemingly on one idea only, the need for consensus. Through a focus on small marginal adjustments, it cannot explain either major changes or the persistence of dominant ideas over time.

The public choice approach usefully challenges the meaning of what the "public interest" is, rather than assuming its existence in any automatic self-evident way. It is flawed, however, in that it reduces virtually all behaviour to self-interest and to remorseless electoral calculus and hence ignores broader ideas. Its prime reformist concern seems to be the efficient construction of the proper incentives to make decision makers behave properly. It also virtually denies the existence of structure and organization, its advocates apparently believing that the latter can be summed up by what organizational leaders do.

The class analysis approach focuses in a critically important way on how relations of political power are set in the basic system of production and property inherent in capitalism. It forces one to deal with the idea of equality and the redistribution of power and income. Its weakness is that it asserts economic determinism in as calculating a way as does the public choice approach. In the Canadian case, the class analysis approach has an extraordinary tendency to treat virtually all other ideas except redistribution and inequality as "distortions" and as being, in a sense, unreal. Regionalism and nationalism, the territorial bases of policy, are given short shrift and/or reduced to veiled expressions of suppressed class politics. The idea of stability and the existence of uncertainty seem to be only indirectly acknowledged. While the class analysis approach now recognizes the relative autonomy of the state and hence concedes some two-way interplay, it is evident that not much autonomy is conceded, since this would invite notions that the state was not as subject to the forces of capitalism as the model and its underlying beliefs require.

Thus, for each of these approaches there are limits beyond which their advocates cannot allow themselves to go without invalidating their ideology, core idea or the model of human behaviour which they hold. This tendency is neither to be applauded nor cursed. It is merely inevitable and is itself an expression of the existence of ideas in public policy and in how policies are evaluated. The same can be said in some degree about our approach. All of the major approaches reviewed in Chapter 6, however, are inadequate in a further way, namely in their failure to deal in any realistic way with the relationships among institutions and structures, and with the critical role of governing instruments, all of which also embody diversity of ideas.

The logical and empirical aspects of our approach are related. The major empirical evidence of a two-way interplay between society and economy on the one hand and government on the other is found in the growth of governing instruments chronicled in Chapter 6 and examined further in Chapters 11 and 12. While other approaches may be inclined to try to explain this growth in a one-dimensional way as either caused by a capitalist economy in crisis or by expansionary bureaucrats, we think there is ample evidence to support the view that a dynamic interplay is a more plausible explanation, especially when policies and decisions are viewed over longer periods of time. The state undoubtedly makes decisions in response to its environment, but these decisions, in turn, affect private behaviour. The growth of social regulation in the health and safety field in the 1960s and 1970s was in part a response to social pressure, but it also produced decisions and policies to which private interests had to and did respond. The ebb and flow between economic and social priorities examined in Chapter 10 reflects both responsiveness to pressures and a society reacting to previous governmental policies. The growth in the complexity of the tax system is a reflection of actions by the state and of private sector reaction to it.

Other major individual policy examples also suggest the plausibility of the two-way direction of causality. The entrenchment of a Charter of

Rights in the Canadian Constitution was an act of political will. There had been some social pressure to enact such a charter, but it was hardly overwhelming in the context of other priorities in the late 1970s and early 1980s. The evolution of Canadian energy policy shows that the National Oil Policy of 1961 was promoted by the multinationals, but it can hardly be said that it was forced upon government decision makers. The latter made the decision to adopt it and the policy was not widely opposed at the time. The adoption of the National Energy Program in 1980 was an act of aggressive intervention to which energy interests were opposed but had to respond. It must be remembered that it was preceded by a decade of international, public-private, and partisan federal-provincial pressure, conflict and decisions.

In the agricultural and transportation sectors there is also evidence of mutual interdependence and influence. The initial Crow grain transportation subsidy was a product of a strong farm and agrarian lobby. It lasted a century but was changed in the early 1980s by a governmental decision that was not triggered by strong external pressure per se but, as we saw in Chapter 11, by a combination of governmental and private forces. Indeed, transportation policy as a whole has resisted pressure to adopt a pure competitive model and has instead opted for a controlled, stable nation-building approach to transportation.

In the field of foreign and defence policy there is evidence of two-way causality. The first post-World War II decade provided an international environment conducive to an expansionary foreign policy, but the moment had to be seized by Canada's foreign policy decision makers and structures. It was, and Canada's Pearsonian internationalism exerted an influence and gave foreign policy a unique if temporary configuration. Both environmental opportunity and executive action were necessary. Later foreign policy initiatives such as the "third option" confronted a stiffer set of international realities and showed a greater amount of Canada's dependence on the United States, particularly, as we saw in Chapter 15, in the realm of industrial policy.

The overall plausibility of the interplay approach is increased precisely because it involves an historical time frame rather than only a short-term period. Its validity is strengthened, moreover, when one explicitly recognizes the importance of structures and processes and when one understands the increasing bilateralization of federal-provincial relations. Structures in part institutionalize and entrench ideas and agency philosophies and hence resist many external demands and pressures. We saw this in several instances throughout the book, including the Department of External Affairs' defence of the overall nonmilitary importance of the NATO alliance, the Ministry of State for Economic Development's salesmanship of the economic development concept, the Department of Labour's defence of its "labour-management" referee roles, and the Department of Finance's defence of Keynesianism in the face of evidence that it was not an adequate guide to policy. It is also in evidence in more general ways as the tax, expenditure, regulatory, public enterprise and exhortation instruments generate their own dynamics and politics. Part of the inherent task of the overall resource allocation processes examined in Chapters 10, 11 and 12 is to screen out certain demands, adopt others and initiate still others. This does not mean that structures determine policy in a unidirectional way. They initiate and react, lead and respond not just at the margin, but cumulatively in substantial ways.

A further reason why causality is not merely one of society to government is found in the nature of federal-provincial relations. In Canadian federalism governments react to other governments. This cannot be considered as merely a minor form of political jockeying akin to interagency relationships within a bureaucracy. It is a highly competitive and partisan process and, though personalities are a large factor, so too are the ideas inherent in federalism and in the widely varying economies and physical or geographic attributes of each region in Canada. These relations are all the more dynamic when one recognizes the need to characterize them as a series of bilateral relations rather than as aggregate relations between Ottawa and "the ten." We have stressed that earlier characterizations of federalism as executive federalism, or even province-building federalism, are no longer sufficient to characterize policy formulation. Aggregate bargaining over such items as tax and equalization arrangements of course remain important, indeed critical policy occasions, but evidence increasingly shows the bilateral nature of federal-provincial relations. This phenomenon is all the more likely when the economic pie is shrinking and zero-sum politics are present, but even a shrinking pie is not the ultimate cause. It is the underlying physical/economic realities aided and abetted by partisanship and expanding and more expert bureaucracies, as well as the inherently uneven impact of Ottawa's policies that also cause the bilateralism to increase. This is not ultimately because Ottawa is always unfair, but rather because there is inherent conflict in ideas such as equity (treating all provinces the same versus treating them differentingly) and regional sensitivity. The evidence of bilateralism is not found just in the intensive bargaining over the constitution in 1980 and 1981 but in particular policy fields explored in this book. It was evident in the regional policy field where Ottawa downplayed the general incentives to companies and opted for general development agreements with each province; in energy policy where consumer versus producer provinces, as well as widely varying energy resource endowments, required a mixture of policies to satisfy different needs; and in transportation and agricultural policy, where on issues such as the changes in 1982 to the Crow agreements, Ottawa acted knowing that the decision favoured some provinces and not others.

The above defence of an interplay approach, as is the case with those who defend other approaches, cannot deal in a fully satisfactory way with the critical problem of the time perspective one is using to reach judgements about evidence and causality. We have stressed the need to view policies over a significant historical period, but problems of interpreting these temporal dimensions remain. One can ask, for example, whether one is dealing with a single event on a longer policy road or just a simple policy case study. In the review in Chapter 14 of social security policy, one can ask whether the adoption of the innovative and redistributive Child Tax Credit was merely a curious episode or part of a longer-term pattern toward greater targeting and less universalism in social policy that will continue to unfold in the 1980s and 1990s. An interplay approach would suggest that, as a single decision, it reflected a largely governmental bureaucratic initiative in the short run but was also affected by the social and economic realities of the 1970s.

Our approach does not allow us to formulate laws of public policy causality in specific cases at specific times. Such scientific aspirations are impossible and arguably are partially undesirable in any macro democratic social setting such as that encompassed by Canadian public policy. This is because causality in human affairs must confront two kinds of definitions. The first is found in social science and seeks to establish methodological and allegedly objective causal connections among specific events on the assumption that one can hold other events constant in some experimental or statistical way. Such causal aspirations are not unimportant, and we have stressed how public-policy theory and practice are linked by such an aspiration. But a second, more important kind of causality exists in political and social life, namely, the existence of a social and political *will* to advocate and partially see the realization of certain ideas.

Democratic politics and, hence, public policy is not merely a mechanistic process of initiation, formulation and implementation, but also a process of expressing hope and of moving peacefully toward an amalgam of ideas and ideals, some of which do conflict with each other. Public policy involves purposeful democratic behaviour. This is true even when one finds that ideas are in conflict and that some Canadians do not always agree with or achieve the ends they seek. It is in the light of these connections between the two definitions of causality that we advance our approach.

Our emphasis on structure also flows from the purposeful behaviour of organizations. Structures are formed to institutionalize and entrench ideas and legal and other mandates. These structures develop capacities, liabilities and weaknesses. They are capable of promoting ideas and change and of stalemating and preventing the adoption of other ideas. Accordingly, they cannot be viewed as mere bureaucratic "toing and fro-ing." Even when such structures take a series of small marginal decisions, such decisions can result in significant change over time.

Similarly, our emphasis on "process" is essential. Process includes both the uncertainties and the dynamics of public policy. Public policy makers make policies about an uncertain future even while they are keeping a close eye on the collective perceptions of the present and memories of the past. Such uncertainties are found everywhere—in the capacity to forecast oil prices or rates of inflation, in the capacity to anticipate partisan critics, and in the capacity to know how interests might react to or counteract policy decisions. Politicians and senior bureaucrats generally do not like making and do not like to be *seen* making large errors any more than other Canadians do, and so they hedge their bets and covet predictability and a sharing of risks and blame. Process also flows from the dynamics of public policy. We have therefore pointed to the various processes that exist and which must somehow be "coordinated" but which also lead lives of their own. These include both policy field processes (the social versus economic policy process) and instrumental processes (the tax versus regulatory process). These processes are also based on ideas.

Our intent in the light of these realities has been a modest one—namely, to provide some basic concepts, centred on the relations among ideas, structures and processes and to suggest the overall validity of the dual interplay referred to above. In this context we also find ourselves in agreement with Vickers in regarding public policy as a series of governing relations rather than merely as discrete decisions which yield "solutions." There is more to be learned about the pattern of continuity and change over time through such an approach than by examining only individual decision case studies. Governing relations are not a tidy means-ends chain but rather embrace a series of ideas, the dominant ideas emphasized throughout the book, and the ideas that are central to key political and other institutions. We have, of course, examined some individual decisions as well, since it is also intellectually necessary to appreciate the way ideas impact at the margin, especially as past cumulative agreements and understandings confront an uncertain future.

Our approach obviously has implications for our view of the role of the modern Canadian state and for how other approaches characterize the state. The class analysis approach has most explicitly dealt with the state arguing that the capitalist state performs three functions: capital accumulation, legitimation, and coercion. It asserts that the state has some (though not much) autonomy. Though this approach forces one to view policies differently in the light of these "functions," it fails to deal with reality in any fully satisfactory way. Moreover, it seemingly tests policy against one simple trade-off—that of redistribution and equality versus the efficiency fostered by the private accumulation of capital. Public policy clearly deserves to be and must be tested against this trade-off, but it is not the only one that should serve as the litmus test of social progress. Similarly, the public choice approach, though helpful in examining the expansion of the state, is weak in explaining why the state acts in the first place. Like class analysis, the public choice approach is forced to subsume all or most public activity at the altar of economic determinism. Incrementalism, or its larger political counterpart, pluralism, is also inadequate, not only if one defines pluralism as interest group pluralism in which the state allegedly acts as a fair and benevolent referee but even if one defines it as brokerage politics, a Mackenzie King style of political operation.

The role of the state in Canada can only be characterized with some degree of accuracy if it is shown that it must deal with the explicit existence of *several* dominant ideas, the territorial, spatial and geographic realities of Canada, several institutions and structures and the ideas inherent in them, and provided one is prepared to acknowledge the existence of an uncertain future. Such a state has a considerable amount of autonomy and has little choice but to lead and react. But such a state can scarcely be understood by assigning it three functions only or by characterizing its people and its bureaucratic apparatus in monolithic ways. The Canadian state embraces many ideas, which is why it satisfies few for very long and must constantly adjust and learn not just in marginal ways but cumulatively in major ways as well. In the next section we offer further observations about why the role of the state in Canada must embrace this larger and more dynamic view of reality.

Public Policy in Practice: The Canadian Experience and the Trudeau Era

The requirement to link ideas, structures and processes also suggests to us a number of other concluding observations or themes about the practice of Canadian public policy in the past twenty years in general and in the Trudeau era in particular. Sheppard and Valpy assert in their excellent and comprehensive account of the historic 1980-81 constitutional deal that political science without biography or a focus on individual personalities is merely taxonomy.[1] It can equally be said that biography without taxonomy is often little more than sophisticated gossip about who did what to whom. While we draw attention in several ways to the role of individual leaders, we have, to use the terminology above, erred on the side of taxonomy and of developing basic concepts, since the ultimate analytical task is to try to understand the persistence of ideas that transcend leaders or the incumbents in office.

The eleven themes we identify below emerge by linking the analysis in several of the chapters. In general, they all suggest issues that cannot be explained ultimately by the personal traits or habits of Prime Minister Trudeau or any other individual leader. Some of them are obviously coloured by the virtues and the vices of the Trudeau era, but most are centred in the broader interplay between ideas, structures and processes.

The Foreign-Domestic and Economic-Social Policy Connections: Why Canadian Policy Is Ineffective in Promoting Either Efficiency or Redistribution

The study and practice of public policy are influenced by the mental and organizational categories and images in which we put public policy and by the specialized experts who guard the policy cubby holes. Some of this compartmentalization is undoubtedly necessary since reality must be carved into digestible chunks. But much of it is also patently dangerous and stultifying. The fundamental tasks in governing Canada are to indirectly or directly facilitate the creation of wealth and employment while preserving individual liberty, to redistribute income and wealth in an acceptable way, both regionally and among income groups, to give people reasonable stability and predictability in their lives, and to do all of this while maintaining a significant degree of national independence and regional and international sensitivity. Thus, economic policy, social policy and foreign policy are part of a seamless governing web. They are a composite summary of the dominant ideas that govern Canadian political life.

We have seen ample evidence that Canada's public policies are not very effective at producing either efficiency or redistribution. Public policy has helped produce a truncated and vulnerable industrial structure. The pattern of social expenditure and taxation has provided a considerable amount of social stability though universal social and welfare programs, marketing boards, subsidies and the like, but has not redistributed resources between rich and poor in a significant way. Critics from the political left attribute the failure to achieve greater equality to capitalism. But Canada is not particularly efficient either.

The answer has to lie in a more complex explanation and understanding of Canada and of its public policy institutions and structures. At the level of ideas, the fact remains that efficiency and redistribution or equality *are* only two of the major ideas in Canadian political life. Important though they may be, they are not the only ideas and hence they are not wholly or consistently supported. Equity, individual liberty, stability, national identity and regional sensitivity are also present in large doses. These other ideas are not rhetorical disguises or distortions of the efficiency and redistribution ideas. These ideas are partly reflected in and reinforced by major political institutions, including federalism. Federalism, almost by definition and certainly in the light of the linguistic, cultural, and varied geographic and economic base of Canada's regions provides opportunities to stabilize relations, in short, to *demobilize* the factors of production and to create strong and enduring allegiance to spatial and territorial (national and regional) ideas and conceptions of policy. The choice is not a simple trade-off between efficiency and equality or redistribution.

The dominant ideas of Canadian public policy suggest that neither of the often heard propositions about future public policy milleniums are persuasive. One, emanating from the political right suggests that efficiency and economic development must come first so that redistribution can be *later* afforded. The second, emanating from the political left, suggests that social equality is a precondition for the enjoyment of individual liberty and a vibrant, efficient growing economy. Both of these propositions ignore the presence of the other contending ideas in Canadian political life and contain utterly heroic assumptions about the *temporal* realities of public policy. Thus the "efficiency and growth now and social reform later" school of thought glosses over the question of whose lives will be mobilized, that is, "destabilized," and in what regions and for how long. Similarly, the "equality now, efficiency later" school of thought utterly ignores the existence of a competitive and changing world.

Canadian public policy is complex and even contradictory not because elected politicians are necessarily less rational or less caring than the rest of us, but because each of the ideas are in some very real sense "good" and desirable, and governing Canada involves a need to steer a course among them.

Public Policy and Purposeful Democracy in the 1980s
In somewhat more specific terms the 1980s and beyond present three overriding challenges to Canadians. First, redistribution cannot be abandoned. The country's social spending dollars must be more genuinely redistributive. This means that social policy should stand more squarely with the pursuit of greater equality. This requires an honest and open challenge to the idea of universality and to the vague "quality of life" and "targeting" notions of social policy, examined in Chapter 14. This

will take some political courage, especially by the two major political parties whose instincts are to slither around this issue in an effort not to unduly offend the bedrock middle class voter. The Canadian social fabric cannot withstand a decade of postponed redistribution while worshipping only at the altar of efficiency.

However, major steps to improve efficiency are *concurrently* necessary and indeed unavoidable. Understated terms such as industrial "adjustment" policies do not convey the urgency or magnitude of the task of industrial reconstruction. As pointed out in Chapters 14, 15, 16 and 17, even the projected and probable *domestic* dimensions of the task are daunting, namely, the westward flow of labour, the greater role of women in nontraditional jobs, the demise of industries and the geographical movement of others, and the technological competitiveness of world trade. They require immense amounts of honest public debate, high levels of social trust and interaction, and major institutional reforms.

These industrial, and therefore social and economic dimensions, are inextricably tied to persistent foreign and trade policy issues and the need for international cooperation. Chief among these is the need to find full access to at least one of the world's industrial markets with a population of 200 million people or more. The most probable, but not necessarily the only exclusive option, is the United States market, but it is evident that a debate on this issue will be difficult to conduct honestly and openly since paradigms will emerge immediately, from continentalism to imperialism, to attempt to foreclose debate. The debate cannot, however, be avoided, since, as we saw in Chapters 14 and 15, virtual tariff-free access is evolving rapidly in any case but without explicit thought about the economic or political consequences. Familiar and persistent questions and ideas must be faced again. Can Canada have greater economic penetration of U.S. markets and still preserve and/or increase its political independence, including its preference for a different array of social programs than found in the United States and including some degree of cultural independence in the face of a revolution in telecommunications? Can viable "third options" be constructed to cultivate greater trade and exchange with other trading blocks such as Japan, the Pacific Rim and Western Europe? What will be the domestic regional impact of these various alternatives? Which regions of Canada will reap the benefits, take the risks, and bear the burden of change?

All of these major policy challenges and the ideas inherent in them present both opportunities and dilemmas for Canada's major political parties. Since each party has different ideological roots and historical legacies and since each is a regional party rather than a truly national party, the opportunities and dilemmas are very real. Will they protect their regional base or take risks to win support in other regions? The Progressive Conservative party may explicitly lean more towards efficiency and a market ethos, but it cannot ultimately govern on that basis alone, since it will not only defy its own historic traditions but face continuing dissension within its ranks of an intolerable kind. The Liberal party can no longer glibly disguise its policies in the clothing of either narrow federal visiblity and anti-provincialism or alleged pragmatism. Its practice in the last decade of supporting neither efficiency nor equality cannot continue in the wake of the new international economic order. The New Democratic party cannot avoid dealing with the issue of universal social programs and of how precisely one gains access to and actually sells products in new international markets.

Institutions, Consensus, Conflict and Consultation

Each of the above macro dimensions of public policy cannot be addressed, let alone be dealt with, in a democractic way in the absence of institutional change, particularly involving federalism, Parliamentary-Government and business-government-labour relations. The key question is one of determining whether Canada has reached a dangerous level of institutional stalemate.

In the 1980s there is a growing sense of malaise about basic political institutions and about how one can reform them to meet the serious challenges ahead and to find the golden mean between planning and remorseless incrementalism of the politics of stalemate. But those who design or advocate new or reformed institutions cannot escape the need to explicitly or implicitly rank the ideas embedded in the core institutions. For example, a renewal of institutions could focus on a greatly strengthened Parliament, including the representation of the regions through an elected Senate. The central claim for overall Parliamentary legitimacy would be a familiar and democratic one, an elected majoritarian governing system restrained and influenced by stronger regional representation in Parliament. Alternatively, reform could centre on some form of real tripartism in recognition of the "real politik" of the division of industrial power between business, government and labour. Or reform could focus on the redesign of federal-provincial executive institutions, including mechanisms to coordinate in real ways the fiscal, capital market and regulatory policies of the two levels of government.

Each institutional reform emphasis leans toward a different institutional idea and basis of legitimacy. Each would be strongly opposed by those who have a preference for other ideas. Thus, choices must be made among institutional reforms. If Parliament is significantly strengthened, it will be at the cost of federalism and new business-labour-government consultative institutions. If federalism is strengthened, Parliament will probably be weaker, and business and labour will feel as frustrated as they have been in recent years. If new business, labour and government institutions are given real power, then federalism and Parliament will decline in influence. If all three are strengthened, it is likely that not much would change.

All of the above reforms would have to face, in addition, the *temporal* realities of public policy, namely, the need to anticipate and deal with an uncertain future and the need to be responsive to the present realities. All of them would have to ensure that a balance is struck between suitable amounts of free discussion, debate and consultation, and a capacity to act in a reasonably decisive way.

The trade-offs in institutional reform ideas and in political power reinforce our emphasis that the role of major institutions in public policy formulation cannot be understood by looking at each of them in isolation. Though federalism, Cabinet-Parliamentary government, political parties and elections, interest groups, the bureaucracy, the media and capitalism separately reflect and embody core ideas, they must also interact with each other. Though governed by an overall constitutional framework, the major institutions in effect represent partially different bases of political legitimacy and each claims to have a right to be consulted or involved. Institutions are related, but they are also in a constant state of tension and partial distrust of each other. As we have seen, this has been most in evidence in the elusive search for consultative forums to help design the long-coveted industrial strategy. But it was also plainly evident in fields such as competition policy, labour market policy, energy policy and transportation, as well as in the debate over tax, expenditure and regulatory "reform."

The importance of *relations* rather than just *choices* shows up in the very names accorded the institutional dynamics. Consensus, conflict and consulation embrace international, intergovernmental, intersectoral, intergroup and interdepartmental *relations*. Integration and fragmentation, coordination and freedom, centralization and decentralization occur simultaneously, but each episodically. Canada thus remains inevitably a partially integrated as well as fragmented society.

This institutional tension and interdependence is aided by other more particular characteristics which the evolving institutional relations generate. Thus, relations between the partisan nature of Parliament, the media and the Cabinet exacerbate the tendency examined below to create policies "for show" and to respond symbolically to short-term perceptions. Interest groups often distrust other institutions and bases of legitimacy, especially federalism and Parliament. Newer social interest groups or collective rights associations distrust older established producer groups and professions. Federal-provincial relations, especially in an age of greater fiscal scarcity, can no longer be characterized by just multilateral executive federalism in which Ottawa and "the ten" bargain. As we stressed above, such relations embrace bilateral issues of consensus and conflict as specific provinces or groups of provinces in particular policy fields attempt to strike bargains or take partially counteractive measures that accommodate not only diverse ideas but also partisan conflict and the need to garner political credit or avoid political blame.

The diverse institutional features of Canada's political system undoubtedly provide opportunities for all institutions to try to stabilize relations or to prevent or stalemate change. As we stressed above, this, combined with the presence of the dominant ideas, affects the capacity of Canadians to wholeheartedly pursue either the idea of efficiency or the idea of equality. Stability is of course itself a dominant idea and is an all the more powerful one when the future is uncertain, and when institutional relations promote stalemates to an excessive degree.

Priority Setting and Institutional Consensus and Reform: The Need To Plan Without Calling It Planning

Despite periodic aspirations by governments to be more rational about priority setting and to take a longer-term view of things, our analysis shows the episodic nature of priorities and planning. This is a direct reflection of the normative and institutional imperatives identified throughout the book as well as other political realities identified in Chapters 4, 5, 10, 11 and 12. The very nature and magnitude of the social, economic and foreign policy challenges highlighted above shows that there is a need for some kind of planning both within government and between the public and private sectors and at the macro and micro levels. But the ideological and normative rhetoric of Canadian politics will not allow politicians to call it planning. It must be called something else— hence the elusive search for industrial and employment "strategies," better economic "management," "adjustment" policies and superior "consultative" forums.

Canadians must have some sympathetic understanding of the double-edged sword their politicians face in the priorities and planning conundrum. Politicians must somehow lead (but not by too much) and at the same time be responsive (but not be weak, too flexible or unaware of the costs of their flexibility). As we showed in Chapters 10, 11 and 12, priorities in the Trudeau era show the ebb and flow of social and then economic leanings as domestic and international circumstances change and as governments respond to and try to anticipate their Parliamentary opponents. Thus, at a macro level the Trudeau government has had to deal with the Nixon shocks of 1971-72, the OPEC shock of 1973, wage and price controls in 1975, the further doubling of energy prices in the wake of the 1979 Iranian revolution, United States' high interest rate policies in 1981 and falling oil prices in 1982 and 1983. As we showed in detail in Chapter 10, the internal priority-setting exercises were almost never "normal." Numerous special priority-setting exercises had to be devised to interrupt the allegedly normal one. These problems were related to and exacerbated by the inability to have general budgetary priorities and the fiscal framework coincide with expenditure priorities or with the overall priorities expressed in Throne Speeches. Over the 1970s and early 1980s there was an increased tendency to have more than one Budget Speech per year. This was, in turn, related to continuous opposition party and often provincial government pressure for a new budget, *now*! The magnification of these pressures by the media only adds to this "revolving door" notion of priorities. It creates greater uncertainty for many while it is promoting stability for others. The episodic nature of priorities reveals the continuous and persistent re-emergence of the dominant ideas, as well as the presence of uncertainty.

It is also, however, a product of the dynamics of individual and collective ministerial behaviour.

Prime Ministers, Ministers and Personalities: The Paradoxes of Power and of Getting Things Done

Much of our detailed account of priorities in this book deals with the Trudeau era. We have made a point, however, of dealing with other eras as well since this helps put the Trudeau period in a larger context. As Chapters 8 and 9 in particular pointed out, no one can deny the importance of personalities and individuals in policy formulation nor fail to recognize the power and preferences of prime ministers and key ministers and advisors. It is a mistake of the highest order, however, to treat leaders in isolation from ideas or to assume that charisma translates into unrestrained power. Prime ministers and key ministers are on top of the structures of policy making, but they are also in the middle of the very ideas and processes we have focused on.

Prime Minister Trudeau in particular evokes stereotyped views partly because of his complex personality, his longevity in power, and his regionally concentrated power base. He and some of his key advisors such as Michael Pitfield have undoubtedly fostered the view of rational and technocratic government. It was a part of the initial philosophy of the early Trudeau regimes. But the reality of the Trudeau era in practice is very diffeent from the initial philosophy. We have seen this in Chapter 10, not only in the priorities adopted, but in the processes used to devise them once the allegedly "regular" rational processes succumbed to the mysteries of politics. Abstract rationality, which is at best a wooly concept to begin with, is the last label we would use to summarize the reality of the Trudeau period. Once again this is because the realities of *governing*, as opposed to merely advocating policy priorities and solutions, conspired in Trudeau's time, as in previous epochs, to limit a leader's powers and degree of flexibility.

Prime ministers embody different dominant ideas and concerns reflecting their regional and economic origins, as well as broader circumstances. Prime Minister Trudeau's concerns with French-English relations and national unity were reflected in language policy, the October crisis of 1970, and later the Charter of Rights and, to a lesser extent, the National Energy Program. But on the other issues Trudeau was more selective about how and when to invest and mobilize his power. As we saw in Chapter 8, Prime Ministers Clark, Pearson and Diefenbaker were similarly selective. There were also ideological differences present, particularly between Prime Minister Joe Clark and Trudeau, not only over items such as Petro-Canada but also about the growth of government in general. In both cases this reflected not only personal views but the different ideological bases of the Progressive Conservative and Liberal parties and of party judgements about where they were most vulnerable electorally and where they had the most to gain.

Assessments or prime ministerial power and policy preferences must obviously deal with two levels of power, power over Cabinet colleagues and power to change human behaviour in a sustained way. With respect to relations of power between the prime minister and ministers, our analysis suggests a number of concluding observations. First, in a large unwieldy Cabinet a prime minister must allow some key ministers to have considerable amounts of power. The charge that Prime Minister Trudeau could not brook other powerful ministers does not stand up to serious scrutiny or historical comparison. He certainly wielded power in many areas but often gave or had to give ample room to others. In the early Trudeau years this was certainly the case in respect of ministers such as Jean Marchand and Gerard Pelletier, and in the later years, Marc Lalonde, Jean Chretien and Allan MacEachen had considerable room for manoeuvre. In between, ministers such as Donald McDonald and John Turner, though they both left politics, could hardly be considered to be wilting flowers.

Thus, in any given period there are always three or four ministers to whom a prime minister has to "give their innings." This is because Cabinet relations are ones of considerable mutual need and support, as well as suspicion and leadership threat. In this respect Trudeau does not seem to be remarkably different from other prime ministers examined in Chapter 8. While no Trudeau minister enjoyed the sustained influence of a C.D. Howe in the King and St. Laurent Cabinets, it is a moot point if any single minister, including Howe, could withstand the criticism and scrutiny levelled at ministers in the modern television age.

It must also be appreciated that "getting things done" in a modern Cabinet is decidedly different from the St. Laurent or early Diefenbaker eras. As we saw in Chapters 7 and 8, central planners used to worry about the proverbial "end-run," proposals that arrived at Cabinet suddenly and without "proper" scrutiny. To those who wanted central control this was the epitomy of political sin. To the minister engaged in the end-run, the same act was the essence of Cabinet democracy, not to mention political creativty. Things get done, in part at least, by breaking the rules.

Perhaps what is needed are more up-to-date football metaphors which reflect the variety of ways in which Cabinets must accommodate the needs of individual ministerial initiators. Cabinets, for example, have to allow individual ministers at least some small victories and short gains. Thus, in modern football parlance one could speak of this kind of ministerial power more accurately in terms of the art of "splitting the seam" of a zone defence. The trick is to find a spot among the Cabinet and central agency defenders where one escapes momentary detection. The "seam" may be between envelopes, among committees, or at a moment of opportunity when public opinion or a crisis creates a climate of receptivity. The Cabinet must also accommodate, albeit less fre-quently, somewhat larger initiatives by individual ministers. The number of these is usually limited by the sheer costs of the medium-size projects, programs or legislative changes. One could liken these to a screen pass where both political and football success depends upon having some blockers in front of you. Bryce Mackasey's unemployment insurance initiatives in the early 1970s, Eugene Whelan's considerable influence in agricultural policy, and Jean Luc Pepin's Crow's Nest transportation reform in the early 1980s could perhaps be seen in this metaphorical light. Finally, there are the even more infrequent but obviously critical occasions when those already at the centre call a surprise play or, as we said in Chapter 16 regarding the National Energy Program, take the football and move to another stadium. The NEP, the constitutional initiatives of 1980-81, and the wage control program of 1975 could be viewed in this light.

The Cabinet must somehow accommodate all of these kinds and levels of "getting things done" because it is both an intensely human place and a locus of power. However, all of the above metaphorical examples deal with only one dimension of power, that of power among ministers. There is also the second and much broader dimension of power, namely, that of changing private behaviour. We discuss this in relation to another important theme of modern Canadian public policy, the emergence of what could be called the "levered society," the emergence of a society where private behaviour is increasingly "levered" or influenced by numerous governing instruments embedded in conflicting policy purposes.

The Levered Society and the Overloaded Policy Instruments of Government

Throughout the book we have stressed the importance of understanding the links between governing instruments and ideas, structures and processes since instruments are another way to view the public policy link between public and private behaviour. Each instrument—taxation, expenditures, regulation, public enterprise and exhortation—has been loaded in numerous policy fields with policy ideas and tasks each intended to induce or require a certain form of behaviour by private citizens, companies and organizations. In the early 1980s this phenomenon was often referred to as policy leverage. For example, following the imposition of the federal "6 and 5" restraint program in 1982, Prime Minister Trudeau announced a policy that "every grant and every accord and every subsidy that the government is paying out of taxpayers' money" will be negotiated with a view to levering the private sector into compliance with the "6 percent world" of the federal anti-inflation policy.[2]

Whatever one may think of the "6 and 5" program as an anti-inflation policy, the Trudeau statement symbolized larger questions about the degree to which Canada has become a levered society and about the related issue of the increasingly overloaded policy circuits of government. The decision to use expenditure grants and subsidies, initially set up for other policy purposes, as a lever of bargaining to meet incomes policy purposes is merely one example of a longer-term tendency to turn the major instruments of governing into a supermarket of carrots and sticks intended to make Canadians behave in certain desired but ever changing and finely tuned ways.

It results increasingly in a bewildering array of cues and contradictions, which contribute to the even greater uncertainty that such leverage measures are supposedly intended to ameliorate. It makes the management of government more difficult that it already is as bureaucrats scurry to carry out the latest marching orders from the top.

Several other examples emerge from previous chapters and show the growth of this tendency to attach multiple conditions in such a way as to increasingly overload the circuits of government and of private decision makers.

- The tax system has become a veritable Christmas tree of complex benefits, incentives and loopholes, so much so that its overall capacity to raise revenue and redistribute income has been seriously compromised. Moreover, the 1981 Budget debacle showed that, once in place, the winners and beneficiaries ensure that many of these benefits can be removed only at great political cost.
- The procurement instrument on major projects and/or other less visible government purchases is increasingly loaded with multiple conditions—from Canadian content, to regional benefits, to affirmative action. Agencies with statutory or nonstatutory persuasive powers are created to become "negotiating chambers" into which one enters to "do a deal," but from which one exits not knowing quite what deal has been made. Such agencies include the Foreign Investment Review Agency, the Canada Oil and Gas Lands Administration, the Office of Industrial and Regional Benefits, several environmental assessment agencies, and regulatory boards.
- Federal research and development policies increasingly reject tax breaks for R&D in favour of direct grants because these increase the leverage quotient and allow the incentives to be better targeted. Moreover, they facilitate the growing political need to obtain visible credit for favours granted.
- Government regulatory boards and agencies are ordered to apply the "6 and 5" rule on prices alongside a host of existing purposes.
- Canada Manpower offices become a veritable supermarket of labour market services, but also become increasingly unable to perform their primary information role in the labour market.
- Statutory controls on public sector wages are accompanied by severe limitations on collective bargaining. Thus, the program becomes an unprecedently draconian one and a none too subtle Trojan horse for the permanent elimination of the right to strike.
- Crown and mixed enterprises are intended to meet an ever widening range of social, regional and commercial purposes, some hidden in cash flow and others overtly subsidized.

Each of these developments, when judged on its individual merits, can be seen to be desirable in a number of ways from the point of view of some interests, regions, officials and ministers. In total, however, they increasingly contribute to confusion and greater problems of coordination. The effect is to create an advanced case of social and organizational constipation, both within government and outside it. The doers and coordinators increasingly stalemate each other.

As was the case in our discussion of ideas and institutions, none of the above is intended to argue that we can embrace a world in which each government program has only one objective, or where no intervention by government is justified. The programs of line departments and agencies are often given or assumed to have multiple objectives in keeping with the complex nature of the country and of the program's impacts. As to intervention, it must be stressed that it is not always governments that initiate the new leverage proposals. As often as not they emanate from private interests seeking protection from the freedom and vagaries of the market. But Canadians must become much more aware of the increasing absurdities and costs of the overly levered society. It is a growing halfway world between public policy and private decision making, where perpetual bargaining and contradictory arm-twisting become the basis of a growth industry. The country is becoming like a giant FIRA, a nether land where much is tried but nothing is done.

Prime Minister Trudeau is fond of saying that Canada is not a confederation of shopping centres. In fact, in one sense, it is fast becoming one—not in the federal-provincial sense of his metaphorical reference, but in the sense of a 1980s version of an ancient bazaar where Canadians are perpetually levered into making deals with the state.

There are no easy answers to the instruments and leverage question raised since it is linked to all of the themes examined above. Many of the medium and smaller "seam splitting" exercises by ministers metaphorically referred to above result in the additions to the instrument package. Conservatives may see the "solution" to the leverage problem simply in less government and less bureaucracy. NDP supporters or left-wing critics may see the leverage mess as evidence of why "half-way" Liberal measures do not work. Others may call for more careful and rational analysis to make sure that instruments "optimally" match goals. There can be little doubt, however, that the malaise reflected in the excessive practice of leverage politics is exacting a heavy cost and could lead to a stronger call for a prime minister who can "discipline" his ministers. While such a prime minister may be found, his discipline will be hard to exercise for a long and sustained period since he too must manage a Cabinet of diverse men and women.

Central Agencies: Damned If You Have Them and Damned If You Do Not

If there is one feature of the structure of executive government that the Trudeau era is most noted for it is the growth of central agencies examined in Chapters 7, 11 and 12. An expanded layer of bureaucracy was inserted between individual ministers and departments and the Cabinet as a whole. Intended to serve the expanded system of Cabinet committees in an improved and more rational way and later adapted to include the envelope system, the apparatus showed in a different way the imperatives and the contradictions inherent in the simultaneous need to centralize and decentralize, to exert better control over bureaucrats while getting better advice, to promote individual ministerial responsibility while strengthening collective Cabinet accountability, and to coordinate the tasks of government horizontally without impeding the vertical delivery of programs, goods and services. Since many ideas about both policy and process collide in such a system, it is not surprising that many are frustrated, indeed angered, by the Trudeau central agencies.

It is certainly plausible to argue that the present system should be dismantled. Indeed, it may well be that a future prime minister will want to do precisely that, perhaps propelled by a desire for a smaller, leaner Cabinet where individual ministers rather than elaborate committees are given a freer reign. Such a pruning exercise may not only see a severe reduction in the number of analysts at the centre but also a concentration of central analytical power in a refurbished Finance-Treasury Board alliance—in short, almost a return to the situation in the early 1960s.

Such a change would signal, as does any change in structure, a desire to emphasize some ideas over others. Accordingly, it would be done at the expense of other ideas that would be de-emphasized by the change. In this sense the central agency question is a permanent one—governments are damned if they have them and expand them and damned if they do not. The possible change noted above may help signal a desire to encourage greater ministerial autonomy and influence and ensure more focused economic scrutiny of government decisions. If so, it would undoubtedly sacrifice, relatively speaking, the concern for a broader-based horizontal coordination and for ensuring, as the envelope system was intended to do, that ministers individually and collectively had to face the economic consequences of their decisions rather than leaving such matters to one or two of their colleagues. Greater departmental freedom may also lead not only to more ministerial power but also to greater deputy-ministerial power and hence to another version of the perpetual concern for bureaucratic influence.

In short, questions about central agency structures inevitably deal with matters of power, about "top-down" versus "bottom-up" planning and coordination, about the ideas that will prevail, about temporary personalities, and about bureaucratic and political leadership.

Bureacrats and Policy: The Continuing Ambivalence

The relationship between bureaucracy and democracy is always stressful. On the one hand, Canadians want their major decisions made by elected politicians. At the same time they want bureaucrats to give good advice in a competent and conscientious way and to implement programs efficiently and effectively. This dual view reflects the ambivalence that is inherent in the issue, namely, that bureaucracy is both a threat to democracy and a necessary but not sufficient condition for its realization. Layered over this dual ambivalent view are more recent concerns about bureaucrats that arise because the bureaucracy itself has become increasingly the object of public policy in fields such as language policy, decentralization, incomes policy and collective bargaining. Perception and reality also clash in perplexing ways. The greater bureaucratic growth since the mid-1960s has occurred at the provincial level, but it is Ottawa's bureaucrats that are most often portrayed as aloof, insensitive and out of control.

Senior bureaucrats undoubtedly have great influence. Their influence should always be the object of great concern. At the same time it must be increasingly acknowledged that in many spheres, unless their critics are prepared to fundamentally restructure the system, including the essence of Cabinet-Parliamentary government, the legitimate right of senior bureaucrats to influence policy must be more candidly acknowledged. This "right" is obviously a question of some delicacy. The principle that ministers make policy and that bureaucrats implement it is clearly the right principle. But the equally valid duty of officials to warn and advise, to uphold current laws and to exercise the delegated power given to them, when examined in the greater context of the reality of policy and decision making, also implies a bundle of obligations which bureaucrat bashers conveniently ignore.

These realities must be kept in mind when assessing proposals to reform the bureaucracy in order to obtain greater ministerial control. The next Progressive Conservative government in Ottawa will likely make a major effort to extend the partial politicizing of the senior bureaucracy begun by the Liberals. As we saw in Chapters 7, 8 and 9, this reform may be especially attractive to a new government because it is something that it can be seen doing immediately on taking office and thus signals its determination to put its own imprimatur on policy direction. This may well have a salutory effect, but it does not in any way deal with the other underlying bases of bureaucratic influence which are rooted in the bureaucrat's expertise, the overall permanence of official-dom and the complexity and contradictory ideas involved in public policy. Sooner or later the new breed or Tory-appointed bureaucrats will take on the hue of officialdom and there will be demands from elected ministers to control the new troops.

Ultimately, of course, the essential institutional feature that has most to do with the bureaucratic ambivalence is found not in the internal entrails of the executive structure but in the larger political system. It is one-party dominance by the Liberal party which ultimately defines the overall malaise. This in turn is tied to the regionalization of Canada's parties. Concerns about bureaucratic power would obviously not disappear totally if Canada's parties alternated in power more frequently, but the issue would be somewhat more sanguine if the "ins" were not in for so long, and the "outs" were not so obviously out.

Beyond Envelopes: The Imperatives of Resource Allocation

The "bureaucratic" questions inherent in the role of central agencies and in the democratic control of bureaucrats are linked to the imperatives of resource allocation. While the fascination in the early 1980s was with Ottawa's envelopes, our analysis hopefully shows why it is always necessary to penetrate beneath the rhetoric of whatever the current "systems" are to the underlying ideas and temporal dimensions of resource allocation. Not only must the functional and regional policy fields, however defined, be both integrated and delegated simultaneously, but so also must the tax, expenditure, regulatory, and other instruments be aggregted and disaggregated. These are not just questions of bureaucratic "to-ing and fro-ing." They go to the very heart of the ideas inherent in political life and to the degree, nature and effects of the exercise of the state's coercive powers.

The temporal aspects of resource allocation cannot be avoided.

Choices do have to be made between the need to allocate resources for current consumption on the one hand and for longer-term investment on the other. But the political determination of what an investment is, as our review of industrial, energy and labour market policies has shown, is not necessarily the same as the economic determination of an investment. In the real world of resource allocation where economy and politics meet, an investment incentive given to one person is often viewed by others as a subsidy. This is merely another way of saying that the compartments of budgeting are not at all watertight. Spillovers abound as the ideas compete for attention. The "economic" committees of Cabinet make social decisions and the "social" committees make economic choices.

The resource allocation processes also encompass concerns about the ideas inherent in Cabinet-Parliamentary government, including the tensions between individual ministerial responsibility and collective Cabinet responsibility. As we saw in Chapters 11 and 12, the resource allocation processes must leave room for special envelopes or special funds within envelopes to meet special problems that arise, to accommodate the power of individual ministers, and to speed up the decision process. We saw as well how the envelope cannot treat the instruments of policy as neutral devices. Taxes and tax expenditures are treated differently because ministerial power and diverse ideas are involved.

Federal-provincial fiscal relations also impose realities. The lack of financial manoeuvrability is primarily not a function of weak politicians unable to undertake "decisive" action, but is also due as much to the reality that an agreement has been struck and some kind of minimum predictability must be established. These bargains are all the more difficult to sustain, however, because they not only encompass agreements among the eleven governments but also bilateral understandings that reflect the fact that provincial economies, and individual Ottawa-provincial partisan relations, are each different. Resource allocation implies the frequent need to treat everybody equally and differently, since both are desirable concepts rooted in the idea of equity.

Policies "For Show" and Policies Without Resources

Our analysis has also depicted both the need and the dangers inherent in the political system's tendency to produce policies "for show" and policies without resources. This tendency shows again the operation of the double-edged sword of policy making. Policy makers always face the need to express concern about issues, to respond and communicate symbolically about problems, and to respond with widely varying degrees of commitment of resources. Thus, in a very real sense there is always a need for policies "for show" and policies without (or with at least only a minimum) resource commitment. The danger of this tendency is obvious. When done excessively it produces cynicism and alienation, sometimes against the party in power and sometimes against the system as a whole. Many symbolic gestures such as a speech showing concern or an offer to consult and talk can be viewed as either the epitomy of democratic leadership or a "cop out" by an indecisive minister or prime minister. A reorganization of a department or the creation of a new one can be viewed as a useful signal of concern, or a bureaucratic smoke-screen.

The increased tendency in the 1970s and 1980s to produce more policies for show cannot be attributed to citizens pounding on the door of government for "quick solutions," since there is increasing evidence that citizens generally do not expect governments to be capable of solving many problems. We place greater emphasis here on the relations between the mass media, the government and Parliament and the perceived need to be seen doing something which their relations with each other engender. These are aided and abetted by the automatic triggering of events such as the monthly unemployment and inflation statistics which, as we showed in Chapters 2 and 13, propels further the partisan hothouse of Parliamentary question period. When added to the apparent scarcity of real resources (tax, expenditure, or regulation) these elements produce an excessive binge of policy symbolism, fine tuning and tinkering, as politicians sometimes respond to reality, and some-times to perceptions of reality. In the Trudeau era this phenomenon can also undoubtedly be attributed to the prime minister and his key advisors' fascination with reorganization and with their tenacity for partisan political survival that generates far more than the normal or desirable share of governing by gestures.

Knowledge, Power, Ideas and Paradigms
At a more detailed level our analysis points out the need to be aware of the severe limits of the "knowledge is power" thesis. Knowledge is not necessarily power, not only because of the many types of knowledge and

information outlined in Chapter 13 but because, as we have stressed, power operates at two levels in the policy process. There is the power of one minister over another, but there is also the power to change actual human behaviour, especially given that interests have a capacity to exercise some countervailing power. There are limits to both. When prime ministers and Cabinets issue new marching orders, not everybody marches, not only in the bureaucracy but in numerous private institutions and markets as well.

It is probably closer to the truth to say that those with frequent access to decision makers and *some* knowledge have influence and power, but again this is often only power of the first kind—that is, over some other persons but not necessarily over private behaviour. It is in this sense that the trade-offs between written versus verbal advice discussed in Chapters 4 and 13 is essential to appreciate. There is a need for a proper flow of Cabinet documents containing good analysis and alternatives. But there is a paradox as well. The greater the volume of written material in the face of limited ministerial time, inclination to read and use it, and ability, the higher the premium on verbal advice to economize on the transmission of the written material.

Because of the need to understand the integrative nature of Canadian public policy and its underlying ideas, we have tried to caution the reader about other related limits of rationality and of formal episodic analyses and evaluations of policies and programs. We have stressed that evaluation involves both mental analysis and social interaction and that, far from being the missing link in the accountability chain, there is ample evidence to suggest that Canada has numerous institutions that engage in such activity. Moreover, it is an illusion to expect to find any single magical locus to determine whether we have succeeded or failed.

It is essential in examining all policy fields to look for the presence of the dominant ideas regardless of the language, or indeed the rhetoric, of the law, the regulations, or last week's ministerial speech. Evaluation and analysis occur at several levels, in numerous institutional contexts and in relation to different professional knowledge groups with a variety of orientation in values. At the macro level these can include Throne Speeches, Budget Speeches and other major speeches by political leaders. At the micro level it can include several task force, advisory council or royal commission reports. While the major recommendations of these bodies may not be adopted, they can have a cumulative impact and help create a climate for change as the psyche of decision makers is "massaged." In institutional terms evaluations also vary. To evaluate for accountability to Parliament is not the same as conducting evaluations that are useful to bureaucrats who must manage programs. This does not mean that it is pointless for the bureaucratic and political managers of public programs or the interest groups and interests who benefit from them to try to set more specific objectives, but it does suggest that there are severe limitations to such objective-setting exercises. Moreover, these limitations do not ultimately or necessarily reflect the irrationality or "failure" (or success) of these *individual* managers, but rather reveal the complex reality of political life.

It is in this context that we also suggest the need to look for and understand the existence of paradigms in particular policy fields. We have seen the presence in several policy fields of policy paradigms of varying degrees of rigour and coherence. These include Keynesianism and monetarism, and even thoughts of Galbraithianism in economic policy; universal versus targeted, and primary versus residual social policy categories and concepts; truncated industrialism, staples and free trade paradigms in industrial policy; growth and supply-oriented versus conserver paradigms in energy policy and education; and training paradigms in labour market policies. The paradigms are related to ideologies and ideas, but they often take on lives of their own. These groups of ideas are important because they may help guide policy in particular fields, and because they are usually entrenched in the education of professional specialists and hence change slowly over time, even when challenged by contending paradigms or new evidence of their inadequacy.

Why There Is No Single "Bottom Line" to Government

Despite mounds of evidence to the contrary, including their own political behaviour, businessmen, accountants and others often search longingly and lovingly for government's "bottom line," the one all-inclusive indicator or measure that will provide the same degree of simple evaluative satisfaction that profits or measures of rate of return supply for the operation of business. This "bottom line" syndrome reflects and melds a genuine concern for efficiency as well as a faith in rationality (provided the latter is not defined very precisely). It also reflects an often justified suspicion of bureaucrats and bureaucracy. Since efficiency is an idea that deservedly strikes a resonant political chord, the existence of a bottom line syndrome should not be surprising. It is an important idea. We have seen it in relation to the Glassco Commission of the early 1960s where efficiency was associated with decentralization and with letting departmental managers manage, and in the Lambert Report where efficiency was associated with the need for greater central control and with rational evaluation. It was evident in the debate examined in Chapters 11 and 12 on tax reform and regulatory reform, as well as on expenditure reform and the reform of Crown corporations.

It ought to be made clear, however, that the presence of ideas other than efficiency means that there are and must be several "bottom lines" in government. Thus, for example, the bottom lines for tax reform hinge on judgements about whether the tax system is efficient, equitable, redistributive, and so on. Bottom lines are also associated with different knowledge groups, including accountants who sell the idea of comprehensive auditing and value for money, economists who urge the value of cost-benefit analysis, scientists and engineers who often want objective planning, and social workers who oscillate between concerns for equity and redistribution. And then there are the bottom lines that emerge from the ideas inherent in the core political institutions, including the desire for consultation.

Our intention in this book has not been to develop and use an approach which shows that there are *always* democratic choices to be made as different dominant and institutional ideas interact. In each of the above concluding themes one can discern the numerous ideas and partial contradictions that exist in public policy making and in governing Canada. But the underlying relations among ideas, structures and processes must be understood since they affect the limits of choice. Democratic public policy making is above all purposeful activity intended to deal with and resolve conflict, foster acceptable and peaceful social relations and offer hope and confidence about Canada's capacity to face the future.

NOTES

1. Robert Sheppard and Michael Valpy, *The National Deal* (Toronto: Fleet Books, 1982), p. 5.
2. Quoted in the *Globe and Mail*, July 24, 1982, p. 1.

Appendix A

A Guide to the Study of Public Policy Fields

In Part III of the book we examined the evolution of the three umbrella policy fields—economic, social and foreign policy—and three major fields—industrial policy, energy policy and labour market policy. There are obviously dozens of other policy fields in which the reader may be interested, or the student of public policy may wish to conduct research and pursue further reading. Even the following list of policy fields does not exhaust the list:

- fiscal
- economic
- agriculture and food
- consumer
- competition
- transportation
- immigration
- Indian
- unemployment insurance
- regional
- northern development
- economic development
- foreign investment
- defence
- cultural
- interest rate
- labour relations
- education
- pensions
- small business
- forestry
- fishery

- monetary
- banking
- housing
- science
- women
- prices and incomes
- energy
- industrial
- foreign
- foreign aid
- communications
- corrections and justice
- youth
- trade
- multicultural
- occupational health
- health care
- the aged
- mining
- resources
- labour market
- environment

The purpose of this appendix is to provide some guidance on studying other policy fields and to suggest how the approach used in the book could be applied to policy fields not examined in the book. The notes are organized in four sections. The first section discusses primary descriptive sources. The second deals with policy-oriented journals and related sources. The third section presents brief references and comments on books on policy fields. Finally, we suggest a list of research questions which evolve out of the approach used in the book and which could be used when studying other policy fields and when reviewing basic books in these fields.

Primary Descriptive Sources

The first introductory task is to develop not only an appreciation of recent events but also a sense of the historical evolution of the policy field in question and of the structures and processes involved. A *brief* decade by decade portrait should be developed. The main primary sources here include:

- *The Canada Year Book* (Government of Canada)
- *The Canadian Annual Review*
- Federal and/or Provincial Departmental Annual Reports in the Policy Field
- *The National Finances and Provincial Finances* (data published annually by the Canadian Tax Foundation)
- Estimates of the Government of Canada (especially the Part III separate departmental reports)
- *How Ottawa Spends Your Tax Dollars* (includes data on departments and trends over previous decade prepared annually by School of Public Administration, Carleton University)
- *Year End Review: Intergovernmental Relations in Canada* (published annually by Institute of Intergovernmental Relations, Queen's University)
- Throne Speeches and Budget Speeches
- Ministerial Speeches
- Departmental/Ministerial Presentations to House of Common and Senate Committees
- Major Royal Commission and Task Force reports on the policy field (usually contains brief historical description)
- Statistics Canada Data and Reports

Analytical and Evaluative Sources

Some of the above primary sources are also evaluative and analytical (for instance, the *How Ottawa Spends Your Tax Dollars* books and the Royal Commission and Task Force Reports). So also in their own "advocacy" way are speeches by ministers. In the broader context, however, there are numerous sources of analysis and evaluation, as Chapters 13 and 18 pointed out.

> *Academic and Opinion Journals.* The major policy-oriented journals are *Canadian Public Administration, Canadian Public Policy, Policy Options, Canadian Forum, Studies in Political Economy, Canadian Tax Journal* and *Canadian Taxation. The Canadian Journal of Political Science* and the *Canadian Journal of Economics* are also important sources. Relevant foreign and comparative journals include *The Public Interest, Regulation, Public Budgeting and Finance, Public Administration Review, Public Administration* (U.K.) and *Policy Sciences.*
>
> *Studies and Reports by Advisory Councils, Royal Commission, Task Forces and Policy Institutes.* The policy institutes include the: Economic Council of Canada, Science Council of Canada, C.D. Howe Research Institute, Conference Board of Canada, Institute for Research on Public Policy, Fraser Institute, Canadian Institute for Economic Policy, Centre for Policy Alternatives, Ontario Economic Council and Western Canada Foundation.
>
> *Financial Press and Other Journalistic Sources.* Useful and essential for week-by-week developments and events. These sources include the *Financial Post,* the *Financial Times of Canada* and *Canadian Business,* as well as business sections and other analytical articles in sources such as *The Globe and Mail, Toronto Star, Saturday Night, Alberta Report* and *Maclean's* magazine.
>
> *Trade Journals and Interest Group Briefs and Publications.* These are too numerous to list but are important sources of opinion.

Major Books on Policy Fields

Where there is a major book on a policy field one should obviously consult it early in the study process, since the better ones present the historical evolution and chronology, and offer an assessment and a way of viewing the policy field in question. Listed below by policy field are several such books. Our list is confined *to fully integrated books.* It does not include other multiple author edited volumes. Other such references may be found in the selected Bibliography. We include very brief annotated notes about their key attributes. Since these notes are perilously brief, the reader should consult the books to form your own opinion.

Agricultural and Food Policy

The classic and still essential reference here is V.C. Fowke's books, *The National Policy and the Wheat Economy* and *Canadian Agricultural Policy: The Historical Pattern*. These analyses build on the Innis' staple theory and on centre-periphery relations. They have great historical depth but do not concern themselves much with policy structures and processes. Don Mitchell's *The Politics of Food* examines from primarily a class analysis perspective the larger politics of both agricultural production and food distribution. It does not deal adequately with either policy structures or with the breadth of ideas inherent in this field. Persons interested in agriculture and food policy should consult sources on transportation policy as well.

Communications and Broadcasting Policy

Woodrow, Woodside, Wiseman and Black's *Conflict Over Communications Policy* provides a good critical review of the ideas inherent in communication policy especially as revealed through federal-provincial conflict. Only limited treatment of structure and other institutions. Frank Peers' *The Politics of Canadian Broadcasting* presents a comprehensive analysis of broadcasting policy, but not one informed by an overall approach to public policy.

Competition Policy

W.T. Stanbury's *Business Interest and the Reform of Canadain Competition Policy* uses an interest group and quasi-public choice approach to view the business community's lobbying in the competition policy field in the early 1970s. Has some historical treatment but somewhat incomplete in relating competition policy to the larger politics of industrial policy. Chris Green's *Canadian Industrial Organization and Policy* is also an essential reference for competition policy, particularly because it is set in a broader industrial policy context. Irving Brecher's *Canada's Competition Policy Revisited: Some New Thoughts on an Old Story* does not deal much with structure and process but offers wise counsel on the old dilemmas.

Economic Policy

Phidd and Doern's *The Politics and Management of Canadian Economic Policy* relates economic policy to the issues of economic management from the post-war to mid-1970s. The focus is on structure and process with much less explicit treatment of ideas. Ingrid Bryan's *Economic Policies in Canada* focuses on economic policy per se including both macro policy and policies and effects on particular sectors such as agriculture, fisheries, natural resources, etc. Provides a useful general review but with only very limited attention to structure and process.

Environmental and Occupational Health Policy

Doern, Prince and McNaughton's *Living With Contradictions: Health and Safety Regulation and Implementation in Ontario* provides a comparative analysis of policy and regulation in three sectors, environmental, workplace and buildings. The relationships between ideas, implementation and compliance philosophies are stressed. Manga, Broyles and Reschenthaler's *Occupational Health and Safety: Issues and Alternatives* deals more with the economics of intervention but also compares different structural models and ideas in British Columbia, Saskatchewan and Ontario.

Energy Policy

Larry Pratt's *The Tar Sands* and Francois Bregha's *Bob Blair's Pipeline* provide comprehensive analyses of macro energy isues as seen through a focus on two major mega-projects of the 1970s and 1980s, the Syncrude project and the Alaska Pipeline. These should be read with William Kilbourn's book *Pipeline* which chronicles the 1956 Pipeline debate. All three are good on the broad politics but weaker on structure and the role of ideas per se. John N. McDougall's *Fuels and the National Policy* traces the historical evolution of policies for coal, oil and natural gas. It uses in a very general way a form of interplay model of public policy. Extremely good in stressing the underlying physical, geographical realities of energy policy. G. Bruce Doern and Glen Toner's *The NEP and the Politics of Energy* basically applies the idea, structure and process approach to energy policy, including the implementation of major NEP program elements. G. Bruce Doern's *Government Intervention in the Canadian Nuclear Industry* focuses on the normative and institutional determinants of government intervention. Only limited treatment of structure per se.

Foreign Policy

Michael Tucker's *Canadian Foreign Policy* comes closest to linking ideas, structure and process in an integrated way, both in general and in selected foreign policy issues. Bruce Thordarson's *Trudeau and Foreign Policy* is similarly integrated, except that it deals with a more limited time period, from 1968 to 1972. Stephen Clarkson's *Canada and the Reagan Challenge* presents an extensive review of foreign policy, especially in the wake of the National Energy Program in the early 1980s. It covers several foreign policy issues quite well but is far from complete in rating these to structure and process. Lyon and Tomlin's *Canada As an International Actor* is a necessary companion piece and complement since it focuses less on structure and process and more on other empirical forms of evidence, including data on voting, perceptions of foreign policy issues and actual foreign policy capabilities. Another useful source is David Protheroe's *Imports and Politics*. Though lacking an overall framework it supplies helpful insights into trade policy structures and processes in the 1970s.

Health Care Policy

Malcolm Taylor's *Health Insurance and Canadian and Public Policy* (McGill-Queen's Press). Has historical breadth and awareness of institutional roles and partisan political dispute. Uses basic systems approach but also tests his approach against other models of analysis.

Immigration Policy

Freda Hawkins' *Canada and Immigration* is historically quite comprehensive and good in presenting some aspects of immigration policy structures and the interests involved. Not very complete on the economic underpinning and dynamics of immigration. Therefore, Alan Green's *Immigration and the Post War Canadian Economy* is an essential complement to the Hawkins' book.

Incomes or Wage and Price Control Policies

Allan Maslove and Gene Swimmer's *Wage Controls in Canada 1975-1978* examines briefly the decision to establish the 1975 controls program. Its focus is on the behaviour of the Anti-Inflation Board, where a public choice approach is used.

Income Security and Social Welfare Policy

Keith G. Banting's *The Welfare State and Canadian Federalism* provides a comprehensive review of Canadian income security policies set in a comparative and historical context. It places a greater causal emphasis on social and economic variables than on political institutions per se. Contains an excellent analysis of relationships between centralization and redistribution. Important to stress that the book really only examines one major institution in any complete way, namely, federalism. Banting is careful not to translate his conclusions to other policy fields. Andrew Armitage's *Social Welfare in Canada* provides a good overview of policy evolution and ideas, but is much less complete on structure and process.

Indian Policy

Sally M. Weaver's *Making Canadian Indian Policy* examines the processes and issues surrounding the Trudeau government's White Paper on Indian policy in the 1968 and 1970 period. Though it articulates no overall framework, it in fact deals well with both ideas (e.g. about equality and participation) and with stuctures, including the power of central agencies. The book concludes that ultimately ideas and values outweighed individual personalities, but the latter are fully examined. The analysis is somewhat incomplete in that it does not adequately locate Indian policy in the context of other priorities of the period. Ponting and Gibbin's *Out of Irrelevance* is less complete on structure and policy dynamics but superior to the Weaver book in examining the actual social condition of Canada's native peoples.

Industrial Policy

There are several excellent books on industrial policy, albeit with different perspectives and covering different time perspectives. Rick French's *How Ottawa Decides*, despite its title, is about industrial policy in the 1970s. Very good on structure and dynamics, but its industrial policy focus is often lost because of an excessive emphasis on the three central agency "planning systems." Allan Tupper's *Public Money in the Private Sector* provides a perceptive examination of industrial assistance policies in a federal-provincial context, including the foreign policy dimensions of such policies. Glen Williams' book, *Not for Export: A Political Economy of Canada's Arrested Industrialization*, uses a quasi-class analysis approach to trace the historical evolution of trade and industrial policy. The analysis is excellent in relating broad historical ideas and interests to the structure of the Department of Trade and Commerce and its successor organizations. Rianne Mahon's *The Politics of Industrial Strategy in Canada: Textiles* uses a class analysis perspective to examine the decline of the textile industry and the domestic problems of adjustment. Especially good at linking the new international economic order to domestic national and regional industrial policy concerns. Peter Morici, Arthur Smith and Sperry Lea's *Canadian Industrial Policy* is useful in laying out the numerous dimensions of the field and because it provides primarily an American view of Canadian industrial policy. Arthur Smith, a former chairman of the Economic Council of Canada, developed only the historical chapters, so it is largely an American view. Uri Zohar's *Canadian Manufacturing: A Study in Productivity and Technological Change* presents a sophisticated time series analysis of nineteen industry groups, focusing on their capacity for productivity and change. Its findings are informative, but the policy prescriptions and analysis are not well handled precisely because ideas, structure and process are not examined.

Language Policy (and Transportation)

Sandford F. Borin's *Language of the Sky* is one of the best single case study types of policy study. It dissects the dispute involving language use, public safety and the air traffic controllers. Good at melding broad issues with short-term policy tactics and at analyzing how issues are perceived regionally and by conflicting interests.

Manpower Training Policy

Dupre, Cameron, McKechnie and Rotenberg's *Federalism and Policy Development* focuses on the federal-provincial dimensions of the development and implementation of the 1967 Adult Occupational Training Act. A good analysis of ideas, structures and process, including an appreciation of the role of education versus training paradigms or "grand designs."

Pensions

Kenneth Bryden's *Old Age Pensions and Policy Making in Canada* is also one of the best single books. Examines historical evolution of pensions for the aged. Good analysis of the market ethos and tests his analysis against a policy model he calls the "policy spiral." Not as complete on structures and detailed processes. Richard Simeon's *Federal Provincial Diplomacy* is stronger in the latter context, since in one of his case studies he analyzes federal-provincial bargaining over the 1965 Canada Pension Plan.

Regional Policy

Several books provide complementary perspectives. Anthony Careless's *Initiative and Response* focuses on the adaptation of Canadian federalism to regional economic development. It provides a breadth of perspective on the chronology of regional policy and shows the two-way impact between regional economic variables and federal-provincial structures and relationships. Various ideas about regionalism are well explored. Harvey Lithwick's *Regional Economic Policy: The Canadian Experience* is an essential complement to the Careless book, since it focuses on economic theories of regional development and examines the effects of policies on reducing regional disparities. John Richards and Larry Pratt's *Prairie Capitalism: Power and Influence in the New West* is a seminal work both in regional policy and resource and energy policy. Using what must be called a quasi-class analysis approach, it traces the changing impact of resource staples on the economic base, class structure and political institutions of the prairies with the focus on the emergence of province-building states in Alberta and Saskatchewan. Though it has historical breadth, it does not deal fully with the evolving national agenda that sets the context for resource and regional issues, nor does it recognize the full play of ideas in existence. Edgar J. Dosman's book *The National Interest* deals with a further territorial dimension of policy, namely, northern development in the 1968 to 1975 period. Though not informed by an explicit framework, the book deals well with the foreign and domestic dimensions of northern policy and the inter-connections between energy, environmental and native peoples' issues. The discussion of structures is good as is the analysis of large projects such as pipelines. Ideologies and ideas per se are not thoroughly examined. Gurston Dack's *A Choice of Futures: Politics in the Canadian North* brings northern policy into the 1980s and into energy policy issues in a more explicit way. It deals with ideas in a more complete way than Dosman's earlier work.

Science and Technology Policy

G. Bruce Doern's *Science and Politics in Canada* examines science policy until the early 1970s. The focus is on the relationships between scientific interests and policy structures. The relationship to broader industrial policy is not fully developed. Peter Aucoin and Richard French's *Knowledge and Power* focuses almost exclusively on the structure of science policy, especially the Minister of State for Science and Technology.

Tax Policy

David Good's *The Politics of Anticipation: Making Canadian Federal Tax Policy* critically examines the tax policy process using a model of policy making "by anticipation." Douglas Hartle's *The Revenue Budget Process* utilizes Good's analysis extensively but reaches somewhat different conclusions. Both books are somewhat narrowly focused in that they do not explicitly deal with broader economic or industrial policy dimensions. They should both be read, therefore, in relation to economic and industrial policy sources cited above.

Transportation Policy

John Langford's *Transport in Transition* reviews the broad param-eters of transportation policy, but its focus is primarily on structure and on the problems of establishing a "ministry" of transport in the 1970s. Howard Darling's *The Politics of Freight Rates* has quite a good historical analysis and links transportation policy to agricultural and regional policy in both Western and Atlantic Canada. David Harvey's *Christmas Turkey or Prairie Vulture?* presents a basic, primarily economic analysis of the Crow's Nest arrangement and transportation subsidies.

Key Questions To Pose When Studying Any Public Policy Field

Listed below are several groups of questions that emerge from the approach used in the book. We do not list them in the unrealistic expectation that one can answer them all, especially given the time constraints, the access to sources, and the limited resources of academic or even applied study. We do believe, however, that these questions convey the intellectual dimensions of the field and the need to address the policy field in relation to ideas, structures and processes both historically and in the current context. Moreover, although many of the books listed in the previous section reflect other approaches and the particular insights of their authors, they can nonetheless be partially re-examined by posing, discussing and attempting to answer the questions posed below. The questions are posed, generally speaking, in the order in which they are discussed in the book, beginning with ideas and concepts and then proceeding to structures and processes.

1. What *ideologies and dominant ideas* (see Chapter 2) are present in the policy field in question? How have they changed over time? What ideas are ranked highest by the prime minister, minister and Cabinet? By the opposition parties? By the interests affected, including provincial governments? What rhetorical language is used to express these ideas or to cloud them over?

2. What *institutional ideas* (see Chapter 2) are present? Which institutions must be consulted? What is the purpose of the consultation?

3. What are the spatial and *territorial aspects* of the policy? In short, what foreign policy issues and ideas are involved and what regional issues are involved?

4. What policy *paradigm(s)* exist in this policy field? Which paradigm is dominant and which is a contending one? Which knowledge groups or experts are identified with these paradigms?

5. What *statutes and laws* are involved in the policy field in question and what are the constitutional limits and constraints? Is new legislation required or could action be taken by executive action?

6. What *instruments* are used in the policy field? In what sequence were instruments used as the policy field evolved over time? What preferred instruments are being advocated as the primary basis of reform by the government? By the interests affected? What ideas are

involved in these instrumental preferences? How, if at all, does the proximity of an election affect instrument choice or the instrument being advocated? What groups, classes or sectors of society are being coerced by the policy or by new policies being advocated?

7. Are the policy changes being advocated major or minor in nature, that is, *fundamental or incremental*? From whose point of view? Who or which interests and agencies are advocating and pressuring and who is reacting?

8. What *risks and uncertainties* are involved in the policy options being advocated, including the status quo? Who must take the risks and who absorbs the consequences?

9. Where does the policy field in question *rank among* the government's and the opposition's *priorities*? High? Low? Medium? To what extent is current policy characterized by a strong Cabinet consensus? Or by a temporary vulnerable consensus?

10. What *structures* are involved in the policy field, directly and indirectly? Of what ideas and/or paradigms are these departments and agencies the prime custodian or defender? Which interests do they view their clientele to be? What policy instruments do they control?

11. What are the *time-related factors* involved in the policy formulation process? Are physical/capital projects involved? Current consumption versus medium- or longer-term investments? Are the policies intended to show short-term concern or other symbolic needs? How much time is there for consultation? Which interests want consultation and which ones want "decisive action"? What legal or political deadlines are involved?

12. In *implementing* the policy change, to what extent is implementation dependent on private behaviour, as opposed to things that officials can do? Who is the clientele for the policy and how does one deliver the policy to them? To what extent can everyone be treated equally and to what extent do different beneficiaries have to be treated differently?

13. How has the policy been *analyzed and evaluated* in the past? What formal studies have been carried out? Are there cumulative studies conducted or "one-shot" analysis? How has the policy field been evaluated through social interaction as opposed to cerebral analysis? What policy-related causal knowledge exists about the field? What information is needed and whose privacy must be invaded to obtain it?

APPENDIX B

CABINET COMMITTEES AND POLICY SECTOR RESOURCE ENVELOPES[1]

Cabinet Committee—Priorities and Planning

1. Financial Arrangements Envelope

Finance

Subsidies under BNA Act

Federal-Provincial Fiscal Arrangement

Utilities Income Tax Transfers

Reciprocal Taxation

Public Works

Municipal Grants

2. Public Debt Envelope

Finance

Public Debt—Interest & Amortization

Cabinet Committee—Economic and Regional Development

3. Economic and Regional Development Envelope

Agriculture

Department

Canadian Dairy Commission

Canadian Livestock Feed Board

Farm Credit Corporation*

Communications

Department

Consumer and Corporate Affairs

Department

Economic Development—Ministry of State

Energy, Mines and Resources

Minerals

Earth Sciences

Environment

Forestry

Fisheries and Oceans
   Department
Industry, Trade and Commerce
   Department
   Canadian Commercial Corporation
   Export Development Corporation*
   Federal Business Development Bank
   Foreign Investment Review Agency
   Standards Council of Canada
Labour
   Department
   Canada Labour Relations Board
Regional Economic Expansion
   Department
   Cape Breton Development Corporation
Science and Technology
   Department
   National Research Council
   Natural Sciences & Eng. Research Council
   Science Council of Canada
Supply and Services
   Unsolicited Proposals for R&D
Transport
   Department
   Air Canada
   Canadian Transport Commission
4. Energy Envelope
Energy, Mines and Resources
   Energy Budgetary
   Energy Nonbudgetary
   Petroleum Compensation Program
   Sarnia-Montreal Pipeline
   Canadian Home Insulation Program (CHIP)
   Atomic Energy Control Board
     Atomic Energy of Canada Limited
     National Energy Board
     Petro-Canada*
Economic Development
   Northern Pipeline Agency

Cabinet Committee—Social Development

5. Social Affairs Envelope

Communications
  Arts and Culture
  Canada Council
  Canadian Broadcasting Corporation
  Canadian Film Development Corporation
  Canadian Radio-Television & Telecommunications Commission
  National Arts Centre Corporation
  National Film Board
  National Library
  National Museums of Canada
  Public Archives
  Social Sciences & Humanities Research Council
Employment and Immigration
  Department
  Advisory Council on Status of Women
  Immigration Appeal Board
  Status of Women—Office of the Coordinator
Environment
  Environment Programs
Indian Affairs and Northern Development
  Department
  Northern Canada Power Commission
Labour
  Canadian Centre for Occupational Health & Safety
  Fitness and Amateur Sport
National Health and Welfare
  Department
  Medical Research Council
Public Works
  Canada Mortgage & Housing Corporation
Secretary of State
  Department
Social Development—Ministry of State
Treasury Board Canada
  Student, Youth & Other Employment
Veterans Affairs
  Department

6. Justice and Legal Envelope
   Justice
   Department
   Canadian Human Rights Commission
   Commissioner for Federal Judicial Affairs
   Law Reform Commission of Canada
   Supreme Court of Canada
   Tax Review Board
   Solicitor General
   Department
   Correctional Services
   National Parole Board
   Royal Canadian Mounted Police

Cabinet Committee—Foreign and Defence Policy

7. External Affairs Envelope
   External Affairs
   Department
   Canadian International Development Agency
   International Development Research Centre
   International Joint Commission
   Finance
   Official Development Assistance—Loans & Investments*
8. Defence Envelope
   National Defence
   Department

Cabinet Committee—Government Operations

9. Parliament Envelope
   Parliament
   The Senate
   House of Commons
   Library of Parliament
10. Services to Government Envelope
    Finance
    Department
    Auditor General
    Insurance
    Tariff Board

Governor General & Lieutenant-Governors
National Revenue
  Department
Post Office
  Department
Privy Council Office
  Canadian Intergovernmental Conference Secretariat
  Chief Electoral Officer
  Commissioner of Official Languages
  Economic Council of Canada
  Public Service Staff Relations Board
Public Works
  Department
  National Capital Commission
Secretary of State
  Public Service Commission
Supply and Services
  Department
  Statistics Canada
Treasury Board Canada
  Comptroller General

---

*Nonbudgetary.
[1]Envelope expenditures are identified by department (eg., Finance) and, as required, by agency (eg., Canadian Dairy Commission) in relationship to the appropriate department (eg., Agriculture). Where the programs of a single department are in more than one envelope, both the department (e.g., Finance) and the programs (e.g., Subsidies under BNA Act, etc.) are identified.

BIBLIOGRAPHY

Though the bibliography is organized into four sections, some of the books obviously overlap several of the sections. The four sections are: Concepts, Ideas and Institutions; Structures and Processes; Policy Evaluation and Analysis; and Policy Fields.

Concepts, Ideas and Institutions

Acheson, K. and J.F. Chant. "The Choice of Monetary Instruments and the Theory of Bureaucracy," in J.P. Cairns, H.H. Binhammer and R.W. Boadway (eds.). *Canadian Banking and Monetary Policy*. Second Edition. Toronto: McGraw-Hill Ryerson, 1972, pp. 233-252.

Aitken, H.G. "Defensive Expansionism: The State and Economic Growth in Canada," in W.T. Easterbrook and M.H. Watkins (eds.), *Approaches to Canadian Economic History*. Toronto: McClelland and Stewart, 1967.

Allison, Graham T. *The Essence of Decision*. Boston: Little Brown, 1971.

Art, R.J. "Bureaucratic Politics and American Foreign Policy: A Critique," *Policy Sciences*. Vol. 4. (1973), pp. 467-480.

Atkinson, Michael M. and K.R. Nossal. "Bureaucratic Politics and the New Fighter Aircraft Decisions," *Canadian Public Administration*. Vol. 24, No. 4. (19810, pp. 531-562.

Axline, Andrew, Maureen Molot, J. Hyndman and Peyton V. Lyon (eds.). *Continental Community: Independence and Integration in North America*. Toronto: McClelland and Stewart, 1974.

Bird, Richard M. *Financing Canadian Government: A Quantitative Overview*. Toronto: Canadian Tax Foundation, 1979.

Bird, Richard. *The Growth of Government Spending in Canada*. Toronto: Canadian Tax Foundation, 1970.

Black, Edwin R. *Divided Loyalties*. Montreal: McGill-Queen's University Press, 1975.

Black, Edwin R. *Politics and the News*. Toronto: Butterworths, 1982.

Blais, Andre. "Le Public Choice et la croissance de l'etate," *Canadian Journal of Political Science*. Vol. XIV, No. 4. (December 1982), pp. 783-808.

Bothwell, Robert, Ian Drummond and John English. *Canada Since 1945: Power, Politics and Provincialism*. Toronto: University of Toronto Press, 1981.

Bothwell, Robert and William Kilbourn. *C.D. Howe: A Biography*. Toronto: McClelland and Stewart, 1979.

Braybrooke, David and C.E. Lindblom. *A Strategy of Decision*. New York: Free Press, 1963.

Breton, Albert. *The Economic Theory of Representative Government*. Chicago: University of Chicago Press, 1974.

Brodie, M.J. and Jane Jenson. *Crisis, Challenge and Change: Party and Class in Canada*. Toronto: Methuen, 1980.

Buchanan, James. "An Economist's Approach to 'Scientific' Politics," in M.B. Parsons (ed.). *Perspectives in the Study of Politics*. Chicago: Rand McNally, 1968, pp. 77-83.

Buchanan, James M. and Richard E. Wagner. *Democracy in Deficit*. New York: Academic Press, 1977.

Cairns, Allan. "The Governments and Societies of Canadian Federalism," *Canadian Journal of Political Science*. Vol. X, pp. 695-725.

Cameron, David. *Nationalism, Self-Determination and the Quebec Question*. Toronto: Macmillan of Canada, 1974.

Campbell, Robert. *Grand Illusions: The Keynesian Experience in Canada*. Trent University. Manuscript in press.

Canadian Federation of Independent Business. *A Decade of Action*. Toronto: Canadian Federation of Independent Business, 1979.

Canadian Manufacturer's Association. *Agenda for Action*. Toronto: 1977.

Chandler, Marsha A. and William M. Chandler. *Public Policy and Provincial Politics*. Toronto: McGraw-Hill Ryerson, 1979.

Christian, W. and C. Campbell. *Political Parties and Ideologies in Canada*. Second Edition. Toronto: McGraw-Hill Ryerson, 1983.

Cook, Ramsay. *Canada and the French Canadian Question*. Toronto: Macmillan of Canada, 1976.

Courchene, Thomas J. *Money, Inflation and the Bank of Canada*. Vol. II. Montreal: C.D. Howe Research Institute, 1981.

Courchene, Thomas J. *The Strategy of Gradualism*. Montreal: C.D. Howe Research Institute, 1978.

Creighton, Donald. *Harold Adams Innis: Portrait of a Scholar*. Toronto: University of Toronto Press, 1978.

Creighton, Donald. *John A. Macdonald: The Old Chieftain*. Toronto: Macmillan of Canada, 1955.

Dahl, Robert A. and Charles E. Lindblom. *Politics, Economics and Welfare*. New York: Harper Torch Books, 1953.

d'Aquino, T.G., Bruce Doern and C. Blair. *Parliamentary Government in Canada: A Critical Assessment and Suggestions for Change*. Ottawa: Intercounsel Ltd., 1979.

Dawson, R.M. *The Government of Canada*. Revised by N. Ward. Toronto: University of Toronto Press, 1970.

Diefenbaker, John G. *One Canada*. Toronto: Macmillan of Canada, 1975.

Dion, Leon. *Quebec: the Unfinished Revolution*. Montreal: McGill-Queen's University Press, 1976.

Donner, Arthur W. and Douglas D. Peters. *Monetarist Counter-Revolution*. Ottawa: Canadian Institute for Economic Policy, 1979.

Dror, Yehezkel. *Design for Policy Sciences*. New York: Elsevier, 1971.

Dror, Yehezkel. *Public Policy Making Reexamined*. San Francisco: Chandler, 1968.

Dwividi, O.P. (ed.). *The Administrative State in Canada.* Toronto: University of Toronto Press, 1982.

Dye, Thomas. *Understanding Public Policy.* Fourth Edition. New York: Prentice-Hall, 1982.

Easton, David. *A Systems Analysis of Political Life.* New York: John Wiley and Sons, 1965.

Edelman, Murray. *Politics as Symbolic Action.* New York: Academic Press, 1971.

Edelman, Murray. *The Symbolic Uses of Politics.* Champaign-Urbana: University of Illinois Press, 1967.

Etzioni, A. *The Active Society.* New York: Free Press, 1968.

Friedman, Milton. *Capitalism and Freedom.* Chicago: University of Chicago Press, 1962.

Friedman, Milton. *Inflation and Unemployment: The New Dimension of Politics.* 1976 Nobel Lecture. London: 1977.

Galbraith, John K. *The New Industrial Estate.* New York: Signet Books, 1967.

Giles, Anthony. *The Politics of Wage Controls: The Canadian State, Organized Labour and Corporatism.* Masters Thesis, School of Public Administration, Carleton University, 1980.

Grant, George. *Lament for a Nation.* Toronto: McClelland and Stewart, 1965.

Guindon, Hubert. "The Modernization of Quebec and the Legitimacy of the Canadian State," *Canadian Review of Sociology and Anthropology.* Vol. 15, No. 2. (1978), pp. 227-245.

Hardin, Herschel. *A Nation Unaware: The Canadian Economic Culture.* Vancouver: J.J. Douglas, 1974.

Hartle, Douglas. *Public Policy Decision Making and Regulation.* Montreal: Institute for Research on Public Policy, 1979.

Hockin, T.A. *Government in Canada.* Toronto: McGraw-Hill Ryerson, 1976.

Hodgins, Barbara. *Where the Economy and the Constitution Meet in Canada.* Montreal: C.D. Howe Institute, 1981.

Hofferbert, R.I. *The Study of Public Policy.* New York: Bobbs Merrill, 1974.

Horowitz, Gad. *Canadian Labour in Politics.* Toronto: University of Toronto Press, 1968.

Innis, Harold. *Essays in Canadian Economic History.* Toronto: University of Toronto Press, 1956.

Irvine, Willian P. *Does Canada Need a New Electoral System?* Kingston: Institute of Intergovernmental Relations, 1979.

Jenkins, W.I. *Policy Analysis.* London: Martin Robertson, 1978.

Jones, C.O. *An Introduction to the Study of Public Policy.* New York: Wadsworth, 1970.

Kwavnick, David. *Organized Labour and Pressure Politics.* Montreal: McGill-Queen's University Press, 1972.

Lakoff, Sanford A. (ed.). "The Third Culture: Science in Social Thought," *Knowledge and Power.* New York: Free Press, 1966, Chapter 1.

Langille, David. *From Consultation to Corporatism? The Consultative Process*

Between Canadian Business, Labour and Government, 1977-1981. Ottawa: Master Research Essay, Department of Political Science, Carleton University, 1982.

Lewis, David. *The Good Fight.* Toronto: Macmillan of Canada, 1981.

Lindblom, Charles E. *The Policy Making Process.* New York: Prentice-Hall, 1968.

Lindblom, Charles E. *Politics and Markets.* New York: Basic Books, 1977.

Lipset, S.M. *Agrarian Socialism.* New York: Anchor Books, Doubleday, 1968.

Lowi, Theodore. "Decision Making Versus Public Policy: Toward an Antidote for Technocracy," *Public Administration Review.* Vol. 30. (1970), pp. 314-325.

Lowi, Theodore, "Four Systems of Policy, Politics and Choice," *Public Administration Review.* Vol. 32. (1972), pp. 298-310.

MacPherson, C.B. *Democracy in Alberta.* Toronto: University of Toronto Press, 1953.

McKenzie, Richard B. and Gordon Tullock. *Modern Political Economy: An Introduction to Economics.* New York: McGraw-Hill, 1978.

Miliband, Ralph. *The State in Capitalist Society.* London: Quartet Books, 1973.

Moniere, Denis. *Ideologies in Quebec.* Toronto: University of Toronto Press, 1981.

Morton, R.L. *The Canadian Identity.* Second Edition. Toronto: University of Toronto Press, 1972.

Morton, W.L. *The Kingdom of Canada.* Toronto: McClelland and Stewart, 1963.

Morton, W.L. *The Progressive Party in Canada.* Toronto: University of Toronto Press, 1950.

Neatby, Blair. *The Politics of Chaos: Canada in the Thirties.* Toronto: Macmillan of Canada, 1972.

Niskanen Jr., William A. *Bureaucracy and Representative Government.* Chicago: Aldine-Atherton, 1971.

O'Connor, James. *The Fiscal Crisis of the State.* New York: St. Martin's Press, 1973.

Olson, Mancur. *The Logic of Collective Action.* Cambridge, Mass.: Harvard University Press, 1965.

Panitch, Leo. *The Canadian State.* Toronto: University of Toronto Press, 1977.

Panitch, Leo. "Trade Unions and the Capitalist State," *New Left Review.* No. 125. (Janurary-February) 1981, pp. 43-92.

Panitch, Leo. "Corporatism in Canada," *Studies in Political Economy.* Vol. 1, No. 1. (Spring, 1979).

Paul, Ellen F. and Phillip A. Russo Jr. *Public Policy: Issues, Analysis and Ideology.* Chatham, N.J.: Chatham House, 1982.

Perlin, George. *The Tory Syndrome.* Montreal: McGill-Queen's University Press, 1980.

Porter, John. *The Vertical Mosaic.* Toronto: University of Toronto Press, 1965.

Pratt, Larry. *The Tar Sands: Syncrude and the Politics of Oil.* Edmonton: Hurtig, 1976.

Presthus, Robert. *Elite Accommodation in Canadian Politics*. Toronto: Macmillan of Canada, 1973.

Pross, Paul A. "Governing Under Pressure: The Special Interest Groups," *Canadian Public Administration*. Vol. 25, No. 2. (Summer, 1982), pp. 170-182.

Pross, Paul A. *Pressure Group Behavior in Canadian Politics*. Toronto: McGraw-Hill Ryerson, 1975.

Rea, K.J. and J.T. McLeod. (eds.). *Business and Government in Canada*. Second Edition. Toronto: Methuen, 1976.

Richards, John and Larry Pratt. *Prairie Capitalism*. Toronto: McClelland and Stewart, 1979.

Rose, Richard and Guy Peters. *Can Government Go Bankrupt?* New York: Basic Books, 1978.

Russell, Peter H. (ed.). *Nationalism in Canada*. Toronto: McGraw-Hill, 1966.

Schumpeter, Joseph A. *Capitalism, Socialism and Democracy*. Third Edition. New York: Harper Torch Books, 1962.

Schwartz, Mildred. *The Environment for Policy Making in Canada and the United States*. Washington: National Planning Association and C.D. Howe Research Institute, 1981.

Sharkansky, Ira. *Public Administration: Policy Making in Government Agencies*.Chicago: Markham, 1972.

Sheppard, Robert and Michael Valpy. *The National Deal: The Fight for a Canadian Constitution*. Toronto: Fleet Books, 1982.

Shonfield, A. *Modern Capitalism: The Changing Balance of Public and Private Power*. London: Oxford University Press, 1965.

Simeon, Richard. "Studying Public Policy," *Canadian Journal of Political Science*. Vol. 9 (December 1976), pp. 547-580.

Simeon, Richard. "The 'Overload Thesis' and Canadian Government," *Canadian Public Policy*. Vol. II, No. 4. (Autumn, 1976), pp. 541-552.

Simeon, Richard. *Federal-Provincial Diplomacy: The Making of Recent Policy in Canada*. Toronto: University of Toronto Press, 1972.

Simeon, Richard. "Regionalism and Canadian Political Institutions," *Queen's Quarterly*. Vol. 82. (Winter, 1975).

Simeon, Richard and David J. Elkin. "Regional Political Cultures in Canada," *Canadian Journal of Political Science*. Vol. VII. (September 1974), pp. 397-437.

Simon, Herbert A. *Administrative Behavior*. Second Edition. New York: Free Press, 1965.

Slayton, Phillip and Michael J. Trebilcock. *The Professions and Public Policy*. Toronto: University of Toronto Press, 1978.

Smiley, D.V. *Canada in Question*. Third Edition. Toronto: McGraw-Hill Ryerson, 1980.

Smiley, Donald. "Canada and the Quest for a New National Policy," *Canadian Journal of Political Science*. Vol. 8. (March, 1975), pp. 40-62.

Stevenson, Garth. *Unfulfilled Union*. Toronto: Macmillan of Canada, 1979.

Stigler, George J. *The Citizen and the State.* Chicago: University of Chicago Press. 1975.

Taylor, Charles. *Radical Tories.* Toronto: Anansi, 1982.

Thorburn, H. (ed.). *Party Politics in Canada.* Fourth Edition. Toronto: Prentice-Hall, 1979.

Thurow, Lester C. *The Zero-Sum Society.* New York: Penguin Books, 1981.

Trebilcock, Michael. "The Consumer Interest and Regulatory Reform," in G. Bruce Doern (ed.). *The Regulatory Process in Canada.* Toronto: Macmillan of Canada, 1978.

Trebilcock, M.J., R.S. Prichard, D.G. Hartle and D.N. Dewees. *The Choice of Governing Instruments.* Ottawa: Ministry of Supply and Services, 1982.

Trudeau, Pierre Elliott. *Federalism and the French Canadians.* Toronto: Macmillan of Canada, 1968.

Van Loon, Rick. "Reforming Welfare in Canada," *Public Policy.* Vol. 27, No. 4. (Fall, 1979), pp. 469-504.

Van Loon, R. and M. Whittington. *The Canadian Political System.* Third Edition. Toronto: McGraw-Hill Ryerson. 1981.

Vickers, Sir Geoffrey. *The Art of Judgement.* New York: Basic Books, 1965.

Vickers, Sir Geoffrey. *Value Systems and Social Processes.* London: Tavistock, 1968.

Whitaker, Reg. "Images of the State in Canada," in Leo Panitch (ed.), *The Canadian State.* Toronto: University of Toronto Press, 1977, Chapter 2.

Whitaker, Reg. *The Government Party.* Toronto: University of Toronto Press, 1977.

Wildavsky, Aaron. *The Politics of the Budgetary Process.* Third Edition. Boston: Little Brown, 1979.

Wilson, V. Seymour. *Canadian Public Policy: Theory and Environment.* Toronto: McGraw-Hill Ryerson, 1981.

Winn, Conrad and J. McMenemy. *Political Parties in Canada.* Toronto: McGraw-Hill Ryerson, 1976.

Structures and Processes

Anderson, Robert D. "The Federal Regulation-Making Process and Regulatory Reform, 1969-1979," in W.T. Stanbury (ed.). *Government Regulation: Scope, Growth, Process.* Montreal: Institute for Research on Public Policy, 1980, Chapter 4.

Aucoin, Peter and Richard French. *Knowledge, Power and Public Policy.* Ottawa: Science Council of Canada, 1974.

Bailey, A.R. and D.G. Hull. *The Way Out; A More Revenue Dependent Public Sector and How It Might Revitalize the Process of Governing.* Montreal: Institute for Research on Public Policy, 1980.

Bond, D.E. and R.A. Shearer. *The Economics of the Canadian Financial System: Theory, Policy and Institutions.* Toronto: Prentice-Hall of Canada, 1972.

Borins, Sandford F. "World War Two Crown Corporations: Their Wartime Role and Peacetime Privatization," *Canadian Public Administration.* (Fall 1982), pp. 380-404.

Brown, Douglas and Julia Eastman. *The Limits of Consultation.* Ottawa: Science Council of Canada, 1981.

Campbell, Colin and George Szablowski. *The Superbureaucrats.* Toronto: Macmillan of Canada, 1979.

Canada. *The Budget Process.* Ottawa: Minister of Finance, April 1982.

Canada. Privy Council Office. *Cabinet Paper System.* Ottawa: 1977.

Canada West Foundation. *Regional Representation.* Calgary: Canada West Foundation, 1981.

Dodge, William (ed.). *Consultation and Consensus: A New Era in Policy Formulation?* Ottawa: Conference Board of Canada, 1978.

Doern, G. Bruce (ed.). *How Ottawa Spends Your Tax Dollars 1981.* Toronto: James Lorimer Publishers. 1981.

Doern, G. Bruce (ed.). *How Ottawa Spends Your Tax Dollars 1982.* Toronto: James Lorimer Publishers, 1982.

Doern, G. Bruce. *The Peripheral Nature of Scientific and Technological Controversy in Federal Policy Formation.* Ottawa: Science Council of Canada, 1981.

Doern, G. Bruce (ed.). *The Regulatory Process in Canada.* Toronto: Macmillan of Canada, 1978.

Doern, G. Bruce and Peter Aucoin (eds.). *Public Policy in Canada.* Toronto: Macmillan of Canada, 1979.

Doern, G. Bruce and Allan Maslove. *The Public Evaluation of Government Spending.* Montreal: Institute for Research on Public Policy, 1979.

Doerr, Audrey. "The Role of Coloured Papers," *Canadian Public Administration.* Vol. 25, No. 3. (Fall, 1982), pp. 366-379.

Doerr, Audrey. *The Machinery of Government in Canada.* Toronto: Methuen, 1981.

Economic Council of Canada. *Responsible Regulation.* Ottawa: Minister of Supply and Services, 1979.

French, Richard. *How Ottawa Decides*. Ottawa: Canadian Institute for Economic Policy, 1980.

French, Richard. "The Privy Council Office: Support for Cabinet Decision Making," in Richard Schultz, O.M. Kruhlak and J.T. Terry. *The Canadian Political Process*. Toronto: Holt, Rinehart and Winston of Canada, 1979, pp. 369-382.

Good, David. *The Politics of Anticipation: Making Canadian Federal Tax Policy*. Ottawa: School of Public Administration, Carleton University, 1980.

Gordon, Marsha. *Government in Business*. Montreal: C.D. Howe Research Institute, 1980.

Government of Canada. *Powers Over the Economy: Securing the Canadian Economic Union in the Constitution*. Ottawa: Government of Canada, July 1980.

Granatstein, J.L. *A Man of Influence: Norman A. Robertson and Canadian Statecraft 1929-68*. Ottawa: Deneau Publishers, 1981.

Granatstein, J.L. *The Ottawa Men: The Civil Service Mandarins 1935-1957*. Toronto: Oxford University Press, 1982.

Gwyn, Richard. *The Northern Magus*. Markham, Ontario: Paperjacks Ltd., 1981.

Hartle, Douglas. *The Expenditure Budget Process in the Government of Canada*. Toronto: Canadian Tax Foundation, 1978.

Hartle, Douglas. *The Revenue Budget Process of the Government of Canada*. Toronto: Canadian Tax Foundation, 1982.

Heclo, Hugh and Aaron Wildavsky. *The Private Government of Public Money*. London: Macmillan, 1973.

Hockin, T. *Apex of Power*. Second Edition. Toronto: Prentice-Hall, 1980.

Hodgetts, J.E. *The Canadian Public Service*. Toronto: University of Toronto Press, 1973.

Humphreys, David. *Joe Clark: A Portrait*. Ottawa: Deneau and Greenberg. 1978.

Jackson, Robert J. and M. Atkinson. *The Canadian Legislative System*. Second Edition. Toronto: Macmillan of Canada, 1980.

Johnson, A.W. "Public Policy: Creativity and Bureaucracy," *Canadian Public Administration*. Vol. 21, No. 1. (Spring, 1978), pp. 1-15.

Kernaghan, W.D.K. "Politics, Policy and Public Servants: Political Neutrality Revisited," *Canadian Public Administration*. Vol. 19, No. 3. (Fall, 1976), pp. 431-456.

Kernaghan, W.D.K. (ed.) *Public Administration in Canada*. Fourth Edition. Toronto: Methuen, 1982.

Langford, John. "The Identification and Classification of Federal Public Corporations: A Preface to Regime Building," *Canadian Public Administration*. Vol. 23. (Spring, 1980), pp. 76-104.

MacDonald, Flora. "The Minister and the Mandarins," *Policy Options*. Vol. 1, No. 3. (September/October 1980), pp. 29-31.

Matheson, W.A. *The Prime Minister and the Cabinet*. Toronto: Methuen, 1976.

McCall-Newman, Christina. *Grits*. Toronto: Macmillan of Canada, 1982.

McCall-Newman, Christina. "Michael Pitfield and the Politics of Mismanagement," *Saturday Night*. (October, 1982).

McCamus, John D. *Freedom of Information: Canadian Perspectives*. Toronto: Butterworths, 1981.

Newman, Peter C. *The Distemper of Our Times*. Toronto: McClelland and Stewart, 1968.

Newman, Peter C. *Renegade in Power*. Toronto: McClelland and Stewart, 1963.

Office of the Prime Minister. "Reorganization for Economic Development." Ottawa: January 12, 1982.

Pearson, Lester B. *Mike*. Toronto: Signet, 1976.

Pickersgill, J.W. *The Mackenzie King Record*. Vol. I. 1939-1944. Toronto: University of Toronto Press, 1960.

Pritchard, R. (ed.). *Crown Corporations in Canada: The Calculus of Instrument Choice*. Toronto: Butterworths, 1982.

Radwanski, George. *Trudeau*. Toronto: Macmillan of Canada, 1978.

Russell, Peter H. "The Effect of a Charter of Rights on the Policy Making Role of Canadian Courts," *Canadian Public Administration*. Vol. 25, No. 1. (Spring, 1982).

Simpson, Jeffrey. *The Discipline of Power*. Toronto: Personal Library, 1981.

Smith, Denis. *Gentle Patriot: A Political Biography of Walter Gordon*. Edmonton: Hurtig, 1973.

Smith, L.G. "Canadian Participation Mechanisms," *Canadian Public Policy*. Vol. VIII, No. 4. (Autumn, 1982), pp. 561-572.

Stanbury, W.T. (ed.). *Government Regulation: Scope, Growth, Process*. Montreal: Institute for Research on Public Policy, 1980.

Stanbury, W.T. and Fred Thompson. (eds.). *Managing Public Enterprises*. New York: Praeger, 1982.

Stanbury, W.T. and Fred Thompson. *Regulatory Reform in Canada*. Montreal: Institute for Research on Public Policy, 1982.

Tupper, Allan. "Public Enterprise as Social Welfare: The Case of the Cape Breton Development Corporation," *Canadian Public Policy*. Vol. IV, No. 4. (Autumn, 1978), pp. 530-546.

Tupper, Allan and G. Bruce Doern (eds.). *Public Corporations and Public Policy in Canada*. Montreal: Institute for Research on Public Policy, 1981.

Van Loon, Rick. "Stop the Music: The Current Policy and Expenditure Management System in Ottawa," *Canadian Public Administration*. Vol. 24. (Summer, 1981), pp. 175-199.

Vining, Aidan R. "An Overview of the Origins, Growth, Size and Functions of Provincial Crown Corporation." Study prepared for the Institute for Research on Public Policy. Vancouver: University of British Columbia, 1979.

Vinning, Grant. "Regulation and Regulatory Modes in Canadian Agriculture." Ottawa: M.A. Thesis, School of Public Administration, Carleton University, 1978.

Weaver, Paul H. "Regulation, Social Policy and Class Conflict," *The Public*

Interest. Vol. 50. (Winter, 1978), pp. 45-64.

Zussman, David. "The Image of the Public Service in Canada," *Canadian Public Administration.* Volume 25, No. 1. (Spring, 1982), pp. 63-80.

Policy Evaluation and Analysis

Auditor General of Canada. *Annual Report 1980.* Ottawa: Minister of Supply and Services, 1980.

Benveniste, Guy. *The Politics of Expertise.* Berkeley: University of California Press, 1973.

Bossons, John. "The Analysis of Tax Reform," in L.H. Officer and Lawrence B. Smith (eds.). *Issues in Canadian Economics.* Toronto: McGraw-Hill Ryerson, 1974.

Cheveldayoff, Wayne. *The Business Page.* Ottawa: Deneau and Greenberg, 1980.

Daub, Mervin. "Economic Forecasting in the Federal Government." Ottawa: Ministry of State for Economic Development, 1982.

Desjardins, D.J. "Sharpening a Public Policy Tool: The CPI." *The Canadian Business Review.* (Summer, 1982), pp. 36-38.

Dickson, Paul. *Think Tanks.* New York: Ballantine Books, 1971.

Dobell, Rodney and David Zussman. "An Evaluation System for Government: If Politics is Theatre, Then Evaluation is (mostly) Art," *Canadian Public Administration.* Vol. 24, No. 3. (Fall, 1981), pp. 404-427.

Laframboise, H.L. "Here Come the Program-Benders," *Optimum.* Vol. 7, No. 1. (1976).

McCracken, M.C. and E. Rudick. *Toward a Better Understanding of the Consumer Price Index.* Ottawa: Economic Council of Canada, 1980.

Meltsner, Arnold J. *Policy Analysts in the Bureaucracy.* Berkeley: University of California Press, 1976.

Nachmias, D. *Public Policy Evaluation Approaches and Methods.* New York: St. Martin's Press, 1978.

Phidd, Richard W. "The Economic Council of Canada 1963-1974." *Canadian Public Administration.* Vol. 18, No. 3. (1975).

Prince, Michael. "Policy Advisory Groups in Government Departments," in G. Bruce Doern and Peter Aucoin (eds.). *Public Policy in Canada.* Toronto: Macmillan of Canada, 1979. Chapter 10.

Ritchie, Ronald. *An Institute for Research on Public Policy.* Ottawa: Information Canada, 1971.

Rogers, Harry, M.A. Ulrich and K.L. Traversy. "Evaluation in Practice: The State of the Art in Canadian Governments," *Canadian Public Administration.* Vol. 24, No. 3. (Fall, 1981), pp. 371-386.

Royal Commission on Financial Management and Accountability. *Final Report.* Ottawa: Minister of Supply and Services, 1979.

Rutman, Len. *Planning Useful Evaluations.* Beverley Hills: Sage Publications, 1980.

Salter, Kiora and Debra Slaco. *Public Inquiries in Canada.* Ottawa: Science Council of Canada, 1981.

Schooler Jr., Dean. *Science, Scientists and Public Policy.* New York: Free Press, 1971.

Scioli Jr., P. Frank and Thomas J. Cook. *Methodology for Analyzing Public Policies.* New York: D.C. Heath, 1978.

Sinclair, Sonja. *Cordial But Not Cosy: A History of the Office of the Auditor General.* Toronto: McClelland and Stewart, 1979.

Smith, David C. (ed.). *Economic Policy Advising in Canada.* Montreal: C.D. Howe Research Institute, 1981.

Sutherland, S.L. "On the Audit Trail of the Auditor General: Parliament's Servant 1973-1980," *Canadian Public Administration.* Vol. 23, No. 4. (Winter, 1980).

Wildavski, Aaron. *Speaking Truth to Power: The Art and Craft of Policy Analysis.* Boston: Little Brown, 1979.

Policy Fields

Abella, Iriving and H. Troper. *None Too Many.* Toronto: Lester and Orpen Dennys Ltd., 1982.

Armitage, Andrew. *Social Welfare in Canada.* Toronto: McClelland and Stewart, 1975.

Anderson, John and Morley Gunderson (eds.). *Union Management Relations in Canada.* Toronto: Addison-Wesley, 1982.

Banting, Keith. *The Welfare State and Canadian Federalism.* Montreal: McGill-Queen's University Press, 1982.

Barber, Clarence L. and John C.P. McCallum *Unemployment and Inflation: The Canadian Experience.* Ottawa: Canadian Institute for Economic Policy, 1980.

Bertrand, Robert. *Canada's Oil Monopoly.* Toronto: James Lorimer Publishers, 1981.

Best, Robert. "Youth Policy," in G. Bruce Doern and V.S. Wilson (eds.). *Issues in Canadian Public Policy.* Toronto: Macmillan of Canada, 1974.

Biggs, M. *The Challenge: Adjust or Protect.* Ottawa: The North-South Institute, 1980.

Blake, David H. and Robert S. Walters. *The Politics of Global Economic Relations.* Englewood Cliffs: Prentice-Hall, 1976.

Boadway, Robin W. and Harry M. Kitchen. *Canadian Tax Policy.* Toronto: Canadian Tax Foundation, 1980.

Borins, Sandford F. *Language of the Sky*. Montreal: McGill-Queen's University Press, 1983.

Brecher, Irving. *Canada's Competition Policy Revisited: Some New Thoughts on an Old Story*. Montreal: Institute for Research on Public Policy, 1981.

Bregha, Francois. *Bob Blair's Pipeline*. Second Edition. Toronto: James Lorimer Publishers, 1981.

Britton, John N.H. and James Gilmour. *The Weakest Link: A Technological Perspective on Canadian Industrial Underdevelopment*. Ottawa: Science Council of Canada, 1978.

Brooks, David. *Zero Energy Growth for Canada*. Toronto: McClelland and Stewart, 1981.

Bryan, I. *Economic Policies in Canada*. Toronto: Butterworths, 1982.

Bryden, Kenneth. *Old Age Pensions and Policy Making in Canada*. Montreal: McGill-Queen's University Press, 1974.

Burns, R.M. and L. Close. *The Municipal Winter Works Incentives Program*. Toronto: Canadian Tax Foundation, 1971.

Canada. *Agenda for Cooperation*. Ottawa: Minister of Supply and Services, 1977.

Canada. *National Energy Program*. Ottawa: Minister of Supply and Services, 1980.

Canada. *Report of the Federal Cultural Policy Review Committee*. Ottawa: Minister of Supply and Services, 1982.

Canada. *Report of the Mackenzie Valley Pipeline Inquiry*. Ottawa: Minister of Supply and Services, 1977.

Canada. *Royal Commission on Conditions of Foreign Service*. Ottawa: Minister of Supply and Services, 1981.

Canada. *NEP Update*. Ottawa: Minister of Supply and Services, 1982.

Canada. *The Way Ahead*. Ottawa: Minister of Supply and Services, 1976.

Canadian Council on Social Development. *Social Policies for the 1980s*. Ottawa: Canadian Council on Social Development, 1981.

Careless, Anthony. *Initiative and Response*. Montreal: McGill-Queen's University Press, 1977.

Clarkson, Stephen. *Canada and the Reagan Challenge*. Ottawa: Canadian Institute for Economic Policy, 1982.

Connaghan, C.J. *Partnership or Marriage of Convenience: A Critical Examination of Contemporary Labour Relations in West Germany*. Ottawa: Labour Canada, 1976.

Copithorne, L. "Natural Resources and Regional Disparities: A Skeptical View," *Canadian Public Policy*. Vol. V, No. 2. (Spring, 1979), pp. 181-194.

Council of Ministers of Education. *Report of the Federal-Provincial Task Force on Student Assistance*. Ottawa: Minister of Supply and Services, 1981.

Crane, David. *Controlling Interest*. Toronto: McClelland and Stewart, 1982.

Currie, A.W. *Canadian Transportation Economics*. Toronto: University of Toronto Press, 1967.

Dacks, Gurston. *A Choice of Futures: Politics in the Canadian North.* Toronto: Methuen, 1981.

Daly, Donald J. "Weak Links in 'The Weakest Link'," *Canadian Public Policy.* Volume V. No. 3. (Summer, 1979), pp. 307-317.

Darling, Howard. *The Politics of Freight Rates.* Toronto: McClelland and Stewart, 1980.

Davies, Gordon W. and S. Sharir. "Towards 'A Rational Immigration Policy': Comments and a Proposal," *Canadian Public Policy.* Vol. II, No. 3. (Summer, 1976), pp. 492-496.

Department of Industry, Trade and Commerce. News Release. "Major Projects Benefits Board to be Formed." Ottawa: May 20, 1982.

Department of Reconstruction. *White Paper on Employment and Income.* Ottawa: King's Printer, 1945.

Diebold, W. *Industrial Policy as an International Issue.* New York: Council on Foreign Relations, 1980.

Dobson, Wendy. *Canada's Energy Policy Debate.* Montreal: C.D. Howe Research Institute, 1981.

Doern, G. Bruce. *Government Intervention in the Nuclear Industry.* Montreal: Institute for Research on Public Policy, 1980.

Doern, G. Bruce. *The Politics of Risk: The Identification of Toxic and Other Hazardous Substances in Canada.* Toronto: Royal Commission on Matters of Health and Safety Arising from the Use of Asbestos in Ontario, 1982.

Doern, G. Bruce. *Science and Politics in Canada.* Montreal: McGill-Queen's University Press, 1972.

Doern, G. Bruce and R.W. Morrison (eds.). *Canadian Nuclear Policies.* Montreal: Institute of Research on Public Policy, 1980.

Doern, G. Bruce, Michael Prince and Garth McNaughton. *Living with Contradictions: Health and Safety Regulation and Implementation in Ontario.* Toronto: Ontario Royal Commission on Matters of Health and Safety Arising from the Use of Asbestos in Ontario, 1982.

Doern, G. Bruce and Glen Toner. *The NEP and the Politics of Energy.* Toronto: Methuen, forthcoming.

Doern, G. Bruce and V. Seymour Wilson (eds.). *Issues in Canadian Public Policy.* Toronto: Macmillan of Canada, 1974.

Dosman, Edgar. *The National Interest.* Toronto: McClelland and Stewart, 1975.

Dow, James. *The Arrow.* Toronto: James Lorimer Publishers, 1979.

Dupre, S., D. Cameron, G.H. McKechnie and T.B. Rotenberg. *Federalism and Policy Development.* Toronto: University of Toronto Press, 1973.

Economic Council of Canada. *Eighth Annual Review.* Ottawa: Queen's Printer, 1968.

Economic Council of Canada. *Financing Confederation.* Ottawa: Minister of Supply and Services, 1982.

Economic Council of Canada. *Living Together.* Ottawa: Minister of Supply and Services, 1980.

Economic Council of Canada. *Looking Outward: A New Trade Strategy for Canada*. Ottawa: Information Canada, 1975.

Economic Council of Canada. *People and Jobs*. Ottawa: Information Canada, 1976.

Economic Council of Canada. *In Short Supply: Jobs and Skills in the 1980s*. Ottawa: Minister of Supply and Services, 1982.

Employment and Immigration Canada. *Labour Market Development in the 1980s*. Ottawa: Minister of Supply and Services, 1981.

Employment and Immigration Canada. *Unemployment Insurance in the 1980s*. Ottawa: Minister of Supply and Services, 1981.

Fayerweather, J. *Foreign Investment in Canada*. Toronto: Oxford University Press, 1973.

Forbes, J.D., R.D. Hughes and T.K. Warley. *Economic Intervention and Regulation in Canadian Agriculture*. Ottawa: Economic Council of Canada and Institute for Research on Public Policy, 1982.

Foster, Peter. *The Blue Eyed Sheiks: The Canadian Oil Establishment*. Toronto: Collins, 1979.

Foster, Peter. *The Sorcerer's Apprentices: Canada's Super Bureaucrats and the Energy Mess*. Toronto: Collins, 1982.

Fowke, V.C. *Canadian Agricultural Policy: The Historical Pattern*. Toronto: University of Toronto Press, 1946.

Fowke, V.C. *The National Policy and the Wheat Economy*. Toronto: University of Toronto Press, 1957.

Fraser Institute. *The Illusion of Wage and Price Controls*. Vancouver: Fraser Institute, 1976.

Gander and Belaire. *Energy Futures for Canadians*. Ottawa: Minister of Supply and Services, 1978.

Gillespie, W.I. "The State and Income Redistribution," *Canadian Taxation*. Vol. 3, No. 3. (Fall, 1981).

Gillespie, W.I. "On the Redistribution of Income in Canada," *Canadian Tax Journal*. Vol. XXIV, No. 4. (1976).

Gillespie, W.I. *The Incidence of Taxes and Public Expenditures in the Canadian Economy*. Ottawa: 1964.

Globerman, Steven. "Canadian Science Policy and Technological Sovereignty," *Canadian Public Policy*. Vol. IV, No. 1. (Winter, 1978).

Gordon, David. *Theories of Power and Underemployment*. New York: Heath, 1972.

Government of Canada. *Statement on Economic Development for Canada in the 1980s*. Ottawa: November 1981.

Green, C. *Canadian Industrial Organization and Policy*. Toronto: McGraw-Hill Ryerson, 1980.

Grubel, H.G. and M.A. Walker (eds.). *Unemployment Insurance: Global Evidence of Its Effects on Unemployment*. Vancouver: Fraser Institute, 1978.

Guest, Dennis. *The Emergence of Social Security in Canada*. Vancouver: University of British Columbia Press, 1980.

Harvey, David R. *Christmas Turkey or Prairie Vulture?* Montreal: Institute for Research on Public Policy, 1981.

Harvey, H.H. "Inflation: A Powerful Tool in Government Science Policy," *Canadian Public Policy.* Vol. II, No. 3. (Summer, 1976), pp. 439-450.

Hasson, Reuben, "The Cruel War: Social Security Abuse in Canada," *Canadian Taxation.* Vol. 3, No. 3. (Fall, 1981), pp. 114-147.

Hawkins, Freda. *Canada and Immigration.* Montreal: McGill-Queen's University Press, 1982.

Heclo, Hugh. *Modern Social Politics in Britain and Sweden.* New Haven: Yale University Press, 1974.

Heilbroner, Robert and Lester Thurow. *The Five Economic Challenges.* Englewood Cliffs: Prentice-Hall, 1981.

Helleiner, G.K. "Canada and the New International Economic Order," *Canadian Public Policy.* Vol. II, No. 3. (Summer, 1976), pp. 451-465.

Hooker, C.A. and R. MacDonald. *Energy and the Quality of Life: Understanding Energy Policy.* Toronto: University of Toronto Press, 1980.

House of Commons. *Fiscal Federalism in Canada.* Ottawa: Minister of Supply and Services, 1981.

Issalys, Pierre and G. Watkins. *Unemployment Insurance Benefits.* Study prepared for the Law Reform Commission of Canada. Ottawa: Minister of Supply and Services, 1977.

Kaliski, S.F. "People, Jobs and the 'New Unemployment'," *Canadian Public Policy.* Vol. II, No. 3. (Summer 1976), pp. 497-503.

Kilbourn, William. *Pipeline.* Toronto: Clark Irwin, 1970.

Langford, John. *Transport in Transition.* Montreal: McGill-Queen's University Press, 1976.

Leis, William (ed.). *Ecology Versus Politics in Canada.* Toronto: University of Toronto Press, 1979.

Leslie, Peter M. *Canadian Universities in 1980 and Beyond: Enrollment Structural Change and Finance.* Ottawa: Association of Universities and Colleges of Canada, 1980.

Lithwick, Harvey. *Regional Economic Policy: The Canadian Experience.* Toronto: McGraw-Hill Ryerson, 1978.

Lucas, Alistair R. and Trevor Bell. *The National Energy Board: Policy Procedure and Practice.* Ottawa: Minister of Supply and Services, 1977.

Lyon, Peyton V. *Canada in World Affairs 1961-1963.* Toronto: Oxford University Press, 1968.

Lyon, Peyton V. and Brian W. Tomlin. *Canada as an International Actor.* Toronto: Macmillan of Canada, 1979.

MacEachen, Hon. Allan J. *Fiscal Arrangements in the Eighties.* Ottawa: Department of Finance, 1981.

Mahon, Rianne. *The Politics of Industrial Strategy in Canada: Textiles.* Toronto: University of Toronto Press, 1983.

Manga, P., R. Broyles and G. Reschenthaler. *Occupational Health and Safety: Issues and Alternatives.* Ottawa: Economic Council of Canada, 1981.

Manzer, Ronald. "Social Policy and Political Paradigms," *Canadian Public Administration*. Vol. 24, No. 4. (Winter, 1981), pp. 641-648.

Marsh, L. *Report on Social Security for Canada—1943*. Toronto: University of Toronto Press, 1975.

Maslove, Allan M. and Eugene Swimmer. *Wage Controls in Canada 1975-1978*. Montreal: Institute for Research on Public Policy, 1980.

Mathias, Philip. *Forced Growth*. Toronto: James Lewis and Samuel, 1971.

Maxwell, Judith. *A Time for Realism*. Montreal: C.D. Howe Research Institute, 1978.

McDougall, John. *Fuels and the National Policy*. Toronto: Butterworths, 1982.

McInnes, Simon. *Federal-Provincial Negotiation: Family Allowances 1970-1976*. Ottawa: Ph.D. Thesis, Department of Political Science, Carleton University, 1978.

McNaughton, Bruce D. *Public Finance for Political Profit: The Politics of Social Security in Canada 1941-1977*. Ottawa: Ph.D. Thesis, Department of Political Science, Carleton University, 1980.

Meng, Ronald, Charles Seeto and Jim Sentang. *A Reconsideration of Canadian Universities and the Redistribution of Income*. Ottawa: Centre for Policy and Program Assessment, School of Public Administration, Carleton University, 1982.

Mitchell, Don. *The Politics of Food*. Toronto: James Lorimer and Publishers, 1975.

Morici, Peter, Arthur Smith and Sperry Lea. *Canadian Industrial Policy*. Washington: National Planning Association, 1982.

Muggah, Betty. "A New Perspective: The Making and Fate of a New Paradigm for Health Policy," *Ian Macdonald Essays*. Ottawa: School of Public Administration, Carleton University, 1981.

Odell, Peter. *Oil and World Power*. 6th Edition. London: Penguin, 1981.

Office of Industrial and Regional Benefits. *Major Capital Projects Inventory*. Ottawa: Industry, Trade and Commerce, October 1981.

Osbert, Lars. "Unemployment Insurance in Canada: A Review of the Recent Amendments," *Canadian Public Policy*. Vol. V, No. 2. (Spring, 1979).

Palda, Kristian S. *The Science Council's Weakest Link*. Vancouver: Fraser Institute, 1979.

Panitch, Leo and Donald Swartz. "From Free Collective Bargaining to Permanent Exceptionalism: The Economic Crisis and the Transformation of Industrial Relations in Canada," in E. Swimmer and M. Thompson (eds.). *Public Sector Industrial Relations in Canada*. Montreal: Institute for Research on Public Policy, 1983.

Parliamentary Task Forces on Employment Opportunities for the '80s. *Work For Tomorrow*. Ottawa: House of Commons, 1981.

Perry, Ross. *The Future of Canada's Auto Industry*. Ottawa: Canadian Institute for Economic Policy, 1982.

Phidd, Richard W. and G. Bruce Doern. *The Politics and Management of*

Canadian Economic Policy. Toronto: Macmillan of Canada, 1978.

Plumptre, A.F.W. *Three Decades of Decisions: Canada and the World Monetary System 1944-75.* Toronto: McClelland and Stewart, 1977.

Ponting, J.R. and R. Gibbons. *Out of Irrelevance.* Toronto: Butterworths, 1979.

Pratt, Larry. "Energy: The Roots of National Policy," *Studies in Political Economy.* No. 7. (Winter, 1982), pp. 27-59.

Pratt, Larry. *The Tar Sands: Syncrude and the Politics of Oil.* Edmonton: Hurtig, 1976.

Prices and Incomes Commission. *Inflation, Unemployment and Incomes Policy.* Ottawa: Information Canada, 1972.

Protheroe, David R. *Imports and Politics.* Montreal: Institute for Research on Public Policy, 1980.

Report of the Committee of Inquiry into the Unemployment Insurance Act. Ottawa: Queen's Printer,1962.

Reshenthaler, G.B. *Occupational Health and Safety in Canada: The Economics and Three Case Studies.* Montreal: Institute for Research on Public Policy, 1979.

Reuber, Grant. "The Impact of Government Policies on the Distribution of Income in Canada: A Review," *Canadian Public Policy.* Vol. IV, No. 4. (1979), pp. 505-529.

Rice, James and Michael Prince. *Social Policy and Administration in Canada.* Ottawa. (Manuscript).

Rickover, R.M. "The 1977 Bank Act: Emerging Issues and Policy Choices," *Canadian Public Policy.* Vol. II, No. 3. (Summer, 1976); pp. 372-379.

Safarian, A.E. "Foreign Ownership and Industrial Behaviour," *Canadian Public Policy.* Vol. V, No. 3. (Summer, 1979), pp. 318-336.

Savoie, Donald J. *Federal-Provincial Collaboration: The Canada-New Brunswick General Development Agreement.* Montreal: McGill-Queen's University Press, 1981.

Scarf, B.L., J.F. Helliwell and R.N. McRae. "Energy Policy and the Budget," *Canadian Public Policy.* Vol. VII, No. 4. (Winter, 1981), pp. 1-27.

Schultz, R. *Federalism, Bureaucracy and Public Policy: The Politics of Highway Transportation Regulation.* Montreal: McGill-Queen's University Press, 1980.

Science Council of Canada. *Canada as a Conserver Society.* Ottawa: Science Council of Canada, 1977.

Science Council of Canada. *Forging the Links: A Technology Policy for Canada.* Ottawa: Science Council of Canada, 1979.

Senate Committee on National Finance. *Government Policy and Regional Development.* Ottawa: Minister of Supply and Services, 1982.

Skinner, Mel. *The Federal 'Make or Buy' R and D Policy: A Preliminary Assessment of Policy Development and Implementation.* Ottawa: Masters Thesis, School of Public Administration, Carleton University, 1979.

Stanbury, W.T. *Business Interests and the Reform of Canadian Competition*

Policy. Toronto: Carswell Methuen, 1977.

Swainson, Neil A. *Conflict Over the Columbia*. Montreal: McGill-Queen's University Press, 1979.

Swimmer, G. and M. Thompson (eds.). *Public Sector Industrial Relations in Canada*. Montreal: Institute for Research on Public Policy, 1983.

Taylor, Malcolm. *Health Insurance and Canadian Public Policy*. Montreal: McGill-Queen's University Press, 1978.

Tomlin, Brian (ed.). *Canada's Foreign Policy: Analysis and Trends*. Toronto: Methuen, 1978.

Toner, Glen. "Oil, Gas and Integration," in Jon Pammett and Brian Tomlin (eds.). *Canadian Politics in the 1980s*. Toronto: Methuen, 1981.

Toner, Glen and F. Bregha. "The Political Economy of Energy," in M. Whittington and G. Williams (eds.). *Canadian Politics in the 1980s*. Toronto: Methuen, 1981.

Tucker, Michael. *Canadian Foreign Policy: Contemporary Issues and Themes*. Toronto: McGraw-Hill Ryerson, 1980.

Tupper, Allan. *Public Money in the Private Sector*. Kingston: Institute of Intergovernmental Relations, Queen's University, 1982.

Van Loon, Rick. "Reforming Welfare in Canada," *Public Policy*. Vol. 27, No. 4. (Fall, 1979), pp. 469-504.

Watkins, G.C. and M.A. Walter (eds.). *Reaction: The National Energy Program*. Vancouver: The Fraser Institute, 1981.

Waverman, Leonard. "The Distribution of Resource Rents: For Whom the Firm Tolls," In P.N. Nemetz (ed.). *Energy Crisis: Policy Response*. Montreal: Institute for Research on Public Policy, 1981.

Weaver, Sally M. *Making Canadian Indian Policy*. Toronto: University of Toronto Press, 1981.

West, E.G. "The Political Economy of American Public School Legislation," *Journal of Law and Economics*. Vol. 10. (October, 1967).

Wilensky, Harold and Charles Lebeaux. *Industrial Society and Social Welfare*. New York: Free Press, 1968.

Williams, Glen. "The National Tariffs: Industrial Underdevelopment Through Import Substitution," *Canadian Journal of Political Science*. Vol. 12. (1979), pp. 333-368.

Williams, Glen. *Not For Export: A Political Economy of Canada's Arrested Industrialization*. Toronto: McClelland and Stewart, 1983.

Wilson, James Q. "'What Works' Revisited: New Findings on Criminal Rehabilitation," *The Public Interest*. No. 6. (Fall, 1980), pp. 3-17.

Wirick, R.G. "The World Petroleum Market and Canadian Policy," *Canadian Public Policy*. Vol. VIII, No. 4. (Autumn, 1982), pp. 5343-553.

Zohar, Uri. *Canadian Manufacturing: A Study in Productivity and Technological Change*. Volume 1. Ottawa: Canadian Institute for Economic Policy, 1983.